VAN NOSTRAND POLITICAL SCIENCE SERIES

Editor

FRANKLIN L. BURDETTE
University of Maryland

WILLIAM G. ANDREWS—*European Political Institutions,* 2nd Ed.

WILLIAM G. ANDREWS—*Soviet Political Institutions*

BETTY B. BURCH and ALLAN B. COLE—*Asian Political Systems: Readings on China, Japan, India, and Pakistan.*

HARWOOD L. CHILDS—*Public Opinion*

R. G. DIXON, JR., and ELMER PLISCHKE—*American Government: Basic Documents and Materials*

WILLIAM GOODMAN—*The Two-Party System in the United States,* 3rd Ed.

GUY B. HATHORN, HOWARD R. PENNIMAN, and MARK F. FERBER—*Government and Politics in the United States,* 2nd Ed.

SAMUEL HENDEL—*The Soviet Crucible: The Soviet System in Theory and Practice,* 3rd Ed.

WALTER DARNELL JACOBS and HAROLD ZINK—*Modern Governments,* 3rd Ed.

WILLMOORE KENDALL and GEORGE W. CAREY—*Liberalism versus Conservatism: The Continuing Debate in American Government*

LANE W. LANCASTER—*Government in Rural America,* 2nd Ed.

P. M. A. LINEBARGER, C. DJANG, and A. W. BURKS—*Far Eastern Governments and Politics: China and Japan,* 2nd Ed.

RUSSELL W. MADDOX, JR.—*Issues in State and Local Government: Selected Readings*

RUSSELL W. MADDOX, JR., and ROBERT F. FUQUAY—*State and Local Government,* 2nd Ed.

MARTIN C. NEEDLER—*Dimensions of American Foreign Policy*

MARTIN C. NEEDLER—*Political Systems of Latin America*

ELMER PLISCHKE—*Conduct of American Diplomacy,* 3rd Ed.

ELMER PLISCHKE—*International Relations: Basic Documents,* 2nd Ed.

H. B. SHARABI—*Governments and Politics of the Middle East in the Twentieth Century*

HAROLD and MARGARET SPROUT—*Foundations of International Politics*

WILLIS G. SWARTZ—*American Governmental Problems,* 2nd Ed.

HAROLD ZINK, HOWARD R. PENNIMAN, and GUY B. HATHORN—*American Government and Politics: National, State, and Local*

D. VAN NOSTRAND COMPANY, INC.
Princeton, New Jersey • Toronto • London • Melbourne

ASIAN POLITICAL SYSTEMS

Readings on China Japan India Pakistan

Edited by
BETTY B. BURCH
Department of Political Science
Tufts University

ALLAN B. COLE
The Fletcher School of Law
and Diplomacy Tufts University

Van Nostrand Regional Offices: *New York, Chicago, San Francisco*

D. Van Nostrand Company, Ltd., *London*

D. Van Nostrand Company (Canada), Ltd., *Toronto*

D. Van Nostrand Australia Pty. Ltd., *Melbourne*

Published simultaneously in Canada by
D. Van Nostrand Company (Canada), Ltd.

Library of Congress Catalog Card No. 68-20916

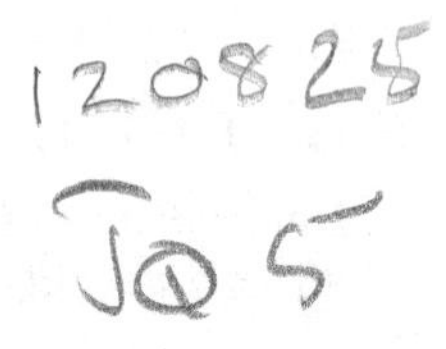

PRINTED IN THE UNITED STATES OF AMERICA

To our students whose interest and comments have been a continuous source of stimulation

Preface

This book presents Asian politics from the point of view of Asians themselves. The selections are by authors whose national origin is that of the country about which they write. Western scholarship concerning these countries is impressive and in some cases admittedly more sophisticated than that of some of the included essays. However, the editors felt that it would be most useful and revealing to draw exclusively from authors whose analyses and comments are derived from their own cultural point of view and experience. This approach should best preserve the indigenous attitudes and flavor so essential to the understanding of any political system.

Asian nations other than China, Japan, India and Pakistan—such as Indonesia and Burma—could have been included, but the editors decided that it was better to cover four representative systems as fully as space allowed than to include a larger number in a more cursory fashion, even though the latter would illustrate other important and distinctive variations. As the Introduction indicates, the four countries examined in this volume present interesting contrasts and similarities. The inclusion of the People's Republic of China hardly needs justification at this time in world history; furthermore, its totalitarian system represents revolutionary communism in Asia. The Japanese polity is of special interest because Japan's phenomenal success in modernization and in economic development represents the aspirations of all Asian countries, and because it now seems to be approaching a stage of stable democracy after an authoritarian past. India, like China, is important because of the global impact of its massive population; also of concern is the fact that India, in contrast to Japan, has recently been showing signs of decreasing political stability after two decades of seemingly stable democracy. Pakistan was chosen because it seemed to represent most clearly a political phenomenon found elsewhere in Asia: the successful military take-over which, unlike China, is reforming rather than revolutionary in nature.

The choice of an analytical framework that is meaningful both for any given country and for purposes of comparison is difficult. The editors decided to group the selections on each of the countries under five headings or topics: political culture (that is, forces and conditions shaping politics); political institutions, or structures; political leadership; political parties, factions, and interest groups; and political processes, or behavior. The readings can thus be read country by country, or for comparative purposes can be read horizontally by topic. Concise headnotes and citations give background, perspective, and source for each piece.

Many of the selections are from public documents such as constitutions and legislative acts, or authoritative statements by heads of state or party chairmen. Commentaries and articles are for the most part written by politicians, political scientists, historians, sociologists, and the like, working and writing within their own countries. A few selections by authors who have resettled abroad, as in the case of some Chinese, have been used to illustrate essential points. All the writers, however, derive their national and cultural origin from the country with which they are chiefly concerned.

The general work of planning and shaping this volume was the responsibility of the editors. However, credit and appreciation are given to Freeland K. Abbott, Chairman of the History Department at Tufts University, who prepared the section on Pakistan.

BETTY B. BURCH

ALLAN B. COLE

Contents

PART III. INDIA

PART IV. PAKISTAN

ASIAN POLITICAL SYSTEMS

Readings on China Japan India Pakistan

Introduction

Profound revolutionary change has marked the four countries with which this volume is concerned, and while contrasts are becoming increasingly apparent, there remain significant similarities. All are concerned with bettering the condition of their peoples through higher productivity and welfare, social and economic justice, cultural advancement, and the like—at least these are the avowed goals. As usual, ends tend to be more comparable than means. Societies with very different characteristics and cultural momentums, but with some features and problems in common, are being transformed from traditional folkways and agricultural predominance to modern, ever-changing technologies and variants of industrial production. How could their politics be immune from change?

Men, groups, and mechanisms are on the move, and it is worth noting the different attitudes among the elites and the wider publics. How aware, comprehending, and activated are villagers and urban dwellers in these countries which have both national and provincial loyalties and objectives? A television aerial above a thatched roof and the newspaper at the door in Japan; the loudspeaker and the ubiquitous study group in China; gossip at the village wells and the few collectively used radios in almost every hamlet in India and Pakistan—all symbolize the contrasts.

Factors shaping the expression of similar goals and the means to attain them have varied according to indigenous historical experience and cultural attitudes. Contrasts between these Asian countries stem not only from different prevailing attitudes and means of communication but more fundamentally from such factors as (1) their social and cultural composition; (2) the patterns of their revolutions; (3) their political systems, whether totalitarian or more liberal; and (4) their stages of economic modernization.

In Edward Shils' classification of alternative courses in political development in the new states, four of his five types are represented in this volume.[1] Japan is in most senses a maturing democracy. India and Pakistan are in some respects tutelary democracies and in others can be called modernizing oligarchies. The People's Republic of China is obviously a totalitarian oligarchy. The declining group not represented here includes more traditional monarchies like those of Afghanistan, Nepal and a few other Himalayan principalities, and some of the Malayan states; most of these are accelerating their pace toward modernity.

In China since reunification under the Communist party, directives and propaganda from Peking can reach every village, every comrade. But pressures arouse anxieties, and the Chinese are past masters at footdragging under absolutist regimes, including the present one which, although capable of effective central

[1] These five political types are discussed by Edward Shils, *Political Development in the New States,* (New York: Humanities Press, Inc., 1965), pp. 47–85.

planning and policy implementation, is determined to make any sacrifice for Communist party control, national power, and progress toward a socialist—ultimately a Communist—society. Mao has admitted the inevitability of "contradictions among the people" while socialism is abuilding; nevertheless most Chinese by will or compulsion consciously identify with the goals and processes of revolution. They have had a concept of where their society is headed and the relation of their roles and achievements to the manifold program, although recent events have obscured the clarity of values and goals and reduced consensus.

India and Pakistan are stirring. Literacy is growing and the radio and movies have some impact. But Indians—leaders and the millions—share less consensus than do Chinese regarding fundamental political objectives. Should the polity of India be that of a genuine parliamentary republic or an authoritarian system with a liberal gloss, a Hindu raj or a decentralized confederation of component agrarian communities with stress on cottage industries? Despite these questions, national elites and segments of their colleagues on the state level are committed to enlargement of the public economic sector and to industrialization, in some fields on a large scale.

In Pakistan the villager has been brought, as never before, into a political role through the Basic Democracy system. While there is a danger that this might be manipulated into a device merely to support the existing regime, such a forecast would be premature. Meanwhile, villagers are learning that a vote is meaningful, that their locally elected bodies can be useful.

Though there is both apathy and partisan collision in Japan, there is widespread understanding of, and participation in, local aspects of national programs and some common grasp of national perspectives. One suspects that many Japanese would like to have national goals which could evoke sacrificial zeal. However, having lost an empire, with China now unified, and new nations arising elsewhere in Asia, the Japanese seem content to participate and often excel in such fields as science, economic innovation and growth, trade, interstate and United Nations diplomacy, the arts, and athletic competitions.

Not only does the degree of national consensus vary, but even unity itself. We need not accept the earlier stereotype of a uniform Japan to recognize its marked degree of social and national cohesion based on linguistic and racial homogeneity. In contrast, China, India, and to a lesser degree Pakistan are veritable empires with ethnic, linguistic, and regional diversity; such pluralism is inevitably reflected in their governmental structures and political processes. In China from 1949 to 1966 procrustean ideology, a commanding party, "democratic centralism" (each level of government and mass organization controlled by and responsive to authorities above), bureaucracy, and military and investigative services all imparted discipline and unified direction to groups, areas, and peoples. Since intensification of the Cultural Revolution in that country from September 1965, questions about national unity have been revived, especially in regard to regional autonomy of action; but it may be, after a tense period of transition, that centralism will again prevail.

Modernizing, revolutionary change had progressed in each of these countries before 1945–49, but in different patterns. Japan was able to extricate itself quickly from the unequal treaty system and to modernize according to institutions and principles of conservative nationalism. This suited not only its self-appointed elites but also the prevailing traditionalism of most Japanese. Thus, Japan became first a constitutional but authoritarian state and more recently a liberal parliamentary monarchy, its Meji and MacArthurian transitions having been controlled and guided from above.

Modernization, in the case of Japan, was achieved by the initiative of native elites. More recently the Japanese have experienced democratization *à l'Américain,* and this is as close as they come to a legacy of political institutions, intellectual traditions, and economic patterns akin to what the British left to India and Pakistan. But Japan's modernization had already been accomplished, so it has had a longer independent basis on which to sift and shake down the Occupation-sponsored reforms.

China's revolution agonized through successive phases during which forces external to China impinged on its traditional society. Modernization was to a considerable extent initiated under the European treaty port pattern which in some ways stimulated and in others impeded Chinese efforts. Japan tried and failed to make it an exclusive colony. Then came drastic revolutionary change, the Soviet Union providing models and experience for the Chinese Communists.

Meanwhile, the Chinese Communist party (CCP) was developing formulae to release and channel indigenous forces of peasant discontent. By stages the Communists captured national power, proceeding to build a revolutionary bureaucracy armed with a modern ideology and administrative means never before available to any emperor or scholar-official. Moreover, the Chinese Communists have been able to harness long dammed-up forces for change, and through dynamic revolution, to cut through the "cake of custom," transforming the values of Confucianism and of folk traditions into incentives encouraging productivity. There are prices for such traumatic change—for such manipulative militancy and politicism—but if one is to consider sheer formulation and execution of policies, the thrust and competence of Chinese government, at least until the Cultural Revolution and in some respects despite it, are in glaring contrast to the situation in India.

Evolutionary moderation has so far been chosen over revolution in India, Pakistan, and Japan. While this has real advantages in some senses, many cultural patterns from the past, for example the Hindu caste system, persist in ways not always conducive to functional efficiency in a modern economic and political order. Furthermore, the new China with its Orwellian qualities is again out of step with most of its neighbors. It has been willing, both internally and in foreign strategies, to stir and exploit the great chasms and tensions in Asian societies, initially so that Communist parties can gain power, and in the longer run to attain new socialist "harmonies."

The congeries of peoples and entities comprising India became the colony of Great Britain, whose institutions and liberal concepts left a significant heritage to the new state. National unity was, however, still fragile at the time of independence. As a consequence, independence came to the subcontinent in the form of partition into two states, India and Pakistan, each with critical problems of political integration and both affiliated in an amorphous Commonwealth once predominantly British in character. The subsequent rate of modernizing change has been tempered by prior problems of national mobilization within each of the two segments.

In contemporary China political style and institutions have grown from a fusion of Chinese nationalism and revolutionary socialism, whereas in Japan,

India, and Pakistan degrees of detachment have been possible because totalitarian ideologies have not prevailed and competing centers of influence have been able to persist.[2] This helps to explain the contrasting and less doctrinaire patterns of socialism in these three countries. In Japan socialism is in opposition; its adherents can precipitate crises, but their main contributions are as political allies of organized labor and as pressures toward the policies of a welfare state. The Indian Congress party has officially advocated a somewhat vague socialism which has found its way into laws and policies affecting economic regulation, taxation, investment, and social legislation, but has not precluded a mixed economy and a rather desultorily enforced social egalitarianism. Pakistan seems to have adopted either a modified capitalism or a modified socialism, depending on one's point of view. Where investment funds in the private sector have been scarce, the government has had to fill the gaps, but it has not, as in India, made socialism the official policy of the ruling party.

Main Political Contrasts

Political and administrative structures

Turning now from shaping factors to political institutions and processes, the emphasis here will be on interpretations and contrasts rather than on comprehensive descriptions of systems. In China the salient political feature is the dictatorship of the Communist party (although the army has played a new role in the Cultural Revolution), allegedly on behalf of the workers and peasants, and despite the actual emergence of new strata, with the avowed aim of proletarianizing the whole society. Party, state, and mass organizations have pyramidal structures, and the electoral process is conducted on the basis of single slates of candidates at various levels. Bodies elected, indirectly from the county (*hsien*) upward, are more for deliberation and approval than for genuine legislation. They help to encourage a sense of participation and provide one of the channels for upward reporting of local and regional conditions. Other avenues for popular participation include the People's Political Consultative Conferences (paling since 1954 as a structure of the United Front), the great mass organizations incorporating nearly all adult Chinese, and the small study groups. Derivative policies and directives can originate in the State Council, Communist China's nearest approximation to a cabinet, and from ministries, but primary policies are determined by the Politburo and/or by the Central Committee of the party. In all vertical structures, "democratic centralism" has been practiced; no institutionalized political opposition has been possible; criticism has been prudently corrective rather than fundamental.[3] Criticism and opposition, though more overt since 1965–66, are still muffled and occur in the context of factional and regional crises; hence they are of uncertain duration.

In Japan, India, and Pakistan there have been various authoritarian tendencies: single-party hegemonies, executive aggrandizement, bureaucratic power and arrogance, military take-over or resurgence in Japan and Pakistan, yet none of these tendencies approaches the totalism of China's web before the Cultural Revolution. Despite considerable centralization of executive power, ministries on both national

[2] During the period 1932–45 this was less true of Japan.

[3] In China a few "kept" parties exist for ideological and manipulative purposes, but they may not compete with the CCP for members or power.

and state (in Japan, prefectural) levels are responsible to corresponding legislatures. Those bodies are directly elected and do indeed legislate. The dominant ruling parties in India, Japan, and, with a lapse, in Pakistan have rested on electoral consent. Losses by the Indian Congress party in 1967, reducing it to a slim majority in Parliament, have emphasized the importance of electoral support. Especially in India and Japan, parties are subject to influence from factions, pressure groups, and lobbies.[4] Hegemonial parties in both these countries pay special attention to the interests of big businesses and farmers, but in India the picture is complicated because of surviving landlord influence which is focused on state governments. Also New Delhi, with varying cooperation from the states, approaches economic programs in the context of underdevelopment, and so emphasizes the public sector. Long-range planning at the center has recently become much more difficult, and unlike the situation in Japan, the policies of state governments grow increasingly important.

The political situation in Pakistan cannot be stated with equal certainty. The Muslim League has not been able to dominate the political scene since the late 1950's, and there has been an excessive fragmentation of parties resulting in the heterodox Combined Opposition party with Miss Fatimah Jinnah, the sister of the nation's founder, as its standard bearer. Never very strong, this unification weakened after the election of 1965 and now, following the death of Miss Jinnah, is having difficulty finding another unifying leader. Meanwhile, the raj of Ayub Khan seems to have an approach similar to that of the British in India. Other sources of opposition may be sought for in such groups as refugees or students, but such a development does not seem likely in the near future.

There are many other political features in Japan, India, and Pakistan which contrast with those of China. Their judicial systems are supposedly (and on the whole actually) independent, and higher courts have the power of review. Communist China has never completed its legal codes; its system of jurisprudence is still immature with no promise of autonomy. Moreover, in normal times, freedom of communications and the press is respected in the non-totalitarian systems; in Pakistan, however, the press remains weak in its influence.

Regarded constitutionally and administratively, Communist China's centralization derives from the nature of the party and from the regime's character as a revolutionary dictatorship. In 1954 a regional echelon was eliminated, and strengthened central control over the provinces was made direct.[5] However, during communization in 1958 the party-government sought to distinguish between controls and administrative discretion, and to delegate more of the latter to regional and local entities in order to encourage initiative and innovation. India's *panchayati raj* system and Pakistan's Basic Democracy have also been experiments in greater local autonomy, but their purpose has been to foster democratic participation. Historically China has been plagued with resurgent regionalism

[4] It is interesting to find national party leaders in China warning cadres against becoming so concerned about local conditions that they may lose sight of national perspectives and strict compliance with directives from above. That such parochial interests have persisted and have grown unevenly is indicated by developments in a number of provinces and border regions in the course of the continuing Cultural Revolution.

[5] Regional bureaus were reestablished for the CCP in 1961, but that level of civil administration was not revived.

whenever the central government has weakened, as when the Nationalists lost their hold on the mainland; more recently, factional conflicts and attendant unrest have caused the weakening and partial breakdown of central controls.

The federal system of India assigns extensive formal and residual powers to the central government, but increasingly the real centers of power lie in the seventeen states. Some fear that the recent schisms in the Congress party and its loss of control of important state governments may endanger national integrity. Linguistic and historical differences, especially between north and south, may imperil national loyalty. In Pakistan the President, Ayub Khan, moves carefully, because he must try to keep both wings of the bifurcated nation happy and please the religious traditionalists while developing a modern state. Regionalism exists, and East Pakistan continues to be hypersensitive to any imagined or real slight. But the common threat posed by India, and adoption of a single political entity rather than perpetuation of essentially tribal units for West Pakistan, have kept such tensions within bounds.

Nothing of this sort exists in Japan. Despite democratization under the Occupation, Japan's political and administrative structure remained unitary and somewhat centralized, formerly along Prussian lines but, since 1946, more comparable with the British pattern. Governors of prefectures are no longer centrally appointed as are those of Pakistan and the states in India, but the police system and other leverages on local governments have been considerably recentralized.

In India the response to the removal of British rule and the spread of representative government has been increased involvement of caste rivalries in state and local politics. The autonomy of clans and joint families in China has been swept away by the revolution. Japan has an *eta,* or special hamlet, minority; but its problems and quest for equality have not been as widespread and serious as those of India's millions of untouchables or outcastes. Although Muslim society in Pakistan and India does not recognize overt castes, there are entrenched distinctions between certain classes and other groups.

Parties, factions, and parliamentary politics

When absolutism prevailed in Asia before importation of the representative principle, factions rather than genuine parties vied for influence and power. It should not be surprising, therefore, that parliamentarianism is faring differently there than in the West and that factionalism persists within parties, especially in Japan and India. Even in China, where legislative institutions have become mechanisms for mobilization and disciplined communication, factions within the CCP have become much more significant and divisive than have the circumscribed groups in the United Front. Although the party's élan and national grid have been shaken, the latter may in time be largely restored. Whether adherent to the Mao-Lin militant orthodoxy or not, party leaders commonly hold offices on various levels of government.

Elitism characterizes parties in these countries, but the CCP is the only one with a massive membership and the organization to control and impel a tremendous population. Although their forms are not directly comparable, parties in Japan, India and Pakistan have very small memberships, while approximately 19,000,000 members belong to the CCP. There is a sectarian aura to party membership in China, and, of course, the discipline is exercised vigorously from the apex.

The conservative Japanese Liberal Democrats (LDP) and the Indian Congress party have been perennially in power and have provoked among frustrated minorities complaints about "the tyrannous majority." [6] In Japan this has caused many in leftist opposition forces to resort to direct extra-parliamentary action. Except for Hindu "ultras" and "decentralist" Gandhians, Indian Congress leadership seems more committed to parliamentary processes and their implications than do conservative politicians in Japan. This aspect may reflect the British legacy. It remains to be seen whether normal, stable parliamentary processes can be restored in Pakistan or whether this will be prevented by authoritarianism and party fragmentation.

On the national level, rivalry between Liberal Democratic factions of Japan causes somewhat more instability within the government party than in the Indian Congress establishment. National factions in Japan also interfere more with central party collection of funds and with the building of local organizations having all-party identification. However, in India on the state and local levels intraparty factionalism is rampant, and the loyalty of the voter is primarily to a local leader rather than to the party itself. Here, the cleavage and tensions between the ministerial and organizational wings of the Congress party are more pronounced, though modified versions can be found in Japanese parties, and even in China, where officials sometimes have difficulty reconciling the demands of official roles with party orthodoxy. Funds, new members, and recruitment of younger leaders are derived from more vigorous organizational elements of the Congress working in and from the states. The Liberal Democratic party in Japan, with less national support, is striving for similar expansion. In strengthening local and regional organizations, efforts are not as fraught with problems for national unity, because prefectures in Japan are not as autonomous as Indian states. Since the achievement of agrarian reforms, the objectives sought by Agricultural Cooperative Associations in Japan are not usually as narrow as those of entrenched caste, landlord, and small farming proprietors in India. There, a serious question is whether representative institutions based on a national party system can endure effectively as competition becomes increasingly shaped by regional forces.

Opposition forces in Japan are fairly strong in national politics; but only since 1967 in India has a meaningful opposition arisen in Parliament to which the Congress majority must be answerable. Opposition in Japan is led by the left-oriented Socialist party, whereas in India comparable parties are weak and find strength only in fragile coalitions. Indian Socialists, more bourgeois in background than those in Japan, are concerned to a greater extent with village problems and with organization from below. While the Indian Communist parties (one favoring the Soviet Union and the other the People's Republic of China) and the organizational wing of the Congress party had been the most effective critics of the government in the Lok Sabha, that role is now played by the new oppositional coalition. Communist parties in these two countries have not synchronized their choices between violent and parliamentary methods. In both countries they are

[6] The Congress party retained a small parliamentary majority after the 1967 elections, but it is no longer the dominant party. The LDP in Japan, in different circumstances, may also soon have to seek coalitions with other moderate parties.

gaining more independence as a result of polycentrism—more specifically the Sino-Soviet rift and the turmoil in China—but the issues which roil each of them are rather different.

Organized labor plays a more sharply political and ideologically affected role in Japanese opposition politics than in India. The right-wing labor federation in Japan is less political and supports the weak Democratic Socialist splinter, whereas the moderate federation in India is Congress-sponsored. The Indian Communist party is the strongest political influence in the leftist trade union federation; but in Japan, Communist factions, while able to influence Sōhyō (the General Council of Trade Unions), must watch it support and powerfully influence the Left Socialists. One can say that such federations in India are the arms of political parties, whereas in Japan it has often been charged that the Socialist party is the agent of Sōhyō. There, too, socialist parties and national movements in support of labor, various causes, and other interests have cooperated more spectacularly in nationwide waves of protest action. Actually, Tokyo is more of a focus for such demonstrations than is New Delhi, because state capitals also attract attention on the subcontinent. In Pakistan, universities have thus far been the main foci for demonstrations.

Regarding electoral differences, it must suffice here to mention only the contrast between Japan's nearly complete literacy and the fact that in the 1962 elections 160,000,000 of India's 212,000,000 eligible voters were illiterate. We have seen pictures of Indian voters casting ballots in boxes under party-designating symbols. The eastern wing of Pakistan is known to have a higher rate of literacy than does West Pakistan; even so, it is not higher than 20 per cent.

Leadership

Mao Tse-tung himself as well as the party and bureaucratic leadership have special problems of aging personnel and succession, but so do the other countries here considered. More in China than in India by this time, the old guards are still prestigious for their records as heroes of liberation movements. In Japan, senior conservative leaders, especially, are survivals from a period now partially discredited. Shigeru Yoshida, five times premier, came as close as any postwar Japanese to the towering eminence of Jawaharlal Nehru or Mao Tse-tung; perhaps the imperial institution militates against such figures.

For these historic reasons there are today more secondary charismatic leaders in China and India than in Japan. Ayub Khan's dominance in Pakistan deters the emergence of other leaders of national prominence. It remains to be seen whether the system of Basic Democracy will change this situation. In each of these countries the rising generation of prime leaders will probably have arrived by more institutionalized routes. Because of the CCP's structure, monopoly of power, and doctrinal issues, a sharper struggle for top succession has preceded the death of Mao. A study of the full and alternate members of the CCP Central Committee elected in and since 1945 indicates layers of proven loyalty and ability in relation to periods of party and revolutionary experience. Thus, Mao's core group dates back before the Long March, most of them to early years before the split from the Kuomintang. Another group joined during the Yenan stage and served in the anti-Japanese "liberated areas." Still another has had slightly less prominent party careers since the Kiangsi Soviet republic in Southeast China.

A fourth layer emerged toward the end of World War II, followed by a smaller number of activists who forged ahead later, some even since the gaining of national power in 1949.[7] Further recruiting for these high policy-making positions will probably be from among provincial party secretaries, top military commanders and political commissars, major department heads in the People's Liberation Army Headquarters, chairmen of mass organizations, perhaps party leaders from various security services, and at a later stage some from engineering and industrial management.

Even before Indian independence, Congress party elites had moved into ministries and administrative offices under British rule; they continued their functions after 1947. In Japan, however, the Occupation's political purge affected politicians more drastically than bureaucrats, and the latter have come to comprise more than one-quarter of the Liberal Democratic party in the Diet. About half the members of this whole delegation have strong business backgrounds or connections, while an equal proportion of the Socialist party's delegation come from leftist labor unions. None of the Indian parties is so dominated by groups exerting such highly organized pressures.

For years there was doubt whether the dominant parties in India and Japan could expand their local organizations and recruit able new leaders worthy of the highest positions. Some successes have been achieved in recent years. Able leaders of young middle age have emerged in a number of Indian states where they have rejuvenated party organizations; now some of them are being promoted to national offices. The former Chief Minister of Gujerat succeeded Krishna Menon as Minister of Defense; another has become President of the Congress party. Prime Minister Indira Gandhi herself is from a younger generation and is politically to the left of her father's former positions in a number of fields. Lower echelons of the Liberal Democratic party in Japan are also having some success, and it is partly because of advancing younger leaders that progressivism and greater attention to programs have made modest gains. The main opposition parties in Japan are also on the threshold of farewell to a generation of veterans in political experience dating back to the mid–1920's.

The founding elite of Pakistan is mostly passing from active service on account of age or is limited by the moderate authoritarianism of the regime. Many of the ablest younger people are in bureaucracy and in state administrative services. Leaders will continue to be recruited from the universities; in the longer run, industry, business and the professions—including the military—will continue to be sources.

Administrative Contrasts

Political leaders and bureaucrats in China, India, and Pakistan have turned from earlier emphasis on revenue collection and maintaining order to activities

[7] For fuller treatments of CCP present and future leadership, see Chao Kuo-chün, "Leadership in the Chinese Communist Party," *The Annals of the American Academy of Political and Social Science,* Vol. 321 (January 1959), pp. 40–50; Donald W. Klein, "The 'Next Generation' of Chinese Communist Leaders," *The China Quarterly,* No. 12 (October-December 1962), pp. 57–74; John W. Lewis, *Chinese Communist Party Leadership and the Succession to Mao Tse-tung: An Appraisal of Tensions* (Washington, D.C.: U.S. Department of State, Bureau of Intelligence and Research), January 1964.

necessary for economic development and social welfare. In Japan, the national ministries boast some of the most competent economists and legal talent in the nation, the former—in touch with private planners and executives—striving to lift productivity and national income still higher. Japan's bureaucracy is obviously the most mature of the four. Each of the systems reflects its background and milieu. China's administration bears the marks of a revolution still in process; India's and Pakistan's have advanced much since 1947 but have been influenced by British methods and traditions; Japan's is one of the governmental branches least altered by Occupation reforms and continues some traits from the eras when officials ruled on behalf of a sacred Emperor rather than as servants of the people.

Hierarchy, a principal hallmark of bureaucracies, has developed even in would-be egalitarian China; it is more accepted and pronounced in Japan and India. The Chinese Communist elite keeps urging administrative cadres to identify with and "learn from" the people. Doubtless there have been tensions between the Chinese people and party cadres who keep impelling them to transform patterns of life and fulfill programs of work, but in general Chinese administrators seem to have reduced significantly the historic gulf between ordinary people and officials. In most countries bureaucracies do the bidding of the prevailing party or coalition, but in non-totalitarian India, Japan, and Pakistan, administrative agencies can be more non-partisan, have greater autonomy within civil service establishments, and can exert more modifying influences in the execution of policies. They are more legalistic and conservative than their Chinese counterparts, but they do not have such serious problems of orthodoxy in following a "general line." Ideology and politicism are much less obtrusive than in China. Although government in Pakistan is strongly supported by the military, it remains essentially civilian in character. As in India, the military are thoroughly imbued with the English tradition that politics is not for the soldier.

Status consciousness and problems of relations between cadres of different types and ranks exist in China; however, they seem to raise more serious impediments in the other countries. Patriarchal and factional tendencies are much stronger in Japanese and lower-level Indian officialdom. Higher Indian officials, notably in the prestigious civil services, tend to come mainly from the upper middle classes. Japanese recruitment is socially broader, but by the time officials rise to high positions, they tend to assume oligarchic airs. Even the CCP warns against "commandism" and "meritism" (the proud expectations of peasant cadres who are veterans of the revolutionary struggle). In Japan cliques (*batsu*), often determined by common university backgrounds, are prevalent in bureaucratized companies as well as in governmental offices. Professional specialization was developing markedly in Chinese administration, but this trend has been challenged and at least temporarily checked by the Great Cultural Revolution which expresses the anxieties of the Mao-Lin faction that revolutionary ethos was giving way to bureaucratic professionalism. Mao has emphasized the need for revolutionary men capable of versatility, and on class grounds he has long been suspicious of specialists and officialdom.

The study of public administration along Western lines is coming of age in Japan, India, and Pakistan. In China this field has been more closely associated with specific revolutionary and development programs. The other governments place more emphasis on exacting, substantive examination of those destined for higher official careers, and on most levels personnel are given more security of tenure. To some extent they apply merit systems, but promotion according to seniority is stressed. Although veterans of the Long March (1934–35) and the Yenan period (1936–47) are given preference, there has been considerable mobility up and down Chinese official ladders. Where the single party permeates bureaucracy as in Communist China, it is difficult by now to distinguish between party and administrative routes to the topmost positions in government. However, the party (and now possibly the army and security services) is the primary route upward. In India either route may be taken. Japanese conservative parties are vehicles for bureaucrats ambitious for ministerial posts. Most of the premiers in Japan since 1945 have been former administrative officials, and from one-third to one-half of their cabinet members have had similar backgrounds. As for the availability of adequately trained public servants, Japan is the only one of the four which is amply supplied. China has many who need much more training. At lower echelons of administration, India and Pakistan lack personnel sufficiently experienced to overcome by persuasion the popular reluctance to change.

Planners and administrators in underdeveloped countries with massive, rapidly growing populations know that no political system can long survive which does not gain in the grim race between human fertility and food production. Japan's haunting problem, on the other hand, is its paucity of natural resources and the need to finance their importation. Foreign experts are frequently used in India and Pakistan, and were employed in China from 1950 to 1960; Japan, on the contrary, has been an exporter of technical skills. In planning and experimentation, India has perhaps more freely than the others borrowed selectively from the experience of both planned and freer economies. In matters of nationalization, India occupies a middle position between China and Japan.

Role of Military Aims

Of all the political contrasts which could be treated, one of the most striking has been the much greater stress on military power by Communist China than by Japan, India, and Pakistan since 1945. Indeed, the major orientation of China toward power is reminiscent of the Meiji slogan: "rich country, strong army." One cannot say that all tensions and aggressions latent in Japanese society have vanished, but even the most conservative wish to prevent military encroachments in politics and the heavy taxation which ambitious rearmament would entail. The Japanese mood may be changing now that China is producing nuclear weapons; certainly, ambitious and advanced economic development anywhere affects war potential. But the chastened Japanese seem still reluctant to develop more than minimally deterrent forces.

As India and Pakistan industrialize, they too will gain in basic power; but even considering the Indo-Pakistan and Sino-Indian border hostilities, India would prefer to continue investing heavily in productive sectors. It has tripled the defense budget but deplores the greatly increased tax burden and the distraction from vital economic development. Despite humiliation in the Himalayas, India did not adopt a full war footing nor institute conscription. (China has had compulsory military service since 1954.) Nothing like the commune's people's militia is contemplated for India and Pakistan.

Militancy permeates Chinese official attitudes and policies. Most programs in revolutionary China become "heaven storming" campaigns. The meanings of existence and direction are understood in terms of struggle between mutually opposed forces; class conflict and man's efforts to reshape his physical and social world are seen in this context. This pattern, so deeply ingrained by Marxism-Leninism and China's civil wars, colors the regime's outlook in its foreign relations. In such totalitarian systems, military personnel are regarded and used as normal components of society. Much attention is devoted to their political indoctrination, and they are employed on economic projects when not otherwise needed. Although Mao has insisted on CCP primacy and leadership, the struggle for power in the Cultural Revolution has increased the reliance of his faction on the army, which itself has suffered some splits.

In India and Japan the army is subordinated to the principle and practice of civilian supremacy, and in Pakistan Ayub Khan now rests the legitimacy of his government on the ballot box rather than the army. But civilian supremacy could be eroded in any of these countries by the tensions and pressures of internal conflicts of interest and international rivalries. India's official policy of non-alignment has been weakened by its dependence on arms from the United States, Britain, and the Soviet Union. Pakistan, uneasy about the geographic separation of its two wings by India, seeks more arms from various sources, including Communist China. But none of these countries is likely to become as militarized as China.

If genuinely representative polities are to prevail in the long run in these non-communist Asian countries, a few more decades are needed to strengthen their foundations. Already in Japan there are signs of an expanding and somewhat stronger middle class, of more adequate social security, and of an emerging generation of leaders less schooled in the authoritarian features of the Meiji system. Probably far more serious than the external threat to India are problems of regionalism and the need for increasingly vigorous economic growth. Pakistan's Basic Democracy also needs more time to take root. The cost of failure could lead either to division or to more authoritarian regimes; the reward for success could be more political stability in that subcontinent and elsewhere in Asia.

Part I

Communist China

SECTION ONE

Political Culture

1 • C. K. Yang: *The "Family Revolution" Before and After Communist Attainment of National Power* *

Solidary patriarchal family systems seem to characterize most traditional societies, and the family system of China has been particularly intense in its qualities and pivotal influence. Professor Yang, a noted Chinese sociologist, emphasizes here the manifold changes occurring in Chinese family life during the decades preceding Communist assumption of national power.

Some Westerners believe that the Chinese Communist Party (CCP) is "opposed to the family institution." Although the party is nationalistic and insists on the perpetuation of the society and state, it is determined to lead in pruning the functions of the family and to release the individual from many family claims so that he can identify with and participate in other collective associations. Until most parents know only the revolutionary society, there will be continuing Communist suspicion of the family as a seedbed of the earlier values. By 1980, however, the socialist revolution may have been in effect for a full generation, and the family will become a perpetuator of the new social values. If this occurs, the party's attitude may change.

The communes at first involved drastic efforts to limit family functions and significance. This may have been one of the reasons for massive peasant foot-dragging. Since 1960–61, mess halls have become optional except at midday for working people. Puritanism, later marriages, and family planning are being encouraged. There has been a widespread addition of women to the labor force, and they are rapidly moving toward equality of political, legal, and economic rights. Doubtless these are transitions to modernity, but whether such changes can be regarded as genuine "emancipation" depends on the pattern of new freedoms and coercions women experience.

This form of family organization, centering upon parental control of married sons and structuring the membership rigidly according to sex and age, produced in the past a stable family and contributed substantially to the long stability of the

* "The Chinese Family in the Communist Revolution," *Chinese Communist Society: The Family and the Village* (Cambridge, Mass.: M.I.T. Press, 1965), pp. 10–20. By permission.

traditional culture. In the traditional society dominated by the kinship factor it seems to have served social needs well with its multiplicity of functions.

But the impact of Western ideas and industrial influences since the closing quarter of the last century increasingly altered the picture. In the traditional family a strong authoritarian character is inherent in the rigid parental control and the stratification according to sex and age. Pressure and tension bore down heavily upon the women and the young. The introduction of the Western idea of individual liberty and rights inspired the women and the young to review and to reject their traditional roles of submission in the family. . . .

But this pattern of social organization became increasingly incompatible with the new needs that arose with China's gradual integration into the modern industrial and nationalistic world. The past three-quarters of a century of floundering efforts at transferring the family and kinship relations to modern economic and political undertakings produced endless contradictions between the particularistic and the universalistic patterns of social life. From such contradictions developed the accelerating trend of change in the traditional family and its old role in the organization of social life, a change that proceeded by popular demand from the educated young for a "family revolution" from the second decade of the present century. There was little success in overcoming the incongruity between the kinship tie as an organizational requirement in the traditional order and the need for objective qualifications for individuals as components of modern economic and political structures. Moreover, the particularistic nature in the kinship-oriented pattern of social organization divided the population into numerous small, self-confined, and loosely interrelated kinship units, while the mass organization of modern industrial society and the national state demanded intimate integration between the social and economic organs based on universal standards for the individuals. . . .

Some students underestimate this revolution as merely a change of political formality from monarchy to a nominal republic, devoid of any serious social significance. Actually, it started the trend toward destroying the theoretical applicability of Confucian kinship ethics to the operation of the state, thus undermining the traditional dominance of the family in social and political life. . . .

. . . The institution that had withstood some two millennia of dynastic changes and foreign invasions and all their political and economic devastations now came to be viewed as symbolizing all of China's sins and weaknesses. The new demands and the proffered solutions, however untried and incoherent in some respects, were pictured as the road to happiness and strength. Nationalistic sentiments which began to surge forth with increasing force in the decade following World War I in China as well as elsewhere helped to impress these arguments on the minds of the public. . . .

The call for skepticism toward the old cultural heritage and a new orientation for the future found the most attentive listeners among modern educated young men and women, who felt the most strain from the rigid sex and age stratifications in the traditional family and society. The rise of the youth movement and the women's movement, as phases of the May 4th Movement (1919), lent important support to the family revolution and in fact became inseparable parts of it. In a sense, the family revolution developed as a rebellion of the educated young of both sexes against the traditional social order.

Such a rebellion, breaking out within the family circle, was naturally viewed with alarm and even terror by the older generation, who found the process increasingly difficult to stop. Under the driving and infectious demand for freedom and equality, and in the growing destruction of unquestioned conformity to traditional institutions in general, many traditional families, mainly among the urban upper and upper-middle classes, were forced to undergo certain fundamental changes by the mid-1920's; and the family problem was pushed into the fore of the nation's attention along with other vital political, social, and economic issues of the day. . . .

It was true that this trend mainly affected the modern intelligentsia, the majority of whom stemmed from the upper and upper-middle classes in the cities. The importance of this group could not be measured entirely by its small numerical size because of its strategic function in giving direction to the social change and its dominant position in such mechanisms of social control as the government. But the influence of the family revolution in this period was definitely spreading, though slowly, to the urban middle class and a small portion of the city workers. The younger generation of the well-to-do landowners in the countryside also became increasingly affected by the new ideological trends as they went to the cities for a modern education, but, as they soon became identified with the urban intelligentsia and no longer remained members of rural communities, the countryside was not much affected by modern ideological movements.

It is obvious that the gradual change of the traditional family was not the result of ideological agitation alone without the operation of other supporting social and economic factors. The confinement of the family revolution and its related ideological movements mainly to the cities was due precisely to the presence of collaborating social and economic forces in the urban areas and the weakness or absence of such forces in the rural communities. . . .

Growing population mobility, with frequent prolonged physical separation of some members from the family, affected the continued operation of the traditional family organization, which required constant, close contact among the members. Increased population mobility stemmed from a number of social situations, notably the steady deterioration of the handicraft and agricultural economy, the expansion of urbanization, and the high frequency of famines and wars. In the eight years of war against the Japanese invasion (1937–1945), there was no new ideological wave on the reform of the family, but the pouring of millions of modern-minded coastal refugees into the hitherto isolated Southwest undoubtedly aided the disintegration of many traditional families and the formation of new ones on the model promoted by the family revolution. When the curtain of enemy occupation was lifted by the Japanese surrender of 1945, the cities revealed a scene of family life marked by physical separation of members and deviation from the traditional standards, departing further from the Confucian pattern than in any preceding period.

In 1949, four years after the Japanese surrender, when the Chinese Communists took over the reins of national political power, China entered upon a period in which drastic political revolution was but one phase of a comprehensive movement aimed at recasting the entire traditional social order by coordinated plans and compulsory measures. The reform of the Chinese family, along with the remaking of other major social institutions, became a part of an over-all drastic social change.

This crisis for the family institution contained no new substance. As already shown, this institution had been changing under constant stress and strain for the preceding three decades; and the Communist crisis, so far as the family was concerned, represented but a more drastic development of the same process, which was now being urged on under a different leadership and in a different manner.

Neither was the effort at altering the family institution anything new with the Communists. Long before the establishment of the Communist regime in 1949, members of the Communist movement had been playing a vital part, along with other reformers and intellectuals, in developing the family revolution and its supporting ideological movements. Ch'en Tu-hsiu, one of the founders of the Chinese Communist Party, ranked with Hu Shih in the New Culture Movement and in the relentless assault against the ideological and institutional citadel of Confucian orthodoxy. Particularly vital was Ch'en's place in initiating and developing the youth movement and the women's movement. Communists in general had been strategic in the agitating and organizing efforts of these movements. The Chinese Communist Party was co-author with the Kuomintang of the Second Revolution, which had serious effects on the development of the family revolution. (Present Communist interpretation of modern Chinese history claims Communist Party leadership in the May 4th Movement and the Second Revolution.) The actual development of the family situation in the "red areas" that came into existence after 1928 has remained largely unrecorded, but scattered information has indicated uncompromising Communist endeavor in changing both the traditional family institution and the kinship-oriented pattern of social organization in those areas.

Many sources of popular information in China for the past thirty years have pictured the Communists as iconoclasts toward the family as a social institution. Ch'en Tu-hsiu was charged by his political enemies with advocating the practice of "communal property and communal wives;" and the charge of practicing "communal wives" was directed against the "red areas" in the early 1930's. There was a disquieting rumor of "forced assignment of wives" by the Communists in 1948 and 1949, a rumor so persistent and widespread that it caused a marriage boom in localities in the paths of the advancing Communist columns in their southward conquest because parents were hurriedly marrying off their daughters in an effort to save them from becoming "assigned wives."

It is probably true that relatively light restrictions were placed upon marriage and divorce in the "red areas" before 1949. This can be seen in such available documents of the period as the Marriage Regulations of the Chinese Soviet Republic and the Temporary Marriage Regulations, both promulgated in 1931 by the Chinese Soviet Republic, and the Marriage Regulations of the Border Area of Shansi, Chahar, and Hopei provinces. But there seems to be no substantiation to the charge of either the practice of "communal wives" or the discarding of the family as a social institution.

Facts as observed in Communist China after 1949 indicate no evidence for any of these allegations. The promulgation of the new Marriage Law on May 1, 1950, and the nationwide efforts at its enforcement by the Communist government through the network of organizations under its command seem clear indications of a Communist policy toward the family which insisted upon drastic reform of the traditional family but fully retained the family as a basic social institution. Even under the people's commune, the family remains the basic social unit, though vastly reduced in its functions. An unmistakable sign of Communist policy was seen in the complex responsibilities involved in divorce by the new Marriage Law, responsibilities that weigh particularly heavy on the husband. . . . Hence the drastic reform of the traditional family demanded by the Communists should not be taken as an iconoclastic view of the family as a social institution.

The reason for the Communist policy of reshaping the traditional family seems plain. The Communist regime is bent on building an industrial society on the socialistic pattern, and it is fully aware of the incompatibility between such a society and the kinship-oriented structure. Also important for the political purpose of the regime is the incompatibility between the individual's traditional loyalty to the family and the new requirements of his loyalty to the state and to the Communist Party.

Up to the Communist accession to power, the family revolution had proceeded largely as a part of a process of spontaneous social change in modern China. The inauguration of the Communist regime, particularly after the promulgation of the new Marriage Law, brought a different development. Change of the traditional family is no longer left to a spontaneous process but is subjected to the compulsory power of law and the pressure of a powerful, well-organized mass movement; and it is coordinated with other aspects of the Communist social, economic, and political revolution.

2 • C. K. YANG: *Changes in Village Socio-Politics* *

Objectivity marks this interpretation of changes in Chinese village society; it was written in late 1957 or early 1958 before the "Great Leap Forward" and the efforts toward communization of peasant society.

The CCP gained national power chiefly by generating and harnessing power in the populous countryside through reforms and organized movements. Its cadres were overwhelmingly from rural origins in 1949, but these have since been reduced in relative proportions. From the fall of 1947 to readjustments in 1960–62, emphasis came to be more on urban workers and on industries. After 1962 came revived attention to the needs of agrarian producers.

Communists have distrusted peasant proprietary and conservative tendencies. As Professor Yang explains, by 1956 most Chinese farmers had lost personal or family title to land and had become organized on collective farms—the third stage after redistribution of lands. The first stage had been mutual-aid teams farming compact rather than fragmented areas; the second, lower-stage followed by advanced agricultural producers' cooperatives. Without consolidating any of these precursive phases, party radicals launched the communization program in 1958. This coincided with the massive mobilization of rural and urban labor in the drastic "Great Leap." Communes were congruent with what Westerners might call townships (hsiang), *which were jurisdictions subordinate within counties* (hsien). *At the height of the movement there were some 26,000 of these, but in the adjustments that ensued, they were increased in size and decreased in number to about 24,000. After 1961 they*

* "A Chinese Village in Early Communist Transition," *Chinese Communist Society: The Family and the Village* (Cambridge, Mass.: M.I.T. Press, 1965), pp. 254–259. By permission.

were reduced in size for the sake of efficiency and were increased in number to about 74,000. As part of these changes, commune functions were much reduced to over-all planning and coordination and certain types of investment. The "three levels" include the commune, "production brigades" (corresponding to the previous higher stage cooperatives), and primary roles performed by "production teams" which are village-based units.

. . . Turning our attention to the political aspect of the village community, we discern trends of similarly drastic change which began after the Communist assumption of power but became intensified by the collectivization process which united the political and economic powers in the hands of one ruling group on a systematic basis. When the entire village became one big farm under a centralized management controlled by the party machinery which also controlled the village government, the mono-center power structure imposed a routinized systematic economic grip over the political behavior of the peasantry in addition to military and political coercion. Aside from directly determining the income of the peasants, the co-operatives controlled local hydraulic projects that concerned not only agricultural production but also the safety of the community from inundation by floods, distributed welfare funds to families with insufficient labor power to earn the minimum income, lent money to needy cases in the form of loans or overdrawals in excess of one's share of the collective output of production, and by paying surtaxes supported local schools and a variety of public undertakings. When the real power of directing such an organization rested with the same party apparatus which governed the local political order, it strongly reduced the chance for any successful organized dissension to rise from the different economic levels and interest groups. The new situation effectively destroyed the old multi-center pattern of village power structure in which there was no centralized control or formal co-ordination over the local interest groups.

During the land reform period, there was obvious instability in the emerging mono-center power structure as observed in Nanching and as indicated in events happening in villages in many parts of the country. One of the leading reasons was the lack of indigenous party members to form a stable core for the new power structure. Since then, the political order in the countryside has gained general stability resulting from, among other reasons, the vast expansion of party membership. Repeated membership drives were vigorously launched after 1953. Such drives tapped two leading sources of membership among the peasants. One was the New Democratic Youth League, which was renamed the Communist Youth League in 1957 and has 23,000,000 members in that year. With plastic minds and inclination toward idealism and adventure as characteristic of youth, league members were standing candidates for selection as party members. Another source of prospective members were the poor peasants, especially those who had participated in the struggle against landlords during land reform, for they were the ones most dissatisfied with past conditions and looked to the new economic order for salvation. Fed from these two sources as well as from urban workers, the Communist Party attained a national membership of 12,000,000 in 1957. This phenomenal growth was likely to have produced local party members in every village community, including Nanching, and contributed to the stabilization of the new political order.

We have previously observed the replacement of the semiautonomous village community with a functional and structural integration of the village into the national political order. The vastly expanded membership of 12,000,000 in the Communist Party and 23,000,000 in the Youth League, in addition to some 1,500,-000 officials in government services, further reflects an intensified change in structural relationship between the village and the national system of government.

In surveying the change in the relationship between the village and the national political order, it is relevant to consider the fact that the party and league members are functionally comparable to the traditional gentry in the sense that both Communist membership and the gentry have a national political consciousness believing in a single ideology, both are intimately related to the national bureaucracy, and both serve as the extended arm of the formal national political power. But the two differ markedly in numerical size and in organizational strength.

In the second half of the nineteenth century, there were about 1,500,000 members in the gentry group in China, giving a statistical average of 2.14 per cent of the population. This gentry group, plus the bureaucracy which filled the some 40,000 official positions in the entire empire, constituted the ruling class for the vast country. Organizationally, the gentry had its local literary societies, fraternal bodies and supporting kinship systems, but as a ruling group, it had no systematic structure integrating the individual members for collective operation on either local or national levels. The small size and the lack of broad organization of the gentry were limiting factors in any effective and close integration between the national system of government and the innumerable village communities throughout the land. During the Republican period, the bureaucracy grew somewhat, but the number of educated rural leaders with national political consciousness shrank, and the integration of the village to the state was no closer than in the imperial times.

In contrast to this, the 12,000,000 members of the Communist Party and the 23,000,000 members of the Youth League add up to a total of 35,000,000. This is 5.83 per cent of 600,000,000, the 1957 Communist figure of China's total population, as compared with 2.14 per cent of gentry in the population of the last century. In addition, the 1,500,000 Communist officials represent an immeasurably larger bureaucracy than the 40,000 official positions in nineteenth-century China. The numerical growth of the Communist ruling group is apparent. Both the Communist Party and the Youth League, as well as the large number of popular organizations under their control, are rigidly structured into a formal system for collective action. It is thus easy to see the relation of the expansion and organization of the Communist political leadership to the closer integration of the village community with the state.

With closer integration of the village community to the state, the Communist political power was being felt by the villagers more intimately than under any previous national political power. With the drastic reduction of local autonomy, the individual freedom of the peasants has been visibly curtailed in many ways. But individual political freedom has not been an outstanding demand among the peasants. To them, the struggle for economic security has been more significant than a quest for political freedom in the Western sense of the term, which has been lacking in their group-minded tradition. It is the problem of adequately feeding the peasants rather than the granting of individual freedom that will determine the stability of the new political order. In this lies the strategic importance of the success or failure of agricultural collectivization.

The economic and political upheavals deeply affected the class structure in the village community through alteration of the economic levels of a sizable proportion of the peasantry. Land reform and collectivization were two forces from the Communist revolution that had the most potent impact on the village community, and both forces had a leveling influence on the old rural class structure. Under the policy of general equalization of land ownership, land reform eliminated the economic status of the whole top class, the landlords and a part of the rich peasants. Most of the landlords were reduced to the poor-peasant status, and some even lost their lives in the struggle. In the few years that followed, a small group of new rich peasants rose from the former rank of poor peasants. They were industrious efficient farmers, after the land reform gave them the principal means of production land. Therefore, in the post–land-reform village, the rural class structure had rich, middle and poor peasants as before the land reform, but without the landlords and those rich peasants who rented out a substantial amount of land.

With collectivization, the economic status of the rich peasants was depressed through the pooling of their land and major equipment into the co-operative and

TABLE 1

CLASSES	*HOUSEHOLDS*		*PERSONS*		*1956 NET INCOME (yuan)*	
	Number	Percentage	Number	Percentage	Per Household	Per Capita
Total	*422*	*100.0*	*1,578*	*100.0*	353.1	94.4
Poor peasants	68	16.0	193	12.2	218.3	76.8
Lower-middle peasants	*181*	*43.0*	*621*	*39.4*		
new	59	14.1	209	13.2	291.7	82.3
old	122	28.9	412	26.2	337.0	99.8
Upper-middle peasants	*164*	*39.0*	*734*	*46.5*		
new	32	7.6	142	9.0	436.0	98.2
old	139	31.4	592	37.5	455.9	101.8
Others	9	2.0	30	1.9	184.1	55.2

the abolition of their efficient independent farm organization. As a consequence, there were only poor and middle peasants in the co-operatives that now embraced 97 per cent of the nation's peasant households. A glimpse of this new pattern of class structure may be had by re-examining the case of two co-operatives in Haiyen county of Chekiang Province, mentioned in the last chapter. Table 1 shows the class distribution of the members of these two co-operatives.

Any attempt to analyze this sample of class structure is limited by two facts: that the locality represents one of the richest in rural China, and that no standard of income is provided in the classification of the peasants. That the locality is unusually rich may put the percentage of poor peasants lower than that which may be found in other sections of the country; there is no comparable data to check against this possible distortion. However, we can partly overcome the second limitation by taking the lower-middle peasant's annual income of roughly 300 yuan per household or 85 yuan per capita as the absolute minimum for subsistence in this locality—a minimum that leaves a very small margin for comfort or savings against sicknesses, births, deaths, or a poor crop. In the table, the small group of "others" may be merged with the "poor peasants" who were without sufficient food or clothing.

With this in mind, we may say that 46.5 per cent of the collectivized peasantry in this sample had the status of upper-middle peasants, who had an annual surplus of roughly 100 to 150 yuan per household or 10 to 15 yuan per capita for small items of comfort or for meeting crises. Life on this scale may be considered satisfactory in rural China. The rest of the peasants in this sample, 61.0 per cent of the households and 53.5 per cent of the population, were in a range from tolerable living to insecure subsistence. With the status of landlords and rich peasants eliminated, what distinguishes this class structure from the pre-Communist one is that the social distance between the well-off and the poor has been considerably reduced. The leveling influence of collectivization has produced a relatively egalitarian pattern of economic status.

This sample also provides limited data for analysing the vital problem of class mobility under the violent impact of the revolution. The figures show that the turbulent upheavals left a large proportion of the peasants, 60.3 per cent of the households and 63.7 per cent of the population, in their old middle-peasant status. The revolutionary process also brought 21.7 per cent of the households and 22.2 per cent of the population in this sample into the new status of middle peasants. For the poor and the destitute, comprising 18.0 per cent of the households and 14.1 per cent of the population, no indication is given as to whether they were old or new.

There is no information on the origin of the group of new middle peasants. Being in a middle position, they could either have risen from the poor peasants or been reduced from the status of rich peasants. Circumstantial evidence strongly suggests that this new group represented for the most part an upward mobility from the bottom. Rich peasants in pre-collectivization days usually constituted a small percentage of the total village population, and thus could not supply so many candidates for the new group of middle peasants in a downward movement. On the other hand, the pre-Communist stratum of poor peasants was large, much larger than the 16.0 per cent of the households and 12.2 per cent of the population as represented in the sample. Thus numerically they could supply candidates for the group of new middle peasants. Furthermore, the newcomers constituted 38.5 per cent of the lower but only 19.3 per cent of the upper middle peasants, suggesting the characteristic process of step-by-step rise from the bottom. On this assumption, keeping in mind that a few newcomers might have come down from the rich peasants, we may say that some 20 per cent of the village population made their way up to middle-peasant status, while 63.7 per cent successfully cushioned the revolutionary shock and held their old economic status. Many households of orphans and widows which formerly might have been among the middle peasants now sank to the status of the poor and destitute through loss of land to the cooperatives without remuneration and by lacking sufficient "labor power" to draw a middle peasant's share from the collective income. Many former landlords were also depressed into the class of poor and destitute in the downward class movement.

Class mobility of considerable proportion was thus a part of the structural change in the village community. The leading cause in the downward mobility was the abolition of property ownership as a major source of income. The factors in upward mobility were more complicated. A large family with an abundance of "labor power," together with other labor factors such as skill and diligence, could certainly enhance their income and class status. Government scholarships and the many free training classes opened the door of education wider than before as a channel of self-advancement for the common peasant. A new channel of status improvement were the many new organizations, including the co-operative farm, the women's association, the peasants' association, and the Youth League, which supplied a relatively free opportunity for the attainment of local leadership and power for the ambitious and capable who were willing to accept the Communist way of life. The rise in power and prestige of the new elite generally brought them improvement of economic position.

Closer integration of the village with the region and the state and operation of the large collectivized farm required literacy and many types of modern knowledge on the part of local leaders. This new requirement tended to place the institution of formal education in a role of increased importance in the institutional framework of the village community, for both literacy and modern knowledge are transmitted not informally at home and in the neighborhood but formally in the classroom. This institutional change was being effected by many Communist educational measures such as the vigorous campaign to eliminate illiteracy among peasants, increased state subsidy for local schools, granting of large numbers of scholarships to the politically loyal and socially deserving, operation of innumerable short-term training courses for political and economic purposes; all these would compel a change in the relative role of formal education which had only limited significance for the common peasant in the pre-Communist village.

3 • MAO TSE-TUNG: *Antagonistic and Non-Antagonistic Contradictions in Relation to the People's Democratic Dictatorship* *

This excerpt is from the famous secret speech made by Chairman Mao to the enlarged Eleventh Session of the Supreme State Conference on February 27, 1957. Actually that speech was revised, and an important section—probably including the portion located in Section Five on Chinese political processes—was added before publication on June 18, 1957. The Supreme State Conference has met infrequently, mainly during times of crisis. The occasion for this speech was the launching of the "hundred flowers" campaign (see also pp. 27 and 90) which soon backfired. Reading No. 22 comprises what are probably Mao's afterthoughts defining the limits within which criticism would be permissible.

Here, where essays or documents illustrate forces and conditions shaping politics, this part of Mao's essay On the Correct Handling of Contradictions Among the People *admits that contradictions do continue, even within Chinese society. There is not only realism in this observation but also the Hegelian-Marxist dialectical analysis. The revolution is seen as destined to move by wave-motions and by confrontations and new syntheses until it comes to rest in a new harmony—the utopian classless communism.*

* *On the Correct Handling of Contradictions Among the People,* 3rd printing (Peking: Foreign Languages Press, 1959), pp. 7, 9–19, 22–23, 25–27.

Our general subject is the correct handling of contradictions among the people. For convenience' sake, let us discuss it under twelve sub-headings. Although reference will be made to contradictions between ourselves and our enemies, this discussion will center mainly on contradictions among the people.

1. *Two Different Types of Contradictions*

. . . Unification of the country, unity of the people and unity among our various nationalities—these are the basic guarantees for the sure triumph of our cause. However, this does not mean that there are no longer any contradictions in our society. . . .

The contradictions between ourselves and our enemies are antagonistic ones. Within the ranks of the people, contradictions among the working people are non-antagonistic, while those between the exploiters and the exploited classes have, apart from their antagonistic aspect, a non-antagonistic aspect. Contradictions among the people have always existed. But their content differs in each period of the revolution and during the building of socialism. In the conditions existing in China today what we call contradictions among the people include the following: contradictions within the working class, contradictions within the peasantry, contradictions within the intelligentsia, contradictions between the working class and the peasantry, contradictions between the working class and peasantry on the one hand and the intelligentsia on the other, contradictions between the working class and other sections of the working people on the one hand and the national bourgeoisie on the other, contradictions within the national bourgeoisie, and so forth. Our people's government is a government that truly represents the interests of the people and serves the people, yet certain contradictions do exist between the government and the masses. These include contradictions between the interests of the state, collective interests and individual interests; between democracy and centralism; between those in positions of leadership and the led, and contradictions arising from the bureaucratic practices of certain state functionaries in their relations with the masses. All these are contradictions among the people. Generally speaking, underlying the contradictions among the people is the basic identity of the interests of the people.

In our country, the contradiction between the working class and the national bourgeoisie is a contradiction among the people. The class struggle waged between the two is, by and large, a class struggle within the ranks of the people. This is because of the dual character of the national bourgeoisie in our country. In the years of the bourgeois-democratic revolution, there was a revolutionary side to their character; there was also a tendency to compromise with the enemy, this was the other side. In the period of the socialist revolution, exploitation of the working class to make profits is one side, while support of the Constitution and willingness to accept socialist transformation is the other. The national bourgeoisie differs from the imperialists, the landlords and the bureaucrat-capitalists. The contradiction between exploiter and exploited, which exists between the national bourgeoisie and the working class, is an antagonistic one. But, in the concrete conditions existing in China, such an antagonistic contradiction, if properly handled, can be transformed into a non-antagonistic one and resolved in a peaceful way. But if it is not properly handled, if, say, we do not follow a policy of uniting, criticizing and educating the national bourgeoisie, or if the national bourgeoisie does not accept this policy, then the contradiction between the working class and the national bourgeoisie can turn into an antagonistic contradiction as between ourselves and the enemy.

Since the contradictions between ourselves and the enemy and those among the people differ in nature, they must be solved in different ways. To put it briefly, the former is a matter of drawing a line between us and our enemies, while the latter is a matter of distinguishing between right and wrong. It is, of course, true that drawing a line between ourselves and our enemies is also a question of distinguishing between right and wrong. For example, the question as to who is right, we or the reactionaries at home and abroad—that is, the imperialists, the feudalists and bureaucrat-capitalists—is also a question of distinguishing between right and wrong, but it is different in nature from questions of right and wrong among the people.

Ours is a people's democratic dictatorship, led by the working class and based on the worker-peasant alliance. What is this dictatorship for? Its first function is to suppress the reactionary classes and elements and those exploiters in the country who range themselves against the socialist revolution, to suppress all those who try to wreck our socialist construction; that is to say, to solve the contradictions between ourselves and the enemy within the country. For instance, to arrest, try and sentence certain counter-revolutionaries, and for a specified period of time to deprive landlords and bureaucrat-capitalists of their right to vote and freedom of speech—all this comes within the scope of our dictatorship. To maintain law and order and safeguard the interests of the people, it is likewise necessary to exercise dictatorship over robbers, swindlers, murderers, arsonists, hooligans and other scoundrels who seriously disrupt social order.

The second function of this dictatorship is to protect our country from subversive activities and possible aggression by the external enemy. Should that happen, it is the task of this dictatorship to solve the external contradiction between ourselves and the enemy. The aim of this dictatorship is to protect all our people so that they can work in peace and build China into a socialist country with a modern industry, agriculture, science and culture.

Who is to exercise this dictatorship? Naturally it must be the working class and the entire people led by it. Dictatorship does not apply in the ranks of the people. The people cannot possibly exercise dictatorship over themselves; nor should one section of them oppress another section. Law-breaking elements among the people will be dealt with according to law, but this is different in principle from using the dictatorship to suppress enemies of the people. What applies among the people is democratic centralism. Our Constitution lays it down that citizens of the People's Republic of China enjoy freedom of speech, of the press, of assembly, of association, of procession, of demonstration, of religious belief and so on. Our Constitution also provides that organs of state must practise democratic centralism and must rely on the masses; that the personnel of organs of state must serve the people. Our socialist democracy is democracy in the widest sense, such as is not to be found in any capitalist country. Our dictatorship is known as the people's democratic dictatorship, led by the working class and based on the worker-peasant alliance. That is to say, democracy operates within the ranks of the people, while the working class, uniting with all those enjoying civil rights, the peasantry in the first place, enforces dictatorship over the reactionary classes and elements and all those who resist socialist transformation and oppose socialist construction. By civil rights, we mean, politically, freedom and democratic rights.

4 • Li Shu-li: *A Professor Speaks Out Against Controls During the "Hundred Flowers" Episode in 1957* *

After the revolts in Poland and Hungary in 1956, and after de-Stalinization had begun to raise crucial questions, Chairman Mao Tse-tung and the Communist party's Politburo evidently decided that the growing complaints against the party and its cadres should be allowed valves for escape. Not long after his secret speech inviting "the hundred flowers" to bloom and differing viewpoints to contend, a series of forums were fostered and critics like Professor Li Shu-li, quoted here, were encouraged to speak out. Those few weeks in April–May 1957 provided the only fully candid statements we have from Chinese who continued to live under the Communist dictatorship.

The resulting accusations were so severe and began to spread so rapidly that the party clamped down again in what was called a campaign of "rectification" of critics and party personnel who were acknowledged to need disciplining. Since then other promptings to voice criticisms have met with extreme caution; in the middle 1960's the satires of certain writers and artists have been oblique and veiled.

Refugees constitute another critical source of information. They are regularly interviewed and can speak freely (though some of them have relatives on the mainland to protect), but such people are often poorly educated and may be atypical or biased.

Li Shu-li [Professor, North-West University; Vice Chairman, Chinese Association for Promoting Democracy, Shensi Province]:

To be quite honest, old teachers like us are today scared stiff, due to the accumulated experience of the past few years. . . .

The remarks I have had the courage to make at this forum I would not dare to make when I am back at North-West University. There seems to be an invisible pressure which compels people to say nothing. Among the democratic parties, so far as I know, it has become very difficult to understand what the masses really think. Whenever we are out to gather people's reactions, the interviewee will either nod his head saying "Good! Good! Good!" or shake his head saying nothing. . . .

In our University there is a batch of so-called positive elements who make a point of eavesdropping on other people's conversations and jotting down points in their small notebooks, which will be used as evidence to "rectify" people in the future. The secretary of the Department of Economics is one of those men. Snooping around, he overheard a remark made by a certain professor. "One can't be too careful about what one says these days." During a campaign he seized upon this remark and made much of it. Was the professor wanting to stage a revolt, he asked. Some of the people in our University in their pursuit of Communist membership, for the sake of demonstrating their "Party" aptitude, toady to the

* *Kuang Ming Daily,* May 11, 1957. Quoted in Roderick MacFarquhar, *The Hundred Flowers Campaign and the Chinese Intellectuals* (New York: Frederick A. Praeger, 1960), p. 98. By permission.

Party and are full of adulation. They also make it their business to deal blows to the "backward" elements so as to create opportunities of showing their own "party" aptitude. . . .

. . . The attitude of certain leaders on the Party committee of North-West University towards the professors is extremely crude. For instance, attendance at the extra-curricular political school should be voluntary, but the Party committee member will insist on personally taking the roll-call and pointing out who have failed to turn up. . . .

5 • CHOU YANG: *The Tasks of Worker, Peasant, and Soldier Writers* *

The culture of China was so sophisticated and strong that it long resisted transformation and ultimately bowed only to drastic revolution. Such a legacy has caused the Communists to be sensitive to currents of thought and expression among the nation's intellectuals. Especially during this transitional generation, when bourgeois tendencies persist among many of the intelligentsia, the party has shown preference to youth from peasant and working class backgrounds in recruiting for educational opportunities.

There is a great thirst for learning, even though it is impregnated with politicism and propaganda. These typical qualities are evident in the following selections from a speech by the "czar" in charge of literary and artistic expression. Chou Yang, the Deputy Director of the Propaganda Department in the party's secretariat, under the Central Committee, was speaking to the All-China Conference of Young Activists in Spare-Time Creative Writing. It met in Peking late in 1965.

In keeping with Mao's concept of revolutionary versatility—a proletarianized intelligentsia and an educated proletariat—there has been much stress on allied work and study. This speech is an example of guidelines for youthful expression.

Within less than a year, and despite several powerful talks in which Chou had been quite orthodox and militant, he was accused of trying to protect writers and artists who were seeking "fewer clichés and more realism." He was removed from his post and was denounced by publicists and other members of the Mao-Lin faction. Mao Tse-tung, the aging Chairman of the CCP, is an extremely idealistic socialist who has disapproved of growing specialization, professionalism, and bureaucratism in the party and government. Moreover, he deplores the compromising of socialism and the partial retreats from the communes and industrializing emphases made after failure of the "Great Leap Forward." By 1965–66, with the support of the more radical faction, including Minister of Defense Lin Piao, who was elevated to second place in the party hierarchy, Mao launched an intensified, manifold campaign to revive revolutionary spirit and programs.

* *Peking Review,* No. 11 (March 11, 1966), pp. 12–17; complete text in *Chinese Literature,* No. 3 (1966).

This literary conference differs from all previous ones in that the participants are a new contingent on our literary front. You come from the masses of workers, peasants and soldiers. You can work as well as write; when you take up guns you are fighters, and when you take up pens you are fighters too. You are a production force, a combat force, and also a creative force. The appearance of such a force on our literary front is an event of unprecedented importance in the history of our literature.

You are new people who have grown up in the age of socialism, educated by the Party and the thinking of Mao Tse-tung, steeled in the class struggles and production struggles of the masses. The aim of your writing is clear: You write for the workers, peasants and soldiers, for the revolution. With strong class feeling you describe in your writing the new life, new struggles and new men and women of the working class, the peasantry and the army. To you, writing is a kind of battle, a battle to win ideological positions.

Some of your works, both as regards ideological content and artistic form, have reached a fairly high standard achieved by few of our writers in the past. Of course, your achievement is not confined to your writings. What is even more important is that by conducting spare-time cultural activities on a large scale among the masses in factories, villages and army units, by telling revolutionary stories, singing new songs, putting on new plays, and fighting the backward old culture to serve contemporary politics and production, you have really popularized socialist art and literature among the workers, peasants and soldiers, and occupied strategic positions among them. In this way you have really turned our art and literature into a strong fighting front with workers, peasants and soldiers participating in it. You have infused fresh blood and revolutionary spirit into our writing and into the cultural life of China's millions. This is a fresh victory on the literary and art front, a victory for the socialist cultural revolution, a victory for Mao Tse-tung's line on art and literature.

There are various kinds of art and literature in the world today, progressive and reactionary. The art and literature which serve imperialism and capitalism are reactionary, decadent and moribund, a poison to corrupt men's minds. Modern revisionist art and literature have degenerated to the point where they ape the bourgeois art and literature of the West. While still posing as socialist, in fact they oppose socialism and the people, and are a turncoat art and literature. They slander the revolution, revolutionary wars and proletarian dictatorship, preach bourgeois humanism, pacifism, fear of nuclear weapons and the philosophy of "survival at any price," along with all kinds of decadent bourgeois ideas and the shameless bourgeois way of life. Art and literature of this sort have become instruments for the imperialists to engage in ideological subversion in the socialist countries, to prepare the way for the restoration of capitalism.

Our art and literature are diametrically opposed to those of imperialism and revisionism. They inspire our people to go forward all the time, to carry on the revolution continuously. They arm the people with socialist and communist ideas, with ideas of the class struggle and the people's war, and with proletarian internationalism. As Comrade Mao Tse-tung once said, they are "powerful weapons for uniting and educating the people and for attacking and destroying the enemy." . . .

The Struggle on the Literary and Art Front, and the New Situation in the Cultural Revolution

After the establishment of the People's Republic of China, literary and art workers in our country have had five great debates and criticisms in connection with whether we should carry out the proletarian line or bourgeois line in literature and art.

There are two main reasons for the frequency and fierceness of these struggles on the literary and art front. In the first place, they are an objective reflection of the domestic and international class struggle, which is inevitable. Art and literature are extremely sensitive organs of the class struggle. It is bound to find reflection in them, and indeed is often first reflected here. Art and literature are like antennae which instantly sense each movement by any class. Every time the situation in the class struggle changes, every time the working class meets with difficulties, every time the working class carries out self-criticism, the bourgeoisie will seize the chance to attack. And often the attack is first launched in the literary and art field, since this is the most sensitive field and the weakest link. In the second place, the bourgeoisie still possesses certain advantages in the literary and art field; so they believe that they are still powerful enough to challenge the working class there. The great majority of intellectuals, including intellectuals who are Party members, have had a bourgeois education. They retain a good deal of what belongs to the bourgeoisie in their world outlook and literary and art outlook. When people do literary and art work, they can easily be contaminated by bourgeois ideas, by bourgeois concepts of fame and profit, especially if they cut themselves off from the workers, peasants and soldiers, from manual labour, from the actual struggle. Then it is even easier for them to be influenced by bourgeois ideas, to become enslaved by these ideas or act as their spokesmen.

It is evident then that the struggle on the literary and art front is inevitable. Unless we wage this struggle, our art and literature, our artists and writers, are liable to degenerate politically. Our economic base is socialist, our political system is proletarian dictatorship. If art and literature, which are part of the ideological superstructure, propagate bourgeois or revisionist ideas instead of working-class, socialist ideas, far from helping to consolidate the socialist economic base and proletarian dictatorship they will help to undermine them, paving the way and preparing men's minds for the restoration of capitalism.

By waging the struggle continuously on the literary and art front, not only can we avert or minimize the danger of revisionism in our art and literature, we can also greatly speed up the development of socialist art and literature. Our proletarian art and literature advance in the course of struggle. Criticism and struggle clear the way for their development. . . .

Write First and Foremost About Socialism, Write First and Foremost About Heroic Characters

. . . In creative writing the problem is mainly what to write about and how to write. Our literature today should: first, write first and foremost about socialism; secondly, write first and foremost about heroic characters.

The transition from the democratic to the socialist revolution involves two historical stages, two different eras. During these two stages our revolutionary, proletarian art and literature have had certain common features but certain differences too. One common feature is that the art and literature in both periods were created to serve the workers, peasants and soldiers and revolutionary politics, guided by proletarian and communist ideology. The difference is that in the stage of the democratic revolution the main task of our art and literature was to propagate the national democratic revolution and oppose imperialism, feudalism and bureaucrat capitalism; while in the stage of the socialist revolution their main task is to propagate the socialist revolution and socialist construction, oppose capitalism, and at the same time together with the revolutionary people of the world to oppose imperialism and revisionism. Because the economic basis of our society and the world situation have changed, there must necessarily be changes in the tasks and content of our art and literature too. In the stage of democratic revolution, our aim was to establish the politics, economy and culture of new democracy; and although these contained socialist elements, which were the decisive ones, the politics, economy and culture as a whole belonged to new democracy and not to socialism. After 1949 the situation changed. The proletariat won political power over the whole country. After the three great socialist transformations our whole economic base became socialist, which meant that our entire culture must also become socialist to correspond to the economic base. This is a fundamental change. Since the completion of the democratic revolution, the main contradiction within the country has become that between the proletariat and the bourgeoisie, between the road of socialism and the road of capitalism. The main task of socialist art and literature is to oppose capitalism. True, they must also oppose imperialism and feudalism, and from the world viewpoint opposing imperialism is still a most important task, yet at home our main task is to oppose capitalism. For quite a long time a number of our writers and artists lacked a clear understanding of the change in our art and literature during these two different historical stages. Today, to propagate socialism and oppose capitalism, to uphold proletarian ideology and eradicate bourgeois ideology are the foremost tasks of our entire ideological, literary and art front. . . .

Bringing Up a New Generation of Writers for Socialist Literature

. . . Special importance attaches to the problem of bringing up a new generation of workers in socialist art and literature. This is because:

First, these new artists and writers will succeed the older generation, but they will not take entirely the same road and may even have to take a fundamentally different road. We should inherit the revolutionary spirit of our many predecessors in revolutionary art and literature from the May Fourth Movement onwards. We should also respect and learn from the rich experience of the older generation of writers. But we cannot take it over wholesale; we must study and analyse it critically. You are living in a different age; you are living, working and fighting in the basic units of factories, rural communes and the army as new workers, peasants and soldiers of the socialist age; you have experience in productive labour and fighting. You have been brought up and educated from the very start by the Party and Mao Tse-tung's thinking. The great majority of you will never leave your work on the production front or in the basic units, but will continue to write and work at the same time, and this is fundamentally different from the older writers. So you will take a new road, one which makes you genuine revolutionaries and labourers, which will gradually lessen the difference between mental and manual labour and lead eventually to communism.

Secondly, this problem is important because the intellectuals, including those in the field of literature, art and science, are one of the chief targets of the imperialists and bourgeoisie, who are trying to win them away from the working class. In addition to attempting to overthrow the proletarian dictatorship by force, the class enemy is plotting hard to bring about a "peaceful evolution." This dastardly plot has already achieved results in the Soviet Union under the rule of the Khrushchev revisionist clique. Since the imperialists and the bourgeoisie have few illusions about our revolutionaries of the older generation, they have put their hope in our younger generation, especially in our young intellectuals. They hope you will change colour, hope that once you have knowledge you will despise the labouring people, cut yourself off from them and learn bourgeois way. . . .

The fundamental way to ensure that our literary and art workers do not degenerate politically lies in not cutting ourselves off from the workers, peasants and soldiers, not cutting ourselves off from labour—not just for the time being but for all time. The aim of our socialist cultural revolution is to make intellectuals who are at the same time labouring people, and workers and peasants who are at the same time intellectuals, to create the conditions for the gradual lessening of the difference between manual and mental labour until finally it is done away with altogether. Only then can we successfully build socialism and go on towards communism. We must therefore continue to carry out the system of cadres' participation in manual labour, and experiment further with the educational system of "part-work, part-study" and "part-farming, part-study." This is basic in constructing our country. Only in this way can we guarantee that our state will not change colour. Our young writers must always retain their revolutionary spirit, they must not lose their revolutionary colour. The most important way of ensuring this is by not cutting ourselves off from labour or from the workers, peasants and soldiers.

SECTION TWO

Political Institutions

6 • *Constitution of the People's Republic of China* *

Revolutionary fathers of the constitution which is still formally valid in mainland China do not generally regard such a basic law as necessarily destined for great longevity. Rather it was designed for the period of "building socialism." In 1967 there were rumors that the Mao-Lin radicals were considering drastic constitutional changes; if so, their intention was probably blunted by the need to compromise with opponents. The experiment with commune government in Peking and Shanghai has apparently aborted. China has had many constitutions since the republican revolution in 1911; another one, adopted in 1947, is formally effective in Nationalist-held Taiwan.

Only parts of the first chapter of the Communist-shaped constitution of 1954 are included here. These portions embody general principles and provide indications of major orientation. Other chapters are also worth reading. This constitution superseded the Organic Law of October 1, 1949, under which the central government and its agencies had been operating. The period of consolidating the new regime was largely over; the first Five-Year Plan had recently been started, and the "general line" had shifted from "new democracy" and an emphasis on the United Front with non-communist elements to "socialist construction," that is, the socialization of the socio-economy.

Prior to election of the first National People's Congress (NPC), which was to adopt this constitution, China's first modern census was taken in 1953, and elections on each lower level were conducted according to a new Electoral Law. Above the county jurisdiction "people's congresses" are indirectly elected from immediately subordinate levels. The first NPC had more than 1200 members who met in a vast new hall in the capital.

General Principles

ARTICLE 1. The People's Republic of China is a people's democratic state led by the working class and based on the alliance of workers and peasants.

ARTICLE 2. All power in the People's Republic of China belongs to the people.

* Chapter I, "General Principles," revised translation (Peking: Foreign Languages Press, 1961), pp. 9–10, 12–14. This constitution was adopted by the First National People's Congress, September 20, 1954.

The organs through which the people exercise power are the National People's Congress and the local people's congresses at various levels.

The National People's Congress, the local people's congresses and other organs of state practise democratic centralism.

ARTICLE 3. The People's Republic of China is a unitary multinational state.

All the nationalities are equal. Discrimination against or oppression of any nationality, and acts which undermine the unity of the nationalities, are prohibited.

All the nationalities have the freedom to use and develop their own spoken and written languages, and to preserve or reform their own customs and ways.

Regional autonomy applies in areas where a minority nationality live in a compact community. All the national autonomous areas are inseparable parts of the People's Republic of China.

ARTICLE 4. The People's Republic of China, by relying on the organs of state and the social forces, and through socialist industrialization and socialist transformation, ensures the gradual abolition of systems of exploitation and the building of a socialist society. . . .

ARTICLE 6. The state sector of the economy is the socialist sector owned by the whole people. It is the leading force in the national economy and the material basis on which the state carries out socialist transformation. The state ensures priority for the development of the state sector of the economy.

All mineral resources and waters, as well as forests, undeveloped land and other resources which the state owns by law, are the property of the whole people. . . .

ARTICLE 13. The state may, in the public interest, requisition by purchase, take over for use or nationalize both urban and rural land as well as other means of production on the conditions provided by law.

ARTICLE 14. The state prohibits the use of private property by any person to the detriment of the public interest.

ARTICLE 15. By economic planning, the state directs the growth and transformation of the national economy in order to bring about the constant increase of productive forces, thereby improving the material and cultural life of the people and consolidating the independence and security of the state.

ARTICLE 16. Work is a matter of honour for every citizen of the People's Republic of China who is capable of working. The state encourages the working enthusiasm and creativeness of citizens.

ARTICLE 17. All organs of state must rely on the masses of the people, constantly maintain close contact with them, heed their opinions and accept their supervision.

ARTICLE 18. All personnel of organs of state must be loyal to the system of people's democracy, observe the Constitution and the law and strive to serve the people.

ARTICLE 19. The People's Republic of China safeguards the system of people's democracy, suppresses all treasonable and counter-revolutionary activities and punishes all traitors and counter-revolutionaries.

The state deprives feudal landlords and bureaucrat-capitalists of political rights for a specific period of time according to law; at the same time it gives them a way to earn a living, in order to enable them to reform through labour and become citizens who earn their livelihood by their own labour.

ARTICLE 20. The armed forces of the People's Republic of China belong to the people; their duty is to safeguard the gains of the people's revolution and the achievements of national construction, and to defend the sovereignty, territorial integrity and security of the state.

7 • *Leading Party Members' Groups in Non-Party Organizations* *

In 1956, as the socialization and collectivization of agriculture, commerce, and industry were nearing completion, the Chinese Communist party supplanted its constitution of 1945 with a new basic document. We quote here only the two articles which describe how party members in governmental organs are responsible to, and subject to discipline by, echeloned party committees. Of course, authoritarian and hegemonial parties infuse their members into key offices throughout the political system. Despite their responsibilities for surveillance and loyalty, such party functionaries sometimes experience tension between obligations to the party and to professional qualitative demands of their positions in civil government.

ARTICLE 59. In the leading body of a state organ or people's organization, where there are three or more Party members holding responsible posts, a leading Party members' group shall be formed. The tasks of such a group in the said organ or organization are: to assume the responsibility of carrying out Party policy and decisions, to fortify unity with non-Party cadres, to cement the ties with the masses, to strengthen Party and state discipline and to combat bureaucracy.

ARTICLE 60. The composition of a leading Party members' group shall be decided by a competent Party committee. The group has a secretary, and may, in case of need, also have a deputy secretary.

A leading Party members' group must in all matters accept the leadership of the competent Party committee.

8 • *On Strengthening Political and Ideological Work in the Army* †

Prolonged economic crisis followed the disastrous "Great Leap" and the drastic communization efforts of 1958–59. Material shortages became acute, and dissatisfaction began seriously to affect even some military units. The Defense Minister and some of his fellow officers had not only resented excessive use of army personnel on economic projects but also favored greater emphasis than did Mao's faction on military professionalism and technological upgrading. There is some evidence that such officers favored halting the polemic with the Soviet Union and repairing the alliance. They were defeated, and Lin Piao succeeded P'eng Teh-huai as Minister of Defense.

* Chapter IX, *The Constitution of the Communist Party of China* [1956] (Peking: Foreign Languages Press, 1956), p. 49.

† "Resolution Made by the Enlarged Meeting of the Military Affairs Commission of the Chinese Communist Party," Peking, October 20, 1960. Reprinted from J. Chester Cheng (ed.), *The Politics of the Chinese Red Army*, pp. 75, 77-82, with the permission of The Hoover Institution on War, Revolution, and Peace.

The party, which had steadily asserted its dominance over military forces according to the slogan "politics in command," must have been gravely concerned about these trends. The People's Liberation Army (PLA) was its ultimate defense and instrument for enforcing policies. The importance which the CCP has attached to military affairs is indicated by the special Military Affairs Commission kept separate from the party secretariat and attached to the Central Committee. In the fall of 1960, an enlarged meeting of this body adopted a lengthy resolution (a confidential but captured document) from which we have chosen significant passages. This called for what became a rigorous reindoctrination of military personnel in the familiar canons of Maoist thought emphasizing orthodox militancy, voluntarism (that is, reliance on ardent human will), and other concepts and practices developed during the epic guerrilla experience. Thus, the PLA was the first sector to undergo rather extensive "rectification" and so to be prepared for the role it was to play during 1966–67 in the "Great Proletarian Cultural Revolution."

III. Develop in All Workers the Three-Eight Working Style

A. Under the leadership of the Party and Comrade Mao Tse-tung, and through the long period of hard revolutionary struggle, our Army has developed an excellent working style. This working style was summarized by Comrade Mao Tse-tung in three sentences and eight characters, namely: Firmly maintain the correct political direction; preserve a hardy and plain style; carry on a flexible and mobile system of strategy and tactics. Then to fortify the above, he brought out eight characters [four groups of two characters each] which may be rendered as unity, intensiveness, seriousness and agility. These are called for short the "three-eight working style." This doctrine is an important component of Mao Tse-tung's military thought, a concentrated expression of the essence of the People's Army, a criterion of our Armys' training, operation and action, and an important means of unifying ourselves and defeating the enemies. . . . Such a working style gives enormous spiritual strength to our Army and once transformed into the masses' self-conscious action, will become a mighty material force. With such an excellent working style, we are able in time of war to overwhelm all enemies; to resist attacks without suffering defeat; to prolong a war without suffering deterioration; to capture the enemy's position in offense; to consolidate our position in defense; and to achieve a big victory at a small price. . . .

B. The methods to cultivate the three-eight working style:

1. By repeated education and the development of greater self-consciouness. The formation of the three-eight working style is chiefly dependent upon political and ideological education and the development of the self-consciousness of the masses. The process of developing the three-eight working style is the process of enhancing the proletariat and exterminating the bourgeoisie, of promoting class awareness. . . .

2. Cadres will take the lead and make themselves examples for others to follow. . . .

3. Constant development and practical training. . . . In the course of executing combat duties, military training and conducting daily life, we must frequently take

the lead, examine the situation, raise our requirements, tighten our control, and take hold of the practice and development of the three-eight working style. . . .

IV, A, 6. Decadent liberalism. Some cadres do not expose, reflect, check or struggle with bad tendencies, bad persons, and bad matters. They do not keep their stand firmly or remain steadfast in matters relating to principles. In matters involving no principles, however, they are unyielding and often indulge in unprincipled disputes. . . .

B. Methods of overcoming these difficulties:

1. We must educate all cadres to know the long-range nature, the intensity, and the complexity of the class struggle within and without the country so that they will be able to hold their stand in storms, to distinguish right from wrong, and to be eternally loyal to the Communist enterprise, the Party, the motherland and the people, the lines of the leader of the Party and the people, Comrade Mao Tse-tung. We must cause them to be always concerned about politics, the great events of the nation, the great events of the Party and the people, as well as public enterprises, and to give consideration to the people, Socialism, and Communism. Individual interest must be subordinate to collective interest, partial interest to the whole interest, and temporary interest to long-term interest. We must always maintain sharp vigilance over imperialism and have a strong will to fight. We should always preserve our political youthfulness, follow our revolutionary steps, and never stop halfway. . . .

4. All reactionary ideas should be resolutely checked and eliminated. Reading yellow journalism and reactionary literature and receiving broadcasting from enemy countries should be strictly prohibited. Those persons who are politically impure must be carefully examined and their cases examined and judged. Bad elements and counterrevolutionaries must be liquidated.

5. It should be made clear to Party organizations at all levels that it is very important for them to control their cadres. All Party cadres (including senior Party cadres) should participate in the Party's organizational life, obey the Party's organizational control, and accept the supervision of Party organizations. The role of the Party's supervisory committees should be brought into full play so that they can really become helpful to Party committees in opposing bad tendencies and preserving discipline.

V. Placing the Emphasis of Ideological Work on the Mastery of Living Ideology

B. Methods of improvement:

1. . . . Party lines, programs and policies as well as Comrade Mao Tse-tung's instructions must be transmitted at the proper time. The study of important editorials and articles in Party newspapers must be organized. Leadership cadres should periodically make reports to the Army units on current affairs and policies. Such a practice ought to be developed into a system and sustained. Investigation should be frequently made to find out the ideological effects on Army units in the execution of the directives of the Central Authorities and the Military Affairs Commission in order to control their ideological activity. The method of class analysis should be applied to conduct experimental surveys, and the essential problems of ideology ought to be firmly grasped. We must prescribe the right

medicine to cure the disease and concentrate our strength on fighting a successful ideological war. . . .

3. The method of conducting living ideological teaching:

a) We should combine political movements with regular education, simultaneously giving attention to the movements and to education. We should not pay attention to ideological problems only when the movements arrive, and afterwards forget about them. The conduct of ideological work should be carried out continuously and without interruption.

b) The political organs at the divisional level and above should from time to time write some lectures and slogans to be recited at the time of roll call according to the state of conditions and the nature of duties in their respective units; or they can call preparatory meetings to arrange programs for practical ideological education.

c) We should strengthen our viewpoints about the masses and labor, promote our class awareness, advance the level of our theoretical and policy understanding, broaden our vistas, and enrich our intelligence through such activities as participating in state construction and mass movements, inspection and interview, social investigation, productive labor, and rescue work.

d) We should extensively and flexibly make use of such means as blooming, contending, debating, arguing, and big-character newspapers for posting on bulletin boards. We should also rely on facts, talk to others in terms of reason and justice, and firmly retain the principle of convincing people with reason.

e) The form of our political education must be varied. Besides classroom lectures, collective training, and discussion meetings, we should also adopt such forms as inviting leaders to give lectures; recalling accidents of our past as compared with the present; individual interviews; calling slogans at the time of reveille and retreat; issuing wall bulletins and big-character newspapers; organizing lecture meetings, exhibitions, and evening parties; and inviting local cadres and masses to make reports.

f) All literary and art work as well as cultural activity in Army units, such as the plays of the cultural work troupe, amateur literary activities, motion pictures, broadcasting, arts, and library work, should serve the purpose of enhancing the proletariat and exterminating the bourgeoisie, of consolidating and promoting combat strength, in combination with the state of ideological conditions and the nature of duties in the Army units. . . .

VI. To Develop Party Branches as Strong Bulwarks for Combat

A. The Company is a primary unit for the execution of combat, training and all other duties. Political work must therefore take root in the Company, and the basic problem of strengthening the work in the Company lies in the leadership of the Party branch in the central rôle in the Company. . . .

1. The failure of some Party branches to develop collective leadership. A few cadres placed themselves above the collective leadership of their Party branches and often made important decisions by themselves. . . .

3. The shortage of Party members. At present, about one third of the companies

(primary units) have no Party branch committees; many platoons have no Party cells; and quite a few small technical units have no Party members at all. . . .

5. The frequent misuse of time intended for observing the Party Day so that very few lectures on the Party were given, and Party organizational life was not strong or robust.

B. Measures for improvement:

1. To strengthen the collective leadership of the Party branch committee. All major problems in the company, including the arrangement, examination and summing up of those important operations assigned to it by Party resolutions and orders from above, the investigation of the cadres' ideological activity, the promotion and installation of cadres, the question of reward and punishment, etc., should be discussed and then decided by the Party branch committee. The secretary of the branch committee should rely on his own exemplary behavior to form the nucleus of the branch's collective leadership by faithfully executing Party policies, strictly observing Party discipline, and intimately associating himself with the masses. The Party branch should from time to time study the ideological activity of cadres and soldiers, conduct a complete investigation of their thoughts, and adopt active measurements to resolve their ideological and practical problems through the activity of Party members and activists. . . .

3. To develop actively the work of recruiting Party members so that the company will always be able to preserve a group of robust Party members. The recruiting of Party members first of all requires that we direct our attention to the political quality of the candidates. We must carefully observe and educate them. It is not until they have fully met our requirements that we can accept them as Party members. . . .

4. To make Party life robust and strong. The assembly of the Party branch should really become the highest leading organ of the company. Generally the assembly's agenda should include the following items: transmission, arrangement and execution of the decisions and directives from the Party and the superiors; hearing and discussing the work reports of the Party branch committee, the commander of the company and its political director; discussing the general situation and the state of political and ideological conditions within the company; developing criticism and making proposals. Each Party member should from time to time report to the Party branch about his own ideological and operational conditions and report the sentiments and demands of the masses. Those leading Party members who have shortcomings or have committed mistakes should be examined and criticized within the Party so as to place cadres under the strict control of the Party.

5. To make each Party member a model to serve as an example for the masses to follow. Politically, ideologically, and in his action, each Party member should set a pattern of behavior as an example for the masses to follow. He should act like this: to be in front of the masses in case of an attack and at the rear of the masses in the case of a retreat; there should be no tears when he is seriously wounded and he should remain in the firing line when lightly wounded; to be ahead of the masses when suffering hardship and behind the masses when enjoying pleasures; to do more work without regard to reward; to go ahead in the face of difficulties and to yield in the case of glories; to learn from the advanced and to give assistance to the backward; to give comfort to other persons and to keep

difficulties for himself; to be concerned with the masses' political progress and their hardships in life; to learn humbly from the masses; to become bosom friends with the masses; to lead the masses to accomplish all tasks. On the basis of different duties, the Party branch should present concrete requirements to Party members in the display of their roles as examples to the masses, and frequently examine and evaluate their achievements.

9 • Lêng Shao-chuan: *Post-Constitutional Development of "People's Justice" in China* *

Revolutionary China under the CCP dictatorship has been slow to develop and codify a new system of laws and jurisprudence. This has been criticized both internally and abroad. What at first surprises many Western observers is the use of laws and legal processes for education, propaganda, warning, and intimidation, as well as for their more accustomed purposes.

Professor Lêng Shao-chuan, the author of this article, is Professor of Government and Foreign Affairs at the University of Virginia and Research Associate of Duke University's World Rule of Law Center. He is a native of Szechwan Province and was educated in China before Communist seizure of national control.

The adoption of the Constitution in 1954 inaugurated a new period in the People's Republic of China. Having sufficiently consolidated their power, the Communists took a significant step to launch China into the stage of socialist transformation and construction. During the years immediately following the promulgation of the Constitution, Communist China appeared to be moving in the direction of a stable legal order and a strong judiciary. This trend, however, suffered a serious setback in mid-1957 when a nation-wide drive against the Rightists was staged. In this article we shall examine the development of "people's justice" from 1954 to the present. Special attention will be given to the legal debates carried on between non-Communist jurists and official spokesmen during the "Blooming and Contending" and Anti-Rightist Movements.

Move Toward Legal Stability, 1954–1957

In an effort to generate popular support and enthusiasm for the Constitution, the Communist regime employed an extensive propaganda campaign in 1954 to mobilize the masses to participate in the discussion of the draft document before its official adoption. Bearing a striking resemblance to the 1936 Constitution of the U.S.S.R., the Chinese Constitution that was promulgated on September 20, 1954 signified a shift from the arbitrary and repressive processes of the "people's tribunals" to a more orderly development in the legal life of the country. A comprehensive bill of rights, for example, was contained in Chapter III of the Constitution. Among other things, it guaranteed equality before the law, freedom of

* *Journal of the International Commission of Jurists* (Geneva, Switzerland), Vol. VI, No. 1 (Summer 1965), pp. 103–111, 119–124, 126–128. By permission.

speech, of the press, of association, of demonstration, and of religion, as well as the right to work, to leisure, to education, and to social assistance. Protection against arbitrary arrest was specifically insured by Article 89, which reads: "Freedom of the person of citizens of the People's Republic of China is inviolable. No citizen may be arrested except by decision of a people's court or with the sanction of a people's procuratorate." Based on this article, the Regulations on Arrest and Detention were promulgated in December 1954 to provide further safeguards in the form of concrete and detailed procedures.

The Constitution, along with the Organic Laws of the People's Courts and the People's Procuratorates (September 21, 1954), also gave the judicial system in Communist China a permanent structure. Under the National People's Congress and its standing Committee, two separate but interlocking judicial hierarchies were set up. The "people's courts," headed by the Supreme People's Court, were given the sole authority to administer justice; the "people's procuratorates", culminating in the Supreme People's Procuratorate, were to exercise the supervisory

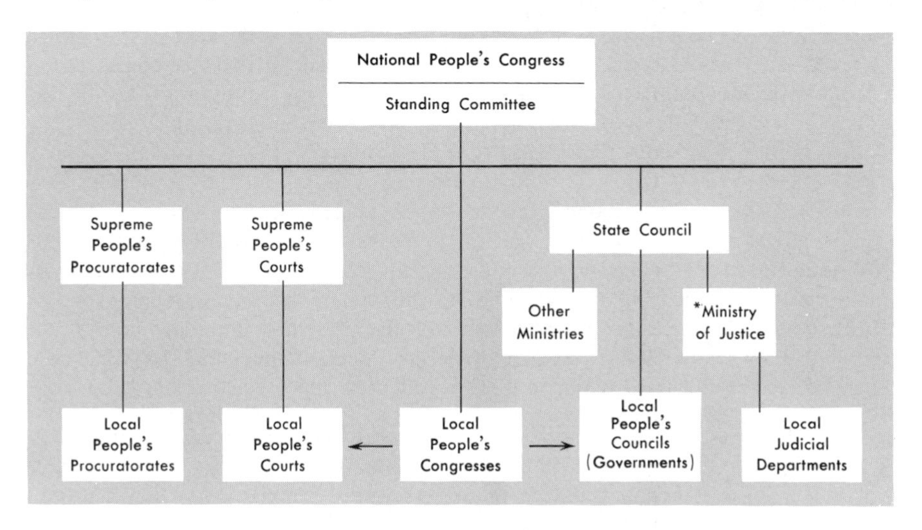

* Abolished in May 1958

Judicial Structure of Communist China

power over the execution of the law. In addition, there were within the State Council certain executive departments, such as the Ministries of Justice, Supervision, Public Security, and Internal Affairs, charged with responsibilities relative to the maintenance of law and order. Until its abolition in 1959, the Ministry of Justice and the judicial departments at local levels handled matters pertaining to the staff and internal administration of the courts.

A number of democratic features of the new judicial system were introduced by both the Constitution and the Organic Law of the People's Courts. These included the right of legal defence, the institution of People's Assessors, and the principles of public (open) trials and withdrawal of judges. Probably more significant was the fact that for the first time the Chinese Communists seemed to accept in a limited form the concept of judicial independence. With identical tones, Article 78 of the Constitution and Article 4 of the Organic Laws stipulated: "In administering justice the People's Courts are independent, subject only to the law."

Article 80 of the Constitution stated that the courts should be responsible to the "people's congresses" at corresponding levels and should report to them. This was in clear contrast with the previous laws which required the subordination of the courts to the leadership of the "people's governments." In other words, under the new system the courts were granted greater freedom in exercising their authority, with no interference from the local executive organs. To be sure they were still subject to other types of control and their independence had to be a qualified one. Writing on this subject, Communist spokesmen were quick to point out that in administering justice the "people's courts" not only must obey the law but must follow the guidance of the party, submit to the control of the people, and accept the supervision of the higher courts and the procuratorates.

Following the promulgation of the Constitution and the Organic Law of the People's Courts, the Communist authorities proceeded to carry out the projected changes in judicial organizations and procedures. At the Judicial Seminar of November 1954 and in a joint directive on December 7, 1954, the Supreme People's Court and the Ministry of Justice repeatedly call upon judicial workers throughout the country to study and implement the Organic Law of the courts. During the years between 1954 and 1957, steady growth and "democratization" of the judicial system had been reported by Shih Liang, Minister of Justice, and Tung Pi-wu, president of the Supreme Court. As of 1957, there existed in Communist China more than 2,700 "people's courts." The number of "people's assessors" increased from 127,250 in 1955 to 246,500 in 1957. Starting from scratch, the number of "people's lawyers" also reached 2,100 by 1957.

The efforts made by the Peking regime to strengthen the judicial system reflected the importance it attached to the courts as useful instruments for stabilizing the new order and ensuring the socialist transformation of the national economy. In their joint directive of December 1954 on the study and implementation of the Organic Law of People's Courts, the Supreme People's Court and the Ministry of Justice clearly defined the major task of the judiciary:

> The enforcement of dictatorship and the protection of democracy are the two inseparable aspects of the basic mission of the people's courts. The work of the judiciary must be made to serve the political mission of the State. During the transitional period, the judiciary's general task is to safeguard the smooth development of social construction and the socialist transformation of the State. The people's courts must not only punish people but also educate them. They must carry out their proper functions to serve socialist construction and the central task of the State through the medium of judicial activities.[1]

In view of the above, small wonder that many of the cases handled by the judiciary were those involving economic construction and the counterrevolutionaries. According to incomplete figures, the "people's courts" of all levels dealt with 364,604 cases of such nature between January 1954 and May 1955 alone. Along with the procuratorial and public security organs, the courts were reported to have struck severe blows to counterrevolutionary and other criminal elements engaged in activities harmful to the programme of socialist construction and transformation. Just preceding the introduction of agricultural cooperativization, a new drive was launched by the Chinese Communists in July 1955 to liquidate the

[1] *Jen-min jih-pao,* December 11, 1954.

counterrevolutionaries. On July 30, in a resolution on the First Five-Year Plan, the Second Session of the National People's Congress called upon all state organs and the entire population to "heighten their revolutionary vigilance in order to uproot all counterrevolutionaries, open or under cover, and smash all subversive activities." Based on the traditional policy of "combining punishment with leniency," this new movement was carried out with great vigour and wide publicity. As a result, numerous counterrevolutionaries were exposed and arrested, and many others gave themselves up and confessed their guilt. In the Political Report of the Central Committee of the Chinese Communist Party on September 15, 1956, Liu Shao-ch'i praised the movement as a great success for breaking the back of the counterrevolutionaries. At the same time he urged the continuation of the fight against internal enemies within the framework of the law:

> Our public security organs, our procurator's offices and our courts must continue to wage a determined struggle against conterrevolutionaries and other criminals. But . . . this struggle must be conducted with strict observance of the law, and, in accordance with the new situation which obtains today, further steps must be taken to put the policy of leniency into practice. The Central Committee of the Party holds that, with the exception of a handful of criminals who have to be condemned to death in response to public indignation caused by their atrocious crimes, no offenders should be given the death penalty, and, while serving their terms of imprisonment, they should be accorded absolutely humane treatment. All cases involving the death penalty should be decided upon or sanctioned by the Supreme People's Court. In this way step by step we shall be able to achieve our aim of completely abolishing the death penalty, and this is all to the good of our socialist construction.[2]

It may be noted here that the question of observing the law was frequently referred to by Communist spokesmen during the years of 1954–1957. This actually reflected two opposite trends. One was the genuine move on the part of the Peking regime to establish socialist legality; the other the persistent tendency of government workers and party cadres to ignore laws and regulations. Some newspapers, for instance, reported the use by the courts of public notices, judgment-proclaiming meetings, and other propaganda devices to educate the people to obey the law and discipline. Others cited the punishment of law-breaking officials as a reminder that there was no exception to the observance of the laws by all citizens. An article in *Hsüeh-hsi* (Study) took the position that the Communist party members should be required to serve as a model for the Chinese people in obeying the law: "Party members are the vanguard of the proletarian class and have as their responsibilities the liberation of the working people, elimination of the classes, and establishment of a socialist society. As the Party is the leading force of national life, law-abiding has a special meaning for every Party member. . . . Failure to obey the law is to violate the Party constitution and the obligations of Party members. The Party demands all its members to obey the Party discipline and to set an example in observing the law. No exception can be made to anyone."

[2] *Eighth National Congress of the Communist Party of China,* Peking 1956, Vol. 1, pp. 83–84.

Probably more revealing were writings and reports by top judicial officials with reference to the observance of the law. In an article for *Cheng-fa yen-chiu* in 1956, Ma Hsi-wu of the Supreme People's Court pointed out that some judicial personnel openly violated the provisions of the Constitution and the Organic Law of the Courts by disregarding the legal rights of the accused in court proceedings. They even used illegal methods ranging from threats to corporal punishment to deprive the accused of the rights of defence and appeal. In his report to the Eighth National Congress of the Chinese Communist Party on September 19, 1956, Tung Pi-wu admitted as a serious problem the existence in China of a small number of Party members and government functionaries who did not pay attention to the legal system of the State. According to him, cases of violating the law and infringements of the people's democratic rights had been discovered in some places and departments. Accidents had occurred in factories and mines due to violations of the labour protection regulations; disputes had arisen from failure to fulfill contracts on the part of certain economic departments; proper legal procedures had not been fully observed by judicial organs; maltreatment of criminals had taken place in prisons and labour reform units. One major reason for these occurrences, Tung said, was the profound hatred in the party and among the masses for the old system of law, which tended to breed contempt for all legal systems. It was possible, he added, that this contempt was increased by the mass revolutionary movements that swept the country in the early period after liberation, because such movements did not entirely rely on laws. He also referred to the "petty bourgeois background" of the overwhelming majority of the Chinese people as another reason for the general contempt for the legal system. For the future, however, all such law-breaking tendencies must come to an end he stressed. As demanded by the Central Committee of the Party,

> all the laws must be strictly observed. No violations of the law should henceforth be permitted. Particularly all the judicial bodies should abide by the law more strictly. . . . We are opposed to all lawbreaking practices as represented by doing work not in accordance with the laws. In future any person who deliberately violates the law must be prosecuted even if he is in a high position and has rendered meritorious service to the state. As for those who are ignorant of the laws, we must not only teach them what the laws are but also educate them to abide by the laws. To demand everyone to do his work in accordance with the law is one of the chief methods to end the occurrence of violations of the laws of the state.[3]

Closely related to the question of observing the law was that of a complete legal system in Communist China. Although the Communists could boast in the mid-1950s a few important laws and regulations covering marriage, land reform, trade unions, agricultural producers' cooperatives, suppression of counter-revolution, penalties against corruption, etc., they nevertheless had to concede that "people's legality" still left something to be desired. One Chinese writer, for example, pointed out that the laws and decrees promulgated by the state were mainly in the form of provisional programmes and were not "well-developed" laws. Two other authors stated that there was much confusion in the Chinese legal system, resulting from the combination of vague terminology, conflicting

[3] For the text of Tung's speech on the legal system of China, see *New China News Agency*, Peking, September 20, 1956.

provisions, and uncertain procedures. Even Tung Pi-wu admitted in his report cited above that China was lacking in some urgently needed basic laws, such as a criminal code, a civil code, a law of procedure, a labour law, and a law of utilization of land. And many existing laws and regulations, he added, had to be revised in the light of changed political and economic conditions. The following passage from Liu Shao-chi's 1956 Political Report provided an official explanation for the absence of comprehensive codes and at the same time underlined the Peking regime's move to build up a complete legal system:

> During the period of revolutionary war and in the early days after the liberation of the country, in order to weed out the remnants of our enemies, to suppress the resistance of all counterrevolutionaries, to destroy the reactionary order and to establish revolutionary order, the only expedient thing to do was to draw up some temporary laws in the nature of general principles in accordance with the policy of the Party and the people's government. During this period, the chief aim of the struggle was to liberate the people from the reactionary rule and to free the productive forces of society from the bondage of old relations of production. The principal method of struggle was to lead the masses in direct action. Such laws in the nature of general principles were thus suited to the needs of the time. Now, however, the period of revolutionary storm and stress is past, new relations of production have been set up, and the aim of our struggle is changed into one of safeguarding the successful development of the productive forces of society. A corresponding change in the methods of struggle will consequently have to follow, and a complete legal system becomes an absolute necessity.[4]

Indeed, there were signs during 1956–1957 that certain fundamental codes were being prepared or ready for adoption. According to *Kuang-ming-jih-pao* on November 24, 1956, the Supreme People's Court had for some time taken steps to summarize the civil and criminal procedures of the "people's courts" at all levels. The draft summary had been sent to the Standing Committee of the National People's Congress for reference and to the Lower Courts for experimental purposes. The same source also reported that the Law Section of the Standing Committee of the NPC was about to complete a draft criminal code of 261 articles. On July 15, 1957, as reported by another source, the People's Congress authorized the Standing Committee to discuss and amend the draft criminal code in consultation with all concerned and then to have it published and put into effect on a trial basis. Writing in the June 1957 issue of *People's China* Shih Liang also stated that both the civil law and the law of procedure were actively taking shape. All this indicated that until the Anti-Rightist Movement got into full swing in late 1957 there had been noticeable efforts made by the Peking regime to build up a more stable and complete legal system despite the obvious gaps existing between juridical niceties and political facts in the Chinese mainland.

The Reversal in 1957

The period of 1956–57 in Communist China was one of relative political freedom and intellectual ferment, characterised by the official policy of "letting one hundred flowers bloom and one hundred schools contend." During this

[4] *Eighth National Congress of the Communist Party of China,* Vol. I, pp. 81–82.

period and especially in the spring of 1957, a good many liberal-minded jurists took advantage of the opportunity to criticise the government for the lack of basic laws and the defective administration of justice. Suggestions were made to restore certain legal concepts and judicial procedures of Western tradition.

Alarmed at the strong criticism evoked by the 'Blooming and Contending" Movement, the Peking Regime launched an Anti-Rightist Campaign in the summer of 1957 to counter-attack its outspoken critics. On the legal front this meant a serious setback for the development of a stable system of justice. In the course of the Campaign, those who had criticised the irregularities of "people's legality" were branded as "rightist" and their ideas as "anti-socialist" and "reactionary." . . .

Recent Development, 1958—The Present

While 1957 marked the official reversal of the trend toward legality, the years that followed were also not conducive to the development of the stable legal order in Communist China. During the period between early 1958 and the present, the Peking regime had been preoccupied with the problems of socialist construction ranging from the Big Leap Forward to the resulting economic failures and retrenchment. At the same time it has been engaged with vigour in ideological struggles against both the "rightist" and "revisionist" influences at home and on the international scene. In the context of this political climate, most of the new laws and regulations adopted have been mainly concerned with economic matters and the work of the judiciary has been primarily geared toward the repression of opposition and advancement of the interest of socialism.

One noticeable feature of Peking's policy during the period under discussion has been its repeated stress on absolute Party leadership in judicial work. At the Fourth National Judicial Work Conference in August 1958, the principle was reaffirmed that "the people's courts should be absolute in their submission to Party leadership, and there could not be the least negligence and vacillation. . . . Only in this way could court work be made to meet the change of situation as well as to implement concretely the lines and policies of the Party under the guidance of the correct lines." "Politics must assume command," and "obey the Party Committees" were also among the conclusions reached by the National Conference of Advanced Public Security, Procuratorial, and Judicial Workers, held in May of 1959. . . .

The pursuit of the mass line in judicial work has, too, been strongly emphasised by the Communist authorities since the beginning of 1958. Several major features of this policy may be noted in the following. (A) Under the direction of the mass line, the courts have been brought directly to the people, judicial procedures have been simplified, and justice has been carried out on the spot. This was particularly evident during the years of the Big Leap, when the "5 goes" (go to factories, go to mines, go to communes, go to streets, and go to markets) and the "3 on-the-spots" (investigation on-the-spot, mediate on the spot and try and sentence on the spot) became a standard practice for judicial workers to "improve the quality of their work" and to "create closer ties between the people's courts and the masses." In the province of Liaoning the "people's courts" reportedly tried and judged on the spot more than 80 per cent of the total number of cases handled from January to October 1959. Judicial personnel in Hopei province adopted during the Big Leap the slogan: "When cases come up at daytime, they shall be disposed of during the day; when cases come up at night, they shall be dealt with under lamplight; and if they cannot be settled in one day, then work shall be carried on continuously." A 1960 report from Honan province exalted the success of the mass line in elevating the legal outlook of the vast masses and in improving the quality of trial work. Not only were all kinds of civil and criminal cases handled with speed and accuracy, but some perplexing old cases were settled and the accumulation of cases was cleared up, so it reported.

(B) Another important aspect of the mass line is the integration of judicial work with productive labour. Since the start of the ill-fated Big Leap, judicial cadres have been sent to lower levels for labour training and for productive work in all forms. . . .

(C) As a part of the mass line style of judicial work, the Communists have put a premium on the use of mediation for resolving disputes and on the "integration of court trial with mass debate." Specific efforts have been made to encourage the masses to enter into "socialist patriotic pacts" with the professed purposes of promoting voluntary observance of law and social discipline, strengthening internal solidarity among the people, and maintaining socialist peace and order. Letters and personal visits to the authorities have also become important channels for the masses to make complaints and report wrongdoings. . . .

The courts being instruments of the People's Democratic Dictatorship, struggle against counterrevolutionaries has also continued to be a focal point of the judicial work during the period under discussion. Such a struggle was waged with special intensity in the 1958 campaigns for the Big Leap Forward and for the communization of agriculture. . . .

The Central Committee of the Chinese Communist Party pointed out in September 1962 that "throughout the historical period of proletarian revolution and proletarian dictatorship, throughout the historical period of transition from capitalism to communism, there is class struggle between the proletariat and the bourgeois and struggle between the socialist road and the capitalist road. . . This struggle is complicated, tortuous, with ups and downs and sometimes is very sharp." Following the same line, many newspaper editorials and journal articles were written in 1963 to play up the incessant class war during the socialist era. Typically, the Chinese people and various state organs were urged to maintain their vigilance in the face of the combined threat of foreign and domestic enemies. Abroad, they should wage the class struggle against the "imperialists, reactionaries, and modern revisionists of different countries who have raised a hue and cry in the grand anti-Chinese chorus"; at home, against "those landlords, rich peasants, and bourgeois rightists who have not reformed themselves and the remnant counterrevolutionaries who are still seeking the restoration of the feudalist rule in China."

Our discussion of the legal life in the post-1957 China would be incomplete without mentioning the fact that in the last few years the Peking regime has taken occasional steps to soften the prevalent rigidity of "people's justice" and to allow the return of some legal discussions among the juridical circles. One sign of this limited relaxation may be seen in the amnesty granted to the reformed "war criminals" and the removal of the "Rightist hat" from the reformed Rightists. . . .

More illustrative of Peking's limited retreat from the harshness of the Anti-Rightist and Big Leap Campaigns has been the reappearance of legal discussions in juridical circles. In the last few years legal forums have been held and textbooks and journal articles have been written on such subjects as "philosophy of law," "state and legal theories," "history of Chinese laws," etc. Reference again has been made to the implementation of the 1956 slogan "let a hundred flowers bloom, let a hundred schools contend." There has been a basic agreement among jurists that law is the expression of the will of the ruling class and that although subservient to the party policy, law has important functions to perform in the stage of socialist construction. Different opinions, however, have been expressed as to what are the specific characteristics of law, which organs have the law-making authority, and whether legal coercion applies to all citizens or to the enemy only.

As a result of the Peking-Moscow split, juridical circles in Communist China have understandably begun to show more interest in legal systems other than that of the Soviet Union. This is reflected in the new attention given to the legal traditions of China by individual researchers and academic institutions. Interesting essays, for instance, have been published on the development of criminal legislation and criminal procedure in old China. Major works have been undertaken to edit with annotations the laws of the imperial dynasties in general and the law of the T'ang dynasty in particular. Law schools at Peking and Kirin Universities have organised scholarly discussions and prepared teaching material on topics like "the T'ang Law," "political philosophy of Han Fei-tzu," and "relations between *li* and *fa*." The current official line is "critical inheritance of the cultural legacy." According to it, one should not cut off history and must understand the past in order to serve the present. Consequently, it is a duty of legal scholars today to examine the entire process of development of Chinese law in a scientific, objective and realistic manner. Only through the use of the Marxist-Leninist method of historical analysis, can one differentiate the elixir from the dregs and decide on what to accept and what to reject in the legal legacy.

In a similar manner the Chinese have shown guarded and yet discernible interest in Western legal theories and institutions during the last few years. As an example, the well-known Commercial press has recently published a new translation of Montesquieu's *Esprit des Lois*. A *Cheng-fa yen-chiu* writer points out that since Montesquieu's theory holds an important place in bourgeois jurisprudence his writings should therefore be appropriately introduced. Another author writes with considerable enthusiasm about Rousseau, calling the latter an outstanding liberal of the 18th Century despite his "class and historical limitations." Towards the contemporary jurists of the West, particularly those of the United States, the Communist Chinese attitude has been less sympathetic. Hans Kelsen's "pure theory of law" is described as a bourgeois trick and his concept of international law a tool of American imperialism." Roscoe Pound's "sociological jurisprudence" is also pictured as reactionary and serving only the interest of the monopolistic capitalist class. Even all this, however, must not be viewed as purely negative. The fact that Chinese jurists now can go to some length to *describe* the "reactionary" theories of the West is a marked improvement over the total absence of any meaningful legal discussion during the Anti-Rightist and "Big Leap" Movements.

10 • Chao Kuo-chün: *Rural Organization and Administration* *

The late Dr. Chao Kuo-chün, a leading authority on Chinese agriculture and agrarian administration, was affiliated for years with Harvard University and then with the School of International Studies in New Delhi. Here he describes the congruence of commune and hsiang *(township), a situation which prevailed during 1958–61 but then was changed. The* hsiang *still has three leading institutions: the people's congress for discussion and local legislative enactment; a people's council for administrative affairs; and a Communist party committee for policy guidance, surveillance, intervention when necessary, and follow-up checking.*

During the effort to make the commune the major jurisdiction for administration, economic planning, accounting, management of labor and local defense, the hsiang *seems to have been largely eclipsed. But, during the readjustments which followed the excesses of 1958–59, the communes were first pruned in functions, then (1961) in size so that they have come to approximate in area the former advanced producers' cooperatives (APC or collective farms) of the years 1956–58. This change followed the shift of emphasis from commune to production brigade and accompanied the further retreat to production teams as basic units for ownership, management, and accounting. Thus, a* hsiang *came to include a number of commune-production brigade areas, each supporting about two hundred households, and it recovered some of its governmental functions. The paled commune came to have only certain responsibilities for surveillance, coordination, planning and investment, while production brigades have become more important in planning and administration. Production teams—one to a very few in a single area—are basic for ownership, cultivation, and (singly or jointly) for the operations of auxiliary industries. These units have not reverted quite to the status of combined private holdings of the pre-1953 mutual aid teams. Local means of production have remained socialized, but small private garden plots have been permitted.*

There existed in the rural areas of China prior to mid-1958, four major centres for the planning and implementation of tasks handed down from the central or provincial government. They were: the local branch of the CCP; the *hsiang* administrative structure (the *hsiang* people's congress and the *hsiang* people's council); the cooperative system (APC, credit cooperative, and in some cases handicrafts cooperative); and the mass organizations, particularly the Youth League and the Women's Federation. The structure and functions of the many of these organizations such as the Party branch and the cooperatives, have been discussed in previous sections (see II D 3 and III 3 and 4). Here the discussion will deal in a summarized manner with the administrative set-up and its functions at the *hsiang* level and the major mass organizations. A *hsiang* (or nationality

* *Agrarian Policy of the Chinese Communist Party, 1921–1959* (Bombay: Asia Publishing House, 1960), pp. 231–236. By permission.

hsiang) is the basic (lowest) administrative unit generally comprised of several villages (or one very large village). Since the collectivization movement in 1955, the size of many *hsiang* has been enlarged through amalgamation, and the unit *ch'ü* (between the *hsiang* and the *hsien* or county) has been abolished in general. There were, in 1958, about 80,000 *hsiang* based on townships and 1,748 *hsien* or the equivalent units. After mid-1958, the *hsiang* administration has been combined with the people's communes.

The *hsiang* people's congress and the *hsiang* people's council are organized according to the Organic Laws governing these two bodies promulgated in September 1954. The people's congress of *hsiang,* consisting of 15 to 20 members if the *hsiang* has less than 2,000 in population and 20 to 35, if there are more than 2,000 people, is elected by direct ballot of all eligible voters 18 years old or above, either by secret voting or by show of hands. The tenure of the deputies of *hsiang* people's congress is two years, subject to re-election or recall by the congress. The power and functions of the *hsiang* people's congress include the following:

(1) To ensure the observance and execution of the laws, decrees, and the resolutions of the people's congresses of the higher levels;

(2) To adopt and promulgate resolutions within the limits of their functions and power;

(3) To approve agricultural and handicrafts production plans and decide on concrete plans of mutual-aid and cooperative work and other economic work;

(4) To plan public works;

(5) To decide on enforcement plans for cultural, education, health, pension and relief measures;

(6) To examine financial receipts and expenditures;

(7) To elect members of the people's council of the *hsiang*;

(8) To elect deputies to the people's congress of the next highest level;

(9) To hear and examine work reports of the *hsiang* people's council;

(10) To revise or annul improper decisions and orders of the *hsiang* people's council;

(11) To protect public property, maintain public order and safeguard civil rights;

(12) To ensure the equal rights of minority nationals; and

(13) To remove, in case of necessity, members or the chairman of the *hsiang* people's council.

The *hsiang* people's congress, according to legal stipulations, should be held once every three months. But it is not clear whether this provision is strictly observed in all the *hsiang* in China.

The legal centre of administrative power at the basic level of course is the *hsiang* people's council. It consists from 3 to 13 persons, depending on the size of the *hsiang,* all of whom are elected by the *hsiang* people's congress. The functions and power of the *hsiang* people's council are described as follows:

(1) To promulgate decisions and orders on the basis of the laws, decrees, the resolutions of the people's congress of the *hsiang* and those of the administrative organs of the state of the higher level;

(2) To sponsor election of deputies to the *hsiang* people's congress;

(3) To convene the *hsiang* people's congress and bring forward bills before it;

(4) To administer finance of the *hsiang*;

(5) To direct agricultural and handicrafts production and direct mutual-aid and cooperative enterprise and other economic work;

(6) To manage public works;

(7) To administer cultural, educational, health, pension, and relief work;

(8) To administer military service work;

(9) To protect public property, maintain public order and safeguard civil rights;

(10) To ensure the equal rights of minority nationals; and

(11) To carry out other business assigned by the people's councils of the higher level.

The *hsiang* people's council is stipulated to meet twice a month. It elects a chairman and several vice-chairmen. It may, according to needs, organize work committees of civil affairs, public security, military affairs, production and cooperation, finance and taxation, culture and education, and mediation. It can call on the deputies of the *hsiang* people's congress and "other suitable persons" to serve on such committees. These organizational divisions are subject to the approval of the people's council at the higher level. After the establishment of people's communes in 1958, the *hsiang* administration is incorporated in the communes, as stated previously.

The question regarding the role and problems of the basic-level administrative system in China is a complex one. It cannot be deliberated fully here. A few observations which have a more direct bearing on the current agrarian programmes of the CCP may be made: First, after the basic completion of the communization movement at the end of 1958, major functions of the *hsiang* people's council such as the direction of agricultural and handicrafts production, the management of public works, and the administration of educational or health work have been taken up by the communes. This may be both advantageous and unavoidable, as the commune leadership is in more direct contact with the rural conditions and problems in a *hsiang*. Second, the economic and technical aspects have significantly become increasingly important at the *hsiang* level in China. Both in the *hsiang* administrative system and in the basic commune production teams, many new tasks have come to occupy important roles—such as the agro-technical study group, the accounting section, the rural credit department, the training class for new farm implements, and the work regarding the government purchase of agricultural products. In a survey of a *hsien* in southern Shantung in 1956, among the 3,900 cadres, 2,809 were engaged in economic and financial work. Third, the existing organizational problems in the *hsiang* are both quantitative and qualitative. Quantitatively, there were, at least up to 1957, in many rural districts too many functionaries who had to be supported by the producing peasants. A survey of two counties in Shantung (near the end of 1956) revealed that on the average there was one cadre in every 200 rural inhabitants. That a similar problem exists in many villages is reflected by a speech of Teng Tzu-hui at the end of 1957 calling on the APCs to reduce their administrative staff from 1·5 to 2 per cent of the total membership to one per cent. At the same time cadres in a number of localities were burdened with too many tasks assigned by the superior organs and by too many meetings. Qualitatively, the rapid development in many agro-technical fields increased the need for better trained men in the *hsiang* administration. The movement to transfer millions of students and urban government employees to the rural areas (started in the fall of 1957) was partly designed to cope with the above problem.

The important role played by the leading mass organizations like the Youth League (14 to 28 age group), the Women's Federation and the Children's Pioneer Corps (9 to 15 age group) in rural China has been discussed previously. It may be desirable to point out again their significance because they play a decisive as well as unique part in the organizational structure of China today. The activists in these mass organizations serve as a rule as the nucleus and vanguard of many an agrarian programme in China (or in the cities, for that matter). The total membership of the Communist Youth League (in April 1958) numbered more than 25 million, and most of them belonged to rural branches. According to a report of Chang Yun at the Third National Congress of Chinese Women on September 9, 1957, half the number of *hsiang* in China were headed by women chiefs or deputy chiefs and 70 to 80 per cent of the APCs had women directors or women deputy directors who numbered more than 500,000. The Children's Pioneer Corps of China had a total membership of 35 million in 1959. The weighty part performed by these organizations is partly seen in the following examples. In 1955, under the initiation of the Youth League, an estimated 120 million young people participated in a nation-wide afforestation campaign which resulted in the planting of trees on six million acres of land. In the winter of 1955–56, 70 million rural youths joined the "accumulate fertilizer" movement and made 400 million tons of native fertilizer. In 1956 the harvest-season nursery organizations took care of more than 6 million children and babies, thus helping considerably the agricultural production. Millions of "advanced agricultural workers" came into existence each year, most of them members of the youth and women organizations. . . .

The various organizations at the *hsiang* (now the commune) level are often coordinated directly or indirectly by the Party branch of the CCP, which serves as the engineer, supervisor and adviser of almost all the major programmes. The role and functions of the Party in the rural areas have been discussed in section III. 4. Party cells were organized in 70 per cent of all *hsiang* in June 1954, 90 per cent at the end of 1955, practically in all the 80,000 *hsiang* in early 1958, and in about 24,000 communes in 1959.

SECTION THREE

Political Leadership

11 • CHAO KUO-CHÜN: *Leadership in the Chinese Communist Party* *

One of the best articles to date on Chinese Communist leadership is this one by Dr. Chao Kuo-chün. Here we have omitted tables which provide statistics about members of the Eighth Central Committee—their ranking, ages, native provinces, education, foreign training, and party seniority; but patterns in these respects are summarized in the text. We have also omitted certain paragraphs which emphasize the unusual solidarity among CCP leaders.

This observation, made in 1959, was partly true, though where so much power was sought and developed, there have been cliques, rivalry, and "rectifications." Party discipline and secrecy have denied outer observers much information about heated debates in policy-making bodies, chiefly the Politburo and Central Committee. Inferential fragments have been learned about the purge of the party heads of government and administration in Manchuria and East China, along with their coteries, in 1954. Five years later came the purge of Defense Minister P'eng Teh-huai and most of his close associates. But never before 1965–66 had the CCP been so openly and seriously wracked by factional rivalries and dissensions. These tensions may be eased and the crevasses repaired, but it is unlikely that the party will fully regain the degree of solidarity and élan that it had previously attained.

The Power Structure of the Chinese Communist Party

The central locus of political power in Communist China is the Chinese Communist Party (CCP), now the largest single Communist organization in the world. As the CCP is the prime mover behind both the domestic and international policies of Communist China, an appraisal of its power structure is of basic importance.

> The Communist Party of China is the vanguard of the Chinese working class, the highest form of its class organization. The aim of the Party is the achievement of socialism and communism in China.

* *The Annals of the American Academy of Political and Social Science,* Vol. 321 (January 1959), pp. 40–50. By permission.

Thus the opening paragraph of the present party constitution adopted in 1956 sets forth, simply and starkly, the official view which the CCP has of itself. Organizationally, the CCP is built in accordance with the fundamental Leninist precepts of elitism, organization, and control. Rigid hierarchy, disciplined subordination of inferior to superior, obedience to authority, sustained control—such are the essential elements in the structure. At the top, the real leadership of the CCP consists of the smallest practicable group of veteran Communists of proven ability and reliability. Control is conveyed downward through a pyramidal organization to the party groups and individual party members at the lower levels. At the bottom, the party makes a continuing attempt to preserve its integrity through strict control of the gates of membership and through stern and unceasing discipline of its members. The entire organization is built on the principle of "democratic centralism," officially defined as "centralism on the basis of democracy and democracy under centralized leadership."

The organization of the party structure is based on the National Party Congress, which elects the Central Committee of the party, which in turn elects the Political Bureau.

According to the revised (1956) party constitution, the Central Committee is the supreme organ of the party during the intervals between meetings of the National Party Congress. Thus, through its group decisions, through the positions held by its individual members, and through the activities of its key central departments—Organization, Propaganda, Rural Work, and United Front Work, for example—the Central Committee has a dominant influence upon the political, military, economic, and social life of the country. The present, Eighth, CC elected in the autumn of 1956 now includes 97 regular members and 96 alternates (the alternate membership was increased from 73 to 96 in May 1958), and is headed by Mao Tse-tung as Chairman and by five Vice Chairmen: Liu Shao-ch'i, Chou En-lai, Chu Teh, Ch'en Yün, and Lin Piao. It includes virtually all members of the previous, Seventh, CC elected in 1945 (with the prominent exceptions of Kao Kang and Jao Shu-shih, who were purged in 1954–55, and a few other individuals who had either died or slipped in importance) together with a greatly expanded group of second-level party leaders who have become important since 1949.

The enlargement of the CC membership in 1956 indicated both the relative stability of the party leadership and its adjustment to new circumstances. Yet membership in the CC is not ipso facto equivalent to a position of real authority. The present large size of the CC combined with the relative infrequency of its meetings has made it more and more difficult for that body to play a major role in the day-to-day decisions of the party.

Power loci

In practice, therefore, the Political Bureau is the central directing and decision-making organ of the party. The Political Bureau was enlarged at the Eighth Congress from 13 to 17 members and again to 20 members in May 1958. The apex of political power in Communist China today is the Standing Committee of the Political Bureau created at the Eighth Party Congress to take over the former functions of the Central Secretariat. The Secretariat is now in charge of top-level administrative work of the party under the direction of the Politburo and its Standing Committee, and the post of general secretary—held by Teng Hsiao-p'ing—remains a very strategic position in the party high command.

From this central core, Communist political power revolves outward through a series of concentric rings which link the party and the nation. Since the abolition of the regional administrative areas and the transfer of top regional party leaders to Peking in 1954, the important local centers of authority have come to be found in the secretariats responsible for provincial party affairs. At the Eighth Party Congress, Chou En-lai spoke of assigning "more powers to the local administrative organs and a better division of labor between the central and local authorities." (Report on the Second Five-Year Plan, September 16, 1956.) The increased importance of local leadership could be noted in May 1958, when two of the three newly elected Politburo members were provincial party secretaries; at the same time, five provincial party secretaries were elected as alternate members of the Central Committee.

Other major loci of power in Communist China include the top military command and political commissar positions, major departments in the headquarters of the People's Liberation Army, and chairmanships of leading mass organizations such as the Young Communist League, the All-China Federation of Trade Unions, and the All-China Women's Federation. Strictly speaking, these positions are not part of the party mechanism. Functionally, however, they are occupied by top party leaders and form an integral part of the total power mosaic of the party. Changes in the leadership of these nonparty organs often suggest changes within the party itself. For example, the removal of Li Li-san from the chairmanship of the Federation of Trade Unions in 1953 indicated his political decline even though no formal party disciplinary action was taken against him.

The Top Leadership

The Standing Committee of the Politburo now consists of seven members: Mao Tse-tung, Liu Shao-ch'i, Chou En-lai, Chu Teh, Ch'en Yün, Teng Hsiao-p'ing, and Lin Piao (Lin was elected in May 1958). The most significant change at this top level of leadership is that registered by Teng Hsiao-p'ing, who has emerged during the past few years as a key figure.

The seven members of the Standing Committee are also the top-ranking members of the Politburo itself which is now constituted as follows:

Members: Mao Tse-tung, Liu Shao-ch'i, Chou En-lai, Chu Teh, Ch'en Yün, Teng Hsiao-p'ing, Lin Piao, Lin Po-ch'ü, Tung Pi-wu, P'eng Chen, Lo Jung-huan, Ch'en Yi, Li Fu-ch'un, P'eng Te-huai, Liu Po-ch'eng, Ho Lung, Li Hsien-nien, K'o Ch'ing-shih, Li Ching-ch'üan, T'an Chen-lin

Alternate members: Ulanfu, Chang Wen-t'ien, Lu Ting-yi, Ch'en Po-ta, K'ang Sheng, Po I-po,

The composition of the Politburo of the Chinese Communist Party indicates both continuity and expansion in leadership. Nine new names have been added to the regular membership of the Pilitburo during the past two years: Lo Jung-huan, Ch'en Yi, Liu Po-ch'eng, Ho Lung, Li Fu-ch'un, and Li Hsien-nien (all elected in September 1956), K'o Ch'ing-shih, Li Chiang-ch'üan, and T'an Chen-lin (elected in May 1958).

The increased weight of military leaders at the top levels of the party structure is suggested by the fact that four of the six members of the Politburo newly elected at the Eighth Congress and seven of the total of 20 members are Marshals of the People's Liberation Army. Yet the available evidence does not indicate that the military is now the dominant power group in Communist China. Five of the seven members of the all-powerful Politburo Standing Committee are civilians, and Marshal Chu Teh, the fourth-ranking member, is now 72. The military still constitutes a minority in the Politburo, and none of the six alternate members of the Politburo is a military man. There are only two generals in the nine-man Central Secretariat. And, finally, the definition of a military leader in the Chinese Communist context is unique, for the Chinese Communist forces have for many years been developed on Mao Tse-tung's concepts which accord major weight to political as well as purely military elements in warfare. Almost all the key army personnel belong to the Kiangsi-Yenan group, and they appear to form a disciplined and cohesive group long associated with the Mao Tse-tung leadership. . . .

While the current greatly expanded Central Committee of 97 regular and 96 alternate members is far less significant than the Politburo as a decision-making organ, a member's ranking within the Central Committee is still generally indicative of his political importance. In order to contribute to an understanding of the top leadership of the Chinese Communist Party, the backgrounds of the 97 regular members of the Eighth Central Committee are analyzed below. Not every one of the current CC members may be considered a top leader, although all key party figures are on the CC. Due to incomplete or inexact information regarding a number of CCP leaders, observations drawn from this background analysis serve largely to indicate the general pattern in the leadership structure.

Background

As an elite group, the leaders of the CCP are relatively young. Of the 97 regular members of the present CC [1959], about 80 per cent belong to the age group from 46 to 60, with the age group 51–55 constituting approximately 35 per cent; 56–60, about 26 per cent; and under 50, about 21 per cent.

Regarding their geographical origin, 30 (31 per cent) are from Hunan province; 12 (12.3 per cent) from Szechwan; 6 each from Hupeh and Shansi; 5 each from Fukien, Hopei, Kiangsu, Shantung, and Shensi; and 4 each from Anhwei, Kiangsi, and Kwangtung. The remaining 6 are distributed among five other provinces (including Inner Mongolia), while eight provinces or areas (including Sinkiang and Tibet) are unrepresented. A substantial portion of the CC membership thus comes from the interior provinces in the hinterland, from areas relatively removed from the Western influences of the port cities and coastal districts. This contrasts sharply with the membership of the Central Executive Committee of the Kuomintang in the prewar period, when about 40 per cent of its membership came from six coastal provinces.

In comparison with the great majority of the Chinese population, the members of the Chinese Communist hierarchy have had much better than average education. Of the 97 CC members, 51 probably received education in a college, normal school, or professional institution, while 22 were trained in military academies (here defined to include Communist military training schools in Juichin and

Yenan). The high proportion of leaders with military training is a reflection of the military environment of modern Chinese politics and of the long years of "armed struggle" against both National Government armies and Japanese forces during the period between 1928 and 1949.

The indigenous roots of the present leadership are suggested by the fact that 56 out of 97 CC members are not known to have had any training outside China. Of the remainder, 25 received training in the USSR, 9 in France, 5 in Japan, and 1 in Germany. Some, of course, visited more than one foreign country (two received brief training in the United States, for example), but in this computation only the country where the individual received his major training is counted.

Available data also indicate that almost all members of the present CC have relatively long party membership. About 70 per cent joined the party between 1921 and 1927; virtually all the rest appear to have joined before 1938. It is almost certain that none of the 8 unknown, with one possible exception, acquired party membership later than 1937.

Other background factors, while significant, are not considered in this analysis because of lack of adequate information. For example, the social background of the majority of the CC members is not definitely known. Of the 40 per cent about whom there are some reports, the largest number comes from peasant families, followed by gentry-official, and working class families.

Characteristics

Many characteristics of the Central Committee membership reflect those of the Chinese Communist Party as a whole. The party as a political organism is relatively young, and its origins are still predominantly rural. Data released at the time of the Eighth Party Congress in September 1956 stated that, of the (then) 10.7 million party members, 67.5 per cent were between 26 and 45 years old, while only 7.6 per cent were over the age of 46. As of 1956, peasants reportedly constituted 69.1 per cent of total party membership; workers, 14 per cent; intellectuals, 11.7 per cent; and others, 5.2 per cent. During the Sino-Japanese war period, 1937–45, over 90 per cent of the party membership consisted of peasants. Women appear to be underrepresented on the present Central Committee. While some 10 per cent of the party members are females, only four women—Ts'ai Ch'ang, Teng Ying-ch'ao, Ch'ien Ying, and Ch'en Shao-min—are among the 97 regular members of the CC and none appear on the Politburo. . . .

In general, however, despite the expansion of the top apparatus, the leadership of the CCP is still dominated by veterans of the pre-1949 struggle for power in the countryside of China. . . .

12 • Liu Shao-ch'i: *The Communist Party Cadres* *

One is entitled to wonder whether Liu Shao-ch'i, the veteran mentor of CCP cadres, labor organizer, political commissar, Central Committee and Politburo member, and (since 1959) Chairman of the People's Government,

* *On the Party*, 4th ed. (Peking: Foreign Languages Press, 1952), pp. 102–105, 107–109, 110–111, 113–114, 120–121.

himself realizes how good a sublimated Confucian he is in some respects. Communists, somewhat like Confucians, regard government as a theater for practical morality. Exponents of this secular faith often express ideas in heavy moralistic tones. Despite the veil of secrecy, we can learn much about problems of revolutionary China from the admonitions of leaders and the self-criticisms of those constrained to air in public their defects and the imputed causes.

The recruiting, indoctrinating, training, and employment of cadres has been one of the keys to the Communist party's rise to and retention of national power. Even if the CCP had fared better in its attempted coups in 1928–30, it could not have done more than hold small territorial pockets because of its paucity of disciplined personnel. It was during the anti-Japanese war (1937–45) in the nineteen so-called "liberated areas" that sufficient bodies of cadres were developed. In May 1945, shortly before that war ended and as the civil conflict was about to be resumed in its decisive phases, Liu made a long speech to the Seventh CCP Congress, from which we have chosen important passages. This has been repeatedly published and somewhat revised, but until 1966 it continued to be widely used as a bible for cadres. Since August of that year, attacks have been made on Liu by the Mao-Lin-led radicals—at first obliquely, then directly. Criticisms have also been directed against certain of Liu's writings, including his booklet On the Party. *These have not been really on grounds of content but rather have been factionally motivated and related to other subsequent issues. In 1967, the Mao-Lin faction and the Red Guards compelled Liu to make a public self-criticism, which he did with some skill. At year's end he was still under house arrest in Peking. But the radicals were apparently not sure enough of their hold on the country to convene the National People's Congress. By the constitution, only that body could remove the Chairman of the People's Republic from office.*

In this piece, Liu wrote about the merits and problems of the cadres from rural and intellectual backgrounds, of veterans and the newer recruits, of the military and civilian cadres, of local cadres, and of cadres from other areas who might come to participate in programs. After the Communists came to national power, more activists from urban working strata were inducted. Many of the tensions to which Liu referred still persist.

Coming from different walks of life our cadres generally are of two categories: those of worker and peasant origin and those of student and intellectual origin. However, both categories fight and work for a common goal. Of these two categories, the first makes up the majority of our cadres. In the first category itself, the cadres of peasant origin constitute the majority. These facts prove that our party is the vanguard of the Chinese working class. In the entire history of China only a party like ours has been able to educate and train up thousands upon thousands of distinguished cadres from among the ordinary workers and peasants. It is only under our Party's education and encouragement that they have achieved such a development today as heroes of the nation's cause. This is to the credit of Marxism-Leninism and Mao Tse-tung's theory of the Chinese revolution.

Each of these two categories of Party cadres has both merits and defects which need to be developed or eliminated as the case may be. The worker and peasant cadres should endeavour to maintain and broaden their connections with the masses and their popular style of work. Meanwhile they should overcome their cultural and theoretical deficiencies. The cadres from the intellectuals on the other hand should, foster the spirit of seeking truth from the facts and the mass standpoint, eliminate their idealistic standpoint and their lack of regard for labour, for workers and peasants, and strive to mix with the masses of workers and peasants.

Both categories are indispensable to the success of the cause of the Chinese people's emancipation and neither can be dispensed with. Therefore it is just as wrong to disregard and despise the worker and peasant cadres as it is wrong to disregard and despise or even discriminate [against] cadres from the ranks of the intellectuals. Both categories must respect each other and learn from each other. Close unity and cooperation between them in all circumstances is decisive for the progress and victory of our cause.

In each of these two categories there is a distinction between old and new cadres, with the latter in the majority. Most of the cadres who joined our Party after the beginning of the War of Resistance to Japanese Aggression have done splendid work for the people, undergone excellent training, and become well experienced in the struggle. Our Party has been constantly reinforced with large numbers of new cadres. It is only with such reinforcements of new cadres that the cause of our Party can succeed. The relationship between the new and old cadres, that is, the proper attitude to be adopted by each toward the other, is a problem of constant importance within our Party.

Comrade Mao Tse-tung has repeatedly called attention to the importance of this problem, pointing out that "all old cadres should welcome the new cadres with the utmost enthusiasm and take good care of them," and that "new and old cadres should respect and learn from each other, and acquire each other's merits and remedy their respective defects so that they can unite as one man and fight for the common cause." However, it must be pointed out that some comrades have not yet paid sufficient attention to this important directive of Comrade Mao Tse-tung. It still happens that new cadres have a poor opinion of the old cadres, who in turn look down upon and fail to welcome and look after the new cadres. From now on they must reflect upon this and correct this once and for all. Only if the old and new cadres unite and cooperate on all matters can we carry out our tasks.

Cadres also differ from each other owing to the difference in the nature, record, and location of their work in the course of the revolution, resulting in the distinction between the military and the civilian cadres, between the cadres of one army and those of another, between the cadres of one place and those of another, between the cadres of one department and those of another, between local cadres and those from outside, etc. Each of these cadres is versed in a certain field of revolutionary work but weak in others, and each has his merits and defects. Therefore, they ought to respect, help, and learn from each other, instead of meeting each other with disdain, complaint or friction. Comrade Mao Tse-tung has stressed the proper relationship between these cadres in his report on Rectification of Three Styles, and every cadre and Party member must act accordingly. Only with a high degree of solidarity and cooperation between these cadres under all circumstances can our common cause be advanced. . . .

In spite of the fact that the most serious sectarianism in the Party has been basically overcome through several years of the Rectification of Three Styles and studies of Party history, a tendency to blind mountain-top-ism which undermines inner-Party solidarity still exists in certain sections of the Party. There are objective and historical causes for the birth of this kind of blind mountain-top-ism:

1) The big percentage of petty-bourgeois elements both inside and outside the Party;

2) The prolonged separation of the different sections of the Party under conditions of rural guerrilla warfare, resulting in special backgrounds, connections and styles of work which are different from each other;

3) Insufficient Marxist-Leninist education in the Party. Hence comrades in different sections of the Party with a mountain-top-ist sentiment often unconsciously display the following typical undesirable phenomena. They relish solely their own glorious history but fail to appreciate or simply ignore those of other sections. They appreciate only their own achievements, knowing nothing about their own shortcomings. Consequently comrades in other sections are permitted only to sing praises to their achievements but not to criticize their defects even though they are real and obvious. On the other hand, they see nothing but defects in the other sections of the Party, hence they have nothing but criticism for others. Nor do they take into account and appreciate the difficulties of others. In their own company they talk and joke, and get along together perfectly, looking after each other and conversing without reservation. But they are inaccessible, aloof, indifferent and inconsiderate to others not of their group. In their inner-Party relations they tend to act together as a group and even join in holding others back.

There are some people in the Party who are overbearing, compelling others to be cautious.

This typical tendency to mountain-top-ism often exists in certain sections of the Party, e.g., between local and outside cadres, between Army and civilian cadres, between cadres of one section of the Army and those of another section, or between the cadres of one district and those of another, thus weakening solidarity and giving rise to discord and friction which ought not to take place. This tendency to mountain-top-ism is in most cases blind and unconscious. Therefore people who display this tendency invariably fail to admit their mistake until they have been properly talked to and convinced about it. The blindness of this tendency, when utilised by some elements with ulterior motives, may cause serious disputes in the Party.

The blind tendency to mountain-top-ism is a special type of sectarianism without an apparently mistaken political programme, but with numerous incorrect political and organisational views, serious tendencies of exclusionism and conservatism and serious isolation from the masses. It is anti-Marxist and anti-Leninist. It weakens the solidarity and unity of the entire Party and it represents a tendency toward factionalism. Hence, it must be opposed and eliminated. This is a principle which must be clearly understood and there must not be the slightest doubt on this point. . . .

For instance, worker and peasant cadres are often proud of their social origin and look down on the cadres from the ranks of the intellectuals. The latter on their part, because of their knowledge, "return the compliments." The old cadres on account of their seniority and longer record of struggle often look down on the new cadres and the new cadres, considering themselves more intelligent and capable, look down on the old cadres. The army cadres by virtue of their ability in warfare look down on the civilian cadres and the civilian cadres on account of their richer experience look down on the army cadres. The cadres of one army unit on account of having won more battles look down on the cadres of another army unit and vice versa. In addition, the cadres of different regions and departments often look down on each other on account of their respective accomplishments and knowledge.

Because of carrying a "knapsack" on the back some comrades look down upon others. This inevitably arouses resentment and engenders disunity among the cadres. This is the reason why Comrade Mao Tse-tung calls upon our cadres to examine their "knapsacks" and get rid of them in order to free themselves spiritually, in order to enable them to establish connections with the masses and commit fewer mistakes, and in order to unite the whole Party. . . .

In regard to the cadres policy, Comrade Mao Tse-tung told us at the Sixth Plenary Session of the Central Committee that the criteria for our cadres policy were, among other things, "resolute carrying out of the Party line, observance of Party discipline, intimate connections with the masses, ability to work independently, willingness in work, and unselfishness."

In short, the best cadres are those who can best serve the masses of the people.

All our comrades know that the criteria mentioned here are correct. Yet there are some comrades who have brought forth other criteria. They suggest that a cadre's Party standing and his qualifications be the primary and sole considerations in selecting and promoting cadres. There are also those who think only of a cadre's ability to speak and to write irrespective of whether he is a practical person or not. Other criteria are blind obedience and personal connections. These criteria for selecting and promoting cadres are obviously incorrect.

Then how shall we appraise cadres?

It should be done along two lines. Firstly, a cadre should be examined minutely and intrinsically by the leadership as to his capabilities and his limitations, his merits and defects, his whole personal history and his work. Secondly, a cadre should be examined at the place where he does his work and through the rank and file under his leadership. Only by combining both of these can there be a relatively comprehensive and correct appraisal of a cadre and in this way avoiding many deviations.

Some comrades hold that cadres can only be examined from the top. In other words, it means the examination of the subordinates by their superiors, according to the former's reports on their work. This idea is incorrect. Such examination is of course necessary, and it is one of the effective means. But it is far from sufficient. Cadres must also be examined from the bottom up. This is to say, the leading cadres must be examined by the masses, by those whom they lead. This is the most effective way.

The Party Constitution provides for measures for examining, selecting and promoting cadres by the masses, and by the rank and file. This consists of examination of the leaders by the rank and file of the Party membership in different Party meetings, conferences, and congresses, by hearing the reports of the leaders on their work, by criticizing their defects, and by electing the leading bodies. The principle of democratic centralism as laid down in the Party Constitution must be effectively enforced in the Party. The setting up of the Party machinery by the elective method, the right to nominate and to reject candidates, and the freedom of criticism and self-criticism—all these must be effectively carried out.

We believe that the appraisal and selection and promotion of cadres both from the top down and from the bottom up will yield correct results in this respect. This explains why it is stipulated in the Party Constitution that all leading bodies of the Party should be established by the elective method and approved by the higher Party committees. . . .

Although considerable achievements and progress have been made in recent years in absorbing and promoting non-party cadres in different fields of the people's cause, and in bringing about solidarity and cooperation between Communist and non-party cadres, much remains to be desired. Here shortcomings still remain among our cadres, such as their lack of serious attention to absorbing different categories of talented non-party elements in the people's service, their lack of skill in working with non-party cadres or helping them in their work, or, as among certain comrades, the survival of sectarian, monopolistic or exclusive styles of work. Consequently in some places it still happens that non-party cadres hold only nominal positions with no actual power to act, and that they are dissatisfied with their work. In this connection, all Communist cadres must strictly examine themselves, and get rid of their defects in order to achieve success in absorbing and uniting non-party cadres. Communist cadres must know how to stimulate the initiative of non-party cadres and assist them in achieving success in their work and in building up their prestige in working for the people's cause, thereby attracting the broad sections of the best elements of the people into serving the people. In dealing with non-party cadres' errors in principle and their political differences with us, patient persuasion should be used. Only thus can the cause of the Chinese people triumph and the devotion of the Communists to the service of the people and their unselfishness be manifested.

13 • TING CHU-YUAN: *The Problem of Revolutionizing the Leadership of the County Party Commissar* *

Although the proportion is gradually declining, still more than 80 per cent of mainland China's population lives in the countryside, mostly in villages with populations of less than 2,000. Since the failure of the "Great Leap" and the onslaught of severe economic crisis (1959–62), the CCP and its regime have devoted more investment and attention to agricultural production and related problems. Compromises have been made to encourage revived peasant cooperation in campaigns and programs. Much attention has been given to rural leadership.

* *Issues and Studies,* II, No. 6 (March 1966), pp. 14–22. By permission.

In the fall and winter of 1965–66, as the Third Five-Year Plan was supposedly beginning, a spate of articles appeared in newspapers about the party secretaries or commissars in the more than 1700 counties (hsien) *throughout the People's Republic. Many cadres wrote in about their activities and problems. This protracted discussion, among others, was one of the subjects followed closely by Chinese observers in Taiwan. Here is a summary interpretation by one of them, a researcher in the Institute of China Mainland Problems in Taipei, Taiwan.*

Shortcomings of the Leadership of the County Party Commissar

The discussion of the leadership of county party commissar has continued for more than five months. During this period many cadres have expressed their viewpoints in scores of special column reports published by the *People's Daily.* The discussion is now featuring reviewals, criticisms and patterns-studying. The problems disclosed in these discussions can be summed up as follows:

1. "Service for whom?"

This does not seem to be a problem. However, "bureaucratism," "formalism," and "paper-work-ism" still exist at the level of county party commissars.

Reflections from the secretary at the Chiliyin People's Commune at Hsin Hsiang in Honan: This commune had to make a great effort to cope with such matters as preparing reports, outlines and tabulations and attending conferences called by many higher agencies. For instance, in September 8–9, 1965 seven units notified this commune to send people to the county for conferences. The multifarious conferences have made it necessary for a considerable number of comrades to stick around the higher echelons. On a certain day, the Communist Youth League county commissar sent to the commune seven investigation questionnaires containing some 120 items including the marital status of inhabitants. This necessitated a great deal of work on the part of a great number of cadres. Cadres at the commune have said that the CCP is a "topsy-turvy" organization and must be improved.

Reflections from the secretary at the Shang Chia People's Commune at Chao Tung in Heilungkiang: The county party commissar exercised his leadership through conferences, documents, tabulation reports and telephone calls. Whenever a mission was assigned by the provincial or local commissar, a meeting would be convened by the county commissar. As the meeting was often lengthy and participated [in] by many people, opinions of lower echelons could hardly be gathered. All the year round the county commissar was busy with this or that conference ordered by a higher echelon. And the party commissar at the commune was also accustomed to sitting in office, listening to reports and directing production through the conference. He would follow the representatives of the county commissar to make inspections here and there as if he had gone deep into the lowest echelon. As a matter of fact, all the precious time of the cadres at the production group was wasted.

Reflection from the Farm Political Department of the Party Committee of Wukung in Shensi: The county commissar was busy in recent years but has achieved nothing. He would do what had been called for but could not take the initiative.

Reflections from the county commissar of Tungtai, Kiangsu: Some county commissars have discussed the so-called "hard" and "soft" missions. They think the "hard" mission is one that is designated by the higher echelon, the "soft" mission, by people's demands. They have emphasized the performance of the "hard" mission but neglected the "soft" one.

Reflections from the county commissar of Lantien, Shensi: Some cadres just do the job perfunctorily. They do not care if the mission has been carried out successfully in the light of the actual situation.

2. *"Too much control"*

Reflections from the assistant secretary of the party committee on Chufu in Shantung: The committee has always been busy with such administrative matters as "agricultural urge." Actually, the production groups and farmers know better than we do when they will sow or plough. In this respect, we are apt to mislead them. And we are too critical. This has made the people reluctant to be responsible for any task. As a result, they would ask for the secretary's instructions on any work, as if nothing could be done without the secretary.

Reflections from the acting secretary of the party committee of Ning-an, Heilungkiang: The party commissar is always busy with the farming seasons. He draws people from various departments to organize a "heterogenious working group" to push farming work in the rural areas. The departments said that this kind of practice amounts to "dismantling a machine for its spare parts." Moreover, the farmers and cadres do not welcome this group because many group members know nothing about farming. Some cadres said: "We don't like to listen to your nonsense about farm production." This centralized control on the part of the county party commissar could only make things more confused.

Reflections from the party commissar of Lantien, Shensi: Some county cadres have asked to be sent down at the same time. Even the people at the basic echelon wouldn't agree to this. The farmers did the farming according to the plan formulated by the higher echelon. When the sprouts did not come out well, the cadres would say: "How could they do the work well when they were in bad humor." The commune members would retort: "You people at the county level have all the reasons. You have asked for dense plantation. The result is low yield and waste of seeds."

3. *"One good act to cover up a hundred bad acts"*

During the discussions, the Chinese Communists have advocated that "the work of revolutionizing the leadership of the county party commissar must be based on production." The following are reflections from the acting secretary of Ning-an in Heilungkiang: In implementation, the county commissar has not done enough about "political prominence." He thinks outstanding production results can cover other shortcomings. It is said that in leadership, the county commissar emphasizes substantial production. But he has failed to materialize fully the so-called "Mao Tse-tung's thoughts taking command." When the party calls for increased production, he simply concentrates his efforts at making things appear "good" and disregards everything else.

4. "Three-self and five-old"

Reflections from the assistant secretary of the party committee of Kuanghan, Szechuan: The county party commissars are generally "not ambitious and satisfied with the status quo." Their ideas are represented by the "Three-Self and Five-Old." The three-self includes "self-styled conservatism, self-complacency and self-conceit." The five-old includes "old ideas, old-fashioned practices, old and stereotyped measures, old seed varieties and old low-level production." There will hardly be any long-range plan if these ideological barriers are not eliminated.

The secretary of the party committee of Fu Ching in Fukien said that the leading cadres at the party committee should get rid of their assuming air.

Reflections from the secretary of the party committee of Hsuancheng in Heilungkiang: The cadres would not change their methods of guiding in production which they had learned from the mutual assistance team. These methods are only applicable to handicraft production for petite agricultural economy. Now the production of the people's commune is geared to a "great socialist agricultural economy," which "combines the agricultural machinery station under the all-people ownership system with the collective economy of the people's commune under the collective ownership system." But those who are accustomed to the old pattern of leadership would say: "Even if we had sat in a house for three years, we would also know what to do in which season." In other words, the "administrative orders" can be used, instead, as measures for inspiring masses ideologically.

5. "The overwhelming fear"

Reflections from the party secretary at Pi Hsien in Szechuan: In carrying out the revolutionary work, one must have the spirit of "rushing forward." One must be afraid of nothing. If you are afraid of this or that, you cannot do the revolutionary work. Some people have warned: "You should not give misleading orders." Yes, To mislead others is not right. But you cannot give up the job because you are afraid of committing mistakes. The mistakes committed during the great leap forward period are really alarming and deterring.

Reflections from the party commissar at Ta Min in Hopeh: In doing the revolutionary work, one must get rid of fear. Without a sound ideological basis, one is apt to be afraid of mistakes and of criticisms. But nobody seems to be afraid of failing in the work of socialistic reconstruction.

A short article appearing in the *People's Daily* of November 26, 1965 disclosed that many county party commissars have pointed out in their letters that revolution cannot succeed if fear is not eliminated. The paper quoted an old saying: "Once bitten by a snake, one is afraid of rope for ten years," to describe the Communist cadres after the failure of the great leap forward. The Chinese Communist leaders had asked them to "release the burdens" and "get the motor running." They also said: "Good work performance is often preceded by mistakes."

Reflections from the party secretary at Hsiangtang in Hunan: We have exaggerated our defects and mistakes in our work. Hence we are indiscriminating, confused and timid. Under this spiritual influence, we can hardly raise high the red banners of the general line and advance with bold steps. As a result, we are too careful in our operations and afraid of making further mistakes and of being criticized. It is therefore imperative to get rid of fear which is the biggest barrier of the revolutionary work.

Reflections from the acting party secretary at Meng Hsien in Shansi: Some people have placed too much emphasis on "keeping within the bounds of duties." This is the first important ideological problem the work of revolutionization of the leadership of county party commissar has to face. They would say: "Several years ago we got into trouble because we failed to keep within the bounds of our duties. Now that we have just come back from our deviations, we cannot afford to go too far." Others would say: 'We ran into trouble in the past because we wished to learn new experience. Now we cannot do this any more." This is the conservatism which they have described as: "being satisfied with the status quo, doing nothing and fearful of revolution."

6. *"Three ways of work emphasis"*

Reflections from the party commissar at Tungtai in Kiangsu: "Work emphasis" must be placed on leading people to rural areas. An analysis of the 18 "types" of work emphasis shows that they can be classified into three categories: In the first category, the leading cadres are in full control of the work in which technicians participate. This is called the "genuine prototype." In the second category, the leading cadres are nominal in function, giving instructions on principles. This is called the "nominal prototype." In the third category, for displaying their achievements, the leading cadres exert special efforts and create special conditions. But people would say: "This is not attainable." This is called the "special prototype."

Reflections from the secretary of the party committee at Yingkuo in Liaoning: The cadres "conduct more superficial inspections than investigation of work emphasis." They just look around without using their hands and brains. And they often visit only progressive communes and groups. As there are less problems with the progressive groups, the cadres do not have to exert much effort at solving problems. They keep themselves away from those groups which have more difficulties and problems simply to avoid troubles.

Reflections from Chisha in Shantung: Many cadres prefer the city life. Some think farming is a laborious work and does not yield results as industry. Cadres are not interested in arduous ideological work. Many have gone to the city. Some people don't want to use their brains to find out the main contradictions, and in most cases they have to ask for approval from the higher level from [for?] making any decision. It seems that they have a strong "organizational concept." In reality, they are simply lazy.

7. *"The spirit of excessive dependence"*

Reflections from the acting party secretary at Chi Hsien in Shansi: The spirit of "learning from the bigger headquarters" is in fact over-emphasis on "keeping within the bounds of duty." That accounts for the lack of achievement.

Reflections from the party commissar at Aigun, Heilungkiang: Some people lack a revolutionary spirit. In production they wish to learn from the bigger headquarters. But they tend to depend on the higher levels to make decisions and develop a spirit of excessive dependence.

An editorial in the *People's Daily* said that with a non-progressive spirit the county party commissar tends to be satisfied with the status quo. It insisted that such low spirit must be seriously reviewed.

Reflections from party commissars in various regions: The basic problem of revolutionizing the leadership lies in poor "mental conditions." Before the problem of world outlook is solved, we must first solve the problem of the many mental problems such as "whether to be an 'official' or a 'people's servant,' " Whether to be painstaking, whether to change our limited ambitions, negative working spirit, narrow-mindedness and the tendency to underestimate, whether to quicken the work tempo and to become more progressive with far-sighted ideas and ambitions.

"Necessary Changes" Required

A short article appearing in the *People's Daily* of October 13, 1965 concluded that "necessary changes" must be made toward revolutionization. In 1965 all the operations of various departments of the Chinese Communist regime are going to change as decided by the party policy-makers. Therefore, the party cadres at low levels are required to change their leadership first. The methods of change include exposing contradictions, and developing ideological struggle into class struggle. The class struggle is supposed to be the guidepost of this revolutionization movement which is actually a large-scale "party rectification."

It is said that the revolutionization of the leadership of the county party commissar is "to revolutionize the core of the leadership." That is to say the county party standing committee must first be revolutionized. The problem involves not only the leading individuals but also the leading group. Also, revolutionization concerns the ascertainment of the main contradiction as well as the relationship between ideology and work, between politics and production, between the leadership and the basic echelon, between the central work and departmental operation and between "work emphasis" and area control. It is problematical that the Chinese Communists could effect a radical change within a short period of time. . . .

Learn from County Commissar Chiao Yu-lu

The CCP "Socialist Education Movement" is an all-out party and non-party rectification campaign. The documents of the working conference of the CCP Central Committee discloses: "the emphasis of this movement is to rectify those who are in power and who are following a capitalistic line, in order further to strengthen and develop the socialist position in cities and rural villages." This reveals that cadres who are "anti-socialist," who are "following the capitalist line" are occupying key positions. These "key" persons "are either on the stage or behind the scene." "Those who support these key persons are either higher-ups or down lower." "The higher-ups include those anti-socialists in departments of the Central Committee." Therefore the Chinese Communists demanded that in the "Socialist Education Movement, the main task was to conduct a four-purify movement among the cadres. (The four-purify means purification of politics, economy, party organization and ideology.) The fourth of the six requirements as demanded by Mao Tse-tung of the "Socialist Education Movement" was "that a good leadership nucleus be established." This "leadership nucleus" is exactly the county commissar. It was decreed that derelict cadres be reassigned or reformed; that sub-quality cadres be advised to withdraw from the party membership; and that cadres involved in serious condition be "deprived of their power—struggle first, then deposition, extradition or even detainment."

The Chinese Communists consider that revolutionization of the county involves practical as well as ideological problems. The practical problem means "deprivation" of those "anti-socialist key persons," and struggle against cadres characterized by "fear" and "three-self-and-five-old" mentality. Actually the underlining theme is "Mao Tse-tung's Thought Commands." The so-called revolutionization of county party leadership is virtually a problem of Mao Tse-tung-ization. Therefore the present-day development of the "socialist education movement" features discussion of Mao Tse-tung's works, listening to Mao Tse-tung and "working as Mao Tse-tung would like." At the beginning of 1966, a climax of "learning from Mao-Tse-tung" was created by the Chinese Communists, sceptering the "Mao Tse-tung's works as the supreme guide for all tasks," requiring cadres of county and higher level to "study them constantly" and "study them for life." . . .

14 • Li Tien-ming: *The Problem of Leadership in the Second Revolutionary Generation* *

Through the last few years, as Mao's health has shown signs of impairment and the top stratum of China's revolutionary party has also advanced in age, governmental and other spokesmen in the West have expressed hope that a rising younger generation, which has not known first-hand the bitter years of struggle for power, would produce leaders less militant and increasingly revisionist. That the present high CCP élite is quite sensitive to such wishfulness is indicated by the report that hired translators in the Foreign Languages Press in Peking have instructions to give high priority to the translation of such utterances abroad.

Mao Tse-tung and many other spokesmen have been paying much attention to the problem of keeping China on the militant revolutionary road even as and after younger leaders assume decisive responsibilities. Actually, those who will increasingly take over the highest positions will seldom be young activists; most of them will be approaching or will have reached middle age. One of the themes of the "Great Cultural Revolution" (1962–65–67) was a precipitated new revolutionary situation which would temper the rising generation in conditions of struggle.

The following observations by a scholar on Taiwan treat some aspects of the developing anxiety on this score and the consequent campaign. Some of the names mentioned (for example, T'ao Chu and Lu Ting-yi) soon came under criticism by the Mao-Lin group of doctrinaire extremists. The author of this article, Lee Tien-ming, a Chinese graduate of Waseda University in Tokyo, has specialized in biographical studies of Communist Chinese leaders and on peasant problems in mainland China.

* "Who Will Succeed Mao Tse-tung?" *Issues and Studies,* II, No. 7 (April 1966), pp. 5–7. By permission.

While conducting a broad research on Mao's successor it is almost impossible not to touch upon the next generation. To specialists on Chinese Communist affairs, study of the next generation is in vogue today. The fact that it is so has arisen from an assumption that Peiping may change in the future. Speaking of the present and next generation, it is rather difficult to draw a clear demarcation between them. By "next generation" we mean a few people who are under the age of 60 with party seniority and at the meantime seemingly enjoying a good deal of Mao's favor at the moment, such as T'ao Chu, Lu Ting-yi and Chiang Nan-hsiang or the future committeemen after the election of ninth Central Committee of Chinese Communist Party. It is difficult to figure out who are in the list, to say nothing of a detailed individual and comparative study. Needless to say, the next generation on the Chinese mainland is already in existence. Some of them are even among the namelist of semi-finals. As to who is going to be the champion of the next generation, it is too early to say yet. Since no really reliable information is available, all we can do is to direct our attention to some of the most noticeable and outstanding Chinese Communist cadres.

Nevertheless, some of the measures taken by the Chinese Communists in recent years may enable us to study this particular problem from another angle. On June 11-29, 1964, the Young Communist League of the Chinese Communists held its ninth national congress. One of the main issues on the agenda was the principal role of the League during the socialistic period. They stressed "the need to strengthen the class-consciousness of youth, to keep their regime fit for revolution for another five or even ten generations to come without changing its course, as it was pointed out at the tenth plenary session of the eighth Central Committee of the Chinese Communist party in 1962. It was clearly mentioned in the revised regulations of the League that Marxism, Leninism and Maoism be observed as the guiding principles. There are 178 Central Committeemen newly elected in the ninth session of the Young Communist League as compared with 149 in the previous session, with an increase of 29. Among them only 32 were incumbents; 147 were new, of whom 17 were elected from the alternate members in the previous session. There were 74 alternate committeemen in the ninth session as compared with 63 in the previous session with an increase of 22. There was only one incumbent, the rest being all newly elected. This shed light on one thing in particular: as early as two years before, Peiping began a vigorous project of building up cadres for the new generation. Later, an editorial entitled "The Cultivation of Our Successors—A Long-Term Revolutionary Enterprise" appeared in the 14th issue of *Red Flag,* July 31, 1962. On August 3 the same year, another editorial "A Cultivation Project for Hundreds of Millions of Proletarian Revolutionary Successors" appeared in the *People's Daily.* On September 23, an article entitled "Cultivation of Revolutionary Successors, A Strategical Role of the Party" by An Tzu-wen, Director of the Organization Department of the CCP Central Committee, appeared in the combined 17th-18th issue of *Red Flag.* All these indicate that the so-called project of cultivating revolutionary successors is not only one of the major policies of the Peiping regime, but also one of the long-range tasks. Maoism and Maoism alone is definitely the yardstick for the cultivation of the revolutionary successors. This was exactly so interpreted in the article "The Revolutionary Successors Are Beginning to Grow" which appeared in the *People's Daily* on January 21, 1966: "To take turn means to take over Mao's theoretical doctrine first." In other words, the cultivation project for revolutionary successors is especially designed for the sole purpose of taking over Maoism, and nothing else.

On January 15-27, 1965, two conferences were held in Peiping. One of them was the second meeting of the fourth national committee of "All-China Youth Federation" while the other was the eighteenth conference of the "All-China Students' Federation." Resolutions were passed concerning the revision of the charters of the federations as well as the restoration of student associations at provincial, district and municipal levels. The Youth Federation reelected Wang Wei as the chairman to replace Liu Hsi-yuan. The number of vice chairmen was increased from 11 to 14, of whom only two were incumbents, the rest being all new faces. The Student Federation re-elected Wu Shao-chu as the chairman to succeed Hu Chi-li. All the vice chairmen were new appointees. The emphasis on new faces in these two conventions conforms with that during the ninth session of the "Chinese Young Communist League:" From March 29 till April 19 the same year, the Young Communist League held its second plenary meeting of the Ninth Central Committee in Peiping. A resolution was passed to "Raise high [the] Maoist Red Banner," and urge the youths to dedicate themselves to" . . . bringing up juveniles and children as successors of proletarian revolution. It also urged that examples and groups of "young pioneers" be formed on administrative village basis at various levels of the Young Communist League so that every child may be integrated into the corresponding level of organizations under the direction of the youth and children organizations, which are, in turn, established under the branches of the Young Communist League so the Peiping regime is not only moulding its second, but the third and possibly the fourth generations as well. The Chinese Communists consider that their revolutionaries should remain qualitatively safe up to the fifth and even the tenth generation. So in their mind the cultivation project should not stop short at the second generation.

The purpose of the Communist cultivation project for the second generation successors is that there shall be no change in the future. The reason why Peiping is making such laborious efforts in this direction is simply because there is really a possibility of qualitative change. With this understanding we can easily see how worried and hesitant Mao must have been in handling the second generation. On the one hand, in Mao's jargon, the youths are just like the early morning sun on whom his hopes can be entrusted. On the other hand the top leaders of Mao's regime have expressed their worries about the youths that they have been brought up in a stable environment thus lacking experience in weathering storms, as reflected frequently in their speeches. When asked by Edgar Snow in an interview on January 9, 1965, about what the youths on the mainland thought of and how they looked at things, Mao replied: 'I don't know anything about them either. Nevertheless there are two possibilities that I can imagine: either the revolution is to continue marching towards Communism, or the youths negate the Communistic revolution and look at it rather passively." Mao can cultivate a man as his successor or some men as a nucleus of collective leadership but cannot cultivate people by the myriads as his second generation. Without the backing of the second generation the successor problem remains unsolved. Recently, in order to set up examples for the youngsters, much publicity has been given to personages such as Lei Feng, Wang Chieh and Chiao Yu-lu. Granting that these persons were in existence and that they were really up to the alleged saint standard, the models for the second generation should be selected by that generation itself. "Saints" are not screws which fit anywhere. It is no problem to vigorize [sic] a man's body or to improve his technique. But the whisper of one's conscience can never be subdued by external force. Some cadres of their first generation such as Hsi Chung-shun, Tang Cheng, Lee Weihan [Li Wei-han] and Yang Hsien-chen could not avoid being purged or stripped of power for one reason or another in the recent past. That means Mao cannot even unite the hearts of the first generation. How can he expect to unite the hearts of the second generation? . . .

SECTION FOUR

Parties, Factions, and Interest Groups

15 • MU FU-SHENG: *The Pervasive Influence of the Communist Party* *

Mu Fu-sheng is a broadly educated engineer who had twelve years of training and professional experience in Britain and the United States before he chose to return to his native China in 1957. There he hoped to make contributions to modernizing development, but he later changed his mind about the possibilities and was allowed to depart.

In this excerpt from his insightful book he describes the pervasive authority and influence of the Chinese Communist party and how intimately it can control the lives of millions.

This gigantic system, the Chinese Communist Party, works, in spite of its size—twelve million members in 1957—like a precision machine tool. The recruiting, training and final screening of the cadre are not much publicised, but through the numerous contacts everyone must have with Party members it is clear that close watch is kept on the family background, social connections and 'political consciousness' of the members of the cadre before and after they join the Party, and that weak links are promptly expelled. During the 'anti-rightist' movement in 1957 some young expelled members committed suicide, and in 1956, as reported in the *People's Daily News,* owing to the refusal to grant permission to a Party member to marry a member of the Communist Youth Corps whose father was a landlord, a double suicide resulted. This showed the Party's vigilance over its purity and discipline. Every member of this political machine knows of nothing except the infallibility of its leaders and the importance of carrying out their directives. Inside the cadre members are always exhorting each other to 'fulfill and over-fulfill' the objective given them by the Party. When enthusiastic laymen make some suggestion concerning national policy they usually get the answer, 'The Organisation, we need not doubt, has adequate measures [for] dealing with such matters.' 'The Organisation' means the Party.

* *The Wilting of the Hundred Flowers* (London: William Heinemann Ltd., 1962), pp. 149–151. By permission of the publisher and The Sterling Lord Agency.

The Party spreads its control system over the entire Chinese society, entering into every nook and corner. There was on the average one Party member among every fifty Chinese in 1957, the aged and the young included. Party members are placed in every Government office, commercial co-operative, farm co-operative, school, research institute, army unit, hospital, bank, city block, womens' association, artists' association, Y.M.C.A., labour union, other political party, pedlars' co-operative, cab co-operative, theatrical company, and so on. There are few forms of organized social life which are not nationalised and placed directly under the Party's control, and the loose ends, such as religious bodies, homes and hawkers are given special attention. It is hardly possible to live in China without being under the 'leadership' of Party members through one or more channels. Where there are Party members there are committees of Party members, which 'guarantee the achievement of the objective set by the Party for the particular organisation'. Usually, but not always, these Party members are placed in strategic positions, such as vice-president, general manager, treasurer or personnel manager, and sometimes a Party member holds no post, but is in an organisation just 'to lead the staff'. Regardless of their position the committee of Party members is always the most powerful part of the organisation and its secretary the most powerful person. Everyone who works is advised to 'stand close' to the Party, that is, to the Party members. The committee of Party members holds its own meetings and keeps its own records which non-Communists cannot attend and read and it 'leads' in the 'study' meetings to which we will refer presently. In fact, the Party representatives are normally referred to with the impersonal designation of 'the Leadership' or 'the Organisation.' When a man is in difficulties or in doubt in public or private affairs he would do well to seek the advice and help of the Party members, because all other channels would either lead to the Party or nowhere; in the latter case he has later to face the question from 'the Leadership,' 'Why did you not come to us?' Party members can speed up the issue of a travel permit or get extra tickets for a theatrical performance or obtain temporary ration cards. When a Party member asks a man to go to a meeting or parade or to read a pamphlet or to a private talk, that is an order which supercedes all other orders and duties, except particularly urgent ones, which have to be explained to 'the Leadership.'

With these simple tools the Party can make and has made the people do practically everything it wants, far more than modern democracy or ancient despotism. . . .

16 • Li Wei-han: *The Characteristics of the Chinese People's Democratic United Front* *

The United Front is a term used in differing historic circumstances for calculated alliances by Communist parties with other, even bourgeois, groups. The CCP had entered such cooperative truces twice before it captured national power, in 1923–27 and 1937–41; it might have done so again—with the Kuomintang (Nationalist party) still dominant—if the mediation and coalition

* *Hung Ch'i* (Red Flag), No. 12 (June 16, 1961); transl. in *Selections from China Mainland Magazines,* No. 268 (July 3, 1961), pp. 1, 17–22 *passim.*

effort of 1946 had succeeded. In convening a National Assembly without the CCP and Democratic League late in 1946, the Kuomintang was attempting a sort of controlled United Front. Within three more years the Communists emerged victorious, and, realizing need for the cooperation of many other groups, sponsored their version of a United Front.

During the years of consolidation, the United Front and its echeloned bodies, called at the apex the People's Political Consultative Conference, were fairly significant. But after the Electoral Law of 1953 and the constitution in the following year, this structure of appointed, and on higher levels indirectly elected, delegates was largely eclipsed by the indirectly elected National People's Congress.

For years, until his dismissal in 1965, Li Wei-han headed the United Front Work Department of the party's secretariat. Here are portions of one of his better known speeches. The whole treatise is wordy, repetitious, and full of clichés. The last section, unused here, reveals how the CCP tries to prescribe its own experience and the United Front tactic for the "bourgeois democratic" anti-imperialist stage in the building of other new nations.

Li was one of the earliest Chinese Marxists who studied in France, and it was there in 1922 that he helped to found the Chinese Communist Youth League. He has been an able intellectual and one of the party's best organizers.

The Chinese people's democratic united front has a history of 14 years. Having triumphantly gone through the stage of democratic revolution, it is now triumphantly going through the socialist stage. Many characteristics have been formed in the long course of its historical development. The following are its principal and basic characteristics:

(1) The united front led by the Chinese Communist Party;
(2) The united front based on the alliance of workers and peasants;
(3) The united front based on alliance with and struggle against the bourgeoisie;
(4) The united front with the armed struggle as its mainstay at the stage of democratic revolution and based on the dictatorship of the proletariat at the socialist stage;
(5) The united front shouldering the revolutionary tasks at the democratic stage and the socialist stage;
(6) The united front of self-education and self-remolding; and
(7) The united front supporting the great unity of the world people.

These characteristics reflect the important laws for the development of the Chinese people's democratic united front. Now let us dwell on these characteristics in the above order.

I. *The United Front Led by the Chinese Communist Party*

The most fundamental characteristic of the Chinese people's democratic united front is leadership by the Chinese Communist Party. All the other characteristics of the people's democratic united front are inseparable from this fundamental characteristic, i.e., the leadership by the Communist Party.

Who ought to act as the leader if China's bourgeois democratic revolution was to win a complete victory? Was it that only the working class and its vanguard, the Communist Party, can and must act as the leader, or that the bourgeoisie and petty-bourgeoisie and their political parties might act as the leader? Over this fundamental question that decided the destiny of China, a protracted struggle has been waged both in theory and in practice. History is the best witness. The old democratic revolution led by the petty-bourgeois and the bourgeoisie could not win victory despite several decades' efforts. The New Democratic revolution led by the Chinese working class and the Chinese Communist Party eventually won victory after twenty-eight years of efforts. Why is it that only the working class and the Communist Party, and not the national bourgeoisie and their political parties, can and must be the leader of the Chinese revolution? "The reason is that the social and economic position of the national bourgeoisie determines its weakness; it lacks foresight and sufficient courage and many of its members are afraid of the masses." "Only the working class is most far-sighted, most selfless and most thoroughly revolutionary." ("On People's Democratic Dictatorship"—*Selected Works of Mao Tse-tung,* Vol. 4, People's Publishing House, 1960 edition, p. 1484, 1483). . . .

V. The United Front Entrusted with Revolutionary Tasks of the Democratic and Socialist Stages

Our country's people's democratic united front has victoriously passed the historical stage of democratic revolution and is now victoriously going through the stage of socialist revolution and socialist construction. This shows that it is a united front entrusted with the revolutionary tasks of two stages, a united front of thorough and uninterrupted revolution.

The historical conditions of the Chinese revolution and the correct leadership of the Chinese Communist Party were responsible for the smooth transformation of our country's people's democratic united front from a united front of the New Democratic revolution into a united front of socialist service. What we mean by historical conditions here are the following. In the world, after the first imperialist world war and the October Socialist Revolution of Russia, capitalism fully exposed its corruptness, the time for a world socialist revolution of the proletariat came, and the national and democratic revolutions of colonial and semi-colonial countries became part of the world socialist revolution of the proletariat. In the nation, the national bourgeoisie forfeited its qualification for leadership over the revolution, and, in the bourgeois democratic revolution, old democracy resigned its place to new democracy. This revolution could be consummated only under the leadership of the working class. What we mean by correct leadership of the Communist Party in the same passage is mainly the following. Leading the Chinese revolution under such historical conditions, the Chinese Communist Party had to handle correctly the relations between the democratic revolution and the socialist revolution, to win and secure for the working class leadership over the democratic revolution for the purpose of carrying through the New-Democratic revolution to the end, and then to proceed immediately and without pause to the socialist revolution, thus bringing about China's transition from capitalism to socialism. The whole practice of the Chinese revolution shows that the correct handling of the relations between the democratic revolution and the socialist revolution and the correct solution of the problem of the realization by the working class of leadership over the democratic revolution were inseparable from each other. The correct solution of these two basic questions in the democratic revolution could turn the people's democratic united front into a united front entrusted with the revolutionary tasks of two stages.

After the victory of the October Revolution of Russia, Lenin and Stalin propounded many times the view that the revolutions of colonies and semi-colonies had already left the category of old bourgeois revolution. This view became part of the theory on the socialist revolution of the world proletariat. On the basis of this theory, the Chinese Communist Party put forward, as far back as the First Revolutionary Civil War, the proposition that China's bourgeois democratic revolution was "part of the October Revolution of the world" and was to "fight for non-capitalist prospects." This proposition was correct. However, as Comrade Mao Tse-tung pointed out, its theoretical significance was not made fully manifest in those days with the result that people could only vaguely understand the question at issue. The correct proposition was opposed and distorted by opportunists. Ch'en Tu-hsiu the right opportunist, representing those who opposed it, regarded China's bourgeois democratic revolution as an old-democratic revolution, considered it necessary for a stage of capitalist society and bourgeois democratic republic to be gone through before the democratic revolution could change to a socialist revolution, and so regarded leadership over the democratic revolution as the business of the bourgeoisie and the victory of the democratic revolution as a victory for the bourgeoisie, and assigned to the working class the role of coolie to the bourgeoisie. His doctrine completely negated the Marxist-Leninist theory of uninterrupted revolution, put a great wall between the democratic revolution and the socialist revolution, and thus, from the right side, opposed proletarian leadership over the democratic revolution. The "left" opportunists during the Second Revolutionary Civil War represented those who distorted the correct proposition. They erased the distinctions between the democratic revolution and the socialist revolution, negated the Marxist-Leninist theory of the phased development of revolution, were subjectively impatient to pass beyond the democratic revolution, and so regarded as targets of the revolution the whole bourgeoisie and even the upper strata of the petty bourgeoisie and underestimated the decisive role of the peasants' anti-feudal struggle in the Chinese revolution, and thus, from the "left" side, seriously impaired proletarian leadership over the revolution. These two kinds of opportunists respectively failed to understand the connections and distinctions between the democratic revolution and the socialist revolution. For this reason, neither of them could solve the problem of proletarian leadership .

On the basis of the theory of Lenin and Stalin that the revolutions of colonies and semi-colonies had left the old category, and on the basis of China's historical characteristics, Comrade Mao Tse-tung explained repeatedly that after World War I and the October Revolution of Russia, China's bourgeois democratic revolution ceased to be an old democratic revolution under bourgeois leadership and became a New Democratic revolution under proletarian leadership and ceased to be part of the old world democratic revolution of the bourgeois and became part of the new world socialist revolution of the proletariat; that taking the nature of its social economy, the revolution was still a bourgeois democratic revolution and not yet a socialist revolution; but that its development and victory were sure to clear a broad way for the socialist revolution and leading to socialist prospects. In this way, he dialectically united the theory of uninterrupted revolution with that of the phased development of revolution, correctly settled the question of the connections and distinctions between the democratic revolution and the socialist revolution, and, in essentials, founded the thought of winning and realizing leadership over the revolution for the proletariat. Comrade Mao Tse-tung said:

"The whole Chinese revolutionary movement led by the Chinese Communist Party is a complete revolutionary movement embracing the two revolutionary stages, democratic and socialist, which are two revolutionary processes differing in character, and the socialist stage can be reached only after the democratic stage is completed. The democratic revolution is the necessary preparation for the socialist revolution, and the socialist revolution is the inevitable trend of the democratic revolution. And the ultimate aim of all communists is to strive for the final building of socialist society and communist society. We can give correct leadership to the Chinese revolution only on the basis of a clear understanding of both the differences between the democratic and socialist revolutions and their interconnections." ("The Chinese Revolution and the Chinese Communist Party"—*Selected Works of Mao Tse-tung,* Vol. 2, People's Publishing House, 1952, 2nd edition, p. 646).

"The present stage of the Chinese revolution is a transitional stage between putting an end to the colonial, semi-colonial and semi-feudal society and establishing a socialist society—a process of New-Democratic revolution." (*Ibid,* p. 642).

"The first step in, or the first stage of, this revolution is certainly not, and cannot be, the establishment of a capitalist society under the dictatorship of the Chinese bourgeoisie; on the contrary, the first stage is to end with the establishment of a new-democratic society under the joint dictatorship of all Chinese revolutionary classes headed by the Chinese proletariat. Then, the revolution will develop into the second stage so that a socialist society can be established in China." ("On New Democracy"—*Selected Works of Mao Tse-tung,* Vol. 2, People's Publishing House, 1952, 2nd edition, p. 665).

After the Tsunyi Meeting [of the Political Bureau of the Communist Party] in [January] 1935, the Party, guided by the theory of New Democratic Revolution of Comrade Mao Tse-tung, made a clear distinction between the democratic revolution and the socialist revolution, on the one hand, and opposed the skipping, subjectively, of the stage of democratic revolution. On the other, it linked up the democratic revolution with the socialist revolution and, in the course of the former, made as good preparations as possible for the latter. Here the principal tasks were: first, to constantly strengthen Party building so that it could become a strong vanguard armed with the Marxist-Leninist theory and closely connected with the broad masses; second, to consolidate and expand the worker-peasant alliance, so that the peasants can be made a great ally of the working class, and to unite with all forces that can be united on the foundation of worker-peasant alliance; third, to build and develop revolutionary bases for armed revolution and people's democratic dictatorship, and to enforce on such bases the various New Democratic policies, thereby protecting and encouraging those capitalist elements who are beneficial to the national economy and people's living on the one hand, and developing as much as possible the socialist political and economic factors, on the other, and as the various New Democratic policies are put into practice, to gradually train Party cadres so that they could gain experience in state administration in the fields of political, economic, military and cultural affairs; fourth, to implement thoroughly the mass line, giving [cadres] a free hand in leading the masses to wage by themselves revolutionary struggles from which to constantly educate themselves and to raise their own consciousness. "The mass line of the Party is the fundamental political line of our Party and also the fundamental oragnizational line of our Party." (Liu Shao-ch'i: *On Party,* p. 37). Thanks to the implementation of this fundamental line, our Party was able to fully mobilize the masses and succeeded in carrying the revolution to the end. Our experience proved that in the course of democratic revolution, the more extensively and deeply the various revolutionary forces, particularly the workers and the peasantry, are mobilized, the more thoroughly the revolution can be carried out. And the more thoroughly the democratic revolution is carried out and the various democratic forces enabled continuously to maintain their broad unity as they enter the socialist revolution, the more properly the socialist revolution can be carried out. By following such a path, the result of the New Democratic revolution is a development not only bearing capitalist factors but also socialist factors. The socialist factors in the New Democratic revolution "are the growing political influence of the proletariat and the Communist Party in the whole country; the leadership of the proletariat and the Communist Party that has been or may be recognized by the peasantry, the intelligentsia and the urban petty bourgeoisie; and the state enterprises of the people's republic and the cooperatives of the laboring people." ("The Chinese Revolution and the Communist Party"—*Selected Works of Mao Tse-tung,* Vol. 2, People's Publishing House, 1952, 2nd edition, p. 645). Pursuance of this path made it possible for the proletariat and the Communist Party to win and consolidate the leadership over the Chinese revolution, lead the democratic revolution to a complete victory, establish the people's republic of democratic dictatorship (factually, proletarian dictatorship), and make the New Democratic revolution immediately change to socialist revolution. Facts prove that the complete victory of the New Democratic revolution and the change to socialist revolution are unified and inseparable from each other.

It is just because the people's democratic united front in a front led by the Communist Party and built on the foundation of worker-peasant alliance that it can become a united front which fulfills completely the democratic revolution. Just because it is a united front which fulfills fully the democratic revolution that it can shoulder the tasks of two revolutionary stages or, we can say, the united front which stands for complete revolution and uninterrupted revolution. Comrade Mao Tse-tung pointed out in 1949, "This united front is so solid that it possesses the resolute will and the inexhaustible capacity to conquer every enemy and overcome all difficulties." ("Speech at the Preparatory Meeting of the New Political Consultative Conference"—*Selected Works of Mao Tse-tung,* Vol. 4, People's Publishing House, 1960 edit p. 1469-1470). It is so in the stage of democratic revolution and also in the stage of socialist revolution. For the past ten years, the people's united front has successfully stood again and again socialist revolution on the economic, political and ideological fronts. It now continues to unite the broadest social forces to successfully carry to completion the socialist revolution and to serve the building of socialism with greater, faster, better and more economical results. It is to be predicted that it will continue to exist for a long period to come and it will continue to grow until socialist society is successfully built and class is completely eliminated. Is there still any doubt about it? No, there should be no doubt.

VI. *The United Front of Self-Education and Self-Remolding*

The people of China, through the people's democratic united front led by the Party, got united not only in the struggle against the enemy but in carrying out self-education and self-remolding. When this work of self-education and self-remolding is well accomplished, it will make the people's democratic united front further developed and consolidated and the better fulfill the revolutionary tasks of the two stages.

During the New Democratic revolutionary period, we used the unity-criticism (or struggle)—unity method to carry out self-education and self-remolding within the Communist Party, in the revolutionary army, among the masses at the revolutionary bases, among the entire cadres and part of our allies, thus having a strong, politically unified, revolutionary rank and file organized. At the stage of socialist revolution, the Party and Comrade Mao Tse-tung gradually introduced the method among the entire people, including the national bourgeoisie, and obtained a great result.

Socialist revolution is an unprecedentedly broad and deep revolution. It is necessary not only to change the social system, do away with private ownership of the means of production and eliminate all exploitations but also to fundamentally remold, politically and ideologically, all exploiters and private owners and educate the people of the whole nation. Comrade Mao Tse-tung said: "In the course of the building of a socialist society, everybody needs remolding, the exploiters need remolding, the laborers need remolding" ("On the Correct Handling of Contradictions among the people," People's Publishing House, 1957 edition, p. 20). Only when this remolding work is well done, can the great historical task of eliminating class and of complete emancipation of the whole people be realized. Marx and Engels pointed out: The proletariat must liberate themselves and at the same time liberate the whole mankind. This is a great ideal. It teaches us that only on the foundation of development of socialist construction, only when all the people are remolded, only when the bourgeoisie and other exploiting elements are fundamentally remolded, and only when all the laborers are helped to carry out further self-remolding, will it be possible for class differences to be eliminated and for us to reach the communist society. Therefore, in the socialist society the work of remolding man, including the remolding of the bourgeoisie and other exploiting elements, is a noble cause in the struggle for the realization of the communist ideal. By subjecting the exploiting class to fundamental remolding we mean to turn the bourgeoisie, the bourgeois intelligentsia and other exploiting elements into laborers and make them part of the working class. This is a difficult and stupendous task. The nation's experience proves that it is comparatively easy to change the ownership of exploiters, but it is truly hard to remold the exploiters, which is ten times as hard as to remold the ownership system and demands efforts to be made for a long period of time.

The realization of this great and difficult task depends on one fundamental condition, namely, the state power led by the Communist Party and the people's democratic dictatorship. With a state of their own, the people can then, through the method of dictatorship, force those of the reactionary class and reactionary cliques which have been toppled to remold themselves through labor; they can then in a nation-wide scope and on a national scale conduct self-education and self-remolding by the unity-criticism (or struggle)—unity method, i.e., starting from the desire for unity, through criticism or struggle, to distinguish between right and wrong and to achieve new unity on a new foundation. Comrade Mao Tse-tung said: "Only when the people have a state of their own can they in a nation-wide scope and on a national scale use democratic methods to educate and remold themselves, enable themselves to get rid of the influence (which is quite deep at present, will exist for a long time to come, and cannot be wiped out quickly) of the reactionary cliques both internally and externally, remold themselves by doing away with the bad habits and bad thinking inherited from the old order, guard themselves against the wrong path led by the reactionary cliques, and march forward toward socialism and communism." ("On People's Democratic Dictatorship"—*Selected Works of Mao Tse-tung,* Vol. 4, People's Publishing House, 1960 edition, p. 1481). The democratic method, i.e., the "unity-criticism (or struggle)-unity" method, is the method for the handling of contradictions among the people and is also the united-front method. Through the people's democratic united front, we can adopt a great variety of forms through which to most widely unite the people of all democratic classes and through which to help people carry out self-education and self-remolding. Over the past ten years or more, the Chinese people's democratic united front and its organization—the Chinese People's Political Consultative Conference and its committees at all levels have played a tremendous role in organizing the bourgeoisie and bourgeois intelligentsia for self-education and self-remolding.

Comrade Mao Tse-tung said: "The struggle of the proletariat and revolutionary people in changing the world consists in achieving the following task to remold the objective world as well as their own subjective world—to remold their faculty of knowing as well as the relations between the subjective world and the objective world." ("On Practice"—*Selected Works of Mao Tse-tung* Vol. 1, People's Publishing House, 1952, 2nd edition, p. 285). The various strata of people of China participating in the people's democratic united front, guided by the Chinese Communist Party, have ceaselessly waged revolutionary struggles in the transformation of China, fulfilled the revolutionary tasks of different periods, and at the same time as revolutionary struggles are waged to transform China, constantly remolded themselves. We believe that if the people taking part in the people's democratic united front, under the guidance of the Communist Party in future, will continue, uninterruptedly and thoroughly, to achieve the tasks of socialist revolution and socialist construction, as well as the tasks of self-education and self-remolding, they can surely enter together the communist society of boundlessly bright and beautiful prospects.

17 • Têng Hsiao-p'ing: *On Communist Party Members* *

The Chinese Communist party has always emphasized the importance of well trained, faithful members. When possible it has recruited carefully, and when this has not been feasible, it has followed rapid expansion with periods of weeding and reindoctrination.

* *Report on the Revision of the Constitution of the Communist Party of China* (Peking: Foreign Languages Press, 1956), pp. 91–98.

Two leaders, Liu Shao-ch'i and Têng Hsiao-p'ing, have—next to Mao himself—become the mentors par excellence of party members, by the 1960's numbering at least seventeen million. The strength of their supporters within the party network was demonstrated in 1965–67 when, though denounced for bureaucratism and opposition to extremist policies of the Mao-Lin faction, they were able to conduct muffled but rather effective opposition and perhaps will compel compromises that will be clarified only later.

During the Seventh Congress of the CCP in 1945, Liu had lectured on policies concerning and qualities of party members.[1] *As Têng explains here, conditions had changed considerably by 1956 when the party constitution, which is still in effect, was adopted on September 26. From Têng's long discussion of the revised basic party document, we select and somewhat abridge this section on membership. As in the case of Liu, but thus far less overtly, Têng's writings have been under official disfavor since 1966. Here again disapproval is based less on content than on other issues and rivalries. As well as outside observers can discern, the writings of these two leaders are quite orthodox and may later be reestablished.*

Until the "Great Cultural Revolution," Têng's was the fastest rising star in the Chinese Communist hierarchy. Since 1952 he had been a Vice-Premier and had held many other important posts as political commissar with major military units, regional bureau positions, and in financial administration. But his strong influence in more bureaucratic aspects of the party stems from his role as Secretary-General of the Central Committee and thus of its large secretariat since 1954. Since 1956, he has been the only official to hold concurrently with this post a seat on the Politburo and on its Standing Committee. Têng is a Szechwanese who apparently still has strong connections in the Southwest. He, too, was one of the young converts who studied in France after World War I.

The most significant change about the Party is that it is now in the position of leadership throughout the country. The Party's programme for a democratic revolution has been carried out in most parts of the country, and its programme for a socialist revolution has in the main been successfully carried out. The present task of the Party is to complete the socialist revolution and bring about, in not too long a period, the socialist industrialization of the country, building China into a mighty socialist industrial country. Organizationally, the composition of the Party has changed both in numerical strength and in the social status of its members. According to figures provided by the Organizational Department of the Central Committee, at the end of June 1956, the Party had a total membership of 10,734,384, which is 1.74 per cent of the total population. Of this, 1,502,814, or 14 per cent of the total membership, are workers; 7,417,459, or 69.1 per cent, are peasants; 1,255,923, or 11.7 per cent, are intellectuals; 558,188, or 5.2 per cent, are of other social status. Women constitute about 10 per cent of the total membership.

The triumph of the Party's cause, the increasing weight of its responsibility

[1] See *On the Party*, 4th ed. (Peking: Foreign Languages Press, 1952), pp. 63–77.

towards the people, and the rise of its prestige among the masses—all this demands that our Party should set higher standards for its members. Moreover, in the past a person's decision to join our Party generally meant that he was prepared to struggle, at the risk of his personal freedom and even his very life, for the interests of the masses and for the supreme ideal of human society. Nowadays, however, it is more likely to find people who have joined the Party for the sake of prestige and position and who do not safeguard the interests of the masses, but harm them instead. To be sure, such people are rather rare in our Party, but we cannot overlook the fact that they do exist. The struggle to raise the standards of the Party membership is one of the Party's important political tasks for the present.

With this end in view, new provisions are made in the draft Constitution regarding the qualifications for Party membership.

In the first place, the draft demands that Party members must be people who work and do not exploit the labour of others. In our day everything that brings honour is the result of labour, and to exploit the labour of others instead of working oneself is a deep disgrace in the eyes of the people. With the development of socialist transformation, exploitation and living on the fruits of other people's labour are dying out in our country. However, in present-day Chinese society there are still exploiters, overt and covert practices of exploitation, and ideas of the exploiting class. We must not allow such people, practices, and ideas to find their way into the ranks of the Party, and we must see to it that every Party member draws a clear line between labour and exploitation.

It is provided in the draft that Party members must energetically fulfill the tasks assigned them by the Party, because this is the concrete guarantee for the carrying out of Party policy and decisions.

The draft Party Constitution requires every Party member to strictly observe the Party Constitution and the laws of the state and behave in accordance with communist ethics, no exception being made for any Party member, whatever his services or position. Here, the Central Committee considers it of special significance today to stipulate very clearly that no Party member, whatever his services or position, is allowed any special privilege to act against the Party Constitution, the laws of the state, or communist ethics. Some Party members who have rendered meritorious service and hold responsible positions have the idea that it is their prerogative to act as they please, discipline or no discipline. There are even Party organizations which have given tacit consent to this view. In actual fact, anyone who entertains or supports this view is helping the enemy to corrode our Party. People who conduct themselves like "overlords" all tend to think that they are indispensable to the Party. The fact, however, is quite the contrary. Our Party, far from having any use for such persons, definitely does not permit the presence in its ranks of any "overlords" who in the matter of fulfilling the duties of Party members may act in a way different from ordinary members. Respect is due to service and position only if the person possessing such standing and record does not get conceited about them or consider them as something entitling him to special privileges, but, on the contrary, becomes ever more modest, prudent and conscious of his responsibility to set a good example. If he does not do this his conceit and insolence will be the ruin of him. The Party will never tolerate such people at the risk of isolating itself from the broad masses.

The draft Party Constitution stipulates that it is the duty of every Party member to practise criticism and self-criticism, expose shortcomings and mistakes in work and strive to overcome and correct them; and that it is his duty to report such shortcomings and mistakes to the leading Party bodies, up to and including the Central Committee. Without doubt this provision in the draft will help to stimulate the political activity of all Party members, promote inner-Party criticism and facilitate the exposure and elimination of shortcomings and mistakes in Party work. . . .

Every applicant for Party membership must undergo the procedure of admission individually. The draft Constitution stipulates that an applicant must be recommended by two full Party members, and is admitted as a probationary member after being accepted by the general membership meeting of a Party branch and approved by the next higher Party committee, and he may become a full Party member only after the completion of a probationary period of a year.

In the draft the term "probationary period" has been adopted in place of "candidature" which has long been employed, and the term "probationary member" in place of "candidate member." This is because the term probationary is more accurate in meaning. The change was suggested by a non-Party personality and we have accepted the suggestion.

During the discussion on the draft, many comrades raised the question: "If it is our purpose to raise the standards of the Party membership, why have we discarded the original provisions about different procedures of admission for applicants of different social status? Might not this affect the purity of the Party?"

The distinction that was hitherto made in the procedure of admitting new members has been removed because the former classification of social status has lost or is losing its original meaning. Both before the Seventh Congress [in 1945] and for a considerable period afterwards it was essential to have different procedures of admission for applicants of different social status and this served a very good purpose. But in recent years the situation has basically changed. The difference between workers and office employees is now only a matter of division of labour within the same class. Casual labourers and farm labourers have disappeared. Poor and middle peasants have all become members of agricultural producers' co-operatives, and before long the distinction between them will become merely a thing of historical interest. With the introduction of obligatory military service,[2] revolutionary soldiers no longer constitute an independent social stratum. The vast majority of our intellectuals have now come over politically to the side of the working class, and there is a rapid change in their family background. The conditions in which the city poor and the professional people used to exist as independent social strata have been virtually eliminated. Every year, large numbers of peasants and students become workers, large numbers of workers, peasants and their sons and daughters join the ranks of the intellectuals and office-workers, large numbers of peasants, students, workers and office-workers join the army and become revolutionary soldiers, while large numbers of revolutionary soldiers return to civilian life as peasants, students, workers or office-workers. What is the point, then, of classifying these social strata into two different categories? And even if we were to try and devise a classification, how could we make it neat and clear-cut?

It has already been stated that only those who work and do not exploit the labour of others, and only those who are fully qualified to be Party members, can

[2] In 1955.

be admitted to the Party. Therefore, the question of different procedures of admission for applicants of different social status has ceased to exist.

Practice has shown that what we should chiefly do in order to purify the ranks of the Party is as follows: strengthen supervision over the work of recruiting new members; see to it that the general membership meeting of the Party branch and the Party committee of the next higher level check up carefully on applicants for admission and on probationary members at the end of their probationary period; subject probationary members to careful observation and give them education during their probationary period; give timely education to Party members who are not fully up to the standard, and expel whatever bad elements who have wormed themselves into the Party. Purity does not depend on the number of Party members required for recommending different types of applicants, the length of Party standing of such members or the length of the probationary period of the applicants.

The present membership of our Party is nine times what it was at the time of the Seventh Congress. How were these new members admitted into the Party? Are they really qualified for Party membership? Judging from the results of the Party rectification campaigns of the past years, the overwhelming majority of them were admitted according to the procedure laid down in the Party Constitution and are qualified for Party membership. On the whole, the Party organizations have grown up in the course of mass revolutionary struggles, and the very fact that those who were admitted were people active among the masses and tested in struggle forms the chief guarantee for the quality of the Party membership. But mistakes were made on many occasions in the matter of admitting new members. During the War of Liberation, new members were recruited in the rural districts of some liberated areas by means of so-called "Campaigns to Join the Party," or through a process of so-called "self-recommendation, public discussion, and approval by the Party organization." In the two years just before and after liberation of the whole country, the membership of the Party grew with undue speed, and in certain areas it grew practically without guidance and without plan, while Party organizations in some areas even went about recruiting new members in large numbers and setting up Party branches before the masses were aroused. The result was that certain Party organizations were at one time impure to a high degree. On the other hand, the mistake of "closed-door" sectarianism was also committed in admitting new members. For instance, at one time the Party failed to attach importance to recruiting new members from among industrial workers; at another time it neglected to recruit new members from among revolutionary intellectuals; in certain rural districts, the Party organizations neglected to recruit the more active youths and women.

Nevertheless, it is an obvious fact that 90 per cent of the present 10,730,000 members have joined our Party since the Seventh Congress. Experience has shown time and again that many members, although they have joined the Party organizationally, have not joined ideologically or at least not fully joined ideologically. It is, therefore, the task of the Party organizations at all levels to be conscientious about educating the vast numbers of new members more effectively, to take practical measures to organize and guide their study of Marxism-Leninism, Comrade Mao Tse-tung's writings and the history and policy of our Party and to strengthen their education in proletarian internationalism, so as to raise the level of their understanding and enable them to become really qualified ideologically as Party members.

18 • *Extracts from the Sixteen-Point Decision Concerning the Great Proletarian Revolution, August 8, 1966* *

In early August 1966 the Mao-Lin radical faction apparently packed an enlarged session of the party's Central Committee, and against opposition, passed the sixteen-point resolution from which key paragraphs are quoted here. This was the signal for acceleration of the "Great Proletarian Cultural Revolution" which had been gathering momentum for many months. Under Lin Piao's direction, reindoctrination of the People's Liberation Army had begun as early as 1961, and military cadres were to be used as models and agents for spreading the movement.

That this was a struggle for power was indicated not only by other published explicit admissions but also, as seen in this document, by criticisms of and warnings to persons of authority who were accused of losing revolutionary militancy, of bureaucratic conservatism, and of revisionism. The "cultural" components of the movement were partly to screen the actual power struggle, but they also constituted part of the serious intent of the radicals. In this and other statements they revealed a number of anxieties: that intellectuals and artists would revert to learning and expression mainly for individualistic expression and with professional emphases; that students would become specialists without practical identification with workers, farmers, and soldiers; that the younger generation would become enmeshed in revisionism which they feared had already affected many party leaders and their supporters; that the economic concessions made since the failure of the radical "Great Leap" and communization campaigns would permanently dilute orthodox doctrines; that bureaucratism was growing in party and government; in short, that the Chinese revolution was increasingly departing from its direction toward a classless society.

Strenuous methods were used in attempts to alter such trends and restore applications of pure doctrine. Although Mao and members of the special revolutionary committee which he established seemed to score regional but inconclusive successes, they were compelled to limit the struggle both because of stubborn resistance and lest prolonged confusion lead to another major economic crisis.

At the Tenth Plenary Session of the Eighth Central Committee of the Party, Comrade Mao Tse-tung said: To overthrow a political power, it is always necessary, first of all, to create public opinion, to do work in the ideological sphere. This is true for the revolutionary class as well as for the counter-revolutionary class. This thesis of Comrade Mao Tse-tung's has been proved entirely correct in practice.

Although the bourgeoisie has been overthrown, it is still trying to use the old ideas, culture, customs and habits of the exploiting classes to corrupt the masses,

* *Peking Review,* No. 33 (August 12, 1966), pp. 6–11.

capture their minds and endeavour to stage a come-back. The proletariat must do just the opposite: it must meet head-on every challenge of the bourgeoisie in the ideological field and use the new ideas, culture, customs and habits of the proletariat to change the mental outlook of the whole of society. At present, our objective is to struggle against and crush those persons in authority who are taking the capitalist road, to criticize and repudiate the reactionary bourgeois academic "authorities" and the ideology of the bourgeoisie and all other exploiting classes and to transform education, literature and art and all other parts of the superstructure that do not correspond to the socialist economic base, so as to facilitate the consolidation and development of the socialist system. . . .

3. *Put Daring Above Everything Else and Boldly Arouse the Masses*

The outcome of this great cultural revolution will be determined by whether the Party leadership does or does not dare boldly to arouse the masses.

Currently, there are four different situations with regard to the leadership being given to the movement of cultural revolution by Party organizations at various levels:

(i) There is the situation in which the persons in charge of Party organizations stand in the van of the movement and dare to arouse the masses boldly. They put daring above everything else, they are dauntless communist fighters and good pupils of Chairman Mao. They advocate the big-character posters and great debates. They encourage the masses to expose every kind of ghost and monster and also to criticize the shortcomings and errors in the work of the persons in charge. This correct kind of leadership is the result of putting proletarian politics in the forefront and Mao Tse-tung's thought in the lead.

(ii) In many units, the persons in charge have a very poor understanding of the task of leadership in this great struggle, their leadership is far from being conscientious and effective, and they accordingly find themselves incompetent and in a weak position. They put fear above everything else, stick to outmoded ways and regulations, and are unwilling to break away from conventional practices and move ahead. They have been taken unawares by the new order of things, the revolutionary order of the masses, with the result that their leadership lags behind the situation, lags behind the masses.

(iii) In some units, the persons in charge, who made mistakes of one kind or another in the past, are even more prone to put fear above everything else, being afraid that the masses will catch them out. Actually, if they make serious self-criticism and accept the criticism of the masses, the Party and the masses will make allowances for their mistakes. But if the persons in charge don't, they will continue to make mistakes and become obstacles to the mass movement.

(iv) Some units are controlled by those who have wormed their way into the Party and are taking the capitalist road. Such persons in authority are extremely afraid of being exposed by the masses and therefore seek every possible pretext to suppress the mass movement. They resort to such tactics as shifting the targets for attack and turning black into white in an attempt to lead the movement astray. When they find themselves very isolated and no longer able to carry on as before, they resort still more to intrigues, stabbing people in the back, spreading rumours, and blurring the distinction between revolution and counter-revolution as much as they can, all for the purpose of attacking the revolutionaries.

What the Central Committee of the Party demands of the Party committees at all levels is that they persevere in giving correct leadership, put daring above everything else, boldly arouse the masses, change the state of weakness and incompetence where it exists, encourage those comrades who have made mistakes but are willing to correct them to cast off their mental burdens and join in the struggle, and dismiss from their leading posts all those in authority who are taking the capitalist road and so make possible the recapture of the leadership for the proletarian revolutionaries. . . .

10. *Educational Reform*

In the great proletarian cultural revolution a most important task is to transform the old educational system and the old principles and methods of teaching.

In this great cultural revolution, the phenomenon of our schools being dominated by bourgeois intellectuals must be completely changed.

In every kind of school we must apply thoroughly the policy advanced by Comrade Mao Tse-tung, of education serving proletarian politics and education being combined with productive labour, so as to enable those receiving an education to develop morally, intellectually and physically and to become labourers with socialist consciousness and culture.

The period of schooling should be shortened. Courses should be fewer and better. The teaching material should be thoroughly transformed, in some cases beginning with simplifying complicated material. While their main task is to study, students should also learn other things. That is to say, in addition to their studies they should also learn industrial work, farming and military affairs, and take part in the struggles of the cultural revolution as they occur to criticize the bourgeoisie. . . .

12. *Policy Towards Scientists, Technicians and Ordinary Members of Working Staffs*

As regards scientists, technicians and ordinary members of working staffs, as long as they are patriotic, work energetically, are not against the Party and socialism, and maintain no illicit relations with any foreign country, we should in the present movement continue to apply the policy of "unity, criticism, unity." Special care should be taken of those scientists and scientific and technical personnel who have made contributions. Efforts should be made to help them gradually transform their world outlook and their style of work.

19 • *Young Communist League Resolution on Strengthening the Role of Primary League Organization in Rural Areas as the Core Among Young People* *

Communist parties always stress the organization and revolutionary direction of young people. During 1920–25 there was a Chinese Socialist Youth Corps; its name was then changed to the Chinese Communist Youth Corps. During the anti-Japanese war, and in the "liberated areas," this was called the New Democratic Youth League, a name that was retained until the title Young Communist League (YCL) was adopted at a congress in May 1957.

This massive organization for youths age 14 to 25 is the main vestibule to party membership. There is some overlap, for young men and woman can join the party at age 18. The YCL accepts top leadership from the Central Committee and on local levels that of the corresponding party committees.

These committees exercise guidance, give encouragement, lead in ideological and organizational work, instruct in Marxist-Leninist-Maoist theories, and help to select leaders for the League. Branches and members of the League cooperate in propaganda activities, campaigns of work and organization, improvement of production, in criticism and struggles, and in supervising the Young Pioneers (ages 9 to 15).

Naturally, as the following resolution indicates, most YCL branches are in rural localities. It was significant during 1966–67 that party extremists circumvented the YCL in mobilizing Red Guards and later Red Rebels as special political shock troops. Obviously in many areas YCL branches must have been loyal to the more practical-minded opponents of extremist methods. On August 13, 1966, the Central Committee of the YCL was reorganized along Maoist lines, and its organs for propaganda were at least temporarily stilled.

(1) The more than 600,000 primary organizations of the Young Communist League in rural areas, under the leadership of the Party and closely united with the great masses of the youth, have played an active part in fulfilling the tasks of socialist construction. Since the big leap forward, particularly since the establishment of rural people's communes, the work of the primary organizations of the League in rural areas has become more active and their role has become more conspicuous. However, owing to the fact that, in the course of the great changes in social organization and production organization, some leading organs of the League failed to take effective measures to adjust and perfect the primary organizations of the League and that a section of the League cadres neglected the basic-level work and the organizational role of the League, part of the primary organizations of the League have become somewhat loose with unsound leading core and are

* New China News Agency, July 24, 1959, reproduced in *Current Scene,* Research Backgrounder, "The Young Communist League (1959–1960)" (Hong Kong, 1962), pp. 13–15. This resolution was adopted by the Third YCL Central Committee at its Fifth Plenary Session, July 18, 1959.

unable to expand their work in a normal way. This lowers to a certain extent the role of the primary organizations as the core among the youth and practically affects the Party leadership over the youth work. This state of affairs must change immediately. . . .

(2) The fundamental problem of League-building is to build an advanced and militant Young Communist League maintaining close ties with the masses. In building the League, the basic principles prescribed in the League Constitution must be adhered to and regularly made clear to the rank-and-file of the League. The League-building must serve the political tasks and central work of the Party and go on in practical struggle. We should proceed from the actual conditions of the League and take long-range measures to increase the fighting strength of the primary organizations of the League and improve the quality of the League members. Both the ideological construction and the organizational construction of the League must be given equal importance, the political advancement and organizational soundness of the League must be insured.

(3) The Young Communist League is a close subsidiary to the Party and a transmission belt between the Party and the masses. The primary organizations of the League in rural areas must give full expression to this role, strengthen the political and ideological work among the youth, actively enlarge the influence of the Party, and genuinely serve as an instrument of the Party to unite and educate the youth. They should regularly organize and lead League members to study, carry out and propagate the policies of the Party and to publicize the situation and tasks. They must actively respond to the calls issued by the Party in each period, and take effective measures and immediate action. . . .

(4) The Young Communist League has been formed in accordance with the principle of democratic centralism, and must at all times carry out its activities in accordance with this principle. Within the League, there should be an ample amount of democratic life on one hand, and centralized leadership and relatively strict discipline on the other. Only this will prevent laxity in League organizations, enable the cadres and members of the League to carry out their work and participate in collective life in accordance with the principle of democratic centralism, enable the members to display their activism and initiative, and insure the League's uniformity in ideological and organizational matters and other activities. . . .

(5) . . . Basic-level League Organizations should, in accordance with the League Constitution, regularly conduct political-ideological work among the youth, publicize Marxism-Leninism and the policies of the Party, organize youth for engaging in various kinds of production activities and cultural and technological studies, manifest an interest in the life of the youth, educate League members, receive new members, and direct the work of the Young Pioneers. . . .

(6) Perfect the core of leading cadres in basic-level organizations and admit new members. Vacancies in the staff of leading cadres of basic-level organizations should be speedily filled. When the core of leading cadres weakens, prompt steps should be taken to readjust and reinforce it. In selecting cadres for leading posts in basic-level organizations, the requirements should be: a firm stand, sincere and honest, willing to study and work hard, and good at associating with the masses. . . . League organizations should regularly stress the increase of membership so as to inject new blood into the League. In some production units where the number of League members is relatively small or where there are no League

members at all, there is the special need for plans to admit a number of new members. Basic-level League organizations should map out plans for developing membership and periodically inspect the implementation of these plans. . . .

(7) To insure the Party's leadership is the life-line of the League. Basic-level League organizations in the rural areas must place themselves closely under the leadership of the Party, consider the main current tasks of the Party as the main current tasks of the League, map out their respective work plans under the centralized leadership of the Party and in line with the Party's work plan, and carry out their work among the masses of youth actively and on their own initiative. Basic-level League organizations should report conditions regularly to the Party, ask for instructions, and present suggestions on related matter.

20 • LIU KO-P'ING: *Anti-Chinese Feelings Among the Minorities* *

Limitations of space do not permit inclusion of essays or statements setting forth the conditions or views of the many interest groups in revolutionary Chinese society. Even to list various strata and groups would be excessive here. So let us select one type—the "national minorities"—and quote the rather candid comments by the Chinese (Han) Chairman of the Nationalities Committee of the National People's Congress early in 1958, when "rectification" was under way after suppression of the blooming flowers.

The minorities population of China by 1967 must be approximately forty-five million—about 6 per cent of the total. Mao Tse-tung and party-dominated administrators have adapted Stalinist nationalities policies. They have tried to reconcile the granting of significant degrees of local autonomy with overall "democratic centralism." This has been more permissible in cultural than in political and administrative matters. Politico-administrative jurisdictions ranging from large autonomous regions to counties with non-Chinese majorities have been established. Communist party organizations have been fostered in these areas. Minority peoples and their agencies have not been free to conduct their own foreign relations; they must cooperate in economic planning and programs, with national conscription and military policies, in matters of transportation, and in revolutionary principles of education and information.

Many have been the glowing reports of satisfaction and progress being made in minority regions. There have also been reports by party functionaries about persistent problems. Accounts reach other countries about recurrent revolts, particularly by groups in Sinkiang and Tibet. When the dust has settled, it may be seen that certain minorities have been able to do some bargaining during the turmoil of the "Great Cultural Revolution."

* *Jen-min Jih-pao,* January 11, 1958, quoted in Roderick MacFarquhar, *The Hundred Flowers Campaign and the Chinese Intellectuals* (New York: Frederick A. Praeger, 1960), pp. 255–257. By permission.

Liu Ko-p'ing is a Moslem who has been a prominent representative of the Northwest since 1949 and an administrator of policies particularly for Ninghsia and Sinkiang. Since 1956 he has been a full member of the party's Central Committee and has served as Chairman of the China-Pakistan Friendship Association.

In the past year or two, and especially since our Party decided to launch a rectification campaign and carry out the policy of "blooming and contending," a considerable amount of reactionary or extremely erroneous views and activity has been brought to light among small sections of the upper strata of the national minorities. Of these views and activities the main ones are:

(1) *Separatist ideas and activities*—The most noticeable examples are those who, claiming that a nationality has the right of self-determination, want to establish a union of republics or autonomous republics. A few of these openly want independence, declaring that "we want independence even if that means we have to forgo socialism" and that "if Han settlers continue to come, we will close the borders!" Meanwhile, separatist or secessionist activities have been brisk among the Mongols, principally among a small number of intellectuals and students who belong to families of feudal princes, aristocrats or high officials of the former puppet Mongolian Government, or who are corrupted by bourgeois ideas. They have tried to organise their own party and government. A small number of students even organised themselves in preparation for a flight to some foreign country where they might continue to engage in activities aimed at dividing the motherland. Some students and intellectuals of the Korean nationality, too, would not recognise China as their motherland. . . .

(2) *Repudiation of Central Government and Party leadership and effort to exclude Han cadres under the excuse of autonomous rights and "nationalisation"*—Some cadres of the local nationalities in Sinkiang have vociferously expressed their disapproval of Han cadres and openly told them to "go home." They said: "This will be genuinely an autonomous region only if the Han cadres are gone. So long as they remain here there will be no real autonomy." Huang Hsien-fan, a rightist of the Chuang nationality, says: "So long as Han cadres remain (in autonomous areas), the national minorities will not be able to exercise their powers. All Han cadres should be evacuated from national minority areas." These rightists especially object to the occupying of leadership posts by Han cadres inside and outside the Party in the autonomous areas.

(3) *Opposition to the coming of Han peasants and workers to national minority areas*—In order to attain the object of exclusion of Han people some people in Sinkiang urge mechanisation of agriculture at full speed. Some Mongols advocate a partitioning into a "purely Mongolian area" and a "purely Han area," so as to separate the Mongolian nationality from other nationalities, even if the Mongols have to do without the Paotow steel complex, the modern industries and the railroad. There are also those who advocate the setting up of industrial and mining enterprises by single nationalities. There are also those who oppose the learning of the Han language, both spoken and written, and the language of other nationalities. They also oppose cultural exchanges between different nationalities.

(4) *Opposition to socialist transformation*—Rightists among the national minorities allege that the co-operative movement has been bungled and that the

co-ops. are not superior in any way, that the system of unified purchase and sale is ruinous and has brought misery to the peasants, and that the movement for the suppression of counter-revolutionaries was also bungled, and that it victimised all the good men. These views are identical with those held by the rightists of the Han nationality. All the anti-socialist arguments of the rightists of the Han nationality are echoed by the rightists of the national minorities.

(5) *Hatred for and opposition to the Party*—The rightists say that "Party members are a privileged class," and that "Party leadership is rule by Great Han nationalism," and that "the national minorities are not yet liberated and are waiting for another liberation," and that "the national minorities could have liberated themselves and built socialism even without Party leadership." Rightists Wang T'ien-shi, Ou Pai-ch'uan, P'eng Po, Pu Lin, Ma Sung-t'ing and others all have organised their own groups for the purpose of opposing Party leadership. They hate especially the Party and Youth League members of their own nationalities, calling these Party and Youth League members traitors, black sheep, sycophants, and degenerates and scapegraces, and praising on the other hand the anti-Party elements as national heroes. Party leaders of the national minorities are attacked with particular vigour. Ma Sung-t'ing, a Hui rightist, declares that none of the Hui Communists know anything about their own nationality, that they have all eaten pork, and that they make the Hui girls marry the Han people. . . .

As most of these views are expressed under the banner of the nationalities and appear to support the interests of these nationalities, they have succeeded in capturing the imagination of some people and hoodwinking them. . . . Therefore, even though these views are held by a handful of men of the national minorities, we must not minimise their dangerous possibilities. These views must be seriously and resolutely criticised.

First, the rightists of the national minorities have been declaring loudly that present conditions are worse than the past and that the Communist Party is not so good as the Kuomintang. . . .

Secondly, concerning separatism or secessionism, that is, the agitation for republics and a federation of republics. The idea exists principally among young non-Party intellectuals of the Mongolian, Korean, Hui, Uighur and other nationalities. But it exists in more serious proportions in a few national minorities where it is entertained not only by those outside the Party, but also by some within the Party, and not only by Party members in general but also by some high-ranking cadres. They also seriously influenced a considerable part of the Party and non-Party cadres with the idea.

SECTION FIVE

Political Processes

21 • T. A. Hsia: *Sloganeering and the Jargon of a Mass Campaign* *

Language, so central to psyche and culture, can no more escape the implications of profound ideo-social revolution than can minds and persons. Indeed, shapers of the new Chinese society and polity have deliberately reformed and manipulated language, coining new terms and slogans, infusing new connotations, using language in the processes of propaganda and mobilization.

Dr. T. A. Hsia has written a terminological and semantic study of the Hsia-Fang, *or "downward transfer," movement of 1956–57. This compulsory trend of cadres and intellectuals from urban and institutional settings back to attempts at living closely with peasants has recurred in subsequent waves. The aims have been mainly anti-bureaucratic and have included improved relations between party and common people, an intermixture of social strata, and interfusion of different cultural levels. During* Hsia-Fang *those being moved were instructed to educate rural people with "revolutionary spirit" and to learn about homespun qualities, points of view, and methods.*

But this selection from the early part of Dr. Hsia's study is not limited to Hsia-Fang. *It calls attention to the semantic concomitants of all great mass movements, doubtless in all great revolutions. These trends seem to be particularly rich in a changing Chinese culture where language has long been intensely and elaborately basic.*

The author is a researcher on the Current Chinese Language Program, Center for Chinese Studies, Institute of International Studies on the University of California's Berkeley campus.

The mass movement imposes its own rules and assigns roles to the people. It speaks its own language, too, over and above the general Communist jargon. This people have to learn. Indeed, to go into a new mass movement entails as many difficulties as learning a new game or trade, with a different set of rules and a special jargon to be kept in mind. First of all, there is the "king-size term" which

* *A Terminological Study of the* Hsia-Fang *Movement,* Studies in Chinese Communist Terminology, No. 10 (Berkeley, Calif.: Center for Chinese Studies, Institute of International Studies, University of California, 1963), pp. 4–6. By permission.

is an abbreviated slogan, the label for the mass movement, or the designation of a policy. It summarizes for the people a certain phase of revolution receiving proper emphasis at the proper time. But before the propaganda machine reaches them with a full elucidation, the poor people may be at a loss to know either the meaning of the "king-size term" or that of the movement itself. . . .

When a mass movement sweeps over the nation, the language catches the general tone of life. It shows the symptoms of monomania, an obsession with one supreme task. This is perhaps excusable, since such features are also observable in the propaganda literature that came out of the mass movements before 1949. A mass movement is a response to an emergency, and one's power of speech must be handicapped when one is busy putting out the fire that threatens to burn down one's house. But there are differences between the mass movements before 1949 and those after. Whereas formerly a mass movement arose only when there was a real crisis, now the sense of emergency is created by the Communist Party to justify the movement. The masses involved in the movements of the old days, such as those of May 4th of 1919 and May 30th of 1925, never represented a very large percentage of the national population, but now a mass movement can be literally participated in by *ch'üan-min* (all the people). The people's "political consciousness" has no doubt undergone a change during the interval, but in addition the power of control that the Communist Party has come to enjoy is greater than ever before. So it is possible for the Party to launch a mass movement with a true uniformity of purpose—and a true uniformity of language.

When Communist China is in the grip of a mass movement, the "king-size term" dominates the speech of those whose life is dedicated to the supreme task. Its auxiliary terms also become the most useful expressions in daily life. The mass movements, whatever the declared purposes in each individual case, all provide a verbal environment which acts most violently upon the people's language habits. Amidst the built-up sound and fury, the people will hear the same slogans and politically fashionable phrases repeated so often that they can hardly suppress their desire to imitate, not to mention the practical necessity for them to imitate. Their ears are kept open to the theories, promises, cheers, threats, and flattery from the radio broadcasts and the lips of their supervisors and mentors, the cadres. If they can read, they will encounter the same theories, etc., in newspapers, pamphlets, and hand-written bulletins. There are certain documents—a speech by Mao, or an editorial in the *Jen Min Jih Pao,* for instance—that form a theoretical guide to the current mass movement. These the people must study and discuss, or at least, in the case of the very dullest, they must have the patience to hear them read and explained. They may not understand every word in the tremendous amount of propaganda dinned into their heads. They will perhaps never be able to use masterfully certain words and phrases, which, after much repetition, have become familiar. But the little they assimilate, even a few phrases from one movement, forms the core of what Mao regards as a "common language" and marks the success of Communist propaganda. . . .

22 • MAO TSE-TUNG: *Criteria for Distinguishing Between Corrective and Antagonistic Criticism* *

Evidently when Chairman Mao observed that the invitation for a "hundred flowers" to bloom (and schools to contend) had resulted in a crop of critical "poisonous weeds," he revised his initiatory secret speech of February 1957, adding in June—we can safely assume—the following definition of the limits within which criticisms would be permissible.

There has been much debate as to whether Mao and the party hierarchy mainly intended to "smoke out" critics. The present editors incline to the view that Chinese leaders were quite aware of the great pressures that had been exerted on people in the course of rapid and often concurrent reforms, including stages in the process of socialization. They were informed about discontents in Eastern Europe which had produced revolts. They themselves were dissatisfied with many aspects of the cadres and their performance. Freer criticism could and did provide cues for "rectification" of party personnel. That leaders were surprised by the virulence and extent of criticism and their loss of "face" ensured that those who had been outspoken would be disgraced and disciplined.

"Let a hundred flowers blossom," and "let a hundred schools of thought contend," "long-term coexistence and mutual supervision"—how did these slogans come to be put forward?

They were put forward in the light of the specific conditions existing in China, on the basis of the recognition that various kinds of contradictions still exist in a socialist society, and in response to the country's urgent need to speed up its economic and cultural development. . . .

On the surface, these two slogans—let a hundred flowers blossom and a hundred schools of thought contend—have no class character: the proletariat can turn them to account, so can the bourgeoisie and other people. But different classes, strata and social groups each have their own views on what are fragrant flowers and what are poisonous weeds. So what, from the point of view of the broad masses of the people, should be the criteria today for distinguishing between fragrant flowers and poisonous weeds?

In the political life of our country, how are our people to determine what is right and what is wrong in our words and actions? Basing ourselves on the principles of our Constitution, the will of the overwhelming majority of our people and the political programmes jointly proclaimed on various occasions by our political parties and groups, we believe that, broadly speaking, words and actions can be judged right if they:

(1) Help to unite the people of our various nationalities, and do not divide them;

(2) Are beneficial, not harmful, to socialist transformation and socialist construction;

* *On the Correct Handling of Contradictions among the People,* 3rd printing (Peking: Foreign Languages Press, 1959), pp. 48, 55–56.

(3) Help to consolidate, not undermine or weaken, the people's democratic dictatorship;

(4) Help to consolidate, not undermine or weaken, democratic centralism;

(5) Tend to strengthen, not to cast off or weaken, the leadership of the Communist Party;

(6) Are beneficial, not harmful, to international socialist solidarity and the solidarity of the peace-loving peoples of the world.

Of these six criteria, the most important are the socialist path and the leadership of the Party. These criteria are put forward in order to foster, and not hinder, the free discussion of various questions among the people. Those who do not approve of these criteria can still put forward their own views and argue their case. When the majority of the people have clear-cut criteria to go by, criticism and self-criticism can be conducted along proper lines, and these criteria can be applied to people's words and actions to determine whether they are fragrant flowers or poisonous weeds. These are political criteria. Naturally, in judging the truthfulness of scientific theories or assessing the aesthetic value of works of art, other pertinent criteria are needed, but these six political criteria are also applicable to all activities in the arts or sciences. In a socialist country like ours, can there possibly be any useful scientific or artistic activity which runs counter to these political criteria?

23 • Liu Shao-ch'i: *On Self-Criticism* *

Aside from expressing the moral and secular religious character of Chinese Communist formulae for social catharsis, the emphasis on self-criticism and on evaluations of "working style" are the principal forms in which middle- and lower-level persons can safely discuss problems. Prestige-conscious leaders do not indulge in self-criticism unless compelled to do so by irresistable disciplinary action. Even then, as in some cases during the "Great Cultural Revolution," such recantations are likely to be perfunctory or guarded. Lesser individuals may have to be quite abject; occasionally half a dozen or more verbal self-flagellations may be required before cadres or aroused "struggle groups" [1] *are appeased. The theories on which this emphasis is based included the dialectical concept of "unity-criticism-unity" and the Communist-espoused process by which an individual can confess, receive absolution by the masses, and as a redeemed member of the new society find the way to renewed life. The potentialities for subordination, discipline, and manipulation are obvious. In practice the associated processes are often both socially crude and psychologically quite sophisticated.*

* *On the Party,* 4th ed. (Peking: Foreign Languages Press, 1952), pp. 91–92.

[1] Such groups may be small ones for study and discussion, or large public assemblies; in either case they typically remonstrate, accuse, denounce, humiliate, and persuade—or, if satisfied, encourage and applaud.

A crucial factor in broadening inner-Party democracy lies in the fostering of criticism and self-criticism among Party members and the cadres. Comrade Mao Tse-tung stresses self-criticism in his report, pointing out that serious self-criticism is an outstanding feature which distinguishes us from other political parties. We must develop a positive sense of responsibility among our Party members and cadres in regard to Party policy and Party work, thus enabling them to use their reasoning power, raise problems boldly and properly and express their views. Those in charge of the leading bodies of the Party at all levels must be the first to practise thorough-going self-criticism on the defects and errors in the work carried out under their leadership. They must set an example to the Party membership and the cadres and be fully prepared in their minds to accept criticism from others, never becoming impulsive or insolent when so confronted, or resorting to repressive or punitive measures. Only in this way can the development of inner-Party democracy be encouraged. Otherwise, Party Congresses and Conferences, even if held regularly, may yet be just lifeless and undemocratic gatherings filled with dull and repetitious speeches, while listening to reports and voting may be nothing but pure routine.

24 • THEODORE H. E. CHEN: *Efforts to Remould Mentality and Attitudes* *

Those in the West who may be tempted to dismiss mainland Chinese processes as those of totalism and of a police state may underestimate two factors: the penetrative depth of this totalism, and the many forms of social pressures that often obviate the use of direct coercion by agencies of state. As is well known, Communists—and this is true even more in China than elsewhere—are not only intent on transforming society, they also insist on changing individuals. Internalization of regeneration is continually stressed. In these circumstances agents and instruments of the party and state not only lay down a barrage of controlled information but also have developed techniques for "remoulding thought." No former dynasty in China ever had such instruments available, though many of them used propaganda; religious and philosophical traditions had also developed means for the cultivation of spirit and self. The Communists, however, have carried politicism much further than did the Confucian system.

Among the numerous interpretations of "thought remoulding," the following essay by a Chinese professor, who has written much about educational developments in the People's Republic of China, is one of the most concise. Dr. Theodore H. E. Chen has long been Professor of Asiatic Studies at the University of Southern California.

* *Thought Reform of the Chinese Intellectuals* (Hong Kong: Hong Kong University Press, 1960), pp. 74–78. By permission.

3. *Thought Reform Must Be Self-Reform*

The Communists make a fetish of voluntarism. Whether it is enlisting for the Korean War, subscribing to state bonds or joining the agricultural co-operatives, while pressure is exerted by propaganda and 'persuasion', the Communists still want the individuals to yield 'voluntarily' at the last moment. There is no doubt that 'persuasion' often becomes mandatory in nature, but the Communist method is to avoid direct, undisguised coercion whenever possible. Though force or compulsion is always around the corner, to be exerted when necessary, the preference is to resort to different forms of persuasion, at times semi-coercive or covertly coercive, until resistance is overcome and the victim 'chooses' to submit. His submission can then be hailed as 'voluntary' action. This kind of pressure is more subtle than direct, undisguised coercion; it is less likely to arouse a violent reaction; and, furthermore, it enables the Communists to boast that they use 'democratic' instead of dictatorial methods on the people. . . .

If action can be compelled, a person's inner thoughts cannot. To be sure, the stage should be—and is—set in such a way that thought deviations are subjected to prompt and sharp criticism as soon as they are detected, but the Communists realize that the transformation takes time and the final change from old to new must be made by the subject himself. This is especially true of intellectuals who are not easily shaken from their established mode of thinking. Ideological remoulding is neither accomplished over-night, nor is completed once for all. Hence the frequent rectification campaigns.

4. *'Positive Elements' Set the Pace*

The most effective indirect compulsion comes from group pressure. While the original source of pressure is the Communist agitator who works behind the scenes, the immediate pressure comes from the group of which the individual is supposed to be a member. The group is the medium through which the Communist Party or the state controls the people; though the control is sure and firm, it is nevertheless indirect; and the Party can claim that the individual submits to the majority of his own group and the procedure is 'democratic'.

The groups range from the small discussion groups for political 'study' to such 'voluntary people's organizations' as the women's organizations, the trade unions, the teachers' federation, the writers' union, and so on. Within each group, a select number of 'positive elements' (also called 'progressive elements' or 'activists') are chosen as leaders who call upon their fellow members to rally to a worthy cause. These 'positive elements' may be genuinely inclined to Communism, or they may be opportunists on the bandwagon. Under the suggestions or the instructions of the Communists and their cadres, they set examples of ideological conversion or 'revolutionary action' and endeavour to create an atmosphere in which lukewarm or indifferent members feel the heat to move with the group. They are often the most articulate members of the group and are actually the voice of the Party or the state, but since they are not Party members or state officials but speak as members of their group, they help to maintain the myth of 'voluntarism' and minimize the feeling of direct Party or state control. . . .

5. *Thought Reform Must Be Concrete and Specific*

To talk in generalities is not enough; to declare that one is turning a new leaf in life and to confess that one has been wrong in the past is not enough. One must confess specific offences and give concrete examples of one's reactionary ideology in the past. Personalized targets, as shown in Chapter VI, make thought reform concrete and specific. The attack on the personalized targets is directed against the specific offences of the condemned persons. In the same way, 'models' or 'heroes' are set up as personalized examples of virtue—both in thought reform and in the emulation drives in farming and industry. The good and bad characteristics must be made tangible and visible in personalized targets.

6. *The Group Pressure on the Individual*

The mass meetings and the big rallies arouse the emotions and set the stage, but the real job of 'soul searching', of 'examining' one's own background and one's own thought is done in small groups, in which 'positive elements' 'help' each individual to see his past errors, to muster 'courage' to confess before his comrades, and to declare his determination to mend his ways. In this process of 'free' discussion in small groups, day in and day out, the individuals are caught off their guard and are led to reveal their inner thoughts. It is extremely difficult not to do so in the long sessions which continue until everyone comes to speak his mind. The Communists do not accept neutrality or indifference, and refusal to speak is considered as a hostile act. If there is no 'freedom of silence' in Communist China there is a *compulsory* 'freedom of speech' from which none are exempted.

The 'small group' usually consists of no more than ten or fifteen persons, and is further subdivided into 'mutual aid study groups' of three or four persons each. It may be engaged in the study of Marxist theories or in the discussion of current events or in the examination of individual 'thought conclusions' growing out of 'study'. In each and every instance, every member is given his turn to talk. The group analyses the thought of each person and 'exposes' his errors. This, it is said, is the 'democratic way'. Moreover, it is an expression of 'collective living', and to refuse to participate is to commit the offence of 'alienating one's self from the group'.

This is, in essence, the technique of criticism and self-criticism. The group criticizes the individual and helps him to criticize himself. Members criticize one another and they criticize themselves. In the name of mutual aid, they take up the task of mutual surveillance. Since some Party member or cadre is likely to be present in the group or drop in and, since everyone knows that all that happens within the group is fully reported to the authorities, anyone who opens his mouth at all has no alternative but to practise criticism and self-criticism in the approved manner. He criticizes his own past background, he relates in detail his past enslavement by bourgeois and imperialist ideology, and he is full of praise for the New Democracy and the Chinese Communist Party. Many adopt this 'line' at the beginning to keep themselves out of trouble; as time passes, by repeating the same stereotyped statements 'progressive ideas' take hold slowly under the hypnotic spell of brainwashing. Not a few experience an ideological conversion, for the duration of the 'study' period at least.

The leader of every 'mutual aid study group' makes regular reports on the 'progress of the thought struggle' of each member to the 'small group' to which the subgroup belongs. The 'small group' in turn reports through its leader to the 'central study group' for each institution or area. On appropriate occasions, the 'small groups' join in large mass meetings either to hear important speeches or reports or to participate in more formal 'discussions'.

The 'thought conclusions' which everyone submits as tangible evidence of his 'thought change', after they have been discussed and analysed in the small groups, are carefully scrutinized by the higher authorities. It is not uncommon for a person to rewrite his 'thought conclusion' six or seven times: he has not gone far enough in the denunciation of his past; sometimes, he has not yet 'completely' told the story of his failings and now must fill the gaps discovered; at other times he lacks thoroughness in criticism and self-criticism. Many cry and suffer sleepless nights before they reach satisfactory 'thought conclusions'.

7. *Reform and Revolutionary Action*

Reference has been made to the Communist emphasis on the 'unity of thought and action' and the Communist disdain of book knowledge or what they consider to be theory unrelated to action. They maintain that change in thought must be tested and reenforced in action, and vice versa. Thought reform, therefore, is not merely an intellectual process. The intellectuals are 'mobilized' to take up actual tasks in the revolutionary struggle, from participation in mass movements to menial projects such as scrubbing floors, washing windows, laying pavements, etc. In these tasks, so the theorists claim, the intellectuals come to appreciate the dignity of labour and to learn to work in teams and to experience the satisfaction of 'collective living'. They cease to be onlookers; they learn to discard their 'objectivity'; they become direct participants in the class struggle.

25 • WANG CHANG-LING: *Peiping's "Great Cultural Revolution" and "Red Guards"* *

Those few researchers and intelligence officers on Taiwan who have regular access to sources of information about trends on the nearby continent have naturally been following the "Great Cultural Revolution" in detail. The following article relates ideological imperatives and the struggles of cliques in the fields of literature, the cinema, and politics to contention for power and doctrinal orthodoxy on the mainland. This was part of the showdown between militant advocates of Maoism in the army and its General Political Department, on the one hand, and factions in the party's Peking Municipal Committee and the secretariat's Propaganda Department, on the other. After the denunciation and dismissal of P'eng Chen's faction and of Chou Yang and Lu Ting-yi as well as some of their associates in the Propaganda Department, the "Cultural Revolution" was further escalated. From early August 1966, the Red Guards began to be mobilized. Later "Red Rebels" and even military

* *Issues and Studies,* III, No. 2 (November 1966), pp. 14–23. By permission.

forces were used. Little is said in this article about the muffled resistance to these pressures by powerfully intrenched party groups.

In referring to Wu Han's historical operatic play Hai Jui's Dismissal, *Mr. Wang has selected the most controversial of a number of writings by several authors who sought obliquely to criticize the CCP and some officials during 1961–63 by treating sympathetically literary characters who had suffered from arbitrary injustice in earlier times.*

While the interpretation of the "Great Cultural Revolution" chosen here is far from thorough, and though a few paragraphs containing value judgments have been omitted, most of what it does include is sound and perceptive.

The author is a scholar and political commentator who occasionally writes for the Nationalist journal Issues and Studies.

The Chinese Communist "Red Guard" movement is a derivative of the "cultural rectification" movement and the "great cultural revolution." Basically, it is an ideological struggle launched by the Chinese Reds for the suppression of the anti-Mao, . . . clique. It is also an intra-Party power struggle involving political and military powers and the right to succeed Mao Tse-tung. Since 1963, the struggles have gone through the stages of the "cultural rectification," the "great cultural revolution" and the "Red Guard" movement, and have increasingly intensified. . . .

1. "Cultural Rectification"—Prelude to the "Great Cultural Revolution"

The Chinese Communist "great cultural revolution" is a derivative of the "cultural rectification" movement. The rectification movement started after the second enlarged meeting of the third national committee of the "All-China Federation of Literary and Art Circles," held in May, 1963. At that time, writers in either mainland China or in other Communist countries showed strong tendencies toward freedom of expression. For instance, many writers in Yugoslavia and the Soviet Union sought freedom and truth, and opposed blind obedience and the handicap of tradition. They were reluctant to follow the line of "socialist realism" in their writings, but advocated "peace-ism," "humanitarianism" and "personal happiness." They were represented by such Soviet writers as Ilya Grigoryevich Ehrenburg, Evgeny Aleksandrovich Yevtushenko, Viktor Platonovich Nekpasov, Alexander I. Solzhenitsyn, and Valery Tarsis. On the Chinese mainland, literary and art workers' desires to seek freedom, truth and free development of individualism were even stronger than those of Soviet and Yugoslav writers. In both the "meeting of dramatic film writers" of June, 1961, and the "Darien forum on literary writings" of August, 1962, the mainland writers fully expressed themselves. Works of these writers were not only divorced from the realm of politics, they expressed individualism, and also indirectly attacked Mao Tse-tung's literary thinking and the tyrannical "three Red flags." Meanwhile, mainland intellectuals in general also started an anti-Mao, anti-Communist movement. Mao Tse-tung, being aware of the seriousness of the situation, made the appeal, "never forget the class struggle," at the tenth plenary session of the Eighth Central Committee of the Chinese Communist Party in September, 1962. He pointed out that "some people are using the writing of novels to carry out anti-Party activities. . . . They are preparing the public opinion for the comeback of capitalism." It was for this reason that the "All-China Federation of Literary and Art Circles" was ordered by Mao to hold an enlarged meeting to arrange for a "cultural rectification" movement.

The figure in charge of the cultural rectification movement was Chou Yang, deputy director in charge of literature of the Propaganda Department of the Party Central Committee. He made a speech in the enlarged meeting, entitled "Strengthen the Literary Front and Oppose Modern Revisionism." This title alone shows that the speech was a clearcut assault on "modern revisionism" and was therefore fully in line with Mao Tse-tung's thinking.

As early as 47 years ago, Chou Yang was already "executioner" of another Chinese Communist cultural rectification movement. Holding high the banner of "Mao Tse-tung's literary thinking," he struck down writer after writer. Those purged by his bloody hands included Yu Ping-po, the "Hu Feng clique" and the "Ting Ling-Chen Chi-hsia clique." Forty-seven years later, however, his attitude changed. He started to advancing his own "Chou Yang's literary thought," denouncing Lu Shun and snubbing "Mao Tse-tung's literary thinking." He tried to establish himself as the "founding father" of the "literature of the 1930s." At the same time, he also positively advocated the "four-good" motion picture (good story, good cast, good shooting and good music; nothing was said about good politics) and the "star system." He boycotted "modern plays," recruited old actors and old writers, carried out the "elimination of clichés" and the "creation of new things," attacked the "three Red flags" tyranny, and advanced "Three freedoms and one contract." His remarks and actions apparently began to run counter to Mao Tse-tung's thinking.

Chou Yang had been subjected to attacks from various quarters 47 years ago for his arrogance. His antagonists included Hu Feng and Ting Ling. Thanks to the protection of Liu Shao-ch'i, he successfully fended off the attacks. Forty-seven years later, the internal struggle within the Chinese Communist Party and regime has not stopped, and Chou Yang's detractors continue to pop up. The following are two instances.

One is the conflict between the Chinese Communist Party, Shanghai branch, and the "Chou Yang clique." In Shanghai literary and art circles Chou had many followers, including Yuan Wen-shu and Chu Pai-yin, deputy director of the Motion Picture Bureau. In early 1961, Chou visited Shanghai and gave a tea reception marking the Spring Festival. Many old actors and writers attended. At the reception, he emphasized his idea of "elimination of clichés and creation of new things." Later, Chu Pai-yin, wrote an article, "Monologue on the Creation of New Things in Motion Pictures," based on Chou's views, which was published in the *Motion Picture Art* magazine. In the name of the Shanghai branch of the "Union of Chinese Cinema Workers," he held several "forums on the creation of new things," so as to enlarge the influence of his views. Then the Shanghai branch of the Party came forward to intervene. Chu, with support from higher places, was not the least chagrined. Based on the demand to "create new things," he drafted his "Views concerning the Screening of artistic motion pictures and draft regulations governing the censorship of scripts and work prints" to counter interference from the CCP Shanghai branch in motion picture production and directing. The draft regulations were later approved by the "Ministry of Culture" and officially promulgated. The Party Shanghai branch was naturally offended. The conflict between Chou Yang and the Shanghai Party branch can be traced back to an even earlier date. In 1959, Chou's right-hand man Yuan Wen-shu was dismissed for political reasons and was forced to leave Shanghai. Through the help of Chou Yang, Yuan was transferred back to Peiping and got a post in the "Union of Chinese Cinema Workers." Since 1964, he had been in charge of the union, replacing Hsia Yen and Chen Huang-mei.

Another instance is the conflict between the Chou Yang clique and the Kirin branch of the Party. In China's northeastern provinces, there was a Changchun Motion Picture Studio. The Party commissar stationed in that studio was a staunch member of the Kirin Provincial Committee. Because of the Commissar's intolerant interference in the work of other cadres of the Changchun Motion Picture Studio, Chou Yang went to Changchun in July or August of 1962 and summoned all studio cadres for a lecture. He admonished the party commissar for "resorting to might" and "treating intra-party difficulty as a problem between the enemy and the State." Later, he positively supported some people inside and outside the Party in opposition to the leadership of the Party's Kirin Provincial Committee. Under his direct manipulation, the party commissar of the Changchun Motion Picture Studio was replaced by Lin Shan, one of his trusted aides. Thus, the studio fell under Chou's complete control. (Editor's Note—First Secretary of the Kirin Provincial Committee was Wu Teh; after the purge of P'eng Chen, Wu was transferred to the post of Second Secretary of the Party's Peking Municipal Committee).

The above is evidence that in 1962, the struggle between the Chou Yang clique and its antagonists was already vehement. After Mao Tse-tung made his warning in the tenth plenary session of the Eighth CCP Central Committee, Chou, in order to carry out Mao's orders, called an enlarged meeting of the "All-China Federation of Literary and Arts Circles" to start the fifth "cultural rectification" movement. In the initial stage of the movement, however, no concrete action was taken except for the publication of a few articles of critical nature. In December, 1962, Mao came forward again. He pointed out that "Quite a number of persons and problems are involved in various kinds of artistic forms such as drama, folk-songs, music, art, dance, motion picture, poetry and literature. The socialist reform has reaped little results in many departments. Many departments are still being controlled by 'dead men'. Many Party members enthusiastically advocate feudalistic and capitalist arts instead of socialist arts. This is indeed perplexing." Mao's remarks created a heavy pressure on the Propaganda Department of the CCP Central Committee, yet Chou Yang didn't seem to be convinced. It was at that time that Chou's antagonists began to direct the spearhead of the rectification toward him and his followers.

Chou's adversaries adopted an old tactic which they had used once before against Hu Feng: They collected as much data and information as possible, to prove that the literary and art circles under Chou's leadership were against "Mao Tse-tung's literary thought." Thus, they could at least charge Chou with failing in his leadership and depose him. They used another trick which they didn't use against Hu. That is, to establish themselves as faithful followers of "Mao's literary thought" in order to curry Mao's trust. It is said that T'ao Chu was the best one in so expressing himself. T'ao at that time was a staunch promoter of the "modern play." Under his direction, a play, "The Red Signal Lamp" was put on stage in south-central China, and later became a stage sensation from Canton to Peiping. With this play, he proved that the "modern play" might be presented in the form of the Peiping opera, and he wrote many theoretical articles on this. That was a heavy blow to Chou Yang who didn't care much about the modern play. When an exhibition of modern plays was held in Eastern China in January, 1964, Chou and Lin Mo-han both boycotted it. When a similar exhibition was held in Peiping in June of that year, Chou not only shunned the preparatory work, but also exerted every effort to undermine the exhibition.

The tide was against Chou Yang in his covert struggle with T'ao Chu. When the modern play exhibition was being held in Peiping, Mao Tse-tung again pointed out that "for the past 15 years, the literary and art circles have basically (not entirely) failed to carry out the Party's policy, have become overlords, refusing to be integrated with workers, peasants, and soldiers. . . . In recent years, they have drifted to the very brink of revisionism. Unless they carry out this reformation, a Petofi Club-type group will emerge." These remarks of Mao, in the Communists' own words, "came like a thunderbolt out of the blue." Chou Yang, who was director of the CCP CC Propaganda Department in charge of literary and art work, naturally felt the pressure.

In July, 1964, Chou began to plunge himself into the "cultural rectification" movement. First to fall victim to the movement was Shao Chuan-lin, Vice chairman and concurrently party secretary of the "Union of Chinese Writers." Shao was charged with writing two articles: "Middle Characters" and "Deepening of Realism" thus opposing "Mao Tse-tung's literary thinking" and "writing about heroic figures." However, Chou Yang's opposers pointed out that this was "sham criticism and self protection; fighting while retreating, last-ditch resistance." They said that when the Dairen meeting on writing was held under the leadership of Shao Chuan-lin, Chou Yang also attended and made a report, opposing the "three Red flags" and advancing "three freedoms and one contract."

In the month following Shao's purge (August), the local Party organization of Dairen declared that it would "take back a copy of someone's speech in the Dairen meeting." That greatly shocked Chou Yang, who was said to be "very upset, and hurriedly had someone make telephone calls to stop this." In spite of Chou's efforts, the secret was exposed and he was forced to make self-criticisms admitting that "I have committed errors of bureaucracy and failed to maintain close contact with the masses," and that "I have failed to grasp my subordinates." After the purge of Shao Chuan-lin, Chou Yang and Lu Ting-I again initiated the purges of Hsia Yen and Tien Han, and the reorganization of the "Ministry of Culture." After reshuffling the ministry, Lu Ting-I took over the post of Minister of Culture from Mao Tun. In November, 1965, Chou Yang attended a meeting of amateur writers, and talked about the cultural rectification and literary theories. He was still able to fend off blows and retain his post. That showed how strong his influence was.

II. Climax of the "Great Cultural Revolution"—Intra-Party Struggle

The situation changed drastically at the end of 1965. In September of that year, Mao Tse-tung pointed out in a meeting of the CCP Central Committee that "the reactionary ideology of the bourgeois class must be criticized." In November of the same year, Yao Wen-yuan published his article "Comments on the New Historical play *Hai Jui's Dismissal,*" starting criticisms of Wu Han. It was said that Yao's article was backed by the Shanghai branch of the Chinese Communist Party. Immediately afterward, the article was reprinted in the *Liberation Army Daily,* which branded *Hai Jui's Dismissal* as a "great poisonous weed."

The publication of Yao's article greatly alarmed Chou Yang, who immediately arranged for a discussion behind closed doors with "a major figure of the CCP Peking Municipal Committee" (presumably P'eng Chen), to work out counter measures. Their tactic was: to mobilize all newspapers and magazines under their control to make criticisms of *Hai Jui's Dismissal,* but from another angle. Their purpose was to channel the public opinion into treating the criticism as an academic topic, to avoid the involvement of the political aspect. Teng To, secretary of the CCP Peking Municipal Committee, even exercised his influence to transfer back a part of the "sent-down" literature or history-majoring students of Peiping colleges to work in the *Peking Daily* and *Frontline* magazine, so as to enhance the strength of their side in the theoretical polemics. Teng To, using the penname of "Hsiang Yang Sheng," published an article entitled "From *Hai Jui's Dismissal* to the Theory of Succession of Morality" in the *Peking Evening News* of December 12, 1965. Chou Yang himself also wrote a series of articles using the penname of "Fang Chiu," dealing with the topic of "good officials" but avoiding politics. At the same time, Wu Han published his articles "Self-Criticism Concerning the Discussion on Morality" and "Self-Criticism Concerning *Hai Jui's Dismissal,*" admitting his mistakes in the morality view, historic outlook and thinking methods, but refusing to admit any political errors. All these maneuvres aimed chiefly at pulling Wu Han from the hands of his hostile attackers. Their efforts were in vain. Wu's opponents increased their pressure as a result of resistance put up by Teng To and company. Beginning in late February, 1965, *Red Flag* published articles by Yin Ta, Kuan Feng and Chi Peng-yu, bringing the polemics to a white-hot stage. On April 18, the *Liberation Army Daily* published an editorial "Hold High the Great Red Banner of Mao Tse-tung's Thinking; Actively Participate in the Great Socialist Cultural Revolution," pointing out that "National defense literature" is a bourgeois slogan while "popular literature of the national revolutionary war" advanced by Lu Hsun is a proletarian slogan. This was upholding Lu Hsun's cause and condemning Chou Yang. From then on, the cultural rectification movement, triggered by the "three household-village" incident, suddenly changed into a heated power struggle within the Chinese Communist Party.

On June 3, the reorganization of the Communist Party Peking Municipal Committee was officially announced. P'eng Chen, Teng To, Lu Ping and others fell as victims. Later, the purges took on increased velocity, resulting in the reshuffling of the CCP-CC Political Bureau, Secretariat, Propaganda Department, official Party newspapers and magazines, the "Ministry of Culture" of the State Council, the General Staff Department and the Cultural Sub-department of the General Political Department of the "People's Liberation Army," cultural, educational and propaganda departments at various levels of Party, political and military organizations of the provinces, colleges and universities, and such mass communications media as newspapers, printing presses, motion picture studios and broadcasting stations. Up to the end of August, a total of 124 major cadres of these organizations had been exposed and purged. Hundreds of publications were ordered to close because of anti-Mao, anti-Communist articles. Scores of literary writings were also criticized.

At the same time, the Communists mobilized the masses to take part in the struggle. One form was to launch criticism by the masses of *Hai Jui's Dismissal* and other anti-Mao and anti-Communist writings. An editorial entitled "The Participation of the Worker-Peasant-Soldier Masses in Academic Criticism is a Matter of Historical Significance" in the sixth issue of the *Red Flag* called for the workers, peasants and soldiers to take part in academic criticism. It declared that their participation is a "matter of historical significance" which is "unprecedented in world history." Another form was to organize and instigate a part of the students of various schools to open fire on the anti-Mao, anti-Communist clique. This brought chaos to the schools. For instance, in the Affiliated Middle School of Peking University, the students divided themselves into two groups; one group, which called itself the "Red Flag Fighting Team," was against Lu Ping, President of Peking University; The Pro-Lu Ping groups once put out 5,000 "big-character posters" to attack the "Red Flag Fighting Team." When Lu Ping was finally purged by the Communist authorities in early June, the "work team" assigned to take over the university had to enter the campus at mid-night. This fact reflects the tension of the situation.

For another instance, when Kuang Ya-ming, President and concurrently first secretary of the Party Committee of Nanking University, was purged, fightings broke out in that university. More than 70 anti-Kuang teachers and students were subjected to "struggles" by pro-Kuang elements. After Kuang was struck down, the *People's Daily* published an editorial entitled "Freely Mobilize the Masses to Thoroughly Wipe Out the Counter-revolutionary Black Gang," pointing out that "in order to win a victory in the struggle, we must freely mobilize the masses." On June 18, the Communists further announced the nullification of the entrance examination system for the enrollment of new students, to be replaced by the "selection and recommendation" system. This was aimed at buying the students over, and fanning up their enthusiasm to join the struggle against the anti-Mao, anti-Communist clique. This measure was quite effective, and in the following months, the whole Chinese mainland was almost turned upside down by juveniles under the Communist instigation.

The eleventh plenary session of the Eighth CCP Central Committee was held August 1-12, 1966. The session adopted the "Decision of the Central Committee of the Chinese Communist Party Concerning the Great Proletarian Cultural Revolution" which pointed out:

> The broad mass of workers, peasants, and soldiers and the broad mass of revolutionary intellectuals and cadres are the main forces of this great cultural revolution. A great number of revolutionary youths who are otherwise unknown to the public have become brave forerunners. They have courage as well as wisdom. They use big-character posters and hold vigorous debates to air their opinions freely and to resolutely expose, criticize, and attack the covert and overt bourgeois representative[s]. . . . Their main revolutionary direction is always correct. This is the mainstream of the great proletarian cultural revolution.

The fact is, this signaled the coming of the "Red Guard" movement.

III. Enlargement of the "Great Cultural Revolution"—Red Guard Attack on "4-Old"

Juvenile organizations set up by the Communists in various schools for the purpose of purging anti-Mao, anti-Communist cliques bore different names. The organization in the Affiliated Middle School of Peking University mentioned above was called the "Red Flag Fighting Team," while that in the Second Middle School of Peking was named the "Red Guard." On August 16, Chen Po-ta, director of the Communist "Great Cultural Revolution Committee," summoned all students coming to Peiping from various parts of China for a lecture. In the evening of the following day, the Red Guards of the Peking Second Middle School drafted a "Declaration of War on the Old World." On August 18, a mass rally was held in the Tien An Men Square of Peiping. Representatives of the Red Guards packed the reviewing stands at the two flanks of the Tien An Gate, and they also kept order at the rally. Later, a representative of the Guards presented a "Red Guard" armband to Mao Tse-tung. Mao, Lin Piao, Chou En-lai and Mao's wife Chiang Ching then received the Red Guards. On the same day, "Red Guards" of the Peking Second Middle School distributed printed "declarations of war" everywhere in the city. The "Red Guard" movement thus formally made its debut.

The "Red Guard" movement bears four special characteristics:

First, the Guards' chief missions are "rebellion" and "making trouble." According to Mao Tse-tung himself, "There may be thousands of principles of Marxism, but in the final analysis, they can be summed up in one sentence: 'Rebellion is justified.' " The Red Guards want to rebel: they want "to rebel against the bourgeois class, against imperialism, against revisionism, against all monsters and demons, and against all ideology of the exploiting class"; they want to turn the "great cultural revolution" into a "storm, which comes with the force of an avalanche or a surging tide, sweeping away all opponents." The Red Guards want to make trouble: They want to "use Mao Tse-tung's thinking as the most powerful weapon to smash old thinking, old culture, old customs and old habits, obliterate the rule of those authorities who walk the road of capitalism . . . and destroy the old rules, regulations and orders of the bourgeois class."

Second, members of the Red Guards are offspring of the so-called "five Red categories"—workers, peasants, revolutionary cadres, revolutionary soldiers, and sons and daughters of "martyrs." Youths not belonging to the five Red categories may also join the organization if they have the courage to "revolutionize themselves," "rebel against their own families" and are willing to "stand shoulder to shoulder with the Red Guards."

Third, the Red Guards "have the right to demonstrate in the streets, freedom of assembly, freedom of association, freedom of speech and freedom of press," and "the power to use Mao Tse-tung's thinking to criticize the errors of Party commissars of their own organizations." "Any one who acts counter to Mao Tse-tung's thinking should be corrected no matted how high his position and how great his authority." Thus, the Red Guards are virtually empowered to interfere with anyone's life. They may hold kangaroo courts, enter and search any house and confiscate property and valuables. They have the right to arrest and punish any official or civilian whom they consider has violated Mao Tse-tung's thinking.

The "big-character posters" of the Red Guards even have power of restriction over the local Party and government administration.

Fourth, the Red Guards have the goal of destroying the "four-old," and setting up the "four-new." The so-called "four-old" includes old thinking, old culture, old customs and old habits. For instance, in Peiping, the names of streets, shops, hospitals and cities were changed; old names that were associated with old ideas were changed. The "Red Guards" also discouraged the possession of U.S. or British records, lunar calendars, fancy labels, palace lanterns, painted screens, flower baskets, fancy furniture, antiques, ancient paintings and calligraphy, hair tonic, cosmetics, silk dresses, fur coats, blue jeans, Hongkong-style dresses, high heels, and other modern shoes. Barbershops were no longer allowed to offer such services as manicures, massages, or make up, and duck-tail haircuts were not permitted. Furthermore, celebration of the Mid-Autumn and Ghost festivals, religious beliefs and the worshipping of ancestors were deprecated.

The so-called "four-new" means "new thinking, new culture, new customs and new habits of the proletariat." To sum up, the Communists aim to "turn the whole old world upside down" and thoroughly "Mao-ize" the individual's thinking and living.

The Red Guards first appeared in Peiping on August 20. Within days, the movement extended to the whole Chinese mainland.

IV. An Analysis of the "Red Guard" Movement

A study of the Chinese Communist "great cultural revolution" shows that two great struggles run through the whole process from the "cultural rectification" beginning in 1963 to the "Red Guard" movement beginning August 20, 1966. One is an ideological struggle and the other is a power struggle.

Let us first look at the ideological struggle:

According to the Marxist-Leninist, any change in the upper social structure is inevitably connected with the change in the lower structure, i.e., economic foundation. Conversely, any change in the economic foundation will inevitably cause a change in the upper structure. Accordingly, when Mao Tse-tung first started the "people's commune" system on the mainland, he also uttered the slogan of "cultural revolution." He not only wanted to confiscate private property and break the family system, so as to thoroughly change China's traditional economic structure, but also to carry out a class struggle in the ideological realm, so as to smash China's traditional cultural structure. With this double-barreled measure, he tried to achieve the goal of establishing a so-called "Communist society." Yet, the people's commune system first turned out to be a fiasco, then the "cultural revolution" met with the intellectuals' resistance. Opposers of the "people's commune" and the "cultural revolution" were found not only outside the Communist Party. In 1962, such anti-Mao, anti-Communist ideological struggles reached a climax. The Communists, fully aware that if the anti-Mao, anti-Communist upsurge was not suppressed, there would be the danger of "perish of our country, our Party and ourselves," adopted such measures as the "four cleanups" and the "cultural rectification movement" with a view to averting the imminent crisis. They didn't expect that the "cultural rectification" would bring conflicts within the Party, which then developed into a situation warranting a "great cultural revolution." The "great cultural revolution," which demands the thorough reorganization of the propaganda system of the Communist Party, the cultural and educational systems of the Red government and such mass communications media organizations as newspapers, printing presses, motion picture studios and radio stations, is one step further in the ideological struggle. When the Red Guards began to launch a "general attack" on the "four-old," sparing not even palace lanterns, commercial brands, flower baskets, antiques, shop signboards, street names and anything that bore signs of the "old thinking and old culture," and trying to "turn the whole old world upside down," the ideological struggle had reached a fanatical stage in terms of scope and intensity. Therefore we are of the view that the "cultural rectification," the "great cultural revolution" and the "Red Guard" movement are all but different names for an ideological struggle.

Now let us turn to the question of the power struggle:

The ideological struggle is not a simple problem involving only elements outside the Communist Party; it is an internal problem of the Party. Ideological differences in the Party gradually developed into an ideological struggle, which in turn brought about a power struggle. The two struggles are inter-related and inseparable. The situation has now become clear: In the literary and art circles, Chou Yang has fallen victim, as Hu Feng and Ting Ling, to attacks, and the struggle against him has been intensified since 1958-59. As Chou was in charge of cultural, literary, historical and educational departments of the Peiping regime, we may say that the big reshuffle of Peiping's propaganda, cultural and educational systems are a consequence of struggle against Chou. However, the power contention in the literary field is only one aspect of the internal struggle of the Red Chinese regime. It is closely interrelated with the contention over the political and military power and the right to succeed Mao Tse-tung. This casts light on the fact that the "cultural rectification" movement has developed into the "great cultural revolution" and that the reorganization of the cultural and educational departments has resulted in the reshuffling of the Politburo, the CCP CC Secretariat, the "People's Liberation Army" and the "Young Communist League." The outcome of the first stage of the struggle has also become clear: P'eng Chen, Lu Ting-I and Lo Jui-ch'ing have been purged and Lin Piao has taken over the No. 2 position of the Chinese Communist Party from Liu Shao-ch'i. As Liu had been in power in the Party for many years, naturally he has followers at various levels and in various quarters all over the country. From the "cultural rectification" to the "great cultural revolution," the purges were all being carried out above the provincial level. To completely wipe out the remnants of the Liu-P'eng clique, Lin Piao has to push the purges to levels below the province. It is probably for this reason that he has initiated the "Red Guard" movement, empowered the Guards to criticize Party commissars, and given them the mission of "smashing the rule of authorities who walk the road of capitalism." The internal power struggle is expanding in scope and scale.

Part II

Japan

SECTION ONE

Political Culture

26 • YOSHIHIKO SEKI: *Japan in Transition* *

By 1955–56, Japan had more than recovered economically from the disasters of war, defeat, and loss of empire. This had been made possible chiefly by the country's available skills and means for training, its expressions of collective will, its deservedly famous social disciplines, and policies of the Occupation which, by 1948, had turned from emphasis on demilitarizing controls to progressive reconstruction. Although conservative trends began before the Occupation ended in April 1952, significant net liberal gains have survived and have since been indigenously strengthened.

Perhaps never before has the economy and society of any country developed and been stimulated as spectacularly as Japan's in the decade following 1952. Psychologically, too, the people as individuals and as a nation have attained a healthy degree of confidence. But life for them has become so modern and complex that it is no longer easy to find a unifying sense of mission or consensus.

Yoshihiko Seki is admirably suited to open our section on postwar Japan with this panoramic interpretation. A political thinker and commentator, he is a member of that socialist movement, now called the Democratic Socialist party, which is so close to Center that it is considered right-wing by some of the other groups on the Left. Persistent, though not strong, this lineage has attracted some of Japan's competent and often more objective intellectuals. The term "progressive" which appears in many Japanese political references has come to mean "reformist" and even "left-revolutionary." Professor Seki teaches the History of Social Ideas at Tokyo Metropolitan University.

The changes that have occurred in Japan during the last ten years are not confined to the physical world; they extend as well to the world of the mind, more specifically, to the ideas one finds in the magazines of the intellectuals. During the ten-year interval between 1953 and 1963, both the subject matter dealt with in these intellectual magazines and the kind of people writing for them changed. The Introductions of previous issues of the *Journal of Social and Political Ideas in*

* "Introduction," *Journal of Social and Political Ideas in Japan,* II, No. 2 (August 1964), pp. 2–10. By permission.

Japan make frequent reference to the postwar Japanese intellectual world being dominated by left-wing thinkers. However, the 1960 demonstrations against ratification of the revised mutual security agreement with the United States were an intellectual turning point of crucial importance, and from that year the solidarity of left-wing intellectuals began to disintegrate. I would go so far as to say that in the last two years Japanese intellectuals have entered their own period of 'Let the hundred flowers bloom,' and that, as a result, their ideological united front dominated by what is called the antiregime group has been destroyed. The articles published in the magazines of the intellectuals reveal clearly that this change was a reality by 1963. In order to provide the reader with a better understanding of the articles that are included in this issue of the *Journal,* I would now like to sketch some of the reasons why and the ways in which these changes occurred.

Summary of the Changes

There were only four monthly magazines of major intellectual importance in 1953, namely, *Chūō Kōron* (The central review), *Sekai* (The world), *Kaizō* (Reconstruction) and *Bungei Shunjū* (Literary annals). *Kaizō* ceased publication in 1955. By 1963, the three remaining magazines were still being published but had been joined by five new monthlies, namely, *Jiyū* (Liberty), *Ronsō* (Debates), *Keizai Orai* (Economic currents), *Ushio* (Tides) and *Gendai no Me* (The eyes of the times), and by a new weekly, the *Asahi Jānaru* (Asahi journal). Most of these new magazines began publication in the five-year period before 1963. Some were undoubtedly started for the purpose of counterbalancing the left-wing editorial policies of *Sekai.*

The second major change between 1953 and 1963 involved the cast of writers. Most articles in the intellectual magazines in 1953 were authored by university professors. Relatively few were written by newspaper reporters and leaders of the socialist movement. In 1963, although the majority of authors continued to be university professors, there was a decided increase in the number of authors drawn from other professions, such as newspaper reporters and journalists, and a surprising number of articles were written by literary critics, members of the conservative party, and business leaders. It would be safe to say that by 1963 relatively fewer articles were being authored by doctrinaire theorists, and relatively more by people with realistic points of view.

This change in the cast of writers coincided with the rise of the new postwar generation. In 1953, the majority of authors were people who had received their higher education before and during the war. Consequently, in the immediate postwar period they went to great lengths in their articles to warn against any revival of conditions that would again entrap them in the dark valley in which they had found themselves before and during the war. By 1963, there was a relative increase in the number of younger people writing articles for the intellectual magazines, people who had no experiences with the prewar or wartime regimes. They judged things more objectively and were far less imbued with hatred and antipathy against Japan's past.

The subject matter and content of the magazines of the intellectuals also changed decidedly between 1953 and 1963. The subjects dealt with in 1953 largely reflected the intensity of the cold war. Most articles were sharply critical of American foreign policy, the mutual security agreement with the United States, and American military bases on Japanese soil. Many articles heaped praise on the 'New China' that had arisen on the mainland. They criticized the Japanese government for what they called its 'reverse course' policies, such as those aimed at revising Japan's 'Peace Constitution' and at altering the educational reforms that had been instituted by the Occupation. *Sekai,* for example, ran a series of articles between July and October 1953, warning that Japan was reverting to fascism.

By 1963, the subject matter dealt with in the intellectual magazines was not only much broader in scope than in 1953, but significantly different in slant. I present here only the briefest outline . . . of these changes. . . . Most authors in 1953 tended to regard prewar Japan in purely negative terms as a militaristic state, but by 1963, a number of authors were at least attempting to be more objective in evaluating Japan's past. Their attempts naturally led to the formulation of new interpretations of history and new methodologies for analyzing social phenomena, interpretations and methodologies quite different from those used by the majority of Japanese intellectuals before and after the war. It is, therefore, not surprising to find that many articles published in 1963 criticized the Marxist-Leninist view of history that idealizes communist nations. Many were also critical of the one-sided view that uses Western Europe as a yardstick to declare that Japan is a backward nation. Many other articles in 1963 accepted the development of mass-society conditions in Japan as a natural by-product of industrialization. They recognized that these conditions are essentially a product of Japan's high economic growth rate, and they strove to identify the additional goals toward which Japan should progress.

Similar changes have occurred in the whole range of mass media, including book publishing, radio, and television. Before the war, certain historical personages of Japan were lauded as ideal representatives of the Japanese people; after the war, however, these same people were often denounced as representatives of Japan's feudalistic militarism. They include the forty-seven *rōnin* of the Tokugawa period, Takamori Saigō, and many political and military leaders of the Meiji period. But by 1963, numerous biographies, stories and historical novels were being published about these very people, and most of such publications attempted to re-evaluate or reinterpret the stands these historical personages had taken on many traditional values such as loyalty and filial piety. The lives of many of these people were also portrayed on stage and television. This emphasis on spiritual values, new to postwar Japan, was found as well in the magazines of the intellectuals in 1963.

Also in 1963, relatively fewer articles were dogmatically left wing in their criticism of the Japanese government and America. Many articles were much more inclined to offer constructive criticism and make realistic proposals on the basis of factual analyses. This represents the third major change that occurred in the magazines of the intellectuals between 1953 and 1963. I do not mean to imply that no left-wing doctrinaire articles were published in 1963; to the contrary, quite a few were published, but far fewer than in 1953. The really noteworthy development by 1963 was the new, more constructive tone of many of the articles. If we can judge the situation in Japan by the magazines of the intellectuals, we can then say that the intellectual climate in 1963 was vastly different from what it had been in 1960. We must now ask why this change occurred.

The Intellectual Climate During the Occupation

The Occupation's policies aimed at the complete elimination of Japanese militarism and the imposition of 'democracy' on the people. Implementation of these policies took concrete form in the Emperor's disclaimer to divinity, in the dissolution of Japan's armed forces, in the prohibition of State Shinto, in the enactment of the land-reform laws, in the encouragement of the labor movement, and in the disestablishment of Japan's mammoth financial combines. Not only did the Occupation authorities punish or purge the national leaders responsible for Japan's war of aggression and condemn the nation's militaristic past, they also tried to build up a new Japan, completely severed from her traditions and history. The implementation of Occupation policies greatly weakened the authority of the central government and tore away the foundations of national identity. The very premises on which Occupation policies were based strongly encouraged the people to belittle or even condemn their own traditional values and history.

People of quite opposing shades of opinion cooperated to a surprising extent with the Occupation authorities. The Japanese people, who had enthusiastically supported their government's war efforts, cooperated fully with the Occupation in the implementation of its policies. The intellectuals who had been denied their freedom of speech during the war years were particularly pleased with these policies because they felt their successful implementation would open a new era for Japan. The Japan Communist Party also cooperated and even called the Occupation forces 'the liberation army.'

Democracy in postwar Japan has faced many difficulties largely because it was imposed on the Japanese people by higher authority; it is not something the Japanese people themselves struggled to establish. Its imposition in the early postwar period made it very difficult for the Japanese to gain a correct understanding and appreciation of what democracy really is. It is not odd, therefore, that ordinary Japanese mistakenly applied the word 'militaristic' to everything that they felt was undesirable and the word 'democratic' to everything that they felt was desirable. People equated democracy with opposition to the state and to all authority, including the authority of parents and teachers. Many intellectuals, including both liberals and communists, differed on many other matters, but they were in full agreement in their condemnation of state authority and Japan's past. These limited areas of agreement, plus the fact that they were not fully cognizant that the kind of democracy provided for in the new Constitution is incompatible with communism, enabled intellectuals who supported the new postwar Constitution and the communists to form a united front.

From around the outbreak of the Korean conflict in 1950, Occupation policy began to shift. Instead of continuing to keep Japan weak, the Occupation now wanted to strengthen her. The Occupation authorities began to consider Japan part of America's defensive ring around the communist bloc of nations. The results of this policy shift were the creation of the quasi-military National Police Reserve which was later transformed into the Self-Defense Forces, the reorganization of the national police system, and the provision of economic assistance to Japan. After signing the San Francisco Peace Treaty in 1951, the Japanese government took over where the Occupation ended and continued to carry out many of these new policies. From that time, the Japanese government began to be strongly criticized by the opposition parties. The voicing of such criticism was greatly facilitated by the fact that the central government did not enjoy the absolute authority that had been wielded by SCAP during the Occupation. The intellectuals became the spiritual pillars of the opposition parties, and with but one major exception, the intellectual climate in the post-Occupation period remained essentially the same as it had been under the Occupation. This exception was that the image of America as the guardian of democracy was lost because Japanese intellectuals became convinced that America was now behind the conservative-party government's attempts to modify many of the democratic reforms instituted immediately after the war. For the intellectuals of Japan, America became the enemy of democracy. After 1950, America encouraged Japan to rearm, and so the intellectuals felt that America was just as much in favor of war as the militaristic government of Japan had been before 1945. The Soviet Union opposed many of America's global policies, and so it was natural for Japan's intellectuals to view the Soviet Union in a favorable light. Even non-communist intellectuals who privately favored the American way of life withheld criticism of the Soviet Union and became vociferous in their condemnation of American international policies. Japanese liberals who disagreed with the thesis that America is the enemy of democracy parted company from the left-wing intellectuals who supported the thesis. Nevertheless, because left-wing intellectuals had gained control of the editorial policies of the magazines of the intellectuals, articles continued to be predominantly left wing in slant and interpretation throughout the 1950's.

Eclipse of the Progressive Intellectuals

The Japanese intellectual climate, so long dominated in the postwar period by left-wing thinking, was destined to change, largely because of the mistaken attitude and approach of left-wing intellectuals themselves. They were often unrealistic and were often not able to formulate concrete recommendations to effect social or political changes because they failed to analyze situations objectively. They were too prone to condemn outright all measures taken by the Japanese government in the post-Occupation period, claiming them to be part of the government's reactionary, 'reverse course' policies. They called for people to resist adamantly what they called the revival of military fascism. Left-wing intellectuals condemned the government for taking measures that I feel were necessary to protect and maintain national independence, measures that included revising the national police law, strengthening the Self-Defense Forces, abolishing the elective and instituting the appointive system for members of local boards of education, and in general modifying Occupation reforms in order to bolster the powers of the central government. In the economic field, they condemned American aid given to Japan under the terms of the mutual security agreement, even though that aid greatly facilitated Japan's postwar recovery. When reform groups within the labor movement began to fight against labor's revolutionary tendencies in an effort to get organized labor to recognize that its primary mission is to protect the individual rights and benefits of laborers, the intellectuals excoriated these groups for betraying the labor movement. But the warnings of left-wing intellectuals went unheeded by the majority of the people because the intellectuals largely opposed the government just for the sake of opposition and failed to make realistic and concrete policy recommendations. They consequently failed to bring to a halt the various modifications being made by the government and certain segments of organized labor. Faced by failure, the intellectuals began to realize how impotent they really were and to reflect on why their past efforts had been so ineffectual.

Added impetus to change in Japan's post-Occupation intellectual climate was given by the reaction that many informed people had to the movements led by left-wing intellectuals against their government and America. As ironical as it may seem, these movements gave rise to the revival of certain healthy nationalistic feelings. Around 1950, the Communist and Socialist Parties of Japan started a popular movement to urge the Japanese government to conclude a peace treaty only if all of the Allied Powers, including the Soviet Union, were signatories. The San Francisco Peace Treaty was finally concluded in 1951, but the Soviet Union was not one of the signatory nations. The popular movement that had been started by the Communist and Socialist Parties over the peace treaty then continued to express itself in various other forms such as opposition to the presence of American military bases on Japanese soil. The stated aim of this opposition was to free Japan from foreign domination. Left-wing intellectuals wrote and published numerous articles loudly calling for national independence. In doing this, many of their articles re-examined Japanese traditions, the very traditions about which the intellectuals had been highly critical during the early part of the Occupation.

When many of the nations of Asia gained independence in the 1950's from their West European colonial masters, Japanese left-wing intellectuals extolled the national liberation movements of the countries of Asia and Africa for being effective anti-imperialist forces. Japanese intellectuals claimed that the people of Japan, by comparison with those of the other countries of Asia, lacked a national consciousness, and that it was this lack that enabled America to maintain military bases on Japanese soil and military control over Okinawa. The rising tide of Afro-Asian nationalism in the 1950's, on which Japan's left-wing intellectuals placed great hope, stimulated the Japanese people into a greater awareness of their own nationalism. Here we have an example of how anti-Americanism in Japan developed into a form of nationalism in which many Japanese came to have a deeper appreciation of their own traditions.

Decline of Marxism-Leninism

Marxism-Leninism has gradually lost its ideological hold over Japanese left-wing intellectuals. This weakening has been one of the most important factors to influence and change the intellectual climate of Japan. Japanese intellectuals, whether consciously or unconsciously, had long placed absolute faith in, and constructed their world views in terms of, Marxism-Leninism. However, the inapplicability of that philosophy to many factors peculiar to Japan, together with the many adverse developments within the socialist bloc of nations, have discouraged Japan's intellectuals and brought ideological disillusionment.

When Stalin was still alive the Soviet Academy of Sciences published a book entitled *Principles of Economics* which pressed the orthodox Marxist-Leninist interpretation that capitalism will inevitably decline because of the impoverishment of the laboring class under that system. The Japanese translation of the book became a best seller and is said to have sold over 700,000 copies. In spite of the claims put forth in this book, Japan's economy continued to prosper, and the standard of living of the average worker continued to rise, with the result that this and other books similarly framed in terms of orthodox Marxist theories began to arouse real skepticism and attract far less the serious attention of the Japanese people.

Khrushchev's denunciation of Stalin in 1956 and the Hungarian revolt in the same year had an enormous impact on Japan's left-wing intellectuals. Until then, our intellectuals had believed, or had pretended to believe, that Stalin and the Soviet Union were infallible. They were stunned to silence by the denunciation and wrote little about the Hungarian revolt. Only later did a number of Japanese Marxist-Leninists begin to criticize the Soviet Union and give more liberal interpretations to Marxist-Leninist theses. In so far as the solidarity of the left-wing camp in Japan is concerned, these developments represented the beginning of the end.

The surfacing of the Sino-Soviet dispute further encouraged Japanese left-wing intellectuals to become more critical of Marxism-Leninism and of the Soviet Union. As early as 1960, Japanese newspapers carried items on the disagreement between China and the Soviet Union, but conspicuously few articles in the magazines of the intellectuals dealt with the subject. At first, the dispute seemed to have little outward effect on Japanese intellectuals, but this does not mean that they were not keenly aware of its ideological implications. Gradually the intellectuals became much more careful in making any pronouncements on ideological matters. This state of affairs lasted until the outbreak of the Sino-Indian border dispute, a dispute that brought tremendous disappointment to all those Japanese intellectuals who had emotionally idealized Asian neutrality. Japanese intellectuals became disillusioned, and their disillusionment undermined the long-standing coalition of pacifists, neutralists and left-wing, anti-American intellectuals.

Resurgence of Self-Confidence

Japanese intellectuals in the immediate postwar period believed that Japan before the war had been both undemocratic and backward and that the government had been thoroughly militaristic in policy and action. Shigeki Tōyama, Seiichi Imai and Akira Fujiwara co-authored a best seller in 1955 entitled *Shōwa Shi* (A history of the Shōwa period). It described the Shōwa period (1926–) as one in which the absolutist Emperor system oppressed the people and forcibly led the nation into an imperialist war. But by shortly after 1955, the economy of Japan had completely recovered from the war and surged ahead to the place today where Japan's high economic growth rate surpasses the miraculous growth rate of West Germany. As Japan miraculously recovered, our nation rose sharply in the esteem of foreign observers, and this approbation by foreigners did much to restore to the people of Japan a strong feeling of self-confidence.

Because of the disastrous results of the war, the Japanese people have hoped in the postwar period that their nation would never again become involved in the dangerous tides of international politics. They have hoped that it would be able to survive as a small nation at peace with the rest of the world. However, with the complete economic recovery of the nation and the creation of a standard of living comparable to that of the advanced nations of the world, she has been increasingly required to play an important international role. Although it is quite the contrary of her original postwar aspirations, Japan is now in the position to assume, particularly in Asia, a greater degree of leadership. Although Japanese intellectuals have not been very enthusiastic about Prime Minister Ikeda's claim that Japan is now a great world power, the claim in itself has also been instrumental in restoring to the average Japanese citizen a feeling of self-confidence.

In the last one-hundred years, Japan has been able to modernize and, except for the Occupation period, maintain her national independence. By contrast, many other countries of Asia have not developed economically in spite of the fact that they have received a great amount of foreign assistance. A number of foreign scholars are now studying the special domestic factors that have enabled Japan to develop and modernize to such an astonishing degree beyond the other countries of Asia. Some American economists attribute a large part of Japan's successful development and modernization to the particular kind of interpersonal relationships that evolved out of the nation's long feudal tradition. A case in point is the peculiar nature of Japanese labor-management relations, relations which Japanese scholars have condemned as backward and premodern. Ambassador Edwin Reischauer, Dr. Robert Ward of the University of Michigan, and other specialists on Japan have pointed to many other specific factors that have greatly facilitated the modernization of our nation. Mr. Reischauer, in particular, has made a number of speeches since his appointment as Ambassador to Japan and has written a number of articles emphasizing that certain democratic traditions are not alien to Japanese soil, that similar traditions had existed here long before the Occupation's attempt to democratize the nation. Although some Japanese progressive intellectuals disagree with a number of his academic positions and damn what they call the "Reischauer ideological offensive," his ideas have done much to free many Japanese of their obsessive reliance on the materialistic interpretation of history.

Whither Japan?

With Japan in its present throes of ideological change, in what direction will the Japanese intellectual world next proceed? Will left-wing ideas again become prominent and influential? Or will the Japanese people go on without a united national goal and continue to enjoy a nonpurposive society in the midst of economic prosperity? If Japan continues as a non-purposive society in which her people think only of their own personal welfare, will her people lose their national vitality? Or will belief in the efficacy of ultranationalism revive and, as the driving philosophy of the nation, again express itself imperialistically on the international scene? Or is it possible that Japan, as the only advanced nation in Asia, will draw upon her experiences of the last one-hundred years of modernization and become a true helper of the underdeveloped countries of Asia? Accurate prediction is not possible, but this much I can say: the antiregime sentiments, long harbored by many Japanese intellectuals, will not easily disappear. Although it is unlikely that Marxism-Leninism will continue indefinitely to be the principal theoretical prop of the antiregime movement, frustration will continue to express itself against both the Japanese government and America as long as there remain dissatisfied elements in our competitive society.

In recent years there has developed a form of nationalistic thought in Japan. One must ask about its future. As I mentioned earlier, by 1963 a number of Japanese were beginning to recognize the positive value of many indigenous ideas, institutions and developments of the prewar and postwar periods. This affirmative evaluation has significantly counter-balanced the negative evaluations made by left-wing intellectuals. I do not think that it is at all fair to claim, as do some left-wing intellectuals, that today's affirmative evaluation of things out of Japan's past constitutes a revival of ultranationalism of the prewar type. I believe that rational modification of some of the excesses of the Occupation's reforms in the fields of education, politics and economics is still required. I feel that it is neither proper nor fair to condemn such modifications as retrogressive.

However, one warning should be sounded: there is always a danger in Japan lest the extremely negative expressions of intellectuals be tied in with the strong, latent feeling of the Japanese people which favors authoritarian leadership.

Should Japan's economic situation deteriorate, or should the country become involved in serious international crises, it is entirely possible that the people of Japan would become disappointed in, and turn against, their democratic form of government. In such an atmosphere, the antiregime sentiments expressed by left-wing intellectuals could well contribute unintentionally to the outward expression of the people's latent authoritarianism. Such a development might well lead to excesses in which all postwar democratic reforms are condemned and discarded.

Careful attention must be paid to an additional important factor, namely, that the mutual security agreement with the United States expires in 1970. Whether Japan renews that agreement in 1970 will depend largely upon the international situation at that time. If the renewal of the agreement in 1970 can be tied to a domestic problem such as constitutional revision, the Japanese intellectual world will again be caught up in a storm of controversy very similar to that of 1960, when a popular front was formed and violent mass demonstrations were made against the government. If this were to happen, a new situation could possibly arise in which the current distinction made between left and right wings would no longer be applicable. At the moment, there is no evidence of such an eventuality, but the direction in which the Japanese intellectual world moves in the next few years will require our careful attention.

27 • Tadashi Fukutake: *The Communal Character and Democratic Development of Farming Villages* *

Prewar Japanese agriculture was one of the most problem-ridden sectors of national life. But among the most successful programs of reform guided by the Occupation was that which redistributed some five million acres to three million farmers, thus making small proprietors by far the most numerous agrarian stratum. Radicalism markedly declined after this redistribution, and peasants became the electoral mainstays of conservative parties. Traditionalism and lingering bossism helped to assure this.

Good agricultural price levels and favorable terms of trade assisted Japan's farmers to improve technology and achieve still higher levels of productivity.

* *Shisō,* November 1960, pp. 44–45; as condensed and transl. in *Journal of Social and Political Ideas in Japan,* II, No. 3 (December 1964), pp. 83–87. By permission.

About two-thirds of them had to rely in part on auxiliary occupations because of their small landholdings. As their levels of education and income improved, they became increasingly integrated into national life and affairs. Compulsory education has been raised to nine years. Newspaper reading and more recently the popular use of television have brought political forums into rural households. Democratization has had varied impact on their local politics.

The surge of the economy since recovery from the war has, for the first time in some decades, significantly altered the rural-urban ratio. By 1965, agriculture, forestry, and fishing accounted for about 29 per cent of the total labor force. Such great changes have inevitably had an affect on politics.

Professor Fukutake is one of his country's leading experts on social, economic, and political changes in the villages. Since the war, he has taught sociology at the University of Tokyo. He is the author or co-author of four books, has contributed to others, and is a director of the Japan Sociological Society.

Japanese farmers have for centuries lived in small communal societies called *buraku.* Even today they have not completely freed themselves from the communal system of production and mode of life that have long been characteristic of *buraku.* During the Tokugawa period (1600-1868) and early Meiji period (1868-1912), *buraku* were identical with *mura* (villages or hamlets). In 1889 they were amalgamated in various combinations to form administrative units in the newly established system of local administration. More than 15,000 administrative villages and towns were thus created. Thereafter, the *buraku* became an integral part of Japan's modern state mechanism and also became increasingly permeated by a capitalist economy. With these developments, *buraku* began to lose their closed, self-contained character, but because they continued to concentrate largely upon wet rice culture, even today they retain their traditional system of communal production. Moreover, most *buraku,* being under the administrative jurisdiction of financially weak town and village governments, are forced to maintain their traditional self-governing mechanisms. Because of the methods employed in the modernization of Japan since the Meiji Restoration, the *buraku* is still largely a communal society in which the existence of the individual is not recognized except as an integral part of the community. This type of communal thinking holds sway not only among *buraku* but throughout the whole of Japanese society, urban areas included. In fact, *buraku*-type thinking and behavior may be said to underlie the whole of Japanese culture. Accordingly, the key to the democratic development of the *buraku* is the key to the democratic development of Japanese society as a whole.

The communal character of *buraku* derived originally from the joint use and management of irrigation water and of the fields and woodlands from which fertilizer, forage and firewood are obtained. Joint use and management inhibited independent farm production, placed individual farming families under communal control, and bound them to traditional norms of living. Anyone deviating from the accepted patterns of behavior was subjected to numerous visible and invisible sanctions. *Buraku* residents therefore developed a type of personality which unquestioningly accepted and followed the traditional customs of the community. *Buraku* society had no room for independent-thinking individuals who rely upon logic and conscience to guide their behavior. Individuals were obedient to the authority inherent in the village as a whole above all others. Even the top-most members of the status hierarchy were bound to the rules of communal life and production; they had no more freedom to put their own private interests above those of the village than did anyone else. Because of this, there was no overt conflict of interest among villagers of different status, and individuals lived and worked together as one body. The principles of democracy, which premise individualism, were completely alien to *buraku* life and thinking.

While Japan was developing a modern capitalist economy following the Meiji Restoration, agricultural communities remained largely feudalistic and premodern. Nevertheless, as a capitalistic money economy became a part of Japanese life, it was inevitable that village community life undergo a gradual change. In the first place, the joint use of fields, woodlands and irrigation water became less of a controlling force within the community. The introduction of chemical fertilizers drastically curtailed the importance of fields and woodlands as a source of natural fertilizer, and the introduction of farm machinery did much to lessen the need for communal productivity by increasing the self-sufficiency of individual farming families. These developments brought about changes within the *buraku* status hierarchy. More and more great landowners, who held the top positions in *buraku* society, moved out of their communities and became parasitic absentee landlords. As they did so, they gradually lost their positions of leadership and became alienated from *buraku* life. The cultivating landowners who succeeded to the top positions in *buraku* hierarchies were not as strong as their predecessors had been. Notwithstanding the central governments' policy of maintaining *buraku* communal order based upon the leadership of landowners, the hierarchical control of village communities became weaker and weaker. There were, of course, regional variations in the process and rate of change, but the cumulative effect was that of weakening the structure of traditional *buraku* society.

The postwar land reform served to weaken the structure even further. It delivered a decisive blow to the power of landlords and converted most of the tenant farmers at the bottom of the status hierarchy into landed farmers. Since the land reform did not adversely affect those landowners who cultivated their own land, such farmers continued to maintain positions of authority in the *buraku* hierarchy, but their authority was considerably less than that wielded by landowners before the reform. Individual farming families began to concentrate upon their own interests, seeking more and more to expand their own productive abilities apart from the rest of the village group.

Regardless of the multifarious changes that have taken place, it hardly need be said that there are still strong communal elements in the Japanese farm-village community. There is still little democratic supervision of communal mountain lands and water supplies, and the degree of productive independence acquired by farming families is still quite low. One cannot expect the personality of people who have been raised in a communal-type society to change overnight. The *buraku* self-governing processes analyzed below are still surrounded by communal elements and are still as undemocratic as ever.

Towns and villages in Japan have been given the status of local self-governing entities, but not the ability to become financially independent. Their hands are kept full just in carrying out the duties assigned to them as remote agents of the central government; they can afford neither the time nor money to plan and carry out their own projects. For this reason, towns and villages utilize the self-governing mechanism of the *buraku* as their basic instrument of administration. This practice serves to perpetuate and even strengthen the control of the *buraku* self-governing mechanism over the members of the community. Although there are numerous variations in the composition of *buraku* self-governing mechanisms, generally speaking, the executive body is composed of a *buraku* headman, a number of councillors, a treasurer, an official in charge of fields and woodlands, an irrigation officer, etc. Since the *buraku* is considered by its members to be a homogeneous unit in which there is little differentiation of function, the chief parishioners of village shrines and local Buddhist temples are also thought of as *buraku* officials. The same is true of leaders of agricultural organizations, fire-fighting squads, youth groups, PTA's etc.

The operation of *buraku* by the above-mentioned officials is generally carried out according to unwritten rules of traditional social practice. Even in cases where rules have been committed to paper, they conform essentially with traditional communal practices. Since most *buraku* officials are chosen from among the older people, leadership tends to be authoritarian and undemocratic. Although younger people now assume the greater part of the responsibility for farm management—due in large part to the postwar advances in agricultural techniques—their voice is inadequately reflected in rural politics. Furthermore, elections for *buraku* officials are rarely very democratic. More often than not, those elected to *buraku* posts are either individuals from well-to-do families who have time and money to spare or else boss-type leaders who are driven by selfish ambition; posts are rarely filled by those people most suited to carry out the responsibilities the positions entail. Of course, general meetings of all *buraku* members are acknowledged to possess the ultimate decision-making authority, and overt dictatorship by *buraku* officials is not allowed. However, general meetings of *buraku* members have no more real power than they did in earlier days when village headmen and other influential farmers used such meetings to clothe their arbitrary decisions in the dress of popular consensus. Even though general meetings give farmers at the bottom of the *buraku* hierarchy a chance to speak out, those people never come forth with any positive ideas or constructive opinions. Moreover, since the vast majority of *buraku* still use the old system of one vote for each household, it can hardly be said that the will of all the people is reflected in *buraku* elections. The *buraku* self-governing process is at best only pseudo- or quasi-democratic.

In theory, *buraku* projects should be financed from the taxes *buraku* residents pay to the city, town or village in which they reside. In actual practice, however, these projects are financed through additional assessments levied unofficially upon *buraku* residents by the *buraku* self-governing mechanism. Naturally, the poorest farmers at the bottom of the *buraku* hierarchy tend to suffer greatest from such assessments. Often a city, town or village government will partially subsidize a *buraku* project, the remainder of the budget being made up by the *buraku* itself. In many such cases, *buraku* residents avoid making cash payments by working off their portion of the assessment as a form of corvée. Under this system, each household is responsible for an equal number of man-hours on any given project. At first glance this may seem to be a fair system, but in reality it is extremely unfair and disadvantageous to the farmers of low income who can ill afford to give up a day's wages in order to work on a project. The basic problem, however, is that this system, by making continual use of the *buraku's* traditional control mechanism, does much to preserve the communal character of rural life.

As changes continue to take place in the social structure of *buraku,* the contradictions inherent in *buraku* self-governing processes gradually become more conspicuous. Most *buraku* can no longer be called pure farm villages. Approximately sixty-five percent of the heads of all farming families engage in some other kind of work besides farming; many *buraku* residents hold down commuting jobs while continuing to engage in agriculture, while many others are not engaged in farming at all. The more *buraku* people engage in occupations other than farming, the less benefit they receive from *buraku* communal projects. Communally maintained farm roads, for example, are seldom used by those who do not engage in farming. Even those farming families who do benefit from *buraku* projects have become more involved in their own interests and are less willing than earlier generations of farmers to serve as corvée laborers on *buraku* projects. However, despite the increasing number of contradictions wrought by these changes, the *buraku* continues as a self-governing unit. This is principally because farmers are not yet completely liberated from the traditional communal methods of farming, and because *buraku* households who are either partially or completely engaged in other occupations are still forced to conform to the traditional pattern of *buraku* life.

The traditional self-governing structure of the *buraku* is preserved in large part because it is forced to carry out the functions and shoulder the financial burdens of local town and village governments. If a *buraku* is to promote its own interests and ensure its receiving subsidies from the local government, *buraku* residents have no choice but to give unanimous support to those people who wield the most influence in petitioning the local government authorities concerned. Claims based upon narrow community interests become particularly vehement and difficult to regulate after towns, villages and *buraku* have been merged into larger administrative units. In such cases, it becomes even more necessary for coercive pressure to be applied on local government authorities by influential petitioners. Efforts are commonly made to regulate the voting behavior of *buraku* residents in order to ensure the election of an influential man of the *buraku* to a town or village council. A town or village council member who succeeds in securing benefits for his own *buraku* becomes a kind of political boss in his community. Then, in order to enhance his own influence, he affiliates himself with some member of the prefectural assembly, and, through him, with a member of the National Diet from the constituency in which the *buraku* is located. Thus, *buraku* interests affect the voting behavior in elections on all levels of government. Support for specific candidates, even in elections for the National Diet, is urged in the name of *buraku* interests. The undemocratic nature of Japanese politics on the national level may be traced to the undemocratic nature of the *buraku,* the basic unit in the Japanese political system.

As pointed out above, in *buraku,* community interests take precedence over all others; occupational and class interests are suppressed in the name of *buraku* peace and unity. If *buraku* are to become democratic, they must be made into simple residential units. To that end, it is necessary that functions within *buraku* be diversified; that is, that the responsibility for various functions within the community be yielded to the groups most qualified to perform those functions.

Such *buraku* groups as agricultural organizations, fire-fighting squads, women's associations and youth groups must be severed from the traditional self-governing mechanism of the *buraku* and treated as independent organizations. These groups must divest themselves of the traditional thinking that has made the *buraku* an all-inclusive and undiversified whole; each functional group must be made up only of individuals who have joined of their own free will for the purpose of helping achieve the goals of that particular group. Only when *buraku* become functionally diversified will the mechanism which allows *buraku* political bosses to control the residents disintegrate. Town and village council members will then no longer be able to represent the interests of *buraku* as complete, homogeneous units; instead they will begin to represent the interests of a particular class, occupation or generation within their constituencies. Petitions to local governments will no longer be made on behalf of entire *buraku;* instead they will be made through the joint efforts of functionally-related groups cooperating across *buraku* boundaries. Rational demands based upon class or occupational interests should serve to bring about the renovation of city, town and village administration.

Eventually, *buraku* residents will be liberated from traditional communal patterns of living and choose their representatives freely and democratically in light of their own class and occupational interests. When this happens, it will be possible to institute democratic reforms not only in *buraku* but also in national politics, where pork barrelling now serves as the dominant method of winning votes. Of course, the task of liberating people from traditional communal patterns of living is not confined to farming villages. Traditional communal principles are still being followed even in the neighborhood associations of large urban areas, particularly in the older sections of large cities. Residents of both farming villages and urban areas seem to live in complete harmony together, but this is because they are bound by strict rules of obligation and duty and because they are afraid of deviating from the accepted norms of the community. Beneath the surface of this seeming tranquility, everyone is in frantic pursuit of his own selfish ends, and, intensely jealous of his neighbors, secretly plots to outdo them all. This selfishness must be converted into the kind of individualism which serves as the basis of rational cooperation for the benefit of all. Only then will our citizens, as free members of their community and free citizens of their nation, grow to be the kind of people who willingly work for the democratization of their local and national governments.

28 • *Political Tendencies of White-Collar Workers* *

All Japanese political parties, including the Communist party, have cross-stratal support. Therefore, analyses of electoral support must strive to explain the magnitude and reasons for the proportions of varied party alignment within a particular class.

* Research Society on Japanese Social Structure, "Special Traits of White-Collar Workers in Large Urban Areas," Chap. 9 in "Howaitokarā no ishiki kōzō," (Tokyo, March 1962), pp. 147–157 (mimeo.); as condensed and transl. in *Journal of Social and Political Ideas in Japan,* I, No. 2 (August 1963), pp. 77–78. By permission.

The actively literate white-collar class in Japan, which first became politically significant in the 1920's, has grown rapidly. Opinion polls and elections have shown that it includes more members of reformist or radical persuasions than most other groups, with the exception of university students. Many such workers are organized, and some of their unions have been among the most militantly active in strikes and demonstrations over postwar issues. This excerpt is from an article which discusses the composition of this rather complex stratum and the patterns of class self-identification which are related to political tendencies. Even non-Marxist Japanese social scientists pay rather more attention to class factors determining political behavior than do their counterparts in most Western countries.

Most white-collar workers are employed in the offices of large enterprises and in various levels of bureaucracy. They have specialized and often technical qualifications. In terms of education, age, income (¥300,000 to ¥600,000, i.e., $833 to $1,666 per year in 1960), and vocational mobility as well as stability, white-collar workers potentially have access to the managerial stratum and so are distinct from blue-collar personnel. They constitute the "new" middle class in large metropolitan areas. In 1961 more than 60 per cent of them consciously identified with their class.

But it is the upper echelon of this stratum, particularly those in major enterprises and agencies, who tend to assimilate to management in outlook, aspirations, and style of living. Assimilation is more marked in economically expansive periods. There are white-collar people in small and medium scale enterprises—in wholesale, retail, and service enterprises—who have less freedom, leisure, and income. Their socio-political tendencies may be more ambivalent. Their greater discontents are commonly offset in part by more intimate involvement with patriarchal types of authority and consonant patterns of obligation. In some ways they tend to assimilate to the stratum of blue-collar workers.

Thus, the white-collar stratum in Japan does not have an independent and distinct social outlook and lacks significant resources for developing a collective identity and influence.

The white-collar worker has a relatively stronger middle status self-identification than the blue-collar worker. Many of them aspire to identifying themselves with the upper middle stratum in ten years' time. In this regard, also, they are distinguished from blue-collar workers. But the self-identification of office workers in medium and small enterprises approaches that of the blue-collar worker. Sometimes they have an even stronger lower status self-identification than laborers in large enterprises.

Members of the industrial management and the upper stratum of owner-management groups, by and large, have a middle class self-identification. There is also a high degree of middle class self-identification among white-collar workers in offices of large enterprises, but as a total group, more white-collar workers have a laboring class, rather than a middle class, self-identification. Although they do not consider themselves to be manual laborers or ordinary workers, they sympathize with the socialists. Professional employees and office workers in large enterprises at the upper echelon of the white-collar worker group strongly identify themselves as being 'the workers' in the sense of the term 'proletariat' as used by socialists. But white-collar workers in small and medium enterprises, who are actually more like members of the proletariat, do not have such a strong class consciousness. They think of themselves simply as salaried workers. This is the unique characteristic of the white-collar worker in Japan as far as class consciousness is concerned.

In their hopes for the future of society, in their support of political parties and in their political thinking, white-collar workers in Japan can be distinguished from members of the managerial stratum by their dualistic thinking. While they have a high education and lead a middle class type of life, they have a class consciousness approaching that of socialist laborers. Of all other types of white-collar workers, office workers in large enterprises and employed professionals make the highest use of various mass media. They have an adequate knowledge of political issues, but their political attitude is very close to that of blue-collar workers. For example, they have a strong tendency to support political strikes called by labor unions, to be opposed to authoritarian politicians and to favor a demilitarized neutrality for Japan. But even in these respects, there is considerable variation among these white-collar workers. The most progressive of them are the employed professional specialists. They are more in favor of a denuclearized neutrality than laborers or blue-collar workers. They lend as much support to political strikes called by labor unions as do the laborers themselves. Most of the white-collar stratum favors and gives support to the socialist parties.

One of the reasons found for the dualism of the new urban middle class is that young white-collar workers who are well educated typically think in the same way as progressive Japanese intellectuals. It remains to be seen whether these young white-collar workers, who presently have relatively low-ranking positions and low salaries, will retain similar thought patterns following advances in age, position and income.

29 • HAJIME TANUMA: *Distribution of Population Among Classes in Japan* *

We often hear that the Japanese are in general hierarchical and class-conscious. They certainly spend much more time studying their own stratal composition than do most peoples whose middle classes predominate. In style of living and some other respects, classes tend to be sharply delineated in Japan, but rather intensive vertical mobility has been experienced during periods of marked techno-economic and political change.

During the last decade of rapid economic growth, the middle strata have been expanded and strengthened. The political import of this is still in process

* "Changes in Factors Conditioning the Urban Middle Class," *Keizai Hyōron* (February 1962), pp. 32–45; as condensed and transl. in *Journal of Social and Political Ideas in Japan,* I, No. 2 (August 1963), pp. 81–82. By permission.

but looks hopeful for the strengthening of representative, progressive politics.

Much has been written about the dual structure of the Japanese economy: on the one hand are highly capitalized, modern industries, department stores and supermarkets, on the other, more than 90 per cent of all enterprises are of small and medium size with numerous handicaps. Many of the latter seek protection as subcontractors of "parent" companies. In recent years marked technical and organizational changes—and in addition, liberalization of tariffs—have exerted greater pressure on small entrepreneurs to change employment or to shift the nature of their production and sales in ways which make them more dependent on the giants. In general there is a prevailing traditionalism-conservatism and proprietary outlook among such venturers and to a lesser degree among their employees. Opposition parties, of course, try to exploit discontents and to win support by advocating remedial policies.

This article provides statistics for 1955 and 1960 on size and composition of the labor force and the urban middle class. However, censual categories are usually inadequate for defining strata within classes. The author of this study, Hajime Tanuma, was graduated in 1948 from the Faculty of Economics, University of Tokyo. As an assistant professor at Hōsei University in Tokyo, he teaches courses on social policy.

To gain an understanding of Japanese society it is particularly important to study the old urban middle class composed of small manufacturers, tradesmen, professionals and individuals who live on the modest income from their investments and savings. It is especially important to study this class because there has been a tendency in Japan since World War II to use again groups in this class to revive militarism. It is also highly essential to study recent changes in factors conditioning the urban middle class in view of the government's policy which tries to divorce it from the working class. I have produced the following tables by using data entitled 'Results of a One Percent Sample Tabulation' contained in Volume II of the *Population Census of 1955* and by using the section entitled 'The Preliminary Report Based on a One Percent Tabulation' from the *Population Census of 1960*. Both documents were published by the Bureau of Statistics, Office of the Prime Minister.

TABLE I. CLASS STRUCTURE IN JAPAN
(estimate)

Item	*1955*	*1960*	
Total labor force	39,910,000	44,000,000	(100%)
Capitalists	810,000	1,020,000	(2.3%)
Urban middle class	6,210,000	6,610,000	(15.0%)
Farmer class	15,060,000	13,490,000	(30.7%)
Working class	17,830,000	22,880,000	(52.0%)
Total non-working population	49,360,000	49,310,000	
15 yrs. of age and over	19,370,000	21,290,000	
14 yrs. of age and under	29,990,000	28,020,000	

These tables provide data on the number of people composing various classes of Japanese society and data comparing the make-up of the urban middle class in 1955 and 1960. Of the 2,750,000 small manufacturers in 1960, only 360,000 of them employed other workers; 1,210,000 employed no other workers; 860,000 employed only members of their own families; and the remaining 30,000 worked on a piece basis.

TABLE II. JAPANESE URBAN MIDDLE CLASS
(estimate)

Item	*1955*	*1960*
Urban middle class (total)	6,210,000	6,610,000
Small manufacturers	2,460,000	2,750,000
Small tradesmen	3,390,000	3,440,000
Professionals	360,000	420,000

30 • SHŌJIRŌ UJIHARA: *Japan's Laboring Class—Changes in the Postwar Period* *

One is well into the following excerpt before finding that an oyakata *is a boss-like foreman, often linked to subordinates not only by authority but by informal relations of obligation (*oya*—parent or patron;* kata*—person).*

The rapid expansion of Japan's industries and services, the bureaucratization of larger enterprises, and technological changes which foster the growth of enlarged categories of technically skilled, self-aware workers have led to further substratification of labor and to changing occupational relationships. In aggregate, these have considerable importance for labor-management relations, for the labor movement, and for politics. The distinction between permanent and temporary employees is not new in Japan but has become more widespread and pronounced. This is one reason for the observation that the most highly organized Japanese workers actually comprise a kind of "labor elite." When one adds the filtering down of economic gains to improved education and changes in the socio-economic structure of modernizing enterprises and sectors, one begins to understand the recent decline of labor militancy and why some socialists have felt compelled to rethink strategy if not basic theories.

The author, a specialist in labor problems, graduated in economics from what was, in 1943, Tokyo Imperial University. He is now a professor at that institution, renamed University of Tokyo, in the Institute of Social Science.

For a long time after the beginning of Japan's industrialization, there were many cases of members of the laboring class becoming small manufacturers and

* *Keizai Hyōron,* Special Supplement (August 1959), pp. 13–22; as condensed and transl. in *Journal of Social and Political Ideas in Japan,* III, No. 3 (December 1965), pp. 66–67. By permission.

vice versa. In a typical modern society, the number of small entrepreneurs usually diminishes rather quickly as industrialization and big business develop, but such has not been the case in Japan. Among the factors which have contributed to the continued presence of a large number of small manufacturers in this country are the small amount of the minimum capital required to start a business and the low productivity of our national economy as a whole. Japan's modern industry can be described as having a 'dual' structure, within which huge and small businesses have existed side by side. In terms of the social class we are examining here, this dual structure meant that Japan's blue-collar workers before World War II showed a high degree of identification with the *petite bourgeoisie,* and the small manufacturers with the laboring class, because those workers and manufacturers together constituted the lower part of the dual structure.

Japan's blue-collar workers and small entrepreneurs together constituted the lowest social stratum in prewar Japan. They were generally uneducated and propertyless and were, in short, 'dropouts' from society. An inexperienced person just starting to work had some small chance of rising to the top of his stratum by accumulating seniority. If he was very lucky, he might become either an *oyakata* worker or a small entrepreneur with his own shop. However, such a person had little chance of rising to the upper part of the dual social structure. The various democratization reforms instituted after the war by the Occupation and the more recent technological innovations have had a great deal to do with changing the situation described just above. In the following I shall simply list four points which seem to be especially relevant to the subject of social stratification.

One, the improved educational standard of workers is depriving the foreman, or the *oyakata* worker, of his educational function and is similarly undermining his over-all authority.

Two, the authority of the *oyakata* worker is being further curtailed by the emergence of a new type of worker who possesses a greater degree of general scientific knowledge than his predecessors. Additionally, the bureaucratization of management has assigned away many of the foreman's previous functions and much of his authority. The disappearance of a practical *raison d'être* for the boss, or *oyakata* worker, means that the foreman is increasingly becoming foreman in name only; he is gradually becoming merely one more link in the bureaucratic chain.

Three, it is much more difficult today than before the war for an enterprising laborer to leave his job in a big business and set up his own shop, however small. This change has been brought on by the 'rationalization' and increased productivity of Japanese industry with the accompanying emphasis on huge investments in equipment. The result is a widening gap in social status and income between the owners of small and medium manufacturing outfits, on the one hand, and their employees, on the other. A much closer identity exists between owners of extremely small shops and foundries and blue-collar workers because such owners are, in effect, manual laborers.

Four, as the subcontracting of labor continues to disappear, a new type of blue-collar worker is appearing in large companies, the so-called 'temporary' worker (*rinjikō*). In contrast to 'permanent' laborers (*honkō,* or *jōyōkō*), 'temporary' workers are assigned work that requires no specific skill or long experience. The 'temporary' laborers, sometimes referred to as 'permanent-temporary' workers (*jōyōteki rinjikō*), are employed with the understanding that their employment is 'more or less' permanent. The term 'temporary' laborer has thus become a euphemism indicating a relatively new group of industrial laborers which is beginning to form a hierarchical level one step below that of skilled laborers. The conclusion is almost inescapable that this group will become defined clearly enough so as to constitute not only a separate, new stratum of labor but an independent social stratum as well.

31 • Shio Sakanishi: *Women's Position and the Family System* *

In Japan there is a fairly numerous type of scholar-journalist called the "critic." The author of this next piece is one of the outstanding postwar women commentators; the widely read women's magazines constitute one of her outlets. Dr. Shio Sakanishi was educated in the humanities and spent considerable time in the United States before the war. Since 1945 she has not only written copiously but has also served on government commissions, testified at Diet hearings, and engaged in a variety of other activities.

Naturally she has been interested in the improved status and rights of women, their admission to suffrage—ahead of France and some other countries—their growing economic competence, and their increasing political awareness. It has been notable that more recent Japanese opinion polls have shown fewer women in the "don't know" columns than in early postwar years. Although female opinions and voting seem specially sensitive about issues of peace, rearmament, and consumer interests, their accession to suffrage has not revolutionized political configurations. It has, of course, broadened the electorate and the methods of campaigning.

The article here somewhat abridged was written for publication in 1956, but most of the conditions and trends described have continued. Flexible conservatism still characterizes much of Japanese family life; changes are more discernible by generations than by half decades. By now a generation has passed since World War II and the proportion of young voters, more strongly influenced by postwar conditions, is impressive.

Japan fought her way out of the feudal system in 1867 through the Meiji Restoration and adopted a Western system in political, economic, and social fields, in which the improvement of women's position was necessarily a part. In 1871 a system of primary education on the basis of sex equality was put into effect. Yet from the first general election in 1890, prewar electoral laws barred women from the franchise, and later legislation forbade their joining political organizations or attending meetings of a political nature. The Civil Law of 1900, prescribing the inferior position of women, provided that a married woman should forfeit rights

* *The Annals of the American Academy of Political and Social Science,* Vol. 308 (November 1956), pp. 130–136. By permission.

enjoyed in spinsterhood and should be subject to the will of her husband as a legal incompetent.

After World War I, as a result of the remarkable emergence of working women due to the development of capitalism, equal rights of the sexes and protection of mothers and children were advocated. In 1922 by an amendment of the fifth article of the Peace Preservation Law that had ruled women out of politics altogether, women received the right to participate in political activities to a limited extent. In 1924, the League for Realizing Women's Suffrage was organized. Meanwhile, the Society for the Study of Politics, composed of leaders of the proletarian parties, was organized, and such progressive women leaders as Akiko Yosano, Natsu Kawasaki, Sumako Fukao, and Kikue Yamakawa joined the group. Abolition of the family-head system, equal opportunity for both sexes, protection of women, equal pay for equal work regardless of sex, abolition of licensed prostitution, were put on the platforms of the proletarian parties. In 1930 the Women's Civil Rights bill passed the lower house of the Diet, but was shelved in the House of Peers. After the Manchurian Incident in September 1931, women's progressive activities were suppressed.

In 1932, a Women's Association for National Defense was organized under the sponsorship of the Army. In addition, the National Council of Women's Organizations was formed under the direction of the Ministry of Education. In this way, both the Army and the bureaucrats strengthened their control over women and prepared the way to war. In 1940 the League for Realizing Women's Suffrage was ordered dissolved, along with the remaining proletarian parties and labor unions, and in 1942 all government-controlled women's organizations were merged into the National Women's Association, which, as a subordinate organization of the Imperial Rule Assistance Association, was to serve the fascistic ends of the Army and the bureaucrats. The government appointed women leaders as commission members or research staff of the Imperial Rule Assistance Association and organized neighborhood associations to aid in mobilizing women and integrating them into the wartime administrative structure. . . .

Reforms of the Occupation

Following unconditional surrender on August 15, 1945, Japan revived as a democratic nation under the authority of the Supreme Commander for the Allied Powers. The late Fumimaro Konoe, the virtual vice prime minister of the Higashikuni Cabinet formed immediately after surrender, opposed women's suffrage because it "would retard the progress of Japanese politics." However, General MacArthur directed the Shidehara Cabinet, formed in October 1945, to emancipate women. On December 15, 1945, the Diet approved a revision of the Election Law to give women voting rights as well as electoral eligibility equal to men. . . .

The first session of the Diet to meet after the new Constitution went into effect on May 3, 1947, approved the revision of the Civil and Criminal Codes and passed the bill to establish a Ministry of Labor. The revised Civil Code, which abolished the family-head system and annulled the legal incompetence of women, provided for freedom of marriage and specified the rights and duties of both husband and wife. It also stipulated equality of husband and wife in parental power, property rights, and the right to seek divorce. The new Criminal Code was also thoroughly consistent with the principle of equality of men and women. Except for the Imperial House Law which does not sanction a female head of state, women came to enjoy perfect legal equality with men. In September 1948, the Ministry of Labor established the Women's and Minor's Bureau, charged with protecting working women and minors and improving women's position in general.

Revision of the Civil Code

Among the many rights given to women in rapid succession, the revision of the Civil Code was the most important and far-reaching in its effects. The old Civil Code defined three types of authority over women. The first was the authority of the family head, who had the right to make decisions regarding marriage, the setting up of a separate family, and the place of domicile of all members of the family. The second was the authority of the parent. Without the approval of parents, one could not marry. The third was the husband's authority over his wife. The relation between husband and wife was that of master and servant. A husband could divorce his wife without her approval and was under no obligation to guarantee her living after divorce. Though the law stipulated monogamy, polygamy virtually prevailed. A husband could recognize, as his own, without his wife's approval, children he had from a woman other than his wife and could have their names entered in the family register. It was quite possible for a legitimate wife who had been childless or who had given birth only to daughters to be thrown out of the house penniless by a bastard son who had succeeded his father as head of the family.

The new Civil Code abolished the family-head system, and in its stead provided for freedom of marriage, equality of husband and wife, equal right to property, equal right to divorce, and equal obligations of chastity. In former days the family council exercised absolute power in case a dispute broke out regarding marriage, inheritance, or support, but nowadays the family courts, 228 subcourts, and 60 local consulting agencies throughout the country are giving advisory services to women. . . .

Women's Political Interest

Looked at from a broader point of view, the situation is more encouraging. That women have become interested in politics and have learned the close relation between politics and daily life is a remarkable advance. They hold a potentially stronger position than men, since according to a report of the election division of the Local Autonomy Board, as of December 20, 1955, there were 26,144,090 eligible women voters, 2,159,902 more than eligible men voters! In the first general election under the new election law (1946), 39 women representatives were elected. Though in the second general election (1947) women representatives decreased to 15, and in the third (1949) to 12, their quality has steadily improved. In the last seven years approximately 1,000 women have been elected to local assemblies; 7 have been elected heads of towns or villages. Though numerically weak, they are playing a noteworthy role in preventing corruption and wasteful expenditures. According to the *Asahi Yearbook* (1956) 4,000 women have been appointed and are serving as mediators in the family courts; 13,682 women have been nominated members of welfare committees and children's welfare committees;

128 women have been elected members of prefectural boards of education; and 10,000 have been elected members of local social education committees.

Mention should also be made of women's rate of balloting. In the first general election, women's rate of voting was 67 per cent, while that of men was 78.5 per cent. In the 1955 House of Representatives election, 72.1 per cent of the women voted compared to 79.9 per cent of the eligible men. Women have shown a keen interest in the elections of local assemblies, which have a more immediate connection with their daily lives: in the first election of those bodies in 1947 their rate of voting was 71.5 per cent as against 82.9 per cent for men, but in 1951, 92.2 per cent of the women voted against 92.3 per cent of the men.

Few feel that life has become better since the achievement of woman suffrage. Yet many women go to the polls, thinking it will help to bring about better days and convinced that merely to do housework diligently is not enough. The political consciousness of Japanese women has begun to awaken. They may talk about politics with no fear of being socially unacceptable, and psychological obstacles to political discussion are notably diminishing. According to a public opinion survey concerning women's voting conducted by the Women's and Minors' Bureau in March 1955, 75 per cent of the women who voted did so dictated by their own judgment without being influenced by anyone else. However, a larger proportion of women in rural areas and of those who voted for the conservative parties apparently did so under the influence of family opinion. It is repeatedly said that since women voters number two million more than men, if they were to unite it would be possible for them to elect desirable representatives and to realize fair politics supported by public opinion. But it will take years before women's political consciousness becomes developed enough to exercise wisely the rights they legally enjoy.

SECTION TWO

Political Institutions

32 • KIYOAKI TSUJI: *The Bureaucracy Preserved and Strengthened* *

Intelligent reformers are critical of the undue influence, conservatism, inadequate responsibility, and inefficiency, as well as the arrogance of bureaucracy; it is rather futile to condemn the structure indiscriminately. We do not observe that socialist regimes become less bureaucratic. Though the above strictures are often applied to Japanese officialdom, some of these attributes are more characteristic of the top echelon than of the "lesser soldiers," and some are shared.

Japanese bureaucrats have had to become somewhat more responsible to the Diet and more sensitive to the press and public opinion than before the new constitution was adopted in 1947. A major trend, which began long before 1940 and has accelerated since the war, has been the intrusion of bureaucrats particularly into conservative parties. They, along with professional politicians and Japan's business leaders, are the three principal elites remaining on the Right. Actually, many younger and mid-ranking officials are known to favor reformist parties, particularly the more moderate socialists; but all public servants except ministers and their deputies are supposed to be publicly neutral in politics. As Professor Tsuji points out in this article, however, much of their activity can and often does imply preferences. When one remembers that Japan is a unitary, not a federal, state, and that the government plays a crucial role in planning for, stimulating, and regulating the economy, it is easy to understand the continuing salience of the bureaucracy.

The author of this article is one of Japan's most distinguished political scientists and writers. He has been a professor at the University of Tokyo and recently was elected to a term as its President. He has also served as Chairman of the Japan Society of Public Administration and as a director of the Japanese Political Science Association.

When World War II came to an end, the Japanese military establishment and financial combines were resolutely dissolved, and other systems established in the

* *Gendai Nihon no seiji katei,* edited by Yoshitake Oka, Iwanami Shoten, 1958, pp. 109–125; as condensed and transl. in *Journal of Social and Political Ideas in Japan,* II, No. 3 (December 1964), pp. 88–92. By permission.

prewar period began to disintegrate. Although the bureaucracy was just as responsible for the war as the military establishment and the financial combines, it was never seriously criticized by either the Japanese government or the people. Shortly after the war, a number of moderate reforms of the bureaucratic system were carried out under the National Public Service Law and the Local Autonomy Law. For example, the old Ministry of Home Affairs was abolished and the police system reorganized, but these actions did not constitute a really drastic reform of the old bureaucratic system. Even the effect of these relatively mild reforms was reduced when, in May 1951, General Ridgeway stated that some of the more excessive reforms instituted by the Occupation could be modified.

The bureaucracy was established by the Meiji government to serve as the main prop of the Emperor-system state. It survived almost eighty years of political difficulties prior to the end of World War II, during which time its influence was pervasive and its authority was enormous. No matter how epoch-making the political changes of August 15, 1945, may have been, it was still no easy undertaking to reform and reduce the power of the bureaucratic system.

From the very outset of the Occupation, the Japanese bureaucracy demonstrated, directly and indirectly, a tenacious ability to preserve itself. This was illustrated by the way in which the new system of local autonomy was implemented. The system became effective on the same day as the new Constitution; its aims were to establish the democratic foundations of Japan and break up the overconcentration of authority in the hands of the central government. Specifically, the Ministry of Home Affairs had symbolized this overconcentration, and the establishment of the system of local autonomy spelled the dissolution of that ministry. However, when local public entities technically acquired autonomy for the first time in history, it turned out that their top positions were largely filled by onetime officials of the old Ministry of Home Affairs. Under the new system, prefectural governorships became elective posts, but vice-governorships remained appointive. A review of the personal backgrounds of the new vice-governors, the ones appointed to carry on the actual administration of the prefectural governments on behalf of the elected governors, shows that twenty-five of the forty-eight vice-governors appointed between 1947 and about 1950 had formerly been officials in the old Ministry of Home Affairs, and four had been officials in offices of overseas governors-general. Only a handful of the high-ranking officials in the new prefectural governments were private individuals recruited from the ranks of the local governments themselves.

I would not go so far as to say that all the bureaucrats who had gained their experience in the old system were unqualified to hold administrative positions in the new autonomous local governments. However, a basic problem was created by the fact that so many of these old bureaucrats were by training accustomed to operating within the prewar and wartime system of centralized control over local areas. In the postwar period, they have continued to administer local self-governments which are built on concepts completely different from those on which local government was based in the prewar period. No one ever questioned these old bureaucrats' understanding of democracy or their ability to administer local public entities under the new system of local autonomy. One cannot avoid the impression that the implicit purpose of the new arrangement was the preservation of the prewar system of centralized bureaucratic control. There is no doubt that many of the efforts made toward greater decentralization of power in the postwar period have been often thwarted by the old bureaucrats who favor centralization.

Under the prewar Emperor system, the police force was controlled by the Minister of Home Affairs. Because the people of the country had no influence or control over the appointment of the Minister, the police system inevitably fell under the strict control of the central government. The prewar Japanese police system was condemned by General MacArthur as a clear-cut proof that Japan had been a modern, totalitarian dictatorship. He demanded a complete reform which, when accomplished, divided the police system into national and local forces, each placed under the administrative control of elected public safety commissions. However, the reform was soon doomed to failure by the 1951 revision of the Police Law. By that revision, the local police units, which had been made autonomous by the initial reform, were placed under the administrative control of the National Rural Police Force. This change was made because the conservative government felt threatened by the frequent labor disputes and by the ever-intensifying cold war conflict. There was an additional reason for the change, namely, the new local public entities had encountered too many financial difficulties in supporting their own local police units. The next step taken was to place the police units at the metropolitan and prefectural levels directly under the administrative control of the National Police Agency. The higher officials of the prefectural and metropolitan police units became appointees of the central government, and a member of the cabinet was appointed the chairman of the National Public Safety Commission. With these modifications, the foundations of local autonomy partially crumbled.

The new postwar civil service system encountered the same fate, although not as rapidly as in the case of the police system. The original aim of the new system was to give life to the self-evident principle of any democratic state, which is incorporated in Article XV of the Constitution as follows: 'The people have the inalienable right to choose their public officials and to dismiss them.' It scarcely needs to be said that the writing of this new regulation was insufficient in itself to sever forthwith the long-standing relationship between official position and the authority of the Emperor, an authority which had long been the fount of all prestige and honor in Japanese society. Nor was its mere writing able to destroy the spiritual structure of the Emperor system that measured one's social worth in terms of the degree of one's access to the supreme authority (i.e., the Emperor). Nevertheless, it was hoped that the new civil service system would constitute a major force for the attainment of these goals. An autonomous National Personnel Authority was established after the war to perform these difficult tasks through the impartial administration of government personnel. However, the true independence of the National Personnel Authority will be guaranteed only when the remaining vestiges of the old bureaucratic system are eliminated and when a new democratic concept of civil service is adopted. There is still no provision for public opinion to make itself felt in the policy formulation of the National Personnel Authority, nor have democratic measures been taken as they have in West Germany, for example, where a representative of civil servants' unions is co-opted as a commissioner in the country's highest personnel authority.

The National Personnel Authority of Japan has no democratic support from the people themselves, and, as might well be expected, it has been attacked by the bureaucratic forces who have been carried over from the old system. The bureaucratic attacks have resulted in the abolition of the system of public impeachment of civil servants involved in graft and corruption, as well as in severe limitations being placed on the freedom of public servants to engage in political activities, participate in strikes, or engage in collective bargaining. Today the point has been reached where attempts are being made to restrict both the size and the competence of the National Personnel Authority. Thus the noble ideals that guided the establishment of the civil service system after the war have been gradually eaten away. Not only has the old prewar bureaucratic system been able to survive in postwar democratic Japan, but, under the pretext that the so-called 'democratic excesses' of the Occupation need correcting, it has even been strengthened.

What has enabled the old bureaucratic system to survive and firmly re-establish its position in the postwar period when other major forces that were just as responsible for the war were either abolished or successfully reformed? I believe that three principal factors have brought about this situation. First, the Occupation authorities used what I call 'indirect rule' to implement the Potsdam Declaration. By this I mean that the Occupation, rather than functioning as a military government, implemented its policies through the Japanese government: the Japanese bureaucracy acted as SCAP's agent for giving effect to the policies of the Allied Powers. SCAP's intent was not to support the old bureaucracy but merely to make use of it; however, in spite of this intention, SCAP was not able to limit its use of our bureaucracy to just technical services. For many years the bureaucracy had occupied too important a political role in the authoritarian pattern of government. The bureaucracy began to reveal its true nature just as soon as it was given the important task of implementing Occupation policies. The ambiguity in the lines of responsibility that inevitably accompany a system of 'indirect rule,' together with the sectionalism between the various departments of SCAP, had the effect of actually supporting the traditional character of the Japanese bureaucratic system.

The second thing that has made it possible for the bureaucracy to survive intact is the deep faith of the people in general that the bureaucracy is by nature neutral. This faith had been nurtured by the government structure established during the early part of the Meiji period. True political stability and a true national order can be realized in a country only when parliamentary politics embrace a wide variety of opinions and partisan interests. But in Japan the belief has prevailed that the only way to secure a national order and political stability is to maintain and perpetuate the established government structure based on bureaucratic paternalism and centered around the hierarchy of the Emperor system.

The Japanese people have always had a vague but obstinate notion that, on the one hand, the government and the bureaucrats are impartial and neutral and that, on the other hand, partisan conflict and party politics are liable to upset the equilibrium of the established order. Even in the period of confusion and chaos that followed Japan's defeat in World War II, this notion strongly influenced the people. Immediately after the war, many people held reservations as to whether the political parties and legislators which had become suddenly active were really justified to hold, or qualified to exercise, their new-found political authority. In reaction to the new political parties and legislators, many of these people sought solace in the seemingly neutral character of the established bureaucracy. This was particularly true in rural areas where people came face to face with the new local bosses who had been suddenly raised to positions of authority after the war.

The August 31, 1946, issue of the *Mainichi Shimbun* gave details on a public-opinion poll it had conducted in major towns and villages throughout the country on the question of what sort of persons should be chosen as governors in the forthcoming local elections. Seventy-five percent of the 130,000 respondents favored 'private individuals,' fourteen percent favored 'party politicians,' and only about eleven percent favored 'government officials.' But when the gubernatorial elections were held half a year later, thirty-one of the forty-six new prefectural governors turned out to be former government officials, most of whom had been appointive governors just before the new system was instituted. (That is, they had been officials of the old Ministry of Home Affairs.—Ed.) These results clearly demonstrate what a high degree of reliance the people place on former representatives of the central government.

The third thing that has enabled the bureaucracy to survive in the postwar period is the fact that political parties, which should have taken over much of the prewar role of the bureaucracy, had neither the knowledge nor the ability after the war to administer the complexities of government. For a long period before the war, the military establishment and the bureaucracy combined forces to prevent our political parties from gaining positions of political authority. When our political parties were suddenly re-established in the immediate postwar period, they were organizationally and numerically weak. All of these factors combined to make the new political parties ill-equipped to legislate the complex and specialized policies required of government; they were not even able to supervise the implementation of such legislation. In the ten-year span between the first Diet in May 1947 and the twenty-sixth Diet in 1957, the government presented 2,520 bills (of which 1,341 were passed), the members of the House of Representatives presented 808 bills (of which 442 were passed), and the members of the House of Councilors presented 224 bills (of which 107 were passed). These figures clearly illustrate how influential the bureaucracy was in initiating the majority of the bills placed before the Diet.

This same bureaucratic influence can be observed today in the way bills are deliberated. The standing committees of the Diet are modeled along American lines; their chief responsibility is to deliberate on bills prior to their submission to a plenary session of the Diet for a vote. Each standing committee corresponds to a particular ministry or agency of the government. A member of a standing committee is very likely to be a former official of the committee's corresponding ministry or agency. Therefore, in the legislative process, he tends to speak in the interest of the section of the bureaucracy of which he is a former official. It is a great asset for a candidate running for a seat in the Diet to have held a high-ranking position in the government. Once such a candidate is elected, he has many opportunities to represent the interests of the particular section of the bureaucracy in which he formerly worked. The criticism one hears today that the standing committees of the National Diet are in fact off-shoots of particular sections of the bureaucracy is solidly grounded.

Throughout the world today politics have become highly specialized and more socially oriented; the formulation and implementation of policy are largely in the hands of bureaucrats who possess a very technical knowledge of the ways of government. In countries which have long democratic traditions, political parties and parliaments are usually on guard against the bureaucracy which, because of its specialization and superior technical knowledge, could take advantage of a situation to further its own ends. While this may be the case in many other countries of the world, what efforts have our political parties and the National Diet made and what have they accomplished in the postwar period to check the expanding authority of our bureaucracy? I regret to have to say that they have accomplished nothing. Our bureaucracy has held a paramount position in the government structure since the beginning of the Meiji period, and, when it became the sole agent of the Occupation for the implementation of Allied policy, it was greatly strengthened rather than weakened. Although to all appearances the bureaucracy was merely being used by other political forces, the bureaucracy was in fact itself using the National Diet and the political parties. In the postwar period, just as in the prewar period, the National Diet and the political parties, though clad in their new, gorgeous gowns, have danced on a stage synchronized by a complex bureaucracy.

33 • NISHIJIMA YOSHIJI: *The Peace Constitution Controversy* *

There are numerous laws of fundamental importance enacted since 1946, but the constitution of the next year is most comprehensive and basic. It declared the Diet to be the supreme organ of state and made the cabinet—which was to include only civilian ministers—responsible to it. It was perhaps significant that a mainly American Occupation favored for Japan a British-type cabinet system with provision for votes of no confidence, dissolution, and elections within the statutory maximum term of four years. It is virtually certain that Japan would not have had such a liberal constitution had it not been for foreign intervention, though the Meiji Constitution—never amended after promulgation in 1889—might have been slightly revised.

Japanese conservatives have longed to revise this rather foreign-sounding basic law, while leftist parties, by barely maintaining a one-third strength in the Diet, have been able to prevent this. They fear that if the door is opened a crack to such change, it will be pushed wide open by a flood of retrogressive revisions. They also recall the oppressions and militarism made possible by features of the Meiji polity. There have been indications that if the Left Socialists should be able to control the state by pressure or attained majority, they might attempt their own form of revised or substituted constitution.

The article which follows gives overwhelming attention to contention over war-renouncing Article IX of the new constitution; it barely mentions some of the other main issues. The author is an editorial writer for the Asahi Shimbun *and head of its Analysis and Research Section.*

* *Japan Quarterly*, X, No. 1 (January–March 1963), pp. 18–27. By permission.

The Activities of the Constitution Research Council

The Constitution Research Council first began work in August, 1957, its task being to study the Japanese Constitution, to investigate and deliberate on the various problems arising in connection with it, and to report on its findings to the Cabinet and, through the Cabinet, to the National Diet. It devoted the whole of the following four years, until the end of July, 1961, to investigating the manner in which the Japanese Constitution first came into being and the manner of its enforcement. Since September, 1961, it has been studying and debating the questions which emerged as the result of its investigations and deliberations, principally those of the need or otherwise for revision of the Constitution and improvements in its operation. It is expected to make its final report to the Cabinet and Diet sometime late this year.

The circumstances underlying the launching of such a large-scale inquiry into the Constitution are, in brief, as follows. The present Constitution was drawn up while Japan was under the control of the Allied occupation forces following her defeat and surrender in World War II, and was based on the so-called "MacArthur Draft." It had passed the House of Representatives and the House of Peers by October, 1946, was promulgated on November 3, and came into effect on May 3, the following year.

From the very outset, there were complaints from conservative elements that the Constitution had been imposed on Japan from the outside. There was considerable dissatisfaction, not only among rightist elements, but within the Conservative parties themselves, concerning certain of its provisions. These included, in particular, the establishment of the Emperor as a "symbol," with the sovereignty resting with the people; Article IX, which renounced war forever in a gesture of absolute pacifism; and certain clauses which, it was claimed, overemphasized basic human rights and failed to make clear the duties of the people as well.

During the Occupation, these dissatisfied elements could do nothing but nurse their grievances in silence, but once the Peace Treaty had come into effect in April, 1953, Japan was truly independent once more, a Constitution Research Association with Kishi Nobusuke at its head was set up within the Liberal Party and drew up a tentative draft of a new constitution considered more suitable for Japan as an independent nation with the right of self-determination. This encouraged the movement toward revising the Constitution, and continued calls for revision within the Liberal-Democratic Party, which succeeded to the Liberal Party, led eventually to the creation of the Constitution Research Council as a consultative agency of the Government.

The Socialist Party and elements farther to the left opposed these moves head-on, and successive general elections from that time on produced heated debates over the pros and cons of constitutional revision. Even the bill providing for the establishment of the Council was, on its presentation by the Liberal-Democratic Government, stubbornly opposed by the left wing on the grounds that the establishment of such a Council would in itself open the way to revision of the Constitution. The bill was passed with the aid of the government party's numerical majority, but when the Council actually started work the nine Socialist members scheduled for inclusion in its total membership of fifty boycotted its meetings, and the Council ever since has consisted of Liberal-Democratic members together with men of learning and experience from outside the political world. On several occasions it has called on the Socialist Party to join in its deliberations, but to no avail.

In order to assuage criticism from the Opposition parties, who claimed that it had been formed to pave the way for constitutional revision, the Constitution Research Council proposed that it should not put forward any final conclusions based on a majority opinion within its own ranks, but content itself with reporting fairly the arguments both for and against revision, leaving the rest to the judgment of the Government, the Diet, and the people. It also adopted an extremely democratic method of conducting its business, the guiding principle being the inclusion of the public in all its deliberations. All meetings of the Council would be open to the public, and the minutes would be put on sale in the same way as official gazettes; the Council would study all information relevant to the question from both home and abroad, as well as referring to experts for their views; and it would hold public hearings in each district of Japan in turn, in order to give as many representatives of the general public as possible a chance to air their views. In addition, the choice as chairman of the Council of Takayanagi Kenzō did something to calm Opposition complaints that the Council represented the thin end of the wedge, since Takayanagi, an expert on British and American law and a former Tokyo University professor, is known for his opposition to any over-all revision of the Constitution, and his moderate, reasonable handling of the question.

Article IX and the Changing Situation

Article IX of the Japanese Constitution runs as follows:

> Aspiring sincerely to an international peace based on justice and order, the Japanese people forever renounce war as a sovereign right of the nation and the threat or use of force as means of settling international disputes.
>
> In order to accomplish the aim of the preceding paragraph, land, sea, and air forces, as well as other war potential, will never be maintained. The right of belligerency of the State will not be recognized.

The original draft of this article was contained in the "MacArthur Note," and despite certain amendments of the phraseology in the course of debate in the Imperial Diet, its essential purport was embodied as it stood in the present Constitution. The government of the day interpreted it very strictly as forbidding even a defensive war, but following the outbreak of the Korean War in 1950 General MacArthur sent a letter to Prime Minister Yoshida seeking the establishment of a Japanese police reserve of 75,000 men. On January 1 of the same year General MacArthur had already issued a declaration which stressed that Article IX did not deny the existence of Japan's right to self-defense, and from that time on the Japanese Government began to take the view that Japan had not renounced her right to defend herself after all.

The U.S.-Japan Security Treaty, signed simultaneously with the Peace Treaty in September of the following year at San Francisco, expressed the hope that Japan would assume increasing responsibility for her own defense against direct and indirect aggression. The buildup of Japan's defense potential went ahead. The police reserve force developed into the National Security Force, and a maritime police force came into being as well. A lively controversy arose as to whether or not these constituted the "war potential" which Japan was prohibited from maintaining under Paragraph Two of Article IX. Then, in March, 1954, an M.S.A. aid agreement was signed between Japan and America, which made legal the outfitting of Japan's land, sea and air forces with mainly American equipment. The outlines became more and more clearly defined. In July, 1954, Japan's land, sea, and air forces were brought together under the title of Self-Defense Forces, and a Self-Defense Agency was set up to administrate them. This arrangement still persists today, but the military nature of the Self-Defense Forces has become increasingly evident with time. In the summer of 1960, the U.S.-Japan Security Treaty was revised in the teeth of opposition so fierce that it forced President Eisenhower to give up his proposed visit to Japan. The revised treaty promised that Japan would maintain and develop her ability to resist armed attack, and the focus of controversy at the time was again, of course, the question of whether or not this provision violated Japan's renunciation of war potential in Article IX of the Constitution.

So far, in the case of the Security Treaty, the emphasis had been on the individual securities of Japan and America. However, Japan's admittance to the United Nations in 1952 gave a new twist to the problem on account of the "right of collective self-defense" stipulated in Article 51 of the United Nations Charter. In applying for membership, the Japanese Government accepted the obligations included in the Charter, promising that Japan would fulfill those obligations with all the means at her disposal. This gave rise to a fresh controversy as to the relationship between Japan's duty to co-operate with the United Nations and Article IX of the Constitution. In other words, could Japan's obligation to co-operate with the United Nations in the military sphere be waived in view of Article IX?

As the government of the day saw it, admittance to the United Nations did not automatically bind Japan to the provision of military forces; it would be sufficient for her to provide "facilities," without any obligation for her to co-operate with the dispatch of Self-Defense forces. The House of Councillors at the time accordingly passed a resolution to the effect that no Self-Defense forces would be sent overseas. Even at the time, however, there were some who argued that though it was right to place a ban on the overseas dispatch of Self-Defense forces as a purely military action, it should be permitted to send them abroad to participate in United Nations contingents organized to maintain or restore peace or for policing purposes. The controversy still drags on, and by now affords the advocates of revision one of the mainstays of their argument.

A number of important changes in the situation at home and abroad have occurred, thus, during the period since Article IX first came into effect, and the keen controversy concerning its interpretation which they provoked now forms the focal point of discussion on the Constitution. How, in other words, should the article be viewed in relation to the defense setup which Japan has, in actuality, evolved?

There are, broadly speaking, two views here. The first holds that the existing defense setup should be maintained, and the gap between the existing reality and the idealistic provisions of Article IX closed either by adding to or revising those provisions. The second holds that the provisions of Article IX must be maintained and protected before anything else, and that the defense setup must accordingly be revised to fit in with this. The former view is held by right-wing elements which insist that Japan's rearmament should be given open constitutional sanction, as well as by advocates of constitutional revision within the Liberal-Democratic Party, while the second is held by the Socialists and others of the left wing.

There is also a middle-of-the-road view, which holds that Article IX is first and foremost a political manifesto proclaiming Japan's rejection of war as a means to attaining her own ends; ideals should be left as ideals, and the existing defense setup permitted as a corollary of Japan's right to defend herself. In other words, this view—which is shared by Chairman Takayanagi himself—sees no necessity for tampering with Article IX.

The views of both pro-revisionists and anti-revisionists exhibit many different shades of emphasis, and it is difficult to define the limits dividing them, but they can still be classified into two main groups according to whether or not they basically approve the course of rearmament on which Japan is now embarked. What follows is an account of the pros and cons of revision as expressed, in the course of the Council's deliberations, by Council members, specialists, and members of the public called on to testify at public hearings.

Conflict Within the Council

The views expressed concerning Article IX by members of the Council show a decided bias in favor of revision. Of those who have given a positive opinion, seventeen are in favor of and nine opposed to revision, as might be expected in view of the overwhelming preponderance of pro-revisionists in the Council as a whole. The principal arguments put forward by the two sides are as follows:

1. Pro-Revision

a. Article IX is at variance with the realities of present-day international politics, and should be revised accordingly. In the light of such realities, Japan has no alternative but to look to the United Nations and other collective security bodies for her defense. For this reason, it is necessary for her to maintain self-defense forces which can co-operate with the United Nations, or other collective security organizations, and Article IX should be revised to permit her to do so.

Justifications for this view, depending on the holder, allow of many different emphases; for example:

- (i) Japan must rely on collective security organizations, especially the United Nations.
- (ii) Japan must be prepared for localized conflicts.
- (iii) Arms cuts, and total disarmament in particular, are still far from being realized.
- (iv) Article IX, which was drawn up on the basis of Allied, particularly American, policies for the control of Japan during the Occupation, is a fiction at any rate.

b. A dispute exists concerning the interpretation of Article IX concerning Japan's right of self-defense and her maintenance of self-defense forces. It should be revised, therefore, so as to remove constitutional doubts on these scores. In other words, although the majority view nowadays is that, legally speaking, Japan could wage a defensive war even under her present Constitution, the theory that the Self-Defense Forces are unconstitutional still has many supporters and considerable persuasive powers. It is imperative, therefore, that the existence and nature of the Self-Defense Forces should be made explicit under the Constitution and all doubts as to the duties of the Self-Defense Forces removed.

c. The existence of Article IX and the controversy as to its interpretation are doing Japan a lot of harm, and the article should be revised accordingly. The controversy divides domestic opinion and deprives the nation's government of its stability. In particular, the theory that the Self-Defense Forces are unconstitutional is lowering the morale of their members.

The advocacy of revision which forms the majority opinion within the Council falls for the most part into one of these three patterns. What is particularly worthy of attention is that all are free from any positive, reactionary advocacy of rearmament such as might lead to a revival of the militarism of the past. For example, view (a), which holds that Japan should rely on the United Nations and other collective security organizations, still agrees that the pacifism which is the basic stipulation of Article IX should be preserved as the ideal guiding the nation, and that pacifism within the framework of co-operation with other nations should be strictly maintained. In a similar fashion, views (b) and (c) confine themselves to insisting that the existence of the right to self-defense and of the Self-Defense Forces should be made explicit so as to dispel constitutional doubts and prevent harm to the nation's affairs. They hold that Japan should keep herself ready to resist aggression from without, and do not argue that Japan should carry out any more positive dispatch of troops overseas. They would hold firmly to the renunciation of war laid down in Paragraph One of Article IX, but would alter the provisions of Paragraph Two concerning the maintenance of a war potential, in order to give the Self-Defense Forces constitutional justification.

2. Anti-Revision

The arguments against revision of Article IX can be categorized as follows:

a. Rather than looking on Article IX as at variance with the actualities of international politics, it should be maintained as it stands, as a basis for dealing with those actualities.

This general view similarly allows of various different emphases in its justification:

(i) Article IX is a declaration of total disarmament, the first to be made by any nation in the world. Japan should be wary of revising it in such a way as to deprive it of its great significance at a time when a road to disarmament is at least being opened up.

(ii) There are a number of factors which make it impossible to agree with revision at the present stage. Among them are the significance of Article IX as a declaration of a peaceful ideal, the strain imposed on the nation's resources by defense commitments, the danger of a revival of militaristic tendencies, the harm done by splitting the nation into two opposing forces, and the possible shock to other Asian nations.

(iii) Though it would be impossible at the present stage for every nation to renounce its right to self-defense, the future aim must be for all nations to give up their war potential. In this respect, Article IX is a pointer to the course to be taken.

b. Since the present interpretation and manner of enforcement of Article IX are in fact permitting Japan a self-defense setup, there is no need for any special revision. Variations of this view are:

(i) The interpretations adopted by the Diet and Government, and the attitude shown by the Supreme Court in its verdicts, indicate that the Self-Defense Forces are not unconstitutional. It is normal for controversies to arise over interpretations of the Constitution, the law, and so on, but it does not follow that they should be subject to constant revision on this account.

(ii) It is a principle of international law that a nation has the right to legitimate self-defense in the same way as the individual. There is nothing in Article IX prohibiting a defensive war. Why, then, should there be any special need to revise it?

(iii) Admitted that the renunciation of the "right of belligerency" mentioned in the latter part of Paragraph Two of Article IX gives rise to a certain number of inconveniences in relation to Japan's co-operation in military measures undertaken by the United Nations, these inconveniences are not such as cannot be reconciled with the United Nations Charter and the U.S.-Japan Security Treaty. If this type of interpretation is possible, then there is no pressing need for revision.

c. Revision of Article IX would not constitute a fundamental solution of the problem, and would in fact cause a lot more trouble instead, since:

(i) It might arouse mistrust and suspicion of Japan among other nations.

(ii) It might serve as a pretext for strengthening Japan's armaments still further.

(iii) It might increase the burden imposed on the public by military expenditure.

(iv) Plans to revise Article IX might lead to a fatal split in public opinion.

(v) It might lead to a revival of the conscription system or spur the nation on along the road to militarism.

(vi) Any revision of the Constitution should be undertaken as a joint action by the three major political parties, and its basic provisions should be left alone so long as no agreement to do so exists.

(vii) Surveys of public opinion, as well as the testimony of witnesses at public hearings of the Constitution Research Council, suggest that the general trend of public opinion and sentiment is against revision of Article IX.

Opinions Expressed at Public Hearings

Since its inception, the Constitution Research Council has held a number of sectional and subcommittee meetings to deal with particular aspects of the question, and has invited scholars, critics, and businessmen to testify at these meetings. In addition, during the 1958-61 period it organized forty-six public hearings in Metropolitan Tokyo and each of the various prefectures and urban prefectures, as well as Hokkaidō. Then, in the period between February, 1961, and September, 1962, it held public hearings in the principal cities of nine districts into which the country was divided for the purpose—Kantō, Kinki, Kyūshū, Hokkaidō, Hokuriku, Shin'etsu, Tōkai, Chūgoku, and Shikoku. The questions on which witnesses testified numbered twenty-four in all, including the position of the Emperor, the renunciation of war, the Diet, and the Cabinet system, each witness choosing whichever subject he wished to speak on. The choice of witnesses was made by taking recommended representatives from various walks of life—the management of large enterprises, medium and smaller enterprises, labor, agriculture, women's organizations, youth organizations, religious bodies, the press, the legal profession, the teaching profession, and so on. Two unusual features distinguished these public hearings. First, they were boycotted completely by the various "defend-the-Constitution" organizations under the wing of the Socialist and Democratic Socialist parties, the reason given being that the Constitution Research Council was itself unconstitutional. Secondly, certain union organizations and student bodies stemming from the Zengakuren (National Federation of Students' Self-Governing Associations) tried forcibly to prevent the holding of the public hearings in every district where they were scheduled. All such demonstrations, however, were cleared away by the police, and the hearings proceeded according to plan.

Since space does not permit a detailed account of each of the local hearings, I will give an account of the main trends at the local hearings, and conclude with a rather more detailed description of the central hearing held in Tokyo.

At the local hearings, two clear trends emerged. The overwhelming majority of speakers responded to questions concerning the Emperor system by advocating maintenance of the Emperor's present position as symbolic head of State. Concerning the crucial issue of Article IX, the advocates of revision were outnumbered by its opponents. A considerable discrepancy was apparent between public opinion and the general trend of opinion within the Constitution Research Council. It is difficult, of course, to give hard-and-fast figures, since there are always delicate shades of emphasis in what witnesses say, but the findings of the Constitution Research Council's secretariat indicate that opponents of revision outnumbered its advocates in the proportion of 6.5 to 3.5. Generally speaking, support for revision seemed to be commoner among representatives of managements, and opposition stronger among representatives of women's, workers' and agricultural organizations, and the press.

The central hearing held in Tokyo on September 28 and 29, 1962, attracted much attention as a kind of summing-up of all the previous hearings. For the hearing, eighteen witnesses were chosen from the various fields already mentioned. According to Constitution Research Council officials, the views of the speakers and the way they conflicted with each other were more or less the same as at the previous local hearings. Here again, the focal point of discussion was the provision of Article IX renouncing war. At previous local hearings, as many as 79% of the women speakers had declared that this provision should be preserved, and in the same way the two women representatives at the Tokyo hearing both came out in favor of "protecting the Peace Constitution." For example, Mrs. Uemura Tamaki, honorary president of the Japanese Y.W.C.A., adopted the idealist standpoint, giving unqualified support for Article IX and declaring, "Unarmed neutrality is the best form of security; the renunciation of war has provided a golden yardstick, an ideal common to all humanity." Wada Haruo, secretary of Zenrō Kaigi (the All-Japan Congress of Labor Unions) declared, "Revision of Article IX should be avoided in principle, in order to maintain a consistent pacifism throughout." "However," he added, "neither a religious rejection of armaments and refusal to resist, nor the extremes of militarism are realistic. The first question, of whether or not self-defense forces should be allowed, and if so how many and in what form, should be decided at a general election or by a special national referendum." Mr. Wada's remarks were noteworthy in that Zenrō Kaigi is the principal organization backing the Democratic Socialist Party.

The two representatives of youth organizations, on the other hand, both favored revision, declaring that Japan's right to maintain the means of self-defense should be made explicit. Their stand was interesting in that previous representatives of youth groups had mostly stressed "protection of the Peace Constitution" in the same way as the women speakers. Kameoka Shigenori of the Central Committee of the Youth Section of the Shūyōdan, a moral training society, declared, "The view that no defense is the best defense is out-and-out selfishness. A people should have the spirit to defend their own country, and Japan should aim at a self-defense force in which, as in Switzerland, the whole nation would participate."

Nagano Shigeo, president of Fuji Iron and Steel Works, declared that, while pacifism should be retained, it was only natural for Japan to maintain the minimum amount of armaments required for her defense—a point which should, moreover, be made quite explicit in the Constitution. Mizukami Tatsuzo, president of Mitsui Bussan, was more cautious: Considering that some sort of self-defense setup had in fact been evolved under the present interpretation of Article IX, it was not worth risking chaos by trying to force through revision.

Finally Ryū Shintarō, Chief Editorial Writer for the *Asahi Shimbun,* who appeared as representative of the press, took the view that revision was unnecessary. His views can be summed up as follows:

"The most serious problems raised by Article IX, which defines Japan's renunciation of war, concern its relationship to the Self-Defense Forces. However, I believe that any nation has the right of self-defense. The Self-Defense Forces today are a reality, and I think that since the Supreme Court does not seem to interpret their existence as unconstitutional they should be permitted within the stringent limitations imposed by Article IX. In other words, I see no reason to revise Article IX. It has been argued that the article should be revised in order to regularize the existence of those forces, but revision would only lead to a succession of new problems at home and abroad, and afford no fundamental solution of the question. It is obvious from the principles underlying Article IX that the dispatch of Japanese troops abroad should be prohibited, a prohibition which would serve at the same time to make clear the peaceful nature of the Self-Defense Forces. Japan can co-operate with the United Nations by other means. Instead of revision, a definite interpretation of Article IX must be established.

"Viewing the situation as a whole, I believe that the requirement at the moment is not to spend time debating the pros and cons of revision, but to find positive policies to embody the essential principles underlying the Constitution. Where international politics are concerned, for example, the nation should rally round the movement to obtain a ban on nuclear arms and disarmament which is proceeding under the present threat of international disaster. The nation should strive toward the goal of world federation; among the constitutions of the world, the Japanese Constitution is unique in making this a matter of national policy."

The above is only the barest sketch of the many different views expressed concerning revision of Article IX, but it should suffice to show why the question forms the central point of controversy in the argument on consitutional revision as a whole. The controversy, of course, was only to be expected. Fifteen years separate the nation which, stripped of its arms after an unprecedented defeat, gave its overwhelming support to the renunciation of war in Article IX, from the nation which today, as a result of a succession of important changes in the international situation involving the Far East, finds itself in possession of Self-Defense Forces which include an army, a navy, and an air force. A gap has inevitably occurred between the law and the reality, and the people who seek to make the law match the reality necessarily find themselves calling for a revision of that law. There are others, however, who would work out some compromise between the law and the actuality by taking a broader view—in the British or American manner—of its interpretation and application, rather than a rigidly literal interpretation in the German manner; such people are doubtless moved by the belief that it would be wiser to avoid the friction certain to be caused by any revision of the Constitution.

After more than five years of activity, the Constitution Research Council is putting the last touches to its final report. It only remains to be seen how the Government and the Diet, not to mention the nation as a whole, will receive is findings. The final judgment on whether to revise the Constitution or not can only come from the people themselves.

34 • Atsushi Satō: *Local Autonomy—Lags and Advances* *

We have already commented on the unitary structure of Japanese government and administration. That is, prefectural jurisdictions are, in relation to the Center, more like British counties than like federated American states. Certain of the Occupation-sponsored reforms attempted to change the high degree of centralization that had existed until 1946–47. These efforts related especially to local government, education, and police affairs. Bureaucratic traditions and fear of subversive radical movements doubtless contributed to degrees of recentralization after 1952, but the weakness of local finance was usually a main contributory factor.

Here is the last and most analytically perceptive part of an article by a Japanese specialist in public administration who has served as consultant to the government's Provisional Commission on Public Administration. Mr. Sato was graduated from the Faculty of Law, University of Tokyo, in 1951 and is now an assistant professor at Seikei University in the capital.

I would now like to review what I believe to be the three major deterrents to the proper functioning of local autonomy in the immediate future. The first is found in the fact that an overwhelming number of governors, mayors and local legislators do not belong to political parties. In Japan one finds that the smaller the administrative unit, the higher the percentage of elected officials without

* *Sekai* (May 1959), pp. 24–32. This article was written prior to the nationwide local elections of April 5, 1959. As condensed and transl. in *Journal of Social and Political Ideas in Japan*, II, No. 3 (December 1964), pp. 72–74. By permission.

party affiliations. A local assemblyman often avoids party affiliation in order to convey the false impression that he represents all of the people within his own village community. But, in truth, he usually operates as the representative of the small political power group which controls the village community; by saying he is neutral and nonpartisan, he is able to camouflage the fact that he represents primarily the interests of a mere handful of influential individuals. Even though a local assemblyman may declare he is politically neutral, he is bound to be conservative because the handful of influential people he represents is always conservative. Since assemblymen are essentially representatives of political power groups within their respective village communities, the local mayor must mediate the assemblymen's conflicting interests. In order to do this effectively, he also must pretend to be nonpartisan and to represent the interests of all sectors of his constituency.

Although this situation is found throughout the country today, the Japan Socialist Party continues to concentrate exclusively on the formulation of national policy; it ignores local constituencies, where national policy is actually implemented. The wellsprings of reform will dry up if the Socialist Party continues to ignore local areas except during elections. The Socialist Party differs from the Liberal Democratic Party in one major respect: it does not have a large number of influential people behind it at the local community level, people to work for it during and between elections. The Socialist Party is like a top-heavy, inverted pyramid: it has many members at its headquarters and in the National Diet but only a few at the level of the local constituency. This situation leads the party to conduct its election campaigns along abstract, theoretical lines which fall far short of the concrete proposals needed for the improvement of local areas. In spite of the lateness of the hour, the Socialist Party is now trying to change its approach to election campaigns by placing less reliance on abstract slogans. For example, the party has adopted a 'Guide to the Writing of a Platform for Local Self-Government,' which is intended for use by party chapters in the next local elections.

The second major deterrent to the proper functioning of local autonomy is the move to merge the administrations of more towns and villages. The central and the prefectural governments have been putting pressure on towns and villages to merge, supposedly for the purpose of creating local-government units of more 'reasonable' size in order to increase efficiency and reduce administrative costs. But the net result of such mergers so far has been merely to reduce the amount of autonomy enjoyed by local governments. After a merger has been effected, the financial burden of the agricultural sector of the expanded self-governing entity often increases because the city-oriented administration of the local-government entity gives priority to the development of the urban areas it encompasses. The relatively small budgetary allotment to the agricultural sector forces the members of village communities to bear additional expenses for the maintenance and development of their own areas. This situation, in turn, leads to the conservative power group's gaining more authority and control over the other members of the village community.

Although town and village mergers impede local autonomy, they do yield some positive results. First, the disputes created by town and village mergers frequently make the residents of the rural areas in a new government entity much more aware of the importance of protecting their local autonomy. Second, town and village mergers frequently decrease the importance of the villages as bases of support for the conservative party. Where a larger administrative entity is created, the farmers often come to constitute a minority because their relative number in the new entity is reduced, and, conversely, the city and town dwellers come to constitute a majority. This change in the ratio between the farming and the non-farming population often leads to a loss of identity between the village community and the boss-controlled agricultural organization in the village. When this happens, the boss-controlled agricultural organization becomes less efficient as a vote-getting mechanism for the conservatives. Third, the enlargement of voting districts better guarantees the secrecy of the ballot, and the secrecy of the ballot weakens the control that village bosses formerly had over the voting patterns of the village electorate. Fourth, the informal and unofficial village assemblies, traditionally composed chiefly of farmers, tend, after merger, to include all types of residents of the community, much like neighborhood associations in urban areas. Fifth, as towns and villages amalgamate, there is usually an increase in the number of labor unions organized by employees of local government. (Note: Most of such unions are affiliated with the National Federation of Local Self-Government Workers Unions.—Ed.)

The third major deterrent to the proper functioning of local autonomy is the growing centralization of power in the hands of the bureaucracy. The central government and the bureaucracy have gradually placed under their authority those aspects of local autonomy that have created problems for them. The move toward greater bureaucratization and centralization has increased in tempo even since the 1955 local elections. A sixth revision of the Local Autonomy Law, in June 1956, empowered higher government offices to increase their interference in the affairs of lower government offices. It also gave prefectural governors and city mayors greater authority over their respective local assemblies. The sixth revision of the Local Autonomy Law made prefectural governments mere branch offices of the central government, with a concomitant loss of autonomy on the part of city, town and village administrations.

In recent years efforts have been made to abolish prefectural governments and replace them with larger, regional governments. Attempts are also being made at the moment to raise the Autonomy Agency to the status of a ministry. (This action was finally taken in 1960.—Ed.) In addition to these problems, local governments now find themselves faced by another very serious situation: the central government has designated many of them delinquent because of the large deficits they have incurred. Because of their large deficits, many local governments now heavily rely upon the central government for subsidies, and the subsidies have strings tied to them. These strings greatly restrict the scope of action that local governments are normally permitted to take.

In spite of the serious inroads made by the central government on local autonomy, a strong and effective defense of local autonomy has yet to evolve. There seem to be only a few concrete attempts being made to protect local autonomy. One is the campaign of the chief executives and assemblies of the twenty-three wards of Tokyo to protect the autonomy they presently enjoy. Another is the work of the National Federation of Local Self-Government Workers Unions, which holds annual seminars for the study of local-government affairs. It must be recognized, however, that these efforts are not really sufficient to prevent the central government from restricting the free exercise of local autonomy.

SECTION THREE

Political Leadership

35 • HAJIME SHINOHARA: *The Leadership of the Conservative Party* *

Professor Shinohara, like most other social scientists on the University of Tokyo's faculty, is a critic of conservative leaders from a pro-socialist point of view. Even though this article is not quite objective in tone and emphasis, it is insightful and accurate as far as it goes. It is in the process of selection and omission of interpretative material—as well as in certain evaluative comments—that his personal views (see further in his next article) are manifested. One can discern his fascination with the traditional, intuitive politician, even though he considers this type to be passé.

Much more could be, and has been, written about the nine (and sometimes more) factions in the Liberal Democratic party (LDP)—how aspirants for the premiership form alliances or coalitions and apportion cabinet posts. LDP cabinets under Prime Minister Hayato Ikeda successively held office from July 1960 to November 1964. The partial autonomy of the groups within the LDP and the methods of their leaders in building personal organizations and cultivating their own financial backing have been described elsewhere.[1]

The author was graduated from the Faculty of Law, University of Tokyo, in 1950 and is now a full professor there. His fields are modern politics and European, especially German, history.

Political leadership in its proper sense means that type of leadership whereby the leader advocates a positive plan of action while maintaining constant two-way communication with the general public. Accordingly, the term political leadership is normally used to refer to democratic political guidance of the type found in the democracies of the West. As an example, one need but recall the leadership of Franklin D. Roosevelt, who, during the 1930's led the American

* *Gendai no seiji rikigaku,* Misuzu Shobō, 1962, pp. 92–124; as condensed and transl. in *Journal of Social and Political Ideas in Japan,* II, No. 3 (December 1964), pp. 40–45. By permission.

[1] See, *e.g.,* Robert A. Scalapino and Junnosuke Masumi, *Parties and Politics in Contemporary Japan* (Berkeley: University of California Press, 1962). This book has recently appeared in a paperback edition.

people under the banner of the New Deal while maintaining close contact with them through his radio fireside chats.

The antithesis of Roosevelt's style of leadership is totalitarian leadership of the type exhibited by Adolf Hitler. Brandishing the sword of antisemitism, Hitler took advantage of the prevailing anxiety over the instability of German society to stir up and inflame the German people. Another type of leadership is authoritarian leadership, such as that of Charles de Gaulle. Although authoritarian leadership bears a superficial resemblance to totalitarian leadership, the former is static and pluralistic, while the latter is dynamic and monolithic. Still another type of leadership is what one may call bureaucratic leadership, which, as I will demonstrate later, is represented by the present Cabinet of Prime Minister Hayato Ikeda. The more bureaucratization comes to permeate society as a whole, the more prevalent this type of leadership becomes. Bureaucratic leadership is characterized by a passivity that prevents it from searching out new approaches to problems. Therefore it may be said to be representative rather than creative. In other words, rather than creating new values, bureaucratic leadership is satisfied merely to represent the old; rather than blazing new trails, it falls into step with the natural development of society and handles all problems through established social mechanisms. Because of this, it is unfit to cope with social upheavals such as those wrought by economic panic. It is effective only when conditions are favorable enough to allow a normal development of society.

Finally, there is a type of leadership which is peculiar to Japan, a country which, despite all its modern technology and institutions, still manifests aspects of a traditional, non-Western culture in all phases of its citizens' conduct. This type of leadership might be referred to as *hara* leadership. A man with *hara* (lit. 'belly') is capable of making quick, nonrational decisions in highly unstable situations of unpredictable outcome. The followers of such a man find him extremely reliable. In Japan's political arena, which is characterized by an irrational tangle of traditional interpersonal relationships, the *hara* type of leader is of great significance. Using extremely vague modes of expression, politicians bargain and make deals with one another in a highly irrational manner. To be able to engage effectively in such negotiations, a politician must have a certain degree of *hara*. In fact, it may be said that *hara* is one of the three prerequisites of a politician's becoming a strongman who heads one of the various conservative party factions; the other two prerequisites being large operating funds and bureaucratic competence.

Let us now look at how Japan's politicians fit into these various leadership categories. Prime Minister Hayato Ikeda's leadership is a typical example of bureaucratic leadership. This is not simply because he is a former bureaucrat who rose through the ranks in the Ministry of Finance but more because his thought and behavior are those of a specialist. When he was Minister of Finance he made highly controversial statements to the effect that if the poor people cannot afford rice they should eat wheat, and that if five or ten small entrepreneurs commit suicide [because they go bankrupt] it cannot be helped. Those statements revealed that Ikeda considers poor people and small entrepreneurs to be only small cogs in the great mechanism of a bureaucratic society. He believes that for the weak to be weeded out by business fluctuations is a natural law of capitalistic, bureaucratic society. Because he has a specialist's absolute faith in the established mechanism of society, Ikeda is what might be called the new-type bureaucrat.

The old-type bureaucrat is represented by former Prime Minister Nobusuke Kishi. When Kishi was driven into a corner during the 1960 demonstrations against revision of the mutual security agreement with the United States, he claimed that he was being supported by the 'silent masses.' By claiming his regime was being supported by all of those who took no part in the demonstrations, he revealed his belief in the old, premodern view that all who are not vocally against a regime are for it.

Another characteristic of Ikeda as a bureaucratic leader is his frequent reference to statistics. For example, he tries to explain away the recent price increases by saying that statistics do not indicate that a significant price rise has occurred. His primary concern is with statistics rather than with the people who suffer as a result of price increases. Bureaucratic leaders like Prime Minister Ikeda quote statistics in their day-to-day pronouncements simply to justify their policies already in force. A real statesman would use statistics as a basis for policy formulation. As a former bureaucrat who specialized in economic affairs, Ikeda never attempts to challenge the fluctuations of Japan's capitalist economy; he merely falls into step with the economic trend of the time. During the early postwar period, when there was an extreme imbalance of government expenditures over revenue, Ikeda, as Finance Minister of the Yoshida Cabinet, was a tough advocate of a tight-money policy. When he became Prime Minister in 1960—a time of great economic prosperity—he announced a double-the-income program. At that time he presented himself as an advocate of economic expansion. Now that a business recession has set in, he is preaching the need of restraint. Because of his almost naive faith in natural economic fluctuations, drastic measures such as are called for at times by the Keynesian school of economics are alien to his thinking.

A specialist's greatest defect is that he has no feeling or sympathy for the masses. Prime Minister Ikeda has so far been able to avoid full disclosure of his cold and impersonal bureaucratic approach largely because of the country's continuing economic prosperity. Ikeda's political future would seem to depend upon two things: whether he is able to accept new economic theories which will allow him to cope effectively with economic deterioration, and whether he is able to develop into a statesman with a broad range of interests and a deep sympathy for the people of the country.

Another outstanding example of a bureaucratic leader is Eisaku Satō, whom many regard as Prime Minister Ikeda's successor. While both Ikeda and Satō are bureaucratic leaders, they represent two distinct variations within that category. If we call Ikeda the 'economic' type, Satō should be classified as the 'political' type. Since Satō rose to prominence in the National Railways Corporation, it is rather difficult to say exactly what his abilities are as a specialist, although I suppose one might well point to his interest in, and knowledge of, police affairs. When he speaks of enriching the lives of the people, he is not speaking from a purely economic point of view; his emphasis is rather upon law and order. In stressing the importance of law and order, the thing uppermost in Satō's mind is the suppression of communism. Concerning communist influence in Japan, Satō has said, 'Ikeda says that there is nothing to worry about because the Communists hold only a few Diet seats and because there is no prospect of the Communist Party growing any larger. My thoughts on this point are somewhat different. I would like to state clearly that I have little patience with communist propaganda.'

In a democratic country all groups should be free to propagandize, so long as they go no further. That Satō should consider propagandizing by any specific group as something to be stopped causes one to feel more than a little uneasy.

Standing in strong contrast to the bureaucratic type leader is the party man (*tōjin*), the party politician of nongovernment background. There are two types of party man, the intuitive type such as Ichirō Kōno and the *hara* type such as Bamboku Ōno. Kōno, who rose to prominence as a journalist, has a sharp intuitive sense. Although intuition is a rather nebulous attribute, when backed by a large reservoir of memory and experience, it is capable of producing very fruitful results. But reliance upon intuition can also cause quick and frequent shifts in a person's viewpoint. Kōno's intuitive sense often stands him in good stead by prompting him to make statements critical of big business and to express concern for such middle-class elements as farmers and small entrepreneurs. In 1960, for example, at the height of the debate over the trade liberalization issue, he expressed reservations over the government's proposed liberalization policy by saying that it would benefit only large enterprises and would adversely affect farmers and people working in small-to-medium enterprises.

In giving his impressions of the Soviet Union and Communist China, Kōno observed that, in those two countries, no detached observers stand on the sidelines and criticize the government. He said that in a small country like Japan it is necessary to cease all infighting and embark on a national movement to achieve great national goals. In Kōno's statements, as well as in his attempts to appeal to the frustrated old middle class, one may detect certain elements that smack of fascism.

Representative of the *hara* type of leader is Bamboku Ōno. A dyed-in-the-wool party man, Ōno gained his political experience as a member of a lobbyist group attached to the now defunct Seiyūkai political party. He has absolutely no use for policy. The Ōne faction which he formed with his own hands, is a closely knit group because it is founded, in the words of Ōno, on the traditional principles of 'humanity and justice.' To Ōno, politics means the dynamics of rival leaders struggling for hegemony; it means an arena where political leaders bargain and deal in the traditional, irrational Japanese manner. It was by using just such *hara* methods that he himself reached his present position. He has said, however, that, rather than seeking to become prime minister, he would like to spend the remainder of his life working for the benefit of the masses. This is one point at which he differs from the bureaucratic-type leaders. When Ōno says 'the masses,' he means 'the disporting masses,' that is, those people who like to spend their time gambling and playing pinball games. His concept of the masses does not include those citizens who take life seriously and work hard to eke out a livelihood. Likewise, he has no concept of government as a public affair which involves constant policy planning and formulation. However human and likable Ōno may be as an individual, he is a leader of a uniquely Japanese type which has no place in a modern government.

Japanese politics today is dominated by one party, a party which in turn is controlled by a polyarchy of faction leaders. The way in which the factions of that party ally with one another determines which one of the faction leaders assumes the semidictatorial positions of party president and prime minister. Theoretically, any one of the various faction leaders within the Liberal Democratic Party can become the party president and, consequently, prime minister.

Since this is the case, I would like to give some attention to the less dominant leaders within the party, leaders who represent orthodox political leadership in the modern sense of the term.

Properly speaking, political parties are power coalitions made along policy lines. Our attention is therefore naturally drawn to those people within the Liberal Democratic Party who emphasize the importance of policy. Representative of this group is Takeo Miki, who supports a policy of social reform. Miki believes that the conservative party should break away from old forms and practices and construct a welfare state in which there is full employment and an expanded social security system. While most of the people of the political, bureaucratic, and financial worlds in Japan hold to the neoclassical school of economics, Miki represents the modern Keynesian school. In view of the fact that the Keynesian school has lost influence both in Japan and abroad, if Miki hopes to achieve his objectives, he will need to cultivate strong backing among intellectuals and a large degree of political toughness. Miki's weakness is that he attempts to side-step any serious contention that arises within the party. His evasive tactics are undoubtedly part of his long-range strategy of working himself into a position of power. They are probably also due in part to the fact that anyone who takes a strong stand on clear-cut principles is liable to be forced out of the conservative power circle. Whatever the reason, the fact remains that Miki's words often contradict his actions.

Another conservative leader who places emphasis upon policy is Kenzō Matsumura. As a postwar Minister of Agriculture in the Shidehara Cabinet, Matsumura introduced the first land reform bill. Later, as Minister of Education in the Hatoyama Cabinet, he took issue with the other Cabinet members when they tried to block the visit to Japan of Kuo Mo-jo, president of Communist China's Academy of Science. A look at these as well as other past actions of this man gives one the feeling that there are definite principles underlying everything he does. I say principles because his ideas do not take the shape of specific policies or reveal a concrete system of thought. In contrast to Miki, Matsumura does not evince out-and-out resistance to communism. Although his approach to China is warm and sympathetic, his interest in the civilization and relics of old China makes his approach cultural rather than political. Considering the fact that he lacks the three above-mentioned prerequisites of a leader of the Liberal Democratic Party, in all probability he will never come to wield real political power.

When speaking of policy-oriented leaders in the conservative party, one should not overlook former Prime Minister Tanzan Ishibashi, even though he is no longer a faction leader. Through his vigorous actions and pronouncements against revision of the mutual security agreement with the United States, as well as against government policy vis-à-vis China and the Soviet Union, he has so isolated himself from the power centers of the conservative party that he is now considered to be something of a heretic. As Minister of Finance in the first Yoshida Cabinet, he protested the national budgets which were forced on the Japanese government by the Allied Occupation authorities. Ever since then he has been highly vocal in his criticism of the government's pro-American policies. As opposed to Ikeda, whose economic policy involves no more than simple adaptation to economic fluctuations, Ishibashi has a systematic understanding of economics and is a long-time advocate of adopting positive measures to expand the country's economy.

His knowledge and insight in the area of domestic policy are closely related to his own fresh and original thinking on foreign policy. In the present Liberal Democratic Party, however, a man like Ishibashi is considered heretical precisely because of his original thought and systematic understanding. It is indeed unfortunate that such men as Matsumura and Ishibashi, upon whom the hopes of the people must necessarily rest, are being shouldered out of the power circles of the conservative party and into obscurity.

As we have seen above, most of the power within the Liberal Democratic Party is held by bureaucratic-type leaders. The next most powerful leaders are party men who depend either upon *hara* or intuition. On the last rung of the party power ladder are those groups which emphasize policy. Most of the party's democratic leadership is to be found among these 'heretic' minority groups. Although there is no totalitarian or authoritarian leadership in the Liberal Democratic Party, no strong democratic leadership—or, for that matter, no real leadership of any kind—can be expected from the leaders who presently dominate the party.

During times of economic stability such as the present, the financial world confidently opposes any and all government attempts to interfere in, or impose any kind of plan on, its operations. It therefore welcomes the election of an economic specialist of the bureaucratic type who will merely 'supervise' economic trends. However, the drawback of this type of specialist is that he does not have sufficient imagination to overcome political and economic disturbances or complications that may arise. Such situations require the leadership of either a politically-oriented bureaucrat, such as Satō, or an intuitive party man, such as Kōno. This is especially true when immediate government action seems necessary. When disturbances or complications arise, the former type depends chiefly upon his ability to exercise authority, while the latter attempts to secure sufficient latitude to act by appealing to the frustrated segments of society.

There are also certain instances in which the *hara* type of leadership is effective. During times of rapid social or political change, the emotional reactions of Japanese people are highly restrained. When faced by crises, rather than thinking out rational solutions for themselves, Japanese tend to look to a *hara* type leader for guidance. Since this is particularly true of Diet members, the *hara* type of politician is able to assert some degree of temporary control during times of confusion.

From the picture I have presented above, the present Liberal Democratic Party does not offer much upon which to place our hopes, but this does not mean that it holds no prospects for the future. I believe the future hope of the conservative party lies in the potential strength of the 'heretic' minority groups which emphasize policy. If the heretics within the Liberal Democratic Party would consolidate their energies and throw all their weight behind their beliefs, their 'heresies' could eventually bring political and economic stability to the country. In order for the heretics to establish a strong position of leadership within the party, it is necessary that their convictions become more widely shared within the party and that the younger conservative politicians and sub-leaders step forward and stand consolidated before the leaders of the party. At present the heretics are scattered, and there are no strong indications that such a move toward a shake-up in the party's leadership is in the offing. If a shake-up in leadership is to take place, the young politicians and sub-leaders must become thoroughly convinced of the importance of emphasizing policy. In addition to criticizing the party executives for their lack of conviction, they must actively cultivate support for their policies among younger members within the party's lower echelons. There is no other way to rid the Liberal Democratic Party of its factionalism.

36 • HAJIME SHINOHARA: *The Leadership of the Progressive Parties* *

In this second essay, Professor Shinohara leaves no doubt as to his Left Socialist sympathies, but on the galaxy of issues debated in these circles since 1960 under the label "structural reform," he is even handed.

After the violent anti-treaty demonstrations of 1960 and the failure of the bitter Miike strike inspired by ideologues of the Labor-Farmer Marxist faction, the pendulum swung again toward reassessments and moderation. Even more important, however, was the impressive economic growth advancing in a capitalist context. Keynesian-type regulatory measures and market expansions had avoided panic and depression. Bourgeois progressivism was enacting measures moving toward more comprehensive social security and other programs of a welfare state. Nearly full employment was being attained, and though gains were unevenly shared, workers were benefiting and becoming less radical. While Chinese Communism was encountering a major economic crisis, Japanese capitalism was achieving a great leap. Important social and technical changes were afoot, including another shift of population from farms to urban occupations. Middle strata were expanding, while union members declined proportionately among all laborers.

European Democratic Socialists had years before faced the implications of these developments for rigid Marxist orthodoxy and had opted for more flexible use of welfare reformism to move toward moderate, parliamentary socialism. In Japan such consideration came late and was opposed more stubbornly by orthodox factions and the fixations, both theoretical and emotional, of their members.

There are two important factors that one must take into consideration in classifying members of the Japan Socialist Party. One factor is the proletarian party to which they belonged before the war, and the other is the faction to which they belong now. When dealing with the older leaders who were active before the war, the first factor is the more important. The older leaders may be classified according to whether they belonged to the Social Democratic Party (*Shakai Minshūtō*), the Labor Farmer Party (*Rōdō Nōmintō*), or the Japan Labor Farmer Party (*Nihon Rōnōtō*). Each of these three prewar parties produced socialist leaders of a distinct type.

* *Gendai no seiji rikigaku,* Misuzu Shobō, 1962, pp. 188–213; as condensed and transl. in *Journal of Social and Political Ideas in Japan,* II, No. 3 (December 1964), pp. 51–55. By permission.

Representative of the type of leader who belonged to the Social Democratic Party is Suehiro Nishio, the charismatic organizer who left the Japan Socialist Party in 1959 to form the Democratic Socialist Party. Nishio believes—as do all of the socialist leaders who had their origins in the Social Democratic Party—that a man's best guide is his own experience. This is revealed in his autobiography, *Taishū to tomo ni* (With the masses, 1951). There he describes how the high, idealistic goals of his youth, after repeated clashes with reality, were gradually replaced by lower, more realistic goals. He concludes that a man's most valuable goals are those which evolve when the high, idealistic goals of his youth have been lowered just enough to become compatible with reality.

This process of determining goals may be sufficient for the ordinary private citizen, but I believe that a socialist leader must construct a comprehensive system of thought and values by analyzing and generalizing his own experience in terms of the basic contradictions in the existing social order. Then, through the application of that system, he must endeavor to resolve the contradictions found in specific life experiences. If he does not do this, if he insists upon treating each specific problem without reference to such a comprehensive system, he will merely be swept along on the changing tide of the times. A good example of just such an instance is to be found in Nishio's own words concerning responsibility for World War II. In his book *Shintō e no michi* (The road to a new party, 1960) he wrote, 'As opposed to people who deal principally in theories and abstractions, politicians must deal directly with reality. Because of this, I was unable to do anything about the great national surge toward war.' It seems to me, however, that one of the necessary qualifications for a leader of the people is the ability to resist, when necessary, the trend of the times.

People like Nishio, who place absolute faith in experience, will have nothing to do with any kind of socialist theory. According to them, any action which opposes their own 'realistic' approach or any person who attempts to observe reality with reference to a theoretical system is 'infected' with ideology. Many people of outlook similar to Nishio's are found among both the leaders of the Japanese Federation of Labor Unions and the present socialist leaders who were connected with the old Social Democratic Party.

Representative of the type of leader who belonged to the prewar Labor Farmer Party is Mosaburō Suzuki, former chairman of the Japan Socialist Party. Suzuki learned about socialism when, as a Japanese newspaper correspondent in Siberia, he observed the Russian proletarian revolution. After that experience he was able to observe reality through enlightened eyes. His association with Itsurō Sakisaka and Yoshitarō Ōmori, coupled with his own independent studies, gave him a firm grounding in Marxist theory.

This grounding was one of the reasons that Suzuki was able to withstand the attempts of the wartime regime to force ideological transformation upon him as a left-wing thinker. An even greater reason lay in his strong orientation toward many of the concepts and values that have evolved within modern bourgeois society, an orientation shared by all members of the Labor Farmer Party. According to Suzuki, 'Proper occupation, normal home life and right living are indispensable to those who devote themselves to the socialist movement.' This modern bourgeois social-value orientation was the major reason that there were fewer cases of ideological transformation among the members of the Labor Farmer Party than there were among other Marxists (i.e., Communists). It was also the principal reason the former members of that party were able to occupy the main stream of the socialist movement in the modern bourgeois society which blossomed after the war.

Suzuki is already thought of as an 'old-timer' because he lacks flexibility in adapting to the new patterns of capitalist development. His belief that capitalism has never changed underlies his opposition to the structural reform theory. Still, his strong anticapitalism and his insistence on the necessity of maintaining the original spirit of socialism will enable him to continue to serve as a steadfast and indispensable pivot within the increasingly divergent circle of socialist leadership.

The Japan Labor Farmer Party was a middle-of-the-road party standing between the Social Democratic Party on the right and the Labor Farmer Party on the left. Many of the leaders of the Japan Labor Farmer Party entered political life through such student political groups as the *Shinjin Kai,* made up mostly of students of Tokyo Imperial University, and the *Kensetsusha Dōmei,* made up of students of Waseda University. Socialist Party members Mitsu Kōno and Shōichi Miyake as well as the late Socialist Party chairman Inejirō Asanuma all entered politics by this route. The present Socialist Party chairman, Jōtarō Kawakami, was also a member of the Japan Labor Farmer Party, although he never belonged to one of the student groups.

Since these former top-leaders of the Japan Labor Farmer Party studied socialism before Marxism was recognized in Japan as an integral system of thought, most of them have never beome well-versed in Marxist theory. Their aims have been encompassed by only a vague, general form of socialism. Since Marxism has long been the prominant socialist theory in Japan, these men, like many other Japanese intellectuals, have suffered from feelings of inferiority toward Marxists. These feelings notwithstanding, they have been Marxist sympathizers ever since the 1920's. The Japan Labor Farmer Party, in its 1927 paper on party activities, defined itself as the party of 'the [proletarian] class and the masses.' This definition clearly demonstrates the difficulties the party faced by assuming an ideological position midway between the right-wing Social Democratic Party, 'the party of the masses,' and the left-wing Labor Farmer Party, 'the party of the proletariat.'

Since the above leaders of the Japan Labor Farmer Party derived from intellectual groups and had no real base of support among either labor or farmers' unions, they have always aimed their activities at the masses. Their well-known propensity for judging situations too opportunistically has been closely connected to the fact that they are adept at appealing directly to the masses and that they have no strong theoretical framework for their policies. Despite these shortcomings, they have been able to display rather effective leadership whenever they have been supplied with theory and organization. Their unique ability to lead the masses politically, coupled with their 'honest poverty' and seriousness of intent, has made them a worthy symbol for the masses. This is probably the reason that the Socialist Party faction which grew out of the old Japan Labor Farmer Party has supplied two successive Socialist Party chairmen.

If we call all the people we have discussed thus far the prewar socialists, then the Wada faction, led by Hiroo Wada and Seiichi Katsumata, would be the postwar socialists. The chief characteristic of the Wada faction is that its top-level leaders are former bureaucrats and its lower-echelon members are former high-ranking officers of the General Council of Japanese Labor Unions

(*Sōhyō*). The top-level leaders, being former bureaucrats, are able policy makers and debaters, but they are overly concerned with who gets what position, and they are too quick to make behind-the-scenes deals through their personal relations with members of the conservative party. Furthermore, with the exception of two or three people such as Setsuo Yokomichi, the members who came from Sōhyō have thus far shown few signs of becoming high-caliber political leaders. This seems to indicate that there is little chance that the faction will be able to furnish any forceful leadership to the Socialist Party.

Although the Wada faction is new in the sense that all of its members have made their political debut since the war, it has produced no new type of socialist leader; its leaders are little different in behavior from the socialist leaders discussed above, who made their political debut before the war. However, it is significant to note that in 1962, Katsumata recommended Saburō Eda, an advocate of the structural reform theory, for the post of Secretary General of the Socialist Party. More recently, the Organizational Problems Study Group, which is made up of labor union activists allegedly most sympathetic to the Wada faction, declared its support of the structural reform theory. From these indications it would appear that the structural reform theory is beginning to take root within the Wada faction and its affiliates, and that the theory is beginning to give the faction a distinctive coloring in the area of policy.

At the January 1962 Socialist Party Convention, Eda vied with Kōzō Sasaki, an opponent of the structural reform theory, for the post of general secretary of the party. The result of this contest was that the party became clearly divided over the issue of whether or not to accept the structural reform theory as part of party policy. Eda and Sasaki have a common background in that they both entered the political arena through their activities in the prewar farmers' movement; however, Sasaki is known as a shrewd behind-the-scenes operator, while Eda is an energetic organizer who has worked to develop the political abilities of the young people around him. The two men differ also on farm policy. Sasaki seeks to ease the financial burden on farmers by assisting them in their annual struggles aimed at securing higher prices for the rice they sell to the government. Eda opposes this policy as old-fashioned and unappealing to younger farmers. His policy is to work for improvements in agricultural management and techniques. His more modern approach is greeted both without the party as a fresh breeze in the area of farm policy. Such men as Tomomi Narita, a policy maker of the Suzuki faction; Tadataka Sata, a former member of the Wada faction; and some of the younger secretaries of the party have ignored factional considerations to gather around Eda. This development may open the way to the ultimate dissolution of intra-party factions.

In the debate over methods to reconstruct the party organization (*Shakai Shinpō,* July 15, 1959), Tomomi Narita stated that the party platform of 1955 furnished insufficient theoretical support for the socialist struggle against the changing aspects of modern capitalism. Narita's statement bares the basic point of difference between those who support the structural reform theory and those who support Sakisaka's position that the original spirit of socialism must always be maintained in the fight against capitalism. Although the Sakisaka position is militantly opposed to capitalism, it lacks the necessary flexibility to confront effectively the changing social conditions within capitalist society. Consequently, it does not furnish its adherents a foundation upon which to formulate practical proposals for converting the capitalist system into a socialist system. The new group centered around Eda and Narita feels that the deficiencies in the Sakisaka theory can be effectively compensated for by borrowing part of the structural reform plan of the Italian Communist Party and some of the theories of mass society which have been produced by the modern schools of political science and sociology. By employing theories of mass society in the analysis of contemporary mass-society conditions, the group hopes to construct socialist policies and programs that will adequately meet those conditions.

The structural reform plan of the Italian Communist Party calls for the labor movement to shed its defensive character and to engage in more than just labor-management struggles; it calls for the working masses to make positive use of present-day bourgeois democracy in order to effect changes in the foundation of the present capitalist system. The accumulative result of those changes would be a democratic, socialistic revolution. In order to bring about the necessary changes, a variety of struggles against monopoly capital should be organized in which a segment of the population much broader than just organized labor would be encouraged to participate. The socialist movement, by thus acquiring the support of the majority of the people, would be able to establish a government of the working masses.

With regard to the possibility of forming a united front with the Communist Party, it is noteworthy that the Eda-Narita group maintains a more flexible, receptive attitude than those who support the Sakisaka theory. In the words of Eda, 'Not that there should be a unified struggle by the Socialist and Communist parties, but the Communist Party should be permitted to take part in all struggles that are participated in by a large number of progressive organizations.' The Eda-Narita group does not aim at establishing itself on either the left or the right in relation to Sakisaka's theory. It aims at adapting to new and changing social situations by widening the scope of its policies. Its attempt to adapt, plus its willingness to accept the criticisms and theories of intellectuals and scholars, indicates that it is endeavoring to maintain a fresh and independent attitude in the struggle to realize a socialist society.

The policy proposals presented by the Central Executive Committee of the Socialist Party to the party's national convention in January 1962 were largely based on the structural reform theory. This precipitated a vigorous debate over the validity of the theory between the mainstream factions, which favor it, and the left-of-center factions, which oppose it. The anti-structural reform factions, headed by Sasaki, argued repeatedly that the Socialist Party should continue to expand and strengthen its opposition to bourgeois democracy. They also argued that if the party were to preach mere reform while still so organizationally weak, it would lose sight of its ultimate goal and lapse into reformism. If we examine these two anti-structural reform arguments, we see that both imply that the party should assume a passive attitude. The first involves merely waiting for the government to make mistakes which can be capitalized on to promote resistance movements. The second means that the party should never attempt any reform as long as it is in a minority position. Although the anti-structural reform group put up a vigorous fight at the 1962 convention, its attitude was basically negative. For this reason the usually powerful left-wing failed to muster enough support to pull the main body of the party back to the left, and the anti-structural reform group was defeated.

Both Sasaki and Suzuki argue that the structural reform theory will not work because capitalism has not changed. However, the question of whether capitalism has changed is not the basic issue. The real question separating the structural reform group and its opponents is one of methods, i.e., how to substitute socialism for capitalism. Thus we see that the 1962 intraparty dispute involved not an ideological difference between the left and right but a difference between dynamic and static approaches. The dynamic approach of the structural reform group gives the group an aura of freshness and positiveness, while the static approach of the anti-structural reform group reinforces the impression that the group is old-fashioned and passive. The 1962 convention was perhaps more important because of the factional realignment which occurred within the party than because of the victory of the structural reform group. Most of the established factions became divided into those members who favor the structural reform theory and those who oppose it.

The Socialist Party today has need of all of the personal qualities of its leaders. The strong-principled, incorruptible leaders of long standing, the politicians with mass appeal, and even the strong men who are accustomed to working behind the scenes all have meaningful roles to play in the party. The task of these men is to contribute their best qualities and their maximum energies toward strengthening the party as a whole. Factional conflict does not necessarily affect the over-all strength of a majority party, but factional struggles have no place in a weak opposition party. Now is the very time when the Socialist Party, under its present new leadership, must maximize all of the energies and abilities at its disposal.

37 • Fukuji Taguchi: *Leadership in the General Council of Japanese Labor Unions* *

Because of the complex history of the Japanese labor movement and the ideological schools which have influenced its leaders, this is an interesting but not an easy article to read. It carries the analysis up to the period 1957–59 but not into or since the critical year 1960, when labor politicism reached a high point. Since the war there has been a series of cycles leading from emphasis on economic aims of organized labor to potentially revolutionary tactics employed by leaders, allied with various kinds of socialist factions and parties; these have moved from multiple discontents and class antagonisms to political actions directed toward "qualitatively" changing the socio-economic (and thereby the political) order. Each of these surges has brought conservative or regulatory counteraction and often legislation. Each has aggravated disputes among labor factions about aims and tactics in the truer interests of labor.

In addition to the Communist party (JCP) with its ideology and infiltrative skills, there has been an autonomous Marxist-Leninist tradition since the

* *Kindai Nihon shisōshi kōza,* Vol. V, Chikuma Shobō, 1960, pp. 339–365; as condensed and transl. in *Journal of Social and Political Ideas in Japan,* III, No. 1 (April 1965), pp. 73–78. By permission. Footnotes within the article have been added by the editors of the present volume.

'twenties called the Rōnō (Labor-Farmer) school which has widely influenced the thought and strategies of labor leaders and leftist intellectuals. It is this tradition which apparently influences the author of this article and certainly the thought of Minoru Takano. The foremost living exponent is the Marxist pundit Itsurō Sakisaka. Takano has denied to this editor any affiliation with the JCP, but the Rōnō influence is reflected directly or indirectly by most of the socialists and labor leaders who stress revolutionary political aims and recurrently press for alliances with the JCP. They sound to foreigners like Communists because they and the Communists draw from the same ideological font, and they both emphasize the need for "qualitative change," i.e., revolution.

During the crisis of 1960 these more radical approaches were defeated both in their opposition to the Security Treaty and in the key Miike strike (in which the striking union specifically tried Sakisaka's guidelines). The results included more restrictive legislation and an increase of "second unions" which strengthened right-wing rival organizations and their nationwide federation. Already the effects of economic boom were moderating the temper of workers and their attitudes toward "excessive politicism." Thus, in the period since this article was written, a new phase of conflict and maneuvering between radical and moderate elements in the trade unions has been developing.

Mr. Taguchi was graduated from the Faculty of Law, University of Tokyo, in 1953. He is an assistant professor of political science at Meiji University in the capital.

It is well known that many of the people who presently constitute the leadership of the Japanese labor movement, particularly of the General Council of Japanese Labor Unions (*Sōhyō*), are either former members of the Democratic Leagues (*Minshuka dōmei*) or, at least, are individuals who were influenced by the thinking that guided those leagues. From 1947, when these leaders began to organize the various Democratic Leagues, down to the present time, they have continued to exhibit certain basic patterns of thinking and behavior. Even though there have been, over the years, transfers of leadership, dissensions among these individuals, and modifications of the function and nature of their leadership, these basic patterns of thinking and behavior have not changed.

The various individuals and groups making up the Democratic Leagues have represented a number of divergent organizational and ideological currents. The individual labor leaders who used to head the Democratic Leagues may be categorized in terms of their prewar or postwar backgrounds in the labor movement. The first type is the professional labor leader who gained his experience in the labor movement before the war. This type may be categorized into three subtypes. The first subtype comprises leaders of unions that were affiliated with the prewar Japanese Federation of Labor (*Nihon rōdō sōdōmei*). Suehiro Nishio and Komakichi Matsuoka represent this subtype. After the war, they supported the right-wing faction of that organization's successor. (Note: *Nihon rōdō sōdōmei* was reorganized after the war as the Japanese Federation of Labor Unions, that is, as the *Nihon rōdō kumiai sōdōmei*; abbrev., *Sōdōmei*.) The second subtype comprises leaders of unions that were affiliated with the prewar National Board of Japanese Labor Unions (*Zempyō*). In the postwar period, these individuals became the leaders of the left-wing faction of Sōdōmei. Minoru Takano is representative of this subtype. The third subtype is represented by Matsuta Hosoya. Before the war, and up until late 1947, Hosoya was a member of the Japan Communist Party. Between 1946 and early 1948, he was the Deputy Secretary-General of the Japanese Congress of Industrial Labor Organizations (*Sanbetsu kaigi*). In February 1948, Hosoya organized a national league for the democratization of Sanbetsu Kaigi.

I would now like to describe briefly some of these various leaders. The first subtype of labor leader mentioned above gained his experience in the labor movement before the war and headed unions affiliated with the right-wing faction of Sōdōmei after the war. The individual of this subtype was born in the 1880's, and usually became a professional activist in the labor movement after having graduated from elementary school and after having gained some practical experience as a laborer. When the government dissolved Sōdōmei in 1940, he not only supported the state-sponsored movement calling for cooperation between labor and industry (*rōshi kyōchō undō*), but even went so far as to become a leader of the movement calling for Japanese industries to render service to the state (*sangyō hōkoku undō*). In the immediate postwar period, he continued to believe that labor and industry should cooperate, and he continued to support outmoded, prewar methods of organizing labor and of bargaining with management. As a consequence, he was not able to meet adequately the new situations that had been created after the war by the urgent demands of organized labor or by the fierce struggles into which organized labor launched. Because he was unable to meet those new situations, Sanbetsu Kaigi was able to take over the leadership of the postwar Japanese labor movement. Most of the individuals in this subtype are now either members of the Japan Socialist Party [1] or officials in that party's headquarters; as a consequence, they have been able to insure a continuing close relationship between the right-wing factions of the Japan Socialist Party and Sōdōmei.

I would now like to deal with the union leaders of the second and third subtypes mentioned above. In the postwar period, the individuals of the second subtype headed unions that were affiliated with Sōdōmei. These individuals supported Sōdōmei's left-wing faction.[2] The individuals of the third subtype headed unions that were affiliated with the communist-dominated Sanbetsu Kaigi. These individuals supported the Democratic Leagues organized within Sanbetsu Kaigi. The individuals of both of these subtypes were active in the anticommunist democratization movement in the late 1940's, and then took the initiative in organizing Sōhyō in 1950. Later, however, they were forced to surrender control of the labor movement to the second type of union leader, which I shall discuss below.

The second type of leader in the Democratic Leagues gained his experience in the labor movement in the postwar period. This type largely comprises individuals who rose through the ranks of unions organized along company and enterprise lines in large industries. This type may be categorized into various subtypes, in terms

[1] More are in the Democratic Socialist Party.

[2] Leaders in the second group are affiliated with more radical factions in the Japan Socialist Party and advocate united fronts with the Communist Party.

of such variables as the time when they rose through the ranks of the labor movement, their age, and their ideological orientation. The take the National Railways Workers Union (*Kokurō*) as an example, the first subtype is composed of relatively older men who, in October 1946, spearheaded the organization of the Anti-Communist League (*Kokutetsu hankyō renmei*) in Kokurō.[3] (In early 1948, the name of the Anti-Communist League in Kokurō was changed to the Democratic League). The second subtype is composed of men who are younger than those in the first subtype mentioned immediately above. These men gained control of Kokurō after the Niigata convention of Kokurō, which was held in July 1952. The individuals in this second subtype constituted the left-wing faction of the Democratic Leagues, whereas the individuals in the first subtype, mentioned immediately above, constituted the right-wing faction of those leagues.

Most of the labor leaders in the first subtype mentioned immediately above were born between 1900 and 1910 and have a rather good education. Unlike the older labor leaders, the men in this category did not have professional experience in the prewar labor movement. During the war, most of them occupied lower managerial posts in various business organizations. After the war, they profited from their prewar business experience and took the initiative in the establishment of labor unions organized along company lines. I classify these particular people as 'the old type of postwar labor leader,' because they have occupied higher positions and have gained more seniority than the people whom I classify as 'the new type of postwar labor leader.' They identify themselves ideologically with the right wing of the Japan Socialist Party. In the early postwar years, they definitely displayed a servile attitude [4] toward the labor policies of the Occupation, the Japanese government, and management.

Younger labor leaders who supported the left wing of the Democratic Leagues are what I classify as 'the new type of postwar labor leader.' This type is found among the members of the Labor Comrade Clique (*Rōdōsha dōshikai*), which was founded in 1951 by the leaders of various unions affiliated with Sōhyō. Many of these individuals were born sometime between 1912 and 1926. Only a few of them have a relatively good education. Because they are so much younger than the old type of postwar labor leader, and because they have had practical experience both as blue-collar workers (*kōin*) and as union activists in the immediate postwar period, they have been able to bring fresh, new ways of thinking to the Japanese labor movement. Although many of these people today ideologically identify themselves with the left wing of the Japan Socialist Party, in some regards they are quite ambivalent. For example, to a degree, they go along with the oppressive labor-union policies of the government and monopoly capital, but, to a degree, they also resist the attempts of the government and monopoly capital to gain complete organizational control of labor unions.

I would like to describe briefly the basic patterns of thinking and behavior which characterize those labor leaders who were active in, or highly influenced by, the Democratic Leagues. The Democratic Leagues won control over the postwar labor movement in the late 1940's, at a time when the Japanese labor

[3] The federation of government workers' unions.

[4] Some are labor boss types who operate in alliances with management, but others have been called "servile" by leftists because they avoid confrontation on doctrinal grounds, arguing that effective production requires rational negotiation and compromise in dealing with employees.

movement itself had begun to weaken and beat a very rapid retreat. That weakening and retreat were brought on by a variety of factors such as the 'reverse-course policies' instituted by the Occupation authorities and the Japanese government, the growing strength and improved position of management, and the increasing alienation of while-collar employees from labor-union activities. The Democratic Leagues took advantage of the situation that prevailed in Japan in the late 1940's, and were, therefore, able to take over the leadership of the labor movement from the Communist-controlled Sanbetsu Kaigi. 'Anticommunism' and 'the democratization of labor unions' were the catchwords that the Democratic Leagues raised up before the labor movement in order to symbolize the nature of their future leadership. Because those symbols coincided with the policies of the Japanese government and the Occupation authorities, they signaled the complete subordination of the labor movement to government authority. In short, those two symbols were inimical to union democracy and autonomy.[5]

The various anticommunist-oriented Democratic Leagues grouped together to form Sōhyō in 1950, but, within one year of its founding, Sōhyō altered its anticommunist stand. A controversy arose around 1951 over the kind of peace treaty Japan should sign with the Allied Powers. As a result of that controversy, the left- and right-wing factions of the Japan Socialist Party split into two organizations, both of which continued to call themselves the Japan Socialist Party. Sōhyō supported the left-wing Socialist Party and became the leader both of the Japanese labor movement and of various popular resistance movements aimed at attaining national independence and peace.

I would now like to discuss the leadership of Sōhyō between 1950 and 1955, with special reference to the thinking of Minoru Takano. Because Takano feels he has a real call to his profession, he stands in sharp contrast to the so-called career, or bureaucratic, labor leaders. In other words, his special kind of leadership is a reflection of his deep sense of mission, a quality but rarely found among the labor leaders who began their careers in the postwar period.

Leadership involves an integral relationship between the leader and the followers. The question therefore arises as to how Takano, with his deep sense of mission, looks upon his followers. An answer to this question is to be found in his concept of the masses. Takano believes that the masses, out of their own personal experiences, can gain an awareness of the fact that they belong to the laboring class. Although many members of the masses today have a strong sense of loyalty toward the companies in which they are employed, Takano expresses his deep trust in the belief that the masses possess an inherent ability to gain an awareness of the fact that they belong to the laboring class. In speaking of the masses' gaining such an awareness, Takano uses the term 'laboring-class morality.' He means by this phrase that laborers have a strong feeling of solidarity and make a sharp distinction between the friends and enemies of the laboring class.

Takano's theses on 'organization' and 'leadership' are both predicated on his interpretation and conception of the masses. The following is my brief paraphrase of Takano's thesis on organization as it relates to the masses: Organization is the process by which common goals are selected and systematically arranged on the basis of the experiences of the masses. At the same time, organization functions as a framework within which the patterns of conduct of its members are

[5] Again, the author's own position on the radical Left is detectable here.

regulated so that the common goals of its members may be realized. Next, what is the function of leadership within such organization? Takano has the following to say: 'Have faith in the masses! Struggle alongside of the masses! Don't abandon them for a moment! Prepare for struggles by carrying a mirror that reflects the demands of the masses, by tying a strong rope around the masses to control them, and by dipping deep into the life of the masses. . . . Make the masses increase their self-confidence, and stress what they can gain if they engage in struggles! Implant in the masses a feeling of sacrifice and heroism! Under the power and authority of labor unions, lead in the struggles of the masses!'

How did the masses accept the Takano type of leadership, and how well did it guide the masses? Actually, it involved a certain risk. The masses were probably too prone to accept it more as a kind of moralistic imperative than as an index for their conduct, an index based on a levelheaded evaluation of the situation. Perhaps it was too charismatic, too much like the type of leadership one often finds in mass movements, a leadership that appeals especially to the emotions of the masses. It was quite different from the type of leadership usually found in such practical organizations as labor unions; leadership in practical organizations is, by nature, more secular and rational because it tries to appeal directly to the interests of the masses. Partly because of the charismatic nature of his leadership, Takano was able to expand greatly the activities of Sōhyō. Sōhyō came to engage in the over-all Japanese labor-union movement as well as in a national movement involving much more than just the labor unions affiliated with Sōhyō. Under the leadership of Takano, Sōhyō became the central pillar of the national resistance movement aimed at attaining national independence and peace. The so-callled Takano line called for 'all the townsmen, all the villagers, and all the families' to participate in that movement.

At the sixth national convention of Sōhyō, held in July 1955, Akira Iwai replaced Takano as Secretary-General. That replacement symbolized the major shift that had occurred in Sōhyō leadership, a shift involving the abandonment of the Takano line and the acceptance of the Ōta-Iwai line. When we study the concept of leadership in the Ōta-Iwai line, we must focus our attention primarily on the thinking of Kaoru Ōta, the guiding theorist of the Ōta-Iwai group. Ōta criticized the Takano line as follows: First, he warned that Takano had underestimated the class potential of Japan's monopoly capitalists. Second, he warned that Takano had overestimated the degree to which Japan's laborers had become aware of their special class interests. Third, he criticized the methods employed by Takano in organizing struggles for the advancement of peace; specifically, he criticized Takano for having involved labor unions in political struggles. Fourth, Ōta claimed that Sōhyō should organize unified struggles throughout a given industry, making specific work-site struggles the foundation for such unified struggles. Ōta made this claim because he feared what would happen as lower priority was placed on the fundamental struggles of laborers and increasingly higher priority was placed on political struggles. Fifth, he pointed out that Japan's class-oriented political parties must be strengthened to the point where they, rather than labor unions, eventually assume full responsibility for political struggles.

The problem posed here is not to determine how sound or appropriate Ōta's criticisms of the Takano line were. The problem is to recognize that when Ōta's theories were applied to practical situations, they neither contributed to a fundamental improvement of Sōhyō's organization nor helped to strengthen Japan's class-oriented political parties. They merely brought about a fusion of the economic struggles being waged by Sōhyō and the political struggles being waged in the Diet by the Japan Socialist Party.

Many people have said that Ōta's patterns of thought are 'realistic,' but I, for one, would like to point out some ways in which they are very peculiar. Ōta's 'realism' relies heavily on leaving things as they are; it does not aim at changing reality. Consequently, Ōta's brand of 'realism' is risky because it encourages a certain amount of opportunism and the abandonment of basic principles. A hard look reveals that Ōta's concept of the masses is quite the opposite of Takano's. Takano treats the masses as a highly ethical entity, while Ōta does not; for Ōta, the masses merely exist. In Ōta's vocabulary, the term 'leadership' means one of two things: it means either the art of making a levelheaded evaluation of the various factors involved in a particular situation, or it means the art of making piecemeal decisions. It can be seen that Ōta's concept of leadership is not anything like Takano's: Ōta's concept does not include 'laboring-class morality.' Ōta's concept of leadership, if strictly applied to political realities, could well form the basis of a flexible tactic for freeing the labor movement from its present overindulgence in dogmatism. However, when it comes to political matters relating to class interests, if the Ōta type of leadership is used over too long a time, it could well cause the labor movement to become highly unstable.

Ōta was the most important leader of the left-wing faction of the Democratic Leagues. By 1957, however, he himself had arrived at the conclusion that the Democratic Leagues had reached their limits of effectiveness, and he, therefore, advocated that the democratization movement be re-evaluated. The Democratic Leagues, when originally established, stood for social reformism, opposition to communism, and cooperation with America. However, because of the inherent nature of the attitude of a labor movement toward government and management, because of the various demands that are usually made by laborers, and because of the ideological orientation of labor-union leaders themselves, the leaders of the Democratic Leagues faced a number of dilemmas. First, those leaders had to try to create a workable balance between the permissible degree of cooperation with, and the necessary degree of opposition to, government and management. Second, the leaders faced the difficult task of how to generate among unionists the necessary feelings of resistance to established authority, but they also faced the problem of how to hold those feelings in check. Over the years, those dilemmas became increasingly insolvable; by 1957, the leaders of Sōhyō had to make it crystal-clear that they stood for opposition to both government and management. Ōta himself announced that the labor movement must have the kind of leadership that is capable of consolidating the laboring class and of making fundamental changes in the Japanese labor movement. He claimed that such fundamental changes in the labor movement were necessary in order to match the fundamental changes that had been made by the ruling class in its attack on the labor movement.

I do not believe that such leadership has yet evolved.

SECTION FOUR

Parties, Factions, and Interest Groups

38 • Toichirō Ichiyanagi: *Electoral Analyses Showing the Plateau Reached by the Japan Socialist Party, 1956–65* *

As we have seen, one reason why a younger group of Left Socialist (JSP) leaders have felt constrained to propose "structural reform"—a strategy of working within liberal capitalism avowedly toward a socialist order—was the need to surmount the "barrier of one-third" strength in the Diet if a socialist regime is ever to be attained by legal means. Khrushchev had asserted in general that this could happen. But during the 1956–66 decade, although Japanese opposition forces were gradually growing in per cent of total vote, they had been on a plateau in number of seats in the Diet and were barely strong enough to block revision of the postwar constitution.

In many ways Japan is being transformed under dynamic capitalist auspices. Orthodox Marxism-Leninism has come to sound rigid and old-fashioned. We have seen that significant changes in the structure of the labor force are under way. Moderation and emphasis on economic aims are increasingly preferred. During reconstruction and recovery, a sizeable majority of youth, including new voters, could be counted on to support "progressive" parties, but studies in the 1960's showed that this pattern is changing.

Socialist parties, except for the JCP, have always been seriously weak in local and prefectural organizations. They have had perforce to rely on labor organizations during electoral campaigns and political demonstrations. But in recent years of prosperity the more moderate unions have been gaining more rapidly in membership than their rivals, though the leftist federation (Sōhyō) is still the larger. So the revisionist-revolutionary parties are likely to continue facing needs for readjustment. Their special appeals have been to unionized laborers, a minority of farmers, students, the more precarious and discontented people in small enterprises, white-collar workers, anti-establishment intellectuals, and peace-emphatic voters.

* "The Socialist Party: The Day of Winning Power Is Remote," *Jiyū* (April 1966). By permission. Translated by Takeo Uchida.

What the Figures Show

People often speak of a gradual increase of votes for the progressives. And, as the JSP is the first of the progressive parties, people think that it is natural that the JSP should be growing.

What the realities reveal, however, is stagnation. Let us first look at the results of the elections for the two Houses since the beginning of the unified JSP.

General elections to the House of Representatives

It is true that the progressives (JSP, Democratic Socialist, and JCP) are increasing, however slowly it may be.

Now, what happens to the figures if we pick up those of the JSP only? Looking at the figures, including the influence of the split by the Democratic Socialists,

TABLE I. FIGURES FOR ELECTION OF PROGRESSIVE CANDIDATES TO THE HOUSE OF REPRESENTATIVES

General Elections	*Successful Candidates*	*Percentage of Votes Won*
1958 (28th)	167	35.7
1960 (29th)	165	39.2
1963 (30th)	172	40.4

TABLE II. FIGURES FOR ELECTIONS OF JSP AND DSP CANDIDATES TO THE HOUSE OF REPRESENTATIVES*

	Number of Candidates	*Successful Candidates*	*Votes Won*	*Ratio of Votes Won*
1958	246	166	13,093,987	32.9
1960	186	145	10,887,134	27.5
	(105)	(17)	(3,464,144)	(8.8)
1963	198	144	11,906,752	29.0
	(59)	(23)	3,023,300	7.4

*Figures in parenthesis are for the Democratic Socialist Party. The votes won by the Liberal-Democratic Party in 1963 amounted to 22,423,910.

(since 1959-60) we cannot help but have an impression that the proportion of votes and seats won by the JSP is rather stationary; the so-called barrier of one-third does exist.

In the election of 1963, there were about five million new voters who were not eligible in 1960. But the votes for the JSP increased only by one million. . . .

Elections to the House of Councilors

The election to the House of Councilors last year (1965) provided rich data, since the LDP lost completely in the Tokyo regional constituency (as a result of a major scandal). Looking back at the results of the four elections since 1956, we find a barrier for the JSP, however, tables III-V show that the JSP is stuck as far as the number of seats is concerned. In ratio of votes of progressives vis-à-vis conservatives, there is a steady rise of progressives, especially in regional constituencies. But this was brought about not by the JSP, but mainly by the JCP. In conclusion, the JSP neither decreased nor increased in regard to electoral

TABLE III. NUMBER OF UPPER HOUSE SEATS FOR CONSERVATIVES VERSUS PROGRESSIVES

	CONSERVATIVES	*PROGRESSIVES*			*OTHERS*	*TOTAL*
	LDP	JSP	DSP	JCP		
1956	61	49	–	2	15	127
1959	71	38	–	1	17	127
1962	69	37	4	3	14	127
1965	71	36	3	3	14	127

TABLE IV. RATIO OF VOTES WON BY CONSERVATIVES AND PROGRESSIVES

National Constituency	*Conservatives* (%)	*Progressives* (%)
1956	49.8	32.6
1959	49.3	28.4
1962	51.1	32.6
1965	47.2	33.7

Regional Constituencies	*Conservatives* (%)	*Progressives* (%)
1956	50.8	41.9
1959	54.4	37.4
1962	47.5	44.9
1965	44.2	45.8

TABLE V. NUMBER OF VOTES AND RATIO OF THE PROGRESSIVES

	Constituency	*JSP*	*DSP*	*JCP*	*Rōnō*
1956	National	8,549,386 (29.9%)		599,249 (2.1%)	181,518 (0.6%)
	Regional	11,156,057 (37.6%)		1,149,009 (3.9%)	120,414 (0.4%)
1959	National	7,734,748 (26.5%)		551,915 (1.9%)	
	Regional	10,265,393 (34.1%)		999,255 (3.3%)	
1962	National	8,667,040 (24.2%)	1,899,738 (5.3%)	1,123,945 (3.1%)	
	Regional	11,917,674 (32.8%)	2,649,422 (7.3%)	1,760,249 (4.8%)	
1965	National	8,729,758 (23.4%)	2,214,275 (5.9%)	1,652,363 (4.4%)	
	Regional	12,346,645 (32.8%)	2,308,860 (6.1%)	2,608,770 (6.9%)	

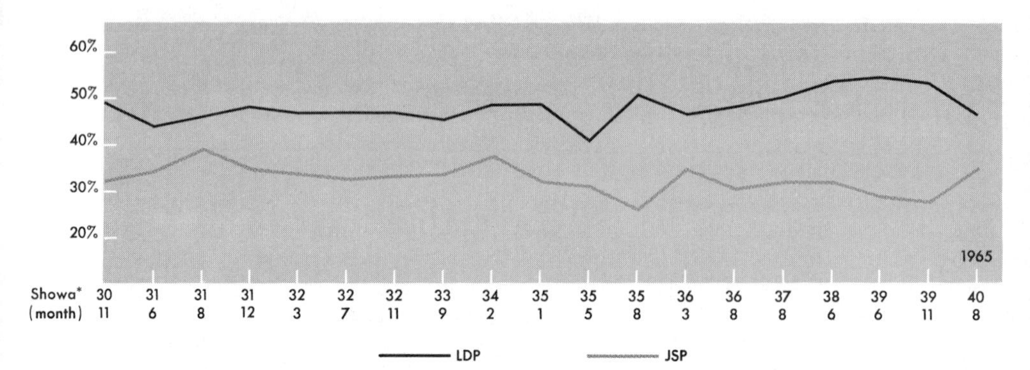

* [*Shōwa* (light and peace) is the Japanese name for the reign (1926-) of Emperor Hirohito. Thus, 1965 is the fortieth year of *Shōwa*.—Ed.]

Graph I. Changes in Support for LDP and JSP

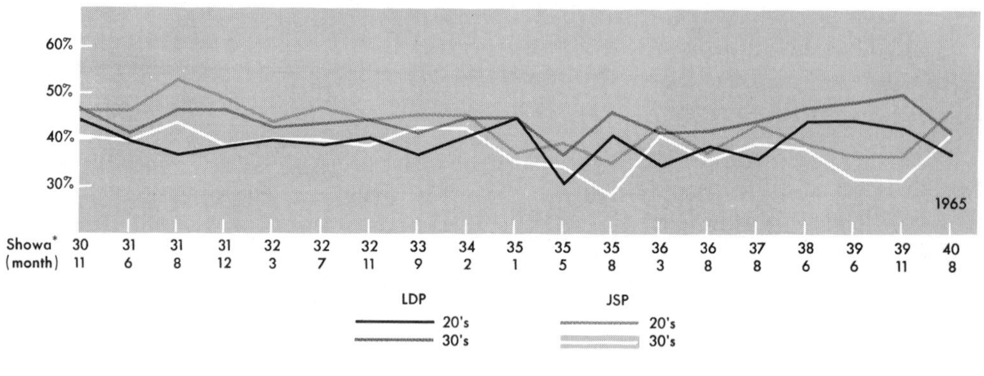

A. 20's, 30's

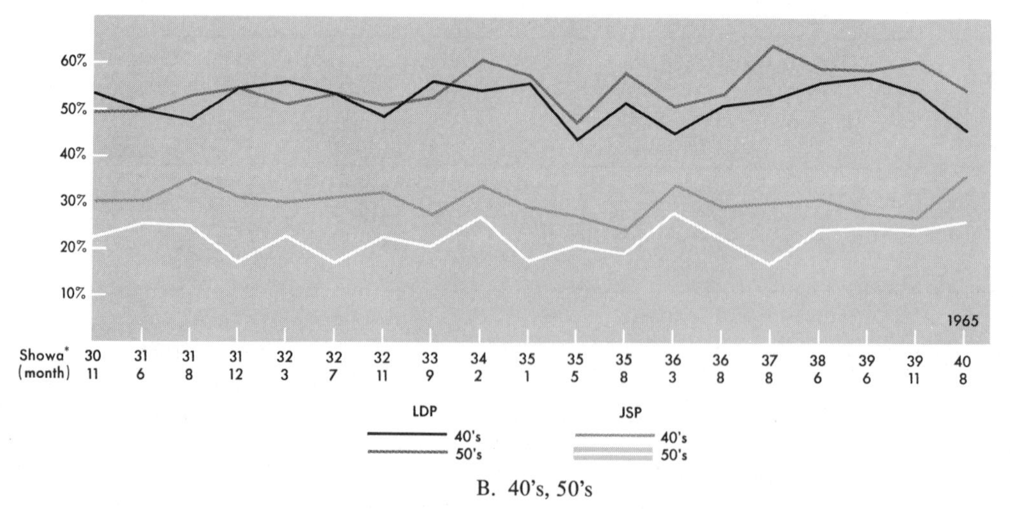

B. 40's, 50's

Graph II. Support-Ratio by Age

achievements during the past decade. Considering the fact that the past ten years saw a great change in the social and economic structure of the country, we may say that the JSP enjoyed (some) plus factors from the changes, but also it was affected by minus factors to the same degree.

It should be noted that the JSP could expand little under such circumstances where movements were carried from cities to villages, from the first industry to the second and third industries, and numerous young voters appeared who were educated under the new educational system.

This period, from the Kishi Cabinet to the Ikeda Cabinet, was a time when the Japanese economy enjoyed rapid economic growth despite some ups and downs. Although there was a struggle against the Security Treaty, did the prosperity of this rapid economic growth and the great flow of international politics from the cold war to peaceful coexistence bring about the stagnation of the JSP? There are views that simply have this kind of understanding (of the impact of) world affairs. If that is true, the conclusion would be that the JSP can only grow during depression and massive unemployment, or, that the party cannot get rid of its dependence on something like a panic. . . .

. . . (According to opinion polls by *Asahi Shimbun*), except in August 1956, when the gap between the LDP and the JSP narrowed to 5% of the votes, the LDP has always retained a margin over the JSP of more than 10%. There have been five times when the percentage of voters supporting the JSP exceeded one-third, including last August (1965). But none of them lasted more than two years. As a whole, as is seen in Graph I, the pattern of support of the two parties is described by a pair of parallel lines. . . .

Next, as to changes in ratio of support by ages, which relate to the question of "conservatization of youth," it is clear that the age strata supporting the conservative party are firm and that there is a high amplitude among voters in their twenties (who fit this pattern) of support. The low supporting-ratio of voters in their twenties for the JSP during 1963-64, when compared with that for the LDP, proves the phenomenon of "conservatization" of young people. . . .

39 • JUNNOSUKE MASUMI: *A Profile of the Japanese Conservative Party* *

Because of strengthened democratic emphases after the World War II, Japan's two revived conservative lineages harked back to the 1880's in assuming the names Liberal and Progressive (alternatively, Democratic). As the following article mentions, these combined in November 1955 to form the Liberal-Democratic party (LDP, Minshu Jiyūtō). Though it has been trying to build a cohesive organization at the center and at prefectural as well as local levels, and in spite of frequent proposals for party modernization, the LDP remains just a few steps beyond a coalition of some nine factions. As described concisely in this article, these factions jockey for candidacies, party, and Diet committee positions, cabinet ministries, and the premiership itself.

* *Asian Survey*, III, No. 8 (August 1963), pp. 390–396. By permission.

The LDP is principally supported by agrarian elements (including forestry and fishing interests), proprietary interests large and small, conservatively inclined civil servants and professional people, perhaps one-third of Japan's laborers (most of them probably non-unionized), and others who prefer the security of the party whose leaders have had overwhelming administrative experience. Parties on the Right have had working majorities in the Diet since 1949; some observers think, however, that conditions may be approaching which will compel the LDP to form extra-party coalitions with lesser, moderate elements. Especially since economic recovery developed into vigorous new growth, contested progressivism has emerged on the part of a few conservative factions, and the party has moved cautiously toward policies of a welfare state.

The author of this article collaborated with Dr. Robert A. Scalapino in the writing of Parties and Politics in Contemporary Japan *(1962); he is an associate professor of political science at Tokyo Metropolitan University.*

Recently the Japanese conservative leaders have been discussing possible reforms of the party organization and electoral system. Various issues have been hotly debated. Among the points under discussion are—the functions of the Party Policy Investigation Board, the present structure of party management, the presidential election system, the method of party approval for official Diet candidates, local party organization, political contributions, intra-party factions, and the method of electing Representatives and Councillors. On occasion, these discussions have led to serious intra-party conflict, but little progress has been made in reaching agreeable solutions. There is no doubt, however, that the conservatives have raised the primary problems requiring resolution. In essence, these issues must be tackled if an integrated party organization is to be created which can cope with the gradual expansion of the Socialist Party. The Socialists also have a "structural reform" plan aimed at strengthening the party so that it may come to power. This plan too has raised internal problems within the party. Thus, both major parties are struggling at the moment to resolve their internal problems.

The struggle between two camps in Japanese politics is not new. The postwar political scene has been dominated by two opposing currents—the conservative and the socialist, often called the "progressive." In the fall of 1955, the conservative elements were finally organized into the Liberal-Democratic Party. This fusion was basically the result of internal and external reactions against the system of political control constructed by Prime Minister Yoshida during the Occupation era. The struggles among the conservatives after the end of the Occupation (1952) were very complicated, but they were mainly concerned with Yoshida—his methods and the questions of his resignation and successor. Yoshida had strong support from the entrenched conservative element in the Diet, especially from those Diet members who had been officials. At the same time, increasing external pressure came from the socialists who had steadily increased the number of seats they held in each parliamentary election after 1949, and were watching for the opportunity to gain power by taking advantage of the internal conflicts among the conservatives. The socialists reunited in October 1955. This stimulated the conservatives into forming a huge, diffuse party in November of that year, with the Big Four—Hatoyama, Ogata, Miki and Ono—as the acting board of directors. With the emergence of a two-party system, there was a perceptible change in the character of the conservative control in the post-Occupation period.

The struggle for increased power between the two parties continues, but the current issue is somewhat different from that of 1955. Concern is no longer limited to the problem of central party organization. Now it includes local organization problems. The basic desire is to integrate local and national organizations so as to prevent the socialists from hurdling the one-third barrier. Consequently the two parties are competitive organizationally in a more complex manner. What are the reasons behind this change? The expanded organizational problem is a product of socio-economic changes that have recently occurred. These changes were not vital to the parties in 1955, but they have grown in importance subsequently. The present essay is specifically concerned with analyzing conservative electoral organization in a changing society.

Local financial expenditures have increased rapidly in the past thirteen years. With 1950 as 100, the rate of increase was 225 in 1955, 382 in 1960, and 438 in 1962. These increases were the result of greatly increased grants-in-aid from the central government, particularly in recent years. Today, more than 40% of the central budget is spent at the local government level.

It is very difficult even for the expert to estimate the extent to which local governments are under the financial domination of the central administration. But, without financial support from the center, the local governments could not afford to enlarge such public programs as road construction, compulsory education and urban renewal. Local governments have full authority only over approximately 30% of their budgets. This is sometimes referred to as "30% self-government."

Therefore, local officials and assemblymen have to be very concerned with the trends of central policy, and have to be adept at maneuvers in obtaining maximum grants for their area. Each prefecture, for instance, maintains an office in Tokyo which has regular contacts with the central government and Diet. In many cases, the personal connections with the official concerned are too intimate. The main task of governors, mayors and local assemblymen is to adapt their programs to the center's policies, and to push the central offices or the Diet into taking favorable action. In this way, they can also strengthen their own "political territories" by the projects they bring to their constituencies. This is also the case for Diet members, who pressure central officials and party officials, in collaboration with local politicians and officials.

Under these circumstances, the importance of ex-officials in the ranks of the conservative party is understandable. Local officials seek to get grants for their "political territories" so as to influence local elections, particularly for mayors or governors. But often, central officials also, particularly those from the Ministries of Agriculture, Finance, and Autonomy, seek to benefit some area in preparation for their own candidacy to the Diet or prefectural governorship. According to the statistics, seventy-eight ex-central higher officials (26% of the conservative Representatives) were elected in 1958, and eighty-four (28%) in 1960. Twenty-one of the 45 governors elected in the April 1963 elections are ex-central higher officials, while seven are ex-Representatives or ex-Councillors.

Thus, local governments are now more dependent upon the central government, and the conservative administration has taken stronger control over local politics through the adroit manipulation of financial-administrative policy. Power seems to be steadily shifting from the local to the central level. This raises a question: is the power shifting to the conservative party or to the central government? The answer is not simple. At least two opposing trends must be considered. The first is that the conservative party dominates the central government. According to an experienced conservative Representative and Diet official, the Liberal-Democratic Party Policy Investigation Board had grown to be a truly powerful force in the policy-making process during 1952-55. Today, the subcommittee members of the Board are very active and are closely related to key central officials. Consequently, meetings of top party leaders which include some ministers can determine government policy, making the final decisions on the budget and other important issues. In general, it can be said that the traditional power of the central government has declined, and that the conservative party has assumed a major decision-making role.

On the other hand, central officials have become increasingly involved in party activities, many of them as members of the Diet. Indeed, most of the leaders of factions within the party, the ministers and top party officials, are ex-central officials of higher rank. In the present government, eight of the sixteen ministers are ex-central officials. The Ministry of Finance alone has provided the present Prime Minister Ikeda, Foreign Minister, Director of the Economic Planning Bureau, Cabinet Secretary General, Director of the Legislation Bureau, Party Secretary General and Chairman of the Party Policy Investigation Board. The influence of ex-officials is now decisive in the conservative government and is a vital factor in strengthening the party. Therefore, it may be concluded that the party controls the central government, but that the ex-central officials control the party.

The conservative government can use financial-administrative policies to strengthen the party's local power. At the Fukuoka election last April, Prime Minister Ikeda urged that "local government [should be] directly connected with the central government." He meant, of course, that the conservative affiliated candidates should be elected as governor and mayors. This general position of the conservatives toward local elections was first articulated in 1955. The Liberal-Democrats, of course, have not been fully successful in effectuating the policy or strengthening the local party organizations.

A major obstacle comes from the intra-party factional struggles. After the Occupation, real power devolved upon the Diet, and Diet members were in a position to pressure the Prime Minister and Cabinet on political appointments as well as on policy questions. The conservative factions, which combined together into a single party in 1955, have maintained an autonomous status, albeit staying within the party ranks. Possibly the survival of the Liberal-Democratic Party is because of continuing socialist pressure. Today, the faction has the status of a semi-official group in the party. Most authoritative sources formally list the members of each faction. Factionalism has weakened the party's cohesion and leadership. It is a primary function of the Prime Minister to create and maintain an alliance among the various factions. In this respect, it should be noted that the factional networks are not limited to the Diet or the national party organization, but also extend to local levels through personal and interest-group connections.

In the 1958 House of Representatives elections, conservatives belonging to more than one faction were successful in 102 out of the 117 constituencies into which Japan is divided. The 56 members of the Kishi faction came from 46 constituencies; the 40 members of the Satō faction, from 36 constituencies; the 38 of the Ikeda faction, from 32; the 22 of the Ishii faction, from 20; the 44 of the Ono faction, from 38; and the 36 of the Kōno faction, from 35 constituencies. But even the faction leaders do not always control their own constituencies. The first constituency of Gifu Prefecture, for example, elected Mr. Ono, but also elected two socialists, and one member each from the Ikeda and Miki-Matsumura factions. The second constituency of Hiroshima Prefecture elected Mr. Ikeda, two members of the Kono faction and one Ono supporter.

In the 1960 House of Representatives elections, the 55 members of the Ikeda faction come from 48 constituencies; the 48 of the Kishi faction, from 38; the 44 of the Satō faction, from 39; the 32 of the Kōno faction, from 30; the 32 of the Miki faction, from 29; the 27 of the Ono faction, from 26; the 26 of the Fujiyama faction, from 24; and the 20 of the Ishii faction, from 19. In this instance, the first constituency of Gifu Prefecture elected Mr. Ono and one of his supporters, but also one member from the Ikeda faction and two Socialists. The first constituency of Kanagawa Prefecture elected Mr. Fujiyama and one Kishi man, together with a Socialist and a Democratic Socialist; and the third constituency of the prefecture elected Mr. Kōno, one Kōno supporter, one Ikeda man and also one each from the Socialist and Democratic Socialist Parties.

The relationship between Representatives and the governors, mayors, assemblymen and local politicians in their constituencies is complicated indeed. For example, an old party politician belonging to the Ono faction, has his "political territory" in the rural area around a prefectural capital city. For the assemblymen from this territory, it is very important to have friendly relations with him when they are running for election and in other activities. Yet the Ono man cannot maintain control over his own territory without friendly relations with the assemblymen. However, the intense personal and interest-group relations produce many cases of disloyalty and double-crossing. Meanwhile, in the prefectural capital, a younger ex-Finance Ministry official, who is a member of the Diet belonging to the Ikeda faction, has consolidated his territory and is usurping part of the Ono man's territory. The assemblymen from the city are naturally connected with the Ikeda man. Additionally, the governor, a member of the Ono faction, is making tentative overtures towards the Ikeda man, but the relationship between the governor and the city mayor, the Ikeda-man's old friend, has not been very close recently. The shift of the governor's position is being closely watched by the urban assemblymen, who are trying to discern where future power lies. Of course, the actual situation here sketched is much more complicated, but the basic outline we have presented is accurate.

The selection of party candidates is naturally important from the factional viewpoint, since this is the first step towards election. The faction controlling the local party prefers to give the nominations to their loyal followers. Questions of total party interest are only rarely considered. A typical case was the gubernatorial election in Nara Prefecture, January 1963, in which two conservatives competed. The present governor was not selected by party headquarters, but was supported by most of the prefectural assemblymen and mayors and was the selection of the Prefectural Liberal-Democratic Party Federation. The rival candidate, a former prefectural assemblyman and Representative belonging to the Ikeda faction, was the nominee of party headquarters. The national and local party organizations were opposing each other, and the national party candidate suffered an ignominious defeat.

Even more striking was the election in Kanagawa in April 1963. The prefectural party split over the choice of the gubernatorial candidate. Mr. Satō supported the incumbent governor who had formerly been in the foreign service, while Mr. Kōno, head of the Kanagawa Prefectural Liberal-Democratic Party Federation, refused to accept his candidacy and supported the Socialist-sponsored candidate. As a result, conservative party headquarters refused to extend party support to either candidate, and the incumbent won as an independent candidate. In addition, Mr. Fujiyama, head of the Yokohama City (capital of Kanagawa) Liberal-Democratic Party Federation, nominated the head of the Chamber of Commerce and Industry as a candidate for mayor, in opposition to the incumbent mayor who was supported by Mr. Satō and the incumbent governor. The result was that the third candidate, a Socialist Representative, defeated both conservatives.

Faction leaders and their networks are more concerned with their own "political territories" and supporters than they are with the party as a whole. Therefore, the efforts to strengthen the local conservative party organization lead to more fierce internal hostilities, rather than to an attack on the Socialists. The loose alliances among the conservative factions tend to break down because of internal conflicts.

The diffusion and shrinking of conservative territory is closely related to recent socio-economic progress. The character of rural areas has been drastically changing. The population is rapidly flowing out of the agricultural sector, resulting in a shortage of labor and a rise in wages. The first as well as the second sons, boys in their twenties and thirties, have begun to commute to non-agricultural sectors, or to leave rural Japan permanently to live in urban areas. This situation, combined with agrarian mechanization, increased cropping and other changes, has drastically altered the traditional rural community life. Moreover, the suburbs of metropolitan centers and medium-sized cities have been shaken by the arrival of salaried people and industrial workers who live in collective housing or apartments separately from the traditional Japanese-style communities. Many big businesses are now building plants with housing attached to rural areas. Generally, the rural areas are rapidly changing due to industrial growth and increased social mobility.

Socio-economic progress has been promoted by the conservative government. For example, the basic agrarian law passed by the Diet in 1961, despite Socialist resistance, is a modern statute in accordance with sound economic principles. The Law of the New Industrial Urban Construction (1962) and the Law of the Industrial Development in Underdeveloped Areas (1961) aim at the construction of industrial centers throughout Japan. These policies were initiated and drafted by big business, ex-officials from the Ministries concerned with economics now in the conservative party, and the central agencies concerned. Meanwhile, national and local politicians and local governments are busily seeking special grants-in-aid, public investments, and plants for their areas under the new policies. To the extent they are successful, they will increase their dependence on the central government and accelerate the dismembering of their traditional "political territories." It is paradoxical that the new conservative policy spoils the traditional conservative wards, but from another standpoint the new policies force those who desire power to create a new type of ward. This may cause antagonism between the progressive ex-officials from the Ministry of Finance and other strongly conservative ex-officials. Probably, this is connected with the conflict between the so-called "Left" and "Right" wings of the party.

40 • Daisaku Ikeda: *For a New Society of Peace and Prosperity—The Vision of the Komeitō* *

Much interest has been stirred within Japan and abroad by the religious and growing political significance of the Buddhist lay movement known as Sōka Gakkai (Axiological, or Value-Affirming, Society). Being an off-shoot of the Nichiren Sect—one of Buddhism's most militant, proto-nationalistic schools—observers have sometimes supposed that the Sōka Gakkai and its political arm, the Komeitō (Clean Politics party), would become conservative and nationalistic.

As this statement by the Gakkai's president indicates, its program is still rather vague. Leading spokesmen reject both capitalism and socialism, envisaging a "third civilization" which would realize both social justice and individual freedoms. They call for the "politics of mercy." They preach patriotism but have so far been moderate in its application. Members of this society and its party are critical of partisan confrontations and of political corruption; as their party's name indicates, they propose to cleanse the political system. The Sōka Gakkai has appealed especially to insecure urbanites—unorganized workers, petty enterprisers, and people near the foot of the social ladder. It has fostered neighborhoods of quasi-apostolic common concern, programs of constructive social service, and its own sectarian ladder for people to climb. Thus it has a religious and political concern for the masses.

By 1965, the society claimed a membership of more than four million families. A decade earlier it first had candidates elected to local offices, and in 1956 it began what has come to be an important minority group in the House of Councilors. In November 1961 the Gakkai founded a preliminary political organization which soon ripened into a party. The Komeitō ran candidates (32) for the House of Representatives for the first time in the campaign of January 1967 and elected 25 of them.

First, I will state the outline of the Komeitō's platform.

We will advance toward the goal of establishing a "peaceful and prosperous new society through our middle-of-the-road policy."

Clean, Democratic Government

To attain this goal, I propose here three major programs.

I. Establishment of clean democratic government.

1. To protect the "Peace" Constitution.

* *Kōmei Shimbun,* January 8, 1967. By permission.

2. To realize ideal parliamentary democracy.
3. To guard freedom of speech, association and religion.

II. Domestic Affairs: Realization of affluent life through public welfare.
1. To establish a "welfare economy" by mutual aids.
2. To establish the best social security system.
3. To create culture on the basis of humanism.

III. Diplomacy: Realization of a peaceful world free from war.
1. To abolish all nuclear weapons.
2. To strengthen the United Nations and realize complete disarmament of the world.
3. To dissolve the Japan-U.S. Security Treaty gradually. . . .

It is regrettable that there are few politicians, if any, who are serious about, responsible for, and convinced in the advancement of the nation.

Unfortunate indeed are the passengers aboard a ship which is being steered by a captain who does not know his destination.

I wish to emphasize that now is the time when we must make vigorous, hopeful and courageous advancement to improve Japanese politics by providing it with good vision.

Humane Middle-of-the-Road Policy

I have so far expounded on several occasions what we mean by the middle-of-the-road policy. Condensed into one sentence, it is a policy of compassion and the respect of humanity which is based on the middle-of-the-road principle of Buddhism.

Therefore, a new society which the Komeitō aims at realizing is a society based on respect for humanity. . . .

However, today both the free competition system as well as communism neglect human beings; thus they are putting the cart before the horse.

In the former society, where the pursuit of profits has taken priority over anything else, individual happiness is inevitably sacrificed. The communist society also curtails individual freedom under its unified economic system and quasi-totalitarian government.

In view of such tendencies, the free enterprise system must be so revised as to reduce the sacrifices of the people.

Communism also is being extensively improved to approve more freedom of individuals.

The international political temper is apparently changing into the middle-of-the-road principle based on humanism and its government. Recent newspapers have reported that there are signs of such moves in Western Europe.

I am fully convinced that we are in this age when mankind is heartily longing to create a new society with peace and prosperity.

Then what kind is the society to be established on the basis of middle-of-the-road policy? We will describe it as a new society with the basic principles of "mutual trust and harmony."

Prime Minister Satō advocates "Social Development." However, there has been some criticism that such "social development" aims at protecting business circles and drawing political funds out of them.

President Lyndon B. Johnson calls for building up the "Great Society." However, critics say that the United States is in the position that they have to intensify the bombing of North Vietnam and to kill people, while slowing down the "Great Society" idea.

The present society, both domestic and international, is dominated by mutual distrust and its resultant disputes and struggles.

First, from the international viewpoint, a total war is being barely avoided, but what is called "peace" is ostensible and is only maintained by the balance of power.

As is seen in Vietnam, partial strife is always going on. What underlines such conflicts is mutual distrust among nations, and the principle of international politics is that "The weak falls a prey to the strong."

Japan's political arena today is plagued with mutual distrust and antagonism between labor and capital, and between the mainstream and the anti-mainstream which is also common in other societies and organizations.

Capitalism so-called is a thought which intends to protect capitalists. Communism arose to rectify the contradictions of capitalism, and its hierarchic theory appeared. It grasps society as the proletariat's struggle against the capitalist class, and insists on proletarian autocracy. After all, what persist are mutual distrust, hostility, antagonism and disputes. Sacrifices and incessant struggles are unavoidable.

The only way to overcome such distrust and antagonism is a middle-of-the-road policy based on respect for humanism beyond national boundaries, racial differences, classes and ideologies. . . .

The Komeitō has published "A Way to a Welfare Economy" in four volumes on its policies . . ., and "Aiming at Public Welfare" in two volumes. In these the Komeitō explains its theoretical justification and systematization of its policies and platforms.

The objective of government should never be such that it protects the interests of some privileged classes or profit-making organizations. It is to establish a society in which all people can fully demonstrate their ability in the right positions and enjoy a superior culture and prosperous lives. Systems, politics and politicians should serve for this purpose. . . .

We call our idea a "welfare economic system," but we certainly do not propose something exorbitant. Its form will be something like, for example, the mixed economy of England, being further strengthened and developed.

What, then, would be the method of reformation? We propose that this should be gradually achieved by establishing a Ministry of Economy or an Economy Coordination Headquarters.

Never will we carry out any radical reformation. We are absolutely opposed to revolution by force.

The Bolshevik revolution neglected the dignity of life and brought misery to the people. We will never employ such a radical method.

Therefore, I think we should resort to gradual reformation with progress, without causing any sacrifices and with the full understanding and supports by the people.

For this reason, I strongly emphasize that what we should do is to reform the present free system into a "welfare economic system," which is the current tendency of the world.

A System of Welfare Economy

Now, to be concrete, what phases do we intend to improve?

The reality of our national economy is that prices have been skyrocketing year after year, and as you know, big business is enjoying prosperity while in the background there are too many cases of bankruptcy of small-to-medium enterprises. In addition, the excessive concentration of wealth in cities has driven agriculture and fisheries into poverty. It is obvious that these have been the results of politics that lacked far-reaching vision and aimed at the interests of a handful of capitalists, disregarding the interests of the general public and the nation as a whole.

In order to dissolve this "Double-Structure" economy, bring about a balanced economic structure and raise the nation's living standard, I think it is vitally important to reform present economic measures which lack planning and coordination as well as to carry out diversified and multi-dimensional measures on an overall basis.

To begin with, I urge that the small-to-medium and mini-scaled enterprises should be intensively protected in financing and taxation. These enterprises deserve every sympathy. They are in too miserable conditions. I must say that politics now is so cold-blooded.

Furthermore, I assert that adjustment of fields should be worked out among big business and small-to-medium business so that the latter may not be sacrificed for the former.

Those which should be kept intact as big enterprises shall continue to develop. However, enterprises which have much influence on the nation's livelihood might better be placed under public management; these include such fields as energy industries, coal mining, and electric power.

As for agriculture, I consider it most important to stabilize the prices of farm products and to set up an elaborate program integrated from production to consumption in order to reform the structure of agriculture and promote the policies best suited for each of the regional peculiarities and scales. . . .

Social Security for Majority

Furthermore, I believe that social security should be widely enlarged to realize "a comfortable society for the public" while striving for the establishment of this ideal economic system.

As you know, in our country, the social security system has been seriously considered and put into effect since the end of World War II. Nevertheless, its standard is yet to reach the international level.

The social security funds comprised 6 percent of the national income of this country in the fiscal year 1965, and in fiscal 1966 it was no more than 6.3 percent; these percentage figures were more than 10 percent below the average in European countries—far lower in comparison to 17 percent in West Germany and France.

Moreover, our system is not based on concrete ideas. It has been set up separately. As a matter of fact, there exist too many imbalances and contradictions between the plans.

For example, let us take a look at the livelihood subsidies. These subsidies cannot keep up with the annual rise in prices. This is making the recipients' lives harder. So they are compelled to do some odd jobs to earn extra money. But they get that much money deducted from their subsidies. We regret that such a cold-blooded measure has been enforced in actuality. . . .

We intend to strive to eliminate the labor tax, establish the system of guaranteeing minimum wages, lighten the burden of educational expenses and so forth, for the betterment of the people's daily lives, based on the "Government of the people, by the people and for the people," while we pledge to extend adequate aid to ensure living, medical security, welfare services and so on. We are determined to win these goals, one by one, steadily for the happiness of the people and the prosperity of the country.

Let us gradually realize a wonderful social security system in every sphere that surpasses those of the Scandinavian countries! . . .

Finally, what is it that we strive for on the stage of international politics? Needless to say, it is ultimately to realize "the world of absolute peace free from war." . . .

Opposition to Nuclear Weapons

Bygone is the age to settle conflicts between nations by force. Hereafter, all mankind must restore their confidence in humanity, and any dispute must be settled by peaceful diplomacy led by the United Nations. We must strive to construct a world where all the countries develop and prosper together through mutual aid. This is the ultimate will of Nichiren Daishonin.

On this fundamental ideology, we propose the following:

1) To plead in the name of all human beings that production, experiments, possession and use of nuclear weapons be completely banned for the safeguard of the human right to live.

2) To strive for the maintenance of world peace by reinforcing the security functions of the United Nations, achieving world-wide complete disarmament, establishing the permanent police of the U.N. in accordance with Article 43 of the U.N. Charter.

3) To dissolve, jointly with above moves, the Japan-U.S. Mutual Security Treaty in the course of ten to twenty years. . . .

Ideal Party Politics

So far, I have given a brief account of our visions on the world as well as Japan.

Some people, however, have misgivings about the Komeitō's intentions, suspecting it of aiming at establishment of one-party autocracy or of forcing the faith of Nichiren Shoshu on the entire nation. Therefore, I would like to clear those suspicions.

As for the idea of one-party autocracy, I declare on this occasion that the Komeitō will never adopt such a system nor any type of fascism.

. . . Up until today we have been fighting against all types of fascism including the wartime military. How can we ourselves become fascists?

The first president of the Sōkagakkai died in prison and its second president was also imprisoned together with him for having opposed the military and the then state religion of Shintoism.

Our party was formed through the true mass movement and has since developed into what it is today. It is the first national or mass party born in Japan.

The Party carries the slogan, "The Komeitō, the Political Party for All of You." . . . This means that the Komeitō is eternally the party for all of you and that it will never exist for the sake of a few party leaders. Nor will it be the party which protects the interests of some specific organizations. It should be the party devoted to attaining peace and happiness for all the people. . . .

If the Komeitō were to aim at one-party autocracy, we the masses would have no reason to support it.

In today's political circles in Japan, the ruling Liberal-Democrats (LDP) won in past elections through its unfair campaigns and in many Diet sessions resorted to "majority-violence" in defiance of parliamentary debates. They are trifling with the people who are not politically enlightened enough, by monopolizing political power within their own clique. As it is, the LDP may well be criticized as the one-party autocrat.

However, the supporters of the Komeitō are not so unprincipled as to exchange their votes for money nor are they indifferent to politics. Are we not the public who, dissatisfied with the conventional government, corrupt and degraded, have stood up with a lofty ideal and philosophy to develop a new political party by ourselves?

This new type of masses with a keen political sense, including the Sōkagakkai members, will never allow the Komeitō to follow a wrong course. Let us confirm this oath of ours at this meeting.

Then I will go on to the concrete idea of the Komeitō's party politics. . . .

. . . In Japan, the growth of a wholesome political sense is hindered by the people's inertia, egoism and indifference to politics stemming from pre-modern traditions. This, to our great regret, is a defect that cannot be overlooked.

Therefore, the LDP indolently retains political power despite its lack of definite principles and all the scandals it has caused. As it is, Japan does not deserve to be called an advanced country. Her politics may well be called that of the 18th century.

I hope every Sōkagakkai member, as a citizen who has embraced the Buddhist philosophy or who distrusts the present government, will become a leader and start a mass movement to awaken the Japanese people from their political inertia and apathy. . . .

It is a matter of regret that in Japan the ruling LDP and the opposition JSP are lacking in a common basis of national interest and consensus. We have few farsighted statesmen. Japanese politicians are too nervous and cunning. Their standard of judgment lies in the immediate benefits of their parties and their own personal interests.

We aim at enlightening the people politically to adapt the parliamentary politics of the United Kingdom to conditions in Japan. With this background we wish to realize fair parliamentary politics and true party politics based on a national consensus.

In the first stage, I think it is necessary for the current two-main-party system which actually results in one-party domination to be replaced by a three-party system joined by the Komeitō. In this way, any unfair practices by either the conservative or progressive party will be checked.

In the second stage, it will be possible gradually to reform the attitude of the parties and politicians pursuing their selfish interests alone into what it should be—giving priority to matters of national interest in any case—through the Komeitō

Dietmen and activities of the public. Then ideal parliamentarism and party politics will doubtless be realized.

For that purpose, let us advance to make all the Diet members of the other parties realize that they should develop themselves, contribute to the people, and act as true party politicians.

Naturally the Komeitō aims at becoming the leading party as much as any other party does. Otherwise it would be criticized as being irresponsible. Whether or not the Komeitō will come to power depends on the choice of the people.

In this light, we wish to declare that even if the Komeitō rises to power, we will maintain and foster second and third parties. If not, it will be affected by corruption and there will be no implanting of the true parliamentarism of United Kingdom into Japan.

Further, I would like to point out the fear held by many that the Komeitō, upon taking power, would force the faith of Nichiren Shoshu Sōkagakkai on all the people, which in reality is nothing but a groundless fear.

The Komeitō, even if in power, will guard the freedom of faith. The idea of Obutsu Myogo (government founded on Buddhism) or the idea of government based on Buddhist compassion denies and divorces itself from authoritarianism.

The freedom of faith is the basic principle of democracy which the people won after their long desperate struggles. Any religion which tries to force it on the people as a state religion would prove that it has neither established doctrine nor real power.

We are of the opinion that the superiority of religion should be decided in the open place through fair religious debates without any restrictions from political power. . . .

Moreover, the supporters of the Komeitō are not only Sōkagakkai members. Irrespective of faith, it strives to win support of the masses through its policies and the character, conviction and political ability of its Diet members. They have to become such statesmen. . . .

We wish to declare that the Komeitō will guard the freedom of faith when it comes into power.

41 • Kyōzuke Hirotsu: *Expansion and Strategy of the Japanese Communist Party in the 'Sixties* *

The Japanese Communist party (JCP) has the largest membership and best organization of any of the leftist opposition parties. Because, however, it has less attraction for non-member voters, it has the smallest representation in the Diet. Its affinity is especially with elements in leftist labor unions. Many major unions have several inner factions, those most to the Left being infiltrated or at times controlled by JCP fractions. The party is also adept at infiltrating and bending movements such as those to support the Peace Constitution and to oppose Japan's development or use of nuclear weapons. In

* "The Communist Party: A Way to Armed Revolution," *Jiyū* (April 1966). By permission.

most such movements JCP elements are just very active minorities; the following article mentions others which are obviously front organizations.

This account of JCP growth was written in the spring of 1966 by the Chief of the First Investigation Section of the Public Security Investigation Agency. Japan had been suffering a business recession (1964–66), and anxiety was growing about possible Japanese involvement in the escalating war in Vietnam. However, the Communists were also having problems, particularly over issues irritating Sino-Soviet relations. A split occurred in the JCP, and by late 1966 even the stronger pro-Peking party had been antagonized by excesses of the Mao-Lin faction in the course of the "Great Cultural Revolution."

Party Construction of the JCP and the Prospect of Revolution

The struggles against the Revised U.S.-Japanese Security Pact during 1959 to 1960 had an epoch-making significance in the history of the JCP's revolutionary movement. The strength of the JCP before the struggles was no more than about 40,000 party members plus 4,000 members of the Democratic Youth League. Despite its official claim to be the vanguard of the proletariat, only 17.8% of the party members belonged to the proletariat (manual workers). Peasants among party members totaled only 10%; laborers in the important basic industries were overwhelmingly allied with the Socialist Party. The majority of the 40,000 members consisted of intellectuals and white collar workers in governmental agencies and public enterprises. It is said that most of them are more than 30 years old. Therefore, the JCP of that time had neither a concrete prospect of revolution nor the power positively to influence real politics in Japan.

At the Central Committee meeting in July 1959, the JCP launched a policy to double membership to 100,000 within one year. . . . Its policy reads as follows:

> At present, the enemy of the working class and the people has become eager to isolate and destroy the Party by attacking and cutting our tie with the masses by all means, fearing our organization of the Party becoming stronger. More important, however, is the fact that American imperialism and Japanese reactionary forces intend to draw Japan into the American aggressive strategy by promoting the Security Pact, eternalizing the bases, cutting Okinawa and Ogasawara from Japan, introducing nuclear weapons, and so on.
>
> In these circumstances, unless we fight on for the expansion of the Party with firm resolution, it will be difficult to survive the immediate attacks of the enemy. . . . Consequently, the Sixth Central Committee decided to build a true vanguard party of the masses mobilizing all powers of the Party.

The following were to be parts of the membership-doubling movement envisaged by the Sixth Central Committee: The JCP responded to the appeal of "neutralism" from the CPR [Chinese People's Republic] and the U.S.S.R. of that time and claimed that "neutralism is the way to independence." It completely changed its strategy and advocated "neutralism" and built many organizations in communities and workshops to fight in the anti-Security Pact movement with the JSP and Sōhyō. Its ninth Central Committee announced a resolution, of the expansion and consolidation of the Democratic Youth League, and ordered intensification of Minseidō activities.

The JCP grew in power to 80,000 party members plus 50,000 members of Minseidō by 1961. As to the composition of these members, the proportion of proletarians and of young people in their twenties increased, and it appears that the JCP has succeeded in its reorganization.

Encouraged by the result of the anti-Security Pact struggle, the JCP, at its 8th Party Assembly, launched "The Over-all Two-Year Plan for the Expansion of Party Power" aiming at 300,000 members, 500,000 subscribers to the periodical *Akahata* (Red Flag), and one million subscribers to the Sunday edition of *Akahata*. The plan is said to be part of "The Long-range Perspective of Revolution." The report of the Central Committee to the 8th Party Assembly stated "that several tens of thousands of people joined the Party in the year 1960. The Party has thus increased its power and membership in a number of ways. The workers have increased in proportion. Laborer party members constitute 42% of total membership, and the number of management cells has doubled." The JCP in launching its two-year plan for the expansion of the party, focused its energy on the managements of important, basic industries and on strategic points in rural areas.

The JCP described the two-year plan as "A plan for victory of the revolution from the viewpoint of the new democratic revolution of the people who will defeat American imperialism and Japanese monopolistic capital that is subordinated to it; it is a plan to establish the united national democratic front based on the class it should properly rely on." It appealed to the whole party "to build the Party patiently with a long-range view of the revolution."

In 1960, the JCP understood that the year 1970, when the next revision of the Security Pact might take place, would be the time of decisive battle. It advocated the necessity to consider seriously the making of non-official organizations (underground organizations) so that the Party might be able to endure under any kind of oppression that would come in 1970's. This is the meaning of the report of the Central Committee that cites "the need for patiently making the organization strong and deep."

. . . In this two-year plan, the JCP emphasized the importance of, first, the governmental agencies and public enterprises and the basic industries which were to become "strongholds of revolution." . . . Secondly, the Party designated several farming villages in the environs of large cities like Tokyo, Osaka, Nagoya, and Fukuoka as strategic points in rural areas in hopes of organizing workers in the villages under its hegemony. . . . Thirdly, the Party said it must appeal to the lower strata of cities, as well as to people in small and medium enterprises, trying to consolidate them around the Party as allies of the revolution.

In sum, it is an historic event that the JCP has launched a concrete idea of a revolutionary coalition government of democratic forces based on the confidence of 100,000 party members, which was (nearly) accomplished during the anti-Security Pact struggle.

Expansion of Party Power and the United Front of the Communists and the Socialists

With the slogan: "Don't be a naked cell!," the JCP has built around its cells such organizations as Minseidō, the New Society of Women, the Association to Protect Peace, the Society to Protect Life and Health, the Democratic Chamber of Commerce, etc. Its circles, such as the *Utagoe* (a chorus group of young people) and *Wakamono* (Young People), are very active. . . .

The Party attaches importance to these forces consolidated in mass organizations as reservoirs of the Party's strength; it canvasses such people for party newspapers and study groups, on the one hand, and it mobilizes them in party meetings and massively in demonstrations for the anti-military base and peace movements, on the other. The reason for the JCP's superiority over the JSP and Sōhyō in mobilizing the masses is nothing but the fact that it has numerous mass organizations in which its cells are embedded.

The first reason for the JCP's expansion shown in the election to the House of Councillors (2,600,000 votes in local constituencies; 1,650,000 votes in the national constituency) is attributable to massive political propaganda supported by the growth of Party power. . . .

Let us compare [in Table 1] the strength of the party as of July 1965 with that of July 1962.

TABLE 1

	July 1962	*July 1965*	*Increase*
Party members	90,000	124,000	34,000
Akhata	120,000 copies	200,000	80,000
Sunday *Akahata*	260,000	710,000	450,000
Minseidō	70,000	133,000	63,000
New Society of Japanese Women	0	57,000	57,000
Democratic Chamber of Commerce	40,000	60,000	10,000
Association to Protect Life and Health	30,000	60,000	30,000

It is true, as the table shows, that the strength of the party expanded greatly during the three years after the 8th Party Assembly. However, the achievement of the JCP is far from the goal of 300,000 party members as envisaged in the two-year plan; even its intermediate goal of 150,000 per year has not been achieved after three years.

Although the main *Akahata* and its Sunday edition have had some success, the expansion of party strength in this respect, too, has occurred more slowly than provided by the original plan. The 9th Party Assembly in November 1965 agreed to launch the "Second Over-all Two-Year Plan for the Expansion of the Party Power," which called for the Party to "expand its strength by 150-200% above the totals for 1965, organize corresponding mass organizations, and train as *kanbu* (cadres) about 10% of the whole membership." These tasks were understood as the emergent ones for the JCP.

The Second Plan seems impractical at this time. Because the recent expansion movement has been enforced by strong pressure from the Party Center, the contradiction within the party is becoming more severe, resulting in deterioration of the quality of members and an increase of drop-outs. . . . Realities do not necessarily call for optimism.

Moreover, the JCP has begun to be isolated within the working class, which is the main force for revolution.

In particular, the attitudes of the JCP toward the April-the-First General Strike ordered by Sōhyō in support of a major increase in wages during 1964 made the JCP's isolation decisive. It opposed the strike vociferously just before it was to go into effect. The JSP and Sōhyō took this opportunity to begin attacking the JCP; thus, the conflict between the JCP and the JSP, which had already surfaced after the anti-Security Pact struggle, worsened.

In these circumstances, the JCP held its Central Committee meeting in September 1965 and concluded that the party's greatest assignment is to overcome delay in party-building in the working class. It adapted such slogans as: "One cell, one union," "Class democracy for all labor unions," "Organize labor unions and party cells in all administrations," and "Establish peasant organizations and party cells in all villages." It also agreed to democratize the existing unions on a class basis and to organize unorganized workers through individual membership in industrial unions. . . .

In brief, the resolution of the Central Committee concerning labor unions proposes to assume hegemony of the labor unions now allied with the Democratic Socialists and organize non-unionized workers along industry-wide lines under its own control. . . .

The JCP makes much of the leadership under chairman Sasaki of the JSP as "a force that aims at a united front (with the Communists)." On the other hand, it is attacking the Eda and Wada factions of the JSP saying that they are anti-Communist right-wing democratic splinters. . . .

As long as the JCP continues such a policy, it is unthinkable that a united front will be realized between the JSP and the JCP in the near future. The reason does not lie, as the JCP claims, in the obstruction by anti-Communist splinters in the JSP and Sōhyō, but rather in the Communist dogmatic understanding of the Social Democrats as "the political troops of the bourgeoisie," and in its policy of attacking the leaders of labor unions who are critical of JCP lines, calling them enemies of the working class. We may say the main reason is the party's "impatient revolutionaries". . . .

SECTION FIVE

Political Processes

42 • Yasuo Watanabe: *The Function of High-Ranking Civil Servants* *

From available essays about the many aspects of political processes and behavior in Japan we have space for only four, the first of these about patterns to be observed in the activities of higher bureaucrats. In the postwar period they became the most influential group in the LDP and in one of its precursors, the Liberal party. Socialists shared only two brief coalitions (1947–48); they have been able to attract only a few leaders with official administrative experience.

The bureaucracy constitutes one of Japan's main reservoirs of economic and legal competence, and it should be no surprise that its practitioners can both play effective roles and reap advantages from operations which involve the linkage of administration, legislation, and business. This article by a specialist in public administration, who teaches at Gakushūin University and has worked for the Cabinet's Administrative Research Council, provides some insight into administrative and legislative processes.

Ever since the Meiji Restoration in 1868, the Japanese bureaucracy seems to have presented two faces. The same bureaucracy which, by its authoritarian methods, has curbed the spontaneous development of the will of the people, has also been enlightened enough to spearhead the nation's drive to achieve rapid modernization. The core of Japan's modern bureaucracy has been composed of men of superior talent recruited largely from the nation's middle class. For better or worse, these men—most of them graduates of the University of Tokyo—have formed the elite providing most of the momentum in Japan's drive toward modernization. In criticizing our bureaucrats, it is of the utmost importance that we seek ways of guiding this momentum in the proper direction.

Since almost all government authority under the old Meiji Constitution was concentrated in the hands of a few powerful leaders, there was little latitude for the proper development of either parliamentary government or party politics. Since World War II, however, the principles of government in Japan have changed; under the new Constitution, promulgated in 1947, the governmental

* *Chūō Kōron,* February 1963, pp. 293–301; as condensed and transl. in *Journal of Social and Political Ideas in Japan,* II, No. 3 (December 1964), pp. 92–97. By permission.

process must take place through the Diet and party politics. Thus, after the San Francisco Peace Treaty was signed and Japan was released from the Allied Occupation in 1952, party politics had to step forth under its own power. Since that time there have emerged numerous interest groups which have endeavored to influence the increasing functions of government. These groups began to multiply particularly rapidly following the establishment of control over Japanese politics by the newly-formed conservative Liberal Democratic Party in 1955. The rapid growth of interest groups naturally led to a tremendous increase in the use of pressure in order to influence government decision-making.

Let us now take a look at the relationship between political parties and the administrative branch of the government. The lower-echelon organization of political parties in Japan is very weak. Parties rely upon outside groups for such essential business as acquiring funds, drafting policy, and securing candidates to stand for election. The party in power also mobilizes the bureaucracy for these purposes. The Political Affairs Research Committee,[1] the Liberal Democratic Party's policy-drafting organ, is made up of subcommittees dealing with the following areas: the cabinet, local administration, national defense, judicial affairs, foreign affairs, finance, education, health, labor, agriculture and forestry, fisheries, commerce and industry, traffic and transportation, communications, construction, etc. Each of these subcommittees has been established to correspond to a ministry or major governmental department. In addition, there are special committees for elections, roads, taxes, etc. All majority-party Diet members belong to one or more of these subcommittees or special committees, the former high-ranking civil servants among them serving as policy experts. These committees and subcommittees usually work closely with their corresponding government offices. No government bill can be sent to the cabinet for presentation to the Diet and no important government policy can be made without the approval of these committees. High-ranking civil servants are frequently obliged to attend the meetings of these committees in order to explain decisions that have been reached by their offices. During compilation of the national budget, each of the various committees apply pressure to the Finance Ministry on behalf of its corresponding government office.

It is quite normal in any party government that the desires of the majority party be reflected in administration. In principle, however, the desires of the majority party should be fully reflected in the cabinet, with influence being brought to bear on the various administrative departments only in the area of basic policy. In the present Japanese party government, the various committees and subcommittees within the majority party, supported by strong pressure groups, maintain close liaison with their corresponding administrative offices, intervening in administration even to the deciding of minute details of policy. This would surely seem to constitute excessive interference in administration by the majority party.

In the summer of 1962, a study group in the Department of Political Science at the University of Tokyo surveyed the social backgrounds and the opinions of high-ranking civil servants, down to and including the level of section chief, in three ministries of the central government. One of the questions put to these officials was 'Under a parliamentary government, do you feel it is all right for

[1] In Selection 39 of this volume this party agency is called the Policy Investigation Board.

political parties to intervene in administration?' To this question, 24 officials answered 'yes' and 193 answered 'no.' Another question put to the officials was 'Do you feel that political parties are intervening too much in administration at present?' To this question, 205 answered 'yes' and 20 answered 'no.' This was only a partial survey, of course, but still it offers insight into the feelings of higher civil servants toward the present workings of party politics.

At present both houses of the Diet utilize standing committees to carry on most of their business. Those standing committees are as follows: Standing Committee for the Cabinet, for Local Administration, for Judicial Affairs, for Foreign Affairs, for Finance, for Education, for Health and Labor, for Agriculture, Forestry and Fisheries, for Commerce and Industry, for Transportation, for Communications, for Construction, for the Budget, for Audit, for House Management, and for Disciplinary Measures. As in the case of the subcommittees of the Liberal Democratic Party's Political Affairs Research Committee, each standing committee of the Diet corresponds to a ministry or major governmental department. Committee deliberations are held throughout the year whether the Diet is in session or not. In addition to regular committee members, these deliberations are attended by bureau chiefs, section chiefs and, in extreme cases, even by assistant section chiefs. These civil servants explain points of policy, present the government's arguments, and answer the interpellations of the committee members. Although their presence is said to be necessary because policy elucidation and defense cannot be fully entrusted to ministers or parliamentary secretaries, their involvement in such Diet business leaves them little time for everyday administrative affairs.

Parliamentary secretaries should be prime candidates for ministerial positions. As such, they should learn the techniques of political pleading and defense in committee meetings, maintain liaison with the majority party, and become experienced in current administration. The responsibility for conducting the affairs of state should fall principally upon the ministers and parliamentary secretaries. Permanent civil servants should consider it most essential to maintain political neutrality and anonymity. At present, however, throughout the process of policy formulation and deliberation, the various subcommittees of the Political Affairs Research Committee and the standing committees of the Diet maintain too close a relationship with their corresponding government offices as well as with outside interest groups. These party and Diet groups tend to serve as representatives of various interest groups and government offices. This naturally encourages sectionalism within the bureaucracy and forces high-ranking civil servants to become involved in politics.

All of Japan's recent cabinets have been built upon a balance of factions. All ministers except the Prime Minister are appointed for terms of only one year. This, plus the fact that they are chosen on the basis of factional considerations rather than personal qualities such as character, insight and leadership ability, means that strong individualities are seldom reflected in administration. To the contrary, ministers are apt to be manipulated by high-ranking civil servants. Furthermore, intraparty factionalism prevents even the Prime Minister from assuming real leadership. The cabinet, the nation's highest executive body, frequently has its hands full just trying to maintain the *status quo*. Since pressure politics tends to bring about policy stagnation, the cabinet is unable to furnish vigorous administrative leadership. In order to prevent sectionalism and ensure over-all coordination in administration, it is necessary to reform the workings of the standing committees in the Diet and of the Political Affairs Research Committee of the majority party. It is also necessary to strengthen the control of the agencies of the Prime Minister's Office over budgeting, planning, personnel management and organization. As for the parties themselves, the most urgent tasks are to tighten internal discipline and order, formulate more clear-cut and unambiguous policies, systematize intraparty workings and structure, and take measures to insure the leadership of party presidents. It is also desirable that the responsibility of cabinet ministers and parliamentary secretaries vis-à-vis policy be clearly defined. As long as the activities of political parties and the workings of the Diet are not overhauled, it will be difficult to make high-ranking civil servants assume administrative accountability.

The handling of administrative business tends to become divided according to areas of specialization. Unifying these areas of specialization under a national vision and clarifying the relationship of each of the whole apparatus of government administration is the function of political parties and the Diet. At present, the factionalism and sectionalism within the majority party prevent unified action in administration and tend to permit excessive expression of special interests. If this situation is allowed to continue, two things are bound to happen. One, bureaucrats will develop a sense of righteous indignation over the loss of stability and impartiality in administration. Two, bureaucrats will become disillusioned and come to look upon party politics with contempt.

Thus far I have dealt with the relationship between government administration and political parties. I would now like to turn to a problem which has to do with administration itself. Items of administrative business, rather than originating in the upper echelons of the administrative hierarchy, have traditionally originated near the bottom and worked themselves toward the top. Such being the case, as administrative functions expand and become more complicated, it is inevitable that the work of ministries and departments proliferate and that areas of jurisdiction become more and more entangled and confused. It is therefore becoming increasingly necessary to constantly adjust and regulate overlapping areas of jurisdiction. As each item of business rises through the numerous levels of authority in any given ministry, the way must be prepared by talks at each level with officials of other ministries having jurisdiction in the matter. In other words, no item is allowed to rise from one level to the next until all the interested authorities on the former level have given their approval. Consequently only those items which have been approved at all levels can be presented to the cabinet for deliberation. Any item that does not have good prospects of being approved at all levels never sees the light of day. Under such a system, even items of extreme importance which demand top-level initiative in making decisions and in coordinating the actions of all the ministries concerned are often pigeonholed if any disagreement over them develops somewhere along their paths between the lower echelons of the administration and the cabinet. Thus, as time goes on, the decision-making process in administration becomes more and more bogged down, and it becomes increasingly difficult to make prompt adjustments to changing situations. Instead of placing all the blame for sectionalism on political leaders and parties, bureaucrats must put forth their own efforts to rectify the present situation and achieve coordination in administration. To the present day, the Japanese government has continued to be administered under the principles of the old Meiji Constitution, in which each ministry was considered to be semiautonomous. The sectionalism which these principles have fostered must be destroyed if the vitality of our bureaucrats is to be utilized effectively. This is one of the great tasks facing the administrative branch of our government today.

Since the idea of total government has no tradition in Japan, administrative sectionalism cannot be eliminated merely by reforming the administrative organization; it is necessary to concentrate upon improving personnel management. The three most important steps to be taken in this connection are to circulate personnel among the ministries, extend the retirement age, and increase salaries and allowances.

At present, our civil servants remain throughout their careers in the ministries to which they were first appointed. Thus, although those people in supervisory positions may be experts within their own small areas of specialization, they lack an over-all *esprit de corps,* a sense of being a part of the whole government. This situation does much to foster sectionalism.

Although there is no definite retirement age at present, it is customary for civil servants to retire gracefully even while still in their forties in order to make way for their juniors. They then either become Diet members or executives in private business and government-subsidized organizations such as public corporations and corporation-affiliated organizations. Thus, while they are still employed as civil servants they must think about what they are going to do after they retire. If, for example, they plan to stand for election to the Diet, they may begin to manipulate government funds in order to benefit the constituencies in which they intend to run. If they intend to go into business, they may help the specific organization they plan to enter. This naturally leads to partiality in government administration. The very fact that vigorous men of outstanding character and judgment must leave administrative posts in the government at such an early age is a great loss to society.

Finally, because of low government salaries, talented young university graduates frequently choose to enter business rather than the civil service. Big business offers not only higher salaries but more allowances. Japan has no tradition of appointing able people from outside government circles to government posts, and, as long as present conditions exist, it will be impossible to recruit such people. It is therefore imperative that more promising young men of progressive spirit and broad outlook be encouraged to embark upon careers in the civil service. This can be done by guaranteeing financial security to civil servants and setting up conditions that will ensure clean government.

Our modern government cannot be allowed to remain clothed in a veil of secrecy; its primary consideration must become the welfare of the people. If rationality, rather than authoritarianism, is to be the hallmark of modern government, then our bureaucracy must accommodate itself to that hallmark. Our citizens, who look upon government bureaucrats as the nation's elite, sincerely desire that the energies of our bureaucracy be put to the most effective use.

43 • SHIGEKI NISHIHIRA: *Are Young People Becoming More Conservative?* *

It has long been known in a general way that in the lives particularly of Japanese males and of eldest sons there are thresholds which tend to lead to conservatism. These include a university graduate's entrance into business management, a less highly educated person's advancement to a company position more closely identified with the elite, a civil servant's attainment of executive rank, and a young man's becoming head of his family.

The following study, however, is based mainly on newspaper opinion polls and interprets the patterns evinced by youth, young adults, and middle-aged respondents with respect to party preference and support, as well as views about two salient political issues. The shaping factors are not described in terms of life thresholds but rather as changes in social, economic, and political conditions, including changes in the leadership and images of major parties. More could have been said about the influence of progressivism on the part of some elements in the ruling conservative party. Intellectual trends have also been important.

Until the late 1950's, it was taken for granted that a distinct majority of new and younger voters supported reformist and revolutionary parties. Economic growth and improved opportunities for employment, prosperity and the desire for capable administration, distance from the war and Occupation, some reduction in the influence of ideological clichés, and increasing pragmatism and professionalism—these and other changes seem to have altered both the progressive-conservative ratio among youth and their political proclivities as maturity advances. In 1965, the Socialist party sponsored a research project in this field conducted by a group of university professors and their students. Somewhat to the concern of the JSP, its findings in the main agreed with those of this analysis.

Mr. Nishihara is a specialist in statistical mathematics who is now a section chief of a special institute in this field. He has conducted research and has published a number of articles about Japanese public opinion and social stratification-mobility.

Some Liberal Democratic Party members in the Diet have written that political conservatism in Japan is destined to decline. More recently, however, some people are beginning to feel that the young people of the country are becoming more conservative. Statistics indicate that the percentage of young people who support the progressive parties is declining. Utilizing available statistics, I would like to attempt an analysis of the political inclinations of Japanese young people and to examine the reasons which lie behind the results of that analysis.

* *Asahi Janaru,* July 26, 1964, pp. 12–19; as condensed and transl. in *Journal of Social and Political Ideas in Japan,* II, No. 3 (December 1964), pp. 137–143. By permission.

Every postwar election for the House of Representatives, with the exception of the first one, in 1946, has given over sixty percent of the seats to the conservatives. The conservatives were at their lowest ebb of popularity in 1946, when they captured only forty-six percent of the popular vote. From that point, they rose in popularity with each succeeding election until 1952, when they gathered sixty-six percent of the popular vote. Each passing election since 1952, however, has seen them gradually dropping in popular esteem. The 1963 elections, in which they won fifty-five percent of the popular vote, marked their lowest point of popularity since 1946. In comparison, the percentage of popular votes garnered by the progressives has been steadily increasing since 1952. The principal reason for this increase, however, is that all three of the progressive parties have been flooding the constituencies with candidates; the increase in popular votes has not resulted in a corresponding increase in the number of Diet seats the progressives have been able to capture. The last three general elections have not produced any notable fluctuations in the progressive-conservative ratio of House seats. The drive by the progressives to increase their holdings in the House has come to a virtual standstill.

In 1963, there were approximately 59,000,000 eligible voters in Japan, about half of whom were below the age of thirty-six. Of these, approximately 5,700,000 had reached the voting age of twenty between the 1960 and 1963 general elections. Notwithstanding this large increase in the number of young people eligible to vote, the progressives won only 1,050,000 more popular votes in the 1963 elections than they had in the 1960 elections. Of course, we cannot overlook such factors as the many people who switched their vote in 1963 from progressive to conservative, the approximately 1,800,000 people who died during the three years between the two elections, and the number of eligible voters who did not vote in the 1963 elections. Still, when we compare the 5,700,000 newly eligible voters, the very group that the progressives are depending upon for their future strength, with the mere 1,050,000 increase in the number of votes cast for the progressives, we see that the progressives are faced with a problem.

Two questions arise from this observation. One, do the young people who are just now coming of age support the progressive parties to the same degree as did young people in the earlier postwar period? Two, do people who support the progressive parties in their youth switch their support to the conservative party as they grow older?

Let us consider the first question with reference to Chart No. 1, below, showing results of a series of nationwide public opinion polls carried out since 1948 by the *Asahi Shimbun*. In these polls the respondents are asked, 'Which political party do you like best?' It is clear from the graph that the progressives have received a higher rate of support from people in their twenties than from the other age groups represented. The progressives reached their lowest ebb of popularity in 1951, just before the Socialist Party split into left- and right-wing independent parties. Their greatest popularity came during the latter part of the Hatoyama Cabinet in 1954, soon after the reunification of the Socialist Party. The poll of January 1960, taken shortly before the signing of the revised mutual security agreement with the United States and the formation of the Democratic Socialist Party by former elements of the Socialist Party, saw a higher ratio of young people in their twenties once again favoring the conservatives over the progressives. According to the poll of May 1960, taken right after the conservatives had rammed the ratification of the revised mutual security agreement through the Diet, the percentage of young people in their twenties who supported the progressives had recovered to thirty percent, but after the Ikeda Cabinet was formed in July 1960, progressive support by that age group again dropped sharply. Since the Ikeda Cabinet has been in power, the rate of progressive support among the twenty to thirty age group has risen again to about thirty-five percent, where it has remained relatively constant. According to the poll of June of this year, the conservatives have a very slight edge over the progressives in this age group. It is clear that the progressives are no longer being supported by young people in their twenties to the same degree as they were during 1955 and 1956.

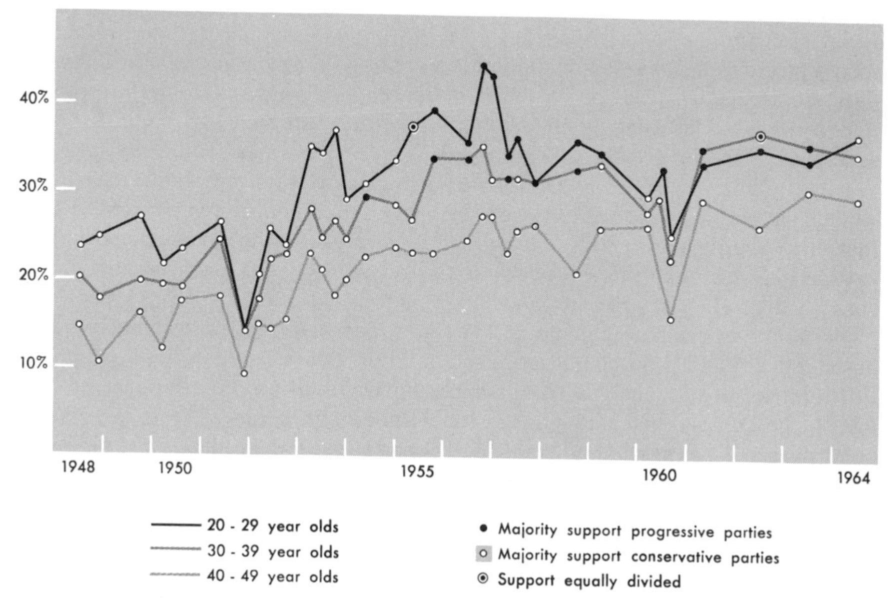

Chart No. 1. Rate of Support for Progressive Parties

Looking at Chart No. 1 once more, we see that at times the line representing the rate of support which people in their twenties give the progressives drops below the corresponding line for people in their thirties. Thus, the present twenty to thirty age group, contrary to what one might expect, at times gives less support to the progressives than do those who passed through the same age group ten years earlier.

The *Mainichi Shimbun* published in its June 4, 1964, morning edition the results of a nationwide poll of twelve- through eighteen-year olds. To the question 'Which do you think is the best political party?' thirty-five percent of the respondents answered, 'the Liberal Democratic Party'; thirty percent, 'the Socialist Party'; six percent, 'the Democratic Socialist Party'; two percent, 'the Communist Party'; two percent listed some other party; and the remaining twenty-five percent gave no preference. The preference of the twelve through eighteen age group seems to be divided fairly equally between the conservative Liberal Democratic Party and the three progressive parties. Thus, in answer to the first question above as to whether young people still support the progressive parties to the same degree as they have in the past, we see that young people today, far from giving overwhelming support to the progressives, tend to favor the conservatives more than did corresponding age groups of several years ago.

Next, let us consider the second question. The Institute of Statistical Mathematics carries out surveys of the twenty-three wards of Tokyo during the spring and winter of each year. Using their figures to compare the opinions held in 1963 by the twenty-five to forty age group with the opinions held by that same group, that is, the twenty to thirty-five age group, in 1958, we find that aging only five years had caused many of these people to switch their allegiance from the progressives to the conservatives. The same institute also carried out a political opinion survey among a nationwide cross section of people in 1953. In interviewing the same people again in 1963, it was learned that approximately forty percent had consistently supported either the progressives or the conservatives, approximately five percent had switched their support from the progressives to the conservatives, and about five percent had switched from the conservatives to the progressives. The twenty to twenty-five age group, the youngest age group interviewed in 1953, showed the greatest change through the intervening ten years. Thus, apropos of the second question above, it can be said that people around thirty show a marked tendency to switch their support from one end of the political spectrum to the other. Whether they become more conservative in their political thinking or not would seem to depend upon the intellectual and political climate of the time. The present climate appears to be pushing them toward the conservative end of the spectrum.

The surveys and analyses with which I have thus far dealt concerned primarily the conservative and progressive parties. Let us now move away from political parties per se and examine the more general political tendencies of young people. In looking over the data available from nationwide surveys, one frequently finds that the proportion of respondents who support no political party is highest in the twenty to twenty-five year old age group. Again, when one checks lists of eligible voters to find which people did not actually vote, he finds that the voting rate is lowest in the twenty to thirty age group. This shows that young people are less concerned with elections than are their elders.

Next, let us look at some opinions concerning concrete issues. Chart No. 2 is the result of a series of polls concerning the revised mutual security agreement with the United States. This series was carried out among the twenty to fifty age group in the twenty-three wards of Tokyo. (The line representing the thirty to thirty-nine age group, omitted here, runs approximately halfway between, and parallel to, the lines representing the twenty to twenty-nine and the forty to forty-nine age groups.) The first poll was being carried out when ratification of the agreement was forced through the Diet on May 19, 1960. According to the data from that poll, there were more people in the twenty to fifty age group who were against ratification than who were for it. By the end of the first year after ratification, the number of those thirty years old and above in favor of the revised agreement had surpassed the number of those still against it. In the twenty to thirty age group, the cons still outnumbered the pros at the end of 1962, although the margin of difference was very small. As can be seen from Chart No. 2, however, the number of those in both age groups who were against the revised agreement decreased rapidly. This decrease was offset by a sharp rise in the number of people who gave a 'don't know' answer. Thus the proportion of young people who are presently opposed to the revised mutual security agreement is higher than that of middle-aged and older people, although the difference is not very great.

Now let us turn to the question of constitutional revision. One must be very careful when dealing with this issue since the conclusions reached on the basis of public opinion polls vary according to the questions asked and the way in which the questions are phrased. Chart No. 3 shows the results of a 1963 poll carried out in Tokyo in which the question asked was 'What do you think of the present Constitution?' The respondents were asked to select one answer from the following

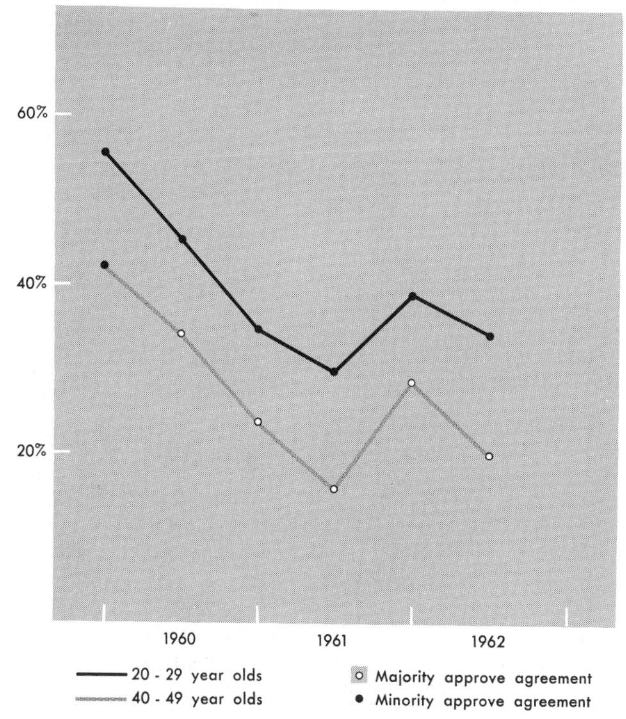

Chart No. 2. Rate of Opposition to Revised Mutual Security Agreement with the United States

list: 1) The Constitution should be revised at some time in the future along socialistic lines; 2) The Constitution should be revised immediately to conform to Japan's present needs; 3) The Constitution should, at an appropriate time, be revised only in those portions which are absolutely inadequate; 4) The Constitution should under no circumstances be revised. It is noteworthy that the majority of young people favored answer number three, the answer which reflects the most realistic, moderate point of view.

The results of the above opinion polls on the revised mutual security agreement and the Constitution indicate that there is no great divergence among age groups when it comes to political issues not directly connected with party support. The opinions of the younger people are slightly more progressive, but even so, the general tendency is away from progressivism toward conservativism. It may also be said that the opinions of young people are neither more radical nor more idealistic than those of their elders. According to data gathered by the Institute of Statistical Mathematics, when one turns to questions concerning everyday life which are distinct and separate from political issues, one finds that differences among age groups become much greater. Younger people tend to be progressive in their attitudes toward life in general; they are more aggressive and individualistic, and the opinions of most go against tradition. However, their generally progressive attitudes toward life do not necessarily prompt them to support the progressive parties. On the contrary, as seen above, young people are in fact tending toward political conservatism. This does not mean, however, that they think about political issues in the same way as the older people do. Young people seem to hope for something new and fresh, realistic and rational; their thoughts seem to be full of dreams for the future, unmixed with tradition.

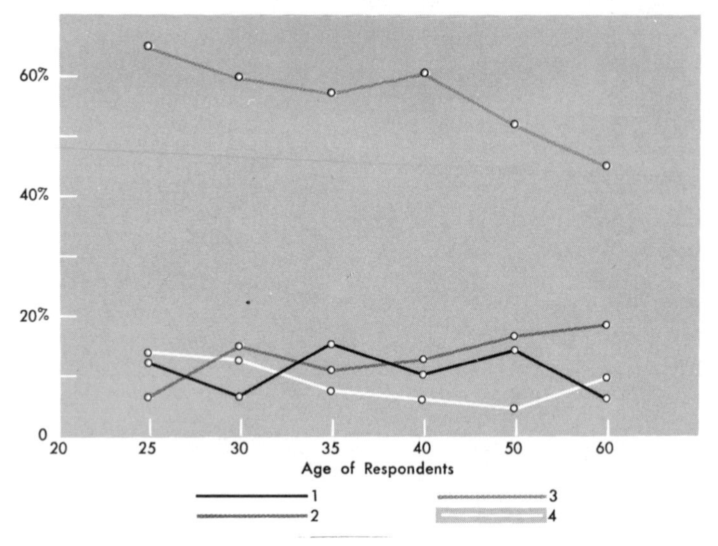

Chart No. 3. Results of the 1963 Poll on the New Constitution

Why, then, have young people today become disaffected with the progressive parties? Thus far voters have supported the progressives for one or more of four reasons: 1) because of various social dissatisfactions; 2) because of the wartime experiences suffered by the people; 3) because of the loyalty of workers to their union organizations; or 4) because of the relative youthfulness and smartness of the image of the progressive parties. According to Sōsuke Mita, a young political scientist who collaborated on this paper, young people today have become disaffected with the progressive parties because the above four reasons no longer appeal to the new generation. That is to say, 1) Japan's accelerated economic growth rate is leading to fewer complaints about lack of food or jobs; 2) the young people of today, who did not experience World War II, tend to feel that the danger of becoming involved in a war is quite remote; 3) according to attitudinal surveys of employees of large enterprises carried out by Professor Kunio Odaka of Tokyo University and his associates, the younger employees have slight feelings of loyalty to either their companies or labor unions and are inclined to be critical of the leadership of both; 4) the progressive parties have lost their youthfulness and vitality in the eyes of young people. The average age of Communist Party and Democratic Socialist Party Diet members is higher than that of Liberal Democratic Party Diet members. The average age of Socialist Party Diet members is lower than that of Liberal Democratic Party Diet members, but, unlike the Liberal Democratic Party, the Socialist Party has no Diet members in their twenties or early thirties.

Strictly speaking, the conservative tendencies of young people today stem from their disaffection with the progressives. This disaffection has caused an increase both in the number of younger people who are critical of the progressives and in the number who are apathetic toward politics. Those who have no interest in politics show a tendency to have faith in, and be satisfied with, the present regime. The greatest task facing the progressives today is to find a way to attract those young people who have become critical of the progressive parties.

44 • RONALD P. DORE: *A Participant Describes an Electoral Campaign in a Yamanashi Hamlet* *

In a society that has modernized as rapidly as Japan's, there are many partial transfers of rural values and patterns of behavior into suburban and urban life. Each village (mura) *characteristically includes a few hamlets* (buraku), *though in recent years administrative consolidation has been under way. Hamlets have been the basic rural communities in all senses, including that of politics. They are the units of local competition and representation in elected village councils. According to peasant tradition and practice, solidarity and harmony are most important ideals; politics on the hamlet level does not, therefore, usually reflect basic stratal and other comparable cleavages of interest.*

The following vivid account describes an election campaign in a sixty-household hamlet in Yamanashi Prefecture. The story was told to Professor Ronald P. Dore by one of the five or six most influential men of the buraku.

Though Japanese farmers see money transactions for votes denounced in newspapers, they feel shame on this account only momentarily or when talking with a reproving person. Their prevailing attitude is that this practice is not so much bribery as it is a customary way of recognizing that a "favor" has been promised in the form of a vote.

Professor Dore is one of the West's most able sociologists interested in Japan. His book is the best we have in English (and probably in any language) on the process and effects of land reform in Japan. He did the field work for this study before becoming a professor in the School of Oriental and African Studies, University of London.

* Ronald P. Dore, *Land Reform in Japan,* published by Oxford University Press under the auspices of the Royal Institute of International Affairs, 1959, pp. 339–341. By permission.

When the election came along it was obvious that we ought to get somebody in the hamlet to stand; there are enough votes here to be sure of electing one member, and one needs somebody to speak up for the hamlet on the Council. The question was: Who? Sometimes the matter is discussed at the annual general meeting of the hamlet, but the elections were not fixed when we had the meeting this year, and in any case it is a tricky business discussing a thing like that unless it is pretty well decided beforehand. Usually somebody drops a hint that he wants to stand, but this time, apart from G who is far too unpopular, nobody made a move. A few of us got together and discussed it, but none of us wanted to stand. I have got enough to do without being a councillor. K said he wanted a quiet life. N [an ex-landlord doctor who had returned to the village after a period as registrar of a medical university] would stand for mayor, but he wouldn't consider being a councillor. T is a good chap, but he gets tight too easily, and too much of that reflects on the hamlet. We thought of several people and eventually decided to try S [also an ex-small-landlord, formerly a railway engineer, since the war an owner-farmer]. He's not much of a man, nobody particularly likes him, and he never says very much, but he said he'd think about it. Apparently, when he went home and told his wife there was a row. She wouldn't hear of it; said they'd lost enough money when he'd been secretary of the local branch of a credit union which had turned out to be a fraud, and a fine sort of councillor he'd make anyway. In the end he walked out of the house in a huff and disappeared.

He didn't come back for days, and nomination day was getting closer. Meanwhile we persuaded his son, and with his support we managed to talk his wife round. Still he didn't come back. We sent telegrams and 'phoned all over the place, but by nomination day we still hadn't tracked him down so we borrowed his seal and went and registered his candidature in his absence. Eventually we found him in one of his old haunts in Tokyo, and he soon came back pleased as a schoolboy to know that he was a candidate.

It was a difficult campaign. Because we were late starting, most of the other candidates had got ahead, and a lot of people in the hamlet had already promised their votes thinking that nobody from here was going to stand—people who'd been asked by relatives in other hamlets, that is. And then there was W down the road in the next hamlet [ex-landlord chairman of the Village Land Committee, who immediately after the war, had started a Socialist Party branch, now defunct]. He was offering 500 yen per vote, whereas most of the candidates were only giving 300, and S decided that was all he could afford.

However, five or six of us divided the hamlet up between us and made sure who would be responsible for whose votes. One trouble was Y. [A landless farmer who makes a precarious living by odd jobbing, unemployment relief work, taking wild bees' nests, and the hiring out of his verbal skills for debt-collecting and other forms of persuasion. These verbal skills are formidable, and combined with the strength of his character earn him the reluctant position of a *yūryokusha* for some purposes.] We decided that we had to let him in on it, since he could do positive harm if we slighted him by leaving him out. However, we only gave him his brother and his other neighbour's household to look after, and handed him the 2,100 yen for the 7 votes. We were a bit suspicious, though, and checked up afterwards. Sure enough, he had only given his brother half the money he should have done, and kept the rest for himself. His brother was angry; he thought he'd been insulted by being offered such a small amount. However, we decided it would do more harm than good to make an issue of it with Y, and S had to take round the extra money to his brother and the other neighbour.

It was hard going, but a lot of people rallied round. The youth group stood on guard at the entrance to the hamlet every night, and just followed round everybody who came soliciting votes from other hamlets—didn't say anything, of course, just stood ostentatiously outside each house they went into to show that they had been observed. In the end we pulled it off. Most people realize, anyway, that unless they have a pretty close relative standing somewhere else in the village their first duty is to the hamlet. The night before the election we totted up the number of votes we'd got, and sure enough, the actual number was within two or three of our estimate. Some people in this hamlet, though, will promise their votes to two or three candidates and take money from them all. It's a dead loss being the official sponsor of a candidate; you get nothing from your own man, because, after all, you're doing it for the good of the hamlet, and nobody else comes near you. Just think what I missed. Five votes in this household; say I collected from two candidates at 300 yen a vote—I could have spent three or four days at a hot spring. And all for S! He's a 'kettle councilor' if ever there was one [*yakan-giin*—one fit only for carrying the *sake* rice-wine kettle and serving drinks at village council parties]. But still, the hamlet had to have somebody.

45 • MASAMICHI RŌYAMA: *Preparing for 1970* *

Last in this section on Japan is an article by the dean of that country's political scientists. Before the war Professor Rōyama taught politics in Tokyo Imperial University. He has since been a university president and a leader of the Social Science Research Institute at International Christian University. He is a prolific writer and commentator and has served on a number of governmental commissions, including ones in constitutional investigation and city planning.

In this broad essay he reinterprets the crisis of 1959–60 over approval of the revised security treaty, describes political trends during the ensuing six years, and looks ahead to what may be another critical year (1970) when the treaty will be reconsidered. Opposition forces are already promising another confrontation on this issue; if the Japanese are then still anxious about becoming involved in the war in Vietnam, such tactics might attract considerable sympathy and support. Professor Rōyama makes suggestions in the interests of sounder parliamentary practices and more rational public discussion.

It is said that the conclusion of the old Security Treaty in 1951 was a necessary condition for the conclusion of the Japanese Peace Treaty which was accelerated by the outbreak of the Korean War. In view of the circumstances which led to the conclusion of this Security Treaty, we can say that the old Security Treaty was not a treaty concluded between the two countries on an equal footing but an

* *Chūō Kōron,* November 1965. By permission.

unequal treaty designed to subjugate Japan to the United States. In several years after the recovery of independence, Japan rehabilitated and reconstructed its economy. It is natural, therefore, that negotiations were started to revise this treaty and make it less unequal. It is also natural and possible, however, that the opinion against revision of the old Security Treaty arose on the ground that such revision would only lawfully extend [such] unequal relationships. Japanese security under the war-renouncing Constitution involved logical and emotional contradictions. Especially those who stood for neutralism or who were opposed to the U.S. military strategy were strongly opposed to the extension of the Security Treaty. The important point which must be analyzed here, however, is how the LDP government, which was doubtless aware of logical contradictions and the emotional opposition, developed its argument for revision. Did the LDP government fail to keep the people from being attracted by the argument against revision because its argument for revision was not convincing to the people and because it did not make sufficient efforts to persuade the people to support revision? Or was the Treaty revision issue of such a character as to make riots inevitable, regardless of the contentions and theoretical grounds for revision?

I cannot analyze these points precisely here. I must point out, however, that judging from the situation within and outside the Diet for about 100 days from February 4 to May 19, 1960, the Kishi cabinet then in office and the ruling party seemed to be in a somewhat easygoing mood because of their belief that the people were supporting the proposed Security Treaty revision out of their nationalistic feelings and that the revised Treaty would also bring economic benefits to Japan. The government and the LDP seemed especially to have failed to pay enough attention to the delicate problem of how antiwar feelings, which had been justified by abstract principles of pacifism and democracy, would resist the U.S.-Japan military alliance. A majority of the Japanese people were not yet trained enough to consider the connection between world peace and national security from a realistic and constructive point of view. They had no mental power yet to settle constructively the relations between world peace and national security through discussions of such problematical points of the Treaty as the "prior consultation" and "consent" clauses and the "scope of application."

Accordingly, the war-renouncing Constitution and national sentiments supporting it were, depending on circumstances, liable to be influenced by the argument for permanent neutrality and the argument against imperialism and the United States. To make the people recognize the necessity of a U.S.-Japan military alliance, therefore, extraordinary efforts should have been made in the field of mentality. The government and the ruling party, however, did not make such efforts. Especially, they failed to clarify the point of contact between the problematical points of the proposed Treaty and ideological views as well as the popular unrest. Some of the lessons to be drawn from this fact were that the confrontation and conflict over national security and defense were fundamental, that ideological antagonism could not be overcome in a short time, and that a majority of the people were not split but restless. This means that the ideological confrontation was not the direct cause for that great political chaos, including mass riots. The direct cause must be sought, therefore, in the process of Diet deliberations on the proposed Treaty and the objective situation at that time.

Secondly, there are established procedures and methods for the determination of policies by the state, especially by the political organs centering around the national

Diet; the question is whether it was right in the political situation in 1960 to apply these established procedures and methods to the revision of the Security Treaty. The political process of policy-making is by no means rational. The institutional procedures, for instance the majority rule principle, are often inapplicable. Hence, the development of spirited political actions in and outside the Diet in a fanatic mass movement, as has often been experienced since the French Revolution. Were the internal and external conditions in 1960 favorable for the rise of such political action? Judgment on this point ought to have been passed by the Kishi cabinet and the ruling LDP. . . . The government and the ruling party put the Treaty ratification bill to vote forcibly on May 19 and rejected the demand for resignation of the cabinet and dissolution of the Lower House. These two actions added fuel to the political frenzy. This was the cause of the extraordinary riots.

After May 19, the Security Treaty revision became an issue between the Kishi cabinet and the general citizenry. The political movement by the citizens at large in the form of their radical participation in politics deviated from the crux of the Treaty revision issue. Generally, the movements before and after May 19 are simply called the "Security Treaty riots." I think, however, that some distinction must be made between the two. Needless to say, there were such events as the breakdown of the summit conference in Paris over the U-2 case and the scheduled visit to Japan of President Eisenhower, which was not unrelated to the said summit conference. These events increased the Japanese uneasiness over the international political situation and consequently the feeling of distrust toward the Kishi cabinet. The crux of the question is why the government, in spite of such complications, put the Treaty to vote forcibly. . . . The judgment by the government and the ruling party was doubtless wrong and unjustified.

The third question is whether resistance of the general citizenry and the popular antipathy against the Kishi cabinet and Prime Minister Kishi had any political connection with the problem of Japan's security based on the Security Treaty. If they had, we must say that the people's views on the Security Treaty were wrong, or at least lopsided, even though the Treaty was approved forcibly by majority rule in the prolonged Diet session. It can be surmised, however, that the peoples' resistance at that time reflected the popular antipathy against the Kishi cabinet, which carried out the ratification of the Treaty forcibly, and against Prime Minister Kishi, rather than opposition to the Treaty itself. This provides the important lesson that national and popular reaction against the behavior and personality of politicians leads to the overheating of political movements.

The Japanese are not used to decision by majority as a formula for making decisions. Usually, however, all conferences have been conducted according to this formula. We must think, therefore, that the majority rule by which the Security Treaty was approved had a fault: the majority represented only a federation of internal factions of the LDP, not the united action of the party as a whole. Moreover, the vote was taken with the intervention of the police and without participation by the opposition parties. Decision by majority under such conditions could not carry any moral authority. Even its legal effect was doubted.

Consequently, the forces, which stood for revolutionary ideology and which were exploiting the parliamentary political structure for their own ends, came to play a leading role in the mass movements. We must say that the forces which were opposing the Security Treaty with a hidden revolutionary design could lead the rather emotional anti-government movement because the government and the ruling party had taken forced action by majority rule, thus committing a blunder in steering the Diet. In brief, the evil bureaucratic tradition existing since the Meji era, which did not regard the Diet as a truly representative organ of the people but treated it and its decisions only as means of legalizing the actions of the cabinet, had not disappeared.

The fourth and last problem was that the anti-Security Treaty riots, though short-lived, represented the most radical form of people's participation in politics in Japanese history. Their scale seemed surprisingly large to those who knew the criticism and opposition movements against the Security Treaty of 1951 and the ensuing Administrative Agreement. Also, the trend of public opinion at the time of the Dulles-Shigemitsu conference in August 1955, which marked the beginning of the negotiations for revision of the Security Treaty, and even at the time of the Dulles-Fujiyama conference in September 1958, were not indicative of the possibility of such great riots occurring within only two years of the latter conference.

In March 1960, when the Diet began its deliberation on the Treaty revision, public opinion surveys were conducted. The *Mainichi* reported on April 5 that the result of its survey was: 15.8 per cent supporting the new Treaty positively, 18.8 per cent accepting it as inevitable, and 27.9 per cent opposing it. According to the results announced by the *Yomiuri* on April 3, 21 per cent supported the Treaty, 28 per cent opposed it, and 51 per cent were without opinions. As can be seen from these figures, opinion against the Treaty was not dominant among the people even after the commencement of Diet deliberations. The majority of the people were unable to decide whether to support or oppose the Treaty.

Thus, it is necessary for us to consider from another angle the fact that the people at large began taking part in a political decision around May 19 in the form of mass uprisings. Probably the factor for such passionate actions, already existing in popular feelings, was coupled with immature Japanese democracy, under which the people's normal participation in politics had not yet been fully established. Under these conditions the orderly movement to file petitions with the Diet, stimulated by successive ocurrences of important political events which led to frontal clashes between the ruling and opposition parties, merged with the mass demonstration movement which had some political designs. Even after the commencement of full-scale U.S.-Japan negotiations for Security Treaty revision in 1958, many political issues in succession came to the fore, such as the rating of teachers' efficiency, revision of the Police Duties Execution Law, and revision of the Defense Agency Establishment Law and the Self-Defense Forces Law, all fanning political fervor outside the Diet. The People's Congress Against Security Treaty Revision was formed, and the first united action against Security Treaty revision was staged in March and April 1959. We cannot but think that people took part in politics through such extraordinary actions because of institutional defects that left no normal, rational formula for their participation in politics, besides which the parliamentary parties were not playing the roles expected of them.

... The problem we must study now is what change has occurred in the historical conditions which led to the riots against the Security Treaty in 1960. In other words, we must analyze the environmental changes since 1960.

First of all, to look back on the internal situation of the country since 1960, the Security Treaty, which the Kishi cabinet rammed through the Lower House, took effect without the approval of the Upper House. Immediately thereafter, the

Kishi cabinet resigned en masse and the Ikeda cabinet came into office. In October of the same year, the Ikeda cabinet dissolved the Lower House and held a general election. The LDP retained a majority in the new Lower House, and a second Ikeda cabinet was formed. It remained in office until the Prime Minister announced his desire to retire in the fall of 1964 because of ill health. In the meantime, the Lower House was dissolved and a general election was held in 1963. The political and ideological conditions of the Japanese, as made known through this election, were almost fixed with little change. The "conservatives vs. renovationists" confrontation persisted, with the "renovationists" narrowly maintaining one-third of the Diet seats.

The Ikeda cabinet maintained what was called a "low posture" during four years of its administration, partly because it came into office just after the great riots against the Security Treaty. It remained prudent at all times, endeavoring not to irritate the opposition and not to take up any question which was likely to cause friction. Its efforts in the field of administration were focused on economic and financial policies, especially on execution of the economic growth plan, or what it called the "income-doubling plan," which was being realized at that time. In the field of international trade, inseparable from economic growth at home, it embarked on liberalization in order to establish Japan's position in the world economy. It also sought to conclude private trade agreements with China and the Soviet Union. Thus, the Ikeda cabinet tried solely to expand Japan's economic strength. It postponed the solution of difficult political questions such as the settlement of Japan-ROK negotiations and also left to the succeeding cabinet solution of such problems as structural distortions caused by economic development, the movement of manpower accompanying the expansion of production, unstable living conditions of the people due to price fluctuations, and the establishment of measures to counter recession. We can say that the Ikeda administration represented a period of relative stability after the anti-Security Treaty riots. Though with some exaggerations, this period may be likened to the period of temporary stability which the Weimar Republic in Germany after World War I enjoyed for four years from the establishment of the Dawes Plan and the Locarno Pact to the year 1929. . . .

The development of the Sino-Soviet dispute also caused a split in the Japan Communist Party and accelerated fission of the pacifist movements as in the case of the Japan Council Against Atom and Hydrogen Bombs. Moreover, it created delicate repercussions in the JSP which had called the United States the common enemy of Japan and China. We should not overlook the fact that this environmental change had a direct bearing on internal conditions in Japan. In other words, we must note that, so long as U.S.-Soviet co-operation lasts, Communist China cannot but demand strongly the neutralization of Japan as part of its policy against the United States and imperialism. . . .

There is another noteworthy change in the world situation. It is the change in relations between France, now led by President De Gaulle, and NATO and the EEC. The core of this change is the change in relations between France and the United States. It can be said that France began altering its foreign policy in 1962 when the Algerian question came to a final settlement. In 1963, France rejected the multilateral nuclear armament plan for NATO, opposed Britain's participation in the EEC and refused to join the Partial Nuclear Test Ban Treaty. By these steps, France revealed its new foreign policy aimed at securing a greater voice in Southeast Asian affairs and improving relations with Communist China. Especially, its recognition of Communist China in January 1964 exerted a direct effect on the Asian situation and on Japan's position. This French-centered tendency toward split in the free camp is called the tendency toward multipolarization of the world. This tendency, which was not yet seen at the time of the anti-Security Treaty riots in Japan in 1960, doubtless, though indirectly, helped the Japanese leftists.

Needless to say, it is Communist China's foreign policy that has a direct bearing on Japan's internal situation. A notable change was caused in Communist China's foreign relations after the anti-Security Treaty riots in Japan by the border dispute with Tibet [India?] in 1962. The Sino-Indian Agreement on Tibet, which had been concluded in 1954 on the basis of the five peace principles, lost its effect due to this dispute. Communist China's policy toward the Himalayan region warrants attention because it has a bearing on India, Pakistan, which is pitted against India over Kashmir, and even on the Southeast Asia policy of the Soviet Union. Furthermore, Communist China's policies toward Afro-Asian countries and non-aligned nations will have an important bearing on the world situation as a whole. Communist Chinese moves toward these countries, which were started after the Bandung Conference of 1955, became active after 1960 and especially after Communist China began endeavoring to display its leadership of these countries in preparation for the Second Afro-Asian Conference scheduled to be held in 1965. Some Afro-Asian countries, however, became wary of these Communist Chinese moves. The breakdown of the Afro-Asian Conference held in Algeria in the spring this year (1965) reflects Communist China's position and the course it was pursuing.

Lastly, we must take up the war situation in Vietnam after the commencement of the bombing of the North in February this year (1965). The Vietnam question is not a new problem but a problem with a historical background. It was not until February 1965, however, that this became a problem for all world powers including Japan. The Vietnam war is no longer a war between North and South Vietnam but a war which is being fought directly between the United States and the National Liberation Front and indirectly between the United States and the Asian communist forces consisting of North Vietnam and Communist China. That is why the movement against the Vietnam war rose suddenly in Japan in connection with the U.S.-Japan Security Treaty. The danger of Japan being involved in war was debated only ideologically at the time of the anti-Security Treaty riots in 1960. It is true that opposition to the proposed revision of the Security Treaty at that time was backed by the fear that the revised Security Treaty might plunge the nation into a war. Now, five years later, a situation has actually appeared which revives that fear. While the Security Treaty itself has been in force without any trouble so far as the internal situation of Japan is concerned, a meaningless but dangerous state of war continues indefinitely in Asia. The present and future Japanese reactions to this new situation are certain to exert a great influence on what is expected in 1970. . . .

The people are rather afraid that the LDP is not united enough in ideology and policy matters to meet an emergency. The opinion for rearmament, which former Prime Minister Kishi published in the U.S. magazine *Foreign Affairs,* even though a personal opinion, will excite popular sentiments apart from the nation's foreign policy, because it is related to the problem of constitutional revision. The LDP must strictly refrain from any such act as may touch off great trouble. Whether or not there will be a repeated version of the 1960 riots due to popular excitement depends on how the people react to the opposition parties' intentional and organized activities rather than on blunders or lack of ability on the part of the government and the ruling party. Especially, the question is what effect the JCP's strategy is exerting on the JSP, Sōhyō (General Council of Japan Trade Unions) and radical men of culture. The JCP was wise enough to regroup its front as soon as the anti-Security Treaty riots were over. Expanding its influence and settling its internal dispute which had been caused by the Sino-Soviet controversy, the JCP has been making steady preparations for 1970, along the anti-imperialist and anti-American line established by Communist China. Its true intention can be seen from the Political Report presented to the eighth Congress in March 1961, that is, the year following the anti-Security Treaty riots, and from the new platform adopted at the same Congress. The JCP intends to develop itself into a vanguard party for the masses with several hundred thousand members, with the "establishment of a government by a federation of democratic forces opposed to the Security Treaty" as its basic goal. Views vary on the extent to which the JCP has attained this goal during the past four years. It may be said, however, that this extent is considerable, in view of the activities of Minseidō (Democratic Youth League) and other peripheral organs of the JCP as well as its showing in the Upper House and Metropolitan Assembly elections held this year.

Success or failure of this strategy of the JCP depends on its co-operation and the attitude to be taken by Sōhyō. As can be imagined from its position hitherto maintained and as can be known from the "one-day joint struggle" which has recently been staged against the Japan-ROK Treaty, the JSP main current faction is led by Chairman Sasaki, and is inclined to accept the JCP's appeal for co-operation because of its enthusiasm for what Secretary General Narita calls a "federated democratic front" which is a united front of a wider range than that envisaged by the JCP. It depends on the moves of the anti-main currenters within the JSP and, to a greater extent, on the popular reaction to the joint struggle, and on whether the Sasaki faction can keep the JSP in line. Especially important is the attitude to be taken by Sōhyō toward joint struggles. The decision to be made by Sōhyō executives will be influenced by the attitude of the government and the ruling party toward the ILO question.

Needless to say, reactions of the people will be too wide and deep to be shaped solely by a federation of the JSP and the JCP, whose ideologies and organizations are biased. Besides the JSP and the JCP, there are such opposition parties as the DSP and Komeitō and organizations of pro-LDP men of culture and intellectuals. Mass media, too, can exert a decisive influence on popular reactions.

In the foregoing I have looked back, as far as space permits, on the lessons of 1960, analyzed the changes which have taken place in the internal and external circumstances during the past five years since that year, and have surveyed the people's reactions to these changes which are reflected mainly in the activities of the government and the political parties. The problem is the conclusion to be reached from these studies. This problem is related to the insight of political science which Bertrand de Jubuneru [Jouvenel], a French scholar of political science, has recently been expounding. It involves foreseeing the future, which is the important but most difficult duty of political scientists. Because 1970 is still five years away, I only want to tell my temporary conclusion for criticism and study by readers. Comparing the lessons gained in 1960 with popular reactions to changes in the internal and external circumstances after that year, we can find a few important points by way of conclusion.

The first point is that to excite and overheat popular sentiments over a peripheral problem not directly related to the Security Treaty issue, or the question of what to do with Japanese security, must be avoided by all means. It is because a dispute over a non-focal matter, even if related to the point at issue, for instance a dispute over Diet proceedings during Diet debates and control over extra-Diet demonstrations, has possibilities of developing into a great storm and of blowing away the focal point itself. What is important in this case as a related condition is not to throw the people's mentality into a state of frustration over economic problems, especially the vicious circle between consumer prices and public charges and wages. If the Satō cabinet, or any cabinet to be installed hereafter, maintains the lukewarm attitude of tiding over the crisis by some means or other, it will be unable to stave off a disastrous "typhoon" in 1970. In relation to that, if the LDP allows the rise within itself of any opinion for constitutional revision for the ulterior purpose of Japan's rearmament, it will invite a violent popular reaction, which will eventually blow away the Security Treaty question itself.

The second point is related to the turbulent situation in Asia, which constitutes the direct background of the Security Treaty question, and its future development. As can be seen from the situation in Vietnam and the dispute between India and Pakistan, the peaceful settlement of the present disturbances in Asia depends directly on the policies of the United States, China, and the Soviet Union, and indirectly on the moves of the UN, not on the Asian countries concerned. Especially, the focal point is the confrontation between the United States and China. Japan is taking a stand of self-restraining neutrality toward their confrontation. It is impossible for the Japanese government, which is backed by such national strength as we see today, to play any positive or constructive role in the settlement of these disputes. Moreover, Japanese public opinion tends to divide, and there are no prospects for forming a national consensus. In such a state of affairs, there is no alternative for any Japanese government but to take such an attitude as has hitherto been taken by successive governments. In such a situation, there can be no belief in the cause of peace nor any hope for lasting peace. The people are dominated by the fear of war, and, concerning national security, they are in a state of mental vacuum.

The anti-Security Treaty riots of 1960 had their fundamental cause in such an unstable mental vacuum of the nation. The repetition of such riots will only betray the foolishness of the Japanese government and people. The government should make all possible efforts to direct the sense of international responsibilty, to which the people began to awaken on the occasion of the Tokyo Olympic Games, to peaceful construction in Asia. Also it must redouble its efforts for the strengthening of the peace-keeping functions of the UN—the efforts it started to make during the 1965 session of the UN General Assembly. If the government finds a bright ray of hope in the skies darkened by war and international disputes, and if it attracts the people's attention to this ray of hope, any organized plot or popular movement will not develop into what may be called a "Revolution of 1970."

The third point is related fundamentally to the Japanese people themselves, though it is not unrelated to the government and the political parties. Although the 20 postwar years are not necessarily long enough to constitute an era in history, the Japanese people during these postwar years have doubtless witnessed numerous events which betrayed the immaturity of their democracy and especially of party politics. This must be attributed solely to passive participation in politics by the people at large, who remain spectators of the confrontation between the established, premodern conservative party and the newly-born, ideologically-biased renovationist parties, and who show their reactions only to the election campaigns of these parties. It was because of this passive attitude that they burst out into a radical and anti-parliamentary form of political participation in 1960. Such being the case, any reform of the electoral system will not bring about democratic, parliamentary politics. The corruption of the conservative party, which has long counted on its numerical strength in the Diet, and the deviation of the leftist renovationist parties, which are unable to draw distinctions between parliamentary political action and revolutionary movements, do not guarantee the normal development of parliamentary politics in Japan nor prepare Japan for 1970, as can be seen from various symptoms. About two general elections will be held before 1970, and the political parties should make the Security Treaty question an election issue and seek the people's judgment on it in these elections. . . .

Part III

India

SECTION ONE

Political Culture

46 • M. N. Srinivas: *The Indian Road to Equality* *

The complexity of Indian political culture makes nation building a difficult task for India's leaders. Its history of foreign invasions, diversity of regional historical experience, multiplicity of languages and religions, and the fissiparous nature of caste continue to divide Indian society. The process of national mobilization begun under the British is still incomplete and perhaps even precarious.

Indian social structure is largely determined by its ancient and unique caste system. M. N. Srinivas, one of India's outstanding anthropologists, has elsewhere defined caste as "a hereditary, endogamus, usually localized group, having traditional association with an occupation, and a particular position in the local hierarchy of castes." Relations between castes are based on concepts of pollution and ritual purity. The origin of caste is unknown, but references are found in early Vedic literature to the four varnas: Brahmin (priest and scholar), Kshatriya (ruler and soldier), Vaishya (merchant), and Shudra (peasant, laborer). These groups were subsequently subdivided into thousands of sub-castes or jati. *Outside and below the caste hierarchy are the untouchables.*

This hierarchical, unequal, ascriptive social system is now undergoing modification through the impact of constitutional norms of legal equality, social mobility through education and new job opportunities, and the political effect of universal suffrage. The modern political role of caste in articulating and aggregating interests, the Westernization of higher castes, and the Sanskritization of lower castes are adapting and modernizing the caste system in Indian society. The following selection discusses both the persistence of the traditional caste system and its adaptation to modernizing pressures.

What makes the Indian experiment at bringing about an egalitarian order so fascinating to sociologists is that it has to take note of that classic expression of inequality viz., caste. It is an ubiquitous institution in India being found among Hindus, Sikhs, Jains, Muslims, Christians and Jews. It is the one institution that cuts across religious, regional and class divisions.

* *Economic Weekly*, Vol. XII (Special Number June 1960), pp. 867–872.

There is a widespread impression among educated Indians that caste is on its last legs, and that the educated, urbanised and Westernised members of the upper classes, have already escaped its bonds. Both these impressions are wrong. These people may observe very few dietetic restrictions, marry outside caste and even region, but this does not mean that they have escaped the bonds of caste entirely. They show caste attitudes in surprising contexts. And they interact closely with relatives who are steeped in caste attitudes. On occasions they are not loth to make use of caste ties. I have known an intercaste marriage of nearly forty years' standing in which the wife continued to have the attitudes of a Brahmin. The son married an American girl, and the Bania subcaste of the father gave the couple a big party to celebrate the occasion. The contradictions in the above situation may be left to the reader's imagination.

Caste is certainly undergoing some changes. For the educated and urbanised middle classes, *jati* is no longer the endogamous unit. There is also a certain amount of interdining with other castes (especially for the men). Occupational homogeneity is no longer there for these groups. But caste is still significant in certain contexts. A Kayasth would like to vote for a Kayasth candidate in preference to a Rajput candidate. The sub-divisions among Kayasths are becoming less relevant for marriage, inter-dining, etc. One may call this horizontal consolidation, though 'horizontal' is not entirely an appropriate term for even the sub-castes of the same caste claim mutual superiority. Harijans are divided into dozens of castes, and even within the same linguistic region, the Harijans usually form a hierarchy. But this has not prevented the Harijans' coming together for political purposes. "Caste" (in the wider sense) ties are significant in modern India and every political party, including the Communists, have to take note of this fact though overtly caste is denounced by important political leaders.

There is a good case for arguing that caste-consciousness and organization have increased in modern India. Witness for instance the proliferation of caste banks, hostels, cooperative societies, charities, marriage halls, conferences and journals in Indian towns. Anyone who wants to study the role of caste in administration ought to pay a visit to Mysore or any other southern State. There caste seems to be the single most important consideration in the selection of candidates to posts and in their promotion, efficiency being a relatively minor consideration. An analysis of the various State cabinets since Independence would show the part played by caste in regional politics. The General Elections of 1957 awoke everyone to the importance of caste in voting. Every party tried to choose a candidate from a locally numerically strong caste. The Communists invented a progressive term for it: "social base". And they made sure that every Communist candidate had a social base.

The concept of dominant caste which has emerged in recent sociological research is important in this connection. A caste is dominant when it wields economic or political power, and occupies a fairly high position in the hierarchy. (In the traditional system, a caste which acquired economic or political power did generally succeed in improving its ritual status.)

The fact that dominant castes exist in many parts of India makes it necessary for us to try to understand the phenomenon. The Lingayat and Okkaliga of Mysore, Reddi and Kamma of Andhra, Gounder, Padayachi and Mudaliar of the Tamil country, Nayar of Kerala, Maratha of Maharastra, Patidar of Gujarat, and Rajput, Jat, Gujar and Ahir of North India, are all examples of dominant caste.

Traditionally, numerically small castes owning land in rural areas, or wielding political power, or inheriting a literary tradition, could dominate. It was these castes which first took to Western education and the benefits which it conferred. Nowadays, with the coming of adult suffrage, numerical strength has become very important and the leaders of the dominant castes help the political parties to secure votes. But the traditional forms of dominance have not entirely disappeared and neither has dominance shifted fully to the numerically strongest castes. There are the beginnings of a shift and this is accompanied by inter-group tensions. But what is significant from our point of view is that there are in many parts of India castes which are *decisively* dominant.

Where dominance is confined to one or a few villages, the locally dominant caste dominates Panchayats. Where dominance is spread over a wider area, the caste becomes significant in the politics of the region and State. For instance, the politics of Mysore State is unintelligible without understanding the part played by Lingayats and Okkaligas. Even the States Reorganization Committee reported that Okkaligas were by and large opposed to merger of Mysore with parts of former Bombay, Andhra and Madras to form a bigger Kannada-speaking State. The Okkaliga leaders were afraid that in the new State the numerical strength of the Lingayats would be greater than that of Okkaligas, and that this would lead to Lingayat dominance. Recently, an ex-Chief Minister of Mysore, an Okkaliga, voiced the opinion that in the present state of affairs in Mysore no non-Lingayat could hope to become Chief Minister.

The leaders of the dominant caste are shrewd and intelligent people. They have a feeling for political power and economic opportunity. They have capital, and a local following. Since Independence, they have shown their enterprise in several ways: they have started bus lines, rice and flour mills, cloth and other shops, taken up contract work for the Government, and built houses in towns for renting. The more adventurous among them have gone into active politics.

The dominant castes have been quick to see that they can benefit from the various development programmes in rural areas. A great amount of money is being spent on rural development, and development officers are under pressure from above to show quick results. They can do this only with the cooperation of the leaders of the dominant castes. No wonder then complaints are constantly heard that the development programmes have helped only the wealthier section of the rural population. The policy of decentralisation has given more power and money to the dominant castes. It would be very optimistic to expect that they will use this power and money for everyone's benefit.

While the leaders of the dominant castes are sensitive to economic and political opportunities, they are socially conservative. They do not, for instance, like the condition of Harijans to improve. They have a vested interest in keeping Harijans poor and ignorant. At the present time, Harijans are their most important source of agricultural labour, and if they become educated and conscious of their rights they will be a threat to the position of the dominant castes. Anti-Harijan sentiments are freely heard in the rural areas: "Today they want to use our wells, and tomorrow they will want to marry our daughters." Attempts by Harijans to exercise the rights given to them by the Constitution, have led to violent reprisals by the dominant castes. Harijans have been beaten up and their huts burned down and they have been subjected to economic boycott. Harijans are among the poorest sections of our agricultural population and many of them are agricultural servants of the land-owning castes. The conditions under which agricultural labourers work are reminiscent of slavery. I have seen boys of 10-16 years of age being made to do all kinds of work from 5 am to 10 pm for about fifty rupees *a year,* two meals two shirts and shorts. This was in a relatively prosperous area and only ten years ago.

It is clear that the Constitutional abolition of Untouchability and the passing of the Anti-Untouchability Offences Act, 1955, will by themselves not help Harijans much. *Harijans must be freed from the economic control of the higher castes.* The best way to do this is to employ them in factories in urban areas. It has been found that ownership of land and membership of the joint family come in the way of their becoming efficient workers. The pull of land, even if it be a quarter of an acre, and the obligations of joint family, prevent the individual from devoting himself to his job. Such a programme will also have the advantage of taking Harijans away from areas where they have been subjected to indignities for a number of years. It will also have the effect of reducing the pressure of population on land.

Implicit in what I have said so far is the assumption that there is, broadly speaking, a coherence between the ritual and economic aspects of the caste hierarchy. That is, the higher castes are generally better off than the lower. Many local exceptions may be cited to the rule, but they do not seriously affect the validity of the general proposition. This has been rendered possible by the fact that, historically, caste has been more flexible than is generally recognised. Castes which acquired economic or political power were able to raise themselves up in the ritual hierarchy. This process, occurring over a long period of time, has resulted in the upward movement of rich and powerful castes. The dominant castes of today are the products of this historical process. With strength of numbers, wealth and following, they occupy a strategic position to exploit the new opportunities for their own advantage.

Western education is the door to higher posts in every line, and an analysis of the social composition of students in colleges and post-graduate institutions would reveal the kind of relation which obtains between the traditional hierarchy and the new hierarchy which is coming into existence. This problem has not been studied systematically on an all-India basis but a few studies which have been made in Poona and Baroda suggest that the traditionally privileged groups maintain a near-monopoly over educational opportunity. The lower groups are not, by and large, taking much advantage of educational facilities, especially at the higher levels.

Generally Brahmins, Kayasths and Banias were the first to take to Western education and these groups still show a keener appreciation of the value of education than others. The values of these castes favour education. A relatively poor Brahmin or Kayasth father may pledge his small house or few acres of land to secure higher education for his son while a rich peasant may discourage his son from proceeding to college because he is needed to help in supervising the cultivation of the ancestral estate. In fact, it appears as though the land-owning non-Brahmin castes have had an initial resistance to education and this resistance began to give way only three or four decades ago.

In many parts of South India, Brahmins were the first to take advantage of the opportunities afforded by Western education. By the beginning of this century they had acquired a near-monopoly of posts in the government and dominated the liberal professions. This was resented by the non-Brahmin castes, and they founded the Justice Party in 1917 in Madras to advance their cause. Dislike, if not hatred, of Brahmin dominance brought together all non-Brahmins, a hospitable category which included not only all Hindus who were not Brahmins but also Muslims, Christians, Parsis, Anglo-Indians, etc. The leaders of the non-Brahmin movement demanded reservation of seats and scholarship in schools and colleges, preference in appointment to government posts and finally, representation in local self-government bodies.

The Justice Party functioned as a political party which cooperated with the British Government when the Congress was leading the struggle against the British. During this period, the non-Brahmin leaders obtained all the concessions and preferences which they were seeking, and several discriminatory rules against the Brahmins were built into the administration. As a result of the joint operation of the concessions and preferences in favour of the non-Brahmins and discrimination against the Brahmins, the latter lost their pre-eminence. In fact it was during this period that Brahmins migrated from South India to towns and cities in the North.

The point which I wish to make is that in south India there was an early reaction against the Brahmin's monopoly of the new opportunities, and as a result, a few non-Brahmin castes have replaced the Brahmins. But it is important to note that the chief beneficiaries of the non-Brahmin movement are the high non-Brahmin castes, usually the land-owning, dominant castes, and *not* the numerically small poor, low castes or the Harijans. It is true, however, that a few individuals amongst the latter rose to high positions, and even more important the castes from which they came became aware, as a result of the Movement, of the importance of education as a means of improving their position.

In Independent India the dominant castes have become even more powerful thanks to the introduction of adult suffrage. And they have used this power to strengthen further their position. Thus, in Mysore, the non-Brahmin movement was at first sought to be justified on the ground that Brahmins had throughout history used their privileged position as makers and interpreters of law to secure for themselves all kinds of advantages and at the expense of the other groups. The main aim of the Movement at this time was to displace the Brahmin. After this was accomplished, the non-Brahmin castes competed among themselves for concessions and preferences. Among the non-Brahmins, only the Harijans were (and still are) treated as a group deserving special treatment, and everyone else was backward. The latter were not distinguished into more and less backward. Under these circumstances each caste was allotted seats in colleges, posts in government and ministerships in the cabinet on the basis of its numerical strength. This has given rise to the widespread complaint that the "two major communities" are collaring all the benefits and the others are made to suffer.

But the Movement has certainly helped to distribute power, position and the means to both viz, education, among several castes instead of confining them to one or two castes as before. And there is less wastage of talent than before though even now there is considerable wastage if we compare India with any developed country. But then the severe discrimination practised against Brahmins was unfair as well as stupid. It led to the immediate lowering of standards everywhere as people were chosen to posts on grounds of caste and not on grounds of ability and character.

Yet another aspect of caste needs to be mentioned here. The association of each caste with one or more hereditary occupations and their gradation into high and low have resulted in most Indians' developing a deep dislike for manual labour. Villagers consider agriculture to be very tough work but manly and worthwhile, but at the same time they envy the man who earns his livelihood sitting in an office chair writing something and issuing orders to all and sundry. When a peasant owns enough land he retires from actual cultivation and confines himself to supervision of others' work. Villagers who have been to school show an aversion to agricultural work. Their aim is to get a white-collared job or to engage themselves in trade.

Villagers consider that an educated man or an official—in fact, anyone whom they respect—should not carry a heavy object, let alone do manual labour. Doing manual labour is the symbol of lowly status, just as not doing it is the symbol of high status. The same attitudes are prevalent in our offices. It would be interesting to make a study of the proportion of peons to other staff in government offices, and also to make a study of how peons spent their 'working' hours.

In the home too, there is a tendency to employ as many servants as possible. This tendency is accentuated by the fact that Indian men are generally illiterate with their hands and also because caste comes in the way of servants doing several kinds of work. The cook will not wash the vessels, the servant will not clean the lavatories, and the *mali* will not sweep the garden.

I am mentioning the above facts to show that hierarchical attitudes are deeply ingrained. They come out in unexpected places. Foreign social scientists are astonished that residential quarters built by the government for its employees in Delhi should observe the hierarchical principle so scrupulously. Granting the need for relating housing accommodation to income-level, should each category of housing be built in compact blocks? Could not the different categories of housing be mixed in each block?

The traditional association between a caste and an occupation has resulted in the prevalence of a certain continuum between rural and urban occupations. Thus rural Barbers when they migrate to towns either work in 'hair-cutting saloons', Washermen start laundries, Smiths work in furniture shops, Oilmen sell, if not press, oil, Malis work as gardeners, Chamars work in shoe shops and Brahmins are teachers, lawyers and cooks. Practising an occupation similar to the traditional, and staying in an area where one's caste-fellows stay, people carry into towns the hierarchical attitudes of the village. (Our towns are usually only demographically towns and not socially.)

This is specially true of the poorer people and of the smaller towns. Residential areas in towns have acquired class values, and as usually there is also a certain amount of association of caste or ethnic group with residential area, castes have a tendency to be pigeonholed, in ordinary talk, into classes. I am not stating here that all members of a caste belong to the same class. Heterogeneity of class affiliation is greater with the better off castes than with the poorer castes. For instance, Brahmins and Kayasthas would show greater heterogeneity than Harijans. The point which I am trying to make here is that because of the traditional association of a caste with an occupation and because of the tendency for migration to occur in groups—either kin or caste—there is a rural-urban continuum. People in towns, especially smaller towns, retain caste attitudes and values. The pattern of settlement makes possible the identification of an urban area with a caste and class. Our urban people continue to live in a hierarchical world contrary to the popular impression that urban occupations, small families and absence of pollution enable people to live in 'freedom'. This impression also fails to take note of the intimate ties existing between people in towns and their relatives in villages. I have earlier mentioned the characteristically urban expressions of caste.

There is yet another feature of Indian industrial life which reveals a close relation between caste and class. There is a tendency for a specialised task in a factory to become the monopoly of a caste or regional group. One may speak of 'workshop homogeneity'. Thus in a Baroda factory, immigrants from UP, non-Brahmin Maharashtrians and lower caste Gujeratis, each tended to be segregated in particular workshops doing the same kind of work. Gujarati Patidars and Maharashtrians from the upper castes preponderated in the white-collar jobs. It is fairly well-known that in appointment to jobs in factories considerations of kinship, caste and region are relevant. Appointments on 'rational' considerations are still not many.

Kin links are a strong feature of Indian life and they go beyond the nuclear family. Indian morality is still very largely made up of kin and caste obligations, and of the rules of religion. Kinship obligations are so strong that they tend to prevail over civic morality. Kinship loyalties tend to perpetuate class and caste differences and work against egalitarianism. Even those who have to profess publicly their belief in egalitarianism have strong kinship loyalties. This results in a divergence between their beliefs and conduct. When such divergence is widespread, people tend to be cynical. And cynicism is not the proper soil for rousing the necessary enthusiasm in the people for the Five Year Plans. It is surprising that Indian leaders do not show keener appreciation of this fact.

In brief, there are today two types of hierarchy, one, which is traditional and the other which is emergent. The traditional hierarchy is articulated in religious terms but it has also an important economic side. Caste system functioned best in a feudal, stationary economy with minimal occupational and spatial mobility. During British rule certain new social and economic forces came into existence which had the effect of making the structure less rigid. The abolition of slavery was followed by the starting of coffee and tea plantations, migration to Africa, Fiji Islands, Malaya and Ceylon, the starting of factories and mills in Bombay, Calcutta and other towns, and the new economic opportunities made possible by the political and administrative integration of the country and the development of communications. Generally the higher castes benefited most from these opportunities, but more rarely, the lower castes also did benefit.

The British started the policy of giving preference to the backward castes. The nationalist forces which were released under British rule, and certain British or European political institutions and ideas favoured egalitarianism. In Independent India several measures, some of them already mentioned, have been adopted which are designed to fight inequality and to further egalitarianism. It must be mentioned here, however, that it was during British rule that there came into existence an Indian middle class, which while not organised on national or regional lines, had its own interests to maintain and further. This class is full of class and caste attitudes and it is this class which has provided the leaders, especially at local levels. The bulk of Indian bureaucracy comes from this class.

There are those who argue that everyone should concentrate on increasing the size of the national cake and that it is obvious that the bigger the cake the greater the chances of everyone having more. This argument is advanced by those who are already getting a good share of the cake. They do not realise that it is not easy to convince workers that a bigger cake will necessarily mean a bigger share for the workers. And unless they are convinced that they and the country are going to benefit from the increased production, they will not put forward their best. Methods which brought about prosperity to Victorian England are slightly out of date in the modern world. Indian workers will certainly compare their conditions with those of their Russian and Chinese counterparts.

There are then two hierarchies in India, leaving aside the 'functional hierarchy' which prevails during working hours. (Every farm, firm, factory and office has its own hierarchy.) The Indian social structure underwent a modicum of liberalisation under the British, and the Indian Government has initiated several measures intended to reduce inequality. But the measures are half-hearted and full of loopholes. Above all there is a failure to realise the magnitude and nature of the problem. Intelligence and commonsense are not harnessed in combating inequality. Good intentions alone are not enough.

Constitutional Safeguards

The Constitution of India prescribes protection and safeguards for Scheduled Castes, Scheduled Tribes and other Backward Classes, either specifically or by way of general rights of citizens with the object of promoting their educational and economic interests and of removing certain social disabilities the Scheduled Castes were subject to. These are:—

(i) the abolition of 'Untouchability' and the forbidding of its practice in any form (Art. 17);

(ii) the promotion of their educational and economic interests and their protection from social injustice and all forms of exploitation (Art. 46);

(iii) the throwing open of Hindu religious institutions of a public character to all classes and sections of Hindus (Art. 25);

(iv) the removal of any disability, liability, restriction or condition with regard to access to shops, public restaurants, hotels and places of public entertainment, the use of wells, tanks, bathing ghats, roads and places of public resort maintained wholly or partly out of State funds or dedicated to the use of the general public (Art. 15);

(v) the right to practise any profession or carry on any occupation, trade or business (Art. 19);

(vi) the forbidding of any denial of admission to educational institutions maintained by the State or receiving aid out of State funds (Art. 29);

(vii) the obligation of the State to consider their claims in the making of appointments to public services and reservation for them in case of inadequate representation (Arts. 16 and 335);

(viii) special representation in Parliament and State Legislatures for a period of twenty years (Arts. 330, 332 and 334);

(ix) the setting up of advisory councils and separate departments in the States and the appointment of a Special Officer at the Centre to promote their welfare and safeguard their interests (Arts. 164, 338 and Fifth Schedule); and

(x) special provision for the administration and control of scheduled and tribal areas (Art. 244 and Fifth and Sixth Schedules).

—*India* 1960.

47 • Congress Working Committee Resolution: *Language Policy, February 24, 1965* *

One of India's most serious problems is the inability of its people to communicate with each other. The dimensions of the problem are indicated by the constitution which selected fourteen major languages from over a thousand as official for Union purposes. Originally Hindi, which is Indo-Aryan or Sanskrit based and spoken with variations by 40 per cent of the population concentrated in the north, was to become the national language in fifteen years. As a concession to the non-Hindi south English was also to be considered official in the interim. Furthermore, a state legislature could designate any regional language for its official use.

Constitutional provisions did not resolve the multilingual problem. Conflict was reduced by the States Reorganization Act of 1955, which redrew state boundaries roughly along linguistic lines. However, the southern states, whose regional languages are Dravidian rather than Sanskrit based, successfully continue to oppose the imposition of Hindi as the national language.

The Congress Working Committee Resolution of 1965, following riots in Madras, was another capitulation to southern linguistic demands in its agreement to continue English as an associate language, as well as agreement that All-India Civil Service examinations may be taken in Hindi, English, or one of the principal regional languages. The establishment of a single national language, with its implications for national unity, is thus postponed indefinitely.

The Working Committee regret to note that there still exist in the minds of our people apprehensions regarding the language policy of the Government and its implementation despite clarifications in the resolutions of the Congress, the resolution of the National Integration Conference, the decisions of the Government of India and the assurances given by the late Prime Minister, Pandit Jawaharlal Nehru and reiterated by the present Prime Minister, Shri Lal Bahadur Shastri.

2. The Congress has always been clear that the stability and progress of this vast country with all its diversities depend upon solutions of all delicate issues by consent and cooperation of the people. Accordingly, it has been working for the evolution of basic principles in relation to the language policy which are just and fair to the people in all the States and are in keeping with the essential unity of the country. In this the country had the benefit of the guidance of Mahatma Gandhi and Pandit Jawaharlal Nehru. As a result, certain consensus has emerged in relation to the language policy.

3. It was in this context that the Constitution of India had laid down that Hindi should be the official language of the Union, at the same time, recognising all the principal regional languages as the national languages of the country. In accordance with this Constitutional provision, it was expected that all necessary steps would be taken to use and enrich these languages. The Committee feel that adequate attention has not been paid to this aspect. The Committee urge upon

* *AICC Economic Review,* Vol. XVI, No. 19 (March 10, 1965), pp. 33–34. By permission.

the Government of India to devote greater attention to the use and development of Hindi and all the other national languages in cooperation with the State Governments. The Working Committee want to make it clear that the country cannot go far enough nor shall we be able to carry our people by the millions to the destined goal of a new, just and prosperous society unless the objective of full development of the national languages is achieved.

4. There is considerable fear, however, in the public mind that Hindi or English is going to be imposed upon them. The Working Committee would like to reiterate the firm resolve of the Congress to adhere to the assurances given by the late Prime Minister, Pandit Jawaharlal Nehru. The Congress stands by these assurances.

5. Section 3 of the Official Languages Act, 1963 prescribes as under:

> Notwithstanding the expiration of the period of fifteen years from the commencement of the Constitution, the English language may, as from the appointed day, continue to be used in addition to Hindi—
> (a) for all the official purposes of the Union for which it was being used immediately before that day; and
> (b) for the transaction of business in Parliament.

6. Apart from this, according to these assurances, every State will have complete and unfettered freedom to continue to transact its own business in the language of its choice which may be the regional language, Hindi or English. Secondly, except as between the States having the same official language communications from one State to another will be either in Hindi accompanied by authentic English translation or in English. Thirdly, non-Hindi States will be free to correspond with the Central Government in English. Fourthly, in the transaction of business at the Central level, English will continue to be used as an associate official language in the intervening period. No change will be made in these arrangements without the consent of the States.

7. The Working Committee note with regret that the three-language formula has not so far been implemented by some of the States. The Working Committee feel it necessary that immediate steps are taken to effectively implement the three-language formula evolved by the National Integration Conference and accepted by the country.

8. The Working Committee also considered the question of the medium for the examination for the All India Services. The Working Committee recommend that as soon as possible examinations for the All India Services should be held in Hindi, English and the principal regional languages and that candidates may be given an option to use any of these languages for the purposes thereof.

9. As this will raise other questions regarding the quality of tests in terms of fair and proper application of the standards of moderation and about the various steps having an equitable share in the All India Services, the Working Committee recommend to the Government of India that this matter should be examined in all its aspects.

10. The Working Committee recommend to the Government of India and the Government of the States to examine the steps that should be taken including amendments to the Official Languages Act of 1963 to give effect to the assurances given by Pandit Jawaharlal Nehru and all the recommendations made in this resolution.

48 • J. C. Sandesava: *Migration and Metropolitan Living—A Study of Indian Cities* *

The following selection illustrates the effect of the growing flood of indigent rural workers into already overcrowded cities which are unable to provide adequate employment, housing, or other welfare services. India's major problem is its vast population of about 500,000,000, growing at an annual rate estimated at 1.5 to 2.0 per cent. The effort to provide food for the additional 5–10,000,000 mouths per year is a formidable task in itself, and one which even with foreign aid leaves total consumption at a bare subsistence level. The population is largely rural, based in some 500,000 villages, but the land can no longer support the increasing numbers. The famine of 1966–1967, centered in Bihar, indicates the dimensions of the problem.

The process of population transfers to cities has been going on in India for years as indeed in the rest of the world. In this urban centres with greater numbers seem to have been bigger gainers. What are the causes of this transfer?

The causes of migration are many. They are often grouped under the broad heads of the *push* and the *pull* factors. Such forces as tend to drive an individual out of a given place are referred to as the push factors and such others as tend to pull an individual to another place are called the pull factors. This distinction, however, is not clear-cut inasmuch as the one may be dependent upon and, in fact, related to the other in a most intricate manner and it is extremely difficult to know which is the initial, independent, motivating factor. Thus, for instance, a push from the village may be operative because there is some pull from the city; on the other hand, it might operate without such a pull.

What were the factors that led migrants to come to the cities in the period of some fifteen to twenty years prior to 1954?

Of the 13,369 families investigated for the Bombay Survey, 2,247 or 17 per cent were families whose heads had come to the city in or after 1941. This number is exclusive of displaced families. These 2,247 families accommodated 2,285 earners. It was found that only 389 or 13.5 per cent of them were lured or pulled to the city—'the prospects of better employment' being the magnet. Causes like 'routine transfer,' 'came with the family' and such other non-alignable factors accounted for 310 or about 11 per cent. This leaves us with a huge balance of about three-fourths of the total migrants who can all be described as having been pushed out of their homelands. 'Unemployment,' 'meagre income,' 'insufficient land to cultivate' and similar other economic causes, and, in a limited number of cases, social factors like 'family differences,' 'class tensions,' etc., acted as the push factors.

About 75 and 70 per cent of the Poona and Kanpur migrants respectively can be classified as having been pushed out. The Calcutta report concluded that about 43 per cent seemed to have been pushed to the city while the pull factors were operative in bringing about 50–51 per cent to the city. The Lucknow Survey which reported the migrants by the pull and the push factors in the tables also,

* *Economic Weekly,* Vol. XVI (May 9, 1964), pp. 807–810.

revealed that whereas the former were operative in case of only 19 per cent the latter accounted for 35 per cent. In a great majority of these cases, economic factors exerted the push.

Faced with a homeland that is hostile and with prospects which promise to be no better, emigrants move to the towns. There is no doubt that the level of living in urban areas is generally higher than in villages. Let us however examine the economic content of the material well-being of urban dwellers.

It is difficult to quantify the exact amount of money that may be considered necessary for ensuring at least a minimum level of living in urban centres. Speaking roughly, if an income of Rs 35 per month per head may be considered to be minimum, families below this line may be deemed to be poor, and families below Rs 25 per month per head may be deemed to be destitute. Accordingly, 37 per cent of the Bombay families would be regarded as poor and 20 per cent destitute. About 5 per cent of the families had a per capita income of less than Rs 15 per month. It is not possible in all cases to classify the families of other cities on these lines of less than Rs 35 and Rs 25 as the groupings differ a bit. But a rough comparative picture may be drawn by relying upon the next best adjacent lines. Here the figures for the city of Calcutta are most telling. At a poverty line of Rs 40 or less about 77 per cent of the multi-households would pass as poor. At a destitution line of Rs 25 or less about 44 per cent of the families would be regarded as destitute. The Kanpur Survey revealed about 57 per cent of the families having a per capita income of Rs 40 or less.

The Poona Survey had the poverty and destitution lines in terms of adult units. If we put a monthly income of Rs 37.50 or less and of Rs 25 or less per month per adult unit as marking poverty and destitution respectively, about 64 per cent of the Poona families would be poor and 41 per cent destitute. The data on the Lucknow Survey relate to the families' total monthly income. Four-fifths of the Lucknow families had a total monthly income of less than Rs 150 and 56 per cent had less than Rs 75.

A significant number of the families in the metropolitan communities are thus destitute. Many more are poor. But even this standard of living, whatever it is, is better than that obtainable in smaller places. For, otherwise, emigration would not have taken place to that extent. . . .

It is difficult to define what precisely constitutes overcrowding. It is obviously necessary to take into account not only the aggregate number of occupants, but their age and sex distribution and marriage relation as well. Also, in addition to the number of rooms, the floor space in the house has also relevance. It is only when all these factors are properly accounted for, assessed and related that one can have a proper index of overcrowding.

The data available from the city surveys do not go into all these niceties. What we have are data on the number of persons per room and the per capita floor space. These indices are admittedly rough but they are fairly reliable indicators.

If more than two persons to a room is taken to constitute overcrowding, three-fourths of the Bombay families were living in overcrowded houses; 47 per cent had between 3–5 persons to a room; 25 per cent between 6–9, 3.4 per cent between 10–13, 0.5 per cent between 14–17 and 0.2 per cent over 17. The Calcutta Survey, on the basis of over three persons to a room, showed that 46 per cent of the multi-households were suffering from overcrowding. On the same basis, 56 per cent of the Poona families were living in overcrowded houses. The Kanpur definition relates the number of rooms to adult units, treating persons under 14 as one-half units. Taking more than two adult units to constitute overcrowding, about one-half of the families were suffering from overcrowding. . . .

This is a general picture of Indian metropolitan housing conditions. There would be, in addition, dependents back at home who could not be brought to the towns for want of accommodation. And there would be still others who could not afford or get even such accommodation. For them shops and restaurants, factories and go-downs, nooks and corners, pavements and public streets are the "homes."

All this may be summed up by saying that whereas for a chosen few metropolitan living may represent a change for the better—involving a change from a bad place to a good one or from a good place to a better one—for the vast majority it is a change which can hardly be described that way. For them it is only a change from a worse place to a bad one. And this fact is of considerable significance.

An area experiences an increase in its population by excess of births over deaths and of immigration over emigration. While the problems presented by natural increase in population in the metropolitan areas are serious enough, the reasons thereof and their implications may be investigated separately. In what follows we confine the analysis to the economic implications of a continued increase in population in the metropolitan areas due to migration, though some of the points discussed below under heads (3), (4) and (5) have relevance even when population undergoes a natural increase.

(1) Migration, it is well-known, is a selective process. It is selective not only in sex and age but in the quality of population as well. It selects more of males, more of persons in the working age-groups. Also it picks the more vital, the more vigorous, the more enterprising of the population.

The loss to village life due to the emigration of these sections of the population can be easily surmised. It is agreed that the availability of good opportunities at home would prevent emigration. But it is equally true that their absence exercises a further depressing influence on the region concerned. More of the dependents and more of the unenterprising lot remain at home. They are either pure consumers or, as compared to those who migrate, perhaps less productive, actually or potentially. Secondly, those who leave the village on reaching adult age also carry with them costs such as those of education, public health, etc., which the village must have incurred. There is also a loss of potential revenue. The city, on the other hand, stands to gain. It receives the productive and the enterprising elements free of cost on whom other communities have incurred the liabilities. These elements represent additional sources of revenue to the city. . . .

Let us now conclude. Many of the metropolitan families have indeed very low per capita incomes, and yet the fact remains that even these are higher than those generally obtainable in rural areas. One wonders though when all social costs like overheads, stresses and strains experienced by the earners and dependents because of low income, bad housing, separation, etc., are duly accounted for, whether there would remain in the overall community balance-sheet much gain, if any.

Most of the migrants to the cities, we have seen, are pushed out their homelands. If, therefore, sufficient economic opportunities are created at home to retain the people who otherwise would knock at the city gates, it would go a long way towards solving many of the city's problems. In the absence of this, attempts to improve the economic and social life of metropolitan communities would provide only short-term relief and would tend to prove to be self-defeating with the passage of time. Increase in the frequency of buses and trains, widening of the streets, creation of separate zones, house-building and slum-clearance, and welfare and community centres are indeed all very necessary for efficient metropolitan life and for increasing its welfare content. But all these won't achieve much unless the problem is tackled from the other end too.

49 • Iqbal Narian: *The Unlocking of Thought Processes—A Study of the Nature of the Western Impact on Modern Indian Political Thought* *

The introduction of Western institutions and norms under British rule had a modernizing effect on the traditional society and culture of India. British nineteenth-century liberalism injected into India's stratified, non-egalitarian society concepts of equality before the law, constitutionalism, secularism, and parliamentary government with a bureaucracy based on achievement rather than ascription. Iqbal Narian discusses the interaction between British and Indian concepts. However, the new generation of leaders moving up from state to national posts are less Westernized and more parochial in attitude, education, and background than Nehru and most of his colleagues. The consequences of this change are as yet unforeseen.

The British rule in India did not provide for just a chance contact between a conqueror and the conquered. It meant essentially the meeting of two different peoples, of two cultures, of two modes of thought and life. What is equally important is that the British rule brought in its wake new means of communion both in terms of modern means of communication and a common medium of thought exchange in the form of the English language. India was thus linked with the outside world and its thought currents which began to invade the country through the system of Western education that the British introduced here. The result was that the Indian genius which has been assimilative through the ages was exposed to an overwhelmingly new set of influences which were not confined merely to the values, ideas and institutions of the British people, whose influence, however, was the most dominating, but also to other peoples of the West. This impact was not short-lived, intermittent and remote. It was spread over a long span of time and was both continuous and close, thereby becoming both vital and living. It was an upsurge that overtook generations of people from Raja

* *Indian Journal of Political Science,* Vol. XXII (Oct.-Dec. 1961), pp. 293–300. By permission.

Ram Mohan Roy to Nehru, becoming most often a mould in which many a thought structure and life pattern were cast. And it came to stay almost through a gradual process of percolation. It should not be forgotten, however, that the Western impact has been a very significant but not the only factor in determining and moulding the thought process in modern India.

The Western impact has been an all-absorbing process. Its span of influence was not confined to any one or more aspects of life, or any community or region. It influenced life as a whole both of the nation and of the individual. Our thought-structure, our value-pattern, our mode of life, our cultural moorings, our education, our industry, our socio-economic structure, our national consciousness and movement, our political horizons, our concepts, our beliefs—all were shaken for a time, as if under the impact of an earthquake. They were shaken but not necessarily uprooted. The shock which has perhaps been phenomenal in the history of India was absorbed in most cases and could not be said to have become a process that uprooted the Indian people from their cultural moorings. Nor could the shock have a uniform effect. It could and did have a greater impact on some aspects of thought and life and less on others. Still the impact has been at once wide and deep and that too on life as a whole, both in its ideals and realities. Not merely this. It has affected the entire people, beginning with the upper strata and slowly filtering down to the lower levels. Again, it has spread over all the regions, primarily, of course, in urban India which became the cultural nursery of a new elite under the impact of the English language, Western education and culture.

We are here concerned, however, with the examination of the nature of Western impact merely in relation to modern Indian political thought.

If one were to view the nature of the impact in this specific context, a few distinctive features would emerge:

First, by and large, this impact was liberal. It unleashed liberalising forces in the thought process of the Indian people who now became conscious of their orthodox bearings and began to question their foundations. Faith began to give way to reason and acceptance was replaced by argument. There was the dawn of a new sense of the dignity of man and his potentialities. This in turn loosened the hold of fate on human psychology and Indian people were imbued with a spirit of self-reliance and an urge for action. It was liberal in a limited political sense also. Indian people now found the foreign yoke galling on their shoulders. They had a new political horizon to achieve—a horizon which promised them liberty, equality and self-government.

Secondly, liberalism brought in its wake the spirit of humanism and progress which had a far-reaching impact both on the thought process and thought structure of the country. Indians now became critics of their own customs, traditions, and institutions. Reform movements came in. Caste structure received its first shock. The process of emancipation of women started. Men began to think in terms of the education of women, curbing of the purdah system, giving up of the *Sati Pratha,* encouraging of widow re-marriage and so on. A vision of unity in diversity was also provided by such movements as the Brahmo Samaj. Service of the community received a premium in such cults as the Ram Krishna Mission. When this is said, it is not claimed that western impact alone was responsible for all this. The contention merely is that it struck the wedge. Many other factors of no less importance stepped in to add to the tempo of the new thought currents. The cumulative result was the birth of a new spirit which expressed itself in the socio-religious movements of the 19th century which may in a way be said to combine the Renaissance and Reformation in the Indian context.

Thirdly, the western impact turned out to be a cohesive force through the English language which became the official language of the people. Language barriers were broken. Regional walls began to collapse. Indian people, irrespective of the region to which they belonged, could now communicate to each other their woes and troubles which they had to undergo in the process of colonial rule with all the exploitation and injustice that are its natural concomitants. Suffering at the hands of a common enemy and a common struggle against the foreign rulers helped the emergence of a national entity to which the western impact in the form of a common official language has no mean contribution to make. One can best appreciate it against the background of the linguistic turmoil and bloodshed in Assam and elsewhere which is one of the potent threats to our national integration today.

Fourthly, alongside the cohesive aspect, the west—*and here the reference is primarily to the British influence*—brought in the communal factor in Indian politics. It is a matter of common knowledge that the British followed *the policy of counterpoise* popularly known as the policy of *divide and rule*. The last and the most devastating phase of this policy assumed the form of Muslim communalism. Thus a new fold was provided in India's political texture. This did not merely infect the course of practical politics but also twisted the thought processes into communal channels as is obvious from the two-nation theory of Mr. Jinnah and equally reactionary concept of Hindu nationalism. Paradoxically enough both the cohesive and the communal have come down to us as a legacy of the British rule, the latter serving as the antithesis and contradiction of the former and, at the present juncture in its added ramifications of caste, region, and language, the last out-balancing the other two.

It may also be added that there were other reactionary aspects of the British rule—such as racial discrimination, economic exploitation in the name of free trade which resulted in discouragement to Indian genius and abject poverty of the masses, political injustice and suppression. All these also left an impact on the Indian mind, giving birth to extremist and revolutionary trends in Indian politics.

The western impact appears to have assumed several forms in its operative aspect. These may broadly be categorised as *positive* and *negative*. In its positive aspect the impact assumed the form of *inspiration* and in its negative aspect that of *reaction*. In the former, western ideas, concepts and institutions became at once the objects of envy and emulation, at once a pathfinder and a battle cry. In the latter, there started in the country revivalist movements and trends. A typical example of a revivalist movement one finds in Arya Samaj with its '*Go back to the Vedas*' ideal. The other revivalist trends also stood for reviving India's pristine glory. These trends represented an effort for rehabilitating the faith of the Indian people in their cultural heritage and in themselves and for providing an anchor to the country's drooping national prestige in the name of her spiritual mission for the west—a familiar cult particularly associated with the name of Swami Vivekanand.

Let us examine here the western impact in its positive aspect at a somewhat greater length, because it provided one of the significant sources of modern Indian political thought. The impact appears to have assumed the following forms:

(*i*) *Ideological:* Intelligentsia in India, which assumed the leadership of the national movements since its inception was bred and nourished in the traditions of western education. Their minds were thus fed on western political ideals. Their intellectual moorings which in turn determined their thought processes could be traced to individualism of Bentham and Herbert Spencer and liberalism of Morley, to the philosophy of the French Revolution with its inspiring banner of liberty, equality, and fraternity, to the fervour of Mill and Bright for representative institutions, to the call of Cavour, Garibaldi, and Mazzini for national unity, national liberation and sane nationalism, to the idealism of Hegel, to the revolutionary fervour and socialist vision of Marx and so on. If one were to pass from the particular to the general, one could say that rationalism, universalism, secularism etc., were the other ideological trends that enthused the Indian mind.

(*ii*) *Conceptual and institutional:* Not merely that. As a corollary to the ideological impact, one finds that by and large West provided the framework both for our concepts and institutions. Our national struggle came to be not merely a fight for freedom but also for western concepts and institutions. We were enamoured of such concepts and institutions as representative government, parliamentary system, rule of law which were obviously British, and Fundamental Rights which we envisaged on the French and the American models. The Nehru Report of 1928 which was the first flower of India's constitutional genius is largely the expression of the Western impact in its conceptual and institutional aspects. Later also, in our quest of federalism and separation of executive and judiciary the source of inspiration was largely provided by the U.S.A. Similar has been the case with our Socialist vision (particularly leftist Socialist vision of earlier days as distinguished from Congress Socialism of to-day) which in its fundamentals can be traced to western sources, more significantly to Marx and Lenin. It may also be noted that western concepts and institutions came to constitute for us criteria of value judgment with regard to constitutional issues—a measuring rod both for the quality and extent of constitutional advance. It was on this basis that we criticised and judged the various measures of constitutional advance, particularly from the days of the Act for the better Government of India almost to the Mountbatten Settlement.

This much about the western impact as a source of *inspiration.* Now let us turn to its role as *a reaction.* Here it assumed the form of a cultural challenge from the West to the East. India found herself in the vortex of a cultural crisis. It was almost in the grip of a Hamlet-like dilemma, with the question *to be or not to be* staring her in the face. The response came almost in the process of Hegelian dialectics. The thesis was provided by the liberals who in their honest infatuation for western concepts and institutions stood for westernisation in their outlook, political vision and methodology of constitutional advance. A reaction, as if by way of an *antithesis,* started in terms of a separate entity of the East equally proud, equally exalting, equally exhilarating. It was in the wake of this reaction that there came in two trends in Indian thought—one the *trend of revivalism* and of reassertion of India's spiritual supremacy and institutions and another of challenging the foundations and decrying the superstructure of western civilization in the name of materialism. Swami Dayanand,

Swami Vivekanand, Bal Gangadhar Tilak, even to some extent Gandhi and to-day Vinoba and Jayaprakash Narain represent this phase. . . .

The western impact has thus been an important factor but not the only factor in influencing the thought processes of modern India. The impact has neither been exclusive nor monopolistic. However, it has certainly been profound and many-sided. Its importance lies in creating an intellectual ferment, in presenting new horizons and throwing new challenges, and in creating a stir from within, whether as an *inspiration* or as *a reaction,* which ultimately unlocked the thought processes. The depth of the impact can be gauged from the fact that the western impact appears to mark almost a dividing line in our thought processes which can hardly claim an organic unity with the thought processes and structure of ancient India, as one can link up the modern Western political thought to its Greek ancestry.

SECTION TWO

Political Institutions

50 • *The Constitution of India* *

The constitution of India, consisting of 395 articles and totaling 392 pages in the official text, is the longest in the world. The articles establishing parliamentary government on both national and state levels were taken largely from the British Government of India Act of 1935. Some aspects of the Presidency and judicial system were borrowed from the United States constitution.

The following selections are sections on the Fundamental Rights of Citizens and the Directive Principles. In the former, citizens are given freedom of speech, assembly, and other rights, but each is limited by the right of the State under certain conditions to restrict their exercise in the interest of the integrity of India, security of the State, public order, etc. Under these restrictions Preventive Detention Acts have been passed, but on the whole the power has been used with restraint. The Directive Principles unlike the Fundamental Rights have moral but not legal force, but they indicate the social and economic goals of the nation.

Part III. Fundamental Rights

14. The State shall not deny to any person equality before the law or the equal protection of the laws within the territory of India.

15. (1) The State shall not discriminate against any citizen on grounds only of religion, race, caste, sex, place of birth or any of them.

(2) No citizen shall, on grounds only of religion, race, caste, sex, place of birth or any of them, be subject to any disability, liability, restriction or condition with regard to—

(*a*) access to shops, public restaurants, hotels and places of public entertainment; or

(*b*) the use of wells, tanks, bathing ghats, roads and places of public resort maintained wholly or partly out of State funds or dedicated to the use of the general public.

(3) Nothing in this article shall prevent the State from making any special provision for women and children.

[(4) Nothing in this article or in clause (2) of article 29 shall prevent the

* As modified up to May, 1965.

State from making any special provision for the advancement of any socially and educationally backward classes of citizens or for the Scheduled Castes and the Scheduled Tribes.]

16. (1) There shall be equality of opportunity for all citizens in matters relating to employment or appointment to any office under the State.

(2) No citizen shall, on grounds only of religion, race, caste, sex, descent, place of birth, residence, or any of them, be ineligible for, or discriminated against in respect of, any employment or office under the State.

(3) Nothing in this article shall prevent Parliament from making any law prescribing, in regard to a class or classes of employment or appointment to an office [under the Government of, or any local or other authority within, a State or Union territory, any requirement as to residence within that State or Union territory] prior to such employment or appointment.

(4) Nothing in this article shall prevent the State from making any provision for the reservation of appointments or posts in favour of any backward class of citizens which, in the opinion of the State, is not adequately represented in the services under the State.

(5) Nothing in this article shall affect the operation of any law which provides that the incumbent of an office in connection with the affairs of any religious or denominational institution or any member of the governing body thereof shall be a person professing a particular religion or belonging to a particular denomination.

17. "Untouchability" is abolished and its practice in any form is forbidden. The enforcement of any disability arising out of "Untouchability" shall be an offence punishable in accordance with law. . . .

19. (1) All citizens shall have the right—

(*a*) to freedom of speech and expression;

(*b*) to assemble peaceably and without arms;

(*c*) to form associations or unions;

(*d*) to move freely throughout the territory of India;

(*e*) to reside and settle in any part of the territory of India;

(*f*) to acquire, hold and dispose of property; and

(*g*) to practise any profession, or to carry on any occupation, trade or business.

[(2) Nothing in sub-clause (*a*) of clause (1) shall affect the operation of any existing law, or prevent the State from making any law, in so far as such law imposes reasonable restrictions on the exercise of the right conferred by the said sub-clause in the interests of [the sovereignty and integrity of India,] the security of the State, friendly relations with foreign States, public order, decency or morality, or in relation to contempt of court, defamation or incitement to an offence.]

(3) Nohing in sub-clause (*b*) of the said clause shall affect the operation of any existing law in so far as it imposes, or prevent the State from making any law imposing, in the interests of [the sovereignty and integrity of India or] public order, reasonable restrictions on the exercise of the right conferred by the said sub-clause. . . .

21. No person shall be deprived of his life or personal liberty except according to procedure established by law.

22. (1) No person who is arrested shall be detained in custody without being informed, as soon as may be, of the grounds for such arrest nor shall he be denied the right to consult, and to be defended by, a legal practitioner of his choice.

(2) Every person who is arrested and detained in custody shall be produced before the nearest magistrate within a period of twenty-four hours of such arrest excluding the time necessary for the journey from the place of arrest to the court of the magistrate and no such person shall be detained in custody beyond the said period without the authority of a magistrate.

(3) Nothing in clauses (1) and (2) shall apply—

(*a*) to any person who for the time being is an enemy alien; or

(*b*) to any person who is arrested or detained under any law providing for preventive detention.

(4) No law providing for preventive detention shall authorise the detention of a person for a longer period than three months unless—

(*a*) an Advisory Board consisting of persons who are, or have been, or are qualified to be appointed as, Judges of a High Court has reported before the expiration of the said period of three months that there is in its opinion sufficient cause for such detention: . . .

(7) Parliament may by law prescribe—

(*a*) the circumstances under which, and the class or classes of cases in which, a person may be detained for a period longer than three months under any law providing for preventive detention without obtaining the opinion of an Advisory Board in accordance with the provisions of subclause (*a*) of clause (4);

(*b*) the maximum period for which any person may in any class or classes of cases be detained under any law providing for preventive detention; and

(*c*) the procedure to be followed by an Advisory Board in an inquiry under sub-clause (*a*) of clause (4).

23. (1) Traffic in human beings and *begar* and other similar forms of forced labour are prohibited and any contravention of this provision shall be an offence punishable in accordance with law.

(2) Nothing in this article shall prevent the State from imposing compulsory service for public purposes, and in imposing such service the State shall not make any discrimination on grounds only of religion, race, caste or class or any of them.

24. No child below the age of fourteen years shall be employed to work in any factory or mine or engaged in any other hazardous employment.

25. (1) Subject to public order, morality and health and to the other provisions of this Part, all persons are equally entitled to freedom of conscience and the right freely to profess, practice and propagate religion.

(2) Nothing in this article shall affect the operation of any existing law or prevent the State from making any law—

(*a*) regulating or restricting any economic, financial, political or other secular activity which may be associated with religious practice;

(*b*) providing for social welfare and reform or the throwing open of Hindu religious institutions of a public character to all classes and sections of Hindus. . . .

29. (1) Any section of the citizens residing in the territory of India or any part thereof having a district language, script or culture of its own shall have the right to conserve the same.

(2) No citizen shall be denied admission into any educational institution maintained by the State or receiving aid out of State funds on grounds only of religion, race, caste, language or any of them. . . .

31. (1) No person shall be deprived of his property save by authority of law.

[(2) No property shall be compulsorily acquired or requisitioned save for a public purpose and save by authority of a law which provides for compensation for the property so acquired or requisitioned and either fixes the amount of the compensation or specifies the principles on which, and the manner in which, the compensation is to be determined and given; and no such law shall be called in question in any court on the ground that the compensation provided by that law is not adequate.

Part IV. Directive Principles of State Policy

36. In this Part, unless the context otherwise requires, "the State" has the same meaning as in Part III.

37. The provisions contained in this Part shall not be enforceable by any court, but the principles therein laid down are nevertheless fundamental in the governance of the country and it shall be the duty of the State to apply these principles in making laws.

38. The State shall strive to promote the welfare of the people by securing and protecting as effectively as it may a social order in which justice, social, economic and political, shall inform all the institutions of the national life.

39. The State shall, in particular, direct its policy towards securing—

(*a*) that the citizens, men and women equally, have the right to an adequate means of livelihood;

(*b*) that the ownership and control of the material resources of the community are so distributed as best to subserve the common good;

(*c*) that the operation of the economic system does not result in the concentration of wealth and means of production to the common detriment;

(*d*) that there is equal pay for equal work for both men and women;

(*e*) that the health and strength of workers, men and women, and the tender age of children are not abused and that citizens are not forced by economic necessity to enter avocations unsuited to their age or strength;

(*f*) that childhood and youth are protected against exploitation and against moral and material abandonment.

40. The State shall take steps to organise village panchayats and endow them with such powers and authority as may be necessary to enable them to function as units of self-government.

41. The State shall, within the limits of its economic capacity and development, make effective provision for securing the right to work, to education and to public assistance in cases of unemployment, old age, sickness and disablement, and in other cases of undeserved want.

42. The State shall make provision for securing just and human conditions of work and for maternity relief.

43. The State shall endeavour to secure, by suitable legislation or economic organisation or in any other way, to all workers, agricultural, industrial or otherwise, work, a living wage, conditions of work ensuring a decent standard of life and full enjoyment of leisure and social and cultural opportunities and, in particular, the State shall endeavour to promote cottage industries on an individual or cooperative basis in rural areas.

44. The State shall endeavour to secure for the citizens a uniform civil code throughout the territory of India.

45. The State shall endeavour to provide, within a period of ten years from the commencement of this Constitution, for free and compulsory education for all children until they complete the age of fourteen years.

46. The State shall promote with special care the educational and economic interests of the weaker sections of the people, and, in particular, of the Scheduled Castes and the Scheduled Tribes, and shall protect them from social injustice and all forms of exploitation.

47. The State shall regard the raising of the level of nutrition and the standard of living of its people and the improvement of public health as among its primary duties and, in particular, the State shall endeavour to bring about prohibition of the consumption except for medicinal purposes of intoxicating drinks and of drugs which are injurious to health.

48. The State shall endeavour to organize agriculture and animal husbandry on modern and scientific lines and shall, in particular, take steps for preserving and improving the breeds, and prohibiting the slaughter, of cows and calves and other milch and draught cattle.

49. It shall be the obligation of the State to protect every monument or place or object of artistic or historic interest, [declared by or under law made by Parliament] to be of national importance, from spoliation, disfigurement, destruction, removal, disposal or export, as the case may be.

50. The State shall take steps to separate the judiciary from the executive in the public services of the State.

51. The State shall endeavour to—

(*a*) promote international peace and security;

(*b*) maintain just and honourable relations between nations;

(*c*) foster respect for international law and treaty obligations in the dealings of organised peoples with one another; and

(*d*) encourage settlement of international disputes by arbitration.

51 • Rajni Kothari: *Parliamentary Government* *

Indian political institutions are still in a state of flux. Parliamentary government is deeply embedded in the constitution and in practice, but political usages or customs which give life and vitality to the system are still in the formative stage. Rajni Kothari, one of India's leading political scientists, discusses below the parliamentary system as it existed under Nehru's firm control as Prime Minister and as undisputed leader of the consistently successful Congress party. The ending of the Nehru era now puts to the test the strength of the system and its ability to adapt to changing political conditions.

Prior to the 1967 general elections, the role of opposition in the Lok Sabha was severely limited by the heavy Congress majority. Recent elections for the

* *Economic Weekly* (May 20, 1961), pp. 783–790.

first time, however, cut the Congress party to a small majority. There is still no other opposition party with a sufficient number of seats to act as a formal Loyal Opposition in the British sense, but the new opposition coalition in the Lok Sabha, tenuous as it may be, of the Jana Sangh, Swatantra, and other parties will oblige the Congress to act with greater circumspection in parliamentary matters in view of the ability of the opposition to question effectively and to propose motions of no confidence.

The Presidency is also in flux. The constitution provided for a President whose powers are considerably more than ceremonial, but it is singularly silent on the crucial issue of whether he may exercise his powers at his own discretion or only, as in the British system, on the advice and consent of the Prime Minister. To date the practice has been to follow the British model. The issue of the Presidency is further complicated by India's federal form of government which gives the President responsibilities to both the states and to the Union. Few problems arose when both central and state governments were controlled by the Congress party, but the 1967 elections, which placed non-Congress coalitions in power in several states, raise new problems and ambiguities about the exercise of presidential power.

It is necessary to emphasise at the outset that the Indian system has worked admirably well *within the limits of its constitutional frame work.* Unlike in so many "new" countries, the essentials of a free polity are preserved. Freedom of speech and association are jealously guarded; political opposition, organised or otherwise, is allowed full scope; new methods of diffusing power are being tried, *albeit* at times prematurely; sectional loyalties are restrained from assuming dangerous proportions. Public opinion, when expressed powerfully, is effective, although very often belatedly. And the party system, although weak and fragmentary, performs the all-important function of maintaining stability and political continuity. It has succeeded in providing a comprehensive frame of reference to the political process, thanks to a subtle dispensation of patronage and an intricate system of "connections" wielded by the ruling party.

The constitutional framework, within which this system works has its limitations. These become all the more serious because the traditions and conventions that enable some other democracies to overcome the shortcomings of their formal order have yet to evolve. The development of the institutional pattern can, however, be looked upon with some confidence. The evolution is on the right lines although it has a long way to go. But for the process to continue, momentary notions about the future institutional order should not be allowed to distract it from the mainstream of development. There is also reason to sound a note of warning about certain recent political developments. The position needs to be examined with a view to distinguish elements which advance democracy from those which impede it. . . .

The institutional assumptions underlying the system of government, based on the British model, adopted in India have been the object of continuous study, starting with the brilliant exposition of Walter Bagehot in mid-nineteenth century. The principal features of this system are representative democracy on the basis of a broad-based franchise, strong government under the guidance of a collectively responsible Cabinet, an independent judiciary, political organisation of the nation through political parties competing for power while agreeing on fundamentals, recognition of the pivotal role of the opposition in the scheme of government, political neutrality of the Head of State and the civil service and the principles of popular mandate, ministerial responsibility, and administrative continuity and anonymity.

Much of this arrangement is based on constitutional conventions and political usage regarding the relationship between the administration and political parties, the government and opposition, and Ministers and civil servants, many of which are lacking in India, as revealed by the experience of the last decade and more. The absence of these conventions and the development of new usages as well as the existence of a different climate of opinion account for the gap between the theory of parliamentary government and the actual practice in India.

Political attitudes like tradition are a product of history and persist through time. It is remarkable that recent developments in ideas regarding the functions of government in India have lent weight to some traditional notions. According to the trusteeship theory, the possession of political power is considered the legitimate preserve of a few who, in turn, look after the interests of the multitude as best as they can. It was considered presumptuous for ordinary people to claim to be able to run the government. That was the natural task of "kshatriyas". Implicit in this prescriptive view of holding public office is an attitude of irresponsibility and fatalism towards political events.

It was to be expected that the institutions of a democratic polity would counter such attitudes by developing new norms of political behaviour. This has not happened. On the contrary, the old norms have found a new lease of life from modern notions of a welfare state, social security and planned economic development. The paternal attitude of the rulers and the apathy of the ruled are the inevitable concomitants of a welfare state. Even in the U K the revival of paternal attitude on the part of the Government reminiscent of the House of Stuarts has been noticed with the coming of the welfare state. In a country like India where 'utilitarian' notions of government have hardly percolated beyond a tiny coterie of nineteenth century liberals and where the traditional attitude towards government as a trust continues, the succession of an alien administration that presumed to "civilise" the natives by a nationalist elite determined to ameliorate the "condition of the people" has led to a position where individuals are not allowed to take decisions for themselves for fear that they will make mistakes. The doctrine of the Real Will takes root and stunts the development of the spirit of adventure and self-reliance. Such a climate is conducive to the growth of a democracy that is collectivist rather than one that is liberal-parliamentary.

The tendency to shirk responsibility is shared also by those in highest political positions. Thus it is not uncommon for Ministers to try to shift responsibility on to civil servants in cases of misgovernment and assert that they had "acted on the best available advice"; the civil servants, in turn, blame party bosses to whose pressure, however, they usually succumb; the organisational wing of the party blames the governmental or parliamentary wing; the States blame the Centre and the Centre blames the States and both blame the Planning Commission; politicians take cover under "party discipline" to explain away embarrassing questions; above all, the Prime Minister himself complains of factions and groups in his own party and administrative inefficiency and careerism in his government.

Cabinet Ministers differ publicly on important policy issues and State Governors spread confusion by thinking loudly in public. It has become a commonplace for Ministers out of office to become hypercritical of the Government even though they never so much as uttered a word of dissent when in office.

The habit of complaining and the tendency to evade responsibility also affect a very important problem of Indian politics—the minority problem. In a democracy, the social or economic minority becomes a political minority. Then by persuasion and public propaganda this political minority strives to become a majority. The consequent alternation between majority and minority lays the foundation of a vigorous party system and checks political authority from becoming arbitrary towards minorities. . . .

The tendency in India is quite the reverse. Minorities remain in a more or less permanent state of minority. There is hardly any attempt to open up minority organisations to outsiders, build up a political movement or create public opinion. The minorities prefer to continue as minorities and ask for special privileges as a group which accepts its minority status as something given and unchangeable. The government reciprocates by pleading greater consideration for minorities on the one hand and by condemning the growth of sectionalism in politics on the other. The result is that political bargaining takes a communal colour and progress toward secularism is frustrated.

This is true not only of communal or economic minorities, but also of political and professional groups. The opposition cites the "political compulsions of a backward economy" and pleads for a share in political authority while their true function is to build up a vigorous opposition and try to capture power. It forgets that the best means of sharing power with the ruling group in a democracy is precisely to build up an effective opposition, by restricting the power of the majority group.

Even more deplorable is the tendency among professional groups to demand special consideration, such as representation on important public bodies. The latest example is provided by the demand made by the Institute of Engineers for special seats in the legislatures. Such demands are made in the belief that opinion in order to be effective must take the form of legislative representation and that official agencies are the only seats of power. There is little attempt at cultivating special "lobbies" on behalf of non-political groups and voluntary organisations representing vital interests.

These, then, are some of the shortcomings of the actual operation of the political process in this country. They should not, however, lead us to neglect some positive developments. While the deeper bases of democracy are largely wanting, certain workable conventions have taken root. The majority rule has not turned into a tyranny; the opposition in Parliament is given more weight than its numerical strength warrants; there are some individualists in the ruling party who do not hesitate to support the opposition when the ruling party is guilty of a distinct breach of the rules of the game; the judiciary, at least at the higher levels, is awake to its responsibilities as a watchdog of the public interest (although there is at times a tendency to stretch the classical doctrine of the liberal state too far); a part of the press has refused to be gagged; and the national leadership restrains fanaticism and jingoism in the ruling party from becoming a menace. Of course, these developments are a result of the presence of powerful personalities steeped in liberal traditions and have not become generally accepted conventions which could effectively prevent the rise of undemocratic forces in the future. There is reason to believe, however, that these values are spreading and, provided there is no major political disturbance in the coming decade, democracy will have struck roots. Meanwhile the cultural climate would also become conducive to the growth of an open and flexible society.

We can now examine the working of parliamentary government in India against the background of ideas, attitudes and the broad institutional matrix analysed above. Only tentative observations on the behaviour of specific institutions can be made here. The ruling party has not given up the position of being the party of the entire Indian people, charged with launching a movement for social and economic reconstruction which is no less significant than the movement for national independence. A large part of the political process takes place within the ruling party and almost the entire political leadership is provided by Congressmen. Public identifies the Congress Party with the government and the administration. The Congress Party constitutes an elaborate party *system* by itself. Political opposition is more effective when it comes from within the ruling party than from other parties. It has succeeded to a remarkable extent in accommodating the most important interests in the country, allowing them to become so many pressure groups and mediating between them to achieve workable solutions. It also provides an efficient channel of communication between the general public and the Central and State governments. The organisational wing of the party asserts itself to take up the cause of aggrieved interests against the government. Not that it always succeeds.

The concentration of power within the ruling party is certainly a cause for concern. This is particularly evident at the time of elections when the party has to rely heavily on the ability of its 'charismatic' leadership. Between elections, however, continuous accomodation and adjustment between the government, the ruling party and the general public can be discerned at the State and district levels, in particular. All this makes for political stability. On the other hand, it also means that the country remains totally unprepared for a political change. The Congress tolerates opposition but it does not consider with equanimity the prospects of the opposition getting into power. The position of the Congress Party in Indian politics is in many respects unique among parliamentary democracies.

This is also reflected in the working of the Cabinet and the government. The principle of collective responsibility is not always observed even though it is laid down in the Constitution and is not a mere matter of convention. This is the result of the fact that the Central and State Ministries lack unity and homogeneity. They resemble more a coalition of regional and political interests than a group united by common loyalties and shared ideas. The eclecticism is more marked at the State level where diverse interests have to be accomodated. At the Centre the powerful personality of the Prime Minister does make for some sort of teamwork and camaraderie. The tendency for individual ministers to continue in office from one election to another, until death, political defeat or the manifest disfavour of the High Command removes him also makes for continuity in political experience. But, again, it creates frustration and a sense of being left out among others.

These characteristics affect the relationship between the executive and the legislature to a marked degree. But the most far-reaching constitutional innovation is the evolution of the office of the Prime Minister. There is no doubt that Shri Nehru's powerful personality is the principal factor in moulding this office. The freedom he enjoys in the choice of his colleagues makes it possible for individuals whose sole support comes from the Prime Minister to hold office for a number of years. The benefit of the Prime Minister's patronage has, more often than not, gone to able men without popular or party support. Membership of the party and a seat in the legislature duly follow on the assumption of Ministerial office. The situation is not dissimilar to that in eighteenth century England when rotten boroughs and the patronage of barons enabled men like Pitt, Burke and Fox to get into Parliament. Shri Nehru has often cast his net wide, including the State Ministries, to get able persons for his Cabinet. He is relatively unfettered in his choice, unlike the British Prime Minister, who has to comply with a number of conventions (such as the rigid division between the Houses of Parliament) and consult important party leaders. Shri Nehru's choice has become even more free with the departure of elderly politicians from the political scene. The stature, prestige and initiative enjoyed by Shri Nehru make his position comparable to that of the United States President rather than the British Prime Minister.

The same cannot be said of the Chief Ministers of various States. Barring a few exceptions, every Chief Minister is under continuous pressure to accommodate men who have a large following in the party in particular regions or among particular interests. Rigid adherence to the principle of seniority in the party and the government further restricts the Chief Minister's freedom to choose his colleagues. There have been innumerable instances of factions within the ruling party having to be appeased by distributing the spoils of office, if necessary by enlarging the Cabinet. The situation is even more delicate in States where a coalition government is in power.

The extent to which the precedents established by Shri Nehru at the Centre will become generally accepted conventions will depend on future events, particularly on the personality of the next Prime Minister and of his colleagues.

The constitutional position of the Union President has been the subject of considerable controversy in this country. The Constitution vests enormous powers in the President, which make him incomparably more powerful than the British monarch. On the other hand, from the debates in the Constituent Assembly it is clear that the framers of the Constitution desired to limit the status of the President to that of a Constitutional figurehead. But the actual limiting of the President's powers has been made to depend on the growth of conventions to that effect. The conventions which will develop in course of time will depend to a large extent on the first half a dozen or so incumbents of the President's office, on their personalities and on those of the Prime Ministers with whom they have to work.

Dr. Rajendra Prasad's impact on the President's office is not clear. It is known, however, that the first President has not been content to remain a silent observer of political events. He has made his weight felt, where necessary by expressing frankly his differences with the Cabinet. This is natural since the President and the Ministers were comrades during the freedom struggle and they now react to each other as individuals, not as institutions. Within the limits of constitutional propriety, therefore, the President may wield considerable influence by virtue of his informal relationship with the Prime Minister and other important ministers.

That, however, is not the whole story. The President is becoming an active factor in politics, lending his support to important factions within the ruling party.

He maintains direct contacts with politicians, leaders of interest groups and even administrators, and wields an influence far in excess of that wielded by the British monarch. The President's support to the Hindi lobby in Parliament and in the government, his close relationship with the Northern group in the Cabinet and his expression of strong difference of opinion on the government's social and economic policies indicate the manner in which Dr. Prasad is trying to assert himself. There may be many other instances that have not yet come to light.

The position of the State Governors is similar to that of the President. Governors have frequently expressed their differences on particular policies of the State Governments. There have also been instances where the Governor has looked more to the Centre than to the elected ministry in the State. The weight he pulls with the Centre has reinforced his position in the State. The appointment of politicians who are not willing to be passive figureheads has also led to the modification in practice of the Governor's role as envisaged in the Constitution.

These developments with regard to the position of the President and the Governors may not be entirely unwelcome. It may effectively check the increasing power of the head of the government. Much would depend, however, on the purposes for which the President's or the Governors' influence is exerted.

The working of the Union and State legislatures during the last fifteen years reveals important trends. The domination of the Congress Party at the Centre and in most of the States has ensured that the legislatures are consulted on all important matters. The overwhelming strength of the ruling party also makes for frank and open discussions by partymen on the floor of the House. M Ps and M L As are aligned on regional lines which cut across party loyalties. The working of Parliamentary Committees reveals a fusion of views of members of opposing parties. These Committees, by their frank criticism of the government have become watchdogs of public interest. Their constant scrutiny has helped to maintain financial propriety and administrative efficiency. Informal contacts between M L As or M Ps and ministers make it possible to sound the government on important movements in public opinion. This process is more noticeable in State capitals than at the Centre. An M L A is much closer to his constituents than an M P. When the State assemblies are in session hectic activity goes on in the corridors, members' chambers and waiting rooms which bears testimony to the opening out of the seat of authority under pressure of democratic politics. Similar contacts between the rulers and the ruled are noticeable when ministers visit the constituencies. Not all complaints are heard, far less satisfied. But it is clear that the contacts are increasing.

Constitutional conventions harden over a period of time. For a precedent to become a convention, at least three conditions must be fulfilled: it must possess the sanction of long usage; it must command general acquiescence; and it must be in consonance with accepted constitutional principles. The most important condition is the sanctity of time which transforms individual acts into conventions. "Those who take decisions create precedents which others tend to follow, and when they have been followed long enough they acquire the sanctity and the respectability of age. They not only are followed but they have to be followed".

Some of the conventions of parliamentary government have been specified in the Indian Constitution. They, therefore, acquire the force of law. Others which have not been specifically mentioned draw their validity from the British experience and the political experience of English rule in India. Still others find their sanction in the debates of the Constituent Assembly. It is about the conventions that have grown since the adoption of the Constitution that doubt prevails.

Institutions in India are still in a stage of flux. Their behaviour does not follow a consistent pattern. The position is made difficult by the fact that the same party has continued in office throughout this period. It is not clear if the precedents it has set would be binding on another party when it comes to power. Again, many recent usages have been the direct result of the impact of dominant personalities. "Charismatic" behaviour can hardly lead to the growth of conventions which must be based on general concensus. Further political decisions, especially those taken within the ruling party's High Command or the Cabinet, were made in an atmosphere of secrecy. They thus become open to different interpretations. Finally, developments in the Centre and the different States are not always uniform.

The progress from monarchial to parliamentary and finally to cabinet government in England has been the result partly of a political revolution but largely of the growth of conventions. In India, however such precedents as have been established must be taken as provisional indicating possible lines of development rather than accepted conventions. . . .

It is clear from the above review of parliamentary government in India that many institutions and processes of political life as they have evolved in practice differ from the forms laid down in the Constitution. Politicians bound together by considerations of expediency and a common loyalty to the Prime Minister who enjoys almost complete freedom in choosing his colleagues, continue uninterrupted in office provided they keep alive, retain the safe seats from which they are elected and enjoy the confidence of their leader. The Head of the State, prominent individuals outside the ministry and the parliamentary committees provide the criticism that keeps the government alert and watchful; and the ruling party which shows the characteristics of a coalition of divergent interests provides the larger framework of political decision-making. This is more an amalgam of the British, American and continental systems of government than an exact replica of the English, although the legal and constitutional rules are largely borrowed from the latter.

The Prime Minister and the close circle of leaders around him in the Congress Party also control the State ministries which follow, with modifications to suit peculiar local circumstances and problems, the pattern established at the Centre. This system has not yet achieved stability. Much would depend on the inter-play of personalities and the fortunes of political parties in the next decade. Provided there is no major disturbance in the ideological balance, there is hope that the substantive pattern that has emerged will be able to meet the demands of a developing polity.

The extent to which future experience will necessitate a modification of political institutions and processes and the extent to which parliamentary government would effectively continue in the existing forms will depend on the resilience of our political institutions and the quality of statesmanship. Confident predictions on these questions are not possible. One can only broadly trace the contours of possible development. This is what has been attempted in this article.

52 • Sant Lal Singh: *The Impact of Planning on the Union-State Relationship* *

Foundations for a federal system were laid down under British rule, especially by the Government of India Act of 1935 which provided for an All-India as well as individual state legislatures. After the absorption of 562 princely states into the Union, twenty-seven states were formed. These were reduced to fourteen by the States Reorganization Act of 1956, which redrew state boundaries along linguistic lines, but the number has since increased to seventeen, again largely under linguistic pressures.

The constitution makes a detailed division of powers between the Center and the states in the Seventh Schedule, but one heavily weighted in favor of the Center. The national government has all residual powers, the power to abolish and create new states, and emergency powers exercised through the President to take over all powers of state government under certain specified conditions. The Planning Commission described below is one of the most powerful bodies in Indian government, and as Sant Lal Singh points out, has done much to shift the balance of power even further in the direction of centralization.

However, in political rather than constitutional terms, recent events have indicated that the focus of political power and activity is increasingly shifting from New Delhi to the state governments. The assumption of power in 1967 by eight non-Congress state governments facilitated this change, and it is unlikely that states will be as passive in the planning process as heretofore.

India has a quasi-federal constitution with a single constitutional document providing for Government at the Union as also in the States, a single citizenship and an unified judiciary, but with legislative powers clearly laid down and demarcated between the Union and the States, with, however, a large concurrent list. The largeness of the Government list with over-riding powers for the Union, the appointment of the Governors of States by the Union President and the enjoyment of residuary powers by the Union, besides the provision for a virtual conversion of the administration to the unitary pattern in times of *emergency* are well-known features of the Constitution that tilt the scales heavily in favour of the Union. . . . The basic idea that is revealed, however, is the concept of an integrated economy transcending the territorial boundaries of the various States. It is in the context of this concept of an integrated national economy that the political significance of the federation has to be appreciated. The modern State with ever increasing functions is a welfare State whose activities involve a large degree of participation in economic life. Through its Directive Principles the Union Constitution virtually inspires this interpretation of the role of the Government. The result has been the Government's decision to plan. The resolution of the Government of India appointing the Planning Commission stated, after referring to the fundamental (economic) Rights and Directive Principles of State

* *Modern Review,* Vol. CXIII (April 1962), pp. 11–12.

Policy laid down in the Constitution, the functions of the Planning Commission in the following terms: The Planning Commission will: (i) make an assessment of the material, capital and human resources of the country . . . . and investigate the possibilities of augmenting such resources . . . . in relation to the nation's requirements; (ii) formulate a plan for the most effective and balanced utilisation of the nation's resources etc.

Over the last twelve years the country has seen the gradual development and unfolding of the processes of economic planning as contemplated in the Government of India Resolution. In course of this economic process significant developments have taken place in constitutional and administrative relations between the component units of the federal Governmental structure of the country. . . .

The Planning machinery of India is headed by the Planning Commission. The Commission is an extra constitutional body created by a resolution of the Government of India in March 1950. It was a body created by the Union Government which also appointed its members. Right from the beginning the Prime Minister has been the Chairman of the Commission, the Finance Minister and the Minister in charge of Planning almost ex-officio members, with one or two other important Union Ministers also featuring as members occasionally. In the beginning the Minister for Planning functioned as the Deputy Chairman. After some time a whole time member, regarded as an expert in administration and Planning, Sri V. T. Krishnamachari, took over as the Deputy Chairman. Since his retirement the Planning Minister has once again taken over the Deputy Chairmanship. From the constitutional point of view, thus, the Planning Commission is entirely a matter for the Union Government, functioning in an advisory capacity to the Government as a body created by it for the purpose. No Act of Parliament has ever sought to regulate its composition, powers or functions. The number of members has varied, with a steady upward trend. While all this has added to the flexibility of the entire arrangement, the Commission has become a constitutional curiosity. With the Prime Minister as the Chairman and some of the most important Ministers in-charge of vital departments as its members, the Commission has become, in matters within its sphere of work, almost synonymous with the Government. Its decisions (technically recommendations to the Union Government) have invariably found acceptance at the Union cabinet. It is not sure that all its decisions even pass through the Cabinet before they are implemented or circulated among the Ministries or executive agencies concerned for implementation. Yet this role of the Planning Commission is not only being tolerated, but it is progressively getting more important. From the constitutional point of view this is an extremely important development. "Legally, it has neither constitutional nor even statutory authority. It is only when the plan formulated by the Commission is approved by the Cabinet that it receives the necessary sanction."

The Secretaryship of the Planning Commission is held, ex-officio, by the seniormost member of the Civil Service, a fact that adds to the informal authority of the body.

Technically the Commission is a planning and deliberative body, discussing broad policies and only *planning out* the details for execution of such a policy; the *execution* of these decisions is a matter entirely for the normal machinery of the executive branches of the Union and State Governments. In reality, however, the two functions must necessarily be close to each other. A body that draws up a scheme of long term economic development of which the individual Five

Year Plans are only separate stages, cannot but get interested in watching the progress of the schemes already in a process of execution. Hence, in due course, the Commission came to have not only an evaluational function, but also some supervisory ones, over not only the Union ministries, but the related departments of the State Governments as well.

It is in this latter context tha he composiion of he Planning Commission comes to have added significance from the standpoint of the States. The Planning Commission has thus strengthened the executive authority of the Centre over the States for which, as noted already, the Constitution had already made certain provisions. What is important is that this growingly important body, which functions legally as an advisor to the Union Government, but on matters that vitally affect the States as well, has no organic link with the latter, whether under the Constitution or as an informal arrangement.

Theoretically, even in the technical realm of planning the Planning Commission is not quite the supreme body. All important and policy decisions, before their presentation to and approval by the Union Cabinet are placed before the National Development Council for its consideration and approval. Like the Planning Commission, the National Development Council has no constitutional or statutory authority. Being composed of all members of the Planning Commission and the Chief Ministers of all the States, however, this is the only body that brings the States into contact with the processes of plan formulation. The National Development Council was formally set up only in August 1952. The Draft Outline of the First Plan, referring to this body, the establishment of which must have been decided upon by then, remarked "In a country of the size of India where the States have under the Constitution full autonomy within their own sphere of duties, it is necessary to have a forum, such as a National Development Council, at which *from time to time* the Prime Minister of India and the Chief Ministers of States can review the working of the Plan and of its various aspects." Thus a National Development Council, apparently, was initially conceived of as *a forum* for reviewing the working of the Plan from time to time. Though, as remarked earlier, it has subsequently been the practice to submit the Plans to this body before final presentation to Parliament, it is doubtful if the body has acquired characteristics significantly different from those of an academic forum. It is, of course, true that the Council passes resolutions both on guiding principles or approaches to particular plans as also on plan documents as a whole, but usually its duties would seem to consist of approving of decisions arrived at by the Commission earlier.

Meeting only occasionally, and under the auspices of the Planning Commission, and without a secretariat of its own, the Council can do little more than function as a conference where, at best, some individual State's grievance can be aired suitably in an atmosphere of general eulogisation and elucidation of decisions already taken. The National Development Council can thus be regarded as a token concession to the federal political structure of the country and can probably serve best the aims of planning, as it appears to have been doing, by rubber-stamping decisions of the really important body, *viz.*, the Planning Commission. . . .

There is an additional factor of importance that accounts for the relatively low impact of the States on the processes of planning, and that is the inadequate development of a planning machinery at the level of the States. We would, therefore, turn now to a brief review of the planning machinery in the States.

The decision to introduce economic planning in the country has been that of the Government of India. The States have been rather passive partners. Naturally, therefore, the State Governments have been slow both in realising the full implications and importance of planning, as also in taking suitable steps, administrative or otherwise, for a vigorous fulfilment of the role that planning in a federal country involves for the Governments of the constituent States. Whatever administrative machinery for planning the State Governments possess have largely been set up under the direction and advice of the Union or the Planning Commission itself. Thus the leadership of the Union is evident even in the formation and functioning of the planning machinery in the States. There is, of course, even today, no perfect uniformity in this respect between the States and in some States the machinery is still in the process of evolution. The general pattern, however, is that under the State cabinet, most States have either a Planning Department, or a still older office of the Development Commissioner. The post of the Development Commissioner is usually occupied by one of the seniormost officers of the State administration (comparable to relative status of the Secretary to the Planning Commission).

The office of the Development Commissioner, or the Planning Department where it exists, is supposed to play, in relation to the various departments concerned of the State Governments, a role similar to that played by the Planning Commission in relation to the different Union Ministries. Normally all communications on matters pertaining to planning from the Planning Commission or the Union Government intended for the State Government is dealt with by the Development Commissioner's office or the State Department of Planning.

The one important thing, however, that distinguishes the State planning authorities in general from the planning machinery in the Centre is the structural and functional weakness of the former. Most State Governments have little more than a skeleton staff to man the planning or development departments, and the staff that exists is poorly equipped from the technical standpoint of planning. The process of plan formulation, resource evaluation, implementation and evaluation of economic plans are today largely technical in nature, requiring a certain amount of economic expertise. The Planning Commission is known to maintain a large band of economists and statisticians—experts in planning technique—who alone can formulate plans—both long term as well as short—that will stand the test of economic scrutiny. Lacking such staff as most State planning departments do, State Governments necessarily lack initiative and have to await guidance from the Centre, or submit to the severest modifications of plans put up by themselves at the hands of the Planning Commission. As the history of the formulation of the last three Five Year Plans of the country, particularly the State plans, provide ample evidence, the majority of State Governments have little awareness of the implications of economic planning, cannot make very reasonable estimates of their resources and formulate a scientific order of priority of their needs, far less possess an idea of the proper relationship between planning at and by the State Governments and planning at the national level. In short, the technical competence of the State Governments in relation to planning is of such an inferior order when compared to the growing size and competence of the planning machinery at the Union Government level, that it is not surprising that the State Governments make little impact on the process of plan formulation.

To compensate for the lack of a constitutional or statutory machinery allowing for an adequate representation of the needs and wishes of the State Governments, reliance has been on the method of consultation. . . . So far as the State Governments are concerned, the process of consultation takes largely the form of summoning of representatives of the State Governments to New Delhi, though recently the practice of senior officers of the Planning Commission visiting the various States has also been growing.

The Indian Planning process involves formulation of a series of Five-Year Plans, consistent with and promoting the long-term objectives as laid down in what is known as the Perspective. The Five-Year Plans, again, are broken up into Annual Plans. . . .

Over the last three Five-Year Plans, the relative importance of the State Plans in the total plan has been increasing. The issues of State are thus getting even more important, with a consequent increasingly favourable reaction on the powers and prestige of the Planning Commission.

'Consultations' between the States and the Planning Commission are thus, in reality, a series of bargainings between the parties, and as these consultations take place only individually for every State, the States as a body have next to no voice in influencing either the total size of the national plan, or the share of the States in it.

Compared to the bargainings and pressures involved in the formulation of the Five-Year Plan, the consultations that take place annually over the size of the State plan for the next financial year are, of course, quite tame. They involve, nevertheless, a substantial inroad into the financial autonomy of the States, a right that is normally valued quite highly in all federations. Indeed, "The annual plan has now become a very important part of the planning procedure in India and has, in fact, evolved into *a very important instrument of federal and State financial relationship.*"

The net position, then, is that the enormous powers that economic planning represents, affecting the destiny of not only the nation as a whole but the relative position of States, is largely concentrated in the hands of the Planning Commission whose legal status is that of an advisory body of experts created by the Union Executive. The decisions of the Commission, technically in the nature of 'recommendations' to the Union Government, are subject to only a formal review by the National Development Council, a body in which the States have also representation. Real power of planning, including planning in the States, vests in the Planning Commission, which only informally consults the State Governments in the formulation of State plans, the National Plan being entirely its own exclusive concern. The rather ineffective organisational equipment for planning that the State Governments generally possess results in the initiative even in State plans lying largely in the hands of the technically much better equipped Planning Commission, and the natural parochialism of State Governments makes a stand for greater autonomy in matters of plan formulation for the States even more difficult to achieve. . . .

The conclusion would thus be clear that the last decade or a little more of economic planning has seen a considerable growth in the influence of the Centre on State policy making and administration. The above survey has largely been concerned with how Central influence is overwhelming in all the three stages of planning in the State sphere, *viz.*, formulation, implementation and evaluation of Plan projects. There is another, and in a sense, a more vital aspect, *viz.*, economic policy making in the widest sense of the term, in which the Planning Commission in particular and the Union Government in general have been imposing their decisions on all concerned. The vitally important economic decisions in favour of a Socialist Pattern of Society, the expansion of the Public Sector, including public sector enterprises under management and control of State Governments, policy towards land ownership and tenurial rights,—to name only a few, are decisions in the making of which the State Governments appear to have had little share. Many of these, *e.g.*, in relation to land revenue and tenures, are subjects in the State list.

53 • Planning Commission, Government of India: *Local Government and Administration* *

Economic development is a major political goal, and the government has the task of reaching and motivating its vast population toward modernizing and increasing productivity. To do so it has experimented with various forms of administrative decentralization. The most important unit of local administration is the District headed by a Collector who, as an officer of the Indian Administrative Service, has both administrative and developmental duties. The Community Development Program in 1952 subdivided the District into Development Blocks, each consisting of approximately one hundred villages. It was hoped that this further decentralization would accelerate rural development, but the result was continuing apathy among the villagers.

The 1957 Balvantray Mehta Report found that assistance from above through the Development Program failed to arouse initiative and self-help by the villagers themselves. In order to stimulate village participation, it proposed an extension of village self-government based on the revival of the traditional panchayat or village council. The result was the system of panchayati raj, or government by panchayat, which now covers most of rural India. It consists of three tiers. The basic unit is the Gram or village panchayat which is directly elected by the villagers and which has some financial, administrative, and in some cases, judicial functions. At the second level is the Panchayat Samiti which corresponds roughly in area to the administrative Development Block. The members are chosen indirectly by and from the Gram panchayats, and they are responsible for the planning and implementation of development projects in close cooperation with the centrally administered Block. At the top is the Zila Parishad, corresponding to the District, whose members are also chosen indirectly by the Samitis and whose functions are largely that of coordination.

* Planning Commission, Government of India, *The New India: Progress Through Democracy* (New York: Macmillan, 1958).

This important experiment in democratic and administrative decentralization is still in the trial and error stage. The following selection from a Planning Commission report gives the political and administrative setting.

District Development Administration

Below the State level, the 300 Districts (roughly comparable to the counties of the United States and Britain), today, as in British India, are considered "the pivot of the structure of administration." These Districts usually contain one or two million people; a few contain as many as four to five million, or a number equaling the population of Norway or Denmark.

The administrative head of each district is called the District Collector or District Magistrate, titles carried over from an earlier period when his chief functions were land-revenue collection and law and order. The Collector is a member of the civil service, not an elected or politically appointed official.

The District Collector's responsibilities are increasing as all development programs—and especially the rural development programs—are intensified. Standing between the State Government with its elected legislature, and the local self-governing groups in the villages, the Collector's position and potential role is of great and, as has been said, pivotal importance in a developing India.

With a strengthened and democratized administration, the Indian Government considers, indeed, the District as an agency of change toward a new social order. It must respond to the needs and aspirations of the people, and in a democratic society will be judged by the ways it finds to achieve these aspirations through the cooperation of the people and their Government.

On the one hand, it is at the District level and below that the development programs directly touch the Indian people, in the villages and countless small towns. On the other, the very choice of democratic means for India's growth, as noted earlier, makes it necessary to strengthen and, where they do not already exist, create local democratic organizations composed of and working with the people, in order to plan and carry out the work of development at the District, sub-district and village level.

Development must be carried out by these local bodies so that strong local leadership may be found and encouraged, and so that the people of each area themselves may assume, under their own leadership, the main responsibility for solving their local problems and developing their own resources.

The need for creating a well organized democratic structure of administration within the Districts is now widely felt. It is believed that local bodies at the District (and in larger Districts, at a sub-district) level should have an organic link with the popularly elected village councils and gradually assume the responsibility for local administration of development programs, with clearly assigned functions. New proposals for decentralizing local administration of development programs along democratic lines were worked out in late 1957 by a team set up through the National Development Council.

During the First Plan the District Collector began more actively to assume the functions of a District Development Officer, in addition to his regulative duties. In some areas a special development or planning deputy was assigned to his office. Under the Second Plan, the Planning Commission has urged further strengthening and staffing of the District administration, to fulfill the urgent local demands for coordination of technical staff in the Districts, to supervise, guide and evaluate all types of development works and programs of the area.

The Planning Commission also recommends District Development Councils to survey and plan for the needs of each District, and to work directly with local village groups through village self-government organizations (*panchayats*) and with the local block and project officers of the national rural development programs.

District Development Committees were established in the First Plan in all Districts for advising on rural development and on other programs. While some were effective, the majority did not function fully, largely because their role of duties and opportunities were not always clearly appreciated.

The Planning Commission suggests that each Council include not only District Collectors and the local development officers, but local representatives of the State Assemblies and national Parliament, leaders of village panchayats and other local bodies, representatives of cooperatives and local social service agencies.

A similar council at a lower or sub-divisional (*taluq*, or block) level is also recommended, with similar representatives. The role and integration of the rural development block in District administration is indeed of great importance for the future.

In general, the functions suggested to these local bodies are: local planning, reviewing and coordinating development activities in the area or District, and very particularly stimulating public initiative, leadership and participation in development activities and small savings drives, and a constant concern that the poorer and disadvantaged people of the area benefit from development programs.

Village Panchayats

In ancient India, it is believed that most villages had a form of local self-government. The common form was one in which elected elders constituted a village council, a panchayat, passing on all public affairs of the village, including private disputes. Many believe, as Prime Minister Nehru writes in his book *The Discovery of India,* that "the strength and perseverance of India in the past seem to have lain in her widespread system of village republics or self-governing panchayats."

Local self-government weakened and finally almost disappeared, as successive waves of alien rulers destroyed the autonomy of the village and imposed new laws and revenues from distant and alien authorities. Every village, however, retained its headman who, together with certain village elders, was by common consent the village's spokesman.

To some extent under British rule, and very particularly since Independence, an effort has been made to revive this old form of village government, and both the First and Second Plans have put a high priority on formation of panchayats.

While local self-government needs no justification in a democracy, it may be useful to summarize why India attaches to it so high a priority.

First, the reasons are frankly practical. If the work of village development is to get done in a democratic society which proposes no all-powerful centrally controlled apparatus, and if it is to be done, too, with maximum financial help from the people themselves, the villages must themselves organize to carry out, and contribute to, much of the work of development—the building of schools, roads, irrigation and similar projects.

The Planning Commission clearly acknowledges that rural progress depends entirely on the existence of an active village organization which can bring all the people, including those at the bottom of the social and economic ladder, into common programs and activities, using assistance from the Government, and their own contributions in labor, cash and kind.

Further, India feels keenly that the nation's strength as a democracy depends to a most important degree on building, in hundreds of thousands of villages, effective local governments through which the people can, as responsible citizens, plan and participate in their own and the nation's progress. As such, these governments are not considered merely as local municipal bodies, performing largely housekeeping or even local development chores. Rather, they are seen as essential means of fitting local and village activities into the over-all pattern of District and State plans, and as the final and essential link in an integrated democratic administrative structure of the nation as a whole.

Further, village society is in a state of transition. Powerful social and economic forces—land reform, wider education, rural development—are bringing great changes. These forces put strains on old village societies which, however backward, had achieved a remarkable social stability and cohesion.

As Mahatma Gandhi, with his great insight, saw so clearly, the social strength and cohesion of the villages is imperative to sustain the new nation. He saw, with equal clarity, the key role of the village panchayats in maintaining that strength, and attached the highest importance to reviving them. His teaching is reflected today in India's recognition that a village panchayat, representing the needs of all groups, can play a considerable part in bringing about a more just and integrated social structure and in developing new patterns of rural leadership. Indeed, India feels the development of local self-government is a key part of the larger process of fundamental reconstruction and reorganization of village social and economic life.

The general purpose is to establish, especially in rural development areas, what is called a "statutory" panchayat to serve every village. A statutory panchayat is one formally set up and registered under State laws which provide some financing, and which permit the panchayat to administer certain civil and criminal suits and adjudicate local disputes. All States now have panchayat legislation.

The number of panchayats increased considerably (40 per cent) over the First Plan, reaching in 1956 to a total of over 117,000. Over the Second Plan, it is hoped to double the number to 244,564—or one for each of nearly half the villages in India. It is suggested that for villages too small or isolated (about half the rural people live in villages of less than 1,000 population), natural groupings of villages may be made to provide a unit of at least 1,000 persons. One panchayat could serve this unit.

Development of village leadership which is representative of the village as a whole is extremely important. There has been concern that the usual election process may not always bring out leaders with the qualities most needed for village development and with constructive interest in the growth of the community as a whole. It is also recognized that unless there is comprehensive village planning, which takes into account the needs of the entire community, those groups with the least economic and social status, such as tenant farmers, landless laborers, artisans, may not benefit sufficiently from Government development programs and assistance.

The Planning Commission urges that States, as many already do, require the elected members to take in, as additional members, representatives of the Harijans (untouchables), the landless or other socially and economically depressed groups in the village; and ex officio representatives of local cooperatives. A means is also now being worked out whereby, by groups of villages, panchayat leaders can be given special training to educate them to their new functions, and to their responsibilities to the community as a whole.

How to finance the panchayats is a special problem if they are to assume wider and more important functions. Most State Governments grant them a portion of the local land taxes; panchayats may also collect small civic taxes; in some few areas they levy land taxes. So far this financing has proved inadequate. The Second Plan recommends that the States grant 15 to 20 per cent of local revenues, plus 15 per cent more if the panchayat itself raises an equal additional amount.

The functions of the statutory panchayat generally conceived today and recommended by the Planning Commission are, in addition to the local planning and development, both administrative and judicial.

Among civic functions, the panchayat is expected under most State laws to act as the local civic authority—maintaining village roads, improving village sanitation (a very important role under India's health program), providing village lighting, and maintaining the village community hall, with its small library and, in some cases, the village battery radio set.

A key function, however, is that of local development—planning the village improvement needs, constructing and maintaining village schools, roads and so on, organizing voluntary village labor and contributions and small savings; development of cooperatives and village livestock improvement; and, very importantly, serving as the village's direct medium of contact with all development programs of the District, State and Center.

The panchayat is also seen as the essential democratic agency to carry out any eventual reorganization of land management. The Planning Commission recommends that panchayats also concern themselves with: development and regulation of use of the village's common land, forests, and reservoirs; assistance in consolidation of holdings; promotion of good land management among the village farmers.

It is also proposed that, on problems of local land reform, the panchayats be associated with decisions on tenants' and owners' rights, on determination of surplus lands and their distribution. As land reform becomes more effective, and more of a direct local issue, these functions may assume a critical significance.

In acting as a judicial body, the panchayat can provide a very real service. Where the panchayats already are active, disputes which otherwise may have dragged through District courts, impoverished the disputants and divided the villages into factions, have in most cases been readily settled. In some States a separate panchayat has the judicial functions.

The potential strength and value of village self-government to India's growth can hardly be calculated. At the very least, it provides the final and integrated link in the chain of administration where vast national and State development programs reach directly to the people to help them rise from the mire of poverty. As it does so, and at its best, it will reflect the ideal of self-governing village republics which Gandhi envisaged: "Here is perfect democracy, based on individual freedom."

SECTION THREE

Political Leadership

54 • Gopal Krishna: *Party Leaders* *

Political leadership in India in recent years has undergone significant changes. Few of the idealistic, selfless leaders of the independence movement remain, and they are being replaced by pragmatic, boss-type politicians. In national as well as local politics, and in the Congress as well as opposition parties, factionalism is emerging. Party loyalty is subordinated to loyalty to individual leaders of factions within the parties, as the following selection makes clear, and voting is largely for personalities rather than policies. While Gopal Krishna is analyzing the one-party dominance of the Congress party in 1966, his discussion of leadership presages the party's heavy loss of electoral support in the 1967 elections caused in part by both internal competition between Congress factional leaders and large scale defections from the party. Nevertheless, the Congress in the past has shown considerable ability to close factional ranks when faced with electoral losses, but failure to do so will further weaken or end its position as the majority party.

In spite of the vast political mobilization that has taken place since independence the leadership of Indian political parties rests with the educated classes. The party leaders have been symbols of power and prestige for party workers and have commanded immense power within the party organizations by virtue of the status conferred upon them by the rank and file followers, by the structure of decision-making in the parties and by their critical importance as collectors of party funds. Their politics has consequently tended to be personal rather than collective, group-oriented, or ideological. In the context of one class politics this has proved to be important for the Indian party system: it has moderated the struggle for power and sectional advantage and has assured respect for institutions which are not rooted in the sentiments of the people but whose rationale is understood and appreciated by the leadership.

The remarkable continuity in party leadership from the pre- into the post-independence period has already been mentioned. Data on 114 contemporary political leaders, reveal that after eighteen years of independence nearly all the leadership positions in the Congress both in the States and at the Centre are

* "One Party Dominance: Developments and Trends," Supplement to *The Indian Journal of Public Administration,* Vol. XII, No. 1 (January–March 1966), pp. 19–24, 52–61. By permission.

still held by men who participated in the freedom movement. Nearly two thirds of the opposition leaders included in this group have been associated with the Congress at one time or the other in the past: all the ten P.S.P. and S.S.P. leaders, five leaders of the Swatantra Party, both leaders of the R.S.P. and both of the Forward Block, two of the independents and seven of the Communists were at one time or the other members of the Indian National Congress and suffered imprisonment. This has an important bearing on the climate of consensus that has provided the framework within which Indian politics has functioned during the past decade and a half.

Our contention that politics is primarily an activity of the educated classes is amply borne out by the educational status of Indian political leaders. Out of the 103 of 114 leaders for whom this information is available, 98 (94 per cent) attended college or University and 17 went abroad for education, while 2 went to school only and 3 have had no formal education. . . .

Politics began as an activity of the new educated professional classes in the latter part of the 19th century. They were joined after 1920 by the full-time functionaries for whom politics was at once a mission and a profession. The same combination of recruits to modern professions and to full-time politics continues to dominate contemporary Indian parties. Of the same 114 leaders 73 (64.00 per cent) are full-time political, social or trade union workers (66, 4 and 3 respectively), while 41 are recruited from the modern professional classes of lawyers (19), teachers (8), journalists (4), civil servants (2), consultants (2), representing the intelligentsia and 6 from business. . . .

Parties dominated by functionaries, when in power, tend to become subordinate to the leadership which controls party funds and access to positions of status and material benefits. After independence politics lost its missionary aspect for the Congress functionaries and as the professional element became dominant, the party of functionaries, dependant upon the favours granted by the leadership whether in the form of candidatures for the State legislatures or Parliament or posts in the organization, became an instrument of those who commanded sources of power and patronage, and the party itself came to depend increasingly upon the utilization of governmental power, prestige and patronage to sustain it in office.

Lack of internal cohesion is the most noticeable characteristic of all the major parties. Factions, inherent in a system of one party dominance where the dominant party draws into its fold divergent elements from a wide range of social groups and economic interests, have become pervasive in the Congress and the absence of a clear ideological bond and of belief in the significance for a larger cause of what they do has caused decay among Congressmen of the sentiment of public purpose in the pursuit of power. Nearly every State unit of the party has suffered deep splits since independence. To keep the factions under control and prevent them from destroying each other and disrupting the organization has been one of the principal concerns of the Congress High Command. It has been able to compel recalcitrant Congressmen to conform to its decisions because of the formidable power of expulsion which it wields: expulsion from the Congress means exclusion from positions of power and authority and loss of access to avenues of prestige and perquisites, so the position of the Congress as the ruling party makes it worthwhile for the dissidents to work within its framework rather than join the ranks of the opposition. Yet this power has not been utilized by the High Command to streamline the organization or to compel unquestioned conformity; no attempt has been made to make the Congress homogeneous by extinguishing all dissent because the diversity of the country, past history and compulsions of power in a democratic polity alike demand that the coalition character of the party be preserved. This has enabled it to admit into its fold, as and when it seemed necessary for preserving its ascendancy in the States, a communal group such as the Akalis in Punjab, caste parties in Madras, a tribal party in Bihar, the leftist-oriented United Democratic Front in Andhra Pradesh, Jagirdars in Rajasthan and a large section of the Praja Socialist Party all over the country. Though this promiscuous accommodation has produced considerable strain in the organization, the cementing element of power and the sagacity of the High Command have enabled the Congress to absorb dissidence, except in Kerala where the strategy of weeding out dissent led to the party's eviction from power.

The opposition parties, with the exception of the Jan Sangh, have also demonstrated marked proneness to factional struggles. The left parties continue to strive for homogeneity that has eluded them throughout their history. Democratic centralism notwithstanding, the ideologically-committed Communists have been violently divided among themselves since 1948 and openly split in 1964. Policy differences, though important, have been aggravated by personal feuds and the party has been shattered from top to bottom by the unrestrained reciprocal invective by the Left and the Right sections of the party: ". . . factionalism, blatant lack of discipline and regional disregard for central authority" have become "permanent features of C.P.I. life, to a degree seen in few, if any, other Communist parties." Regional loyalties have triumphed over national policies, as in the case of the language issue in Assam, and erstwhile comrades have accused each other of being traitors to the country and to the cause of communism. Factional disputes in the party are aggravated by the fierce controversies in the international communist movement, which have been the major cause of the 1964 split.

The socialists too are acutely faction-ridden: every leader has a faction of his own and the party has suffered at least half a dozen major splits since 1947. These had little to do with policy or ideology but more with personality. Mutual jealousy and an exaggerated sense of self-importance on the part of party leaders, the misplaced militancy of the rank and file activists and the unsuccessful opportunistic alliances after the party's electoral failure in 1952 combined to destroy the socialist movement as an effective force in Indian public life.

The other left parties, the Revolutionary Socialist Party, the Forward Bloc and the Peasants' and Workers' Party, have shown the tendency to split into factions characteristic of all the left parties.

The Swatantra Party does not even strive to be cohesive. Acknowledging that there does not exist in the country today a sufficiently large politically homogeneous opposition to the Congress, the founders of the Swatantra Party contented themselves with bringing together local opposition groups which agreed to a minimal programme of opposition to the Nehru-inspired state socialism of the Congress. This party of "property, liberty and democracy" consists predominantly of former Congressmen, a section of landowners in Andhra Pradesh, some of the former Akalis in Punjab, agricultural and feudal interests in Gujarat and some of the Princes of Orissa and Rajasthan and is financially supported by business enterprises in Bombay and Calcutta. The party does not, indeed, pretend to even a broad agreement on national policies and leaves State units free to take their own decisions on major issues. Its primary preoccupation has been to somehow engineer a "conservative" alternative to the Congress.

The spirit of party loyalty thus appears to have weakened in the Congress, has never existed in the Swatantra Party and barely survives to sustain the Socialists and Communists of all descriptions; the Jan Sangh perhaps commands it in the largest measure, though it too has its factional tensions between those closely associated with the R.S.S. and the rest. . . .

Indian politics has undergone more change since 1962 than in the preceding 15 years of Independence. That period was marked by the ascendancy of Nehru; political equilibrium appeared to rest specifically on the skill and charisma of one man. While this provided the nation with a period of stability, it was difficult to evaluate the strength of the institutions of the new political order or how far they would be capable of accommodating themselves to political change and it appeared as though the personal leadership of Nehru had inhibited the institutionalization of the political process. But the events since his death in May 1964 have shown that the end of the Nehru era also marked the end of the tutelary stage of Indian democracy and the manner of choosing his two successors demonstrated that the traditions of the Congress party rather than the merits of an individual, remarkable as they were, are the fundamental element in the stability of the political system.

The style and orientations of the new leadership are different from those of Nehru and more conducive to a healthy growth of institutionalized politics. While Nehru's leadership was entirely personal, the new leadership has of necessity to be more collective and in the gravest crisis of war with Pakistan gave proof of its capacity to work as a coherent team. It is pragmatic in outlook and undramatic in style. It operates in a climate of opinion marked by disillusionment with ideologies.

On the opposition side, the split in the Communist Party following the open rupture between the Soviet and the Chinese parties is of momentous significance. The earlier dispute between the so-called "Right" and "Left" Communists over the attitude to be adopted towards the Congress in a situation of growing challenge from the "reactionary" forces represented by the Swatantra Party and the Jan Sangh assumed altogether different proportions with the imposition on it of the international rivalry between the Soviet and Chinese parties and the crisis of conscience forced on Indian Communists by the Chinese invasion of India in 1962, when the claims of patriotism clashed with sentiments of loyalty to the centre of communist revolution in Asia.

The struggle between the Soviet and Chinese parties has resulted in the emergence of "polycentric" tendencies in the once highly centralized world Communist movement. The fragmentation of this movement which had been at once the source of strength and the undoing of the Indian party offers it its first opportunity to formulate policies and programmes relevant to Indian conditions and best calculated to further its own position. There is little doubt that the Left and Right Communists between them command the loyal adherence of a considerable body of devoted workers and could enlist increasing electoral support if the split in the Party could be healed and if this crucial opportunity were taken to chart out an Indian path to communism. But the split appears to have gone too deep—as far as one can see the Chinese have no incentive to promote a rapprochement between the two groups—and may have left the Party permanently crippled.

The Socialists, impelled by electoral failures, attempted to reunite and in the process lost a sizable number of party workers and leaders to the Congress, without establishing unity. . . . Lacking in leadership of national stature the party has been slow in securing support outside the four northern States. Its championship of Hindi as the national language may prove to be a barrier to its spread in the South.

The local parties such as the D.M.K. in Madras, the Akali Dal in Punjab, the Muslim League in Kerala and sectional parties such as the Republican Party in Maharashtra and Uttar Pradesh have built for themselves pockets of support on the basis of religion and caste, and since these are likely to continue to influence political allegiance in the forseeable future, will probably continue to command a measure of political support. The D.M.K. alone among the local parties may emerge as a powerful opposition party at the State level, and in association with other opposition parties may even compete with the Congress for a majority in the State Assembly. With its emergence as the principal opposition party in Madras after 1962 it has undergone major changes in policy and outlook: it abandoned its demand for a separate State of Tamil Nad and has offered its full support to the Central Government in meeting external threats to the nation; it has moderated its caste hostility to the Brahmins and may even seek their support against the Congress in the next election: the compulsions of electoral politics are already making it non-sectarian, and association with a major opposition party may perhaps make it a part of the national party system.

In terms of conventional democratic theory, a weak opposition seriously impairs the quality of a democracy. A further thesis is that the plurality system of voting and the single member constituency produce a lack of correspondence between the votes polled and seats won by parties and thus distort the choice of the electorate and detract from the political equality of the voters; they artificially inflate the majority of the dominant party and diminish the numerical strength of the opposition parties. These objections, no doubt valid as far as they go, overlook one essential purpose of the electoral system: to produce workable legislative majorities which can sustain stable executive government. Theoretically the present electoral system should induce the opposition parties to pool their resources, ultimately crystallizing into a two-party system. However, the issues that divide the opposition are fundamental and their social and regional support structures are not often negotiable, with the result that temporary united fronts, contrived to defeat Congress candidates in the elections, have not led to the consolidation of even like-minded parties. Parties coming together on specific issues, such as the formation of the linguistic States in Maharashtra and Gujarat or the ousting of the Communist Government in Kerala, fall apart when the issues are resolved and resume their politics of opposition to each other as well as to the Congress. The only partially successful attempt to unite like-minded parties was made by the Socialists in 1953 when the Socialist Party, the Kisan Mazdoor Praja party led by Acharya Kripalani and a section of the Forward Bloc led by R. S. Ruikar merged to form the Praja Socialist Party. But that unity was short lived; indeed, one may date the process of disintegration of the socialist movement in India to the formation of the P.S.P. The proposal for a union of the Swatantra Party and the Jan Sangh did not get off the ground.

Over the years the opposition parties have shown a singular inability to combine against the ruling party on the basis either of principle or of expediency. Instead of aggregating their strength they have chosen to preserve their separate identities, which they value more highly than electoral gains. It is a commonly observed phenomenon that the more distant a party is from a position of power the more rigid it tends to be in its choice of allies, the more puritan it claims to be in its outlook and the more it cherishes its separate identity; it emphasizes incompatibilities rather than points of accord. When electoral failure finally drives it near to destruction it seeks promiscuous alliances and unprincipled accommodations which ultimately destroy its character. This is neatly illustrated by the history of the Socialist Party since independence. Other opposition parties too, and the Congress party in Kerala, have not found the politics of joint fronts worthwhile.

The support base of the opposition parties is very small and shows no sign of expansion. The benefit mainly from negative anti-Congress votes, sometimes spectacularly as during the bye-elections in 1963 following the collapse of Nehru's policy on China, but this does not result in any permanent gain. This is because the voting act is not in any significant manner related either to policy preferences or to the pursuit of interests. Indian political behaviour appears to be peculiarly unrelated to public issues and curiously impervious to performance in office. The electoral failures of the Congress party are often caused by its own internal organizational disruption rather than by failures of policy. The results of 95 by-elections to the State Assemblies and 21 to the Lok Sabha held between April 1962 and December 1964 show that in the former the Congress made 9 net gains and in the latter suffered one net loss. That this was the worst period of demoralization in the country and in the party suggests that the latter possesses great staying power in periods of difficulty and that failures in policy or administrative performance have little impact on the voting behaviour of the electorate. The principal threat to the ascendancy of the Congress comes from its own internal factional disputes, as was clearly demonstrated in the mid-term elections in Kerala held in March 1965. The opposition between the Congress party and its breakaway faction, the Kerala Congress, lost them 13 seats out of 72 which they could have won in a house of 134, and the post-election posture of the Congress High Command opposing accommodation with the dissidents forced President's rule on the State. Factional disruption led to the defeat of a number of Congress candidates in Madhya Pradesh in 1962, depriving the party of a majority in the State Legislature. The dissidents in Mysore have already formed a party of their own and those in Orissa are only precariously in the Congress; the situation in Uttar Pradesh and Punjab is precarious and has only just been patched up in Rajasthan. Unless action by the High Command or good sense on the part of faction leaders or some combination of the two are able to restore a measure of peace and order in the party it may suffer major reverses in the faction-ridden States of north India where the party's position is under serious attack. For just as the possession of power assists the Congress party in maintaining its cohesion, its loss would lead to desertion on a large scale. The sentiment of loyalty is minimal, as is shown in every election by the number of Congressmen who, on failing to get party nomination, stand against official candidates. Meanwhile factions based on personalities and constantly combining in shifting coalitions cause instability in the party and ultimately destroy the sense of public purpose which must govern the pursuit and use of power.

Political stability and orderly progress are not among the gifts bestowed by nature and circumstance upon societies undergoing rapid social and economic change. That India has enjoyed them since independence gives no assurance of their continuation in the future. With the spread of education and the media of communication, population growth and increasing urbanisation, economic development, greater mobility and insufficient employment opportunities the outlook of the politically relevant strata is likely to undergo a measure of change that is today unpredictable. By the end of the seventies, if not before, one should expect the majority of the adult population to be literate and the newspapers and radio to reach all villages. The most conservative estimates place the Indian population in 1975 at 563 million, of which 19.6 per cent would be living in towns of 20,000 or more—which would mean a doubling of their 1961 population. General economic conditions may not, however, be a great deal better than they are today: income inequalities may be somewhat greater and employment opportunities will not keep pace with the influx of new entrants into the labour force, in which case discontent is likely to be much more acute. Regional disparities will probably widen and add to the strain on the political system.

In the past, parties and politicians found it profitable to mobilise caste sentiment in their competition for power and influence and this led some observers to hold that the institution of caste was being strengthened under the democratic political system. By now it is obvious that political competition is undermining caste solidarity; a single caste has never formed a basis of power for any party in India, except possibly in Maharashtra, and the need to construct workable coalitions has successfully corroded parochial loyalties among politicians of all parties. While caste sentiment will persist for a long time, the social coherence it used to supply is likely to diminish, and over a long period Indian society may become progressively atomised, giving rise to conditions productive of anomy, particularly in urban areas.

The next few years will probably see major changes in the leadership of the political parties, though their basic character as entities dominated by urban middle class functionaries is likely to remain largely unaltered as towns will continue to be the principal centres of political recruitment and of the institutional structures of authority. The generation of leaders who came into politics during the freedom movement will give place to men born in the thirties and forties for whom that movement would belong to history and not to their own personal experience. Of the present leadership only about a quarter who are now less than fifty years old should still be occupying leadership positions in the country. . . .

The introduction of the system of Panchayati Raj has for the first time carried the political process to the remotest villages in the country. This has given rise to a new rural leadership, which usually consists of the locally dominant persons who are economically prosperous, belong to higher castes and have linkages with powerful party leaders and administrative officers at the district and possibly State levels. They are taking political parties into the villages and in the process turning them into instruments of their own power at the local level. Parties are thus beginning to acquire an odd combination of features, as instruments of power in the hands of local leaders, of group manipulation in the hands of State leaders and of political integration in the hands of national leaders.

In societies undergoing rapid change stability is provided by an overwhelmingly dominant party rather than by relatively evenly balanced parties and I have no doubt that the stability of the Indian polity will require the continued dominance of the Congress party in the foreseeable future. The prospects in this direction are hopeful but not wholly certain. Its position has been gradually corroded in several districts and in some of the faction-ridden States its legislative majorities may well be threatened in the next election.

As against this it ought to be noted that the Congress commands vastly greater resources than any of the opposition parties and is likely to continue to do so. It enjoys the supreme advantage of being the ruling party, its organization is more wide-spread and institutional penetration deeper: it has thus a far superior capability for mobilising political support. The opposition parties, which are at best regional, have a long way to go before they can challenge its supremacy. In any event they show more signs of decay than it does. Their habitual inability to combine against it is unlikely to give way to purposeful combination in the near future.

The capacity of the Congress party to win adequate majorities in the States and at the Centre rests on a judicious balancing of factions, keeping them under control and preserving the coalition character of the party. The search for clarity and well-defined positions has nothing to recommend it to the Congress. Its amorphousness is indeed the basis of its strength and the source of the country's political stability. Any attempt to make the party artificially homogeneous would make it rigid and incapable of producing workable majorities. As the increasing pace of economic development and political mobilization begins to give rise to new groups commanding resources and influence and seeking a share in the affairs of the State the competition for power could become fierce. If this competition is not to cause political instability it must take place within the organisational framework of the dominant party. The need for accommodation and consensus will increase rather than diminish in the decades to come. To achieve it successfully, the Congress leadership will need all its resources of authority and tact. Above all, it will need to see that the High Command itself is not fragmented by factional loyalties, for it is the only group which has hitherto successfully conducted the policies of this amorphous party and continental society by being above faction and guided by national purpose.

The conditions of the Indian polity preclude the emergence of sharply defined positions. Its leadership, whether of the ruling party or the opposition, must be oriented towards seeking consensus, which necessarily involves compromise. It cannot be radically innovative.

There are, however, obvious limits to coalition-building, and the achievement capabilities of coalitions are notoriously small. The contradiction facing the Indian parties is that while the political system imposes on them the roles of seeking power and influence through loosely constructed coalitions and of integrating the political community by drawing an increasing number of citizens into participation in political processes, the social conditions demand a purposeful, coherent and well-directed effort to harness the resources of the State and society to build stable institutions and achieve economic development and social improvement. The relevant conditions for these are general stability and economic mobilisation, which can best be achieved by limiting the extent of participation in politics in the short run and consciously restricting the area of public life exposed to political pressures, without interfering with the integration taking place through basic democratic processes, thus allowing a balance between social autonomy and public purpose. The dominant position of the Congress party, its legacy of acknowledged authority and the essentially one class character of political leadership have combined to give India a party system that has served these contrary purposes.

Among the major achievements of Nehru was to lay the basis of a consensus in favour of social, political and economic modernization. His successors can build upon it, but the pace will be slow and undramatic. Whether the party system will continue to perform the same useful role—providing stability without stagnation and integrating the political community while restricting the area of issues open to sectional manoeuvering—will depend largely on the Congress party's capacity to hold together its hetrodox elements and assimilate new claimants to status and power, while at the same time supporting a structure of administration and public policy which will enable the nation to achieve an acceptable degree of economic development and social change.

55 • Frank Moraes: *Gandhi Ten Years After* *

Independence from Great Britain under the spiritual but astute leadership of Mahatma Gandhi ceased to be the goal of a few Western-educated elite and became that of a mass movement supported by all segments of Indian society. Gandhi's contribution was his ability to unify, organize, and activate an inert society through his doctrines of "ahimsa" (non-violence) and "saytyagraha" (soul force) which expressed themselves in civil disobedience and passive resistance based on selflessness and self-discipline.

Frank Moraes, one of India's leading journalists, points out in the selection below that while few of Gandhi's social doctrines have survived the impact of modernization and industrialization, his influence still pervades Indian society and continues to be a significant factor in Indian politics. A segment of the Congress party remains devoted to Gandhian ideas; civil disobedience for linguistic or other causes continues to plague the government; his dislike for power politics finds expression in Jayaprakash Narayan's proposals for a non-political, self-sufficient village society and in a lingering popular suspicion of politicians as power-seekers; and decision by unanimous consensus is considered more desirable than decision by majority vote in choosing a Prime Minister or selecting a village panchayat. But above all, Gandhism persists as moral inspiration.

* Excerpted by special permission from *Foreign Affairs,* Vol. 36, No. 2 (January 1958), pp. 253–266. Copyright by the Council on Foreign Relations, Inc., New York.

"In times of crisis and difficulty," I asked Nehru recently, "do you inquire of yourself, 'What would Gandhi have done?' " Nehru reflected a moment before he replied. "It's a difficult question but I'll answer it frankly. In moments of crisis, political or personal, I *do* think of Gandhi but for a somewhat selfish reason. I think of him because I would like to recapture his serenity of mind, the calmness of spirit with which he used to face a crisis. But if you ask me, do I consciously inquire of myself, 'What would Gandhi have done?' well—no."

It was an honest answer and typical of the man. Here was Gandhi's heir whom the Mahatma in his own lifetime had named as his successor confessing that not in every moment of crisis did he turn instinctively for inspiration to the Master.

"And yet," Nehru went on, "Gandhi typified the spirit of India in a curious and characteristic way. He had the same strong core of tradition and thought to which he remained loyal. But outside that he could adjust himself and his views to the impact of others. He was resilient and flexible. He would bend but he would not break."

As I listened to Nehru I felt that that was probably how the Mahatma would have liked it, for Gandhi had never insisted that his followers should live in the image of himself. True, he was an exacting taskmaster who expected and insisted on scrupulous adherence to certain standards of conduct, of discipline and rectitude. But even within the idiosyncrasies of his own personal mode of life Gandhi was prepared to make concessions to others, whether in the way of diet, tobacco, tea or celibacy. It was one reason why he attracted such diverse individuals as the exuberantly extroverted Sarojini Naidu on the one hand and the saintly but astringent Vinoba Bhave on the other.

Looking back over the past ten years from January 30, 1948, when the Mahatma was assassinated, it would be pharisaical to pretend that Gandhi's ideas and teachings survive and shine as vividly as they did in his lifetime. Like Hinduism, Gandhism is much more than a way of life for, just as the mere observance of caste, ritual and the institution of the joint family does not constitute Hinduism, so also the adoption of ascetic habits, verging on the masochistic, does not in itself generate the "soul force" which is Gandhism. Paradoxically enough, while Hinduism is beginning to shed its outer habiliments such as caste and the joint family, the present-day exponents of Gandhism, with rare exceptions, prefer the façade to the faith. The result is a general debasing of Gandhian gold.

Service was the master passion of Gandhi's life, and although he was not the first Indian to preach political liberty he was distinctive in so far as he was the first to identify himself with the people. This quality of never standing apart from the people is what distinguished the Mahatma most clearly from the older school of Indian politicians. An English friend describes how he once asked Gandhi whether his service was done through love of the cause or love of the people. Gandhi's reply was characteristic. "For love of the people," he said, and added. "To serve a cause without serving persons is a dead thing."

To the end of his life Gandhi combined with a basic, often extreme conservatism a heterodox outlook on many matters, and the rebel was as strong as the puritanical streak in him. The rebel in Gandhi drew Nehru to the Mahatma.

"Sometimes," Nehru confesses in his autobiography, "his language was almost incomprehensible to an average modern." Many of his ideas appeared to the younger man to be mediaeval and revivalist. Nehru recoiled from the Mahatma's idealization of poverty and suffering, his doctrine of wealth as a trust, his frequent stress on the religious and spiritual aspect of the civil disobedience movement, his attitude to machinery and modern civilization and his vagueness in defining political and economic objectives.

Yet behind Gandhi's gentle mien Nehru detected a resolute purpose. The Mahatma, he discovered, was different from the older school of Indian politicians in another respect, for while the latter had consisted largely of armchair politicians who delighted in marathon speeches and in the passing of long-winded resolutions, the Mahatma insisted on action. A wrong, he declared, should provoke not only protest but active resistance, and such resistance should be non-violent.

We come here to the core of Gandhi's teaching. Blended in the doctrine of *ahimsa* or non-violence are two of Christianity's outstanding principles—the precept of returning good for evil and the promise that the meek shall inherit the earth. The idea of using moral suasion rather than force is not new to humanity but to Gandhi belongs the credit of employing it as an instrument for political and social regeneration. In this the Mahatma was influenced greatly by the ideas of an American and a Russian, by Thoreau and Tolstoy.

With Thoreau he believed that in a time of injustice the place of the just man was in prison, and from the American he drew strength in his own way of life, in "the joy," as Thoreau put it, "of possessing all and owning nothing." It was to Tolstoy that Gandhi sent an account of his first non-violent campaigns in South Africa. Tolstoy's reply ends on a prophetic note: "Your activity in the Transvaal, as it seems to us at this end of the world, is the most essential work, the most important of all the work now being done in the world, wherein not only the nations of the Christian, but of all the world will inevitably take part."

To many this will seem an extravagant prophecy which indeed it was. But its interest lies in its irony, for there is no notion more mistaken or fanciful than the widespread belief that India and the National Congress Party were at any time, in Gandhi's lifetime or after, committed to non-violence as a creed. The Congress Party, including Nehru and other prominent leaders such as the late Sardar Vallabhbhai Patel, accepted non-violence but only as a method. With them it was an instrument of political practice, not an article of faith. The distinction is important for it explains many of the contradictions, seeming or real, in Indian policies at home and abroad since the Mahatma's death.

To Gandhi non-violence was a dogma, a creed and an article of faith, but the majority of his followers saw it only as a worthy means to a worthy end. They approached non-violence pragmatically whereas Gandhi's faith in it was absolute and immutable. Good means, he insisted, must lead to good ends while bad means could only vitiate and defeat the ends. In so far as he viewed ends as a projection of means he was often wont to regard means *as* ends and thus non-violence became with him a mission.

Most of the Congress Party, more especially Nehru, never shared this view. If they did, it is difficult to reconcile some of their actions with their speeches. Thus on the outbreak of the Second World War Gandhi urged that Indian aid should be given to the British unconditionally but that it should be of a non-violent character. Nehru's view, like that of the majority of his colleagues, was different. India, they felt, should assist Britain in a war against Nazism even to the extent of armed support, but it could do so only as a free nation. Subsequently, differences arose over a later resolution adopted by the Congress Party which Gandhi interpreted as committing the Congress to non-violence, even in external war. With this interpretation the majority of his colleagues, notably Nehru, Patel and Azad, disagreed, explaining to the Mahatma that their acceptance of the principle of non-violence was limited only to the country's internal political struggle and was never intended to be extended to external war. Significantly they also pointed out to him that the Congress had never applied the principle of non-violence to the Indian armed services and police since the Congress Party had frequently urged more rapid Indianization of the army.

Gandhi, having listened to them patiently, was admant. "It is my certain belief," he said, "that only non-violence can save India and the world from self-extinction." But his colleagues would not be convinced, and so—not for the first time—the Mahatma relinquished the leadership of the Congress Party.

The interesting fact that emerges from all this is that neither India nor the Congress Party accepted Gandhi's doctrine of non-violence as a creed. Even the Mahatma's effort to equate non-violence with Hindu teaching was vigorously contested, not least by Hindus themselves, many of whom pointed to the *Mahabharata,* the great epic poem which has as its central theme, the war between the Kauravas and Pandavas. In the *Bhagavad Gita,* which is an interpolation in the *Mahabharata,* Krishna addressing his disciple, Arjuna, urges him to play his part in the destruction of the enemy in war. Gandhi's attempt to explain this as symbolic of the eternal conflict between good and evil, right and wrong in the human soul, is not convincing for it cannot be reconciled with Krishna's address to Arjuna as a soldier whose duty it is to defend the community uninfluenced by fear. Nor in the Mahatma's lifetime was the modern educated middle class easily impressed by non-violence as a political faith. It seemed to them to lack an intellectual basis because violence by any rational thinking was permissible in defense of personal honor and against aggression.

Here Nehru, by rationalizing those of Gandhi's teachings which were not easily acceptable to the sophisticated intellectual, did much to reconcile this class to Gandhi's leadership and induced them to follow him. "A worthy end should have worthy means leading up to it," he observed in commending non-violence. But clearly he himself accepted it as a political weapon not because he respected it as an absolute creed but because he regarded it as the right policy in the conditions which prevailed.

One might almost say in the light of present-day events that Nehru used Gandhi's means to achieve what have proved to be largely his own political and economic ends. But this would be demonstrably unfair since at the time he could not have foreseen the future. That, however, is what has actually happened. The Indian Government of today, headed by Nehru, favors industrialization and high power projects, stands for a socialistic pattern of society, refuses to regard wealth as a trust and has put private enterprise on the defensive—developments at which Gandhi in all likelihood would have looked askance. On the other hand it is attempting to enforce prohibition over wide areas of India, to encourage the handloom, spinning wheel and small-scale industries, and to accelerate land reforms—measures which the Mahatma would have blessed. The Government has also been active in initiating birth-control clinics within ten years of the Mahatma's death. It will be remembered that Gandhi denounced artificial birth control as "sin" and preached the rarefied cult of *brahmacharya* which means chastity or voluntary restraint.

Only a few months ago I asked one of Gandhi's oldest English associates, H. S. L. Polak, who had worked with him in South Africa, how much of Gandhi's teaching he thought survived in India. "Ostensibly a great deal," said Polak. "In reality, very little."

I think he was right. The façade of Gandhism is there and many Congressmen still talk of the Mahatma as "the voice of conscience," but the voice, if ever heard, seems rarely to prevail. . . .

I remember asking Nehru some years ago, when the Mahatma was alive and the Congress Working Committee was meeting for a busy and protracted session, whether he could find time to see me. He puckered his eyebrows fretfully, for his day was very crowded, and then suddenly he smiled. "I know," he said. "Come and see me during Gandhiji's prayer meeting. I'm never there!"

It might have marked the beginning of the secular approach. Yet I feel he is less than just when he describes the foreign policy he now pursues as rooted in Indian tradition and deriving from Gandhi, the Buddha and Asoka. It is true that these great sons of India preached peace and good will to all men, and that in so far as non-alignment represents good will to all men it is in line with ancient tradition. But neither Nehru nor the Congress Party has at any stage accepted non-violence as a doctrine or a creed. Indeed they repudiated this concept of non-violence in Gandhi's own lifetime. Many Hindus repudiate it as contrary to Hindu tradition. Perhaps some might also see significance in the fact that of the three men, one, Gandhi, was assassinated by one of his own countrymen, while the religion preached by another, the Buddha, was gradually edged out of India and mainly flourishes in Thailand, Ceylon, Japan and elsewhere. Prophets rarely flourish in their own country.

Moreover, the Mahatma's conception of non-violence or *ahimsa* was never passive. He certainly never compromised with evil for he insisted that a wrong should not merely provoke protest but that it should be actively resisted. The practical expression of *ahimsa* was *satyagraha* which literally means "the power of truth" but is generally described as "soul force." *Satyagraha,* which came to be known in its political form in India as civil disobedience, was described by Gandhi as the weapon of the strong, not the weak, its motive force arising from a feeling of inner strength and its practice calling for self-discipline. For *satyagraha* inflicted physical injury on none but the exponent who by enduring the maximum suffering without thought of counter-violence sought to shame or inspire the wrongdoer into doing right.

I think Gandhi would have approved wholeheartedly of Nehru's foreign policy of non-alignment, as the majority of thoughtful Indians do; and indeed Nehru proclaimed his policy even in the Mahatma's lifetime. Where Gandhi might—and in all likelihood would—have differed from Nehru would have been in some of the attitudes adopted and emphasis placed in implementing the policy. He would certainly not have approved of carrying non-alignment to the point of being privy to anything wrong or evil. I feel he would have come out as unequivocally against the Soviet butchery in Hungary as the French butchery in Algeria. And not on the ground of violence alone but on the ground of wrongful oppression. Although his belief in the intrinsic goodness of man—which again is at the root of the Christian doctrine of saving souls—led him to appeal equally to Roosevelt and to Hitler during World War II and did not permit him to differentiate between Communists and non-Communists as human beings, he was implacable in his opposition to what he felt was evil.

"I do not know," he told some Indian Communists who tried to convert him as far back as 1924, "whether Bolshevism is for the good of Russia in the long run. But I do know that in so far as it is based on violence and denial of God it repels me. . . . I am an uncompromising opponent of violent methods even to serve the noblest of causes."

Gandhi believed in the spiritual nature of man, and for him a world or doctrine which denied the existence of God was meaningless and abnormal. It is here that modern India departs markedly from the Gandhian tradition, for to the Mahatma individuals were more important than governments and he worked passionately to uphold the individual's right to freedom of opinion and action. In a curious and distinctive way he was more concerned with individuals than causes. On one occasion he held up a meeting of the Congress Working Committee whose members had come hundreds of miles from various parts of India while he listened gravely and earnestly to the pleas of a widow who was there to consult him on a personal problem.

"Who can judge?" remarked a spectator who told me of this incident. "His sense of values is probably more true than ours."

Socialism sees society not in terms of individuals but as a conglomeration of groups, of classes and masses, of workers and capitalists, of peasants and landlords, of various forces operating at different strata to change the face of society. This is how Nehru and the Congress Party view India today, and it is here that they deviate most significantly from the Gandhian outlook and tradition. For to the Mahatma society meant individuals not groups, and he saw India as much in the faces of a peasant or a landlord as in the eyes of a child or a teacher. Gandhi was primarily a humanist and only next a politician. He was more concerned in achieving the ultimate slowly than in seizing on an immediate advantage and exploring it. This explains his weakness as a purely political negotiator. He was more interested in the purpose than in the mechanism of modern politics.

He functioned, it is true, in opposition to an established alien order whereas Nehru and the Congress Party operate today as the government in power. Political, economic and social values tend to change when viewed from different and opposite vantage points. This partly explains the movement of the Congress away from many of Gandhi's teachings, but the divergence is also influenced by the sharp difference in attitude or approach. The Gandhian emphasis was on the individual whereas the present-day Congress stress is on the State. Men appear differently when seen as individuals or as members of groups. The group outlook blurs the individual image. Gandhi put the human personality higher than the leviathan of the State.

On the domestic and foreign planes this difference of approach has led to an imperceptible but none the less definite demarcation between Gandhian precept and Congress practice. Socialism utilizes the machinery of the law and the State to set right what it believes to be an inequitable order of things. The ethical ideal of socialism is not far removed from Gandhism, but according to the Mahatma change should come through conversion and not through compulsion. The same motivation inspires Vinoba Bhave's movement in *bhoodan* or voluntary renunciation of land, the spirit which animates it being in line with Gandhian teaching and tradition. Compulsory acquisition of land with or without compensation would be strictly contrary to Gandhian principles. To state this is not to justify the Mahatma but merely to point out the divergence between his precept and Congress practice, for looked at from a modern point of view Gandhi's attitude seems perilously close to that of England's Victorian Liberals who opposed the Factory Acts on the plea that they infringed the freedom of the individual. . . .

Yet it would be unfair to infer from all this that Gandhism in India today is more honored in the breach than in the observance. The ideals which Gandhi symbolized and which he attempted to impress on his people were uncommonly, even transcendentally high, and not many men were as well equipped as the Mahatma either in experience or character to maintain such demanding standards. Despite the drawbacks and deficiencies inherent in the Indian situation and people, Gandhi has left on his country the stamp of his moral impress. This survives.

56 • Jawaharlal Nehru: *Indian Socialism* *

Jawaharlal Nehru was Prime Minister for seventeen years and dominated Indian politics until his death in 1964. Western-educated and modern-minded, he devoted himself to achieving national unity, a secular state, constitutionalism, and a rising standard of living for the Indian people. His political ideology was eclectic, containing aspects of Gandhism, Marxism, liberalism, and western socialism.

A major contribution to the stability of the new state was his role as unifier and balancer of the wide spectrum from right to left within the Congress party. Nehru held the party together both by the force of his personality and by balancing the numerically stronger conservative right wing with his liberal socialism on the side of the weaker left.

Socialism became the official party doctrine at the Avadi Congress party session in 1955, and was reinforced at Bhubaneshwar in 1964 when the party declared that "the object of the Indian National Congress is the well-being and advancement of the people of India, by peaceful and constitutional means, of a socialist state based on parliamentary democracy in which there is equality of opportunity and of political, economic, and social rights and which aims at world peace and fellowship." Selections from Nehru's speeches as Prime Minister in 1955 to the Lok Sabha give his concept of liberal socialism. The first speech is in support of an amendment to Article 31 (2) of the constitution which would make non-justiciable the amount of compensation paid for private property taken for public purposes.

Now we come to the major and the longest Minute of Dissent, that of the hon. Member Shri N. C. Chatterjee, in which he has quoted from high legal authorities, apart from the fact that he is himself a high legal authority. First of all we must

* *Jawaharlal Nehru's Speeches, 1953–1957* (New Delhi: Publication Division, Ministry of Information and Broadcasting, Government of India), pp. 124–144, 152–154. By permission.

bear in mind exactly what this Bill is and what this attempt to amend the Constitution is. It is odd that words like confiscation of property and expropriation are thrown about when actually what the Constitution—or the amended Constitution, if you amend it—says is that there will be no such thing except by law and except on payment of compensation. The quantum of compensation is to be determined by the legislature. Shri Chatterjee has given many quotations about due process of law. For instance he says a distinguished American judge has observed: "A great desire to improve the public condition is not enough to warrant achieving the desire by a shorter cut than the constitutional way."

I say that this is the constitutional way, and what is proposed is the definite, legal and constitutional way of doing it and we are varying or amending the Constitution in the constitutional way. I do not quite understand this throwing about of words like expropriation and confiscation and doing things apart from the law. Remember that the sole major change proposed is to make clear one thing which was clear to us at the time this Constitution was framed. That is to say, according to the Constitution as it emerged from the Constituent Assembly, the quantum of compensation or the principles governing compensation would be decided by the legislature. This was made perfectly clear. It is obvious that those who framed the Constitution failed in giving expression to their wishes accurately and precisely, and thereby, the Supreme Court and some other Courts have interpreted it in a different way. The Supreme Court is the final authority for interpreting the Constitution. All I can say is that the Constitution was not worded as precisely as the framers of the Constitution intended. What the framers of the Constitution intended is there for anyone to see. All that has been done now is to make that wording more precise and more in accordance with what the framers of the Constitution at that time meant and openly said. I do not therefore understand this measure of excitement and agitation in people's minds—not in this House but elsewhere—about this matter. . . .

Shri Chatterjee has written at length and has begun by referring to the makers of the Indian Constitution having deliberately conferred certain Fundamental Rights. I was one of those humble individuals who had something to do with the making of the Constitution; there are others sitting here who had recorded their views then. I submit that the makers of the Constitution were perfectly clear as to what they meant. What we are putting before the House in this Joint Committee's Report, I submit, is precisely and exactly what they said at that time, so far as article 31(2) is concerned. There is nothing new about it and there is nothing very terrible about it. The whole Constitution is based on the proposition that we must proceed by law and, secondly, that compensation should be paid, except in a certain small number of specified cases. Generally speaking, compensation must be paid, but the determination of what the compensation should be is left to the legislature. To repeat what I said four or five years ago, if anything is done by the legislature which is considered a fraud on the Constitution, then the courts may come in, but otherwise it should not be open to the courts to challenge the decision of the legislature on this point. It is a simple issue. Where does expropriation come in? I really do not understand it. The view in regard to property which Shri Chatterjee has put forward in his Minute of Dissent, and in which he is supported by some high legal authorities, is one with which I cannot agree. It may be that, as Shri Chatterjee says, quoting a great political thinker, "men will sooner forget the death of their relatives than the confiscation of their property." We would rather not encourage such men in this country. It is a monstrous thing that property should be made a god, above human beings. To say that whatever a man may do—he may even commit murder—is nothing, but property is a god and must be worshipped, is a view of property which Government is not prepared to accept at all.

Shri Chatterjee repeatedly refers to the use of the phrase "the sanctity of private property," as though there was something divine or semi-divine about it. The possession of property is a right which we recognize, which we protect, and it is defined here how compensation is to be given if a man is deprived of it. But to talk in terms of sanctity, divinity and so on being attached to property is very much out of date. It has no relation to present-day facts. If Shri Chatterjee quotes something from the judges of the middle of the nineteenth century, I will only say that that may have been the way of thinking then, but that it is not so now.

Again, Shri Chatterjee quotes—rather, he quotes someone who quotes—an eminent English jurist as having said that "the public good is in nothing more essentially interested than in the protection of private property." I should like the House to consider these words. That is what I call an astounding and amazing statement—that the highest public good is the protection of private property, more than everything else. I submit that we should not only agree to it but reject it summarily and absolutely, whoever might have made it.

Shri Chatterjee goes on to say that no one shall be arbitrarily deprived of his property. I agree completely. Who is doing so? Is this arbitrary deprivation of property? First, the law does not do it. Secondly, the law lays down rules and regulations on the principles of compensation. Where does arbitrariness come in? I regret to say some people do not see what is being done. There are even some people who write in newspapers without understanding the purport. They talk loosely and use words like expropriation, confiscation and arbitrary action. There is nothing of the kind.

Shri Chatterjee has referred to the United States Constitution in this respect. The United States Constitution is a great document, but I do not think it is quite appropriate to compare it with our Constitution or to say that our Constitution is based on it. Of course, we have taken a good many things from it and many more things from the Constitution of the United Kingdom. Nevertheless, our Constitution is not the Constitution of the United Kingdom, or, much less, that of the United States. The United States Constitution dates back to some time in the eighteenth century. It is obviously not a recent document. It represents the idea of the fathers of the American Constitution and the American nation at that time and they produced a very fine document, but for us to consider it in another country, in India, in the middle of the twentieth century, is hardly a reasonable proposition.

I should therefore like Parliament to remember these basic things. Here is something that is proposed which in effect clarifies and elucidates the Constitution and brings it completely in line with what the makers of the Constitution intended. Unfortunately, they did not do so in clear enough language, and therefore the courts have interpreted it differently. So, first, it is a matter of elucidation. Secondly, it is wrong to say that we are suggesting any arbitrary action, any confiscatory action or any expropriatory action. In fact, the Constitution has said that there should be compensation by law. But it is true that the quantum of compensation will be determined by the legislature. I cannot say offhand what in a particular case the legislature might do. But, by and large, if you have to govern this country democratically, you have to trust the legislature not only in this but in a hundred other matters of far greater moment. This legislature might decide on some far-reaching change affecting, perhaps, a question of such magnitude as war and peace. Surely the Supreme Court will not decide that. It may decide other questions in ways which directly or indirectly might even affect property. All kinds of decisions may be taken which will have a powerful effect on our social and economic structure, and, for example, on planning. But it is the legislature's will that is bound to prevail in such matters. There is no way out of it. It seems to me a basically wrong approach to single out this question of compensation and to take it out of the purview of the legislature in the sense of somebody else revising the legislature's decision. Such a course can be thought of only if you think that property is something semi-divine and that the protection of private property is to the largest good of the nation, which hardly anyone today will say, obviously. . . .

In this transitional age, to think in a static way and to imagine that property has exactly the same place in human life as it used to have means that we have stopped thinking. These apprehensions and fears therefore appear to me completely unjustified. Far greater developments and disasters might suddenly confront the world and in this context for somebody to be afraid of some mill or plant or factory being acquired seems to me out of proportion. So far as this Government is concerned, my mind is perfectly clear on the subject. I have no respect for property, except perhaps some personal belongings. But I respect the other person's respect for property occasionally. The House will forgive me if I speak in a personal sense; I have no property sense. It seems a burden to me to carry property; it is a nuisance. In life's journey one should be lightly laden; one cannot be tied down to a patch of land or a building. I cannot appreciate this intense attachment to property. But, while not appreciating it, I realize and recognize its prevalence. At the same time I think the proposition that some hon. Members on the opposite side advanced about acquisition or confiscation without compensation seems to me basically wrong. I say so from the point of view of the public good, not because I love property. Except in particular cases, where a person misbehaves and so on, I do not want anything to be acquired except on payment of just compensation. . . .

Coming to industrial property, our approach is that the Government should never acquire any old plant except for the purpose of holding some strategic point for the benefit of planning. The reasons behind this approach are obvious. We are an under-developed country, industrially speaking; we want to industralize the country; we want hundreds of factories to go up. Should I not use all the resources available at my hand to put up new factories—State factories—instead of acquiring old and perhaps worn-out plants belonging to somebody else?

We are not going to acquire anything unless it comes in the way of our planning. The idea which is sometimes put forward by some honourable Members opposite, that a kind of general scheme of nationalization would bring about great equalization, is incorrect. Drastic equalization in that way simply means equalization of the lowest stage of poverty. That is not good enough. We want to raise our country's standards and yet bring about this equalization, so that we can go towards an egalitarian society. The whole idea of nationalization does not come into the picture at all except that when planning requires that some strategic point which comes in its way should be taken possession of, the State should control it. Otherwise the State should go ahead and build up new State plants. The public sector becomes bigger and more and more important and productive, letting the private sector advance simultaneously. If the public sector is nibbling and eating into the private sector, there is no total advance, even though there might be some advantage from the social point of view. We shall only be losing our resources by shifting a factory from the private to the public sector. . . .

If I may, with all respect, refer to Gandhiji, his view was always to activize the lowest strata. We need not now go into how we should do it. The thinking of many of our leading people is that dynamism somehow starts from the top and seeps to the bottom. I think that outlook must change. To activize this base we may have to take numerous social steps like narrowing the big gap between the top and the bottom. That is the right approach. Acquiring property or depriving somebody of his property, or thinking that we are doing good to the country by not paying compensation will not help.

So I would plead with this House that this particular amendment of the Constitution removes a slight obstacle that had come in our way, and clears the path for us to go ahead with the vast schemes of development that we shall have to undertake.

Government and the People [1]

. . . Democracy, as a speaker just now said, is a means to an end. What is the end we aim at? I do not know if everybody will agree with me, but I would say the end is the good life for the individual. What form it should take can be argued about, but the good life certainly must imply a certain satisfaction of the essential economic needs, which will release him from continuous oppression, and which will give him a chance to develop his creative faculties. . . .

In the past, democracy has been taken chiefly to mean political democracy, roughly represented by the idea of every person having a vote. It is obvious that a vote by itself does not mean very much to a person who is down and out and starving. Such a person will be much more interested in food to eat than in a vote. Therefore, political democracy by itself is not enough except that it may be used to obtain a gradually increasing measure of economic democracy. The good things of life must become available to more and more people and gross inequalities must be removed. That process has, no doubt, gone on for some time in countries where there is political democracy. . . .

We believe in democracy. Speaking for myself, I believe in it, first of all, because I think it is the right means to achieve ends and because it is a peaceful method. Secondly, because it removes the pressures which other forms of Government may impose on the individual. It transforms the discipline which is imposed by authority largely to self-discipline. Self-discipline means that even people who do not agree—the minority—accept solutions because it is better to accept them than to have conflict. It is better to accept them and then change them, if necessary, by peaceful methods. Therefore, democracy means to me an attempt at the solution of problems by peaceful methods. If it is not peaceful,

[1] Address to the First All-India Seminar on Parliamentary Democracy, New Delhi, February 25, 1956.

then to my mind, it is not democracy. If I may further elaborate the second reason, democracy gives the individual an opportunity to develop. Such opportunity does not mean anarchy, where every individual does what he likes. A social organization must have some disciplines to hold it together. Those can either be imposed from outside or be in the nature of self-discipline. Imposition from outside may take the form of one country governing another or of an autocratic or authoritarian form of government. In a proper democracy, discipline is self-imposed. There is no democracy if there is no discipline.

The question arises: if people cannot observe discipline, then does not the democratic structure tend to crack up? Something will have to take the place of democracy to enforce discipline. The enforced discipline may come—as it sometimes has—from military dictatorship. If a vacuum is created, external authorities may fill it or some internal authority grows up to fill it. . . .

. . . The nature of government has progressively changed in every country, whether the structure of society there is capitalist or socialist or something in between. Even in countries supposed to be intensely capitalistic the governments perform social functions to a great extent today. Functions normally relegated to private individuals or private enterprise are now performed by governments. The pressure of circumstances is such that the social sector of governments has grown even in countries which normally do not want it to grow. In the other countries which deliberately aim at dealing with this sector governmentally, it will of course grow more. Thus, whatever the basic policy pursued by a country, it becomes inevitable for the governmental structure to become involved in social problems ever increasingly. The old idea of government used to be a police State. I am not using that word in a bad sense but in the sense that the government's chief functions were those of guarding the country, giving security to the country from external invasion and internal disorder, collecting taxes, and so on. These were the main functions of government. Governments must continue to discharge them, but innumerable other functions have come in. How far can parliamentary democracy be adapted to meet these new burdens and functions of government satisfactorily, effectively, and in time? Time is the overriding consideration and that is why the question has arisen whether it is possible to have devolution of authority in parliamentary democracy which ensures that these problems can be dealt with rapidly and effectively. The easiest way to deal with a problem is for an autocrat or dictator to settle it at once, rightly or wrongly. Obviously that is an approach which is bad for the growth of the people. It does not develop that creative energy, that spirit and that sense of freedom which we consider essential. But remember also that creative energy and a sense of freedom do not develop merely by giving a person the right to vote.

Parliamentary democracy is inevitably going in the direction, everywhere, of what might be called economic democracy. It may take different forms, but only in the measure that it solves the economic problems does it succeed even in the political field. If the economic problems are not solved then the political structure tends to weaken and crack up.

Ultimately, all problems concerning human beings and their mutual relations depend on the character of the human beings. The same type of governmental machinery or constitution might be totally unsuited to different conditions, to different backgrounds of people, although certain basic principles may be common. We in India, owing to a very long period of contact with England and with

British parliamentary institutions, were made to think on the lines of wanting British parliamentary institutions in India. When the chance came, we reproduced those parliamentary structures and institutions here in a large measure. I think we have largely succeeded and I think we shall succeed even more. The question that I have put before you is not merely related to India but to every country: how far this parliamentary structure, as it is, is competent to deal with the great problems that come one after another at the beginning of this atomic age.

We talk about the spread of political power, in the sense that everybody has a vote. We have to remember at the same time that there are methods of influencing people in the right or in the wrong direction—methods of propaganda which may excite people, let us say, and bring them up to a high temper and create war conditions. These engines of propaganda may be exploited by democracy or they may break up democracy. We live in such an extraordinary age of change that every old yardstick is too short to measure it.

There is one aspect of democratic government to which we in India must give more consideration than other countries. In Western Europe they developed their parliamentary system gradually, in the course of a hundred years or more. Occasionally there were conflicts; occasionally there was a danger of a crack-up, but somehow they managed to get over it all. Except for these occasional conflicts, it has been a long period of relatively measured advance, and progress has been without too great a stress.

In India, we have certain advantages and certain disadvantages. In the course of the last thirty or forty years, we built up a movement of an unusual type. While it was largely a peaceful movement, it was nevertheless a revolutionary movement. This unusual combination of revolutionary content and peaceful methods changed the character of the people in the course of a generation. Freedom was not suddenly thrown into our laps. We struggled for it; we conditioned ourselves for it; we went through great strain and trouble over it. But the change was far less difficult than in any other country that I can think of because we were conditioned to function peacefully. The trail of bitterness and conflict did not pursue us and we could adapt ourselves mentally and physically to the changed conditions. At the same time, since our whole training has been in opposition, it has not been easy to get our people out of the habit of thinking and functioning as though they are in the opposition. It is a natural feeling, and has developed in all countries, particularly in countries which have had major revolutions. . . .

To sum up, all our institutions, including the parliamentary institutions, are ultimately the projections of a people's character, thinking and aims. They are strong and lasting in the measure that they are in accordance with the people's character and thinking. Otherwise, they tend to break up.

The Opposition [2]

I read yesterday that my friend and old colleague, Jayaprakash Narayan, has said recently that I should help—I forget his words—in establishing or in developing a strong opposition to the Congress. This is a very strange request. I believe completely in any government, whatever it might be, having stout critics, having an opposition to face. Without criticism people and governments become

[2] From a speech at Island Ground, Madras, January 31, 1957.

complacent. The whole parliamentary system of government is based on such criticism. The free Press is also based on criticism. It would be a bad thing for us if the Press was not free to criticize, if people were not allowed to speak and criticize government fully and in the open. It would not be parliamentary government. It would not be proper democracy. I welcome criticism in Parliament. In fact, we welcome criticism from our own party members. The amount of room we have in our own party for criticism of Government's policy is great. But when Jayaprakashji says that I should build up an opposition, does he want me to build up a bogus thing to oppose the Congress? What value or what virtue will that have? He gives the example, I think, of the great Turkish leader, Kemal Ataturk. With all respect to Jayaprakashji, the example is not a good one. There was no democracy in Turkey, real or even unreal. It was a dictatorship. Does he want that kind of thing to happen in India? The point is that the opposition should have the freest opportunity to express its opinion in the Press and on the platform and to fight elections. I cannot canvass for the P.S.P. or the Communist Party. They have the freest opportunity to do so. The Election Commission is independent of Government. It is open to you, to any of you, to vote as you like. You know that there is no question of pressure or coercion. I do submit that we in India have a greater degree of freedom in elections—and in things other than elections—than almost any other country in the world. There may be a few countries which have the same freedom as we have. But a far greater number of countries in the world have no such freedom. We have it and I am proud of it and I am sure it will continue. I want every type of oppositionist to go and apply to the people. If the people are not going to vote for him, am I to coerce them to vote for him?

Jayaprakashji says it would be good for the Congress to be defeated. I might perhaps agree that it might be good for the Congress to be defeated, but surely the question is not for us, but for the people. The issue is what is good for the country, not what is good for the Congress. Our friends like Jayaprakashji have got so entangled in their dislike of the Congress that they have forgotten such a thing as India and the good of India. It is my belief that if by any mischance the Congress was defeated it would be very bad for India. I do not say that Congressmen are better people than others. There are good men in other organizations. There are patriots in other organizations. It is not a question of personal friendship; it is a question of the national good. Suppose in Parliament, instead of the strong Congress Party, we had a dozen or twenty small groups with nobody in a majority. What would happen? There would be no stable government, and each little group would intrigue with the other. There would be offers of ministerships for people who gave up a party to join another. That is what inevitably happens when there are all kinds of parties with none having a majority. I can give you instances where countries are failing because of the failure to get a stable government. At a time when we talk of the Second Five-Year Plan, when the energy of the nation should be put into development, when we have Pakistan shouting itself hoarse about *jehad* and war, are we to experiment with numerous odd groups? It surprises me and amazes me that a person of good sense should suggest something which totally ignores the facts of life in India today. The facts of life are these, that we have to fight a tremendous opposition in India, not any political party, but our own failings, our own liability to go wrong, our disruptive tendencies, our communalism, our provincialism, our casteism, our readiness even to break into violence, and so many other things. Our history shows that we are very prone to disruptive, fissiparous tendencies. And if British rule in India did a good thing, it was to make us united in our fight. But really the first effective mass-scale attempt to build up this unity was by Gandhiji under and within the Congress. It brought results, and yet you see how soon such unity goes to pieces. Take the question of States' reorganization. Whether the decision was right or wrong, is it not fantastic for people to commit murder, arson and violence on that account? Does it not show our inherent weakness? It may be, of course, that this was done for political reasons, because of the approach of elections. I put it to Jayaprakashji because his own party—the P.S.P.—took a considerable part in this agitation. I am not for a moment criticizing their view of the matter or their taking part in agitations with regard to boundaries. But I do submit that by doing it in the way they have, they encouraged the most dangerous thing in India, that is, the tendency to disruption.

SECTION FOUR

Parties, Factions, and Interest Groups

57 • Gopal Krishna: *The Indian National Congress Party* *

Few new states in the modern world have had the advantage of stability of political institutions and continuity of leadership which the Congress party has been able to provide for India. The Congress, founded in 1885, headed the movement for independence and upon achieving its goal transformed itself into the Indian National Congress party. For two decades it was a dominant party within a multiparty system in which oppositional parties before 1967 had little chance for success on either the national or state level. Not only had it been the major agent for mobilizing and organizing the masses for independence, but it had in 1947 a highly articulated, hierarchical organizational structure with considerable experience in decision-making and administration. In addition, it was uniquely blessed with outstanding leaders such as Gandhi, Nehru, Sardar Patel, and others who were able successfully to adapt to their new role of running a modern state. Furthermore, it continued to include within its ranks such a wide spectrum of opinion from right to left that it was able to undercut opposition effectively in terms of policies. The Praja Socialist party, for example, had little to offer in the face of the Congress stand on socialism. Gopal Krishna, in the following section, discusses the origins of the party, the reasons for its dominance, and its ability to maintain a popular consensus for so long and crucial a period in the life of the new nation.

The overwhelming dominance of the Congress party and the numerical weakness of the opposition have been a cause of much concern to all well-wishers of Indian democracy. This failure to conform to the ideal pattern for a democratic polity envisaged by conventional students of politics has produced a certain confusion of thought among the political leaders as well as among the academic students of the Indian party system, which permits competition without it leading to the periodic displacement of the ruling party from office and operates a

* "One Party Dominance: Development and Trends," Supplement to *The Indian Journal of Public Administration,* Vol. XII, No. 1 (January–March 1966), pp. 3–11. By permission.

liberal polity without always subordinating the organizational wing of the latter to the governmental wing. The characteristics of this system have been the continued dominance of the Congress party, claiming to represent the nation and holding the monopoly of power, internecine factional disputes within it, and a persistent tendency for it either to take over the programmes of the opposition parties or to make timely concessions on issues taken up by them, so preventing them from acquiring much permanent strength. The role of the opposition parties has generally been restricted to influencing the policies of the ruling party rather than challenging its monopoly of power. The recent past of national struggle and the broad consensus inherited from it on national aims and the tasks of nation-building combined with the charismatic and skillful leadership of Nehru—who simultaneously filled the roles of Prime Minister and leader of the opposition—have assisted the perpetuation of the dominant position of the Congress party.

More perceptive students of the Indian party system have characterized it as a "one party dominance system." This is distinguished from the more widespread "one party system" by the all-important difference that the former operates within the framework of an open polity but the latter within an essentially authoritarian and closed one. Freedom of opinion and organization is a strong feature of the Indian system and the genuineness of political competition is amply attested to by the fact that more than half the electorate has exercised its right to vote consistently in favour of the opposition candidates in the three elections held since independence. The ruling party, though it enjoys secure dominance, is subjected to unfettered organized opposition, making it responsive to currents of opinion and interests expressed through the instrumentality of the latter. The numerically weak opposition is not only permitted to exist but is looked upon as a legitimate and necessary part of the system, often consulted on matters of public policy and allowed to exercise influence far in excess of its strength in Parliament and the State legislatures. Those holding office are accessible as much to the members of the opposition parties as they are to those of the ruling party. Finally, the constitutional requirement that the ruling party renew its mandate at fixed intervals through free elections makes it ultimately accountable to the electorate.

The conventional classification of political parties on the basis of ideological inclinations or alleged interest representation, which is derived from the European social theory conceiving politics to be a second order activity or organized economic interests in society, will not enlighten understanding of Indian political parties both because the theory in itself is inadequate to explain the phenomenon of political parties and because the historical and social context of party development in India has tended to make the Indian parties highly eclectic in their outlook and amorphous in composition. Political parties are not, whether in India or elsewhere, merely spokesmen for other interest groups, but are in their own right "agencies for formulating, transmitting, and anchoring political opinions." They are autonomous institutions competing for power and towards that end they build "an alliance of substructures or sub-coalitions."

Their social composition and intellectual inclination have prevented Indian parties from stimulating interest group organization outside their folds. In one case where this could have been successfully done—among the urban working class—the parties vied with each other in splitting it in order to prevent the accession of its whole strength to anyone of them. Such articulate interest groups as exist have tended to join the Congress, the only truly "national party," which has thus built up a substructure of all types of groups providing a secure foundation to its power in the country.

The contemporary party system developed originally in the context of the struggle for freedom and since 1950 within the framework of Parliamentary government; both these environments have exerted their influence on the present character and structure of the political parties. The attitudes, the postures, the forms and the style of the political organizations of the pre-independence period have been carried over into the post-independence phase of political development; their evolution has shown a continuity in spite of the change of context.

The origins of political parties in India lie in the process of social and political modernization now at work for well over a hundred years. The changes brought about by the spread of education and modern media of communication, the rise of industry and the new professions, the introduction of new institutions of government necessitating new forms of political organization, the spread among members of modern professions and business of the aspiration to create a new nation encompassing all sections of society and the activization of those who opposed them in the name of separate community identities—all these have been instrumental in shaping party politics in India. Articulate political parochialism—characteristic of a society where primary loyalties continued to centre around caste and community, social and geographic mobility was minimal and attitudes were not enlightened by an awareness of the larger national community—resulted in the early formation of communal and caste parties, seeking in their own way to participate in the process of political modernization. The twenties and thirties saw the rise of parties based on socialist ideology, professing secularism and introducing in Indian society ideas of equality and class antagonism alien to its tradition and repugnant to its social ethos. Thus by 1940 nearly all the major political parties now active in Indian politics, or their parent bodies, had been founded and had taken root.

Historically and sociologically politics in India has been a one class sphere. Political activity, initiated by the educated classes in the latter part of the 19th century, long remained their preserve. They supplied all the leaders and nearly all the activists of all the political parties. The social framework within which the Indian parties have to operate is a complex one, consisting of a small modern sector in which economic classes have acquired marginal significance and a large traditional sector in which caste and religion are the dominant elements; while the former is predominantly urban and in terms of economic activity modern, the latter is rural and its economic organization is dominated by traditional agriculture. In this setting the need to secure maximum electoral support for parties founded and led by urban-educated persons influenced by modern ideas of class and nation and pursuing the interests of their own class has led to a vast and confusing mixture of ideological declamation and unblushing use of sectarian loyalties of caste, community, language and religion, at the expense of rational pursuit both of interest and of national purpose.

The identification of the freedom movement with the Indian National Congress made the latter the dominant entity in Indian politics. The compulsions of the struggle prevented it from becoming a rigidly organized party; it remained a composite movement, permitting the co-existence within its rank of socially distant and ideologically diverse elements held together by their commitment to the national objective of independence. Ideological considerations, unimportant to the vast majority of Congressmen, were in other cases—such as that of the Congress Socialists—deliberately subordinated to this objective. The independence movement also generated a broad consensus regarding the goals of the nation, expressed in the ideals of democracy and social justice.

The Congress directed its efforts towards containing sectarianism in all its forms by resolving or avoiding conflicts, balancing interests, blurring ideological distinctions and allowing social and intellectual pluralism to find a place in its own ranks. This is consistent with its search for a national consensus which lends some pragmatic justification to the subordination of conceptual clarity to purposes of politics.

The Congress developed as an extra-Parliamentary movement, especially after 1920. It shed its devotees of legislative politics in 1918, and though its members were permitted to contest elections after 1923 and formed Ministries in seven provinces in 1937, its essentially extra-Parliamentary character and the consequent ascendancy of the organizational over the legislative wing were preserved. The unchallenged authority exercised over the entire movement by the Congress High Command, whose members never became subordinate partners in the legislative process initiated by the imperial order, entrenched the tradition of centralized leadership.

The unequivocal emphasis on the creation of mass sanctions to achieve political ends placed a premium on demonstrations and defiance of authority, whose claim to voluntary obedience had been corroded over a period of several decades and was finally undermined. The Gandhian insistence on non-violence minimized disorder during the struggle, but the agitational style and extra-Parliamentary aspect of politics have left their legacies to independent India.

The political leadership of independent India was inherited from the independence movement. Its continuity was characteristic not only of the Congress but also of all the other parties. Many leaders of the present-day opposition parties were previously associated with the Congress and their outlook on politics, attitudes to authority and political style were formed or influenced by this association.

With the coming of independence the context of politics was transformed. From being a national movement of protest the Congress emerged as the ruling party. The Parliamentary system erected under the Constitution required for its proper operation a party system to organize the electorate, to form a channel of communication between politics and society and to provide the country with a Government that rested on popular consent. The comprehensive and authoritative organization of the Congress party provided the basis for building a viable political community and the national leadership under Nehru symbolized the unity and progress of the nation. The relatively slow process of penetration of politics in society limited the area of public life exposed to partisan political pressure. In its pursuit of stability and consensus the Congress consciously endeavored to depoliticise the more explosive issues and simultaneously took steps to minimize conflicts and reduce social tensions by introducing agrarian reforms, however tardily implemented, by measures to secure industrial peace, by legislation and social reforms designed to promote welfare and moderate inequality, and by a thoroughgoing re-organization of the States on a linguistic basis. It directed its efforts towards creating a new consensus on national goals based on the ideas of planning, welfare and democracy and also consciously endeavoured to remove the most potent causes of cleavage and dissension.

The process of transforming the Congress from a movement for national independence to the position of a ruling party began with the elimination from its ranks of organized groups not amenable to control by the leadership and ended with the final subordination of the organization to the leadership in 1951. The first to depart, in 1948, following the prohibition on organized groups within the Congress, were the Socialists, followed by Acharya Kripalani and his associates in 1951, and subsequently by a numerous body of persons who were either distressed by the course of Congress politics or found its ideological shifts unacceptable or were disappointed in their search for power and positions. This process, inevitable as it was, did not make the party any less heterogeneous, but only more pliable, because the elimination of ideologically or temperamentally discordant elements was accompanied by a process of absorbing socially dominant elements which had kept away from the Congress in the pre-independence period. Since the Congress was not a revolutionary ideological party and proposed to bring about social transformation on the basis of the widest possible consensus it could not treat any section of the population as deserving to be excluded from it. The need to consolidate its power also recommended this course, and the result was the entry of a large number of caste and community leaders, landlords, businessmen and many of the former opponents of the Congress, which, while it strengthened its power base at least for a time, caused much internal stress and often dismayed the older and more dedicated party workers.

The acquisition of supreme power at the Centre and in the States raised fierce controversy within the Congress over the role of the organization in the changed situation. It was easy enough to assert the supremacy of the organization when the national leaders were outside the governmental system, but in 1946 when they constituted the Government, the organization suffered an eclipse. The considerations of power, along with intellectual notions derived from text-book lessons in Parliamentary democracy, contrived to bring about a thoughtless relegation of the party to a secondary role in the emerging order. At the Centre the leadership of Nehru did not have its basis in ascendancy in the organization and he, therefore, placed greater trust in the governmental apparatus for carrying out the programme of economic and social development; when the party appeared to become a centre of resistance to his leadership he asserted his unrivalled authority to make it firmly subordinate to his own power and purpose. The party, instead of being actively associated with the formulation and implementation of social reconstruction programmes, became a suppliant adjunct to the Government, its only function being to endorse the policies of the Government when called upon to do so by the leader. In the States the machinery of the organization was used by rival factions to gain control over the Government, and then its power and patronage were utilized by the successful faction to control the party.

The achievement of the Congress during the first decade and a half of independence consisted then of drawing into its fold all the socially powerful elements, old and new, for every one of whom it offered some stake in the new order. It buttressed its power by reducing conflict and by building support structures in critical sectors—for example, by founding the Indian National Trade Union Congress in 1947 to neutralize the organized working class. Its ideology was suitably renovated to appeal to the middle classes without injuring the privileged ones. The composite character of the party was preserved, indeed made more heterogeneous by promiscuous accommodation of divergent elements, whose commitment to the new consensus being created around the objectives of economic development, socialism and democracy remained superficial.

It is a necessary feature of parliamentary democracy that competition for power takes place through periodical free elections and where a democratic system is newly established the contending parties participating in this process tend to become increasingly oriented towards organizing themselves for mobilizing electoral support for their candidates. Their capacity to influence decisions, when they do not command power, depends upon the number of seats they win and the proportion of votes they poll and the need to secure the largest number of votes possible imposes on them the effort to cultivate the support of diverse elements in the community. Their emphasis shifts from a select membership to a mass following and every democratic party becomes a coalition of groups commanding some support among different sections of the electorate. This weakens discipline within the party and the attempt to formulate its objectives so as to arouse least opposition makes it ideologically heterogeneous; its consensus rests on the minimal agreement indispensable for either maintaining the party in existence or placing it or keeping it in power. The attractions of power serve as the bond holding the party together. Fifty years ago Robert Michels pointed out: "As organization increases in size, the struggle for great principles becomes impossible. It may be noticed that in the democratic parties of today the great conflicts of view are fought out to an ever diminishing extent in the field of ideas and with the weapons of pure theory, that they, therefore, degenerate more and more into personal struggles and invectives, to be settled finally upon considerations of purely superficial character." Admittedly, a party must exhibit a certain "harmonious direction of wills towards identical objective and practical aims," but the objective and the aims are liable to be sufficiently vague and general in character to enable a large body of persons with divergent interests and opinions to come together and work through a single organization for their achievement.

The introduction of universal adult franchise for the elections to the State and Central legislatures brought the political parties into an intimate and direct relationship with Indian society, whose principal features are the relatively low level of social integration and essentially aglommerative character. Caste and community were never out of Indian public life and even the great reform movements of the 19th century did not transcend them. Formally organized political parties oriented towards communal interests have existed since at least 1906 when the All-India Muslim League and the All-India Hindu Mahasabha were founded; they were followed by the Justice Party, a movement dominated by the non-Brahmin land-owners of Andhra Pradesh, founded in Coimbatore in 1917, and the All-India Scheduled Castes Federation founded by Ambedkar in 1942. Parties based on organized economic interests were few, and the only significant one was the Unionist Party in the Punjab, founded by Fazl-i-Hussain in 1923, representing the Muslim, Hindu and Sikh landlords in the province. The nationalist movement itself was not subjected to those pressures of group interests seeking accommodation normally exerted upon political parties in a democratic society. The plural social structure of India was not allowed to find uninhibited expression in its politics when all efforts were directed towards winning independence. But an important consequence of the process of the penetration of politics into society which accompanied the growth of the national movement was to spread political awareness among increasing sections of a very poorly integrated population and to promote ideas of social solidarity among them. Since the integrative process was far slower than the process of political awakening, it resulted in emphasizing group identities often at the expense of the larger national community. The new constitutional framework introduced in 1950 was designed to promote national integration through citizen participation in politics, principally through the electoral process which when set to work in 1952 accelerated the politicization of the population. But the vast majority of the new electorate was politically illiterate; its social awareness often did not extend beyond caste and community, and by and large it was innocent of issues transcending those of strictly personal interest. Once these persons were brought into the political process, parties had to take into account in selecting their candidates the parochial sentiments and loyalties which alone seemed to have significance for the greater portion of the electorate. Lacking generally direct contact with the voters through their own organizational agencies, parties had to approach them through intermediaries having access to them through their mostly informal traditional organizations. Their formal appeals to the electorate continued to be couched in what Morris-Jones has called the modern idiom, but the candidates knew well enough that the party manifestos exercised little influence on the ultimate choice of the voters. A new dimension thus came to be added to the activities of the political parties making them mediating agencies between the largely traditional and politically diffuse electorate and the modern state system with its emphasis on citizenship, purposive direction of public policy and political integration. The interpenetration of politics and the social order compelled the parties to come to terms with, and in the process help to moderate and modify, the traditional group orientation in Indian public life. Even when the struggle for power and influence appeared to encourage them to make use of group sentiment, thus increasing and solidifying the already powerful parochial tendencies, the parties in effect contributed to the making of the national community by drawing many non-modern groups into the modern sector of political activity.

The process of inducting rising groups into the political society has been working out mainly through the instrumentality of the dominant ruling party, though other parties have also played their part in it. The tension this creates between the "in-groups" and "out-groups," the old possessors of power and the new contenders for it, characterized the later history of the Congress even during the freedom struggle. Since independence the new factor of competition for the distribution of public resources has been added to the contention for power and influence. The parties have tried to utilize social groups for strengthening their own electoral base, while the latter have tried to utilize parties for gaining a share in the resources being made available through State agencies for economic development and social welfare. In the competition for their support the ruling party possessed a great advantage over its adversaries by virtue of its command over the public resources, and it has utilized these to build for itself a firm support base. The opposition parties have tried to secure support by appealing to sectional sentiments, whether over language or over economic claims, and by taking up group causes, though only occasionally with success. In the process, however, every party has become engaged in the dual and seemingly contradictory processes of encouraging sectionalism and integrating the community.

58 • Rajni Kothari: *Party System* *

The continued dominance of the Congress Party meant, according to Rajni Kothari writing in 1961, that effective Indian politics took place within the party itself rather than between parties. The weak and fragmented oppositional parties were unable to form coalitions, and were reduced to acting as pressure points on various Congress leaders rather than as an opposition hoping to win power. In the general elections of 1952, 1957, and 1962 Congress won over 70 per cent of the seats in the Lok Sabha. In 1962 it won 353 seats out of 494, with its closest competitor, the Communist party, holding only 29. With rare exceptions it dominated the state legislative assemblies as well. The following selection discusses the dynamics of party politics under this system.

Nevertheless, two decades of political dominance had an eroding effect on the ageing Congress in the form of corruption, public apathy, and increasingly vicious intra-party factionalism. The fourth general election of 1967 ended the dominant position of the Congress and so ended an era in Indian politics. Electoral losses were unexpectedly large, and left it with a slim majority in the Lok Sabha, the loss of nine and later eleven state legislative assemblies, and the defeat of many of its top leaders including incredibly K. Kamaraj, the president of the party itself. The one-party dominance of the Congress, however, was not replaced by a viable two or multiparty system, but by a series of fragile, unstable coalitions, united momentarily by opposition to the Congress. By 1968 several state coalitions, West Bengal among them, had already collapsed, giving rise to disorders and uncertainty.

The influence of the party system in politics is largely a result of our historical development. In many Asian countries, political institutions have developed under quite different auspices under an administrative bureaucracy or a military elite. In India, the movement for national independence was allowed to be openly organized by the British; second, and this is very important, it was spread over a period; thus there was enough time to build up a well-designed organisational network; third, the need was felt quite early to give the movement a mass basis thus turning a "microscopic minority" of Swarajists into a nationwide organisation. Max Weber's "stages" of party development from aristocratic cliques to parties of notables and finally to mass parties do not apply to the Indian case where almost from the beginning the party had to be consciously organised and given a popular basis at a later stage. The Indian National Congress had emerged as a highly organised party long before Independence, achieving what Sir Ivor Jennings has called "organisation in depth". India was, therefore, in a very fortunate position when Independence came. The leadership of the "movement" took over the government of the country and sustained it at all levels. Along with the administrative hierarchy inherited from the British, this made for political stability, avoided political disintegration and ruled out any possibility of the military taking over.

* *Economic Weekly,* Vol. XIII (June 3, 1961), pp. 847–854.

The "organisation in depth" of the Congress party also ensured that its authority would not be seriously challenged. While acute differences with the official line often developed within the Congress, the dissenting members could either try to influence the party from within or leave the party and go into wilderness. Attempts at bringing about an open split have been frustrated and although each break has meant the withdrawal of some very capable men from the Congress, thus weakening the party, the dissidents have lacked the political support that could make for an effective opposition.

This was so before Independence; it has been even more so since. The position is similar to that in Britain and America where the formation of a new party is an almost impossible task, except that in India the dissidents from the Congress do not have the alternative of joining another equally well-organised party. Besides, differences within the Congress did not always mean a complete and decisive breaking away of the dissidents from the party. Thus, when the Socialists in the Congress differed from the party's official leadership, there was considerable difference of opinion among the socialists, one group advocating a complete break and the other pleading for changing the Congress from within. The argument has continued ever since between those in the Socialist party (now the P S P), who have sought "co-operation" with the Congress, and those who have advocated socialist militancy, in the process further splitting the socialist opposition (for example, the breaking away of the Lohia Group from the P S P). The only major merger among opposition groups (between the Socialist party and the KMP) made for a dilution of the socialist platform and turned the P S P into a feeble replica of the Congress, which could provide no real alternative to the ruling party. On the other hand, the decision of the Kidwai Group to continue within the Congress strengthened the hands of the Prime Minister against the rightists in the Congress.

Many of the weaknesses of the Congress party arise from its eclecticism; so does its strength. The Congress has shown a flexibility in its political programmes which has defeated all attempts at providing real alternative to it. By adopting the socialistic pattern resolution, it stole the thunder from the P S P; by modifying its agrarian policy in practice, it prevented the Swatantra party from mobilising the land-owning classes against it. Even the Communists are forced to choose between "co-operating with Nehru" or going all-out against the parliamentary system. In this latter sense what the Communist party offers is an alternative to the present political system, rather than to the ruling party, the Amritsar thesis notwithstanding. The Congress party (as well as some opposition parties) treats the Communist party as alien to the existing political order and is in no way reconciled to its parliamentary status: the Kerala experience demonstrated this beyond all doubt. The understanding between the parties, which is necessary for the C P I to function as a parliamentary opposition, just does not exist.

Political developments in the Western world have led to the classification of political systems into one-party systems (used widely to describe the dictatorships) and multi-party systems; the latter being further divided into the two-party systems and systems where there are more than two parties. Complementary to this broad classification is the distinction made on the Continent between the party of action and the party of platform, depending upon the degree of proximity to power. There is also the distinction between the party of programme and the party of personages, broadly approximating to the distinction between institutional and personal government. Finally, theorising about the British system has led to a division between the conservative party and the progressive party.

None of these classifications is completely relevant to the Indian situation. Although the opposition parties are remote from the exercise of authority, thus making for much preoccupation with ideological issues, the Congress party is also preoccupied with such issues to a marked degree, largely because of frustration with action programmes. Similarly, the Congress party claims to be as "progressive" as most of the opposition parties. Again, the dominance of personalities and the lack of institutional leadership is evident in a more or less equal degree in all Indian parties. The more general classification into one-party and multi-party systems also loses much of its meaning when applied to India. The fact is that we have neither a one-party system which assumes not only the absence but the illegality of other parties nor a multi-party system which assumes that no party is sufficiently powerful to form the government by itself. Nor is it a 'multi-party system in theory but a one-party system in practice' as it is often described. Attempts to fit facts into a preconceived pattern are misleading as they fail to take into account the most important facts about the Indian situation. The party system as it has emerged is unique and should be analysed in terms of itself. Most important for this analysis is to understand the relationship between the Congress and the opposition parties. We must, therefore, start with the latter.

The role of opposition parties in India is quite distinctive. Instead of providing an alternative to the Congress party, they function by influencing sections within the Congress. They oppose by making Congressmen oppose. Groups within the ruling party assume the role of opposition parties, often quite openly, reflecting the ideologies and interests of the other parties. The latter influence political decision-making at the margin. Criticism from the platform or in the legislature has often found response among Congressmen and been echoed in the deliberations of the party. The political stature of an opposition leader and his personal relations with the high-ups in the Congress have often given him an influence with the Congress which has prevented frustration and bitterness which would otherwise result from his party being in a position of permanent minority. This also explains why there is such a wide gap between the leadership and the rank and file of the opposition parties and partly accounts for the lack of unity among these parties.

The fragmentation of opposition parties has baffled observers. It has been observed that in a social order which is in the process of disruption, militant political parties provide a sense of belonging to the educated youth, who are also more often than not unemployed. This is true to some extent and accounts for the anxiety of the rank and file of opposition parties to maintain the separate identities of their respective parties. The importance of this factor should not, however, be overstressed. For it is also true that political parties in India have failed to inspire young men who are turning increasingly indifferent to politics. Their ranks are being slowly depleted and the opposition parties are becoming top-heavy with much personal rivalry among leaders. The reasons for fragmentation have, therefore, to be sought in other factors.

One reason which has already been mentioned is the position of the Congress and its front-rank leadership in Indian politics. The impression has, therefore, gained ground that only if the Congress breaks up is there any chance for any other party to come up. Rampant factionalism within the Congress has given the opposition hope that such a break up is in the offing. Meanwhile, only by entering into some arrangement with the ruling party can the opposition parties taste power. This is possible in States where the Congress does not have an absolute majority in the legislatures.

This points to another and a more important reason for the continuing divisions within the opposition. The fact that no single party has been able to challenge the Congress led each party think that it is more capable than the others to eventually replace the Congress and that the others should therefore merge themselves. This attitude in turn ensures that no party can really replace Congress. Meanwhile, individual politicians contest the elections to get themselves elected, not to put their party in power. This has led to lack of concern for building up the party; it has also made for the absence of a common outlook among the members of the party in different parts of the country. Instances where regional units of these parties have flouted their national leadership are not lacking. The P S P, for instance, was forced to change its stand three times in two years on the question of coalitions with other parties, and in the end had to approve rather than condemn deviations from the official line in the States. While discipline among the rank and file is stressed with almost totalitarian thoroughness, disunity among the leadership has become endemic. Disunity among opposition parties is reinforced by disunity within each party and the result is to reduce politics to a sort of personal sport for individual politicians. (The Communist Party, however, presents a marked contrast with other opposition groups in all these respects but the Congress is determined to prevent it from coming to power. In this, the Congress can confidently count on the support of other opposition parties.)

Opposition to the ruling party does not take the usually expected form. It takes quite different forms in this country. There is much irresponsible criticism, a chronic habit of complaining and shifting all blame to the Government, sporadic campaigns of personal vilification and an inclination to wash dirty linen in public. The monopolistic position of the Congress, the unorganised and fragmentary nature of the opposition which cannot even adequately ventilate popular grievances, and the atmosphere of corruption and jobbery have given rise to a negative attitude among the general public. It goes further: antipathy to the ruling group turns into antipathy to politics itself. Politics is not for good men and it is only for opportunists and careerists. Such reactions are common among the middle class and more so among the intellectuals. The net result is that organised opposition is discounted and centralisation of power continues unchecked. This is aggravated by opposition politicians who, frustrated with the existing situation, plead for co-operation with the ruling group, in effect refusing to oppose. The "compulsions of a backward economy" thesis is a rationalisation born out of a basic weakness of the opposition. Here too the Communist Party's strategy is very different viz to wait for a general exasperation with the party system that would give it its real chance. Such exasperation is already noticeable among important sections of the people, and is often expressed by men who are till yesterday outstanding politicians. The fanciful plea for "unanimous elections" is another indication of the anti-party bias in recent political thinking. Such an ideology, shared as it is by part of the opposition, means that the latter is withdrawing from political struggle in precisely those areas, such as local government where it has most chances of success. All this adds to the confused and fragmentary state of political opposition in the country. The net result is that the only alternatives with which the country is left are the continuing exercise of power by the Congress which works through an internalised opposition system but which, if continued for long and under the leadership of less scrupulous leaders, would turn totalitarian; and the Communist rise to power which would bring an end to the party system itself. It is an impossible choice.

Today almost the whole of the political process is taking place within the folds of the Congress. The Congress is more than a party, it constitutes an entire party *system*. The conflicts and alignments within the Congress are of greater political import than its conflict with the opposition groups. The operative political categories in India are factions within the ruling party, organised on different lines and interacting in a continuous process of pressure, adjustment and accommodation. The true opposition that emerges is not against but within the Congress. In this, the opposition parties themselves play their part at the margin as indicated above.

This also means that a large part of political conflict and competition for power take place before and after rather than during the general elections. Before, in the selection of candidates and the regional and group pressures that affect such selection and after, in the formation of ministries and the dispensation of patronage. Also in cases where the Congress has not returned with an absolute majority in the legislature, the real process starts after the elections. Attempts are made to obstruct other parties from assuming or continuing in power for long by mustering the strength of the Congress from all sides, by invoking interference from the High Command or the Central Government, by coalitions and united fronts and by the holding of new elections under more favourable circumstances. What the elections (and re-elections) do is to endow such a process with legal sanction. The elections are very important on other counts also. They provide a channel of participation to the general public thus legitimising authority, force the ruling party to make bargains with organised interests, and generally spread political consciousness among the electorate.

The upshot of the above analysis is that the working of factions within the Congress provide the substantive context of the political process that goes on in this country. Further, it is at the level of factions that the true nature of the Congress and its distinctiveness from other parties is also revealed. For it is at this level that one can see how close the Congress is to society: it reflects all the major social divisions and interest groups. It is also at this level that traditional institutions find entry into the political process. The factions have their own structure and lines of communication and constitute an intricate system of decision-making. They give rise to forms of political behaviour that cut across the formally established institutions and provide a clue to the otherwise baffling twists and turns of Indian political life. They can, with some intensive study, be as precisely located as the more formal institutions. Broad and tentative observations can here be advanced.

The faction system (factionalism is an emotive term and has no place in an analysis of institutions) works at all levels of the Congress organisation. Generally, however, the lower down we go, the more pervasive the system becomes in conditioning the political process. It is also found in more unalloyed forms nearer the base. Once we leave the rarefied atmosphere of parliament and administration and the Working Committee and go down, say, to the Mandal Committee level, we see that the whole picture changes. The issues differ; the understanding of politics differ; the norms differ; and although the formal procedures bear resemblance to those found in the higher levels, the actual process of arriving at decisions differs. There is much that the purist would find deplorable at this level but it should not be forgotten that what happens here determines to a large extent the tenor of Indian political life.

Factions at the local level are based on caste, kinship and personal loyalties, the last being the most important. Dominant personalities provide the rallying points of opposing factions. As factional loyalties are, however, based on expediency and are thus inherently unstable, kin and caste ties are brought into play to impart stability to personal followings. These are then reinforced by the dispensation of patronage and the personality of the leader. The result is clear divisions of the party that are openly avowed and that give rise to constant conflicts and adjustments. Of course, the factions sometimes disrupt and make for total frustration. Political adjustments are often confined to the dominant caste within which the faction system operates, thus leaving out the majority and making for much concentration of power. The depressed communities are usually denied any real access to power. Consequently the political process assumes great rigidity. But this is not always so. The electoral system is forcing the higher castes to seek support among the lower strata; the administration's "interference" in local affairs on behalf of the depressed communities opens a way for ventilation of complaints which have to be heard and settled; and the Congress ideology, which is slowly seeping into local politics, makes it difficult to deny elementary rights to men who were hitherto considered as outcastes. Moreover, the dynamics of the faction system itself is obliging local leaders to cast their net wider than their own community and extend their patronage system beyond their own kin. A miniature party system cutting across traditional divisions is emerging within the Congress in most localities.

The Congress organisation has not spread physically to each village; nor is it necessary. Members of the Mandal Congress maintain contact with the politically active villages in various ways, through the Local Board, the District Development Committees; the village Sarpanch does so through the Panchayat Samiti and the Zilla Parishad, and even the local Talati who very often lives in town. Being the ruling party, the Congress has a privileged position among villagers who still look towards political authority in the traditional manner. The faction system penetrates the villages too. Village politics is invariably the cock-pit of local factions; these factions are linked to factions at the Mandal level sometimes and these links may create faction hierarchies; more often, however, the leader of each faction at the Mandal level is influential in a group of villages, mediates in village disputes and helps settle them, in the process building up his own support in the locality. The linkage is often indirect and roundabout but it is nonetheless present.

The really important links of the Mandal-level factions are, however, with groups within the District and the Pradesh Congress. It is a two-way traffic. Good connections with important persons or groups in the Pradesh Congress or the State Government strengthen the hands of particular leaders and the factions they lead at the lower level. Equally, a strong and dynamic leader with a large following in the district carries great weight at the State level. The system of communications between factions at different levels is important and although politicians from above often come to "settle" disputes at the lower level, such attempts are usually soon abandoned, largely because the State politicians are themselves indirect parties to the faction system. In fact, quite often the conciliatory move from above comes at the behest of local politicians in conflict with the ruling group.

To complete the picture, it must be mentioned that the strength of State politicians and their groups depends to a large extent on the weight they carry with the High Command and the Union Government. The process is similar as between the district and the State, except that it is of much greater political import and substantially affects the incidence of political mortality in the States.

The hierarchy of factions outlined above does not exhaust the group process within the Congress. While it is very important for maintaining both the unity and the efficiency of the party, the most important dimension of the faction system is found at the State and national levels. The two-party system that is really emerging in India is made up of the Congress government in power and the organisational wing of the party. The opposition parties marginally influence this struggle; so does the factional hierarchy discussed above. On the other hand, this struggle is largely independent and has its own dynamics, very often affecting the fortunes of politicians at other levels and in other parties.

A marked shift has been noticeable of late in this struggle. The organisational wing of the Congress, till recently dominated by those in the government, has begun to assert its independence quite openly. Those in charge of the organisation constitute a rival faction to those running the government. They use various techniques of competition, traditionally associated with the opposition party. They make representations on behalf of aggrieved interests; they make legislative members make use of the question hour in criticising the government; they even utilise the press to publicise their dissatisfaction with the government; above all, they seek to win a majority in the legislature on their behalf and if the governing group feels it must have its own way, they are prepared to replace it as an alternative government. They use other means also. Motions are passed in Pradesh Congress meetings; representations to the High Command are made and mediation called for; very active canvassing is carried out for elections to the A.I.C.C., the Pradesh Election Committee, the Central Election Committee and the Working Committee.

The organisational wing has been building up its strength by giving greater importance to the affiliated agencies of the Congress like the Seva Dal, the Youth Congress and the Mahila Congress, but even more, by making political use of these agencies. This is a comparatively recent phenomenon. These agencies recruit new and young men who add strength to the Congress organisation and nurse the ideology that field work is more important than the governmental work: the trend of reducing the ministerial VIPs to their proper size was clearly in evidence at the Sardarnagar Session.

All this does not mean that either the organisational or the governmental wing is united against the other; the faction system enters the functioning of each. Again built around personalities, the organisation is made up of a number of groups; so is the government. The strength of the faction system in the highest governmental organs was dramatically evident at the recent contest for the Deputy Leadership of the Congress. These groups interact in an intricate manner, governmental factions seeking support from among organisational factions and vice versa. The affiliated agencies themselves display the same trend, the Youth Congress runs as a parallel organisation to the Seva Dal in many of its functions and constitutes a rival force. Leaders of the Youth Congress and the Mahila Congress are known to build up "connections" with important persons in the party, extending thereby the faction system into these agencies. Thus almost every Congressman belongs to one faction or another; the faction system runs through the entire working of the party and constitutes the substantive party system in Indian politics.

Alongside the directly affiliated agencies, there are a number of organised interest groups close to the Congress that are able to influence the organisational wing and through it, the government. The strength of the Indian National Trade Union Congress as a pressure group, for example, is well-known. There are similar other organisations of students, women, peasants and the professions which are either run by Congressmen or which enter into informal relationships with the Congress. They are also a part of the faction system and exert substantial pressure on the organisation.

The organisational and the governmental wings of the Congress are in some ways not unlike two different parties and the rivalry between them has influenced the conventions of parliamentary government. After a prolonged debate a general agreement has been reached in England that the government is responsible to the electorate as a whole and not only to the party that has put it in power. It follows that to insist on the government's subservience to the party's executive would be to violate a basic tenet of democracy that the most important organ of the party is the parliamentary party and that the primary function of the party organisation outside parliament is to "service" the parliamentary party and work for its success in the governmental process. The situation in India is quite different. Historically, the formation of Congress ministries in the States in 1937 was part of the political strategy of the Congress and the governments formed by the Congress followed the directives of the party, although this caused strains even then. Since independence, the view that the Congress is not merely one among many parties and that it still continues to be a national organisation, the growing realisation that the Congress organisation had lost its former vigour and must be revived, the emergence of the organisational wing as a rival organ and the attempts of this organ to control the government, and the lack of effective opposition from other parties have led to a situation contrary to that found in other countries. The Congress insists, and many in the parliament and the government agree with this view, that the Congress government is accountable to the party. The lack of opposition from outside and the weakness of the legislative and electoral machinery in making government accountable to public opinion have also made the divergence of the Indian from other parliamentary systems inevitable. The faction system is a different type of party system. It accounts for this divergence from the traditional pattern.

The unqualified condemnation of "factionalism" within the Congress by national leaders is often based on an unrealistic appreciation of the political process. It is forgotten that factions have roles to play at the present level of our political development. They prevent the rise of a monolithic state by providing a built-in opposition within the ruling party. In the absence of effective opposition from outside, they prevent excessive concentration of power. Within the party, too, they make for intimate relationships thus modifying the operation of the law of oligarchy found in all organised parties. They make for constant interaction between opposing interests and necessitate the adjustments so vital to the democratic process. They accommodate all the important sections of society, *albeit* in an unequal manner. They lend flexibility to the political process and enable governmental changes to occur without a purge. While they have obstructed the growth of the vital convention of tolerating opposition parties in power when public opinion demands it and has kept the country unprepared for a change in administration, it has prevented the Congress monopoly from becoming totalitarian. On the whole it has made "politics by discussion" both possible and necessary.

On the other hand, factions, if not restricted, can prove dangerous, and lead to instability and intrigues. More important is the danger to the country's unity. It is true that genuine political unity assumes political divisions, but when the emphasis on divisions outstrips the concern for unity, the result is disintegration of the political community. But the worst consequence of factions, one that is inherent in it, is the exaggerated emphasis placed on personalities. The result is exercise of authority based on individual caprices in place of institutions and programmes. "Charismatic" authority is more suited to a totalitarian political order than to a democracy. Unless institutional correctives restrict factions, political instability and the consequent public exasperation would pave the way for dictatorship.

Such correctives exist within the Congress organisation. The Congress has an elaborate conciliation machinery that is prepared to intervene whenever the factions reach a deadlock. There is the Congress Parliamentary Board which mediates between government and party when acute conflicts arise. Deputations from the High Command to the States have become a regular feature of Congress politics. Various standing and *ad hoc* committees are appointed by the Congress President and constitute part of this conciliation machinery. Such questions as corruption among Congressmen, communalism and the neglect of minorities as well as specific charges against ministers are dealt with by these committees. The Central Election Committee and the Pradesh Committees apply themselves carefully to the selection and screening of candidates and settle differences between various organs and interest groups within the party. The conciliation machinery is in almost continuous operation and problems arising from the working of factions constantly call for solution. The dangers inherent in the system are partly avoided by such timely mediation. The conciliation machinery wields considerable influence as it derives its authority directly from the High Command. On the other hand, it is certain that its present efficacy depends on the presence of outstanding leaders who have the interest of the nation at heart. Once, however, the faction system becomes all-pervasive and the power conflicts at the Centre come into open with each leader trying to build up support in the organisation, such a machinery will become ineffective. This tendency would be corrected only by a complete division within the Congress organisation all along the hierarchy which would lead to the formation of a genuine party system free from factions.

Much would depend on the smoothness with which such a development takes place. The faction system has been performing an important function during the difficult period of transition from a national movement in which all sections of opinion joined together to a full-fledged party system in which the public is asked to choose between competing parties and programmes. With the rise of such a party system, each party will have to close its ranks when faced by other parties, although every party would still continue to perform its pluralist function of representing diverse social interests within itself. It is very difficult to trace the steps by which such a development would occur. The fragmentation of the democratic opposition within the country seems to have no sign of ending. The "menace" of the Communist Party adds to this fragmentation by forcing the other opposition groups to work with the Congress, thus preventing the building up of a strong and unified organisation which alone can ensure success at the polls. Such fragmentation leads to the emergence of local parties, which while they can successfully compete with the Congress in selected areas, have neither the leadership nor the organisation to spread their influence. Further, such localised parties, because they do not have to answer to a diverse electorate, tend to be parochial in nature. They cannot represent different interests cutting across the non-secular divisions within society.

The formation of the Swatantra Party has filled an important gap in Indian politics: a rightist party performs a useful function in a democracy. That its programme is largely negative does not matter: such is the politics of the right when in opposition. To condemn the party because it represents "vested interests" is also wrong. All political parties start by representing interests. But the party suffers from the same traits as other opposition parties. It lacks unity, is without sound leadership, is weak in organisation and its appeal is confined to the discontented. It is rigid in its approaches to other parties. The main function it performs at the present is, therefore, of influencing the Congress at the margin through factions within the Congress.

Among parties with narrow local influence, the most prominent seems to be the Jan Sangh which is now trying to free itself from its sectional past, to build up a sound organisation and capitalise on the growing discontent with the Congress party. It may well emerge as a major opposition group in some States. It has not however, succeeded, in attracting progressive individuals, and is too encumbered by its past and lacks dynamic leadership. So long as its successes are largely negative and built upon the discontent of minorities, its future is doubtful and it is dangerous to the political development of the country in spite of its avowed secularism.

There are two great dilemas of Indian politics that are prominently reflected in the party system. One concerns the place of the Communist Party in it. A political situation in which the Communist Party appears as the only alternative to the Congrss is unthinkable. The totalitarian dangers of a communist rise to power are obvious. But this danger also causes the adoption of totalitarian tactics by parties of the right. The communists are prevented from coming to power by unparliamentary tactics. At the same time, continued rule by the same party ultimately leads to a situation where the public begins to crave for a change—any change. The paradoxical situation in which a large number of people who dislike the Congress are nevertheless obliged to vote for it cannot continue for long. Change, when it comes would be catastrophic. The political strategy adopted by other opposition parties in face of the Communist 'threat'—which obsesses them more than it does even the Congress—prevents them from concentrating on building up their own organisations. This prevents any party other than the Communist Party from emerging as an alternative to the Congress.

The Communists, on the other hand, realising that the Congress will not allow them to come to power easily, adopt more roundabout and flexible techniques. They concentrate their efforts on strategic areas hoping to make them pockets of power from where the "movement" can be directed. At the same time they make every attempt to make themselves acceptable to the public. The Dange-line on China, the Amritsar thesis and active participation in legislative activities make the communists appear respectable. At the same time they have also launched on a process of "permeation." Their influence on Congressmen, some in important positions, whose democratic convictions are not strong, is well-known. The acute rivalry between factions within the Congress is also driving leaders of the factions to strengthen their hands by accepting the support of pro-communists and giving them important positions. (This is one of the most disturbing aspects of the working of factions within Congress: the opportunistic alliance of factions with communists and communalists. With this has started a process of Communist "infiltration" in the ruling party, the government and the non-political agencies). Once the Communists succeed in controlling a few key positions in the Congress or the government, the political situation will be transformed.

The other dilemma of Indian politics is closely related. It follows partly from the impact of modern ideas on a traditional society and partly from the means adopted to bring about change. The Congress is pledged to speedy industrialisation and uplift of the masses. The means it has selected to implement its policies are essentially alien to the traditional order. A wedge is drawn between Congressmen preaching "western" methods and the people who respond to traditional modes of thought and conduct. The problems being tackled are, however, real problems. The result is that the masses desire change without comprehending the nature of that change. They expect a sudden transformation of their conditions. This creates tension. While expectations are dramatically aroused, the programmes adopted fall short of fulfilling them. Frustration mounts and the argument for adopting other and more speedy methods of change become increasingly attractive. Such arguments—for example, the case for giving power to a dictator or a disciplined "vanguard" for a few years—find ready response in a traditionally authoritarian society. The Congress may itself succumb to such pressures both from fear of losing power and under the influence of new ideologies.

What is preventing such a development is the presence of a leadership steeped in liberal values. This leadership is now ageing. The ideological convictions of the newly emerging leadership are not yet clear. Meanwhile, institutions continue to be in a state of flux, thus exaggerating the importance of individuals. Much would depend on the development of the party system and the extent to which it imparts stability to existing institutions. In the meantime, in the transition period the factions within political parties are playing an important part. They have made for political mobility within limits, effective opposition to authority and consequent division of power. The dangers they give rise to are also clear: instability, too much emphasis on personalities and political intrigue. What the future holds in store is not clear. But it would largely depend on the extent to which the present system of political power being exercised by factions can transform itself into a democratic party system which would make a smooth change in government possible.

59 • *The Congress Party Election Manifesto, 1967* *

The Election Manifesto of the Congress party issued in preparation for the 1967 general elections was a public statement of its ideology and goals. As a party platform it gives considerable insight into the accomplishments and failures of the Congress party, and also into the formidable problems facing any government in India.

1. It has been the proud privilege of the Indian National Congress to serve the country for over eighty years. These years constitute a unique chapter of India's long history. In this short span India produced a succession of great men and women and felt the impact of revolutionary ideas in political, social, economic and cultural fields. Thus emerged a great revolutionary movement led by the Indian National Congress against the forces of colonialism and imperialism culminating in the Independence of India.

2. With the advent of freedom India entered on a new phase of reconstruction and transformation. This calls for hard decisions, bold innovation and upsetting of many established patterns of thought and living. India under the leadership of the Indian National Congress has deliberately made a choice in favour of an open and democratic society. In proclaiming democracy as our way of life we emphasise not only its central concept of political equality but also its equalitarian implications in social and economic fields. True to the genius of our movement for political emancipation and in the faith that enduring good to society cannot come through violence, we have decided to bring about through the open and democratic process the social and economic changes our society needs.

3. The nation has placed its seal of approval through three successive elections on the basic policies and programmes of the Congress. These policies and programmes were embodied in the three Five Year Plans which were designed to take the country towards a socialist society where the principal means of production will be under social ownership and control, production will be progressively speeded up raising the standard of living of the people and there is equality of opportunity and equitable distribution of the national wealth. In an economically under-developed society like ours, the very structure of political power and its interlinking with command over economic resources make it necessary that the commanding heights of economy shall not be in private hands. For, they who hold the levers of economic power will also ultimately run the political apparatus. The free exercise of the democratic process demands therefore the intervention of the State in the running of the economy of the country.

4. In our country with a vast and growing population and low living standards of the bulk of the people, the existing disparities in wealth and income are especially galling. Without mobilising economic resources and speeding up processes of economic development to the maximum extent, standards of general well-being cannot be raised to a substantial degree. There will, however, be inordinate delays in the redress of inequalities if the leveling standards of the under-privileged in the country is left to the normal course of economic development and the play of market forces. If the people are not able to see for themselves visible and early

* Published by the All India Congress Committee.

advance in the achievement of social justice, the release of new social energy and productive forces will be impeded and this will come in the way of full realisation of our potential of economic growth. It is, therefore, imperative that the State should play an active and dynamic role in planning, guiding and directing the economic development of the country. It is for these reasons that the Indian National Congress has placed before the country the goal of a democratic socialist society. The nation has accepted planned development as the method for the attainment of this goal. Successive five year plans have helped us to move forward in this direction. The Draft outline of the Fourth Plan has embodied policies and programmes which are designed to secure substantial realisation of our objectives.

5. We had in the early stages the guidance of Gandhiji and then the wise stewardship of Pandit Jawaharlal Nehru. They enjoyed in a unique measure the affection and understanding of the Indian people. After the death of Jawaharlalji, it fell to Shri Lal Bahadur Shastri to shoulder the heavy burden. He carried on bravely for 19 months when in an hour of triumph after the conclusion of the Tashkent agreement he left us. The mantle has now fallen on a new generation in the midst of increasing difficulties.

6. When India attained freedom, many were the prophets of gloom and disaster who predicted the disintegration of the Indian democracy. The partition of India placed a heavy strain on the concept of secularism which is vital to the maintenance of our society. There were 500 and odd Indian States with their separate identities. The Congress, thanks to the statesmanship of Sardar Patel, steered the country through these troubled days and built up an integrated India.

7. A new society is emerging in India. The Indian National Congress is proud to play a dynamic role in this process. Over the last twenty years, Governments formed under the leadership of the Congress legislated and implemented many far-reaching changes in our social and economic structure. Measures were adopted to deal a powerful blow to untouchability, a curse which blighted the lives of millions for centuries. However, much more remains to be done in this field. The tribal people who had been cut off from the mainstream of our national life for years are now coming into their own. The door of opportunity has been thrown open for the women of India in all the vital spheres of national life. A new awareness permeates every nook and corner of the country.

8. In the last two decades there have been real beginnings of an industrial and scientific revolution in the country. This has given a new dimension to the awakening and aspirations of our people. The scientific and technical education of our boys and girls on an ever-increasing scale is a significant aspect of this new society. We have today a reservoir of young and talented scientists and technologists with the capacity and ability to foster further growth and progress of scientific research and development. Modern transport and communications are opening up the country, making available new facilities of education and economic opportunity to what were hitherto remote and almost inaccessible areas in the country. Electricity in industry and agriculture is revolutionising the lives of the people who are enjoying its benefits. Our aim is to take it to every village. We are also laying foundations for the use of atomic energy for constructive and peaceful purposes. Establishment of the Panchayati institutions is a revolutionary step promoting mass participation in the administrative process and the economic reconstruction of the country at the village level. . . .

10. In 1962 we faced the unexpected and unprovoked invasion of our motherland by China. Closely following this was the aggression by Pakistan initially in Kutch and thereafter in Kashmir and other parts of the country. Twice during the last five years the people of India rallied in a remarkable way for the defence of the country. The Indian National Congress pays its homage to the valiant jawans and the officers of the Armed Forces and to the police and remembers with gratitude those who died or were wounded on the battle-field. The nation is pledged to vacate aggression on its territories. The Congress stands committed to redeem that pledge.

11. The picture of steady and uninterrupted growth during the last three plans has been distorted by the effects of last year's unprecedented drought and the aftermath of the struggle against the Pakistani aggressors. These setbacks to progress make it all the more necessary that the coming years should see increased and redoubled effort to speed up the full development of our economy. The Fourth and Fifth Plans occupy a crucial place in the perspective of India's development. During the coming few years we must intensify our efforts for a self-reliant and progressive economy.

12. A modern society can only be built on the foundations of science and technology. The men of science and technology will be the kingpins of the economic and social transformation of India. The Indian National Congress has confidence in the young scientists and technologists of India, who have shown that they are second to none in skill, competence and dedication. There is great need for the administrators of the country to place complete trust in Indian engineering, Indian skills and Indian talents. The Indian National Congress hopes that technological self-reliance will be the key-note of the coming years. The Congress also calls on the Government to so alter the conditions of work and service as to attract our best men from whichever part of the world they may be working in now. In an age of science and technology in which we need the best skills and competence, no foreign aid can replace the loss of skills as a result of the drain of some of our ablest students to other countries. The Indian National Congress calls on the Government of India and the Governments in the States and private industry to create conditions to arrest this.

13. While recognising that during the initial stage of economic development external assistance plays an important role, it is essential to reduce the period to the minimum and to diminish speedily the amount and range of external assistance. This can be done only by producing to the maximum, increasing our export earnings, reducing our imports of essentials and eliminating import of non-essentials. Whatever external aid we may obtain should be used wholly for the building up of such sectors of our economy as will accelerate our movement towards self-reliance. Machine building, fertilisers, petroleum, metallurgical industries and development of highly trained personnel are among the steps that will quicken the transition. The Indian National Congress realises that the spirit of Swadeshi needs to be urgently strengthened in the new context of economic and industrial development. The movement for import substitution, which has been facilitated by recent measures of the government and has become even more essential, should be pushed forward to the utmost. The Indian National Congress calls on all sections of the people, and more specially on industry and enterprise and on scientists and technologists, to co-operate actively with the Government in this vital task. . . .

20. The country is rightly anxious and uneasy about the steep rise in prices in recent years. Increased production, the practice of austerity and necessary measures and discipline in the momentary and fiscal field are the essential bases of price stabilisation. But there are other institutional measures which can help this stabilisation particularly for the low income and fixed income groups. Procurement, building of buffer stocks, supplies of basic consumer goods at controlled prices through a chain of consumer cooperatives and other socially controlled channels are obvious means.

21. The pattern of conspicuous consumption and wasteful display which increasingly characterise some of the urban areas are out of place in a socialist society. They also constitute a drain on the resources available to the community for productive investment. There is thus compelling need to impose limitations on urban income and property. Concrete steps should, therefore, be taken for placing restrictions on individual holdings of urban land for preventing racketeering in land in urban areas. The lower middle and working classes should be enabled to secure housing sites at reasonable rates. The problem of slums has not been so far tackled effectively. Among other measures in dealing with this problem the Government should promote dispersal of industries to the utmost extent.

22. Industrialisation is leading to over-crowding in cities. Both the economic and social costs of over-crowding are heavy. Along with rural industrialisation and other schemes for the utilisation of resources in rural areas new townships should be developed so that the large manpower is absorbed increasingly by these new centres. The rapid diffusion of electric power should facilitate the development.

23. The most advanced societies are those in which education receives the highest attention. Particularly is this so in a society committed to socialism. To enable every individual to express his personality to the fullest extent and contribute to the development of society, the maximum facility for education should be provided. Every child of school-going age, whatever his economic or social background, should be enabled to obtain the highest skills which the educational system of the country can provide. A scheme of scholarships which will enable the poorest to go through education should be established. Simultaneously, the country has to realise that no educational system can deliver the goods unless the teachers are respected and receive adequate incentives. The coming years should see a deliberate orientation of resources for their betterment. . . .

25. Labour has a vital role to play in the economic development and reconstruction of the country. There has been a great deal of legislation to ensure that progressively labour has a fair deal. Apart from a fair wage, other reasonable conditions of work and minimum social security there is need for institutionally established facilities to enable labour participation in management.

26. The quality of our planning will be judged by, among other tests, the manner and the degree to which we employ the vast manpower of India. Non-utilisation of our vast manpower is one of the central weaknesses of the economy we inherited at the time of our independence. The whole process of building a new order means providing new opportunities for work and employment. It is now realised that neither agriculture nor large-scale industry nor even both of them together can absorb the growing number of the unemployed and under-employed especially in the villages. Improved methods of agriculture, increase in

the number of crops in the year, work on improvement of minor irrigation, building of social service institutions and large-scale industries will, of course, provide employment on an increasing scale, but that by itself cannot meet the needs of the situation. A comprehensive programme of decentralised industry in the rural area implemented with drive and a sense of paramount urgency can make a large contribution to the solution of the vast problem of unemployment. For the purpose of enlarging the opportunities of employment it is imperative that the level of productivity should rise continuously reflecting increasingly effective use of man power and other resources of the nation. This is also indispensable for raising the standards of living of the people generally.

27. Our land policies have during the period of three plans introduced some major changes in the agrarian structure. The intermediary tenancies which prevailed in many parts of the country have been done away with. Land ceilings have been fixed in most States. Laws for tenancy reforms have also been enacted in many States. It is obvious that the land reforms have in some respects not been implemented effectively. The implementation should improve.

28. An important problem is to give a new deal to agricultural labour. The State should give special attention to their problem. Land availability being limited it will be possible to provide cultivable land only to a fraction of agricultural labour. For the bulk of them other avenues of part or full employment have to be found, such as processing and other industries, animal husbandry, fisheries, labour and construction cooperatives etc. Credit should be made available to them against personal security or assets that are to be created. Minimum wage legislation for agricultural labour should be implemented more effectively. . . .

31. Credit for the rural sector is vital. Today, the money-lender dominates the rural scene in spite of the growth of the co-operative movement. The Indian National Congress recognises that a strong cooperative movement is an important instrument of the socialist transformation of the country-side. For this movement to be effective, exploitation by the vested interests will have to be eliminated. It is primarily for the large body of co-operators to bring about this process of cleansing. It has to be recognized that credit has to be linked with processing and marketing if it is to be truly effective. The Government at the Centre and in the States should increase the tempo of social control over processing and marketing and to link these increasingly with credit. . . .

37. Scheduled castes, scheduled tribes and other economically under-privileged classes have always been a source of special concern to the Congress. Despite increasing amounts set apart for their welfare, levels of well-being among these communities have not risen appreciably. It should be our special effort to see that in addition to special provision for their welfare they benefit increasingly from the general schemes of development. There is also the problem of the relatively underdeveloped areas in the country. Special attention should be given to their needs in the Fourth Five Year Plan.

38. It is of the highest importance that the provision of basic needs of every individual is ensured and a national minimum comprising the essential requirements in respect of food, clothing, housing, education and health is established as speedily as possible. The nation should set before itself a goal in this respect and it would be reasonable to expect that the objective will be substantially realised by the end of the Fifth Plan.

39. The way we conducted our struggle for freedom, the provisions in the Constitution of India, the vital implication of democracy and socialism all affirm the basic equality of Indian citizens regardless of their caste, creed or sex.

40. The essence of the way of life we have adopted is that there is full equality and no discrimination as between one citizen and another. It is India's pride that it is the home of all the important religions of the world. Equal respect for all religions has been one of the distinguished marks of our effort to create a new democratic, socialist society. The Congress must continue to strive diligently for strengthening secular forces so that even the smallest minority in India enjoys a honoured place in the new social order. The Congress would endeavour to see that any impediment to the enjoyment of equal rights and obligations with other citizens of India is suitably dealt with. We have all by our joint efforts to produce an atmosphere of unity and national integration in which caste or communal distinctions cease to have any importance or relevance.

41. The Congress policy of prohibition should be maintained and encouraged. In doing so, while efforts are being made to increase its effectiveness, care should be taken to remove the evils that flow from the manner of its inplementation.

42. There has been a tremendous increase in population (over 78 million) in the first decade of planning. This was the result of a spectacular fall in death rates which in turn was brought about by our successful fight against disease, famine and pestilence. This has also increased the expectation of life. Progress we achieved in the economic field was largely nullified by this high rate of population growth. Every year we have 10 million new mouths to feed. It is of the utmost importance that we take speedy and effective steps to check population growth. . . .

44. The world has been made familiar with the basic foreign policy of the Congress through its powerful advocacy by the late Jawaharlal Nehru. It is in consonance with the best traditions of India's struggle for freedom and the striving for peace in which all thoughtful people in all parts of the world are engaged in this atomic age. Peaceful co-existence, non-alignment and disarmament are important aspects of this policy of peace and friendship with all countries especially our neighbours. The policy includes abstention from the use of threat of use of force for the settlement of inter-State disputes or against the territorial integrity and political-independence of other States.

45. India has also been in the forefront of the movement for the liberation of countries still under colonial rule. The Congress Party has consistently supported the campaigns against racial discrimination generally and in particular in South Africa, South West Africa, Southern Rhodesia, Mozambique and Angola.

46. The Congress Party continues to lend its strong support to the United Nations as an effective instrument of world peace.

47. Our relations with our neighbours, Ceylon, Nepal and Burma, are cordial and friendly but unfortunately we have not been able to reach understanding with China and Pakistan. While it would be our constant endeavour to do so there can be no slackening in our vigilance to ensure the territorial integrity of India.

48. The difficult times we are passing through are a challenge as well as an opportunity to us. The Congress has a tradition of service and a record of achievements of which the people of India may well be proud. Today the nation expects from the Congress a pledge to serve the people with faith and vigour.

The spirit of service and sacrifice, the devoted and dedicated endeavour of Congressmen and the intimate and dynamic contacts with the people which the Congress has built up through decades will, we trust, help it to play the historic role once again in fulfilling the nation's aspirations.

49. With humility and confidence the Indian National Congress seeks the mandate of the nation to work for a social order based on freedom and justice which will ensure that every individual has the means and opportunities for a full life and is enabled to make his maximum contribution to the service of the nation.

SECTION FIVE

Political Processes

60 • V. M. SIRISKAR: *Political Behavior in India* *

The electoral behavior in the city of Poona in Maharashtra in 1962 is the basis of the following generalizations made by a leading political scientist. The role of caste is of particular significance because it colors and often determines the behavior of political parties. While political leaders decry the intrusion of caste into politics, they all make use of these traditional groupings in their efforts to win votes. Parties select their candidates with a careful eye to winning the support of the larger castes, and the traditionally dominant but numerically small castes, especially Brahmin, are losing political advantage to the numerically larger middle and lower castes.

The castes are becoming politicized through growing awareness that numbers determine "who gets what" in the form of patronage, roads, and schools. To increase their numerical strength they are forming caste associations to mobilize their members and even in some cases forming caste federations such as the Gujerat Kshatriya Sabha. Castes acting in self-interest thus approximate pressure groups although their ascriptive basis distinguishes them from the voluntary associations of Western pluralistic politics. Caste and other factors in voting behavior pointed out by Siriskar below continued to manifest themselves in the 1967 elections.

On the other hand, intra-caste rivalries often oblige individual caste leaders, particularly in village and state elections, to seek additional supporters from other castes. This cross-cutting of caste due to factionalism creates a more complex, less caste-based political system.

If an attempt is made to compare the socio-economic variables in the West and in this country, it appears that factors like caste religion, family and to some extent, party-loyalty are more important than age, sex, income and occupation.

In India socio-economic status has caste as a further complicating factor. This factor often overshadows other factors determining the socio-economic status. Education, income and occupation remaining the same, caste decides the status according to the hierarchy. Thus, in any income and occupation bracket, the Brahmin gets the higher status than other castes. Professor J. H. Morris

* V. M. Siriskar, *Political Behavior in India* (Bombay: Manaktala & Sons, 1965), pp. 246–254. By permission.

Jones has remarked: "Caste (or sub-caste or community) is the core of traditional politics. To it belongs a complete social ethos. It embraces all and is all-embracing. Every man is born into a particular communal or caste group and with it inherits a place and station in society *from which his whole behaviour and outlook may be said, in idea at least, to be derived* (emphasis mine)."

This does not mean that caste remains the sole determinant of socio-political behaviour in India. Political parties, pressure groups and political loyalties have cut across caste barriers to some extent. What has been sometimes overlooked, is the sudden strengthening of caste loyalties *vis-à-vis* class and political loyalties. Without decrying this socio-political phenomenon, which is affecting the democratic politics in India, it is necessary to analyse the factors responsible for it.

To believe that the third General Elections were a take-off to a healthy democratic set-up, appears to be a little too optimistic and over-simplified view of a complex situation. The pessimistic interpretation that caste has taken a complete and firm grip on Indian politics is equally an over-simplification. The truth lies somewhere between these two views. The efforts must be directed to find out the political role of caste and to what extent this represents an unhealthy and reactionary trend. "The increasing solidarity of castes over large geographical distances has led in some ways to a strengthening of the caste spirit, a spirit which has a new element in it; it is competitive."

It is obvious that the introduction of universal franchise opened up the field of political power to those majority castes who were left out of the share of power before Independence. In Maharashtra, this meant the shift of political power from the urban areas to the rural areas and from the Brahmin caste to the non-Brahmin castes—mainly the Maratha caste.

The role of caste was to a certain extent over-shadowed by the emotionally surcharged atmosphere of the 1957 elections in Maharashtra. But this could not be considered as a permanent phenomenon. The 1962 elections to a certain extent have indicated the transient character of non-caste voting behaviour witnessed earlier.

In Maharashtra the dominant castes were the Maratha and the Brahmin. Anti-Brahminism is not confined to Maharashtra, but is found all over Southern India in varying degrees. In Poona, there was a microcosm of Maharashtra, but with a difference. Historically, the Marathas and the Brahmins were the ruling castes during the time of Shivaji and the Peshwas respectively. Poona was the centre of political power and influence since those times. Thus conflict between the two castes had historical origins in Poona.

There was a shift in favour of the less privileged classes and castes all over India. This was inevitable to a certain extent owing to the universal franchise. But the tendency was aggravated by two factors. The tendency of withdrawal exhibited by the frustrated Brahmins and the "capture" of the major political (institution) party—the Congress, by the non-Brahmin castes. The non-Brahmin politicians realized that the Congress was the real centre of power and they established their hold on this centre. To some extent the intellectuals from the Brahmin caste found it to their liking the role of opposition. It was of interest to note that most of the leading opposition parties, whether rightist or leftist in Maharashtra have mostly a Brahmin leadership.

If any reference to the role of caste in politics is made, one is considered as doing a disservice to the country by emphasizing a factor of cleavage and not evaluating the elections, parties and politics by modern standards. This charge is further strengthened by the fact that all parties and their leaders speak from house-tops against caste, casteism and casteist politics. But surprisingly enough with all this verbal attack, the caste remains a powerful factor in politics. The reasons are not far to seek. No party seems to be free from the sly caste appeal. Caste has very deep roots in the Hindu social structure and it is wrong to expect that the mere institutionalization of Western political ideals and techniques would automatically do away with this social system of ancient standing.

Caste has been the agency of integration in the traditional society. In the passing of the traditional society, it takes a new significance when it allies itself with the new modern agency of integration, the political party. To bring about a consensus in a modernizing political community, a clever use is made of caste, the traditional integrative agency.

The role of caste in the elections in Poona can be understood from three independent sources—the reactions of voters to the propaganda campaigns of various parties, the press and the polling figures at certain booths.

It was found that the charge of casteist politics and casteism was levelled against the Congress by voters who were predominantly Brahmin. While those who levelled the same charges against the Jan Sangh were predominantly non-Brahmin. Thus, attitudes of voters to political propaganda appear to be conditioned by the fact of their caste origins. A systematic study of political attitudes and caste is an urgent necessity.

The local press reported certain very interesting news items. These related to the resolutions passed by caste panchayats in Poona to support the Congress or other parties in the elections. Without going into the question how far these panchayats could influence its members, the reports are significant enough. Neither the party concerned nor the panchayat felt that it was anything wrong for a caste organization meant for social and charitable purposes to dabble in politics.

The local press indulged in the controversy which arose over an alleged anti-Brahmin statement by Shri More. This again indicates the influence of caste. For in the first instance the controversy would not have arisen, and if it had it would not have received the attention given by the press and the people.

The polling figures at certain booths further strengthened the view that caste played an important role in the elections. There is no use in gainsaying the fact that caste even now plays a significant role in political life. At the same time, there are certain indications that the influence is on the decline under particular circumstances.

It is neither desired nor attempted to single out caste as the factor influencing elections. This is not possible in a fast changing situation where no party could ever remain a one-caste-organization. New caste groups are becoming conscious of the possibility of seizure of political power through the ballot-box. The predominance of Maratha caste in Maharashtra politics is due to the numerical strength of that caste. It is as high as 40 per cent in the total population. No other single caste has such strength of numbers. But this does not rule out a new alignment of two or three caste groups to challenge the Maratha caste. This in turn induces a healthy compromise in the accommodation being given to the other castes.

The democratic processes and the democratic institutions in this country are to some extent distorted, owing to the factor of caste. But at the same time these processes and institutions are undermining the hold of caste. No one can foretell the date when caste would disappear from Indian politics. But the strengthening of parties, pressure groups and political loyalties on the basis of economic programmes would be the way to unloosen the caste from its present position.

The findings of the survey indicated that though the system of elections was running successfully, the independent discriminating rational voter was not very much in evidence. Political philosophy of Western democracy is based on the Lockean notion of rationality of man. He wrote that men entered civil society "only with an intention in every one, the better preserve himself, his liberty and prosperity, for no rational creature can be supposed to change his condition with an intention to be worse."

Rationality of the citizen was taken for granted by the theorists of Western democracy in the eighteenth and nineteenth centuries. This was in consonance with the general tendency of the times, to believe in the human reason to solve all human problems and cure all ills of the society. The doubts about this basic rationality of citizens arose only after 1890. But when India adopted the Western form of democracy, the Western educated framers of the constitution showed a faith in the rationality of citizens, mostly illiterate and ignorant.

How far does the common voter in Poona conform to this test of rationality? "If rationality is defined merely as the possession of the information necessary to make a decision, ratiocination on that information, and the self-conscious evolution of a decision, the voter is, by and large, not rational." In the present study, more than 33 per cent voters did not know anything about the political issues and nearly 25 per cent were ignorant of the candidates and the legislatures for which they were contesting.

This does not mean that the voter is completely irrational. It only means that the voter in Poona does not possess the rationality which Locke expected of him not to speak of Benthamite expectations. There is a tendency in certain quarters in this country and also in the Western world to eulogize the illiterate millions for their "solid" commonsense and proper choice of their rulers. Actually this might be arguing in a circle. The results of the three elections have placed the Congress in power. This has meant stable government. But it is necessary to focuss the attention on how these results were obtained. Any enquiry in the process of elections indicates factors other than rationality. It may be said that India has secured stable government; but the means of mass manipulation, casteist influences, minority fears and charismatic hold of the Prime Minister have played no mean part in this process. A usual slogan to be heard was "A vote for the pair of bullocks is a vote for Panditji; a vote for Panditji is a vote for stability and progress."

"The citizen of classical democratic theory was conceived to be both interested and active in the political discourse." The average voter in Poona lacked both high political interest and an urge to participate in the political discourse.

As regards participation, it is necessary to point out that participation in the manner of totalitarian society is not hinted at here. Such participation is an abject surrender to conformism. Democratic participation presupposes an alert discriminating mind, capable of non-conformism of radical nature, if necessary.

Voting has been regarded as the minimum participation. But it would be wrong to overlook the social meaning of voting in India in general and in Poona in particular. Can we say that the Indian voter, by and large, really understands the "act of voting?" In majority of the cases, he might be performing the act as a surrender mainly to the group pressures. India can be considered as the example of such voting. For instance, "the whole mythology of voting has been transformed; the vote comes to be regarded as a public act of allegiance to an abstract 'democracy' rather than a *private decision* as to what is good and what is bad for the State."

In the sample studied, it was found that in a large number of cases, the act of voting was done as per instructions of the head of the family. In many cases, the head of the family received instructions from his "caste panchayat." In other cases, it was the community-leader—a Mulla, a Church-father, a Panth-leader, who issued the necessary instructions. A prominent Jan Sangh worker told the following experience about .the Muslim voters. When they were approached for vote, they frankly told him that they would vote as per instructions from the Mulla. If the Jan Sangh wanted Muslim votes, the Mulla should be approached. A senior P.S.P. leader in a way corroborated the above, by saying that a large Muslim vote went to the Congress at the last minute, because a certain shady character but influential in the locality, was won over by the Congress. How can our analysis be reconciled with the classical theory of liberal political democracy? "Is the theory 'wrong?' Must it be discarded in favour of empirical political sociology? Must its ethical or normative content be dismissed as incompatible with the nature of modern man or of mass society?" It can be said that without denouncing the classical theory, it would be necessary to understand the act of voting in India as operating in a mixed political culture of a traditional society, experiencing modernizing influence of the Western impact; when even in the Western societies voting does not fully conform to the classical theory.

With greater modernization, due to industrialization, urbanization and spread of education, voting may suume its indivdual character to some extent. But there is no possibility of any approximation with the ideal voter of the classical theory.

The Indian Constitution has adopted universal franchise. This has been hailed as "the fountain spring of India's democracy." Universal franchise was a bitterly contested subject in the Constituent Assembly. But the majority was in favour of the adoption. They believed with Dr. P. Subbarayan. He said "I have no fears for adult franchise. The Indian humanity is such that they have enough common sense, enough horsesense, which will make it possible for them to choose their rulers with discrimination, and to choose the people whom they think would be able to carry on the administration in a manner which will be for the benefit of the common man, of whom we have talked so much in this House."

Universal adult franchise without universal education can be a very dangerous thing. That it has not been so during the period covering the last three General Elections is owing to certain peculiar conditions in this country. The absence of any well developed party-system, meant that with the universal adult franchise, the Congress, the only organized nationwide party, could sweep the polls. Secondly, the franchise has meant political power for the majority caste-groups.

What appears to be urgently necessary is a vast programme of "informing the discretion" of the masses. The mere faith in the horse-sense of our common people will not suffice. The government, the political parties, the press and the educational institutions have to undertake this programme of "educating the masters." In the absence of such enlightenment, the danger to democratic institutions and values would increase. The three General Elections and the successful working of parliamentary institutions are by themselves no guarantee of a democratic society.

It was found that there was a correlation between poverty, illiteracy and political ignorance. From the point of view of any improvement in the present situation, it appeared that illiteracy was the major stumbling block. The disappointing increase in the literacy rates between the crucial decade of 1951-1961 aggravates the malady. Even the sloganized ideals of socialistic pattern did not reach the illiterate voters.

This indicated that the voters were unaware of policies and programmes which were to benefit them more than any other section of the community. Education need not be considered as a panacea for all the ills of the Indian democracy. But an educated electorate is any day preferable to an illiterate one.

The press has been a very important factor in the pre-Independence period. It continues to be a major agency of political education of the electorate. But the illiteracy limits its function to the literate minority. In the present survey, it was found that though the influence of the press could not be decisive, it was marginal but sufficiently significant. It could be said that in general, the press conducted itself well in the election campaign. The growth of the language press depends on the increase in literacy and increase in the reading habits. Planned efforts in these directions are not much in evidence. The importance of a politically educated and conscious electorate in a democracy cannot be exaggerated.

The failure of the opposition parties to have some kind of electoral understanding resulted in the usual dissipation of their limited strength.

It could be said with certain justification that neither the press nor the parties made sustained efforts to educate the electorate. This failure to some extent might have contributed to the candidate-orientation of the voters. Apart from illiteracy, this factor also could be regarded as making the Indian elections less dominated by issues and ideologies and more by personalities. . . .

61 • DEVENDRA PAL VERMA: *Panchayat Elections in a Punjab Village* *

Traditional and modern aspects of the Indian political process exist in a symbiotic, mutually reinforcing relationship. Political brokerage is played in terms of caste and factions, and in turn the latter are reinforced by an electoral system which offers a new form of access to political power.

The following selection illustrates the interaction of the new and old in the election of a village panchayat. Modernization of the political process is seen in the increase of contested rather than unanimous elections; candidacy based on youth and education rather than age; acceptance of adversary politics and political power as valid rather than the Gandhian concept of political

* *AICC Economic Review,* Vol. XV, No. 19 (March 10, 1964), pp. 23–26. By permission.

power as valid only if personally disinterested; and the growing awareness that public office brings prestige and availability of public funds to individuals as well as the groups they represent. On the other hand, traditional aspects are seen in the primacy of caste and community bloc voting; voting for individuals rather than public issues; and overtones of mistrust of politics in general and suspicion of politicians as corrupt in particular.

It was sometime in the month of October, 1963, that the Punjab Government announced its decision to hold elections to the village panchayats in the State in December, 1963. It was to be the third general election for constituting the rural local bodies—second under the scheme of Panchayati Raj. The State Government sanctioned a sum of Rs. 44 lakh for meeting the expenses of these elections and a Panchayati Raj Officer was appointed to process the election details. After the lapse of a few days the election schedule was decided; the elections were to commence on 26th December, 1963, and to conclude on 6th January, 1964. The District and Block authorities were pressed into service and they made all the necessary arrangements for the polling. In November there was just a ripple in the placid rural life. There was hardly any stir in most of the villages of the State.

In the year 1960, with the inauguration of the Panchayati Raj in the State, village panchayats were elected and constituted anew. At that time, the present writer with a group of post-graduate students went to selected villages of Hoshiarpur District and on the basis of a questionnaire contacted the village voters, explained to them the object of our task, asked them the set questions, and noted their replies and reactions. We observed the entire election scene in all these villages and prepared a report on the basis of our study which was highly interesting and instructive.

This time when the announcement regarding the panchayat elections was made, I decided to select two villages and make an intensive study of the electoral behaviour of the people there. Khanpur is a village about 3 miles to the west of Hoshiarpur city. I had gone to this village in the year 1960 and decided to select it again this time. The second choice was Sattaur, about 5 or 6 miles away from the city; it was chosen mainly for the reason that there was intense election activity prior to the polling day. The village was divided into two sharp camps. But a day prior to the polling, the two factions got together and reached agreement, and so no election took place on 6th January. As panchayat polls had concluded on this date throughout the District, it was not possible to choose another village and to go there for the purposes of study.

Thus this field survey is restricted to village Khanpur only. All that has been observed and written pertains to that village and whatever facts have been noted and observations made are purely from an academic angle. The conclusions of this study cannot, in the very nature of things, be made applicable to the whole State. Any such projection would be grossly unfair. However, it will perhaps be useful for us to know something of the "election environment" that prevailed in the rural areas of the State, for that would give us the necessary perspective to understand and appreciate the electoral behaviour of the people of Khanpur.

It was reported that there was little stir in the villages regarding the panchayat elections. Election fever developed earlier in those villages where factional rivalries were intense; these rivalries did not originate on account of the panchayat elections but were of the traditional type which are the bane of our rural life. This initial lack of enthusiasm was attributed to certain factors, the chief being that the panchayats had not become effective instruments of power at the village level and that these continued to be cold-shouldered by the authorities at the Block and the District levels. Another reason that was attributed to such an attitude was that village panchayats on account of lack of financial resources had not been able to accomplish anything substantial in improving the lot of the villages. Moreover, the members of the panchayats had not been accorded a respectful treatment by the various officials though initially much was made of it by the State Government. There had been reports of misuse of funds by the panchayats and this charge, even if greatly exaggerated, provided the people with an opportunity to condemn the whole system. It was pointed out that people in certain villages on account of certain reasons went to the extent of suing these bodies in the law courts. It is said that many of the panches [1] and sarpanches [2] did not contest panchayat elections for a second term because of these reasons.

It was in the second and third weeks of December, 1963 that intensive activities were reported in many places in the rural areas. But mostly the political parties, as in the last elections to the panchayats, remained outside the village election arena. It was only in the Moga Tehsil of Ferozepur District that the major political parties in the State were involved in the panchayat contests. In most of the rural areas of major districts like Ludhiana, Jullundur and Hoshiarpur, village politics remained immune from the influence of political parties.

The main form of canvassing was from door to door. Group meetings were held at frequent intervals, but behind the closed doors. At certain places meetings of the entire male voters of the villages were held with a view to arriving at some agreement so that the sarpanches and panches could be unanimously elected.

The successive elections have provided the villagers with a good deal of political maturity and shrewdness. Barring those who are in the fray and those who are their active supporters the village voter smiles and humours every contestant but reserves his vote to his own choice; of course, it is a different matter as to what his basis of choice is.

The State Government has encouraged, by way of financial grants, unanimous elections to the village panchayats and their motive is laudable. But an overwhelming number of panchayats out of more than 13,000 in the State, have been constituted after keen election contests. It has been reported that only 20% of the village panchayats in the State have been elected unanimously. And in the contest most of the sitting panches and sarpanches who contested the elections have been defeated, either because the people were not satisfied with their work or because the voters felt that these representaives during their tenure of office were primarily concerned with currying favour with the Government officials, almost neglecting the interests of their villages. Another general feature of these panchayat elections has been an increase in the number of educated and young people who have sought to contest these elections. Apart from the amusing report from Patiala that five hundred *sadhus* are contesting elections to the various panchayats, it has been reported from the same city that two scores of the descendants of the former

[1] Member of a panchayat.
[2] Chairman of the panchayat.

chieftains of Punjab who ruled over small principalities offered to contest elections to the village panchayats of their respective areas.

There was brisk and heavy polling throughout the State with 70% to 90% village folks exercising their right to vote; polling was peaceful in the entire State, barring one or two stray cases in Districts of Ferozepur and Bhatinda.

Khanpur is a village, just 2 or 3 miles to the west of Hoshiarpur. At one time the village enjoyed a prominent position in the district for it was the centre of fine handloom cloth that was sent to distant places, even outside the country. With the partition, and migration of the Muslim population Khanpur lost its glory and is now inhabited by about 2,200 people, about 50% of whom belong to scheduled castes, divided into three subcastes: (i) Mahashes; (ii) Balmikis; (iii) Adharmis—in that order. The displaced persons from West Punjab form another major chunk of the population—nearly 20% of the total followed by Aggarwals and Brahmans. The whole population is dependent on the city of Hoshiarpur for livelihood; scheduled castes working as labourers and others either as shop-keepers or doing service. There are very few who own land or are dependent upon agriculture.

The village still bears the scars of the partition days—deserted houses with missing roofs and burnt walls. The village has pucca streets but sanitation is very poor. Right in front of the primary school—where the polling station was located—filthy water in a *kachcha* drain has accumulated with no outlet whatsoever. Candidates had set up their polling offices in the open space bisected by this foul-smelling drain. The voters gathered in groups here and we had to contact them at this very place, thus inhaling an over-dose of the foul smell. In the year 1960, we had had the same experience, so three years made no difference to the disposal of this dirty water.

In Khanpur, the candidates who made up their minds to contest the panchayat elections, started their canvassing campaign just 10 days prior to the polling date. The main form of canvassing was door-to-door. The major communities held separate meetings and it appeared that in these meetings the main stress laid was on supporting without exception the candidate of one's own community. This was more true of the scheduled castes. Last time only one scheduled caste candidate contested the election and he was supported by the entire community; this time there was division in their ranks and Mahashes set up 2 candidates and Balmikis and Adharmis put up one candidate each; so a total of 4 scheduled caste candidates were in the field. The panchayat of Khanpur has 6 elected panches. There were 9 candidates in the field for these offices—4 scheduled castes and 5 belonging to other communities. For the offices of the Sarpanch there were 3 candidates in the contest, none belonging to the scheduled caste.

There was no division between the caste Hindus and the scheduled castes as far as the election of the sarpanch was concerned. This election was fought more or less on non-caste basis. More than 78% of the voters contacted told us that the election of the Sarpanch was free from caste loyalties but they affirmed that the votes for electing the panches were mainly being cast on caste and community basis. About 15% of the voters were of the view that both for sarpanch and panches caste loyalty was a major factor. There were few who would not say anything in the matter. Another factor of importance that divided the village voters is the wedge that still persists between the displaced persons from Pakistan and the so-called local inhabitants of the village. Seventeen years of common habitation has not been able to blend the people into a single village community in Khanpur. We were told by some old and educated people that persons who had rendered service to the village voluntarily and still continued to do so, were not willing to come forward and so the field was left open to those who aspired for power and prestige. About five days prior to the polling a meeting of the male voters of the village was held to explore the possibilities of electing the office-bearers of the panchayat unanimously, but in vain.

Some of the village officials such as the Lambardar and Patwari, it is generally believed, exercise a good deal of influence on the villagers in many matters. It may be so. But as far as elections to the panchayat are concerned the village voters exercise their franchise rights in their own way and do not accept the biddings of these officers. Khanpur provides ample proof of this. Of the three candidates contesting election to the office of the Sarpanch, one was the son of the village Lambardar. This gentleman, though a government official, was more active than his young son in canvassing support for him. The villagers kept him in good humour with promise of full support. But when the election result was declared, his son trailed behind as the poor third. A shop-keeper, about 40 years old and better educated than the other two, was declared elected by an overwhelming majority of votes. This fellow appeared to be very amiable and so was able to curry favour with the Khanpur voters to make their choice and the village Lambardar's influence could not cut much ice. Of the six panches, three panches belonging to the Scheduled Castes—each representing one sub-caste mentioned above—were returned and three belonged to the other major communities in the village. The result of the panches confirms what the people told us about the influence of caste when the polling was in progress.

The old Sarpanch, a village Doctor by profession, and as many as four out of the six out-going panches declined to contest the election this time. We met the outgoing Sarpanch. He told us that the villagers were prepared to re-elect him as Sarpanch unanimously, and this was confirmed by everyone of the voters whom we met. But he was dissatisfied with the working of the panchayat. Firstly, official control and red-tape made the village panchayat an ineffective body. The district authorities were vested with enormous powers of control and the ways of bureaucracy remained unchanged. He told us that the papers referred to the higher authorities were not disposed of and returned for long. The situation with regard to the district offices was hardly different. The activities of the panchayat were stifled on account of the official callousness. Secondly, the poor financial resources coupled with the unwillingness of the village people to pay taxes levied by the panchayat rendered it ineffective to do anything substantial. Thirdly, the village people in the past three years had hardly given any cooperation to the panchayat. Some of panches of the outgoing panchayat also complained that the villagers had not cooperated with them and even did not accord them respectful treatment.

About 80% of the people we contacted and a great majority of these were the male voters, were unequivocal in their condemnation of the outgoing panchayat. According to them, it undertook no developmental activity and did nothing to improve the lot of the village. There seems to be some substance in their grievances. We had visited this village three years ago in 1960. Three years made no visible difference in the village environment. The same dirty lanes, the same heaps of cow-dung, the same filthy drains! The outgoing panchayat had constructed a boundary wall with the Government aid, and put up 8 or 9 handpumps in the village streets to provide drinking water to the village. The villagers expected much more but not much was done. If the Panchayat had raised the primary school to the status of a middle school, the villagers would have been happy. But instead, they grumbled further, the panchayat was merely busy in deciding ordinary cases referred to it. There was some bitterness and sarcasm in the tone of certain persons who narrated the story of how the Khanpur panchayat spent a lot of money and time in suing a landlord of the village in the law courts, for constructing a bund in his fields that diverted the rain waters towards the village. The panchayat lost the case.

More than 62% of the people were of the opinion that even in the performance of its judicial functions, the village panchayat did not satisfy the poor and the weak.

The polling in Khanpur was peaceful. The voters came in groups and there was a lot of enthusiasm. The polling was brisk, males mostly voting in the forenoon, followed by females who came in the afternoon after finishing the household chores. One noticeable fact of the polling day was the active part that a few young educated ladies took in canvassing support for their candidates. Some of these females came to the village primarily to canvass support for their relatives. Most of the female voters did not observe *purdha*. Throughout the afternoon we found young, middle-aged and old ladies coming to the polling station in large numbers. Only the old women persisted in their orthodoxy. But social change in Khanpur has not gone beyond this point. No woman contested to the panchayat as was the case last time. Over 90% of the young and middle-aged females said that they were voting of their own free accord and that their male elders had nothing to do with it. The old ladies made no tall claim like this and over 76% stated that not only they but all the females, young and old, voted at the bidding of their husbands or other senior members.

The total number of voters in Khanpur was 798. Of these 438 were males and 360 females. There were complaints from males as well as females that the village electoral roll did not contain the names of many persons who were fully qualified and eligible to vote. A person who retired as a Havildar from the Army had been living in the village since 1958. He was bitter for the non-inclusion of his name. Most of the people blamed the village patwari for this lapse. This complaint was made at the time of the 1960 election too. People wanted that the Patwari should prepare the electoral roll after ascertaining facts from every house and family.

Out of the total electorate of 798 as many as 645—341 males and 304 females—cast their votes, thus giving a voting percentage of 80.

It is obvious from the foregoing account that the people in the rural areas have attained a good deal of maturity and understanding in the working of the democratic processes. As far as elections are concerned, democracy is fast coming of age, if it has not already done so. But peaceful and orderly elections and high polling percentage is only one aspect of democracy. We can say that it is the exterior of democracy. The inner aspect is of real and vital importance, for we have yet to catch the spirit and the soul of democracy.

62 • Rajni Kothari and Ghamshyam Shah: *Caste Orientation of Political Factions, Modasa Constituency—A Case Study* *

The following case study illustrates on a small-scale constituency level the role of intra-Congress factionalism and its relation to caste. The behavior of Modasa was repeated and accentuated on the national and state level in the 1967 general elections and contributed heavily to the striking decline of the Congress party. As in Modasa there was a large-scale defection from the party of factional groups, dissatisfied because of failure to get nomination tickets, which joined the Swatantra and other opposition parties or formed separate oppositional Congress splinter parties.

Modasa, an Assembly constituency of Gujarat State, is situated in a relatively developed part of the otherwise backward district of Sabarkantha. Modasa town, the headquarters of the constituency and the taluka, has for long enjoyed some locational importance in the economic and social geography of Gujarat. Situated very close to the Gajarat-Rajasthan border and having easy access to important centres of business in both States, it has commanded various trade routes in the area. The Taluka has also occupied an important place in the political geography of the Sabarkantha district. An island of British territory surrounded by native States and Agency areas, it acquired a number of modern features and exerted considerable influence on proximate areas. The prosperous, educated and mobile trading "Baniya" community dominated the town of Modasa and extended its sway in the surrounding villages. In addition, there emerged in Modasa an outstanding political leader and a towering personality known as "Dada," who dominated the entire district for over thirty years. An architect of almost all the people's movements in the surrounding princely States as well as the anti-British agitation in Modasa, he continued to have a dominating role in the politics of Sabarkantha after the coming of Independence.

Two points should be noted straightaway. The commercial importance of Modasa, the position of the Baniya community and the fact that "Dada" himself was a Baniya gave a preponderant influence to this community in the public life of Modasa. Secondly, being part of British India and centre of the nationalist and States people's movements gave Modasa a dominant position in the politics of the district. Both these points—the predominance of Baniyas in Modasa and of Modasa in the district—provide us with a starting point to the changes that have taken place since Independence.

The Baniyas are split into two major castes, the "Nima," a small and largely urban community but much respected and influential, and the "Khadaita," somewhat more numerous and having a much greater pull in the countryside owing to its money-lending and "sahukar" functions. There are other minor castes among Baniyas but not so important. Between all of them, the Baniyas constitute no more than 3.5 per cent of the population. But they dominated the social and political life of Modasa for a very long period. In much larger numbers and mostly of

* *Economic Weekly,* Vol. XV (Special Number, July 1963), pp. 1169–1178.

peasant stock is the "Patidar" community of Modasa. A few Patidar families, the more highly placed in the social hierarchy and prosperous land-owners, have migrated from outside. The large majority, however, have been relatively backward and poor. The latter are known as "Anjana" Patidars. Not much behind these in the social hierarchy are the "Kshatriyas," the most numerous community group in Modasa and comprising of various castes and sub-castes. Socially very backward and politically dormant, the Kshatriyas account for 40 to 50 per cent of Modasa's population. There are many other castes, tribal and "backward" groupings but these are often indistinguishable from the Kshatriyas. There are also other smaller groups of artisan communities, Harijans, Brahmins and Muslims, the latter with a substantial population in Modasa town. None of these, however, is important from the point of view of the constituency as a whole.

Two strains develop in the politics of Modasa after 1952. Firstly, the retirement from active politics and death later of Dada leads to a shift of power within the district from Modasa to Himatnagar, the district capital, from where the new line of leadership emerges. Secondly, within Modasa taluka itself, the hegemony of the Baniyas is challenged; first, the ruling Nima group is challenged by the other group of Baniyas, the Khadaitas, and still later the Baniyas as a whole by the Patidars. At the district level too Dada had cultivated Patidar leaders who took over after him. Thus, both the Baniya preponderance in Modasa politics and the importance of Modasa and its leadership in the district politics are affected, largely as a result of the working of the electoral process. We shall consider these shifts in power in some detail below.

Largely because of the dominant influence of Dada, Modasa remained with Congress for a long time and except for the short-lived victory of the Mahagujarat candidate in 1957 (the election was later declared void and the Congress came back in the bye-election that followed), Modasa has always voted Congress. However, a growing rift has taken place within the Congress, taking the form of clear-cut factions. What is more, this has culminated in considerable defection from the Congress, leading to an impressive performance by the Swatantra Party which lost by a very narrow margin in 1962 and finally to its victory in the Panchayati Raj elections of 1963. In what follows, we shall consider these two aspects of political change in Modasa—the intraparty factionalism in which the selection of candidates for the Congress plays the decisive role, and the shift in popularity from Congress to the Opposition in which caste alignments play the decisive role.

In the crystallisation of factional positions within the Congress, the selection of party candidates has invariably played an important role. In Modasa, the recurrence of this event from one election to another has led, first, to competition for the party ticket between individuals and, secondly, to an attempt by the unsuccessful candidate to build his strength by seeking support from various groups. An examination of the process provides a clue to the first two questions formulated in the beginning: how factions come into being and how they get consolidated.

In both 1952 and 1957 the Congress ticket was given to a worker from Modasa town, a non-Baniya by caste but an ardent follower of Dada and a close associate of the Nima group among the Baniyas. It was denied both times to a Khadaita Baniya, wealthy and very influential in the villages. The former had the whole official organisation of the Congress with him. The latter had to build his strength on the basis of his own social and economic connections. He did this, first, by mobilising the support of his community throughout the constituency and, second, by using the economic hold of this community on parts of the peasantry. Thus came into being the first substantial faction in Modasa politics. How powerful it was, was shown in two elections held in 1957, the general election and a bye-election that followed immediately. In the former, the Khadaita candidate was denied the Congress ticket and he worked against the Congress. Before the bye-election was held, however, he had been given the Congress ticket in another constituency in the district and had become an M L A. In the bye-election, therefore, this faction returned to the Congress fold and worked for it. While the Congress lost in the general election, it won by a comfortable majority in the bye-election. (In both the elections the popular appeal of the Congress was reduced because of the "Mahagujarat" agitation for linguistic autonomy. This accounts for the large vote polled by the Mahagujarat candidate (See Table 2). But the decisive difference was made by the bulk vote held and controlled by the Khadaita Baniyas.)

Thus before 1962 the main cleavage was between the majority group in the Congress organisation controlled by one Baniya caste and the minority group backed by another Baniya caste. The caste conflict that developed was not there from the beginning, but grew from the minority faction's attempt to consolidate its position. The other major caste groups in the Congress, the Patidars and the Kshatriyas, remained outside the main conflict and had not yet taken the form of factions. The Patidars had in 1957 argued for a "peasant candidate" but did not press their claim in deference to the Nima group. It was in 1962 that the selection was bitterly contested by them.

TABLE 2. VOTING IN THREE ELECTIONS HELD BETWEEN 1957 AND 1962
(per cent of total votes polled)

	1957	*1957* Bye-election	*1962*
Congress	49	69	41
Mahagujarat/PSP	51	31	19
Swatantra Party			39
Others (including invalid votes)			9

The Patidars had now become restive, organised themselves into a powerful faction, and put in their claim in opposition to the claims of the Nima and Khadaita Baniya candidates. An intense campaign followed and ultimately resulted in a polarisation, the traditional Nima group and the Patidars presenting a united front against the Khadaita Baniya. The Patidar faction was still prepared to withdraw in favour of a Nima Baniya but was not prepared to make room for a Khadaita Baniya who was getting to be much disliked in the countryside and particularly by the Patidars who were rapidly growing into positions of leadership in the villages.

Most of the Mandal Congress Committees, practically the whole of the Taluka Congress and a majority of the D C C were against the candidature of the Khadaita who was generally unpopular with the local Congress, largely owing to his habit of bypassing the organisation and relying either on his castemen or on "higher authorities" at the State level. But to the surprise of everyone, he managed to get the ticket by bringing pressure from the State level on the D C C where he succeeded in getting a majority.

The sequel to the selection is important. Barring the Khadaitas most of whom were outside the fold of the official Congress organisation, Congressmen all over the Taluka were dissatisfied. The most resentful was the Patidar faction which decided to put up its candidate against the Congress. In these circumstances, it found the newly-formed Swatantra Party a handy instrument to fight the Congress with. The upshot was *en bloc* desertion by the Patidar group from the Congress.

Here is a clear case of party factions becoming irreconcilable and leading to the desertion of a whole faction from the parent party into a new party which, but for the desertion, had no base in the constituency. Party factions, instead of providing a basis for accommodation and flexibility, here became irreconcilable and led to an open break. It was through the Swatantra Party that the resentment could be channelised. Although in the outcome the Swatantra Party was defeated by a narrow margin, its performance was remarkable and would have been impossible without the desertion of the Patidar group from the Congress.

Attitudes to power, however, differ. Both the Nima and the Patidar groups had been deprived of the party ticket by the Khadaita candidate's strategy of "pressure from above." But while the Nima group continued within the Congress, *albeit* with a much reduced enthusiasm and with some of its workers withdrawing from active politics, the Patidars, known for their aggressiveness in politics and not given to taking a defeat lying-down, left the Congress determined to undo it before long. Attitudes of particular groups have much to do with the precise form that political mobility takes. It is only by a combination of an extraordinary set of circumstances, as found in Modasa, that the commercial community of Baniyas has occupied such a predominant political position. With the tone of politics changing from a respectable and paternalistic activity into something acutely competitive, and with the rise of new and aggressive groups, the days of the Baniyas in Gujarat politics are numbered. Modasa is a case in point. Even among the Baniyas, the more urbane and idealistic Nimas are first on their way out. The Khadaitas, money-lenders and mortgage-dealers, are known to be more tough in their management of human affairs and can put their money to good effect in politics. But before the passion for politics of the Patidars and before the overwhelming numbers of the Kshatriyas, even the Khadaitas will be forced to retreat. Considering the cost of politics, they will soon decide to give it up altogether. Though in the 1962 election in Modasa a Khadaita Baniya won narrowly against a Patidar, this was perhaps the last time that this could happen. The future, which was foreshadowed in the election, lay with the numerous and rising Patidars and Kshatriyas, as indeed was to be proved only a year afterwards when the Taluka Panchayat was elected.

The role of factions in the selection of the Congress candidate underlines the importance of caste in the politics of Modasa. We may now ask and recapitulate: how precisely have the various castes grouped themselves in Modasa politics?

Broadly speaking, the first important caste consolidation was that of the Khadaita Baniyas. This, in turn, led to another caste consolidation. The Patidars, deferential so long as Dada and the Nima group were in power, now began to feel uncomfortable. This was largely because whereas the Nimas were largely an urban caste and interfered little in rural affairs, the Khadaitas operated in areas where the Patidars made their livelihood. Moreover, in so many local events—the D L B elections, the composition of the School Board, the election of delegates to the A I C C—these were the two groups that came into conflict. Finally, as we will see below, the

Kshatriya community was advised in 1962 both by their regional organisation, the Gujarat Kshatriya Sabha, and the local Patidars with whom they had close social contacts, to vote for the Swatantra Party. This has since led gradually to a caste alliance between the Patidars and the Kshatriyas against the Baniyas.

Thus starting with the activisation of intra-party groups, the gradual weakening of the ideological heirs of Dada and the rise of new bidders for power, the political contest got organised on the basis of caste, at first within the Congress and then beyond. It is remarkable that in none of the elections did a Khadaita stand against a Khadaita, a Nima against a Nima or a Patidar against a Patidar. What is found in some other places, men of the same caste standing against each other thus enabling politics to cut across caste groups, did not occur in Modasa where the major groups in politics are caste groups. Indeed here it is the caste loyalties that often cut across party affiliations such as the Congress Khadaitas working against the Congress candidate in 1957. Even the Patidar group's joining the Swatantra Party after defecting from the Congress is to be interpreted as continuation of a factional struggle within the Congress that had developed on a caste basis. The new party was no more than an instrument for carrying on the fight.

Our consideration of factionalism has so far been limited to the political elite of Modasa. It should now be seen how such a form of political competition gets structured into the mass of the electorate. More particularly, it needs to be examined how far caste provides the infra-structure of political organisation and makes available to the competing groups the necessary mechanism for electoral divisions and alignments. For us, two questions are involved here: How far do the relationships between various castes of Modasa provide material for politics? In other words, what is the secular potentiality of Modasa's caste hierarchy? Secondly, how actually did these relationships provide a basis for electoral behaviour in 1962?

Modasa is a comparatively backward constituency. The political articulation found here is not one of horizontal differentiation (in terms of various social and political groupings) but of vertical dependence (between a dominant minority and a dependent majority). The developing cleavage is between two or more minority groups, although one minority may be more numerous than the other. The changes that occur are changes in the dominance pattern of politics where one dominant community gives place to another, the large majority of people simply providing a numerical base for the contesting parties, having not yet themselves emerged as active participants in the political process. This is one point. Another point, and one of considerable general significance is that such a change in the dominance pattern is initiated in the sphere of politics which then gets reflected in society. Indeed, to a marked extent the changes taking place in the secular relationships between various groups in Modasa society can be understood largely in terms of the political relationships between those groups. What follows will make this clear.

Where the rival contenders for votes come from minority communities, there is no direct identification in terms of caste, occupation, interest group or political party between the candidate and the voter that could be statistically related. The relation is indirect and can be asserted only because of supporting data collected both from a review of the last few years and other field data on the conduct of the election. But whatever statistical evidence there is, goes to support the assertions we make; which increases our confidence in the analysis.

Let us first state our assertions. The Baniya community has enjoyed long political hegemony in this area, partly owing to its social and economic position and partly owing to its supply of political leadership during the Independence movement. As is usual in the politics of minority dominance, the minority itself gets split into rival factions. In Modasa these factions also took a community base, between the two sects of Nima Baniya and Khadaita Baniya. The Nimas had dominated so long as politics was largely urban-oriented. With adult franchise, this was no longer possible. On the other hand, the Khadaitas, both more numerous and exercising a greater rural penetration, began to dominate a number of local institutions. The Nimas continued to control the Taluka Congress for some time but, lacking the wherewithal by which to control the rural masses, lost in real power to the Khadaitas. But while the Nimas, found mostly in the urban areas, continued to hold certain positions because of the traditional respect in which they were held, it was the Khadaita community, both more numerous and exercising a greater rural penetration, that dominated local centres of power. With years of influence and status in the village community behind him and the wherewithal by which to control the needy and the backward, the (Khadaita) Baniya has enjoyed this position of dominance for a considerable time now.

This position, however, was not left unchallenged. The chief contestant has been the Patidar community of Modasa. Now it is true that in terms of economic power and influence, the Patidars have a long leeway to make up. But they have other qualifications. They are more numerous. They are the farmers, the sons of the soil. Many of them have made a success of farming and have prospered. As politics became more broad-based and peasant-oriented, this increased their confidence and their sense of solidarity, especially against the Baniyas. The upshot was that the Patidars of Modasa were no longer satisfied with a dependent status in politics. Indeed, for a large majority of them, politics provided the only opening for getting out of their "low" and dependent status in society as well. Thus in the 1962 election, the first time the Patidars made a determined bid for power, it was from among the "backward" Patidars (caste Anjana) that a candidate was put up. A year later he became the President of the Taluka Panchayat of Modasa!

Far more numerous than any other caste group, economically exploited and socially handicapped, is the Kshatriya community of Modasa. An incomparable political force in terms of numbers, the Kshatriyas have all along had a dependent status, in politics as well as in society. They have conformed to whichever dominance pattern obtained in their different villages. This was so right up to the 1962 elections. But 1962 did make a difference even to the Kshatriyas. Two factors are important. The Gujarat Kshatriya Sabha, a prominent social organisation of Kshatriyas throughout the State and dominated by outstanding leaders of the community, had openly called upon the community to vote for the Swatantra Party. This was a great influence and made the community for the first time conscious of itself as a political force. Secondly, in the whole of Sabarkantha district, the numerous low caste Patidars (Anjanas) are very close to the Kshatriyas in the social hierarchy and are usually in constant social intercourse. Now that a Patidar—and that too an Anjana Patidar—had at last made bold to contest against the powerful Baniya, the sympathies of the Kshatriyas were naturally for the Patidar. The facts most emphasised by the latter was that he was a *khedut,* a farmer, and that he had joined issue with the Baniya, the traditional usurper.

This provided a manifesto, a sort of ideology and one that readily carried meaning to the uneducated villager. Then there was also the fact that the Swatantra Party had given its ticket in the adjoining constituency to a Kshatriya. The latter also exerted his influence on the Kshatriya vote in Modasa.

With all these factors, however, the Kshatriya vote was decisively split, the Congress and its Baniya candidate still retaining their dominance on the community in a number of places. This accounts for the ultimate victory of the Congress candidate over his Patidar rival from the Swatantra Party. The latter's calculation of a firm Patidar-Kshatriya alliance had to contend with the strong influence wielded by the trading class on the mass of voters that continued to be in a state of dependence, indebtedness, obligation or simply influence hallowed by tradition and usage. On the other hand, by forging such an alliance and turning it into an expanding base of political organisation, the Patidar leaders of the Swatantra Party posed a formidable challenge for the Congress, one that nearly shook her from her fort in the very first encounter and was likely to become a menace for a long time to come. To see it, however, as a Swatantra challenge to the Congress would be misleading. It was essentially the challenge of the Patidars against the dominant Baniyas, in the process also bringing in the numerous lower strata of the population and affecting time-honoured dominant-dependent relationships. . . .

But if the splitting of the Kshatriya vote enabled the Congress to withstand the Swatantra challenge of a rural alliance against Baniya dominance, it was the urban vote that really tilted the balance in favour of the Congress. The vote in Modasa town followed a pattern very different from the pattern in the countryside. Here is was not the persistence or decline of a dominance pattern on social or economic lines but political record and persuasion that influenced voter's decisions.

The interesting thing to note in this connection is that a recent event of explosive significance—diversion of the railway line from Modasa to another part of the district in spite of official and expert advice being in favour of Modasa—, which had led to a great deal of agitation and violence, had turned the people of the town hostile to the Congress. Yet, their dissatisfaction could not be turned to the advantage of the Swatantra Party. There were two reasons for this. Firstly, the P S P which had been in the forefront of the Mahagujarat movement had also taken the lead in the Railway agitation. Hence it was the P S P that derived the most benefit. Secondly the old Nima leadership in the Congress had a good hold over the population of the town. Although thrown out of position within the party by the Khadaitas, the Nima leaders could not, like the Patidars, bring themselves to oppose the Congress or even be indifferent to it. (Some, however, subsequently retired from active politics.) They used all their influence and pressure to save the party's prestige and the name of Dada. The result was that the P S P and the Congress polled between them almost the entire vote of the town, the Swatantra Party making a miserable show. The margin thus secured enabled the Congress to tilt the balance and win the election.

Such are the reasons for the actual outcome of the general elections, the Congress losing substantially but yet retaining the seat.

. . . The upshot is a trend of declining Baniya dominance and rising Patidar-Kshatriya alliance against such a dominance in Modasa politics.

The trend was confirmed in the election of the Taluka Panchayat President that followed in 1963. In this election, the impressive majority of the Patidar candidate of the Swatantra Party against the Congress candidate largely owed itself to the support he got from Kshatriya and Patidar Sarpanches. The caste break-up of the vote is given in Table 7.

The experience of the elections has opened the eyes of a section of the Congress leadership which is aware of the strong position of the Patidar leadership of the Taluka. The only way of regaining the lost position of the Congress in Modasa is to win back this group and this could be done only at one price: the present Khadaita hegemony of the Taluka Congress should go. Such a solution may indeed find favour with the D C C which is also dominated by the Patidars. Moreover, if the D C C can enforce its line of thinking on the Taluka, Modasa too will be in their hands and the rivalry between two centers of power in the district ever since the death of Dada will come to an end. The territorial shift of power from Modasa to Himatnagar (the District capital and home of the D C C group) and the social shift from Baniyas to Patidars would be complete. The enticements for the D C C to enter into this grand design are indeed tempting but any movement on their part would depend upon (i) the success in wooing back the Patidar group of Modasa; and (ii) the ease with which the Khadaita M L A and his group

TABLE 7. TALUKA PANCHAYAT ELECTION

Caste	*Swatantra*	*Congress*	*Total*
Brahmin	1	4	5
Patidar	16	2	18
Kshatriya	27	3	30
Baniya	—	5	5
Others	1	1	2
	45	15	60

can be persuaded or coerced into acquiescence. The latter would depend on the pull of the M L A with "higher level" leadership. Meanwhile, Modasa politics after a long factional process has crystallised along a pattern that seems to augur well for the opposition party.

Conclusions

(1) The political orientation of this relatively backward constituency has been provided by a long period of one-man dominance followed by the political hegemony of the Congress Party since independence.

(2) This led to political competition within the Congress. Opposition got internalised and the outcome was a structuring of the party into a system of factions. Starting with individual competition and frustration the process soon got crystallised along an ongoing structure of ascription, influence and power. In the main, this derived from (a) kinship and caste alignments and (b) economic power.

(3) The process gained shape from a sequence of competitive trials provided by a series of elections over a period of twelve years (1952 to 1963) and even more, by the selection of candidates for the Congress ticket for each of these elections.

(4) Such a structuring of political power along factional lines drew its sustenance from the division of the electorate on the lines of the prevailing infra-structure of Modasa society, although in the process it radically altered the power relationships of this structure by introducing new principles of organisation and affiliation.

These changes in the power relationships of Modasa can be understood in terms of the changes through which the dominance pattern in society has passed. For long this pattern was one of urban dominance in which one section of the trading community of "Baniyas" were all-powerful. With the growing importance of numbers and thus of the rural population, the pattern turned into one in which economic hold and a long period of rural domination gave power to another sect of Baniyas, the money-lenders and the village "sahukars." Meanwhile, the more enterprising and aggressive of the farming communities, the "Patidar" community, was catching up and soon began challenging the dominance of the trading class. They were the new rural leaders and owing to their closeness in occupation and social hierarchy to the numerous small and landless farmers, coming from various "backward" castes but together known as the "Kshatriya," there came about a consolidation of rural power never known before. With this, the hegemony of the urban and trading communities was undermined once and for all.

(5) Such an understanding of politics in terms of an infrastructure of communities also provides a clue to the 1962 election results. The trading community with its traditional hold on the villages on the one hand and the conscious and articulate section of the peasantry on the other provided the basis of the polarisation that came about in Modasa politics. When the faction representing the latter defected from the Congress Party in 1962, the factional cleavage within the party turned into a political cleavage between two parties. Underlying both, however, was the caste cleavage described here.

The decisive influence was, of course, exercised by the large and inarticulate "backward" vote of the Kshatriya communities. This vote was split. The Swatantra Party was a late-comer and had no organisational network to count upon. On the other hand, the candidate of the Congress had vast influence in the constituency, especially owing to his wealth and business links. That the balance was still in favour of the Swatantra Party is owing to the close links of its socially "backward" candidate with the bulk of the farming population of Modasa. It is significant, therefore, that it was the urban vote of Modasa town that enabled the Congress to steal a march over the Swatantra.

(6) More than the outcome, however, it is the trends revealed by the 1962 election that are more important. These point to the emergence of a strong political alliance between the two farming communities of Patidars and Kshatriyas. The days of Baniya dominance in Modasa politics seem to be numbered. Whether the alliance will benefit the Swatantra Party as it appears to have done in the local-self-government election of '63 or the Congress will stage a come-back by winning back the Patidar leadership into its folds cannot be predicted with certainty, although there are great difficulties in the way of the Congress, thanks to the powerful faction chain stretching from the Taluka right to the State and national levels that could be invoked by the present Baniya M L A of Modasa. What is certain is that whichever party wins over this new rural coalition will come out successful in Modasa. The crux of political divisions in Modasa is their community and interest orientation (the latter taking an urban-rural and trader-farmer complexion), caste emerging as the relevant political category and providing the necessary structural basis for mobilisation.

(7) Such a community orientation of politics, however, should not lead to an instrumental view of politics according to which politics is but a reflection of social

cleavages that exist apart from and prior to the play of politics. Such a view of the relationship between society and politics is not borne out by the Modasa study. Indeed, the point that emerges clearly in Modasa is the *political origin of social changes:* politics is the great leveller of social distances and dominance positions found in a peasant society. The distances exist, the antagonisms are also there, but these are largely latent. It is in politics that they are crystallised and given shape. "Baniyas," "Patidars," and "Kshatriyas" were indeed the significant categories of Modasa politics, but they operated not as traditional communal groups but as political groups, in the process passing over important social gradations or creating new gradations. What emerges from Modasa is not so much social conditioning of politics but politicisation of social cleavages and the creation of new identifications and loyalties, although both were involved in the process of change. While caste provided an ongoing structure along which politics got articulated, politics provided events and opportunities by which traditional structures were found to disintegrate or re-shape under the impact of new forces. Modasa is a revealing case study in the polticisation of a traditional society.

63 • *Indian General Elections of 1967* *

The 1967 elections constitute a major watershed in Indian party politics. Above all they mark the end of the era of Congress party dominance and the emergence of new roles and responsibilities for opposition parties on both the national and state levels. Congress' share of seats in the Lok Sabha declined to a small majority of 54 per cent from the 70 per cent or more of the three previous elections. This difference enables coalitions of non-Congress parties in Parliament to act more effectively as an opposition in questioning and holding Congress officials to account. Nevertheless, Congress still remains the largest single party, having won six times as many seats as its nearest rival. Furthermore, as the following tables indicate, its popular vote declined only about 3–4 per cent (44.7 per cent in 1962 to 41.0 per cent in 1967). The ability of non-Congress parties for the first time in 1967 to form viable coalitions for electoral purposes accounts to a considerable extent for the discrepancy between the large loss of parliamentary seats of Congress and its small decline in popular vote. Many party stalwarts including Kamaraj, the party president, were rejected by the voters, indicating popular discontent with party leadership.

Equally significant were the results for state legislative assemblies. Nine of the sixteen state gavernments passed from the control of Congress; post-elections defections from the party have caused the loss of three additional states. The non-Congress governments with the exception of Madras were based on fragile, unstable party coalitions, several of which soon fell due to coalitional defections. With Congress no longer dominating Parliament with an

* "A Post-Election Survey," *Eastern Economist,* Vol. 48, No. 12 (March 24, 1967), pp. 519, 521. By permission.

overwhelming majority, and with over half of the states in other hands, new federal-state relations will have to be worked out based on an even greater devolution of power to the state level.

The following tables present an analysis of the performance of different political parties in the fourth general election held in February this year. These results have been compared with those of the 1962 general election.

PARTY POSITION: LOK SABHA

State	*Seats*	*Con.*	*Swa.*	*CPI*	*CPI (M)*	*PSP*	*SSP*	*JS*	*Rep.*	*Others*	*Ind.*	*Total*
All India Total	520	281	42	23	19	13	23	35	1	37	41	515
Andhra Pradesh	41	35	3	1	...	...	...	...	...	...	2	41
Assam	14	10	...	1	...	2	...	...	...	1A	...	14
Bihar	53	34	...	5	...	1	7	1	...	...	5	53
Gujarat	24	11	10	...	...	...	...	...	...	...	3	24
Haryana	9	7	...	...	...	...	...	1	...	...	1	9
Jammu & Kashmir	6	5	...	...	...	...	...	...	...	1B	...	6
Kerala	19	1	...	3	9	...	3	...	...	2C	1	19
Madhya Pradesh	37	24	1	...	...	...	...	10	...	...	2	37
Madras	39	3	...	...	4	...	...	...	...	25D	1	39
Maharashtra	45	37	...	2	...	1	2	...	...	2E	1	45
Mysore	27	18	5	...	...	2	1	...	...	...	1	27
Nagaland	1	...	...	...	...	...	...	...	...	1F	...	1
Orissa	20	6	8	...	...	4	1	...	...	...	1	20
Punjab	13	9	...	...	...	...	...	1	...	3G	...	13
Rajasthan	23	10	8	...	...	...	...	3	...	...	2	23
Uttar Pradesh	85	47	1	5	1	2	8	12	1	...	8	85
West Bengal	40	14	...	5	5	1	1	...	...	2H	12	40
Andaman & Nicobar Islands	1	1	...	...	...	...	...	...	...	...	...	1
Chandigarh	1	...	...	...	...	...	...	1	...	...	...	1
Dadra, Nagar Haveli	1	1	...	...	...	...	...	...	...	...	...	1
Delhi	7	1	...	...	...	...	...	6	...	...	...	7
Goa, Daman & Diu	2	(Election to be held on March 28, 1967)										
Himachal Pradesh	6	4	...	...	...	...	...	...	...	...	...	4
Laccadive, Minicoy & Amindivi Islands	1	...	...	...	...	...	...	...	...	...	1	1
Manipur	2	...	...	1	...	...	...	...	...	...	...	1
Pondicherry	1	1	...	...	...	...	...	...	...	...	...	1
Tripura	2	2	...	...	...	...	...	...	...	...	...	2

A. All Party Hill Leaders' Conference. B. National Conference. C. Muslim League. D. Dravida Munnetra Kazhagam. E. Peasants' & Workers' Party. F. Naga Nationalist Organization (affiliated to Congress). G. Shiromani Akali Dal (Sant Group). H. Forward Bloc.

PARTY POSITIONS: ASSEMBLIES

State	*Seats*	*Con.*	*Swa.*	*CPI*	*CPI (M)*	*PSP*	*SSP*	*JS*	*Rep.*	*Others*	*Ind.*	*Total*
Andhra Pradesh	287	165	29	10	9	...	1	3	2	...	68	287
Assam	126	73	2	7	...	5	4	...	...	9*	24	124
Bihar	318	128	4	24	4	18	67	26	1	...	46	318
Gujarat	168	92	64	...	...	3	...	1	...	...	7	167
Haryana	81	48	3	...	...	...	...	12	2	...	16	81
Jammu & Kashmir	75	58	...	...	...	...	...	3	...	8**	2	71
Kerala	133	9	...	19	52	...	19	...	...	19†	15	133
Madhya Pradesh	296	167	7	1	...	9	10	78	...	...	24	296
Madras	234	49	20	2	11	4	2	...	...	138††	7	233
Maharashtra	270	202	...	10	1	8	4	4	5	19+	16	269
Mysore	216	126	16	2	...	20	6	4	2	...	40	216
Orissa	140	30	49	7	1	21	2	...	...	...	29	139
Punjab	104	48	...	5	3	...	1	9	3	26++	9	104
Rajasthan	184	89	49	1	...	...	8	22	...	...	15	184
Uttar Pradesh	425	198	12	14	1	11	44	97	9	...	37	423
West Bengal	280	127	1	16	43	7	7	1	...	13@	65	280
Delhi (Metropolitan Council)	56	19	...	...	...	...	1	33	2	...	1	56
Himachal Pradesh	60	33	...	2	...	...	7	...	...	...	13	55
Manipur	30	16	...	1	...	...	4	...	...	...	9	30
Tripura	30	27	...	1	2	...	...	...	...	...	...	30

*All Party Hill Leaders' Conference 9; **National Conference 8; †Muslim League 14, Kerala Congress 5; ††Dravida Munnetra Kazhagam 138; +Peasants' and Workers' Party 19; ++Shiromani Akali Dal (Sant Group) 24, Shiromani Akali Dal (Master Group) 2; @Forward Bloc 13.

HOUSE OF THE PEOPLE (LOK SABHA)
(number of seats won by different parties)

	1951–52		1957		1962		1967	
	Number of seats	*Percentage*	*Number of seats*	*Percentage*	*Number of seats*	*Percentage*	*Number of seats*	*Percentage*
Congress	357(7)	74.5	359(12)	74.5	358(3)	72.9	276(5)	54.6
Socialist	12	2.5	19*	3.9	12	2.4*	13*	2.5*
KMPP	8(1)	1.7					23**	4.5**
CPI	16	3.4	27	5.6	29	5.9	23	4.5
CPI (M)							19	3.7
Jana Sangh	3	0.6	4	0.8	14	2.9	35	6.8
Swatantra	...	...	...	...	18	3.7	42	8.1
Independents, including others	83(2)	17.3	73	15.2	60	12.2	79	15.3
TOTAL	479(10)	100.0	482(12)	100.0	491(3)	100.0	510(5)	100.0

*PSP; **SSP.
Uncontested seats, given in brackets, are excluded from the totals.

LEGISLATIVE ASSEMBLIES
(number of seats won by different parties)

	1951–52		1957		1962		1967	
	Number of seats	*Percentage*	*Number of seats*	*Percentage*	*Number of seats*	*Percentage*	*Number of seats*	*Percentage*
Congress	2207(39)	68.3	1850(43)	64.8	1759	61.9	1690	50.6
Socialist	122(3)	3.9	195*	6.8*	149*	5.3*	106*	3.2*
KMPP	77	2.3					176(SSP)	5.3
CPI							121	3.6
CPI (M)	106	3.3	161	5.6	153	5.4	127	3.6
Jana Sangh	34	1.1	46	1.6	116	4.1	264	8.0
Swatantra	...	...	...	...	166	5.8	255	7.7
Independents including others	683(9)	21.1	606(5)	21.2	499	17.5	600	18.0
TOTAL	3229(51)	100.0	2858(48)	100.0	2842(13)	100.0	3339	100.0

*PSP.
Uncontested seats, given in brackets, are excluded from the totals.

HOUSE OF THE PEOPLE (LOK SABHA)
(percentage of valid votes polled by different parties)

Party	*1951–52*	*1957*	*1962*	*1967*
Congress	45.0	47.8	44.7	41.0
Swatantra	...	...	7.9	8.5
Jana Sangh	3.1	5.9	6.4	9.4
CPI	3.3	8.9	9.9	4.8
CPI (M)	...	...	...	4.5
KMPP	5.8	...	...	5.0*
PSP	10.6**	10.4	6.8	3.0
Independents, including others	32.2	27.0	24.2	24.2
Total	100.0	100.0	100.0	100.0

*SSP; **Socialist.

LEGISLATIVE ASSEMBLIES

(percentage of valid votes polled by different parties)

Party	*1951–52*	*1957*	*1962*	*1967*
Congress	42.2	45.6	44.4	40.1
Socialist	9.7	10.0*	7.0*	3.3
KMPP	5.1	...	...	5.1**
CPI	4.4	7.7	8.6	4.3
CPI (M)				4.6
Jana Sangh	2.8	4.0	6.1	8.8
Swatantra	...	...	7.4	6.6
Independents, including others	35.8	32.7	26.5	27.2
Total	100.0	100.0	100.0	100.0

*PSP; **SSP.

Part IV

Pakistan

SECTION ONE

Political Culture

64 • KHALID BIN SAYEED: *Islam and National Integration in Pakistan* *

Pakistan was ostensibly created to be an "Islamic state"; the 1956 constitution stipulated "the Islamic republic of Pakistan." The 1962 constitution simply referred to "the Republic of Pakistan." The first amendment to that constitution, however, forced upon President Ayub Khan in 1963, was to reinsert the descriptive adjective "Islamic."

But the term "Islamic" is itself in need of interpretation. It is absurdly unfair to Pakistan to interpret it in terms of medieval Islam, just as it would be unfair to define a Christian state as one rigidly based on medieval Christian interpretations.

The following article is complete except for one section, in which the author points out that Islam is not inimical to modernization, and that "the industrial and commercial elite have been modernized to such an extent that they genuinely believe that Islam and modern commerce and industry can coexist" (p. 412). It clearly reveals the internal struggle between traditional and modernist Islamic practices. This division is the basis for much of the political dissension in Pakistan, exemplified in part by the role of Jama'at-i-Islam *(Community of Islam) party of Maulana Muhammad Maudoodi (Mawlana Mawdudi). President Muhammad Ayub Khan has been the most forthright of all Pakistan leaders in facing this problem involving both the nature of Islam and its authority.*

This reading is a slightly modified version of an article which first appeared in the Summer 1963 issue of The Middle East Journal. *Khalid Bin Sayeed is professor of political studies at Queen's University, Kingston, Ontario.*

It is common knowledge that both negative and positive factors brought about the establishment of Pakistan. It was not merely the fear of the Hindu numerical majority in the subcontinent that brought together the Muslims of the two physically separate territories now known as West and East Pakistan. Muslims of these areas feared that the Hindu majority would not allow the Muslims to

* Donald E. Smith, ed., *Politics and Religion in South Asia* (Princeton, N. J.: Princeton University Press, 1966), pp. 398–412. By permission.

establish their unique cultural and political identity. The Qur'an claims that its message of Islam is a vast improvement on what Judaism or Christianity had offered to the world. So the Muslim leaders of India, while trying to persuade their fellow believers about the validity of their demands for a separate state, posed the formidable question: What similarity can there be between Islam and Hinduism, which, to quote Jinnah, "challenged each other at every point of the compass?"

Two of the trenchant contrasts between the two faiths that were stressed were the Islamic oneness of God as opposed to Hindu idolatry, and the Islamic egalitarian brotherhood of believers as opposed to the Hindu caste system. When their opponents pointed out that great numbers of Muslims were descendants of converts from Hinduism such pleas fell on deaf ears, because converts do not like to be reminded of their origins and would do everything to dispel the impression that in religious ardor they lag behind their fellow believers. How Islamic were the Muslim masses? Even in the heart of predominantly Muslim-majority areas in West Pakistan, "the peasantry," wrote Sir Malcolm Darling, "almost to a man confess themselves the servants of the one true God and of Muhammad, his Prophet, but in actual fact they are the servants of landlord, money-lender and pir." And as one moved away from the Indus basin, whatever vigor there was in the Islamic cultural stream was lost in the Hindu sea. Arguments that Muslim peasants differed very little from the customs and manners of their Hindu neighbors were silenced by the claim that the Islamic state of Pakistan would enable Muslims to purify their culture and pursue their beliefs in an Islamic environment.

What are the basic characteristics of the Islamic state? These are to be found in the concept of Islamic law and how it can be amended. According to one of the famous Muslim definitions of law: "The science of law is the knowledge of the rights and duties whereby man is enabled to observe right conduct in his life, and to prepare himself for the world to come," as opposed to the conception of Roman or modern law, which is largely molded by the historical experience of a people. The fundamental principles of Islamic law have already been laid down for all time by God in the Qur'an. These include matters like conduct of war against non-Muslims, treatment of non-Muslims, regulations regarding inheritance and marriage, *zakat* (charity under state or community auspices), penalties and punishment for criminal offenses, etc. Another source of Islamic law is the authoritative tradition of the Prophet. The Prophet himself had put some of these Islamic principles into effect during his lifetime, as a law-giver and head of the state, and had also made authoritative pronouncements as to how they should be interpreted and applied. These are called the Sunnah or Traditions of the Prophet.

A third source is the *ijma* or the consensus of the community. There has been some dispute as to whose consensus the *ijma* represents. Is it the consensus of the learned doctors and divines or the consensus of the entire community of believers? The counterpart of *ijma* or consensus *is ijtihad* which means "exercise of judgment." Modernists would claim that *ijtihad* made Islam a dynamic religion in the sense that Muslims were free to mold their legal and political doctrines according to changing circumstances. The orthodox *ulama* took a stand against this, and pointed out that exercise of judgment did not imply that an individual Muslim or the legislature could stretch the meaning of the Quranic principles in such a way that their spirit was lost or distorted. Some of them would assert that since the gaps in the Muslim legal system had all been filled by the *ijtihad* of successive generations of doctors, supported by the consensus of the community, the "gate of *ijtihad* was closed."

The Politicians and Modernist Islam

What was the state of affairs when Pakistan came into being? It was true that the *ulama* had played a vital role in enlisting the support of the rural masses for the Pakistan movement. But the leadership was largely in the hands of upper middle-class lawyers and merchants and the big landowners of the Punjab and the United Provinces. The most powerful among these were the lawyers and the intellectuals, who had been brought up on the writings of Amir Ali and Iqbal. Both of these writers had said that Islam was a dynamic religion, and that all that was best in modern science and democracy was reflected in the principles of Islam. Practices like polygamy, the right of divorce being available only to men, and the so-called inferiority of women in Islam were distortions or misguided interpretations of the original principles. The Prophet had married widows in order to save them from poverty and social disgrace. Polygamy had been allowed because of the excess of women over men, a result of the death toll in tribal wars. But the Qur'an had explicitly recommended that monogamy was better than polygamy. Similarly, Islam was perfectly democratic because it insisted on the equality of all believers irrespective of their national or racial origins. The first four Caliphs had been chosen in a democratic fashion. The later institutions of monarchy and feudalism which had crept into Islam were a result of the moral and spiritual lapses that Muslims had suffered and therefore they could not be said to have been derived from Islamic principles.

The Muslim League government of Pakistan, dominated by lawyers and university-educated landowners, believed that the parliamentary government that had been established in Pakistan under the adapted Government of India Act, 1935, was by no means at variance with the principles of Islam. The new State Bank of Pakistan, the National Bank of Pakistan and the Industrial Development Corporation were institutions which were necessary for the existence of a modern state. Muslims had lagged behind in banking and other commercial enterprises. They should be encouraged to take to such professions with eagerness and speed. Islam had frowned upon the taking and giving of interest, but this was because interest had originally encouraged usury. It was suggested that Islam was not against interest charged for the services and risks taken by the banking institution.

On the other hand, the rural masses of Punjab and Bengal had been told time and again that Pakistan would mean the establishment of an Islamic state. Their *mullahs* had preached to them during Friday sermons that the modern cinema encouraged sexual laxity and that the current evils of gambling, drinking and free mixing of men and women to be found among Muslim urban classes were reprehensible. They thought that now that Pakistan had come into being, all these evil practices would be prohibited. Nothing demonstrates more graphically the contrast in expectations between the illiterate rural masses and the urbanized and westernized elites, on the question of the Islamic state, than the story of Qaid-i-Azam Jinnah being cheered by the peasants of a Sindhi village as "Long live Mawlana Muhammad Ali Jinnah." It is reported that Jinnah stopped his car and told the peasants not to call him Mawlana as he was not their religious leader but a political leader. The peasants perhaps thought that the founder of the new state would become one of their pious Caliphs.

In March 1949 the famous Objectives Resolution was moved in the Constituent Assembly by the prime minister, Liaquat Ali Khan. It declared that "sovereignty over the entire universe belongs to God Almighty alone," but He had delegated this authority to the state of Pakistan and that this was to be exercised through its people "within the limits prescribed by Him." The resolution also stated that (a) "the state shall exercise its power and authority through the chosen representatives of the people" and that (b) "the principles of democracy, freedom, equality, tolerance and social justice, as enunciated by Islam, shall be fully observed." (c) "The Muslims shall be enabled to order their lives in accordance with the teachings and requirements of Islam as set out in the Holy Qur'an and the Sunnah."

All this suggested that the resolution could be interpreted in different ways. Modernists could say that the resolution guaranteed a democratic constitution and the sovereignty of the people. The orthodox could point out that democracy did not imply, by any means, absolute popular sovereignty because the resolution clearly stated that the people of Pakistan on whom God had conferred His authority were to exercise their power "within the limits prescribed by Him." Further, the fact that the resolution clearly stated that Muslims would be enabled to order their lives in accordance with the teachings and requirements of Islam as set out in the Holy Qur'an and the Sunnah meant that the legislature could not repeal or modify Islamic provisions like the prohibition of alcoholic drinks, interest and gambling, and the severe punishments such as cutting off of hands for theft and stoning to death for adultery.

These, according to a fundamentalist like Mawlana Mawdudi, the head of the Jama'at-i-Islami movement, constituted mandatory legislation which was beyond the purview of any legislature in a Muslim country. Then came the recommendatory provisions. But, according to Mawdudi, there was also the sphere of permissible legislation under which the Muslim society could legislate, keeping in view the ever-increasing requirements of every age. However, he was quite emphatic that the present western-educated Muslim leaders of Pakistan were not competent to initiate legislation even within the permissible field, because they were neither well versed in Islamic doctrine nor good Muslims. On the other hand, there were others like Mawlana Abul Hasanat, president of the Jami'at-al-Ulama-i-Pakistan, who were of the opinion that Islamic law was complete and merely required interpretation by well-qualified experts. This meant that there was hardly any room for further legislation.

One cannot help feeling that leaders like Liaquat were probably temporizing with a difficult situation. They had assured the Muslims that an Islamic state based on the Qur'an and the Sunnah would be established, and the Muslim masses had supported the demand for Pakistan because of these assurances. The leaders still needed the support of the masses and particularly that of the influential *ulama*. In the Constituent Assembly Mawlana Shabbir Ahmad Usmani supported the Objectives Resolution. It is inconceivable that Liaquat and his cabinet would have allowed the incorporation of primitive law into the Pakistan penal code. But the Objectives Resolution had created the impression that Pakistan would move in the direction of an orthodox Islamic state.

National Unity and Sectarian Conflict

On the question of rights of minorities, the Objectives Resolution did suggest that minorities would be entitled to the same fundamental rights "including equality of status, of opportunity, and before law" as Muslims. But Mawlana Shabbir Ahmad Usmani in his speech during the debate was of the opinion that, since an Islamic state was an ideological state, "people who do not subscribe to those ideas may have a place in the administrative machinery of the state but they cannot be entrusted with the responsibility of framing the general policy of the state or dealing with matters vital to its safety and integrity."

It is obvious that Islam has set up a wall between believer and unbelievers. The word *kafir* (infidel) is repeatedly used in the Qur'an. Similarly, *jihad* (holy struggle for the spread of Islam) is recommended, though there are several other verses which stress tolerance and generous treatment of minorities. Then there are other verses which suggest that Islam should be preached by peaceful means and, if unbelievers persist in their beliefs, they should be left unmolested. But the over-all impression is that a community of believers is surrounded by a hostile world, and that the latter will not leave Muslims alone unless they are converted or overcome.

The treatment of certain sects within the fold of Islam who did not accept the beliefs and practices of the Sunni majority became a matter of immediate concern in Pakistan. The community which provoked intense hostility among the orthodox *ulama* was that of the Ahmadis. They number about 200,000, and believe that their prophet, Mirza Ghulam Ahmad (1835-1908), appeared in order to reform and renovate the original religion of Islam. Ever since Mirza Ghulam Ahmad proclaimed his faith towards the end of the nineteenth century, Muslims have felt outraged that one of the cardinal doctrines of Islam, namely, the finality of the Prophethood under Muhammad, who had brought the best and the most perfect faith, was being challenged. Mawlana Shabbir Ahmad Usmani, in a pamphlet called *Ash-shahab,* alleged that the Ahmadis were apostates and showed that in Islam the appropriate penalty for apostasy was death. It was well known that a few Ahmadis had been stoned to death in Afghanistan. Intense feelings of hostility toward them existed even before partition. But after Pakistan came into being and Sir Muhammad Zafrullah Khan, an Ahmadi, became its foreign minister, it was felt that he and others were not only propagating their faith but also establishing themselves in positions of importance in the administrative and political structure of Pakistan.

The campaign against the Ahmadis started soon after the establishment of Pakistan. According to the *Report of the Court of Inquiry Set up to Inquire into the Punjab Disturbances of 1953,* commonly known as the Munir Report, the campaign against them had assumed a clear pattern from 1948 on. Religious leaders would publicly describe Zafrullah as an apostate and a traitor and often justify the killing of Ahmadis. In a number of cases described in the report, enraged individuals would leave these meetings in such a state of fury that they would search out Ahmadis and kill them. This campaign gained steady momentum and several religious leaders combined to demand that Ahmadis should be declared a minority and Sir Zafrullah and other Ahmadis should be dismissed from office. It was significant that both the central and provincial Muslim League governments were aware that this campaign was gathering momentum and watched it with mounting alarm, but until the very end took no clear and firm action against it.

It has been estimated that about 377 Muslim League leaders from all over West Punjab actually supported the movement. The chief minister of West Punjab, Mumtaz Daultana, was most reluctant to take any vigorous stand against it because he felt that it would be politically dangerous. Instead of suppressing it, he tried to direct its main course towards Karachi so that the central government might bear the responsibility. The result was that Muslims in several districts of Punjab, excited by the speeches of the *ulama* and the *imams* in general meetings and mosques, and probably encouraged by the weakness of the government, resorted to lawlessness. In February 1953 martial law had to be imposed and the chief minister, Daultana, was replaced by the central government.

The way Prime Minister Nazimuddin and Daultana reacted to the demands of the *ulama* that Ahmadis should be declared a minority community provides a revealing commentary on the conflict between their moral or religious convictions and their political interests. Daultana, who is reported to have impressed his dons with his brilliance at Oxford, must have felt that it was not proper on the part of the *ulama* and other agitators to display such intolerance towards a religious sect but, guided by his political interests, he thought that he could not suppress such an agitation without incurring unpopularity among the great majority of Muslims in his province. Nazimuddin, on the other hand, though educated in Cambridge, was an intensely religious man. He was probably in sympathy with the demands of the *ulama,* whom he also respected, but thought that it would be politically unwise to accede to them: Pakistan would earn a bad name in foreign countries because the foreign minister, Sir Zafrullah, enjoyed an international reputation. Such actions by the prime minister would have created the impression abroad that Pakistan was acting in a medieval fashion.

Another conclusion which emerges from the religious disturbances and the Munir Report is that Islam, instead of uniting the different sections of the country, could work as a divisive factor. In the case of religious disturbances, one could see that there was not only a conflict between the great majority of Muslims and Ahmadis, but also between the orthodox *ulama* and the western-educated ruling classes. If such controversies were allowed to be raised, there could also be a conflict between Sunni Muslims, who are greatly in the majority, and the small but influential minority of Shi'i Muslims.

We have already referred to the liberal interpretations of Islam by Amir Ali and Iqbal. These two could have been good starting-points for Pakistan's intellectual and political elite, in formulating a liberal and progressive Islamic ideology. Why did not the leaders think along these lines? Perhaps there are two answers. First, there was an acute shortage of talent. The result was that both political and intellectual leaders became absorbed in building and operating the administrative apparatus of the country. Second, perhaps political leaders did not feel that there was any dire need for a political ideology. Merely by mouthing religious slogans and catch phrases, they had been able to mobilize Muslim support for Pakistan, and they thought they could continue to operate in the same way. Such a method of operation, however, was bound to attract political opportunists. Thus, the Muslim League in 1946 appointed a *Masha'ikh* Committee consisting of twelve members, some of whom were well-known religious leaders, to campaign for the Muslim League in the general elections. Others on the committee were highly westernized landowners, who were given fictitious titles of *pir* and *masha'ikh* so that the Muslim masses might be persuaded to vote for the Muslim League. Those who have seen these men either in the Lahore Gymkhana Club or in their luxurious drawing-rooms would find the situation highly amusing; indeed it was of such men that Philip Mason wrote: "It is no doubt a chance association, but if you speak of the ruling class in Pakistan today, I think of men watching the polo in Lahore, the kind of people you'd see at point-to-point races in England, with check caps pulled down over their eyes and horsey coats with slanting pockets."

Education and Islamic Values

When martial law was imposed in October 1958 and the former activities of politicians and civil servants were investigated, astonishing disclosures were made regarding corruption and maladministration. It was ironical that in a state which had been established to demonstrate an Islamic way of life, two of its seven prime ministers were accused of corruption and asked by the martial law regime to return their ill-gotten wealth to the state. Nearly all the educational and political leaders would blame the British system of education for this state of affairs. It had been designed to produce, as Macaulay said in his *Minute,* "a class of persons, Indian in blood and color, but English in taste, in opinion, in morals, and in intellect." Cynics would perhaps further add that these leaders resorted to corruption because they could not maintain their English or American tastes on Pakistani salaries. However, one should not condemn this education out of hand because Indians imbibed Europe's liberal nationalism from it, as indeed the two Nehrus and Jinnah and Liaquat did. But the fact remained that by itself this education had not created a national consciousness among Pakistan's leaders and for a great majority of people it was only a passport to a clerical job.

The Qur'an stresses repeatedly the concept of the *ummah*. It constantly differentiates this *ummah* from the infidels. But how is it, one may ask, that a conference of psychologists in Pakistan held in 1959 declared "that the average Pakistani tends to be selfish rather than cooperative?" "The average Pakistani is preoccupied with his own petty desires and megalomaniac whims because no all-absorbing national interest is within sight." Similarly, Edward C. Banfield, basing his observations on the study of an Italian village, has observed: "That the Montegranesi are prisoners of their family-centered ethos—that because of it they cannot act concertedly or in the common good—is a fundamental impediment to their economic and other progress." These findings apply to a people whose faith, Roman Catholicism, like Islam, offers a total view of the world. All this goes to suggest that abstract ideas are not enough, that they must have an underpinning of group activity reaching down to the lowest unit of society. Obviously this has been missing in Pakistan.

It can be said to the credit of the new regime that at least it has initiated a discussion of these fundamental problems. The *Report of the Committee on National Education* is interspersed with recommendations like these: "That religious instruction be made compulsory throughout the primary and middle stages. . . . Emphasis on activities requiring the subordination of the individual to the team or group. There should be a persistent effort to make the student community-conscious. We want to produce men and women who will work hard because they believe that idleness and slackness are morally wrong, and because they see in hard work a means to their own personal salvation and the salvation of their country." Social studies have been made compulsory from grades VI-X and Islamic studies from grades VI-VIII. It may also be pertinent to point out that emphasis is being laid in schools on Islam in a Pakistani environment. The *Report of the Curriculum Committee for Secondary Education* points out: "Students of Islamic History, as now presented, will develop confidence in themselves and instead of looking for leadership to other Muslim countries, will try to lead others in the presentation of Islam."

What is missing in these recommendations is the role that mosques and religious schools attached to mosques can play in developing group activity and civic consciousness. Children in the villages go to small schools attached to mosques, where the teaching of the Qur'an and elementary religious education are imparted. Village mosques and even those in cities can play a vital role in promoting group activities of various sorts in the way that churches in western countries have done. The Constitution Commission has recommended that the *imams* should be trained, not only in religious studies but also in modern sciences, so that they may explain Islam in the context of modern conditions to both the uneducated and "those who are of the western way of thinking."

When outsiders wonder whether the two physically separated units will remain together Pakistanis proudly state that the cementing force of Islam will overcome the geographical distance and cultural diversities. But obviously this cementing force has not been strong enough to persuade Pakistanis to arrive at a political settlement, and the economic battle has continued unabated both under the martial law regime and the present constitutional autocracy. Many observers have suggested that the elite in both wings are becoming increasingly secularized, and that the impact of modernity and secular forces seem to be different in West and East Pakistan. . . .

Islam and Nation Building

How can one sum up the role that Islam has played in nation building in Pakistan? There is considerable evidence to show that Jinnah, with all his brilliance and forensic ability, could not have achieved Pakistan had not the two cries, "Islam in Danger!" and "Pakistan an Islamic State!" been raised. But we have seen that attempts to Islamicize the constitution have often divided the people of Pakistan. Sunnis versus Shi'as is an old conflict, and in 1953 the *mullahs* and mawlanas instigated riots against the Ahmadis. It has been suggested that East Pakistani Muslims have often been influenced by Hindu culture, that their intellectuals still relish Tagore more than Iqbal and the rural masses still take part in Hindu Jatras. In this case, one can see that Islam rallied the Bengalis and the Punjabis under the same banner for the achievement of Pakistan, but an insistence on a pure Islamic culture can further worsen the relationship between East and West Pakistan.

We have seen that when Pakistan came into being the political institutions the new state had to establish were western in character, and that traditional Islam had nothing to contribute. The new institution of Basic Democracies is not Islamic in origin but dates back to the days of Lord Ripon. Ayub, however, can take credit for the change that he has brought about in the Muslim personal law, in the form of the Muslim Family Laws Ordinance, 1961. The Ordinance places several obstacles to a Muslim male's right to divorce his wife or wives and makes polygamy a difficult proposition. The new regime has also made efforts to educate and modernize the outlook of *imams* of mosques, and in East Pakistan the Bureau of National Reconstruction has organized regular classes for the training of the *imams*. The matter of rewriting sermons to suit modern conditions has also been discussed, and the necessity of Bengali translations of sermons has been stressed.

It is noteworthy that former politicians very largely kept the masses in their apathetic state and attempted to set up parliamentary institutions at the top. Ayub, perhaps for both intellectual and personal reasons, is not in favor of a restoration of full-fledged democracy at the top, but is deliberately disturbing "the placid, pathetic contentment of the masses."

Ayub has made it clear that he is not in favor of traditional Islam. He is acutely aware that in order to defeat the traditionalists he must suggest that Islam is in favor of scientific progress, rationalism and birth control. A clear indication of how his mind is working is provided by the new Central Institute of Islamic Research that has been created under Article 207 of the new Constitution. Its purpose is not merely to undertake research and instruction in Islam but also to assist in "the reconstruction of Muslim society." An article by its director, Dr. Fazlur Rahman, points out that: ". . . to insist that today's commercial bank —with an overall controlled economy—comes under the Quranic prohibition and is banned by the Prophetic Sunnah is not so much historical or religious honesty but an acute crisis of human confidence and uncompromising cynicism. The Qur'an and the Sunnah were given for intelligent moral understanding and implementation, not for rigid formalism." Thus one can see which way the wind of change is blowing. The *ulama* and orthodox people find this wind very chilly indeed.

65 • Hassan Nawaz Gardezi: *Some Social and Economic Characteristics* *

Either Pakistan or Indonesia—another Asian country—has the world's fifth largest population (the United States has fourth largest). The following excerpt from the writings of a Pakistani demographer gives a statistical picture of certain social characteristics that play some role in determining the structure of the government, and it vividly depicts problems that face any government in Pakistan. Literacy, for example, poses a problem of tremendous size—as it does in India. Although responsible government does not necessarily demand a high rate of literacy, there can be no question that it helps, and an increasing industrialization makes its own demands on literacy.

Earlier in this article (which has been rather severely edited) the author points out the growing trend toward urbanization in Pakistan. Although still primarily an agricultural country, both wings of Pakistan showed a percentage

* Anwar S. Dil, ed., *Perspectives in Pakistan* (Abbottabad, Bookservice, 1965). pp. 102–135 *passim*. By permission. The author of this article is head of the Department of Sociology, University of the Punjab, Lahore.

increase in urban dwellers between the 1951 and the 1961 census. Almost a quarter of West Pakistan was urban in 1961, although only slightly more than five per cent of East Pakistan. Half of the urban population live in cities of 100,000 or over (in 1961 there were sixteen such cities, only three of which were in East Pakistan). "On the whole," he concludes, "trends indicate that the role of small towns in the urbanization of the country is decreasing in importance and the emergence of large cities has become an important feature of urbanization in Pakistan today." This growth is largely to be explained by a movement from rural to urban areas, rather than from an increase in the urban birthrate.

Age and Sex Composition

. . . According to the 1961 census of population there were 44.5 per cent of the people in the age group 0 to 14 years, 40.2 per cent in the age group 15 to 44 years, and only 16.3 per cent in the age group 45 and over. Thus it is evident that the population of Pakistan is composed of a very high proportion of young persons, especially those below 14 years of age, and a very small proportion of old people. A large proportion of children, or persons below 14 years of age, is a characteristic of the age structure which Pakistan shares with a number of other economically under-developed countries. In economically advanced countries there tends to be a more even distribution of persons in different age categories of population.

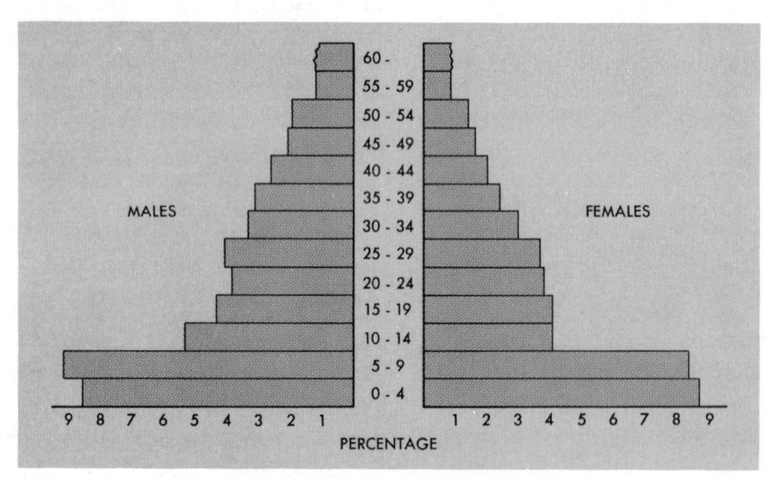

Figure 1. Age-Sex Pyramid, Pakistan 1961.

Figure 1 represents graphically the age and sex distribution of the population of Pakistan. . . . Figure 2 represents the age and sex structure of the population of the United States, an economically advanced country. . . .

The presence of a high proportion of younger people in the population of Pakistan can be explained by reference to the birth and death rates. High birth rates in Pakistan result in constant and large increments to the number of very young people, and thus the base of the age-sex pyramid assumes a very broad shape . . .

It will also be noted by looking at figure 1 that the first two bars depicting the proportions of persons in age categories 0-4 and 5-9 years are much longer than the other bars. This is an evidence of exceptionally high *infant mortality* and child mortality rates in Pakistan. According to one estimate the infant mortality rate in Pakistan during the period 1950-1955 was as high as 200. The infant mortality rate in the United States was 26.9 during the period 1953-55. . . .

The proportion of males improves in Pakistan as they pass from the 0-4 year age category into the 5-9 year age category. For females, however, the case is otherwise. This suggests that females in Pakistan suffer a higher mortality during the first few years of life as compared with males. . . .

The fact that a large proportion of the population of Pakistan consists of children below 15 years of age has the immediate economic disadvantage of

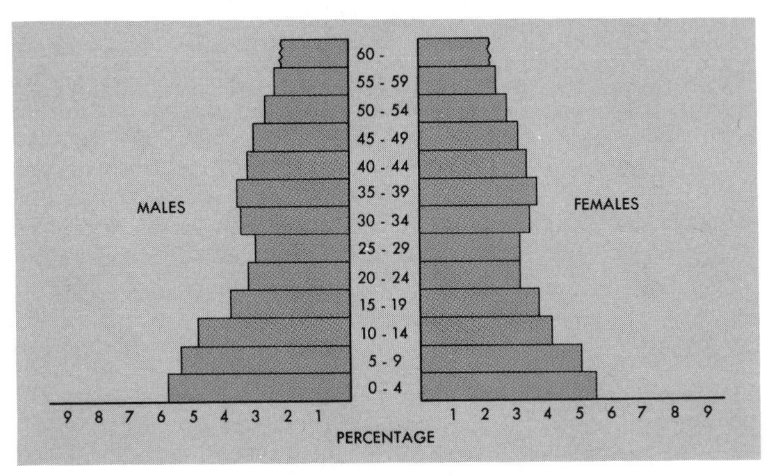

Figure 2. Age-Sex Pyramid, United States 1959.

creating a high ratio of dependents to economically active age groups. Socially this situation may result in forcing children into the acceptance of adult roles, mainly economic roles, at the expense of receiving education and engaging in activities conducive to their unique development needs. The preponderance of children in the population of Pakistan also points to the grave responsibility of providing services and utilities peculiar to the needs of the youth. The sooner this responsibility is realized by government and private agencies, the better it is for the well-being of the nation. In economically advanced countries, as is evident from the example of the United States, a great proportion of the population consists of adult persons and thus the incidence of dependency is minimized. The main burden of dependency in the western populations is constituted by the presence of considerable numbers of old people, 60 years of age and above.

So far attention has been focussed on age structure without taking into consideration the relative distribution of males and females in different age categories. The relative distribution of men and women in a population is indicated by *sex ratio,* usually expressed as number of males per 100 females. In Pakistan there has always been a preponderance of male over female population. In 1961 the sex ratio in Pakistan was 111, and in 1951 the corresponding figure was 113.

It can be observed from figure 1 that there are more males than females in every age category of the population of Pakistan, except in the 0-4 year group. . . .
The high sex ratios in Pakistan are mainly due to the differential impact of mortality on male and female populations. During the first four years of life the difference between the numbers of males and females is only slight, as can be observed from figure 1. In the category of 0-4 years there were approximately 7.88 million males and 7.84 million females in 1961. In the next 10 years, that is, 5-14 years of age, the difference between the numbers of males and females is quite prominent, there being approximately 1.7 million more males than females. This disparity is, in all probability, the result of higher death rates among female children.[1] There being a preference for male children in Pakistani culture, it is feared that the rearing of female children is subject to neglect and consequently a higher death rate prevails among female children as compared with male children.

A marked difference between the numbers of males and females occurs again in the age categories of 30 years and over. This difference can also be attributed to higher death rates among women in adult and old ages. . . . Child birth has constituted a great hazard to the health and life of women in Pakistan, especially in the lower socio-economic strata because of the non-availability of adequate maternity services and prevalence of unhygienic conditions. The undesirable effects of repeated child birth not only take the form of many maternal deaths at the time of child birth but also weaken the health of women during mature adulthood and old age, thereby exposing them to greater hazards of deaths. . . .

Changes in Age and Sex Composition

In 1951 the percentage of population in the age categories 0-9 was 28.36. In 1961 this figure rose to 35.14. This increase in the proportion of Pakistan's young population can be attributed to an unprecedented high birth rate during the decade 1951-61, and a probable decline in infant mortality.

During the same decade a substantial numerical as well as proportionate decrease of population was registered in age categories 10-19. This decrease can be attributed to continued high death rates in the age categories 1-9 during the decade 1951-61. There also took place a decrease in the proportion of persons aged 20-24 years during the decade under consideration, but this decrease was almost balanced by an increase in the age categories 25-44 years. A considerable increase also took place in the age categories 60 years and over during the same decade. Thus, on the whole, while the proportion of Pakistan's population in dependent-age categories, that is below 10 years and over 60 years increased, the proportion of persons in adult age groups decreased. The social and economic problems associated with a preponderantly young population were thus intensified during the decade 1951-61.

A significant change in the sex-wise distribution of the population over the decade under consideration is that the number of females in age categories 25-34 years increased more as compared with the number of males in the same age

[1] It is also believed that in India and Pakistan people are reluctant to report female members of their families to census enumerators. But the extent of the inadequate reporting of females is considered small enough to be neglected for the purpose of broader analyses. *See:* E. H. Slade, *Census of Pakistan 1951,* I., p. 54–56.

category. This may be the result of some improvement in maternity services in the country over the decade 1951-1961, and a consequent lowering of maternal deaths.

Rural-Urban Differences in Age and Sex Composition

. . . An analysis of rural-urban differences indicates that the proportion of males in the urban population of Pakistan is greater than the proportion of males in the rural population. In western countries, such as the United States of America, high sex ratios or male preponderance is a characteristic of a rural population structure. In Pakistan the case is otherwise. Table 6 indicates rural and urban sex ratios in Pakistan and the two wings of the country. It is apparent from this Table that the urban population of Pakistan, especially in the East wing, has a more striking preponderance of males over females as compared with the rural population. While low sex ratios in western countries are being used as indices of urbanization, in Pakistan low sex ratios correlate with rural population structure.

TABLE 6. RURAL-URBAN SEX RATIOS IN PAKISTAN AND THE TWO WINGS, 1951 AND 1961

YEAR	*PAKISTAN*		*EAST PAKISTAN*		*WEST PAKISTAN*	
	Rural	*Urban*	*Rural*	*Urban*	*Rural*	*Urban*
1951	111	133	109	151	114	129
1961	109	129	106	142	112	126

SOURCE: Government of Pakistan, Ministry of Home Affairs, *Population Census of Pakistan, 1961,* Bulletin No. 2.

According to the analyses of Davis, past trends have indicated that the masculinity of the urban population has been increasing in India and Pakistan. Table 6, however, indicates that during the decade 1951-1961 male excess in the urban population of Pakistan and both the wings has been slightly reduced. This is partly a result of a general improvement in the proportion of females in the population of the country as a whole. Furthermore, the phenomenally high sex ratios of urban population indicated by the 1951 census returns are partly attributed to an exceptional under-enumeration of females in the cities of Pakistan. With improvements in the quality of 1961 census, one would expect the figures to show an improvement in the proportion of female population irrespective of the underlying demographic trends.

The striking male excess in the cities of Pakistan can mainly be attributed to sex-selective migration from rural to urban areas. There is reason to believe that more males than females migrate from rural to urban areas. This trend of migration is contrary to the trends in western countries like the United States where more females migrate from rural areas to urban areas. There are a number of cultural factors which discourage the migration of females from the rural areas to the urban areas of Pakistan. Women in Pakistan have been traditionally expected to stay with domestic pursuits and consequently there is a tendency among them to stay back in the village home while their men move to cities in search for employment. The urban opportunity structure in Pakistan does not favour employment of women. The urban industrial labour force has absorbed an extremely small proportion of women. Inadequate urban housing also prevents migrant labourers from bringing their women folk to the cities.

It is also possible that the higher sex ratios of the urban population are partly a result of differential mortality. It has already been observed that in all probability females in Pakistan suffer higher mortality as compared with males. This is perhaps more so in the urban areas. The insanitary conditions and congestion characteristic of the lower class housing in Pakistani cities takes a greater toll of female life especially during critical periods of life such as that of child birth.

Another important aspect of urban sex ratios is revealed when we take the size of the urban locality into consideration. An analysis of the successive censuses

TABLE 7. NUMERICAL AND PERCENTAGE DISTRIBUTION OF PERSONS IN DIFFERENT RELIGIOUS CATEGORIES

RELIGION	*AREA*					
	PAKISTAN		*EAST PAKISTAN*		*WEST PAKISTAN*	
	Number in Thousands	*Percentage*	*Number in Thousands*	*Percentage*	*Number in Thousands*	*Percentage*
Muslim	82,556	88.1	40,890	80.4	41,666	97.2
Hindus	10,002	10.7	9,380	18.4	622	1.5
Christians	733	0.8	149	0.3	584	1.4
Buddhists	376	0.4	421	0.8	8	.01
Others	53					
Total	93,720	100	50,840	100	42,880	100

SOURCE: Government of Pakistan, Ministry of Home Affairs, *Population Census of Pakistan, 1961*, Bulletin No. 2, Karachi, 1961, p. 19–20.

during 1881 to 1941 indicated that male preponderance increases in India and Pakistan with increase in the size of the city. Data from the Pakistan census of 1951 also indicated an increase in sex ratios with increase in the size of locality, except for cities of a half million and over in population, in which case sex ratios were lower than the two immediately preceding categories.

Religious Composition

. . . This partition [of India in 1947] was accomplished on the principle that the Muslim majority areas in the north and east shall constitute a separate independent nation of Pakistan. Thus Pakistan came to acquire a predominantly Muslim population. . . .

In terms of growth the Muslim population has shown a fairly high rate of increase over many decades. During the decade 1951-61 the Muslim population showed a decennial percentage increase of 27.1; the Hindu population during the same period showed a percentage increase of 2.4. The Christian population showed most rapid growth during the same decade with a decennial percentage increase of 35.8. Other religious groups increased during the same decade by 17.5 per cent. The highest rate of population growth among Christians, the considerably high rate of growth among Muslims and the rather low rate of growth among Hindus is a pattern consistent with the previous trends. Davis who analysed fertility ratios in India and Pakistan up to 1941 found that among the three religious groups Christians showed the highest fertility and Hindus showed the lowest fertility. . . .

Literacy and Education

. . . Pakistan is among the countries of the world which have lowest literacy rates. In 1961 only 19.2 per cent of Pakistan's population aged 5 years and over was literate. Strict comparisons between different countries with respect to literacy are not possible because of the lack of comparable definitions. Yet it is revealing to note that in the United States 97 per cent of the population 14 years of age and over could read and write in 1952, in Canada 98.1 per cent of the population over 10 years of age had at least one year of schooling in 1951, and in Sweden 100 per cent of the population aged 7 years and over could read and write in 1947. Among Asian countries the Japanese population aged 7 years and over had 92.7 per cent people who had at least one year of schooling in 1950, and in the Philippines 62.2 per cent of the population aged 10 years and over could read and write in 1948. The higher literacy rate in East Pakistan as compared with West Pakistan is attributed to a relatively widespread existence of *Madrasas* or *Maktabs* in the East wing. In these Madrasas education up to primary level is imparted in addition to religious teaching.

TABLE 8. PERCENTAGE OF LITERATES IN THE POPULATION FIVE YEARS OF AGE AND OVER FOR PAKISTAN AND THE TWO WINGS, 1961*

AREA	PERCENTAGE OF LITERATES		
	Both Sexes	*Males*	*Females*
Pakistan	19.2	28.0	9.3
East Pakistan	21.5	31.5	10.7
West Pakistan	16.3	23.9	7.4

*Literacy is defined as ability to read a simple statement with understanding.

SOURCE: Government of Pakistan, Ministry of Home Affairs, *Population Census of Pakistan, 1961,* Census Bulletin 4, p. vii.

The presence of extremely low rates of literacy among females can be attributed to the fact that forces of social change have not influenced the traditional roles of women to the same degree as the roles of men have been influenced. The observance of *Purdah*[2] by women in some sections of the Pakistani population, restrictions on the employment of women and emphasis on the domestic pursuits

[2] Segregation and/or veiling observed by women.

of women are some aspects of the traditional roles of women in Pakistan which interfere with their attainment of higher levels of literacy and education.

Distribution of literates by rural and urban areas of Pakistan is markedly uneven both in the case of national population and the provinces. . . . The rural population of Pakistan which constitutes 87 per cent of the total population of the country has a strikingly low literacy of 16.6 per cent. The urban population of Pakistan which constitutes only 13 per cent of the total population of the country has a literacy of 35.8 per cent. The same feature of low rural literacy as compared with urban literacy is shared by the two wings of the country. . . . A comparison of the

TABLE 9. PERCENTAGE OF LITERATES* BY SEX, IN URBAN AND RURAL POPULATION FIVE YEARS OF AGE AND OVER, PAKISTAN AND THE TWO WINGS, 1961

AREA	PERCENTAGE OF LITERATES					
	URBAN			RURAL		
	Both Sexes	Males	Females	Both Sexes	Males	Females
Pakistan	35.8	45.0	23.3	16.6	25.0	7.2
East Pakistan	45.7	54.8	31.9	20.2	29.9	9.7
West Pakistan	33.0	42.2	21.2	10.9	17.5	3.2

*Census definition.

SOURCE: Government of Pakistan, Ministry of Home Affairs, *Population Census of Pakistan, 1961,* Census Bulletin 4, p. xiii.

large cities of Pakistan, with a population of 50,000 and over, indicates that the three largest cities of Pakistan are not among the most literate ones. Dacca with 46.9 per cent literates ranks seventh among the large cities, Karachi with 39.3 per cent literates has the fifteenth position, and Lahore with 38.7 per cent literacy has the sixteenth place in order of literacy. Mymensingh, Jhelum and Rawalpindi have the highest proportion of literates, ranking first, second and third respectively.

Trends in Literacy

According to the 1951 census, Pakistan had a literacy percentage of 22 as compared with 19.2 per cent literacy in 1961. There was, however, no actual drop in literacy during the decade, and the difference between the two figures is attributed to the use of two different definitions of literacy in 1951 and 1961. Literates in 1951 included many persons who could read without understanding.[3] Such literates were excluded by definition from the category of literates in 1961.

A more meaningful definition of literacy, which is also consistent with current standards recommended for international usage, would include among the literate category only those persons who can both read and write. Both the 1951 and 1961 censuses distinguish the literates able to read and write from lower level literates. Data comparing the percentages of persons able to read and write in 1951 and 1961 with necessary adjustments by the author of the source table are presented in

[3] In 1951 literacy was defined as the "ability to read any language in clear print," E. H. Slade, *Census of Pakistan, 1951.* Vol. I, Pakistan, Karachi, Manager of Publications, 1955, p. 8–10.

Table 10. This comparison indicates that there was an increase in the proportion of literates during the decade 1951-61 . . . [and] that the increase in literacy during the decade was greater in West Pakistan as compared with East Pakistan.

Levels of Education

. . . In 1961, of all the literates in Pakistan 14.1 per cent or 1.02 million persons had acquired literacy without any formal schooling. The presence of opportunities for acquiring literacy outside the formal institutions is a blessing for an economically under-developed country like Pakistan. This fact also indicates that education as one of the traditional functions of the primary groups like family has not been completely taken over by secondary agencies. However, education so acquired remains of doubtful utility, as complex skills and techniques necessary for an adequate level of performance cannot be taught within the primary group structure. . . .

The highest proportion of literates in Pakistan, 57.4 per cent, had completed 1 to 5 years of school or had not gone much beyond the primary level of education

TABLE 10. PERSONS ABLE TO READ AND WRITE AS PERCENTAGE OF POPULATION FIVE YEARS AND ABOVE FOR PAKISTAN AND PROVINCES, 1951 AND 1961

Areas	*1951*	*1961*	*Increase*
Pakistan	14.0	17.5	3.5
East Pakistan	18.8	19.9	1.1
West Pakistan	7.6	14.4	6.8

SOURCE: Jamila Akhtar, "Literacy and Education: Fifth Release from 1961 Census of Pakistan". *The Pakistan Development Review,* Vol. III, Karachi, 1962.

in 1961. The per cent of literates with 6 to 9 years of schooling was 21.5. Education up to Matriculation and Intermediate level was attained by only 6.2 per cent of total literates. Only 0.6 per cent of the literates had general and professional college degrees and 0.2 per cent had post graduate or higher degrees.

An analysis of data on educational levels leads to the conclusion that the Pakistani population is not only characterised by an extremely low level of literacy, but that the literate population constitutes a very small proportion of persons with secondary and higher levels of education. Ninety-three per cent of the literate population of Pakistan in 1961 had completed education below the matriculation level. Without under-estimating the value of education up to this level, one must emphasize that the tasks of social, economic and technological development before the nation cannot be adequately handled unless the proportion of literates at higher levels of education register revolutionary increases. Table 11 permits a comparison of levels of education between the two wings of the country. It has already been noted that East Pakistan has a higher literacy rate as compared with West Pakistan. The breakdown of the literacy figures, however, indicates that East Pakistan has a greater concentration of literates in the lower levels of educational attainment as compared with West Pakistan. In East Pakistan 16.7 per cent of the literates had no formal schooling and 63.5 per cent had completed one to 5 years of school in 1961. The corresponding proportion for West Pakistan were 10.7 and 47.1 respectively. From this point onwards for each higher level of educational attainment the proportions of literates are higher in the western wing as compared with the eastern wing of the country.

Since educational attainment at secondary and higher levels is more meaningfully related to levels of performance it will not be without interest to take the inter-wing comparison in this respect a step further. East Pakistan with a total population of 50.8 million, had two lakh, 47 thousand (247,000) persons educated up to Matriculate level (10 years of school) in 1961. West Pakistan with 43.0 million people had 4 lakh, 81 thousand (.481 million) persons with the same qualification. The proportion of literates with Degree and higher level of education was 0.4 per cent in East Pakistan as compared with 1.5 per cent in West Pakistan. . . .

TABLE 11. PERCENTAGE DISTRIBUTION OF THE LITERATES BY EDUCATIONAL LEVELS, PAKISTAN AND PROVINCES, 1961

EDUCATIONAL LEVEL	*PERCENTAGE OF LITERATES*		
	Pakistan	*East Pakistan*	*West Pakistan*
Total Literate	100	100	100
Without Formal Education	14.1	16.2	10.7
Class I to V	57.4	63.5	47.1
Class VI to IX	21.5	16.5	79.9
Matriculation and Intermediate	6.2	3.4	10.9
Degree	0.6	0.3	1.0
Higher Degree	0.2	0.1	0.5
Oriental	0.03	0.02	0.04

SOURCE: Government of Pakistan, Ministry of Home Affairs, *Population Census of Pakistan, 1961,* Census Bulletin 4, p. xviii.

Literacy at Specified Ages

In Pakistan literacy among the primary school ages, 5-9 years, is the lowest. . . .

Low literacy among the 5-9 years age group is attributed to a number of plausible factors, such as late entry into school, a high rate of drop outs after the first one or two years of school, and the failure of the first few years of school in making the child literate. These explanations, however, assume that adequate schooling facilities are available for the large proportion of the Pakistani children in the age group 5-9.

The population of Pakistan consists of roughly 16.0 million persons aged 5-9 as against 8.4 million in the age group 10-14 years. Thus, unless the facilities for the education of persons 5-9 years of age are almost twice as adequate as those available to the persons of 10-14 years of age, there will remain a disparity between the proportions of literates among the two age groups. Furthermore, the utilization of existing educational facilities is subject to the relative cultural emphases on different types of roles which the members of a society are expected to play according to their age level and sex. In the Pakistani culture the educational roles of children, as expressed in formal school attendance, are not yet characterized by over-riding emphasis as compared with their roles as breadwinners, helpers in the domestic life, and youthful husbands and active family members. It is a fair assumption that the education of the growing youth including the acquisition of literacy, takes place on the job as and when the need arises among large sections of Pakistan's rural population and some sections of the urban population. . . .

Pakistan is one of the countries of the world characterized by the lowest literacy role, with very small proportions of literates falling in higher levels of educational attainment. Generally such low literacy and educational attainment is accompanied in human populations with low agricultural and industrial production, low per capita income, high mortality and fertility rates and political instability. Greater proportions of literates live in cities, although the overwhelming majority of the Pakistani population lives in rural areas. Literacy among females is much lower in Pakistan as compared with male literacy. Among the rural population female literacy is extremely low. East Pakistan has the higher literacy rate as compared with West Pakistan but higher levels of educational attainment are more common among West Pakistan literates. Literacy among children of 5 to 9 years of age is low in Pakistan compared with persons of higher age categories. Inadequacy of the facilities of education for children of 5-9 years of age may be one of the factors responsible for low literacy in this age group.

TABLE 12. MALE AND FEMALE LITERACY IN SPECIFIED AGE GROUPS, PAKISTAN, 1961

AGE GROUP	*PERCENTAGE OF LITERATES*		
(years)	*Both Sexes*	*Males*	*Females*
5–9	10.7	13.9	7.1
10–14	30.7	39.7	19.4
15–19	27.3	39.1	14.7
20–24	24.5	37.1	11.7
25 and over	17.7	27.4	6.2

SOURCE: Government of Pakistan, Ministry of Home Affairs, *Population Census of Pakistan, 1961,* Census Bulletin 4, p. xvii.

On the whole the attainment of higher literacy and educational levels in Pakistan will be dependent upon both the availability of educational facilities to the people of all economic strata as well as the promotion of cultural definitions favourable to educational roles of men and women at different ages.

The size of the economically active civilian population of Pakistan is indicated by the census category of *civilian labour force.*[4] As enumerated in 1961, the

[4] According to the 1961 Census of Population, the Civilian Labour Force of Pakistan includes persons aged 10 years and above (a) working for profit or earning wages or salary, (b) helping any members of their family on the farm etc., (c) and not working but looking for work. *See:* Government of Pakistan, Office of Census Commissioner, Ministry of Home and Kashmir Affairs, Home Affairs Division, *Population Census of Pakistan, 1961,* Census Bulletin No. 5, Karachi, Manager of Publication, 1963, Introductory pages.

number of persons 10 years of age and over in the civilian labour force was approximately 30.2 million, out of which 17.44 million belonged to East Pakistan and 12.76 million belonged to West Pakistan.

There is evidence that over the decade 1951 to 1961 the size of the labour force in Pakistan and the two wings of the country has increased both in numerical strength and as a proportion of the total population. . . .

TABLE 13. CHANGE IN THE CIVILIAN LABOUR FORCE TWELVE YEARS AND ABOVE, PAKISTAN AND THE PROVINCES, 1951–1961

YEAR	*PAKISTAN*		*EAST PAKISTAN*		*WEST PAKISTAN*	
	Labour Force (millions)	*Population* (per cent)	*Labour Force* (millions)	*Population* (per cent)	*Labour Force* (millions)	*Population* (per cent)
1951	22.39	30.7	12.88	30.7	9.50	30.6
1961	29.41	32.6	16.85	33.2	12.55	31.8

SOURCE: Sultan S. Hashmi, *Main Features of the Demographic Conditions in Pakistan*, Country Background Paper presented to the Asian Population Conference, New Delhi, December, 1963, Karachi, Central Statistical Office, Economic Affairs Division, President's Secretariat, 1963, p. 93.

TABLE A

Country and Year	*Economically Active* (per cent of total population)	*Minimum Age Limit Taken into Account*
United Kingdom (1951)	46.2	15 years
France (1946)	52.1	14 years
U.S.A. (1950)	39.8	14 years
Japan (1950)	43.7	14 years

The proportion of persons in the economically active population of Pakistan is smaller as compared with a number of western and a few Asian countries. Although precise comparisons among proportions of economically active people in different countries are not possible because of lack of strict comparability in data, the . . . figures [in Table A] are indicative of the relatively small size of Pakistan's civilian labour force.

The presence of a high proportion of children in the population of Pakistan, as already discussed, adversely affects the size of the economically active population. Furthermore, the participation of women in the labour force of Pakistan is, to some extent, subject to cultural restrictions, and consequently results in lowering the size of the economically active population.

In Pakistan a relatively small number of women seek employment outside home. In 1961 only 12.4 per cent of the civilian labour force of Pakistan was of the female sex. In contrast a number of western countries and some of the Asian countries show a greater participation of women in the labour force.

As indicated earlier precise comparisons of data from different countries is not possible because of the lack of strictly comparable definitions and procedures of collecting labour force information. The . . . countries [in Table B] have, however, a much greater participation of women in the labour force as compared with Pakistan.

Employment of women outside the home is especially low in West Pakistan as compared with East Pakistan. Whereas 15.1 per cent of the East Pakistan's civilian labour force comprises females, only 8.7 per cent of the West Pakistan's civilian labour force comprises women. The greater contribution of women to the labour supply of East Pakistan is consistent with higher female literacy and generally a lesser degree of segregation of sexes in the East wing as compared to the West wing of Pakistan.

An important feature of the composition of Pakistan's labour force is that a much smaller proportion of females participate in the urban labour force as compared with the rural labour force. In 1961 the proportion of women in Pakistan's urban civilian labour force was only 4.4 per cent as against 13.6 per cent in the rural areas.

TABLE B

Country and Year	*Per Cent of Women in Economically Active Population*
United States (1950)	27.4
United Kingdom (1951)	30.6
Japan (1950)	38.6
Philippines (1948)	40.1

. . . In 1961, 47.8 per cent of the male children in Pakistan between the ages 10-14 years were in the labour force. In contrast 4.9 per cent of children in economically developed countries between ages 10-14 years belonged to the economically active population.

Furthermore, whereas 83.5 per cent of men 60 years of age and above in Pakistan belonged to the civilian labour force, the United States and West Germany had 59.3 per cent and 49.9 per cent of their male population 60 years of age and above in the economically active categories in 1950. In the United Kingdom 51.8 per cent of persons in the same age category belonged to the economically active population in 1951. . . .

The extraordinarily high participation of young males in Pakistan's labour force is partly due to an exaggerated emphasis on the economic roles of the very young population. The low per capita income of the masses of people and lack of educational facilities leave little choice for a majority of parents but to make their children engage in economic roles. Furthermore, Pakistan being a predominantly rural society has a characteristic employment structure conducive to the participation of children in the labour force. Unlike the case of urban-industrial employment structure, in the rural-agricultural type of jobs age of entering occupations and age of retirement are not rigidly specified. Children may enter the labour force as soon as they are able to perform a minimum of unskilled labour by working for wages or helping on the family farm. The lack of mechanical specializations on the farms need not require any prolonged periods of apprenticeship and vocational education prior to entering the jobs.

TABLE 14. PERCENTAGE OF PERSONS BELONGING TO THE CIVILIAN LABOUR FORCE IN THE SPECIFIED AGE GROUPS OF PAKISTAN'S POPULATION, 1961

AGE GROUP	*PER CENT OF AGE GROUP IN CIVILIAN LABOUR FORCE*		
	Both Sexes	*Males*	*Females*
10–14	30.6	47.8	8.9
15–19	45.7	76.7	12.6
20–34	55.1	93.5	15.5
35–59	60.3	95.4	16.0
60 and over	51.6	83.5	10.8

SOURCE: Government of Pakistan, *Census of Population, 1961*, Census Bulletin No. 5, p. xx and *Census of Population, 1961*, Census Bulletin No. 3, p. 40.

The participation in Pakistani labour force of a very high proportion of old men above 60 years of age can likewise be attributed to Pakistan's predominantly rural-agricultural employment structure. Cultural emphasis on the status of old people in Pakistani society can be regarded as an additional factor conducive to the continued participation of people up to very advanced ages in the labour force. The realization by the old people of their controlling position in the family and the community, and the value attached to their wisdom and experience may prevent their retirement before senility.

SECTION TWO

Political Institutions

66 • *The Constitution of Pakistan*

These excerpts are from the second (1962) constitution of Pakistan, as amended in 1963 and 1964. The first constitution, proclaimed in 1956 after nine years of effort—until that time the country operated under the 1935 India Act—was very shortly abrogated by Governor-General Ghulam Muhammad; this abrogation led to the Martial Law government soon dominated by Muhammad Ayub Khan, the present president.

The 1956 constitution was essentially parliamentary in character; the 1962 constitution is essentially presidential in nature. The entire constitution, without appendices, covers approximately 180 pages. These excerpts include Fundamental Rights, that is, Pakistan's Bill of Rights, and Principles of Policy, or a general statement of the basic principles to be followed by the government. It should be noted, however, that the validity of no law can be questioned on the grounds that it is not in accordance with the Principles of Policy (article 8, paragraph 2).

Articles further describing the Islamic character of the state are to be found within the Fundamental Rights and the Principles of Policy. Articles 199 through 206 established an Advisory Council of Islamic Ideology and an Islamic Research Institute. On this subject see the chapter "Pakistan and the Secular State" by Freeland Abbott in Donald E. Smith, editor, South Asian Religion and Politics *(Princeton, 1966), pages 352–370.*

Part I. The Republic of Pakistan

1.—(1) The State of Pakistan shall be a Republic under the name of the Islamic Republic of Pakistan.

(2) The Republic shall consist of—

(a) the Province of East Pakistan and the Province of West Pakistan; and

(b) such other States and territories as are or may become included in Pakistan, whether by accession or otherwise.

2.—(1) To enjoy the protection of the law, and to be treated in accordance with law, and only in accordance with law, is the inalienable right of every citizen, wherever he may be, and of every other person for the time being within Pakistan.

(2) In particular—

(a) no action detrimental to the life, liberty, body, reputation or property of any person shall be taken except in accordance with law;

(b) no person shall be prevented from, or be hindered in, doing that which is not prohibited by law; and

(c) no person shall be compelled to do that which the law does not require him to do.

3. Loyalty to the Republic is the basic duty of every citizen.

4. Obedience to the law is the basic obligation of every citizen, wherever he may be, and of every other person for the time being within Pakistan.

Part II. Fundamental Rights and Principles of Policy

CHAPTER 1.—FUNDAMENTAL RIGHTS

5. In this Chapter, unless the context otherwise requires, "the State" includes the Central Government, the Central Legislature, the Provincial Governments, the Provincial Legislatures, and all local or other authorities in Pakistan.

6.—(1) Any law, or any custom or usage having the force of law, in so far as it is inconsistent with the rights conferred by this Chapter, shall, to the extent of such inconsistency, be void.

(2) The State shall not make any law which takes away or abridges the rights so conferred, and any law made in contravention of this clause shall, to the extent of such contravention, be void.

(3) The provisions of this Article shall not apply to—

(i) any law relating to members of the Defence Services, or of the forces charged with the maintenance of public order, for the purpose of ensuring the proper discharge of their duties or the maintenance of discipline among them; or

(ii) any of the laws specified in the Fourth Schedule as in force immediately before the coming into force of the Constitution (First Amendment) Act, 1963;

and no such law nor any provision thereof shall be void on the ground that such law or provision is inconsistent with, or repugnant to, any provision of this Chapter.

THE RIGHTS

I. SECURITY OF PERSON AND FREEDOM OF MOVEMENT

1.—Security of person.

No person shall be deprived of life or liberty save in accordance with law.

2.—Safeguards as to arrest and detention.

(1) No person who is arrested shall be detained in custody without being informed, as soon as may be, of the grounds for such arrest, nor shall he be denied the right to consult and be defended by a legal practitioner of his choice.

(2) Every person who is arrested and detained in custody shall be produced before the nearest magistrate within a period of twenty-four hours of such arrest, excluding the time necessary for the journey from the place of arrest to the court of the magistrate, and no such person shall be detained in custody beyond the said period without the authority of a magistrate.

(3) Nothing in sub-paragraphs (1) and (2) shall apply to any person—

(a) who for the time being is an enemy alien; or

(b) who is arrested or detained under any law providing for preventive detention.

(4) No law providing for preventive detention shall authorize the detention of a person for a period exceeding three months unless the appropriate Advisory Board has reported before the expiration of the said period of three months that there is, in its opinion, sufficient cause for such detention.

Explanation.—*In this sub-paragraph, "the appropriate Advisory Board" means,—*

(*i*) *in the case of a person detained under a Central Law, a Board consisting of a Judge of the Supreme Court, who shall be nominated by the Chief Justice of that Court, and a senior officer in the service of Pakistan, who shall be nominated by the President; and*

(*ii*) *in the case of a person detained under a Provincial Law, a Board consisting of a Judge of the High Court of the Province concerned, who shall be nominated by the Chief Justice of that Court, and a senior officer in the service of Pakistan, who shall be nominated by the Governor of that Province.*

(5) When any person is detained in pursuance of an order made under any law providing for preventive detention, the authority making the order shall, as soon as may be, communicate to such person the grounds on which the order has been made, and shall afford him the earliest opportunity of making a representation against the order:

Provided that the authority making any such order may refuse to disclose facts which such authority considers it to be against the public interest to disclose.

3.—Slavery and forced labour prohibited.

(1) No person shall be held in slavery, and no law shall permit or in any way facilitate the introduction into Pakistan of slavery in any form.

(2) All forms of forced labour are prohibited.

(3) Nothing in this paragraph shall be deemed to affect compulsory service—

(a) *by persons undergoing punishment for offences against any law; or*

(b) *required by any law for public purposes.*

4.—Protection against retrospective punishment.

No law shall authorize the punishment of a person—

(*a*) *for an act or omission that was not punishable by law at the time of the act or omission; or*

(*b*) *for an offence by a penalty greater than, or of a kind different from, the penalty prescribed by law for that offence at the time the offence was committed.*

5.—Freedom of movement.

Subject to any reasonable restrictions imposed by law in the public interest, every citizen shall have the right to move freely throughout Pakistan and to reside and settle in any part thereof.

II. FREEDOM OF ASSEMBLY, ASSOCIATION AND VOCATION

6.—Freedom of assembly.

Every citizen shall have the right to assemble peacefully and without arms, subject to any reasonable restrictions imposed by law in the interest of public order.

7.—Freedom of association.

Every citizen shall have the right to form associations or unions, subject to any reasonable restrictions imposed by law in the interest of morality or public order.

8.—Freedom of trade, business or profession.

Every citizen, possessing such qualifications, if any, as may be prescribed by law in relation to his profession or occupation, shall have the right to enter upon any lawful profession or occupation, and to conduct any lawful trade or business:

Provided that nothing in this paragraph shall prevent—

(*a*) *the regulation of any trade or profession by a licensing system; or*

(*b*) *the regulation of trade, commerce or industry in the interest of free competition therein; or*

(*c*) *the carrying on, by the Central or a Provincial Government or by a corporation controlled by any such Government, of any trade, business, industry or service, to the exclusion, complete or partial, of other persons.*

III. FREEDOM OF SPEECH

9.—Freedom of speech.

Every citizen shall have the right to freedom of speech and expression, subject to any reasonable restrictions imposed by law in the interest of the security of Pakistan, friendly relations with foreign States, public order, decency or morality, or in relation to contempt of court, defamation or incitement to an offence.

IV. FREEDOM OF RELIGION

10.—Freedom to profess religion and to manage religious institutions.

Subject to law, public order and morality—

(*a*) *every citizen has the right to profess, practice and propagate any religion; and*

(*b*) *every religious denomination and every sect thereof has the right to establish, maintain and manage its religious institutions.*

11.—Safeguard against taxation for purposes of any particular religion.

No person shall be compelled to pay any special tax the proceeds of which are to be spent on the propagation or maintenance of any religion other than his own.

12.—Safeguards as to educational institutions in respect of religion, etc.

(*1*) *No person attending any educational institution shall be required to receive religious instruction, or take part in any religious ceremony, or attend religious worship, if such instruction, ceremony or worship relates to a religion other than his own.*

(*2*) *No religious community or denomination shall be prevented from providing religious instruction for pupils of that community or denomination in any educational institution maintained wholly by that community or denomination.*

(*3*) *No citizen shall be denied admission to any educational institution receiving aid from public revenues on the ground only of race, religion, caste, or place of birth.*

(*4*) *In respect of any religious institution, there shall be no discrimination against any community in the granting of exemption or concession in relation to taxation.*

(*5*) *Every religious community or denomination shall have the right to establish and maintain educational institutions of its own choice, and the State shall not deny recognition to any such institution on the ground only that the management of such institution vests in that community or denomination.*

(6) Nothing in this paragraph shall prevent any public authority from making provision for the advancement of any socially or educationally backward class of citizens.

V. PROPERTY RIGHTS

13.—Provision as to property.

Subject to any reasonable restrictions imposed by law in the public interest, every citizen shall have the right to acquire, hold and dispose of property.

14.—Protection of property rights.

(1) No person shall be deprived of his property save in accordance with law.

(2) No property shall be compulsorily acquired or taken possession of save for a public purpose, and save by the authority of law which provides for compensation therefor and either fixes the amount of compensation or specifies the principles on which and the manner in which compensation is to be determined and given.

(3) Nothing in this paragraph shall affect the validity of—

(a) *any law permitting the compulsory acquisition or taking possession of any property for preventing danger to life, property or public health; or*

(b) *any law relating to the acquisition, administration, or disposal of any property which is or is deemed to be evacuee property under any law; or*

(c) *any law providing for the taking over by the State for a limited period of the management of any property for the benefit of its owner; or*

(d) *any law in force immediately before the coming into force of the Constitution (First Amendment) Act, 1963.*

Explanation.—*In sub-paragraphs (2) and (3), "property" shall mean immovable property, or any commercial or industrial undertaking, or any interest in any such undertaking.*

VI. EQUALITY OF CITIZENS

15.—Equality of citizens.

All citizens are equal before law and are entitled to equal protection of law.

VII. ACCESS TO PUBLIC PLACES

16.—Non-discrimination in respect of access to public places.

In respect of access to places of public entertainment or resort, not intended for religious purposes only, there shall be no discrimination against any citizen on the ground only of race, religion, caste, sex or place of birth, but nothing herein shall be deemed to prevent the making of any special provision for women.

VIII. DISCRIMINATION IN SERVICES

17.—Safeguard against discrimination in services.

(1) No citizen otherwise qualified for appointment in the service of Pakistan shall be discriminated against in respect of any such appointment on the ground only of race, religion, caste, sex, residence or place of birth:

Provided that for a period of fifteen years from the coming into force of the Constitution (First Amendment) Act, 1963, posts may be reserved for persons belonging to any class or area to secure their adequate representation in the service of Pakistan:

Provided further that in the interest of the said service, specified posts or services may be reserved for members of either sex.

(2) Nothing in this paragraph shall prevent any Provincial Government or any local or other authority in a Province from prescribing, in relation to any class of service under that Government or authority, conditions as to residence in the Province prior to appointment under that Government or authority.

IX. CULTURE, SCRIPT AND LANGUAGE

18.—Preservation of culture, script and language.

Any section of citizens having a distinct language, script or culture shall have the right to preserve the same.

X. UNTOUCHABILITY

19.—Abolition of untouchability.

Untouchability is abolished, and its practice in any form is forbidden and shall be declared by law to be an offence.

CHAPTER 2.—PRINCIPLES OF POLICY

7.—(1) The Principles set out in this Chapter shall be known as the Principles of Policy and it is the responsibility of each organ and authority of the State, and of each person performing functions on behalf of an organ or authority of the State, to act in accordance with those Principles in so far as they relate to the functions of the organ or authority.

(2) In so far as the observance of any particular Principle of Policy may be dependent upon resources being available for the purpose, the Principle shall be regarded as being subject to the availability of resources.

8.—(1) The responsibility of deciding whether any action of an organ or authority of the State, or of a person performing functions on behalf of an organ or authority of the State, is in accordance with the Principles of Policy is that of the organ or authority of the State, or of the person, concerned.

(2) The validity of an action or of a law shall not be called in question on the ground that it is not in accordance with the Principles of Policy, and no action shall lie against the State, any organ or authority of the State or any person on such a ground.

(3) The National Assembly, a Provincial Assembly, the President or a Governor, may refer to the Advisory Council of Islamic Ideology for advice any question as to whether a proposed law is or is not repugnant to the teachings and requirements of Islam as set out in the Holy Quran and Sunnah.

PRINCIPLES OF POLICY

1.—Islam.

No law shall be repugnant to the teachings and requirements of Islam as set out in the Holy Quran and Sunnah and all existing laws shall be brought in conformity with the Holy Quran and Sunnah.

Explanation.—*In the application of this principle to the personal law of any Muslim sect, the expression "Quran and Sunnah" shall mean the Quran and Sunnah as interpreted by that sect.*

1A.—Islamic Way of Life.

1. The Muslims of Pakistan should be enabled, individually and collectively, to order their lives in accordance with the fundamental principles and basic concepts of Islam, and should be provided with facilities whereby they may be enabled to understand the meaning of life according to those principles and concepts.

2. The teaching of the Holy Quran and Islamiat to the Muslims of Pakistan should be compulsory.

3. Unity and the observance of Islamic moral standards should be promoted amongst the Muslims of Pakistan.

4. The proper organization of zakat, wakfs and mosques should be ensured.

2.—National Solidarity.

Parochial, racial, tribal, sectarian and provincial prejudices amongst the citizens should be discouraged.

3.—Fair Treatment to Minorities.

The legitimate rights and interests of the minorities should be safeguarded, and the members of minorities should be given due opportunity to enter the service of Pakistan.

4.—Promotion of Interests of Backward Peoples.

Special care should be taken to promote the educational and economic interests of people of backward classes or in backward areas.

5.—Advancement of Under-privileged Castes, etc.

Steps should be taken to bring on terms of equality with other persons the members of under-privileged castes, races, tribes and groups and, to this end, the under-privileged castes, races, tribes and groups within a Province should be identified by the Government of the Province and entered in a schedule of under-privileged classes.

6.—Opportunities to Participate in National Life, etc.

The people of different areas and classes, through education, training, industrial development and other methods, should be enabled to participate fully in all forms of national activities, including employment in the service of Pakistan.

7.—Education.

Illiteracy should be eliminated, and free and compulsory primary education should be provided for all, as soon as is practicable.

8.—Humane Conditions of Work.

Just and humane conditions of work should be provided and children and women should not be employed in vocations unsuited to their age and sex, and maternity benefits should be provided for women in employment.

9.—Well-being of the People.

The well-being of the people, irrespective of caste, creed or race, should be secured—

- (*a*) *by raising the standard of living of the common man;*
- (*b*) *by preventing the undue concentration of wealth and means of production and distribution in the hands of a few, to the detriment of the interest of the common man; and*
- (*c*) *by ensuring an equitable adjustment of rights between employers and employees and between landlords and tenants.*

10.—Opportunity to Gain Adequate Livelihood.

All citizens should have the opportunity to work and earn an adequate livelihood, and also to enjoy reasonable rest and leisure.

11.—Social Security.

All persons in the service of Pakistan or otherwise employed should be provided with social security by means of compulsory social insurance or otherwise.

12.—Provision of Basic Necessities.

The basic necessities of life, such as food, clothing, housing, education and medical treatment, should be provided for citizens who, irrespective of caste, creed or race, are permanently or temporarily unable to earn their livelihood on account of infirmity, disability, sickness or unemployment.

13.—Administrative Offices to be provided for Public Convenience.

Administrative offices and other services should, so far as is practicable, be provided in places where they will best meet the convenience and requirements of the public.

14.—[*Entry into Service of Pakistan not to be denied on Grounds of Race, etc.*] *Omitted by the Constitution (First Amendment) Act, 1963 (I of 1964), section 4.*

15.—Reduction of Disparity in Remuneration for Public Services.

Disparity in the remuneration of persons in the various classes of the service of Pakistan should, within reasonable and practicable limits, be reduced.

16.—Parity between the Provinces in Central Government.

Parity between the Provinces in all spheres of the Central Government should, as nearly as is practicable, be achieved.

17.—Service in the Defence Services.

Persons from all parts of Pakistan should be enabled to serve in the Defence Services of Pakistan.

18.—Elimination of Riba.

Riba (*Usury*) *should be eliminated.*

19.—Prostitution, Gambling and Drug-taking to be Discouraged.

Prostitution, gambling and the taking of injurious drugs should be discouraged.

20.—Consumption of Alcohol to be Discouraged.

The consumption of alcoholic liquor (except for medicinal purposes and, in the case of non-Muslims, for religious purposes) should be discouraged.

21.—Strengthening Bonds with the Muslim World, and Promoting International Peace.

The bonds of unity amongst Muslim countries should be preserved and strengthened, international peace and security should be promoted, goodwill and friendly relations amongst all nations should be fostered, and the settlement of international disputes by peaceful means should be encouraged.

Part III. The Centre

CHAPTER 1.—THE PRESIDENT

9. There shall be a President of Pakistan, who shall be elected in accordance with this Constitution and the law.

10. A person shall not be elected as President unless—

(a) he is a Muslim;

(b) he has attained the age of thirty-five years; and

(c) he is qualified to be elected as a member of the National Assembly.

11.—(1) Before he enters upon his office, a President shall make before the Chief Justice of the Supreme Court an oath in such form set out in the First Schedule as is applicable to his office.

(2) This Article does not apply to a person acting as President.

12.—(1) Subject to this Constitution, a President shall hold office for the period that, under clause (2) of this Article, is his term of office:

Provided that a President shall, notwithstanding the expiration of his term, continue to hold office until his successor enters upon his office.

(2) The term of office of a President is the period commencing on the day on which he enters upon his office and ending—

(*a*) where his predecessor as President completed his term of office—five years after his predecessor ceased to hold office;

(*b*) where his predecessor as President ceased to hold office before completing his term of office—on the day on which his predecessor's term of office was due to expire.

(3) A President may resign his office by writing under his hand addressed to the Speaker of the National Assembly.

13.—(1) Not less than one-third of the total number of members of the National Assembly may give written notice signed by each of them to the Speaker of the Assembly that they intend to move a resolution in the Assembly for the removal of the President from office on a charge that he has wilfully violated this Constitution or has been guilty of gross misconduct.

(2) The notice shall set out particulars of the charge.

(3) The Speaker shall forthwith cause a copy of the notice to be transmitted to the President. . . .

Part X. Islamic Institutions

Chapter 1.—Advisory Council of Islamic Ideology

199. There shall be an Advisory Council of Islamic Ideology.

200. The Council shall consist of such number of members, being not less than five and not more than twelve, as the President may determine.

201.—(1) Members of the Council shall be appointed by the President on such terms and conditions as the President may determine.

(2) The President shall, in selecting a person for appointment to the Council, have regard to the person's understanding and appreciation of Islam and of the economic, political, legal and administrative problems of Pakistan.

202.—(1) A member of the Council shall, subject to this Article, hold office for a period of three years from the date of his appointment.

(2) If a resolution recommending the removal of a member of the Council from office is passed by a majority of the total number of members of the Council, the President may remove that member from office, but a member shall not otherwise be removed from office.

(3) A member of the Council may resign his office by writing under his hand addressed to the President.

203. The President shall appoint one of the members of the Council to be the Chairman of the Council.

204.—(1) The functions of the Council shall be—

(*a*) to make recommendations to the Central Government and the Provincial Governments as to means of enabling and encouraging the

Muslims of Pakistan to order their lives in all respects in accordance with the principles and concepts of Islam, and to examine all laws in force immediately before the commencement of the Constitution (First Amendment) Act, 1963, with a view to bringing them into conformity with the teachings and requirements of Islam as set out in the Holy Quran and Sunnah; and

(*b*) to advise the National Assembly, a Provincial Assembly, the President or a Governor on any question referred to the Council under Article 8, that is to say, a question as to whether a proposed law is or is not repugnant to the teachings and requirements of Islam as set out in the Holy Quran and Sunnah.

(2) When, under Article 8, a question is referred by an Assembly, the President or a Governor to the Council for advice, the Council shall, within seven days thereafter, inform the Assembly, the President or the Governor, as the case requires, of the period within which the Council expects to be able to furnish that advice.

(3) Where the Assembly, the President or the Governor, as the case may be, considers that, in the public interest, the making of the proposed law in relation to which the question arose should not be postponed until the advice is furnished, the law may be made before the advice is furnished.

205.—(1) The proceedings of the Council shall be regulated by rules of procedure to be made by the Council with the approval of the President.

(2) The Council shall, not later than the fifteenth day of January in each year, prepare a report in regard to its proceedings during the year ending on the previous thirty-first day of December, and submit the same to the President, who shall cause it to be laid before the National Assembly.

206. In this Chapter, "the Council" means the Advisory Council of Islamic Ideology.

CHAPTER 2.—ISLAMIC RESEARCH INSTITUTE

207.—(1) There shall be an organization to be known as Islamic Research Institute, which shall be established by the President.

(2) The function of the Institute shall be to undertake Islamic research and instruction in Islam for the purpose of assisting in the reconstruction of Muslim society on a truly Islamic basis.

67 • MUHAMMAD MUNIR: *Constitution of 1962* *

The following description of the 1962 constitution of the Islamic Republic of Pakistan is by a former Chief Justice of Pakistan. It is taken from the introduction to his definitive study of the constitution.

The present Constitution was promulgated on 1st March 1962, and it came into force on 8th June, 1962, when the first meeting of the National Assembly was

* *Constitution of the Islamic Republic of Pakistan* (Lahore: All-Pakistan Legal Decisions, 1965), pp. 53–65.

held at Rawalpindi. Several Orders were issued by the President to remove difficulties in bringing the Constitution into effective operation and four Amendment Acts were passed by the National Assembly to which the President gave assent, the first Act restoring the fundamental rights and the Islamic features of the 1956 Constitution and the second one making some alterations in the order under which first general elections to the office of President and members of the Legislative Assemblies were to be held. The third Act amended Arts. 103 and 104 relating to qualification of members of Assemblies, while the fourth partially removed the disqualification of Judges of Superior Courts to be appointed to an office of profit for two years after retirement, and empowered the President and the Governors to direct the retirement of civil servants serving under them on completion of 25 years of qualifying service or 55 years of age.

The basic institution under the present Constitution is the Electoral College, consisting of 80,000 Electors. Each Province is divided into 40,000 Electoral Units and the residents of each Unit elect for a period of five years from amongst themselves an Elector, on the principle of adult franchise. The Electors so chosen constitute the Electoral College and elect the President, members of the National Assembly and members of the Provincial Assemblies of their respective Provinces. They also have the exclusive right to vote at any Referendum that may be held under the Constitution. In addition to their functions under the Constitution, the members of the Electoral College have to perform such other functions, particularly those relating to matters of self-government, as may be conferred on them by law.

The President, who must be a Muslim, is elected for a period of five years, but he is eligible for re-election. If a person is, and has been for a continuous period of more than eight years holding office as President, he cannot seek further election unless a majority of the members of the National Assembly and the two Provincial Assemblies approve his candidature. Not more than three persons, sitting President excepted, to be selected at a joint sitting of the three Assemblies, may seek election to the office of President. The President is the Supreme Commander of the Defence Services and the executive authority of the Republic vests in him. He may have a Council of Ministers, composed of persons who are not members of the National Assembly, to assist him in the discharge of his functions. He may seek the advice of all or any of his Ministers, but he is not bound to accept it. When the National Assembly is not in session, he may promulgate Ordinances and in a state of emergency, to be formally proclaimed by him, he acquires the power to promulgate Ordinances whether the National Assembly be in session or not. He may dissolve the National Assembly before the expiry of its term but in that event he himself ceases to hold office and must seek re-election. Appointments to civil services of the Centre are made by the President and the persons appointed, subject to certain safeguards against dismissal, removal and reduction, hold office during his pleasure, and as Supreme Commander of the Defence Services he grants Commissions in, and appoints Chief Commanders of those Services. His assent is necessary to the Bills passed by the National Assembly and he can, if a Bill be not readily acceptable to him, require a majority of two-thirds of the total number of members of the Assembly before he gives his assent to it or directs a referendum about it.

Except "new expenditure," the Budget directed by the President to be presented to the National Assembly is not subject to the vote of the Assembly.

On notice, given to the Speaker by one-third members of the National Assembly, the President is liable to be removed for any glaring breach of the Constitution, misconduct, or infirmity if the resolution for his removal is supported by three-fourths of the total number of members of the Assembly, but if at least one-half of such members do not vote for the resolution, those voting for it lose their seats in the Assembly.

In the Constitution, as originally promulgated, though there were fundamental rights, they could not be enforced through Courts, but by the Constitution (First Amendment) Act, 1963, those rights have been made justiciable.

In the Provinces the executive authority vests in the Governor who is appointed by, holds office during the pleasure, and functions under the directions of the President. Each Governor also has a Council of Ministers composed of persons not members of the Provincial Assembly, whose appointment is approved by the President and who hold office during the pleasure of the Governor, subject to the concurrence of the President. The Governor's assent, like that of the President to Central Bills, is necessary to Bills passed by the Provincial Assembly. In financial and other matters a Governor's position is generally similar to that of the President at the Centre.

The executive authority of the Republic extends to all matters in respect of which the Central Legislature has power to make laws. In the same manner the executive authority of a Province extends to all matters in respect of which the Provincial Legislature is competent to legislate.

There are two Provinces, East Pakistan and West Pakistan. The Central Assembly, called the National Assembly, consists of 156 members, of whom 150 are elected, half and half, from the two Provinces, by the Electoral College. The remaining six seats, three from each Province, are reserved for women who are elected by members of the National Assembly of their respective Province. The term of the Assembly is five years, but it may be dissolved earlier. Only a part of the Annual Budget is subject to its vote. Each Provincial Assembly consists of 155 members, of whom 150 are elected by the members of the Electoral College of the Province and five seats are reserved for women who are elected by members of their respective Provincial Assembly. Each Assembly elects a Speaker and its members enjoy the usual privileges of members of Parliament. A Governor cannot dissolve the Provincial Assembly before the expiry of its term, except with the approval of the majority of the National Assembly and the concurrence of the President.

Legislative powers are distributed between the Centre and the Provinces. The Central Legislature has the power to legislate on matters specified in the Third Schedule and the Provincial Legislatures on all other matters: but no Court can question the competency of a Legislature to legislate on any particular matter, and in case of conflict between a Central law and a Provincial law, the former prevails over the latter.

The Supreme Court, with a Chief Justice and as many Judges as may be determined by law, and in the absence of any such law, by the President, is the Court of ultimate jurisdiction in the country. Besides its being a Court of appeal in a limited class of cases, it has advisory and constitutional jurisdiction. It also has original jurisdiction which is confined to inter-Government disputes. Its special jurisdiction to give leave to appeal is restricted to petitions for leave to appeal against the judgments of the High Courts. The High Courts are regular Courts of appeal and revision in the Provinces and also exercise what may be called writ jurisdiction in defined circumstances. The Judges of the Supreme Court and the High Courts are appointed by the President and they hold office during good behaviour until they attain the ages of sixty-five and sixty years respectively. They cannot be removed unless the Supreme Judicial Council, composed of the three Chief Justices and two senior-most Judges of the Supreme Court, after enquiry recommend their removal on the ground of misconduct or infirmity.

Appointments to civil services of the Provinces are made by the Governors. Members of such services hold office during the Governor's pleasure but there are safeguards against their dismissal, removal and reduction in rank.

The Constitution imposes a limit on the area of land which a citizen may beneficially own or possess.

Islamic provisions of the Constitution have been substantially altered by the Constitution (First Amendment) Act, 1963. The original name of the State and the Preamble have been restored to their 1956 form, and a further obligation, namely, that of bringing the existing laws in conformity with the Holy Quran and the Sunnah, has been added to the functions of the Advisory Council of Islamic Ideology. Similarly, to Article 8 has been added the injunction that no law shall be repugnant to the teachings and requirements of Islam as set out in the Holy Quran and the Sunnah and all existing laws shall be brought in conformity with these two primary sources of Islamic law.

There are two Islamic institutions to be set up under the Constitution: (1) the Islamic Research Institute, entrusted with the task of research and instruction in Islam with the object of assisting in the reconstruction of Muslim society, and (2) the Advisory Council of Islamic Ideology, charged with the duty of recommending means to enable and encourage the Muslims to order their lives in accordance with the principles and concepts of Islam, besides the newly-added function of examining the existing laws in order to bring them in accord with the Holy Quran and the Sunnah. The Council has also to advise whether a proposed law is or is not repugnant to the Holy Quran and the Sunnah.

The process of amendment of the Constitution is extremely difficult. No amending Bill can be presented to the President unless it has the support of two-thirds of the total number of members of the National Assembly. The President may withhold his assent to the Bill so passed or return it for reconsideration. If assent is withheld, the Assembly may reconsider the Bill but it cannot again be presented to the President for assent unless it has the support of three-fourths of the total number of members. If the Bill is returned for reconsideration and it is passed by the Assembly, without any amendment or with amendments suggested by the President, by a two-third majority of the total number of members, it may be re-presented to the President who may, if the Bill be still not acceptable to him, dissolve the Assembly or direct a referendum.

Democracy, whatever form it may take, has for its foundation the assumption that ultimate power vests in the people and that, in the last analysis, they are the sovereign authority in a State. . . .

Under the Presidential system, democracy takes a different form, but it is still subject to the principle of popular sovereignty. Under this system, the people choose for a fixed period their representatives for the Legislature and a President who chooses his own Executive. The law-making is done by the Legislature but the executive authority is exercised by the President and the persons chosen by him who constitute a Presidential Executive. These two organs are independent of each other and are accountable to the people by a system of periodic elections.

The President is not responsible to the Legislature and cannot, before the expiry of his term, be removed by a mere vote of no-confidence. In the same manner, the Legislature cannot be dissolved by the President before the expiry of its term. Absolute powers of the President may be restricted by providing that in certain matters, as, for instance, in making appointments to important public offices, the President shall consult the Legislature or a committee of the Legislature. But what is of determining importance is that though the functions of the Executive and the Legislature are different and neither is responsible to the other, the control of finances is entirely in the hands of the Legislature which is thus in a position to cripple the President's policies and projects by refusing him funds without which he cannot function effectively.

The Constitution of 1956 had adopted a Parliamentary pattern. The President was elected for a period of five years by the members of the National Assembly and the Provincial Assemblies. He was the constitutional Head of State but the Parliamentary Executive was headed by the Prime Minister, to be appointed by the President from amongst members of the National Assembly, who was most likely to command the confidence of the majority of the members of that Assembly. If the Prime Minister lost the confidence of the majority, he could be dismissed and replaced by a more popular person by the President. Other Ministers were appointed by the President but with the advice of the Prime Minister. The Cabinet of Ministers was collectively responsible to the National Assembly. The executive authority vested in the President but he was bound to act on the advice of the Prime Minister. The 310 members of the National Assembly were directly elected by the people on the principle of adult franchise for a period of five years but the Assembly was liable to dissolution earlier. All expenditure, except expenditure charged on the Consolidated Fund, had to be submitted in the form of demands for grants to the National Assembly which had the power to assent or to refuse to assent to any demand. An Act, called the Appropriation Act, had to be passed each year to provide for appropriation out of the Consolidated Fund of all moneys to meet the grants made by the National Assembly, and no money could be withdrawn from that Fund except in accordance with the appropriation law.

As the Constitution of 1962 was given by a single individual and not by a representative Assembly, it embodies, like other Constitutions, the political philosophy of its maker. Factors contributing to that philosophy were the past experience of the working of the 1956 Constitution and the generally felt need for stability and a strong Central Government. As politicians and political parties were considered to be responsible for the evils of the past, the Constitution did away with both. They were considered to be the bane of the Parliamentary system which had led to instability, vacillation and corruption. That system had therefore to go, and democracy has no alternative except a Presidential system. But unlike other such systems, the Pakistan system was supposed to work without political parties and politicians. Article 173, therefore, provided that a person who, in connection with an election, holds out himself or any other person as being a member of, or as having the support of, a political party, shall be punishable. But this prohibition was made removable by an Act of the Legislature.

Direct elections for the President were not only expensive but, in view of the disparity between the populations of the two Provinces, they could produce some ugly and anomalous results. Election of the President by the three Assemblies had been an essential feature of the 1956 Constitution but for a Presidential form of Government such an electorate was considered to be too narrow and unsound in principle. An Electoral College was, therefore, set up for the election of the President.

In the absence of, and with a ban on, political parties, which are formed on clashing ideologies and principles, the adult residents of a Unit were to elect, regardless of any political principle, from amongst themselves an Elector for their Unit. A Unit was to consist of about 1,000 persons in West Pakistan, and since there had to be parity between the two Provinces in the number of Units, of a considerably larger number in East Pakistan. For the principle that the ideology of political parties influences the elections was substituted the supposition that the only consideration weighing with the Electors would, and ought to be, the comparative merits of the contesting candidates. The best men, so elected, would vote for the best candidate for the Presidency as well as for the best candidates for election to the Central and Provincial Assemblies. A further assumption underlying the system was that the persons chosen as Electors for the Units would belong to a higher and more enlightened level of society and thus be better able to understand problems which their own electors could not, and that in this way the local interests and the intelligentsia of the country would be more effectively represented in the electorate for the election of the President and members of the Assemblies.

As the Constitution, but for a division of powers and functions, would have been no Constitution, and the concentration of all power by amalgamating legislative and executive functions and assigning them to the same person or set of persons would have produced a naked dictatorship or oligarchy, these two functions were distributed between the President and the Legislature, the President being responsible for administration and the Assembly's functions being confined to law-making. It was expected of members of the Legislative Assemblies that just as the Electors for the Units would vote for the best men, the members of the Legislative Assemblies would vote for the laws that they considered to be in the best interests of the country. But disillusionment came too soon and these assumptions were shattered to pieces with the very first session of the National Assembly which had been chosen by the Electors for the Units. The Assemblies were a hotchpotch of individuals, with groups based on no ideology or principle. Their members were not subject to any party discipline and acted either individually or in loose and incohesive groups. The President had no party of his own, and it was clear from the very beginning that the assumption that the members of the Assemblies would consider each legislative measure from a patriotic and national point of view was unfounded. The President needed legislation to give effect to his own political philosophy of a welfare State. He had also to oppose legislation which he considered to be detrimental to the interests of the country. But political parties being a constitutional anathema, there were no means for him to collect in the National Assembly a following to support and propagate his views. This chaotic condition having become intolerable, the Political Parties Act, permitting collective political activity, had to be passed in the very first session of the National Assembly. The natural result of this law was that the President had to create a party of his own or join one of the old parties.

In a welfare State where the emphasis is on the collective good as distinguished from individual interests, sharply defined fundamental rights do not exist, and if they do, being, unlike ordinary rights, not justiciable, they are more in the nature of directive principles. But no political party in Pakistan can afford to have any such conception of fundamental rights, and when a private Bill for their justiciability was introduced in the National Assembly, no party, including the loose and incoherent party that had collected around the President, had the courage or conviction to oppose the Bill. The President had, therefore, to yield to the popular demand and another link in his philosophy gave way when the Government itself introduced and carried through the National Assembly the Constitution (First Amendment) Bill which became an Act of that name of 1963.

The thoughtfully phrased Islamic features of the Constitution met the same fate. No one in Pakistan could oppose a Bill which was professedly based on religion. The maker of the Constitution had in mind some distinction between the broad principles and concepts of Islam on the one hand and the letter of the Holy Book and the Sunnah, regardless of context and principle, on the other. The private Bill which had proposed restoration of fundamental rights had also moved for restoration of the Islamic features to their 1956 form. This amendment also could not be opposed and was accepted by the Government, with the result that the name of the State, Islamic Republic of Pakistan, was restored, together with the other Islamic features of the 1956 Constitution. Thus, another major principle disappeared from the new Constitution.

If a strong opposition party is ever formed in the National Assembly, the Constitution amendment battles, as far as one can judge, will be fought on two issues, namely, (1) whether the Annual Budget Statement should be substantially subject to the vote of the Assembly, and (2) whether elections to the Assemblies should be direct? A representative and responsible Assembly is an essential and common feature of a democratic Constitution, but indirect elections under the present system fail to give effect to the principle of responsibility and periodic accountability of the elected Executive and Legislature. Direct election of the President may cause some complications but direct elections to the Assemblies, though expensive, present no such apprehension. At present the principle is that the Elector for the Unit is not to have any mandate from his own electorate. But assuming that he is elected with a mandate, it is obvious that under the present system he can ignore, even disobey, it with impunity. By electing an Elector for the Unit, the voter is supposed to surrender to him his own judgment, the Elector becoming a delegate of the voter with the right to exercise his own independent judgment. But the voter, not knowing how his delegate has used his judgment, cannot hold him to account for his action.

The question whether the Governors should also be elected depends upon whether a perfectly federal form of Government is to be preferred to the present unitarian form. The existing system gives a cohesion and stability to administration while any change for a full federation may arouse acute parochial jealousies and may even lead to disruption, profession of a common religion alone having never produced in history a lasting political union.

Thus, though the constitution is founded on drastically altered principles of popular Government, particularly in regard to the powers of the Chief Executive; the inability of the Assemblies to control finance and, on the principle of distribution of powers, to pass Laws in opposition to the policy of the Executive; and unaccountability of the Executive and the Legislature to the sovereign people, it is not to be forgotten that democracy and Constitution are both concerned with the Law of Government and that the question what form and powers various organs of Government should have does not depend upon academic theories but on the actual conditions of society, which in a politically nascent and economically developing country are in a state of constant flux. No Constitution can claim to be valid and final for all times; but the desire to change or improve upon an existing instrument of Government must be the result of forces which take their birth inside the body-politic and come to produce a natural pressure too strong to be resisted. And of this the first Amendment Act is an apt example.

68 • KHALID BIN SAYEED: *Pakistan's Basic Democracy* *

"We have given," President Ayub said in a broadcast, "this scheme the name of Basic Democracies for the obvious reason that we want it to grow and evolve from the very first rung of the political ladder so that it finds its roots deep among the people starting at the village level in rural areas and at the mohalla level in towns." Whatever one may think of the name, Basic Democracies does represent the first step taken by Ayub's government to involve the citizen directly in the government. It has been both jeered at and praised, but it is still too early for one to say clearly whether or not the system works. The author of the following article views the Basic Democracies with a jaded eye, implying that it is an unnecessary dilution of democracy. The Combined Opposition parties are also opposed to the principle of Basic Democracies, arguing in general that it is only a disguise which replaces the real thing. One must ask, however, whether or not democracy without dilution, or indirection, would be a wise form of government in a society where religious impulses surge so strongly.

Basic Democracy comprises a five-tier system of local government starting from Union Councils or Town Committees and proceeding upwards via *Tehsil/Thana* Councils, District Councils, Divisional Councils, to the top tier, the Provincial Development Council. A group of villages with a total population of some 10,000, but varying between 4,000 and 15,000, are represented in the Union Council. Each elected member in the Council represents a constituency of from 1,000 to 1,500 people, the idea being that each representative will be well known to his constituents. In the Union Councils, two-thirds of the members are elected and a third are nominated. There are no officials among the nominated members in the Union Councils. Nominated members come from groups such as women, agricultural labor, and those interests who have been reluctant to expose themselves to the rigors of an election or do not want to take the risk of being defeated with the consequential decline in prestige in their local communities. And, of course, openings should be provided for retired officers and N.C.O.'s who are plentiful in the countryside. The procedure regarding nomination is that heads of departments of Police, Education, Irrigation, Public Works and Revenue at the *Tehsil* and *Thana* levels separately recommend names of suitable persons to the Deputy

* *The Middle East Journal,* Vol. 15, No. 3 (Summer 1961), pp. 249–263. By permission. The author is grateful to the Canada Council whose research grant enabled him to pursue the research involved in this paper in Pakistan during the summer of 1960.

Commissioners. This has probably created the impression that only persons whom officials consider pliable will be nominated. It may also be pointed out that in the Town Committees, that is, the lowest tier in the cities, it has been decided not to nominate any members. They will be entirely elected bodies. According to the Government, this decision was made because the members elected in the Union Councils, *i.e.*, in the rural areas, are usually much less educated than those elected in the Town Committees. Similarly, in the *Basic Democracies Order, 1959,* Town Committees have been given functions, such as family planning, which have not been given to the Union Councils.

Pakistan being predominantly an agricultural country, Union Councils, which consist of rural representatives, are the most important part of local government. It may be argued that for the first time a Union Council consisting usually of 15 members, ten of whom are elected, has been made responsible for activities ranging from the maintenance of law and order to agricultural development. But when one reads the various sections of the *Basic Democracies Order, 1959,* one feels that the Union Councils are expected to play an ancillary role. Leadership and administrative initiative rests with the officials. Thus, both in the matter of revenue administration and agriculture development, the Union Council renders assistance to or acts in consultation with officials or advisory committees of District administration. This goes to show that the educated and official élite in Pakistan feel that they know what is best for the rural people. Perhaps as long as the illiteracy and poverty of the rural areas remain, leadership and initiative will be exercised largely from the top.

In the matter of taxation, only the Union and the District Councils have been empowered to levy and collect taxes. But this power can be exercised only with the previous sanction of the appropriate government authority. For example, a Union Council can levy taxes, rates, tolls and fees on 23 items, the most important of which are value of buildings and lands and import and export of goods. Another interesting feature is the special community tax on all adult males for the construction of works of public utility. A local Council may exempt certain persons from this tax in lieu of voluntary labor performed in the building of such works.

The *Thana* Councils in East Pakistan or *Tehsil* Councils in West Pakistan stand above the Union Councils. A *Thana* Council is constituted equally by representative members and official members. The representative members are the Chairmen of the Union Councils and Town Committees. The Chairman of the *Thana* and *Tehsil* Council is the sub-divisional officer of the area concerned. The *Thana* or *Tehsil* Council does not perform any vital functions, apart from those of co-ordinating the activities of all Union Councils and Town Committees within its jurisdiction and performing such activities assigned to it by the District Council.

The next tier is the District Council which is composed of Chairmen of the *Thana* or *Tehsil* Councils, Chairmen of municipal bodies, Vice Presidents of Cantonment Boards (military areas) in the District, and such representatives of Government Departments appointed by the Commissioner. In addition to these official members, there are non-official members like the Chairmen of the Union Councils and Town Committees. District Councils have been assigned a great number of compulsory functions and 70 optional functions. They range from the maintenance of primary schools, promotion of sanitation and public health, to promotion of cultural and social welfare activities. They are responsible for highly technical functions, such as popularization of improved methods of agriculture, maintenance of crop statistics, establishment and management of industrial schools, establishment and maintenance of cattle farms and dairies and improvement of means of communications. All this implies that the District Councils will be dominated by District officials of technical departments and they are not likely to emerge as Councils where non-official representative members will receive training in responsible government.

The next unit in the hierarchy is the Divisional Council chaired by the Commissioner of the Division. These Councils consist of Chairmen of District Councils (District Magistrates or Deputy Commissioners), representatives of Government Departments, municipal bodies and cantonment boards, all of whom are officials, and an equal number of appointed members. Twenty-five per cent of these appointed members are to consist of Chairmen of Union Councils. The principal functions of the Divisional Councils are to coordinate the activities of all local Councils and municipal bodies within the division, formulate and recommend to the Development Council development schemes, and review the progress made in the various branches of administration.

The Development Council stands at the apex of the pyramid and consists of heads of government departments in the province and appointed members appointed by the President on the recommendations of the respective Governor.

CHART OF BASIC DEMOCRACIES *

PROVINCIAL DEVELOPMENT COUNCILS
Total number two. (One Council in East Pakistan, one Council in West Pakistan).
Chairman—Governor

DIVISIONAL COUNCILS
Total number 15. (13 in West Pakistan, two in East Pakistan).
Chairman—Divisional Commissioner

DISTRICT COUNCILS
Total number 76. (59 in West Pakistan, 17 in East Pakistan).
Chairman—Deputy Commissioner in West Pakistan
District Magistrate in East Pakistan.

TEHSIL COUNCILS in West Pakistan
THANA COUNCILS in East Pakistan
Total number 599. (187 in West Pakistan, 412 in East Pakistan).
Chairman—Sub-Divisional Officer

UNION COUNCILS
Total number 7,117 (3,064 in West Pakistan, 4,053 in East Pakistan).
Chairman—elected

* In addition to these bodies, there are 108 Municipal Committees, 62 Cantonment boards, 219 Town Committees and 880 Union Committees throughout Pakistan.

It is obvious that not only has the principle of nomination been brought in to dilute democracy at the lowest tier, namely, the Union Council, but also that the principle of election has been abandoned in all councils above the Union Councils and Town Committees. And such elected chairmen of the Union Councils and Town Committees who are appointed in the upper layers of the pyramid are outnumbered three to one or five to one by nominees and officials.

As regards appointment of officials, the government argues that the elected members should not feel unduly alarmed by the presence of officials because the officials under Basic Democracy will be officials-in-Council instead of being armed with arbitrary powers. It is needless to point out that, officials being what they are, the possibility of their trying to check popular discontent or enthusiasm is much greater than that of the elected chairmen of Union Councils challenging the awe inspiring and prestige conscious civil servants. The fear still remains that, in Basic Democracy, not even Lord Ripon's objective of substituting outside control for inside interference may be achieved because district officers cannot only control Divisional and District Councils in which the officials predominate, but also Union Councils through their nominees.

The Basic Democracies Order, 1959, has the familiar flavor of former British constitutional Acts. Section 74 of the Order reads:

> Control over the activities of local councils.—(1) If, in the opinion of the Controlling Authority, anything done or intended to be done by or on behalf of a local council is not in conformity with the law, or is in any way against public interest, the Controlling Authority may, by order,—
> (a) quash the proceedings;
> (b) suspend the execution of any resolution passed or order made by the local council;
> (c) prohibit the doing of anything proposed to be done; and
> (d) require the local council to take such action as may be specified.

What is equally disquieting is the fact that local councils, after a governmental inquiry, may be superseded on grounds that they are not functioning efficiently or have acted in a manner contrary to public interest. Ultimately, it is not the letter of the Order but the spirit with which it is likely to be implemented that is important. Firstly, those who have studied the history of district administration of East Pakistan will recall that that administration, thanks to the Permanent Land Revenue Settlement, did not exercise as rigorous or close a control as the administration in West Pakistan. Secondly, the young officials in the Civil Service of Pakistan, who are likely to be in charge of the lower tiers of Basic Democracy, have not yet become infected by the idea that what these illiterate villagers need is not self-government but good government.

The brain behind the campaign to popularize Basic Democracy was that of Brigadier F. R. Khan, former Joint Secretary of the Ministry of National Reconstruction and Information. The President himself went on an extensive mass-contact tour in his celebrated train *Pak Jamhuriyat* during December 14-21, 1959. Elections started on December 25-26. What is interesting to note here were the sort of blessings that Basic Democracy was supposed to usher into Pakistan. According to Brigadier F. R. Khan, Basic Democracy constituted the sheet-anchor of the human rights of the people of Pakistan. The Commissioner of Bahawalpur said that Basic Democracy would create a classless society where political parties would not function and disrupt the *millat*. According to the same authority, the political thinkers in England had also begun to doubt the utility of parliamentary system and its effectiveness in ushering in a welfare state. According to Mr. Ghulam Ahmed Pervaiz, Basic Democracy was akin to the idea of *Shura* (Council of Advisors) in Islām and the type of democracy introduced by Western civilization had no place in Islām. President Ayub also pointed out:

> . . . Basic Democracy was picked up from Islamic injunctions of conscience. In the orthodox democratic system the only function of the Opposition was to oppose the party in power without the least consideration of national good. Communists and Fascists based their system on party rule smashing individual or group opposition. The whole system of Islam was against both these alternatives. There was no place for independent individual in party system of government. This is why Hazrat Omar thought necessary that councils should consist of men of high character and wisdom belonging to no party.

All this goes to show that the Government has planned its publicity campaign in such a way that the system of Basic Democracy will appeal to different sections in different ways. The orthodox are being told that Basic Democracy is Islamic in origin and spirit. The urban groups are being assured that Basic Democracy has all the good features of a democratic system minus its major defect, the party system.

The strategy being followed in order to keep the Union Councils free from the influence of former politicians is obvious. The Government has made it clear that corrupt politicians will be disqualified under the Elective Bodies Disqualification Order before holding elections. In all, nearly 6,500 persons (3,500 in West Pakistan and 3,000 is East Pakistan) have been disqualified from contesting elections to any elective body till December 31, 1966. It is common knowledge that general elections to various Provincial Legislatures, particularly in West Pakistan, have never been free or honest. Elections to various local bodies have been much worse. In West Pakistan, in districts where there were large landowners, tenants could never expect to cast their votes freely. A clear account of how District Board elections were influenced by the landlords is to be found in the *Reports on the Sargodha District Board Elections 1952-53*. Here it was obvious that the struggle was between the supporters of Daultana, led by his brother-in-law, and the supporters of Firoz Khan Noon, supported probably by the Tiwana landowners. Formerly, supporters of the Noon faction were returned unopposed from *Zails* (revenue division) comprising tribes and castes of similar origin. The problem for the Daultana faction was how to get their supporters returned unopposed. They solved it by changing the constituencies in such a way that parts of as many as four *Zails* were included in one constituency. By placing their supporters in the District administrative hierarchy, they had the nomination papers of their rivals rejected. The net result was that by such tactics and by official pressure and terror no fewer than 28 candidates of the Daultana faction out tof the 46 Muslim constituencies were returned unopposed.

What has been the election atmosphere under Basic Democracy? First, there was the problem of holding election meetings. Martial Law regulation No. 55, which made processions or meetings of a political nature illegal, had to be amended. This was done in the beginning of December, 1959. The Government also made it clear that no sectarian, political, linguistic or parochial canvassing would be allowed. The maximum expenditure to be incurred by the candidates in the rural areas was fixed at Rs. 200 and at Rs. 500 in urban areas. Both in East and West Pakistan, polling was much heavier in rural than in urban areas. According to newspaper reports, polling in the interior towns and districts of East Pakistan such as Baraisal and Bogra was as high as 80 to 90 per cent. Similarly, in West Pakistan polling in Lahore was 40 to 50 per cent, whereas in the interior and rural areas like Gujranwala, Sheikhupura, and Sialkot it was 70 to 80 per cent. In Peshawar, the polling again was heavy in rural areas and light in the city. The reports also suggest that the polling was unexpectedly heavy among women voters. For example, in Gujranwala, 80 to 90 per cent of the female voters cast their votes. This suggests that Basic Democracy seems to have attracted more attention among less sophisticated voters than those in urban areas where the demand for the restoration of parliamentary democracy has been persistent. It is significant that polling has been heavy in spite of the fact that candidates were not allowed to entertain voters or convey them to the polling booths in trucks. This goes to show that voters have been attracted by the novelty of Basic Democracy, the promises of the régime that their candidates are going to play an important rôle in improving their lot, and above all, by the personality of Field Marshal Ayub. However, the candidates did not present clear or concrete programs as regards village or social improvement, with the result that the contests were resolved largely on the basis of personal qualifications and group or tribal affiliations of the candidate. The light voting in urban areas brought down the percentage of the electorate who exercised their franchise. Out of 33.7 million registered voters, 20.8 million voted, which meant that 61.7 per cent of the electorate exercised their franchise.

Another interesting factor is the kind of candidates who stood for election. In East Pakistan, the candidates were mainly farmers, *imams* of mosques, small businessmen, social workers, lawyers and medical practitioners. In Lahore, out of 2,415 candidates contesting 98 seats, 2,000 were traders and 300 were lawyers. There was not a single prominent ex-politician among these candidates. In other words, in urban areas like Lahore, alternative leadership could be found. In Lyallpur (West Pakistan), where an average landholder possessed small or medium-sized landholdings and where the *Arian* tribe predominated, most of the 708 candidates for 313 seats belonged to the lower and middle classes. Similarly, it has been estimated that out of the persons elected in the District of Hyderabad (West Pakistan) 1,053 were new leaders and the remaining 67 were former members of the local bodies. Out of the elected members, 18 were landlords and contractors, 521 small landowners, 157 *haris,* 295 merchants and businessmen, 82 tailors, weavers, and domestic servants, 31 lawyers, 16 doctors and *hakims,* and five journalists. As for the whole of Pakistan, the classification of successful candidates based on figures disclosed by Government circles is as follows: agriculturalists, 48,998; lawyers, 288; businessmen, 2,586; ex-government servants, 391; journalists, ten; and the rest are mostly small shopkeepers and tradesmen.

The influence of former politicians, though diminished considerably, has persisted. Former politicians did not campaign openly, but used their influence through agents and sending secret instructions. This influence of ex-politicians can be assessed with some accuracy in West Pakistan. Thus, Qaiyum Khan, former President of the Muslim League and a Frontier leader, advised his friends and agents not to let followers of his rival, Khan Abdul Ghaffar Khan, get elected.

Khuhro and Pirzada used their influence to get their candidates elected in Sind. In Sargodha, it seemed that the former conflict between the Daultana and Noon factions continued to simmer. Malik Noon's son, his personal assistant, and Daultana's personal assistant, were once again in the struggle. The brother of the former Provincial Minister, Fazl-i-Ilahi Piracha, was elected unopposed. Thus, in certain areas of West Pakistan, where large landlords or ex-military officers dominate, it has been difficult to find alternative leadership. In the rural areas of West Pakistan, about 412 landlords have been elected. In the Attock *Tehsil,* the majority of the 770 candidates were ex-politicians and political workers. In Sargodha *Tehsil,* 257 candidates were returned unopposed leaving 229 in the field. In West Pakistan, 3,864 ex-politicians have been elected. Fifty per cent of these successful candidates are former Muslim Leaguers and among the rest may be found members with former Republican, Awani League and *Jama'at-i-Islami* affiliations. In East Pakistan, there are 2,800 ex-politicians among the successful candidates. This means that about eight per cent of the successful candidates in the whole of Pakistan are former politicians.

In East Pakistan, where the Hindu minority represents an important section, 998 Hindu candidates were elected unopposed and 3,967 Hindu candidates were successful out of 9,262.

According to a report published by the West Pakistan election authorities on the elections under Basic Democracy, out of every hundred persons elected, eight belonged to the top income group (over $420 a month), 30 to the upper middle class, 50 to the lower middle class, and 12 to the lowest income group (under $63 a month). The Bureau of National Reconstruction, which is in charge of the working of Basic Democracy throughout Pakistan, has recently published a progress report in which election results throughout the country have been analyzed. The proportion of literates elected in East Pakistan was much higher than it was in West Pakistan. Ninety-nine and seven-tenths per cent of the 40,000 Union Councillors in East Pakistan were literate. On the other hand, only 60.7 per cent of 38,457 Councillors in West Pakistan were literate. On the national basis, 84.2 per cent of the new leadership was literate with 8.1 per cent having studied up to matriculation and above.

Can it be assumed that the local institutions, having been insulated from the influence of politicians, are now likely to function harmoniously and efficiently? When politicians, a great majority of whom came from educated and urbanized groups, could not display an *esprit de corps,* how can better results be expected from the less sophisticated rural leaders? Will the local Councillors cease to be plagued by tribal feuds? Will a Jat or a Rajput sit down with an Arain, or a Jat with a refugee in concert to levy taxes and devise methods to raise the low living standards? Already fears are being expressed that nominated members may combine with some of the elected members to veto the wishes of the majority of elected members. The scheme of Basic Democracy has been constructed on the assumption that local affairs lend themselves to a non-political or technical and rational approach. The Union Councils will be dealing with the building of roads, establishment of health centers, and the problem of finding the wherewithal to finance these schemes. These are concrete problems in contrast to the more abstract political or linguistic controversial issues. Richard Park has argued that perhaps the more local an issue and the more intimate the aquaintance with it, the greater the possibility of feuds and factionalism. G. M. Carstairs has recently demonstrated that mutual mistrust and suspicion is a constant process in the life of the villages and leads to a continual reforming and shifting of alliances, none of which persist for long. Should one be pessimistic and say that the kind of intrigues and squabbles that went on between the Daultanas and Noons or between Talpurs and Khuhros will riddle the Union, *Tehsil,* and District Councils? Will the Deputy Commissioners leave the same kind of handing-over notes that the author has seen in the Deputy Commissioner of Sialkot's office, all of which pointed out that the District Board was riddled with intrigues and factions woven around the personalities of leaders of tribal jealousies?

Much depends upon the kind of leadership that emerges in these new Councils. Lucien Pye, drawing on his experiences in South East Asia, wrote: "Political behaviour is likely to be influenced more by considerations of the source than by the content of the communication." So far as the source of leadership in Union Councils in East Pakistan is concerned, it is not likely to change very much in the near future. The Sayyids, the Choudhuris, the Sheikhs, the Khundakars and the Bhuyans will continue to dominate the village organization with the *mullah* leading the prayers in the mosques or offering prayers to increase the crop output or for the cure of certain diseases of villagers. The problem is probably of a more pressing nature in West Pakistan where, with one stroke of the pen, baked by the full force of the Martial Law, the government has deprived the large landowners of their large holdings. These large landowners were the natural leaders in their areas. It may be pointed out that their *sakht hukum* (stringent orders), though odious in the eyes of the modernists, were sometimes useful from the narrow economic point of view in the sense that the landlord by the twin methods of force and persuasion made the tenants grow certain cash crops even though their cultivation involved harder work. The landlord has also taken the place of the money-lender after the flight of the Hindus. Now that the influence of the long hated landlords is declining, who is going to take their place? The first obvious answer is that the medium-sized landowners continue to be there, as Ayub's régime has not touched their holdings. Secondly, there are the retired Army officers as well as N.C.O.'s, not to mention retired accountants, and headmasters, teachers, and traders. Similarly, if the elected members are faced with disfavor, aroused by a raising of the rates or drastic sanitary improvements, the authority of the District Officer is there to reassure them that all will be well in the end. The rôle of the District Officer should not be condemned out of hand.

What is equally encouraging is that new leadership is emerging among the peasants. In the Kaghan Valley (West Pakistan), the Gujjars have astonished everybody by nominating their own candidates after discussing the suitability of all possible candidates at several informal gatherings of elders. These decisions have produced a large number of unopposed returns among their candidates. Formerly, all seats in the Valley were the monopoly of influential landlords. The writer attended a meeting of the Union Council of Mandra not far from Rawalpindi (West Pakistan) last August and to his surprise there took place a heated debate between a member who had two years of college education and was a manager of an insurance company and another medium-sized landowner who was also a retired military officer. The former was in favor of raising new taxes and undertaking new schemes of social welfare, and was a much more persuasive speaker. The retired military officer, backed by other retired military officers and conservative trade and agricultural elements, resisted the imposition of what he termed "unbearable taxes," which were likely to drive away traders from the Union. There was an equally lively controversy as regards the proposal that there should be a higher tax (one rupee, which equals 21 cents) on those who had male children than those who had female children (tax four annas, which equals five cents). This was resisted by all the members on the plea that the poor people of the countryside, being more virile than urban people, usually had male children.

There is also a tendency to undertake progressive reforms among Municipal Committees. Noakhali in East Pakistan, for long a center of orthodoxy, is moving in the same direction. The Noakhali Municipal Committee has adopted an ingenious device to curb polygamy. Among the 72 approved taxes, the Committee has included a marriage tax. The tax becomes progressively higher as the number of wives that a man marries increases. For the first marriage, the tax is Rs. 2; for the second marriage during the lifetime of the first wife, a tax of Rs. 50 will have to be paid; for the third marriage during the lifetime of either the first or second wife, the tax will be Rs. 500. The tax goes up to Rs. 1,000 for every fourth marriage during the lifetime of any of the first three wives. Under the recent Muslim Family Laws Ordinance, registration of marriages, arbitration in cases of husbands desiring to marry more than one wife, have been brought under the purview of the Union Councils. By measures such as these, it is likely that the influence of the *pirs* and the *mullahs,* who have been very powerful in West Pakistan, is likely to decline.

However, the Government is aware that the District Officers may step into the vacuum before the local leaders consolidate their position. The Deputy Commissioners have been told that instead of holding their usual *durbars* in which the Union Councillors may be summoned from distant places, they should go and meet them. But the District Officers are not the only dominant figures. In District Council meetings, the Chairman of Union Councils play a very submissive rôle and feel inferior to English-speaking lawyers and officials of technical Departments. This was clearly the impression that the writer gathered when he attended the District Council meeting of Rawalpindi last August. Chairmen of Union Councils in this District Council meeting were sitting quiet—clearly because they could not follow the proceedings that were being conducted in English. The agenda was read in English and the rules of procedure, which had been framed by the Government, were all in English. It was only after considerable time had elapsed, and presumably when the Chairmen of Union Councils could not tolerate the situation any more, that some of the Chairmen summoned enough courage to get up and tell the Deputy Commissioner bluntly that the proceedings should be conducted in Urdu so that they could follow the business of the house. At first the Deputy Commissioner was reluctant because he suggested that at least the rules of procedure and financial matters should be discussed in English because the equivalent technical words in Urdu were not available. Secondly, the writer found that the proceedings were being dominated by the officials of various technical Departments who were either displaying their technical knowledge or moving amendments drafted in a legal form. Thus, much depends upon the courage and the initiative of the Chairmen of Union Councils to compel the Deputy Commissioner to hold the proceedings in Urdu, or Sindi, or Pushtu, or Bengali.

We are also familiar with the fact that the Government has opened a number of training centers to provide training to members of Union Councils and Committees. They have been given courses and lectures in the principles of Basic Democracy, their duties as members or Chairmen of Union Councils or Town Committees, co-ordination of Local Councils under Basic Democracy with nation-building Departments, simple ideas of socio-economic planning and development. It seems that some 80,000 elected members of Union Councils and Town Committees are likely to form an electoral college to elect a National Assembly consisting of about 200 members. They were called upon to express their confidence in the present President soon after their election in January, 1960, and also authorize him to take steps to formulate the constitution. This indirect election has been criticized by urban groups on the plea that it may be easier to corrupt an electorate of 80,000 than an electorate of 90 million.

In Basic Democracy, what the Government has done is to take the Pakistani society back to its plural foundations. It may be argued that, formerly, whenever the electorate were asked to decide questions of national importance, they tended to look at them from parochial or emotional points of view and interest. The result was that national questions could not be solved. The argument is: Ask the people only those questions which they can understand and, since they can understand their local problems, let them vote on local issues and set up Councils and Committees to decide local problems. National problems should be left in the hands of an indirectly elected powerful President and a Legislature with limited powers.

Another noteworthy point is that in this scheme of Basic Democracy too much is being expected from civil servants. They are likely to feel that all their technical or professional ability in agriculture or animal husbandry is being wasted in tiresome and tedious arguments with rustics or ill-informed people. This sort of resentment may bring about domination of the local institutions. History will be repeating itself and Union and District Councils, instead of becoming effective instruments of local self-government, may emerge as departments of the government administration. It may also be suggested that the government in its haste to launch the scheme of Basic Democracy has not carefully studied and considered the actual needs and aspirations of the people. All kinds of seemingly idealistic and progressive ideas are being put forward before the people. The danger is that aspirations may be aroused which the economy of the country may not be able to satisfy. Finally, one comes back to the old argument as to whether the new institutions will strike deep roots in the soil of the country. Will they evoke sufficient devotion and affection on the part of the people? In other words, will there be village Hampdens with dauntless breasts to fight for the rights and privileges of the Union Councils and Town Committees? Will the people who have not created these Councils fight for their rights when the more organized urban groups did not fight for the preservation of democracy in the country?

Even if Basic Democracy lays the foundations for strong local institutions, these are not likely to solve the national problems of the country. Linguistic and cultural differences between East and West Pakistan, in addition to physical separation, have proved to be too strong to be kept under firm control by the unifying factors of Islām and a superimposed administrative unity. Moreover, it is not the rural masses, whose interests are being looked after under Basic Democracy, who have created any intractable problems for Pakistan. It is the educated groups from the Punjab and Bengal who have been unable to obtain adjustment of their economic and political problems within a democratic framework. Ayub, like De Gaulle, has denounced these groups and has insulated the governmental machinery from the wranglings of factions and parties. He has so far not devised any alternative system in which provincial grievances can be ventilated, discussed, and settled on a compromise basis. Under Basic Democracy, he hopes to train the rural masses in the art of representative government at the local level. But no system has been put forward whereby the more important group, the educated urban classes, may be trained to operate democracy on a national basis.

Perhaps one should not end all this on such a negative note. It redounds to the credit of Ayub's régime that for the first time an earnest effort is being made towards rural uplift. The Muslim League, with all its claims of having mobilized Muslim support for Pakistan all over the country, never produced a program comparable to that of Gandhi for village development. There is no denying the fact that the villages today are vibrating with a new life which has not been there before. One cannot dismiss scenes of thousands of volunteers constructing roads, new public health centers and schools springing up, and *haris,* who until the other day paid blackmail for their lands and cattle to the local chieftains and for their souls to the *pirs,* winning elections against their own landlords, as things of no consequence.

GLOSSARY

Arain—an agricultural tribe consisting of small vegetable growers, gardeners, tenants or self-cultivating owners in West Pakistan. A few individual members of the Arain tribe became very prosperous and rose to high positions under the British.

Gujjars—an agricultural tribe in West Pakistan.

Haris—tenants in Sind who render compulsory assistance to their landlords by plowing their fields.

Jats—an agricultural tribe of West Pakistan consisting of peasants and landed proprietors concentrated in the southwestern plains of the Punjab.

Pirs—religious leaders who are usually superior to *mullahs,* but not as elevated as the saints.

Rajput—tribe consisting of landlords of noble birth in West Pakistan. Originally the name of a military tribe of Hindus who claimed descent from the ancient Kshatriyas.

Tehsil—a revenue sub-division of a District in West Pakistan.

Thana—a subordinate police station in East Pakistan, the jurisdiction of which embraces a number of villages.

SECTION THREE

Political Leadership

69 • S. M. Ikram: *Jinnah, the Man and the Statesman* *

Muhammad Ali Jinnah is referred to by Pakistanis as Quaid-i-Azam, the Great Leader. He reluctantly came to support partition after he had decided there was no alternative, and he led the Muslim League in its victorious fight for an independent Pakistan. Aloof and austere, he has remained a controversial figure. When independence was established in 1947 Mr. Jinnah became Governor-General, but by this time his health was broken as a result of years of exertion for his cause. Thirteen months later, September 11, 1948, he died. This appraisal was written by a prominent Pakistan official and author.

I

> Let there be no mistake about it. One who wants to understand Jinnah must shed the popular prejudices against him.[1]

Quaid-i-Azam's superb qualities as a political leader are widely recognized. Justice has, however, not been done to him as a man. The grim struggle which he had to wage within a very limited time for the attainment of a near-impossible task left no room for leisurely diplomacy, and the fact that his objectives ran counter to the wishes and sentiments of the British, the Hindus, the nationalist Muslims and the Punjab Unionists was bound to influence their attitude. Even ordinary Muslims have not been much more successful at understanding this gaunt, lonely figure. Inevitably, they have recreated his image according to their own fancy, and forgotten that although in an effort to do his duty to his people, he created for them the largest Muslim state of the day, he was the product of a liberal, cosmopolitan atmosphere. From his early days he had worked with men like Dadabhoy Naoroji, Pheroze Shah Mehta and Gokhale, and although during the later years of his life, the world knew him only as a Muslim leader, he always remained a lofty-minded, noble-souled, far-seeing statesman. His place is not only among the makers of the modern Muslim world, but with the great statesmen of Asia, indeed the world.

About Quaid's basic personal qualities there is not much difference of opinion. He came from a business community, and was business-like, methodical and

* *Modern Muslim India and the Birth of Pakistan,* rev. ed. (Lahore, Sh. Muhd. Ashraf, 1965), pp. 313-326. By permission.

[1] Sharma, M. S. M., *Peeps into Pakistan,* p. 1.

cool-headed. His integrity and incorruptibility have become a byword. . . . He did not give himself up to politics, until he had made ample money from legal practice, and become financially independent. His courage—moral as well as physical—, strength of will and independence of outlook cannot but evoke admiration. Repeatedly his strong nerve was put to severe tests, but he always came out with flying colours. In 1943 he had to face an assassin armed with a dagger. He grappled with the man, and held him, till help became available. . . . Quaid's nerve was also tested in a less violent but, perhaps, more potent manner by Mountbatten. He threatened Quaid that "failing agreement," power may be transferred to the Interim Government. Quaid remained "very calm" and gave a nonchalant answer. "Mountbatten felt that Jinnah's reaction was both abnormal and disturbing. It was certainly shrewd. The *ballon d'essai* has gone up and come down again, providing only the evidence that Jinnah has a very steady nerve."

Quaid has been occasionally accused of showing lack of courtesy. . . . Those who have tried to understand Quaid's mind, have, however, realized that his sharp reaction to certain individuals and on certain occasions was a part of his basic integrity and tendency to call a spade a spade. Lord Pethick-Lawrence's observations on this point give the clue to Quaid's behaviour. In the course of a speech at London in January 1959, he said, "Now he had, of course, immense powers of intellect and also of persuasive eloquence which he used with such effect that the idea, which was at first an ideal only, became in the end a reality. Not only had he those gifts but I realized in him a man of very firm resolution, a man who when he had made a promise always kept it, and *if he felt that anybody else with whom he was negotiating failed to keep their promise he reacted strongly*." [Italics ours]

While many of Quaid's basic personal qualities are recognized, the grim struggle in which he was engaged during the most important years of his life and the animosities which this struggle generated have obscured others. It is not, for example generally realized, that at heart he was intensely humane, intrinsically fair-minded, completely free from ill-will towards other communities, and large-hearted where this did not involve sacrifice of public interests. In order to instil a sense of discipline in the Muslim League he had to take drastic action against some of his lieutenants, and he acquired the reputation of a stern disciplinarian, but all this was done in the public cause. Personally he was large-hearted and fair-minded. . . . Indeed, Quaid never permitted his personal sentiments to come in the way of his public duty.

Other qualities which are rarely attributed to him and of which evidence comes from another unexpected source are his freedom from communal hatred, keenness to safeguard the Hindu interests in Pakistan and his humanity. M. S. M. Sharma who was editor of the "Daily Gazette," Karachi, stayed on in Pakistan till the beginning of 1948. As a journalist, he had always taken a narrow, communal angle, and was so bitter against Pakistan that even the redoubtable Patel had to ask him to shed his "bitterness" before taking up his pen to write about the early days of Pakistan. His *Peeps into Pakistan* was written some years later, but shows that even by then he had not attained an objectivity of approach. The book contains mistakes of fact and inference, but as expressing the thoughts and experiences of a Hindu who stayed on in Pakistan and was not friendly to the new country or to its founder, his remarks about the Quaid are of more than ordinary interest. He reveals that it was at the Quaid's instance that a Minorities' Association was established to safeguard the interests of the minorities. Indeed, he gives the gist of a long conversation which the Quaid had with him, and which deserves to be reproduced at length:

> The long and short of his lecture to me was just this. Now that he had got Pakistan, he had no longer any grudge against the Hindus. In fact, he was anxious to revert to his old and familiar role of "Ambassador of Hindu-Muslim Unity." He proposed that he should continue as the champion of minorities in Pakistan as he had been for several years now, the champion of the minorities in India.
>
> Now, "my dear fellow," he roared, "I am going to constitute myself as the Protector-General of the Hindu Minority in Pakistan. I am going to rely on your help. I am going to take no refusal."

There is plenty of evidence not only in Sharma's book but also in Quaid's public speeches of the period to show that he meant every word of what he said, and did his best to protect the interests of the Hindu minority in Pakistan. When the *Dawn* started publishing what Sharma calls "fearful cartoons of things supposed to have occurred in India" and gave (according to Sharma, wrong) details of the butchery of Muslims, Jinnah encouraged Sharma to give his point of view, and "expose the mischief." Even more revealing is his reaction to the riot which was triggered off in Karachi owing to the arrival of a number of Sikhs, in an atmosphere charged with animosities arising out of the reports from the East Punjab, and further aggravated by the entry of Indian troops in Kashmir. The Quaid tried to put down the trouble with peremptory orders. Sharma gives some important details of his reaction to this tragedy: "In fairness to Jinnah I must record that he was the most shocked individual in Pakistan. He visited the Hindu refugee camps and at least at one of them, the iron-man lost his nerve and shed a few tears."

The account which Sharma gives of the Quaid shedding tears at a Hindu refugee camp will cause surprise. The Quaid had imposed such an iron discipline on himself and was so averse to a show of sentimental weakness, that very few would consider him capable of "tears." Evidence is, however, available from quite a different source to show that he had a tender heart below a stiff exterior. Altaf Hussain, the Editor of *Dawn,* saw things from an angle completely different from that of Sharma, but he also in an article entitled "When Quaid Wept," has recorded an occasion, when he saw Quaid quietly shedding tears over the sufferings of the Muslims in East Punjab. So far as Quaid's shedding of tears at a Hindu refugee camp is concerned, there is another eye-witness. Jamshed Nusserwanji, a former mayor of Karachi, told Hector Bolitho, "I beg you to believe that Mr. Jinnah was a humanitarian (*sic*). He was never generous in tears—oh, no—but I saw him weep, twice. Once was after Partition, in January 1948, when I went with him to see an encampment of Hindus who had stayed on in Pakistan. When he saw their misery, he wept. I saw the tears on his cheek." The second occasion when Nusserwanji saw tears in Quaid's eyes were after his failure at Calcutta in 1928, to which a reference has already been made.

Sharma gives an account of the last meeting of the Council of All-India Muslim League held at Karachi on 15 December, 1947, at which, according to him, the Quaid made a "violent effort to convert the Muslim League into a non-communal and national organization whose membership would be thrown open to all citizens of Pakistan regardless of caste, creed, race or religion." This historic meeting was not open to the public, and it is difficult to assess the accuracy of Sharma's version of the proceedings but there is a fair basis for believing that Quaid was not opposed to the opening, at a suitable time, of the door of the Muslim League to the members of other communities and converting it into a national organization. A few days after the meeting of the Council he was interviewed by the representative of the B.B.C. who asked him "whether the Muslim League would eventually transform itself into a national organization open to members of all religious communities?" Quaid-i-Azam replied: "The time has not yet come for a national organization of that kind. Public opinion among the Muslims of Pakistan is not yet ripe for it." He, however, significantly added, after warning against being dazzled by democratic slogans, "But the decision to form a purely Muslim organization in Pakistan is not irrevocable. It may be altered as and when necessary to suit changing conditions. Nothing is static in politics."

Sharma says that at the Council, the Quaid-i-Azam did not have things in his own way. Even otherwise, according to him, Quaid could not control the anti-Hindu forces in the new state. He says, "Jinnah had greatly over-rated his hold on Muslims whom he could goad into lawlessness but he could not restrain them." He, however, leaves no doubt about the Quaid's own views and the efforts which he made to safeguard the interests of the minorities.

For Quaid-i-Azam—or Pakistan—Sharma is not a friendly or even a fair witness. He has some cheap, fanciful gibes at "the Sultan of Kashmir" and says many other unfair, unfriendly things about the Quaid. But this does not detract from—in fact, it adds to—the value of his testimony regarding the humane side of Quaid's personality which is corroborated not only by Quaid's speeches and actions as Governor-General but also by such evidence as is available. And what a far cry is all this from the popular image of the Quaid-i-Azam!

Apparently Mrs. Sarojini Naidu, whose detailed assessment has been reproduced at length by Bolitho and regarded as "the wisest" of all estimates of the Quaid, was not far wrong, when she wrote:

> Never was there a nature whose outer qualities provided so complete an antithesis of its inner worth. Tall and stately, but thin to the point of emaciation, languid and luxurious of habit, Mohamed Ali Jinnah's attenuated form is the deceptive sheath of a spirit of exceptional vitality and endurance. Somewhat formal and fastidious, and a little aloof and imperious of manner, the calm hauteur of his accustomed reserve but masks—for those who know him—a naive and eager humanity, an intuition quick and tender as a woman's, a humour gay and winning as a child's. Pre-eminently rational and practical, discreet and dispassionate in his estimate and acceptance of life, the obvious sanity and serenity of his worldly wisdom effectually disguise a shy and splendid idealism which is the very essence of the man.

II

The emotional, almost unintelligent manner in which the majority community reacted to the demand for Pakistan, has not only obscured the personality of the Quaid-i-Azam, but also cast a deep shadow on his work as statesman. The real test of his constructive statesmanship came when he became the Governor-General of Pakistan. Unluckily his tenure was too brief, but he worked during most difficult and crucial times, and his performance even within a limited time can give the measure of the man. Some indication of this has already been given. For a proper assessment of Quaid's qualities as a statesman, perhaps, the best method is a study of the slender volume of his "Speeches as Governor-General of Pakistan, 1947-48." They are, all "occasional pieces" and most of the speeches are brief and businesslike, but they breathe cool wisdom, humanity and liberal, progressive ideas.

Quaid's place in history will, however, be determined on the basis of his supreme achievement—establishment of Pakistan. Before dealing with the consequences of this momentous step it is useful to point out the circumstances in which the decision in favour of division was taken. Even the time which Quaid took to make up his mind in favour of Pakistan would show that the decision was not taken lightly. Indeed, the question was too big to be decided easily by any leader of responsibility. Khaliq-uz-Zaman has given an account of his talks with the Quaid on 12 May, 1939 when he expounded the case for Pakistan. The Quaid's remarks were, "Have you weighed the consequences?" His reaction was that he was not opposed to it but, "it had to be examined in all its bearings." Aga Khan has recorded his conviction that as late as 1946 the Quaid had not finally determined his goal. Till the middle of the year, *i.e.*, till the Congress took up a strange and disturbing attitude with regard to the Cabinet Mission Plan—theoretically accepting it, but distorting the meaning of its basic provisions—, he had not made up his mind. Even, as late as 12 May, 1946, when the Muslim League officially placed its demands before the Cabinet Mission, it was prepared to entrust certain subjects to the Centre on certain conditions.

Those who were in touch with the Quaid say that it was the Congress behaviour in the middle of 1946 which made him finally clinch the issue. He argued that if even when the British were in control, the Congress leaders could resort to such "bad faith," what would they not do when they were in full charge of affairs and controlled the army. After the experience of 1946, Quaid's mind was finally made up. He saw that safety for Muslims and the only way to avoid endless squabbles and conflicts between large Muslim-majority areas and Hindu India lay in a division of the sub-continent. He, now, set about his task not only with his usual singleness of purpose, but also in a new spirit of desperation. For the first time in its history, the Muslim League talked of Direct Action. Besides, Quaid made it clear that not only was there to be a division but also an immediate division of the armed forces. This, however, was a decision which was forced on him. All his life he had worked for peace, harmony and freedom of India, subject, of course, to the safeguarding of the Muslim position. Sharma says, "Jinnah's highest ambition in life was a hazy notion that he must be hailed as a born deliverer of men from bondage." If his career is studied dispassionately, it would appear that his principal role in political life had been that of lifting the road blocks from the path of India's constitutional progress. When in the second decade of this century, future progress was likely to be hampered by lack of Hindu-Muslim agreement, he had a hand in drawing up the Lucknow Pact. Fifteen years later when at the Round Table Conference the Muslim delegates insisted that there should be no further discussion of the constitutional proposals, unless their claims were settled in advance, he intervened and successfully urged that proposals for further constitutional progress may be discussed, subject to the proviso that any implementation would be conditional on settlement of the Muslim claims.

Even the creation of Pakistan was, in reality, the lifting of a road-block. The two other alternatives were civil war, or prolongation of the British rule, which, as Attlee has revealed, was being suggested by Viceroy Wavell. The Quaid by successfully advocating a course, by which these disastrous alternatives were avoided, smoothed the path of India's freedom.

Quaid's conflict with the Congress which was in the vanguard of the struggle for Indian independence, has obscured his own passionate devotion to the cause of India's freedom. Menon, for example, has bemoaned that "Jinnah, the hero of my generation, a great nationalist in his time and one who fought many a battle for freedom of his country, should later have fought so successfully against its freedom. . . ." The last part of the sentence is a cruel misreading of the Quaid's role. He and Mahatma Gandhi differed on the mould in which India's freedom from foreign rule should be cast but on the basic goal of freedom there was no difference of opinion. Mahatma's slogan was "Quit India," while Quaid's demand was "Divide and Quit." The common element—"Quit" in the two demands is too obvious to need emphasis. It was this emphasis on freedom by the Muslim League which upset old Indian hands like Ismay. In the Interim Government, League and Congress representatives were at loggerheads, but on the demand for India's freedom, they were united. Lord Ismay, while explaining to Hector Bolitho the need for hastening the independence of India said, "There was another reason; the Viceroy's Executive Council which had been composed of six or eight wise men, had disappeared. We had, instead, a Cabinet of nine Congress leaders and five Muslim League leaders, who could agree on only one thought—that the British should quit India."

One reason for misjudging the Quaid is that the advantages of Pakistan have not been fully realized. It is said, for example, that it has not solved the communal problem. The reference is, presumably, to the communal riots, which continue to take place in India. These could easily be controlled if the local administration is keen and alert. Even as it is, the enormous reduction in the size of the communal problem should not be lost sight of. From the point of view of Hindustan also, Pakistan has been a great blessing. It was not without reason that Vallabbhai Patel and V.P. Menon during "a lengthy discussion in December 1946 or early in January 1947," coolly weighed the relative advantages of the Cabinet Mission Plan and the division of India on the lines which were later incorporated in the Third June Plan and came to the conclusion that the latter course was better.

So far as the advantages of Pakistan to areas which now constitute Pakistan are concerned, they are too obvious to need any emphasis. Even from the point of view of Hindustan, the division has been beneficial, and it may be useful to give a long quotation from the pen of Dr. Sachin Sen, a Hindu scholar:

"In undivided India, there would have been Muslim domination in the army and the utmost extension of provincial autonomy. In the Muslim majority areas, Muslim dominance would have been felt, and it would have spread unhealthy reaction in the Hindu majority areas. The spirit of communal exclusiveness would have been on the increase. The disadvantages of a weak Centre in the exploitation of economic resources of India had to be accepted. The ideals of one language, one citizenship would have been discouraged. In a partitioned India, the army is safe although the frontier is not. Militarily, there is the need for common defence measures and if Pakistan proves hostile and makes the Hindus dominant in the Indian Union, and if the synthesis of Hindu-Islamic culture which was growing in India is arrested, the possibilities of a revival movement in the Indian Union are great. In Pakistan, there is the declared intention of returning to Shariat laws and to the scheme of society proclaimed by the Prophet Muhammad. In divided India the revivalist movement may gain momentum, if there is the lack of vigilance and warning of enlightened, progressive democratic forces. Divided India is more politically and economically integrated. The unification of India with the native States would not have been complete in undivided India. A strong Centre, one language, one citizenship, all these have been possible in a partitioned India."

Subject to the safeguarding of interests of the people who had put absolute faith in him, Quaid-i-Azam acted with moderation, goodwill and true patriotism. Even when Partition came, he bade farewell to India in a friendly spirit. The message which he gave on 7 August, 1947, *i.e.*, at a time when special trains carrying record for the future Pakistan Government to Karachi had been blown up and massacres in the Punjab had commenced, breathes the spirit of goodwill and friendliness. He expressed his hope that "the two Indias are parting as friends for ever." Owing to several factors this dream has had only a fitful realization. The two Governments were able to control the criminal forces which were let loose in 1947, and their relations might have improved but for Kashmir. This dispute virtually created a state of undeclared war and all remaining ties had to be rent asunder. Still Quaid-i-Azam remained cool and in spite of growing bitterness and long after the beginning of the Kashmir dispute—but before India's lack of good faith with regard to her pledge for plebiscite in Kashmir became manifest—he offered Joint Defence and even co-ordination between India and Pakistan "for the purpose of playing their part in international affairs." Prime Minister Nehru's response (as expressed in reply to a question in the Indian Parliament) was positive, but obviously "Joint Defence" could not come about until—as Quaid pointed out—"Pakistan and India can resolve their own differences," particularly the Kashmir dispute. These differences have not been resolved with the result that India and Pakistan remain poles apart, and Pakistan has turned to other directions for friendship and security. The fact that those well-meaning Indian leaders, who want the two countries to be friendly, start talking of a Confederation has not helped matters. The possibility of a Confederation was knocked on the head when Patel and Menon decided against the Cabinet Mission Plan and the Congress asked for a division of Punjab and Bengal. Now the only possibility—in favourable times—is what Quaid called "some sort of a treaty" between two sovereign states, which, in view of the geography and history of Pakistan and India, may be substantial enough to include Joint Defence and other mutually beneficial arrangements. Indo-Pak amity will not be achieved unless India is really keen about it, has a better understanding of Pakistan's positive side, and can keep in check the urge to "get seventeen annas for the rupee." Even then bold and resourceful leadership will be needed in both countries, to reduce bitterness, prejudices and unconscious hostility, and to deal with the negative forces. At present, chances of an understanding are meagre and have been further reduced by Nehru's death just when, following the Chinese invasion of India, he was beginning to realize the perils of the traditional Indian attitude to Pakistan, but if some day the forces of statesmanship gain the upperhand, Quaid's approach to the question will provide a realistic—and adequate—basis.

70 • S. M. Ikram: *Liaquat Ali Khan* *

Liaquat Ali Khan, who served as Prime Minister under Jinnah and after Jinnah's death under Khwaja Nazimuddin, the second Governor-General of Pakistan, was a man who moved slowly and carefully, who gave thorough consideration to problems before he reached a decision. Jinnah, on the other hand, grasped the essentials of a problem quickly and brilliantly. Liaquat was both tolerant and patient—two virtues that were often mistaken by his opponents as signs of weakness. During his tenure as Prime Minister (from August 14, 1947, to his assassination in October 1951) he successfully guided Pakistan through an economic war with India, toured Great Britain and the United States to emphasize that Pakistan was not to be "taken for granted," and smoothed over near-hostile relations with India by journeying to New Delhi to negotiate the Nehru-Liaquat Pact, impressing Indian leaders with his earnestness and sincerity.

The selection which follows emphasizes one of the major internal problems he faced—a problem, in fact, which faces every nation in one form or another. In the Western world it is usually succinctly described as that of "church and state," and in the United States today this involves such matters as public prayers in schools, or the use of public buses for private parochial school students. In Pakistan the problem today looms larger, because the concept of what an "Islamic state" is (or, indeed, what "Islamic conduct" is) still seeks expression in the modern idiom. In the West, medieval concepts of Christianity have largely been left by the wayside; in Pakistan the matter is a live political issue.

The Objective Resolutions quoted in this article were made part of the 1956 constitution; in the 1962 constitution they have been incorporated into the Fundamental Rights and Principles of Policy (Articles 6–8).

Liaquat Ali Khan [1896-1951] was the leader of the Muslim League Party in the Indian Interim Government and his appointment as Premier of Pakistan followed almost inevitably. . . . So long as the Quaid was alive, the ultimate responsibility for matters of highest national importance continued to be his, but the Prime Minister was responsible for carrying out all decisions and in most cases for taking them with the help of his Cabinet. After Quaid's death, Liaquat's responsibilities increased a hundred-fold. Although there was no change in his office, he became, by common consent, the Quaid's successor. He was Quaid's chief lieutenant during his lifetime and so he stepped into his shoes after his death, but it was not an easy task to fill the void created by the death of the father of the nation. Quaid had led the people to their goal and had, therefore, all those advantages which national heroes can command. His word was law. Nobody asked questions once he had pronounced a verdict. Liaquat took over Quaid's responsibilities without the advantages which the Quaid had. He had to work

* *Modern Muslim India and the Birth of Pakistan,* rev. ed. (Lahore, Sh. Muhd. Ashraf, 1965), pp. 329–343. By permission.

hard to display all his qualities of sound judgment and constructive statesmanship before he could earn the confidence of the people. Outside Pakistan the number of those who doubted his—and, in fact, any Pakistani's—ability to fill the void left by the Quaid was much larger. Many newspapers in England and America openly stated that with the architect's death "the house that Jinnah built" would collapse. The fact that the Quaid's death coincided with the downfall of Hyderabad greatly added to the prevailing gloom and increased Liaquat's difficulties. The way he mastered these difficulties and discharged his onerous responsibilities can be seen now by reference to the pages of the same foreign newspapers. A leftist critic, while comparing Liaquat Ali Khan with Pandit Nehru and the Quaid-i-Azam says that "although he lacks their public appeal, his abilities as an administrator and political boss are superior to either of them." "The Manchester Guardian" in a leading article summed up the position by saying about Nawab Liaquat Ali Khan, ". . . for nearly three years he has been building up his present commanding position. Courage, humanity, practical idealism, and skill in handling his political colleagues are the qualities which equipped him for his task in Pakistan. His patient work is now beginning to earn recognition from the world. He is passing from the status of national statesman to an international one. He belongs to the small group of world figures by whom international destinies are decided. *The best testimony to him is the condition of Pakistan today.*" [Italics ours]

Not only was Pakistan able to adjust herself to the death of the Quaid without any political or administrative dislocation, but under the wise statesmanship of his successor, Pakistan maintained a continuous record of progress and consolidation. Her economic strength was put to a severe test when after the devaluation of the pound, almost all countries in the sterling area devalued their currencies and only Pakistan stood out. Very few outside Pakistan thought that she would be able to maintain this attitude for long. It was felt that economic forces would prove too strong, and she would have to reconsider her decision. India, on which Pakistan depended for supply of coal and other necessities, and for sale of her major commercial crops like jute and cotton, was so put out by Pakistan's decision that she refused to recognize the new exchange rate of Pakistani rupee and a trade war started between the two dominions. . . . This economic war lasted for more than a year, and . . . involved great efforts and sacrifices on the part of Pakistan. . . . She found new markets for her produce and was similarly able to purchase elsewhere the coal and other stuff for which she depended on India. Ultimately, on 25 January, 1951, India had to accept the par value of Pakistani rupee, and the 17-month-old trade deadlock was resolved. If Pakistan attained political independence in 1947, it attained full commercial independence 3½ years later and though the two countries, in their mutual interest, resumed a well-regulated trade, Pakistan emerged stronger and economically more independent on account of the "cold war." . . .

The Quaid was very keen to raise the standard of political life in Pakistan. He had no hesitation in dismissing an all-powerful provincial Premier because allegations of maladministration and nepotism were received against him. One of the measures which he brought on the Statute Book within the first year of the inception of Pakistan was the Anti-Corruption Act and he took immediate steps to set up a machinery for enforcing the Act. Liaquat Ali Khan more than maintained Quaid's policy in this respect. At least, in the beginning, his position was not as strong as that of the Quaid in dealing with powerful politicians, who allowed serious abuses to creep into their administration. As a matter of fact, in the opinion of some shrewd observers, he did himself some damage and made powerful enemies for himself when he insisted on the Quaid's policy being followed with regard to certain politicians in the Punjab and Bengal. But it is greatly to his credit that he ignored these considerations and did his best to build up a healthy and clean political life in Pakistan.

One of the major problems with which Liaquat Ali Khan had to deal soon after the Quaid's death related to the adjustment of modernist and traditional viewpoints about the future of Pakistan. This is a problem with which all Muslim states have had to deal and their solutions have differed widely—from secularism of Turkey to extreme traditionalism of Saudi Arabia. In Pakistan the problem assumed a sharp political shape on account of the activities of Maulana Maududi and Jamaat-i-Islami, Maulana Maududi, who was at one time the editor of "Al-Jamiat," is a brilliant writer on religious subjects. Some years before the Partition he settled down at Pathankot in East Punjab, and started urging the establishment of *Hakumat-i-Ilahia* in the pages of his *Tarjaman-ul-Quran*. He took no part in the struggle for Pakistan and in fact he and his companions were generally critical of the Muslim League leadership. Massacres of East Punjab, however, forced him and his companions to seek asylum in Pakistan and he established his headquarters at Lahore. Here, he and his organization started a campaign for replacement of the Pakistan Penal Code and other statutes in operation during the British period by Islamic Law and acceptance of the view that the Constituent Assembly of Pakistan or Muslim legislature had no right to frame any constitution or initiate any laws which were not provided for in the Quran, as interpreted by qualified *ulama*. He made the following four-fold demand from the Pakistan Constituent Assembly in an interview which he gave to a representative of the *Dawn* in April, 1948:

(1) Acknowledgment of the sovereignty of God (as against the sovereignty of the people in democracy);

(2) acceptance of Shariat as the basis of the constitution;

(3) amendment of anti-Islamic laws and an assurance that no law contrary to Shariat will be enacted; and

(4) the Pakistan Government to exercise its power within the limits of Shariat.

In dealing with Maulana Maududi the Government of Pakistan—a League Government—did not allow itself to be influenced by his past attitude towards the Muslim League. In fact, shortly after Partition, Jamaat-i-Islami offered their assistance in looking after certain refugee camps and the Punjab Government gladly accepted this offer of co-operation. Maulana was more than welcome at the Radio Pakistan—a State-controlled organization—and he broadcast a number of talks from Lahore Radio Station.

Soon, however, it appeared that the extremism of Maulana would involve him in a conflict with the Government. He, for example, advised Government servants against signing a pledge demanded by the West Punjab Government, until that Government became Islamic. He also expressed the view that fighting in Kashmir, where a large number of Pathans had gone to the rescue of their Muslim brethren, was not *Jehad,* as Pakistan had treaties with India. This view was severely criticised in the press and action was taken, by the Punjab Government, to detain Maulana under Punjab Public Safety Act in October, 1948. Shortly, thereafter, the question of enunciating the principles, under which Pakistan's constitution should be framed, came before the Constituent Assembly, and Liaquat Ali Khan made it clear that though his Government did not share Maulana Maududi's views about the future of Pakistan, they were determined to give the people the constitution wanted by them. On March 7, 1949, Liaquat Ali Khan brought before the Constituent Assembly what has been known as the Objectives Resolution and delivered a long speech in explaining its provisions. In the course of the discussions that followed the Leader of the Congress Party in the Assembly stated that he had consulted "some Lahore Ulama"[1] and had been informed that a non-Muslim could not hold an office of importance in an Islamic State. Liaquat Ali Khan corrected him and stated that this would not apply to the state which they were envisaging and issued a warning, on the floor of the house, to those Lahore *ulama* who were misleading the public.

The full text of the Objectives Resolution was as follows:

> Whereas sovereignty over the entire universe belongs to God Almighty alone, and the authority which He has delegated to the State of Pakistan through its people for being exercised within the limits prescribed by Him is a sacred trust;
>
> This Constituent Assembly representing the people of Pakistan resolves to frame a constitution for the sovereign independent State of Pakistan;
>
> Wherein the State shall exercise its powers and authority through the chosen representatives of the people;
>
> Wherein the principles of democracy, freedom, equality, tolerance and social justice as enunciated by Islam shall be fully observed;
>
> Wherein the Muslims shall be enabled to order their lives in the individual and collective spheres in accord with the teaching and requirements of Islam as set out in the Holy Quran and the Sunna;
>
> Wherein adequate provision shall be made for the minorities freely to profess and practise their religions and develop their cultures;
>
> Whereby the territories now included in or in accession with Pakistan and such other territories as may hereafter be included in or accede to Pakistan shall form a Federation wherein the units will be autonomous with such boundaries and limitations on their powers and authority as may be prescribed;
>
> Wherein shall be guaranteed fundamental rights including equality of status, of opportunity before law, social, economic and political justice, and freedom of thought, expression, belief, faith, worship and association, subject to law and public morality;
>
> Wherein adequate provision shall be made to safeguard the legitimate interests of minorities and backward and depressed classes;
>
> Wherein the independence of the judiciary shall be fully secured;
>
> Wherein the integrity of the territories of the Federation, its independence and all its rights including its sovereign rights on land, sea and air shall be safeguarded;

[1] The statement was universally taken to refer to *ulama* of Jamaat-i-Islami and this has not been contradicted either by the speaker or by the Jamaat.

So that the people of Pakistan may prosper and attain their rightful and honoured place amongst the nations of the world and make their full contribution towards international peace and progress and happiness of humanity.

The Objectives Resolution is a brief document, but its significance is realized if its background and the acute controversies it successfully resolved are taken into consideration. The basic stand of the Jamaat-i-Islami which had carried on most active propaganda in favour of an Islamic State, but . . . had not joined the struggle for establishment of Pakistan, was that sovereignty (including the law-making power) belongs to God alone and the legislature (or rather, the *ulama*) can only interpret what have been revealed as Divine Ordinances. This would have left no law-making power with the legislature, and completely diluted its authority. The Objectives Resolution attempted to reconcile the conflicting view-points by affirming that the "sovereignty over the entire Universe belongs to Allah Almighty alone" but followed it up by referring to "the sovereign independent state of Pakistan" and stipulated that the authority "within the limits prescribed by Him" was to be exercised by the people of Pakistan. Limitations on the power of legislature were few. They related to the future alone, and excluded only those laws which were definitely "repugnant to Quran and Sunnah." This left a vast field, in fact, the main field of modern legislative activity, to be operated in accordance with the traditions and requirements of the Muslim community and according to sound, healthy principles of Islamic law, under the sovereign authority of legislature.

One demand of Jamaat-i-Islamii was that Pakistan should formally declare itself to be an Islamic state. The Objectives Resolution did not provide this, but the only clause added in 1956 to the Objectives Resolution of 1949 and retained in the preamble to the constitution of 1962, laid down that "Pakistan would be a democratic State based on Islamic principles of social justice."

The other important demand on behalf of the group advocating an Islamic State was that the Muslims of Pakistan should be *compelled* to live in accordance with the teachings of the Quran and the Sunnah. The relevant provision in the Objectives Resolution was that the "Muslims of Pakistan should be enabled individually and collectively to order their lives in accordance with the teachings of Islam as set out in the Holy Quran and the Sunnah." The significance of the omission of an expression incorporating the idea of "compulsion" and selection of the word "enabled" can be realized, if it is recalled that Maulana Shabbir Ahmad Usmani, the leader of the theologians was a member of the Sub-Committee, which drafted the Objectives Resolution, and co-piloted it along with the Prime Minister, in the Constituent Assembly. The entire approach of the Objective Resolution was that while Pakistan should be a progressive, modern state and not a theocratic, medieval government like the former Saudi Arabia or Yemen, yet every attempt should be made to translate the people's dream of an Islamic social order into action. The Constitution of 1956, and following it the Constitution of 1962 maintained the same approach. The idea of "compulsion" in the fields normally left out of the purview of a modern state was not incorporated but elaborate provision was made through directive principles not only for "enabling" the people to order their lives in accordance with the Quran and Sunnah but also for their Islamic education and for propagation of Islamic values.

At least, some Western scholars have grasped the historic importance of the Objectives Resolution. For example, Professor Grunebaum, after reproducing the Resolution *in extenso* (and referring to some provisions of the constitution of Pakistan) remarks, "It would seem to me that on the theoretical level at least, as good an integration of traditional and Western ideas has been reached in this document as one might reasonably expect," and later, he adds that "the attempted bridging of the gap between the Muslim tradition and the Western-inspired idea of the nation-state deserves the greatest attention."

If the balanced and comprehensive approach to the ideological problem which Liaquat Ali Khan had been advocating succeeds and can be worked out in detail by scholars and thinkers, he would have rendered a great service not only to Pakistan but to many other Muslim countries which are faced with the same problem. . . . If it is to be achieved, Pakistan will have to produce another Iqbal —or at least somebody, who working on the foundations already laid by Shah Waliullah, Amir Ali and Iqbal can attempt a new synthesis. This may or may not be possible in the near future, but at any rate Liaquat Ali Khan deserves credit for having maintained a sane and balanced stand—in spite of criticism from those who do not fully realise the implications of Maulana Maududi's original viewpoint. . . .

Under Liaquat's leadership, Pakistan was able to belie the forebodings of those who thought that with Jinnah's death "the house that Jinnah built" will collapse. He consolidated the foundations and began to build up the new edifice. With his charm, intelligence and good sense he impressed all those who came in contact with him and was able to raise the prestige of the country. In March 1950 he toured U.S.A. at the invitation of the government and favourably impressed those he met. Internationally, he was thought a worthy successor of the Quaid-i-Azam. It would, however, be idle to pretend that he possessed the Quaid's authority. He maintained his position more as an arbitrator than as a leader, and met with one or two serious reverses. His dismissal of Mamdot Government displeased many who had faced and brought to knees the Unionist regime in 1947. The Governor-General Khwaja Nazim-ud-Din condemned the Punjab government in strong language, echoing the thoughts and style of Sir Francis Mudie. The fact that Khan of Mamdot was ultimately exonerated strengthened the feeling that he had not received a fair deal, and even Liaquat found it necessary to curb the autocracy of the British Governor. He suggested the appointment of Advisers, in the absence of a Council of Ministers, and considering that after the resignation of the Congress ministers during the War, even the British authorities had appointed Advisers to assist the provincial Governors, the step taken by Liaquat was fully justified. Mudie, however, resisted and Liaquat allowed him to resign and leave. The decision of Liaquat's government to accept the cease-fire in Kashmir at the time it did—"to the army's horror"—has also been criticised. Perhaps a final judgment on this question cannot be passed, till more data is available and all considerations underlying this fateful decision are known. A development which must have caused Liaquat great personal disappointment and which led to delay in the country's progress on the constitutional road was the successful resistance to the Interim Report of the Basic Principles Committee which he submitted to the Constituent Assembly in September, 1950. There was such widespread opposition to these proposals that they had to be withdrawn. This was the low ebb of Liaquat's political career, but there is no doubt that he would have, in course of time, found a solution. Unluckily he was not spared long for the purpose; on 16 October 1951, he fell a martyr to the bullet of an assassin. His death was a staggering blow to Pakistan, and the ship of the new state entered troubled waters, but by then its seaworthiness had been established.

71 • Mohammad Ayub Khan: *Pakistan Perspective* *

In this excerpt President Ayub Muhammad Khan quite clearly expresses his belief in democracy, and his concept of the kind of democracy that will work in Pakistan—an outline of the Basic Democracy scheme (first suggested after World War I by a British colonial officer) which is now operating. It should be noted that President Ayub was forced to surrender his stand against the formation of political parties, as he had earlier been forced to surrender his stand in opposition to democracy in Pakistan. One should also remember that this was written to publicize a particular point of view, and to try to persuade the Western world, specifically, the United States, that it is not only our duty to give financial support to the developing countries, but that this support is necessary for the welfare of the United States itself.

I am not sure if the peculiar strains which confronted Pakistan immediately on its emergence as a free state are adequately understood.

The first strain was ideological. It is a common fallacy to believe that the concept of Pakistan was formed in a poet's dream. The poet, Dr. Muhammad Iqbal, was no idle dreamer. Nor can countries like Pakistan (364,737 square miles; population 80,000,000) spring from the nebulous realm of poetry alone. Iqbal was in fact a philosopher of traditional as well as modern thought who had made a careful study of human affairs, both East and West, and focussed the light of his inquiry on the causes of economic and cultural subjugation to which the Muslims of India had been systematically subjected since their first abortive struggle for independence in 1857. It was in his presidential address to the annual session of All-India Muslim League in 1930 that he spelt out the broad outlines of a plan under which the Muslims of India were led to aspire to an independent state in which they would be free to follow their own way of life.

The All-India Muslim League based its Charter on this idea and, under the leadership of Quaid-i-Azam Mahomed Ali Jinnah, launched a struggle which culminated in the establishment of Pakistan in August 1947.

Iqbal's thesis that in their free state the Muslims were to practice their own way of life posed an ideological problem which was not easy to handle. On the one hand, there were many outside Pakistan who charged us with planning to establish an obdurate theocracy in the mediæval sense of the term. On the other, most of us within Pakistan itself were not quite clear how to go about welding our spiritual ideals into the business of statecraft. The result was a great deal of loose groping which infected our politics and our intellect alike.

* Excerpted by special permission from *Foreign Affairs,* Vol. 38, No. 4 (July 1960), pp. 547–556. Copyright by the Council on Foreign Relations, Inc., New York.

Pakistan was thus involved in the paradox of almost losing its ideology in the very act of trying to fulfill it. This distraction was totally unwarranted, for Iqbal, one of the main creators of our ideology, had taken pains to define it in very clear terms:

> In Islam the spiritual and the temporal are not two distinct domains and the nature of an act, however, secular in its import, is determined by the attitude of mind with which the agent does it. It is the invisible mental background of the act which ultimately determines its character. An act is temporal or profane if it is done in a spirit of detachment from the infinite complexity of life behind it. It is spiritual if it is inspired by that complexity. In Islam it is the same reality which appears as Church looked at from one point of view and State from another.

According to this concept, the State owes a singular and specific duty to it people. "The essence of Tauhid (Unity of God) as a working idea is equality, solidity and freedom," according to Iqbal. "The State from the Islamic standpoint is an endeavor to transform these ideals into space-time forces, an aspiration to realize them in a definite human organization."

It is this sort of human organization which Pakistan aspires to become and one of my endeavors is to clear at least a part of the way by liberating the basic concept of our ideology from the dust of vagueness and ambiguities it has accumulated over the years.

The second strain which befell Pakistan immediately its emergence was economic. Besides more than 9,000,000 refugees who poured over the border in a state of appalling terror and distress, food fell desperately short owing to hundreds of thousands of acres of land going out of use every year on account of salinity and water-logging, a menace which still continues unabated. As much as 10,000,000 acres of good fertile land have already fallen out of cultivation on this account. Moreover, successive governments were unable to control the situation adequately, and large-scale organized smuggling, currency rackets, black-marketing and increasingly plastic standards of honesty and efficiency brought the affairs of the country to the verge of total ruin.

The third strain—which is a continuous one—is geographical. Divided into two wings (West Pakistan: 310,236 square miles, population 38,779,000; East Pakistan: 54,501 square miles, population 42,063,000), there are over 1,000 miles of India in-between without any assured means of land communications. Air travel is heavily subsidized but still too expensive for most people. The sea link involves a journey of about seven days. There is diversity of languages, scripts and social customs. By the very nature of things, these factors are centrifugal and call for a new and bold experiment with political and administrative science to weave unity out of diversity. The situation is often difficult but not baffling, for a common ideology provides a positive base for cohesion. The firmness of this base is strong or weak accordingly as that ideology is understood and practiced rightly or wrongly.

Finally, there is the emotional factor. Till the advent of Pakistan, none of us was in fact a Pakistani, for the simple reason that there was no territorial entity bearing that name. Actually, the boundaries of Pakistan were still being drawn and re-drawn secretly in the Viceregal Lodge at New Delhi when independence was proclaimed. Never had the destiny of so many millions depended so helplessly on the arbitrary strokes of one man's pencil. It was because Mr. Radcliffe happened to make a small dent on the wrong side of the line that over 4,000,000 inhabitants of Jammu and Kashmir have been locked in a life-and-death struggle for self-determination for 13 long and dreadful years.

So, prior to 1947, our nationalism was based more on an idea than on any territorial definition. Till then, ideologically we were Muslims; territorially we happened to be Indians; and parochially we were a conglomeration of at least eleven smaller, provincial loyalties. But when suddenly Pakistan emerged as a reality, we who had got together from every nook and corner of the vast subcontinent were faced with the task of transforming all our traditional, territorial and parochial loyalties into one great loyalty for the new state of Pakistan. This process of metamorphism was naturally attended by difficult psychological and emotional strains which we have borne in full measure—and are still bearing.

Under normal circumstances, it would have required most extraordinary efforts by the best of governments to cope with the problems which have been confronting us. But unfortunately neither have our circumstances been normal, nor did we have good strong governments; and they did not make even ordinary efforts to resolve the problems in front of them.

The founder of Pakistan, Quaid-i-Azam Mahomed Ali Jinnah, was already a sick man on the eve of his triumph. He died within about a year. His Prime Minister, Liaquat Ali Khan, who had been closest to him during the struggle for independence, fell to an assassin's bullet in 1951. This created a vacuum in top leadership; and in smaller hands party politics became a mad scramble for power. Government after government rose and fell and within a period of five years six Prime Ministers presided over precariously balanced cabinets. The real and pressing problems of the country were ignored in this hide and seek for power.

It is now the fashion to blame the politicians outright for this mess. Yes, they were guilty of many misdeeds of omission and commission; but there is one fundamental point in which, I have a feeling, they were rather sinned against than sinning. That is, they were given a system of government totally unsuited to the temper and climate of the country.

The British parliamentary system which we inherited and later adopted in the Constitution of 1956 is largely an unwritten law and takes for granted too many prerequisites which do not really exist in a country like Pakistan. Our rate of literacy is appallingly low. Our means of communication are poor, even primitive. The rural population which constitutes over 80 per cent of the total is hardly touched by the world outside the villages.

Just before independence, when Mr. Jinnah was anxious to put more and more of his party men in the Central and Provincial Assemblies of India to carry on the struggle for the idea of Pakistan, he issued an appeal: "Vote for a Muslim Leaguer even if it be a lamp-post." People complied cheerfully; some even literally! When independence came, the gentlemen thus elected found themselves in a position of vantage to assume power in the new state of Pakistan, and the political system in their hands enabled them to keep delaying the making of a constitution for about eight years. The outgoing Parliament of Pakistan had 80 seats, each member presuming to represent about a million of his countrymen for almost an indefinite period. Even under the Constitution of 1956, a member of the Provincial Assembly was required to be elected by more than 100,000 voters. Now this is the type of electoral college which just cannot work in Pakistan—or for that matter in any country where conditions like those of Pakistan obtain, as they do in many newly independent countries of Asia and Africa. An average villager with little or no education has no means of gaining any personal knowledge about a candidate who is mixed up in a population of 100,000 or more, spread over a large area without any advanced means of communication and contact. Votes cast under these circumstances cannot but be vague, wanton and responsive to fear, coercion, temptation and other modes of misguidance. This is exactly what had been happening in Pakistan. Whenever elections were held, they could be easily manipulated to return candidates with power to influence, money to bribe and nuisance value to coerce. Conditions such as these reduce the practice of democracy to a farce.

But this does not dismay us. Nor should it be taken to imply that we can do—or wish to do—without democracy. The revolution of October 7, 1958, was not aimed against the institution of democracy as such. No, it was only against the manner in which its institutions were being worked. There are two main reasons why we in Pakistan cannot but adhere to a democratic pattern of life and government. In the first place, as Muslims, we are brought up on two basic ingredients of democracy, namely, equality and fraternity. Anything to the contrary would be the negation of our spiritual faith and practice. And, secondly, we have to fight a long and arduous battle for progress and development in which every man, woman and child of Pakistan must participate to the fullest possible extent. Democracy provides the only healthy and dignified way for arousing the willing cooperation of people and harnessing it to a sustained national endeavor.

We must, therefore, have democracy. The question then is: What type of democracy? The answer need not be sought in the theories and practices of other people alone. On the contrary, it must be found from within the book of Pakistan itself.

To my mind, there are four prerequisites for the success of any democratic system in a country like Pakistan:

1. It should be simple to understand, easy to work and cheap to sustain.
2. It should put to the voter only such questions as he can answer in the light of his own personal knowledge and understanding without external prompting.
3. It should ensure the effective participation of all citizens in the affairs of the country up to the level of their mental horizon and intellectual calibre.
4. It should be able to produce reasonably strong and stable governments.

The scheme of "basic democracies" which has been launched in Pakistan is designed to meet most of these fundamental prerequisites. Under this scheme, the two wings of the country have each been divided into 40,000 constituencies with an average population of about 1,000. Every constituency elects one representative by universal franchise. In such a small and well-defined field of choice, voters of the meanest intelligence cannot go far wrong in putting their finger on the right type of candidate.

Ten such constituencies form a Union Council in the rural areas, and this elects its own chairman from amongst the elected members. Provision has also been made for nominated members to ensure, where necessary, the representation of special interests, like women, minorities, etc. In towns and larger municipalities organization follows a similar pattern.

The elected chairmen of Union Councils and Town Committees represent their areas on the next tier of administration, namely, the Thana Council, which covers the entire area under the jurisdiction of a Police Station. From this stage, this system of associating the chosen representatives of the people with local administration travels upwards covering all intermediary tiers, like tehsils, districts and divisions, up to the provincial level. This is designed to ensure a full sense of cooperation between the official and elected agencies at all stages of public administration.

The first elections to basic democracies were held last December and I feel the results were quite heartening. The average percentage of votes cast was 67 per cent by men and 42 per cent by women. Those elected included 14 per cent university graduates, 78 per cent literate and 8 per cent illiterate members. They came from the real hard core of the country, the majority of them being middle-class and lower middle-class agriculturists, lawyers, medical practitioners, businessmen, retired government servants, workers and artisans.

One great lesson which these elections brought out was that, for the first time in Pakistan, it seemed possible for an average citizen to seek election purely on his or her personal merit without the help of any financial, social or political backing. Also for the first time, the elected candidate finds himself in a position to participate effectively and directly in the affairs of the country as they exist immediately around him.

The Union Councils and Town Committees have been given a wide charter of duties and responsibilities ranging from local self-government to national reconstruction and development. Besides this, I am looking to this gigantic instrument of mass representation to achieve three other pressing objectives. First, to help throw up a fresh supply of local and national leaders. Second, to serve as a two-way traffic post between the government and the basic core of the people and to bridge the gulf which under the best of systems is bound to exist between them in countries where education is limited, distances are large and modern facilities for reaching the masses are not universal. And, third, I would personally like this body of 80,000 elected representatives to serve as the electoral college for the Parliament and, possibly, for the President. This is only my personal view, for I do not wish to pre-judge the recommendations of the Constitution Commission which is at the moment seized of this and other allied problems.

The Constitution Commission of Pakistan, consisting of eminent judges, lawyers and other interests, was set up in February this year and has been entrusted with the following terms of reference:

> To examine the progressive failure of the parliamentary government in Pakistan leading to the abrogation of the Constitution of 1956 and to determine the causes and the nature of the failure;
>
> To consider how best the said or like causes may be identified and their recurrence prevented;
>
> And, having further taken account of the genius of the people, the general standard of education and of political judgment in the country, the present state of a sense of nationhood, the prime need for sustained development, and the effect of the constitutional and administrative changes brought into being in recent months, to submit constitutional proposals in the form of a report advising how best the following ends may be secured: a democracy adaptable to changing circumstances and based on the Islamic principles of justice, equality and tolerance; the consolidation of national unity; and a firm and stable system of government.

I trust that toward the end of this year we shall be in a position to determine the broad shape of our future constitutional pattern. I would like to move as fast as possible, but there are many in our country who look askance at this haste. Some of them fear that politicians may return and mess things up once again. Others suspect that reforms and innovations introduced under the Martial Law may backslide and that the development program may slow down with the return of normal conditions.

These misgivings are understandable, but I do not feel they are well-founded. The former politicians are no problem to us now or in the near future. We have taken good care to spare them the usual tragic fate of those overtaken by revolutionary upheavals. On the contrary, we are content to treat them as a big joke, just as they turned a perfectly sound country into the laughing-stock of the whole world. When they are confronted with skeletons collected from their cupboards, most of them wisely prefer to retire from public life for five to six years rather than face the risk of open trial. This saves a lot of dirty linen from being washed publicly, and decent folk prefer this quiet exit of errant politicians.

As regards the suspicion that the return of constitutional rule might undo or retard the progress of reforms launched under the Martial Law, this again is an unreal fear. These reforms were long overdue and have been fully and unequivocally acclaimed by the people. No future government dare retard or obstruct them. The only prerequisite is that the government should be strong enough to resist the pressure of vested interests which have been hit hard by some of the reforms. This, I am positive, the new Constitution must ensure.

Moreover, when circumstances such as our revolution concentrate power in the hands of one person, it is his bounden duty to pass that power on to a more broadly based system without avoidable delay. Individuals are fallible; but institutions stay. That is why I am in such a hurry to ensure the induction of a suitable constitutional system without any loss of time.

While the Constitution is still in the making, there is time to complete the reforms already in hand or give a start to those which are still under contemplation. The meaning of all this activity is to prepare the ground for the growth of a happy and healthy life which, after all, is the end-product of all human endeavor.

An archaic type of feudalism which existed in Pakistan—particularly West Pakistan—had vested the entire political, economic and social might of the country in a limited group of families. It was impossible to make any advance in any direction without first breaking this monopoly of power. Therefore, land reform was one of the first measures to be taken by the new regime. This was a major operation but it was performed peacefully and scientifically and was attended by no manner of tyranny or injustice. This is a far-reaching socio-economic change and its full impact will be felt only with the passage of time.

Other fields in which reforms have been undertaken include education, public health, fiscal systems, law courts, civil administration and the rehabilitation of refugees. The object is to get us to the starting point of development, whence we may be better able to grapple with some of the most pressing and immediate of our problems. These are: fighting the grave menace to the land of salinity and water-logging; curbing the excessive rate of growth of population; and launching the next Five Year Plan for national development, estimated to cost over 19,000,000,000 rupees (about $4,000,000,000). According to experts, these figures are not astronomical but only reasonable.

The next 15 to 20 years are going to be most crucial for Pakistan. Either we "make the grade" in this period or we do not. If we fail to make the grade, we are bound to be submerged under the tidal wave of Communism which is constantly lashing its fury all around us. Since we do not seek this fate we must move forward, and do so quickly. It is here that our eyes turn towards our friends and allies. They have already given us magnanimous aid, for which we are most grateful. But there are reasons of history which entitle us to claim still more.

During the last 20 years or so the area which is now Pakistan was subjected to foreign rule. This stunted our growth immeasurably and all this long period of time was lost to us for preparing ourselves to move with the modern scientific times. We have now to catch up with the fast-moving world—and this will require extraordinary endeavor as well as expenditure.

It was during the period of imperial rule that the British industrial development started and gained momentum with resources which to a large extent were taken from the colonial areas. The British industrial development in a way gave a fillip to the American industrial development. It is common knowledge that up to the Second World War, Britain had enormous investments in both the Americas. Most of the progress in the Commonwealth countries and Dominions was also stimulated by the British industrial development. So far as the area now forming Pakistan is concerned, its manpower was generally employed to man the British Armies to maintain and protect the Empire. For this reason, this part of the Indo-Pakistan sub-continent was purposely kept industrially backward so that the populace would not be diverted into other channels of employment.

Moreover, in the context of present-day world politics Pakistan has openly and unequivocally cast its lot with the West, and unlike several other countries around us, we have shut ourselves off almost completely from the possibility of any major assistance from the Communist bloc. We do not believe in hunting with the hound and running with the hare. We wish to follow, and are following, a clear and unambiguous path.

All these factors lead to one conclusion: that the English-speaking world ought to feel a special responsibility to assist Pakistan in attaining a reasonable posture of advancement. It is not just a claim. It is in fact the dictate of history.

SECTION FOUR

Parties, Factions, and Interest Groups

72 • MUSHTAQ AHMAD: *Political Parties* *

The political system in Pakistan is marked neither by one-party rule, as is the case in many developing nations, nor by the domination of one party, as has been the case in India. Indeed, the Muslim League, which in 1947 approximated in Pakistan the status of the Congress party in India, has itself split up into government (Conventionist Muslim League or Muslim League Pakistan) and anti-government (Council Muslim League) factions.

Pakistan's problems are too great to lend themselves to easy solutions, and dissident elements are always to be found. The strength of the initial Muslim League was largely urban, but the Pakistan it achieved was largely rural. This already apparent urban-rural dichotomy was complicated by the tremendous rush of refugees who swept into the country after partition, and who had claims for land on the one hand and shops and homes on the other. Thus they added to the problems of both the landlords and the government. Dissidents appeared in East Pakistan for a variety of reasons—primarily linguistic and economic. There was objection to the government's proposal to treat only Urdu as the national language and thus ignore Bengali, and to the government's financing of West Pakistan development from the income of East Pakistan's jute and tea. In 1954 a coalition of dissident groups in East Pakistan, known as the United Front, swept the Muslim League from power in that wing of the country. Ten years later an anti-government coalition was formed that reached across both wings: the Council Muslim League, the Awami League, the National Awami party, the Jama'at-i-Islami, and the Nizam-i-Islami party all joined to form the Combined Opposition parties. This coalition advanced Miss Fatima Jinnah, sister of Muhammad Ali Jinnah, as its presidential candidate in the 1964 elections.

In time, something like a responsible opposition could conceivably develop out of the Combined Opposition parties which polled about a third of

* *Government and Politics in Pakistan,* 2nd ed. (Karachi: Pakistan Publishing House, 1963), pp. 281–286. By permission.

the votes in the election. But for this to take place it will be necessary for the Ayub-led government to make some concessions to its political opponents. So far, there has been no evidence that this will happen.

Constitutions are not a panacea for the ills of the country, for even the best Constitution can fail if it is not properly worked. What went wrong with Pakistan democracy was not the character of the 1956 Constitution or the parliamentary system; it was the failure of the unwritten constitution, namely, the political parties without which written constitutions tend to wither away. Being the life-blood of democracy their return was a question of time in spite of the anti-party bias of the new Constitution. Throwing the parties out was like throwing the baby out with the bath water. Legislation was required for their restoration due to the legal restrictions that had been imposed on their revival and not because they could acquire a special sanctity or status through legislative recognition. Even the President, who was opposed to the revival of parties, on the ground that the lifting of the ban would result in a mushroom growth, recognised their necessity soon after the Assembly was convened. The Presidential system introduced by him could itself operate as a check to the multiplication of the parties as the Presidential executive, unlike the parliamentary executive, cannot be shared by more than one party. But now that the ministerial positions have been thrown open to the members of the National Assembly, the multiplicity of parties for which the old system was discredited, might become a feature of the new order also.

The parliamentary parties, both in the Government and in the Opposition are admittedly coalitions which, like all coalitions, carry within them the seeds of their dissolution. Neither the Conventionist Muslim League nor the Opposition, consisting of Councillors' Muslim League and the Pak People's groups, are political parties in the real sense, although each of them has created a machinery for organisation outside the Assembly. Nor can it be predicted with any assurance that other parties, not represented in the House so far, will not soon make their appearance with a considerable following and equal or probably more popular support.

The Conventionist Muslim League is a party behind the power rather than a party in power. The initiative in calling a Convention of the Muslim Leaguers held at Karachi in September, 1962, was taken by the Ministers who were closely associated with its proceedings and decisions. By the fact of being a pro-Government party it is also a pro-Constitution party, staunchly in favour of the Presidential system and its plea for making fundamental rights justiciable did not qualify that support. There was no place in its counsels for politicians disqualified under EBDO, even for Khan Abdul Qayyum Khan who was President of the League before the imposition of the ban on the party. Mr. Daultana and Mr. Khuhro did not attend the Convention and Mr. Nurul Amin had joined hands with other leaders of East Pakistan who were opposed to the Constitution. That Messrs Daultana and Khuhro are big landlords of West Pakistan with claims to the leadership of the landed aristocracy does not mean that the Conventionists are a party of peasants or that they do not rely upon the feudal class in the Province. Most of the members of the National Assembly from West Pakistan are landlords and the great majority of them are sitting on the

Treasury Benches. The industrialists have always been on the side of the government for obvious reasons, and the Conventionists can count on their support in a much greater degree now to finance their organisation. Chaudhri Khaliquzzaman, the Chief Organiser of the Convention, was virtually a nominee of the forces behind the Convention. With age he had not risen in stature, as whatever claim to leadership he had was thoroughly exposed when he was forced to resign the presidentship of the Muslim League in 1951 and to retire from active politics. That the Convention was described as a Muslim Leaguers' Convention and not Muslim League Convention was not wholly ascribable to any legal hitch about the revival of the party, since other parties like the Nizam-e-Islam and the Jamaat-e-Islam had already revived themselves without encountering the charge of illegality. The object was to forestall other Leaguers from using the Council of the organisation as a platform to rehabilitate the League through their efforts.

The Council Meeting in Dacca was more representative of League opinion than the Convention, as it included a large number of porminent League politicians. The election of Khwaja Nazimuddin as the President of the organisation was significant as he was among the few politicians who had an untarnished reputation for honesty and integrity and who had paid a high price for it in being thrown out of office by scheming bureaucrats and intriguing politicians. To bring him out of nearly a decade of retirement was to demonstrate a new determination to uphold the cause of democracy which had suffered at the League's own hands. Democratisation of the Constitution, through the restoration of full powers to the National Assembly, introduction of adult franchise and justiciability of fundamental rights, was the burden of the speeches made at the meeting and the resolutions adopted by it. The organisation was not in a hurry to capture office and was will to bide its time till the next election. After his election Khwaja Nazimuddin declared:

> As long as I remain President of the Muslim League, the party will not be interested in joining the present Government because I feel under the Constitution it is not possible to give effect to all the policies enunciated in the Muslim League resolutions.

The attitudes of the Council and the Convention towards the Constitution and the Government were well defined and there could be no question of rapprochement between them. The Convention could not absorb the Council and was not willing to be absorbed by it. The result was the emergence of two League groups in the National Assembly, one sitting on the Treasury Benches and the other occupying the Opposition Benches. The Council in fact has more in common, as far as political issues are concerned, with the National Democratic Front which consists of various other organizations excluding the Conventionist League, and with which it was ready to associate itself on specific demands to democratise the Constitution.

[*Combined Opposition Parties*]

The National Democratic Front, as its very name suggests, has not even the pretensions of being a political party. Its object is to mobilise support of organisations and individuals behind the demand for the amendment of the

Constitution. Explaining the reasons for his association with his political opponents, the leader of the Front, Mr. Suhrawardy, said:

> We are not working on a party level but we are all united for the cause of democratisation of the Constitution and realisation of a fuller democracy in the country.

Since the demand has been made from many quarters, a collective agitation is deemed to be more effective and at the same time politically more convenient as it holds in abeyance the underlying conflict of interest and attitudes among the politicians. For the EBDOed politicians of different political parties, it provides a common ground to settle their scores with the forces at whose hands all of them feel they have equally suffered. The NDF has its main backing in East Pakistan which had also witnessed the formation of a United Front in the past. Ironically enough the very leaders who formed the Front then and also dissolved it, have once again combined and the Chief Minister of the Province ousted by them in the election of 1954 is also with them. The KSP, the Awami League and the National Awami Party have once again united to launch a campaign against the Constitution, this time with a wider base in which the parties of West Pakistan including the Muslim League (Councillors) and the Jamaat-e-Islami are represented.

The political climate in the post-Martial Law period is not very different from the situation obtaining in August 1955 when constitutional government was restored. In a sense it is more disturbing. The 1956-Constitution, though adopted by the Constitutent Assembly, was not accepted by the Opposition. The Awami League members had not signed it. The new Constitution, framed by the President has the support of the majority in the National Assembly, consisting of the Muslim League (Convention), but not of the Opposition. Within their own ranks the Constitutionalists and the Oppositionists are divided, the alignment of forces being guided by provincial and power considerations rather than economic and social issues.

Provincialism is still an article of faith for the politicians and parties and determines their attitudes in a much greater degree than ever before. The debates in the National Assembly were dominated by provincial demands not only in respect of economic resources and share in administrative services but also in the matter of defence. The demands have their justification but they could hardly be the main raw material for the debate in the National Assembly.

Religion, which was exploited by the parties in the past is still their stock-in-trade. Instead of being looked upon as a moral and cohesive force, it is used as a device to divert the attention of the masses from the central problem of politics. Just as the Ulema have not desisted from dabbling in politics, the politicians consider religion a convenient substitute for a programme and every party, at any rate in West Pakistan, exploits it to its advantage, cold-shouldering the intelligentsia which none of them care to cultivate.

Only in East Pakistan is the intelligentsia actively associated with politics. East Pakistan, it was shrewdly observed by Burton Marshall, was all politics and West Pakistan all government. The politics of the former was a reaction against the government of the latter, precluding the marriage of the two which was essential for the smooth working of the democratic process. East Pakistan is socially egalitarian; its economy is characterised by a sharing of poverty.

West Pakistan is socially stratified, distinguished by extremes of wealth and want with little desire on the part of the wealthy to share their riches with the multitude. The pattern of inequality inherited from its feudal past was further consolidated by the rise of a new industrial oligarchy. As between the leadership of the two provinces there was no permanent meeting ground, their relationship was marred by continuous tensions which compromises could only assuage but could never eliminate so long as economic disparities between the two provinces persisted and inequalities within the Province of West Pakistan showed no signs of abatement.

With diverse problems of geography, politics and economics, the country needed leaders capable of transcending the provincial barriers to a higher plane of nationalism. Such a leadership was provided by the Quaid-e-Azam and to a lesser extent by Liaquat Ali Khan. After them, a leader of national stature did not make his appearance. The field of politics was occupied by men of no national consequence either because they had no gift for leadership or because they were provincial in outlook. Khwaja Nazimuddin, Chaudhri Khaliquzzaman and Suhrawardy belong to the old generation of leaders. The first two are spent forces and the third is ineffective without his lieutenants who control the organisation.

The emerging pattern of politics is just a picture of the past. Too much dependence on leadership that was discredited but not wholly disowned and too little concern for organisations continues to be the bane of political parties. With their limited regional and provincial appeal and personal loyalties, neither the legislatures nor the executive can acquire a fully national and democratic character. The Presidential system, under which the Presidential Cabinet is part of the Parliament, will encourage the multiplicity of political parties, making the candidate to the Presidency a nominee not of one national party but of a combination of several parties acting as an electoral alliance. The future President will, therefore, have to be a compromise man whose political strength will be unequal to his constitutional powers. This precisely is the predicament of President Ayub Khan.

73 • SALMA OMER: *Basic Democracies and Effective Rural Leadership* *

This selection, taken from a handbook prepared for village AID workers in Pakistan, describes the potential of the Basic Democracies Program in terms of creating an effective political grouping. The 1964 and 1965 elections seem to show that at present the Basic Democrats "vote for the government," but the one-third vote Miss Jinnah received indicates this might not always be so.

Salma Omer is the Director of Village AID and Technical Advisor (Development) to the Government of Pakistan Ministry of Health, Labor, and Social Welfare (National Development Organization).

* S. N. Rizui, ed., *Reader in Basic Democracies* (West Pakistan Academy for Village Development, n.d.), pp. 27–38. By permission.

The creation of Basic Democracies has ushered in a new era and infused a new spirit into the apparently calm and quiet life of the thousands of villages of Pakistan. A cursory analysis of the Basic Democracies system brings into prominence two factors hitherto practically unknown to the political structure of Pakistan. The first is the election of one representative from amongst 1,000 people and the other, the harmonious blending of official and non-official elements in running the affairs of tahsil, the district and the division.

Restricted Constituency

The very fact that one representative is chosen from 1,000 people is an assurance that only those persons will be elected who are known to the community as honest, God-fearing individuals who have the interest of the community at heart. The above statement does not envisage a Utopia where everything is done in a perfect manner and where there is no room for human follies. It does not mean that people will always select the best persons and the influence of the wealthy, the traditional leaders and the social pressures will be a thing of the past. We wish to emphasize, however, that this system of electing one person out of 1,000 minimizes to a very great extent the election of wrong people who have vested interests. Re-election of persons who have not been able to win the confidence of the people will be extremely difficult. It is also hoped that as the people's awareness increases due to the working of the Basic Democracies, the influence of educational and land reforms and the impact of the Village AID movement, they will become more conscious of their votes and the moral and social responsibility that they have in voting for the right person.

Blending of Official and Elected Representatives

Another distinguishing feature of Basic Democracies is the happy blending of official and non-official elements. This statement may warrant a lot of criticism and may bring a sarcastic smile to the lips of those champions of democracy, who believe that this very idea is a negation of democracy and all its stands for. In this paper, we do not propose to indulge in an argument of what democracy is, what it connotes and what machinery it needs for free and easy functioning. All that we wish to convey is that the creators of this system have not tried to deceive anybody at home or abroad. The President has announced in clear words that those who are looking for a pure democracy (I am sure this word connotes so many things to so many people) may not find it here. All that he wants for this country is a system which the people can *understand and work*. Thus, keeping this important objective in mind, the Basic Democracies system was evolved.

Historical Analysis

It may be borne in mind that the two very powerful media of communication, the radio and newspapers, are hardly known in the small hamlets and villages of Pakistan in which 85% of our people live. The horrifyingly low percentage of literacy and the break-down of the pre-British village from a cultural, religious, educational and economic unit to a mere concentration of people absorbed in making two ends meet, is not at all conducive to political awareness and consciousness. It was from this 85% population that the 60,000 elected members were to be chosen. It cannot be expected that all the elected members would be politically conscious of their duties, educated and literate enough to administer the functions of local government, with horizons broad enough to comprehend the inter-relation and working of the nation building departments and the repercussions that one particular development scheme can have on others.

Let us look at the other side of the picture. Our literate population is about 18% and they are concentrated in urban areas. Historically, the Muslims were the hardest hit by the British supremacy of undivided India. Their prestige was hurt on the one hand, while on the other hand, because they were the rulers of India, and made several efforts, led by Siraj-ud-Daula, Hyder Ali and Tippu Sultan, to throw off the yoke of the Britishers, they were ruthlessly suppressed and curbed. The last national attempt in 1857 met with a terrific disaster and the Muslims were so shaken and despised by their white rulers that it became almost impossible for them to keep abreast of new developments. The Muslims after 1857, in a way, completely cut themselves off from the political, educational and cultural scene of India and their sense of frustration created a complex in them.

This state of affairs continued till Sir Syed Ahmad Khan came on the scene in the nineteenth century. In the meanwhile, the Hindus had made great strides, specially in the field of education, while the Muslim were still gloating over their past glory completely oblivious of the modern trends of the country.

Sir Syed Ahmad and his able followers—Mohsen-ul-Mulk, Hali, Shibli, Nazeer Ahmad—considered education their first and foremost objective. They infused a new spirit in the Muslim community which resulted in a large number of Muslims getting education in the English language and ultimately joining government service. Government service was the goal that every educated Muslim aspired to, as it brought financial gain as well as prestige, status and much needed security.

In other words, a very large number of the 18% literate or educated people are employed in government service. Even if we were to dispel the argument that in a free and independent Pakistan there should be no gulf dividing the official and non-official, that they should be willing to work hand in hand, the above argument is enough justification for associating government officials with Basic Democracies.

The past 11 years before the present revolution are an eloquent testimony to the fact that the country could not throw up capable, efficient, sincere and honest public leaders who could guide the destiny of this country. Even during this period the senior government official have played a very important role in keeping the warp and woof of this country intact, inspite of pressures by unscrupulous political leaders. The lack of trust and confidence in public servants, therefore, is certainly unfounded and baseless.

Inter-Professional and Inter-Disciplinary Approach

Another factor that needs to be borne in mind is that the affairs of the state in the twentieth century have become so inter-connected and inter-related and are of such a technical and professional nature that they need an inter-professional and inter-disciplinary approach. It would, therefore, not be possible, even for an educated man of one discipline to evolve or comprehend the intricate details of a developmental plan prepared by a person of another profession. The provision, therefore, of a council composed of elected members and representatives of nation building departments would go a long way in evolving technically sound plans which would be appreciated and accepted by the people, and in which, they would enjoy participating. The conclusion, therefore, of this historical analysis is that in our present state of development we cannot afford to disassociate the comparatively more educated, alert and capable sector of our population, the public servant, from the decentralised administration of this country through the institution of Basic Democracies. It may be noted however, that public servants suffer from severe handicaps, which will be described in the following pages, but, in spite of these weaknesses in their training and education, they can play an effective role in the functioning of Basic Democracies if they are willing to change their attitudes.

Effective Rural Leadership a Shared Enterprise

It can, therefore, be stated emphatically that effective rural leadership through Basic Democracies will be shared by the elected and nominated members, on the one hand, and by the public servants of the Basic Democracies councils, on the other hand, although the type and nature of these two leaderships will differ qualitatively and quantitatively. We shall describe this difference a little later.

Start Where People Are

The above discourse emphasising the capability of the public servant should not however be construed as minimising the importance of the elected members. It should not mean lack of faith in the abilities and the dormant potentialities of the people living in the villages. But in spite of our faith in the people's ability to govern themselves we should not lose sight of two very important principles of community development. The first principle is to "start where people are" and not where we want them to be. The second principle states "move at the pace for which people are ready."

A cursory analysis of the two principles stated above shows very clearly that we should take cognizance of the intellectual ability and experience that our people possess before thrusting too many responsibilities on them. For centuries we were neither prepared nor given the opportunity of governing our affairs. Consequently, the experience that comes through doing was not accumulated. Our well meaning and intelligent villagers, therefore, will have to learn slowly and steadily the process of democratic citizenship while they work for the common good through the Basic Democracies institutions. Similarly the pace at which they should be expected to move, or, in other words, the responsibilities that they will be expected to undertake, should be such that they are capable of shouldering.

Go from the Known to the Unknown

Another very important educational principle is to move from the known to the unknown. The experience that the members will get by working at the union council level regarding affairs of the union that are so near to them and about which they are fully aware, will gradually prepare them to shoulder greater responsibilities at the tahsil/thana, district and divisional level, where planning is done at a much higher plane and cognizance needs to be taken of many factors, sometimes conflicting and divergent.

Another factor that needs to be taken cognizance of is the fact that though our people may not have the intellectual ability and the experience of conceptually evolving and understanding intricate schemes of development in various spheres, they are an intelligent, hard-working, sturdy people, who are quite capable of understanding schemes and plans that affect their daily lives. They can also effectively execute plans that they have understood properly and have evolved themselves. If the right approach is made to them, in the right spirit, with the right attitude, their apathy and indifference dwindles away and they are eager to work on projects that can have a salutary effect on their day-to-day lives.

Resources of the People

In short our people have many strengths, in spite of the fact that they are illiterate and not prepared educationally and formally for local self-government. The religion that they profess emphasizes fellow feeling, community living, collective and joint planning and action. It is, therefore, important that we tap the resources that our people possess, both moral and material, and bring out the best in the individual, the group and the community in order that the experiment in local government be made successful.

As stated earlier the leadership that is expected from public servants in the Basic Democracies councils and the elected members in the Basic Democracies will differ both qualitatively and quantitatively.

Leadership—Its Connotation

In this article we take a rather broad view of 'leadership' meaning creating leadership at all levels, helping others to grow, assisting people to shoulder and execute responsibilities. It does not connote a leader who expects his followers to be 'dumb driven cattle.' It, therefore, means that the leader has to be more giving of himself than demanding.

Leadership Role of the Public Servant

How will the public servants give leadership in the Basic Democracies councils? The very fact that at all tiers except the union councils, the public servant, that is, the commissioner, deputy commissioner and tahsildar/sub-divisional officer has been appointed as the chairman of the respective councils, it is incumbent on him to guide and channel the efforts of the members towards constructive and useful schemes.

The above mentioned public servants have in the past conducted the administration of the district and tahsil more or less on their own, without taking into consideration the will of the people. There may have been a progressive element amongst these officers, who considered it important to ascertain the public will and may have done it in their own informal ways. But now the institution of Basic Democracies expects them to take into confidence the representatives of the people and jointly evolve a programme for the development of their respective regions. In other words, it means sharing authority.

The commissioner, deputy commissioner and tahsildar/subdivisional officer have now to give leadership in sharing and delegating such authority to the representatives of the people in the right method and with the right attitudes. If, as chairman of the respective councils, they demonstrate their will to share authority and give a patient hearing to the elected members, consider eliciting their views as necessary in deciding on projects and plans, the other representatives of the nation building departments will be inspired to do the same. It is an extremely easy job to make a statement like this but a very difficult task to change from giving orders to receiving them. A shift of emphasis from the public servant as the monarch of all he surveys to that of perhaps a team leader is an extremely difficult psychological and social adjustment. This entails not only a patient hearing but guiding and helping the representatives of the people in understanding and comprehending problems beyond their scope and gradually assisting them to shoulder more responsibility both individually and collectively.

The chairman of the Basic Democracies councils and the members of the nation building departments may consider themselves more able in general administration and in the technicalities of various development plans and projects, but they have to understand and accept the fact that the representatives of the people are much more closer to the people. The elected members of the Basic Democracies share the happiness and sorrows of the people. They live with them every moment of their lives. Consequently, they are more capable, perhaps, of understanding them and putting their point of view across. The elected members can with greater authority say what projects will meet the needs of the people and on which they are ready to participate. Thus, the chairman should give leadership in putting his trust and confidence in the capabilities of the people. The representatives of nation building departments should also follow this practice. In brief, the public servants should try to create leadership from amongst the elected members. The public servant should help the elected members to express their feelings and sentiments. The public servants should similarly not take over all the responsibilities. Even in work of a technical nature, they should involve the elected members, in order that the representatives of the people gain experience and knowledge.

Leadership Role of the Elected Members

The elected member, on the other hand, assumes leadership vis-a-vis the general public in his particular union, directly, and in the tahsil, thana, district and division, indirectly. The elected member should understand clearly that he occupies a position of responsibility, status and prestige as he is the chosen representative of the people. Once he is elected he should not lose direct and close touch with the people, otherwise, he can no longer act as the spokesman of the people, nor will he be able to convey to the people the vital decisions affecting their lives. His leadership consists in associating himself with as many people as possible on an equal footing.

Another very important leadership role that he has to play is enlisting the active support of communities in local projects. A cursory analysis of the functions of the councils shows that they will undertake many projects for which they will have to harness the moral and material resources of the people. This can only be done if the elected member mingles with the people, knows them well enough to judge the respective capabilities of individuals and groups and, through informal contacts and meetings, associates them in understanding the utility and benefit of a particular project.

Leadership in motivating the people and creating a harmonious, congenial and confident community capable of implementing and executing the decisions taken in the councils will rest with the chosen representatives of the people.

Leadership Role of the Nominated Members

The nominated member in Basic Democracies will also share leadership in developing rural areas. There were two major reasons for keeping the provision of nominated members, first, to give an opportunity to members of minoity groups, representing either different religions or particular affiliations who have not been elected to present their point of view; second, to give an opportunity of serving to capable or professional individuals who fight shy of elections.

In the former case, their leadership role will be that of the elected member, i.e., to keep in close touch with their community and to motivate the community to execute plans prepared by the council. It the latter case, where their selection has been made due to their professional skill or capability, they should contribute to the deliberations of the councils keeping constantly in view the fact that they have to help prepare elected members to understand and shoulder responsibilties. Though they are full-fledged members, they must not lose sight of the fact that their particular skill or competence has been the reason for associating them with the Basic Democracies. They must, therefore, assist the other members in gaining such competence.

Other Rival Groups

There are other groups that exist in the villages which are capable of giving guidance in a specific field. Will such leadership come in conflict with the leadership provided by Basic Democracies members and diminish the prestige or status of the councils? Does the fact that agriculture, industry, community development, etc., are the statutory responsibilities of the Basic Democracies mean that no other group can exist or work without obtaining approval of the councils? These are important questions which must receive objective deliberation from the Basic Democracies members.

Groups That Give Leadership in Rural Areas

What groups are already in operation or are expected to be formed in these rural areas, which can be termed rival groups?

The very fact that V-AID has covered 27.9% of East Pakistan and 40% of the population of West Pakistan means that, by and large, every village covered by a V-AID development area has a village council. The existence of V-AID results in the formation of youth groups, women's groups, progressive farmers associations, health and sanitation committees, etc. Besides the V-AID motivated councils and committees, there also exist in the villages:

(1) cooperative societies; (2) vocational association (like weavers association, etc.); (3) welfare groups; (4) professional associations; (5) sports groups; (6) various *baradaries;* (7) religious groups; (8) tribal groups.

These groups are engaged in specific activities with a particular focus and emphasis. The activities of the V-AID council, the tribal groups and *baradaries* cut across a wider field and encompass many facts of welfare. But can we, by any stretch of the imagination, term them rival groups which challenge the existence of Basic Democracies and diminish their prestige and status? On the contrary, it can be asserted that such functional groups offer a very good channel for communication of ideas, thoughts and decisions of the Basic Democracies councils at the grass-root level. These functional groups can be utilised by the Basic Democracies, not in an authoritarian manner but through a democratic approach for futhering programmes and plans.

This need not be a one-way traffic. Functional groups, especially the Village AID sponsored council of elders, can undertake projects on a self-help basis which can then be placed under the Basic Democracies. Similarly, it can also be possible for the Basic Democracies and the village council to join hands on a common project.

The various groups serve two very important purposes. One is that they can serve as channels of communication through which views and decisions can be conveyed and people's participation sought. Secondly (except for the *baradaries,* the religious groups and the tribal groups), the other functional and professional and welfare groups are a training ground in democratic citizenship where people learn to determine their needs and to work collectively to redress that needs.

If the institution of Basic Democracies is to work, it is important that it be manned by people whose horizons are broad and who can work in the larger interest of the nation. Such persons can respect and appreciate differences of opinion and still work jointly on beneficial projects. But such persons are not created over-night. It takes years of experience, from working in small committees that organise a small function to better organised groups following parliamentary procedure. It is, therefore, in the interest of Basic Democracies that such organisations be formed and develop on healthy lines. Basic Democracies will both strengthen and be strengthened by the existence of such formal, but voluntary, groups.

Is Basic Democracies a Democratic Institution?

Basic Democracies has the potential of evolving into a thoroughly democratic institution. It is closer to the people and associates a much larger number of people with administration and local government than has ever occurred before. It also provides a safe-guard against the despotic public servant becoming a virtual monarch and decentralises administration at every level.

Even the best form and structure can be ruined if placed in the hands of inefficient, insincere and dishonest people. Similarly, a fairly modest and workable structure of government can prove successful if operated by honest, intelligent and sincere people. Basic Democracies is a workable system that the people can comprehend.

The system has placed a tremendous amount of trust and confidence in the public servants. They have to prove worthy of this trust and provide creative leadership. They are equipped with knowledge and experience of administration and local government to discharge their responsibilities in a worthy manner. A great deal of the success of Basic Democracies will depend on the attitude of the public servant, on *his desire to share authority* with the representatives of the people and to delegate responsibilities to them. He has a vital role to play, especially as chairman of various councils, in providing sustained, creative and intelligent leadership.

The elected representatives, on the other hand, should also have a sustained interest and the will to make Basic Democracies a success. If Basic Democracies succeeds, it will be through the joint efforts of the representatives of the people and the public servants, but if it fails, the public servant will be largely responsible. This assertion is not a hypothetical statement, but is based on an analysis of the Basic Democracies Order. Unless the public servants give leadership to the elected members through close association and sharing of responsibilities, the representatives of the people will not be able to motivate the teeming millions living in the villages, and if this is not done, the vast number of problems in the country cannot be solved, either by the government or by the 80,000 elected and nominated members of the Basic Democracies councils.

Basic Democracies institutions have to put into effect a *chain reaction* of effective rural leadership capable of solving its own problems and working for the greatest good of the greatest number.

SECTION FIVE

Political Processes

74 • SHARIF AL-MUJAHID: *Pakistan's First Presidential Elections* *

These two accounts, by the Chairman of the Journalism Department at the University of Karachi, describe the bitter contest by which presidential elections were inaugurated in Pakistan and members were elected to the National Assembly. The presidential election, in accordance with the system of Basic Democracies, was in two parts: first, the election (by universal suffrage) of some 75,000 "basic democrats"—approximately 5,000 others were elected unopposed. This part of the election was completed during the third week in November 1964. Early in January came the second part of the election—that by the duly installed "basic democrats"—of a president for the nation. Between November and January the presidential candidates engaged in a second campaign tour, speaking to audiences made up of these representatives. On January 2, 1965, the "basic democrats" went to the polls and elected Muhammad Ayub Khan president by a wide majority over Miss Fatimah Jinnah, the seventy-one-year-old sister of Muhammad Ali Jinnah, the founder of Pakistan. The Assembly elections were held late in March.

There can be no doubt that the margin of Ayub's victory was enhanced by governmental control of the press and radio, by the fact that his opponent was an elderly woman, and that the Combined Opposition had little in common among themselves. Bearing these facts in mind, one must admit that Miss Jinnah made a fine showing. But for the dismay and discord that marked the Combined Opposition parties after the presidential election, their showing in the Assembly elections could have been much stronger.

For an authoritarian regime, says Tocqueville, "the most dangerous moment" usually comes "when it begins to reform itself." And for the Ayub regime this was that crucial moment. While he considered the lifting of martial law and the promulgation of this constitution as sufficient concession to the protagonists of democracy, the latter took it as only the first of a series of steps toward full democracy. Ayub felt that the goals of "unity," "political stability" and "modernization" were enchanting enough to sell his new constitution—and his regime. The dictates

* *Asian Survey,* Vol. 5, No. 6 (June 1965), pp. 280–294. By permission.

of economic development are such, he argued, that developing countries like Pakistan cannot progress under the "strains and stresses of the western democratic system." Over the years, this argument has been reinforced by the telling fact that Pakistan's economic growth under the Ayub regime has not only been stupendous, but is even considered one of the most impressive in Asia.

As against this is the simple but cogent argument of all democrats in all ages—namely, there is no substitute for freedom, nor is freedom a half-way house. The clamor for the democratization of the constitution thus became increasingly strident, and the opposition for a time seemed to carry everything before it. But, by a stroke of fortune, this "dangerous moment" for the Ayub regime synchronized with the dispatch, in the fall of 1962, of massive western, and especially U.S., arms aid to India which posed a new threat to Pakistan's security. This emergency enabled Ayub to galvanize public opinion in his favor, and gave him the much needed respite to put the former politicians in "their proper place" through a new Political Parties' Ordinance. The fast-rising opposition tide was, thus, effectively stemmed, and a dangerous corner turned—at least for the time being.

"Democracy," according to Disraeli, "is inconceivable without political parties." And, in spite of his dislike of politicians, politicking and political parties, Ayub had to permit the revival of political groupings in the National Assembly. But "the firm policies of the Government and the disarray of the opposition groupings" had largely "inhibited political activity," with the result that the opposition was "reduced to vocalizing in the National Assembly, and there too the chorus" was fast "becoming discordant." The new press laws served the purpose of a leash for the press and took care of "irresponsible" press criticism. The finishing touch to Ayub's control of the country's politics and political activities was given when he assumed in December 1963 the presidency of the Pakistan Muslim League (PML), founded in September 1962 at a convention in Karachi. All this led a good many of even the "old guard" to jump on his bandwagon, and the ruling Muslim League party in the legislatures was vastly strengthened.

By winter of 1964, Ayub was in firm control of the internal situation, and his prestige as world statesman, chiefly because of a Gaullist policy in the context of Pakistan's foreign affairs, had soared high—and with it, the country's prestige abroad as well. The largest nation in Asia was won over to Pakistan's side—and close contact was established with Djakarta and Colombo as well. And with Nehru's death in May 1964, Ayub emerged as an outstanding leader in the region; this status received confirmation at the Commonwealth Prime Ministers' conference (July 1962) where his performance elicited favorable comment from the British press. Yet another plum was conveniently picked up when he initiated the Istanbul Pact of July 1964, by which the three Muslim members of CENTO agreed to launch the "Regional Cooperation for Development" (RCD) on the pattern of the Common Market in Europe. This move, which earned for Ayub the epithet of a "Moslem De Gaulle," was hailed in Pakistan as a concrete step towards the unity of the Muslim world, a goal cherished by all Muslim Pakistanis.

All this was deftly exploited by his enthusiasts—and they were many—to call for Ayub's unanimous election for the next presidential term. Before long, a systematic campaign in its support was launched through speeches and statements which recounted in glowing terms his services and achievements. Ayub, it was argued, should be elected unopposed "in recognition of his unique achievement for the Muslim world," for the sake of "stability of administration and over-all development," for "political and economic stability," for ensuring "a bright and prosperous future for the country and unity in the Muslim world" and for a host of other reasons, some of them quite understandable, even convincing. When his candidature was finally launched by the PML, even *Dawn* lent its enthusiastic support to the unanimous-election plea, since there was "no one else among the living personalities who" could "present anything like the same credentials to the electoral college."

Weak, faction-ridden, and effete though the opposition may have been, its ranks were still not altogether denuded of persons capable of upsetting the "unanimous-election" campaign. The person who accomplished this near miracle was Khawaja Nazimuddin, a former Governor General and Prime Minister, as well as a former Chief Minister of (united) Bengal and East Pakistan, and now President of the Council Muslim League (CML), a faction of the pre-martial law Pakistan Muslim League, dominated by the "old guard" and parliamentary system-oriented politicians. It took him several months of intensive travelling and maneuvering to talk other opposition leaders through their own respective party workers into fighting the presidential elections jointly. Eventually, on July 21, 1964, five opposition parties merged into a Combined Opposition party (COP), adopted a nine-point program as its election manifesto, and agreed to put up a single presidential candidate. Ironically, this development synchronized with Ayub's return from a "triumphant tour" which had occasioned an overflowing of the nation's gratitude and its appreciation of his "singular," "splendid" and "remarkable achievements." The five opposition parties represented in COP were the middle-of-the-road Council Muslim League (CML) headed by Khawaja Nazimuddin; the extreme left National Awami party (NAP) headed by Maualana Abdul Hamid Khan Bhashani; the central-left Awami League (AL) headed by Nawabzada Nasrullah Khan (President) and Sheikh Mujibur Rahman (General Secretary, East Pakistan AL); the central-right Nizam-i-Islam party (NIP) headed by Chaudhri Mohammed Ali, a former Prime Minister; and the extreme right Jamaat-i-Islami (JI), headed by Maulana Maudoodi.

The ruling party reacted quickly, bitterly, even somewhat maliciously to this election alliance. The COP was compared to the Jugto (United) Front, a confused jumble of heterogeneous parties which fought for spoils among themselves once it had toppled the Muslim League Government in the East Pakistan elections of March 1954, and the COP's nine-point program to the Jugto Front's utopian and parochial 21-point manifesto. The COP was characterized as an odd conglomeration of "tried and discredited leaders" and "frustrated politicians" who had brought the country to such "disgrace" in their own heydey, who had now joined hands to "elevate the disgrace to the national level," and who, above all, were actuated by nothing except the desire "to seize power." They were "anti-social," their activities "nefarious," and their mission was "to create chaos." Several ministers, among others, taunted the opposition with having thus far failed to find any national figure to head their ticket.

Nor was this taunt altogether unfounded. The opposition was in fact in search of a candidate for almost two months, and was hard put to find one—for the simple reason that party and petty jealousies had heavily weighed with the five COP components in the consideration and rejection of several names. Finally, on September 19, the name of Miss Fatima Jinnah, the sister of Quaid-i-Azam, Mohammed Ali Jinnah, the founder of Pakistan, was proposed and accepted unanimously. Miss Jinnah, though initially reluctant, finally yielded to the impassioned appeals of both Nazimuddin and his tactical adviser, Fazlur Rahman, in the name of the "nation," "democracy" and "patriotism." She felt compelled "to accept the nation's call," as a matter of "duty" and promised to "spare nothing in devotion, service and hard work in achieving the objectives for which the millions in Pakistan have seen silently and devotedly yearning for the last few years."

Why did the opposition nominate Miss Jinnah? Firstly, they were in search of a national figure whose patriotism, sincerity and integrity were above question, who commanded the respect and devotion of the entire nation, and who had the courage of her convictions. Furthermore, Miss Jinnah had held no office in the past and, therefore, could not be accused of inefficiency, corruption, maladministration, and a host of other charges which were levelled against other opposition leaders, with or without justification. Fearless and undaunted, she had a razor-sharp tongue which had spared none in the past, not even when she spoke on the government-controlled radio. The opposition was also apprehensive that any other candidate might be screened out by the ruling party under the constitutional proviso that there should be no more than four candidates, including the sitting President, in a presidential election. Above all, the opposition felt that it was necessary to "exploit" Miss Jinnah's great emotional appeal with the masses if its "mission" for the restoration of unfettered democracy and civic rights were to have any chance of success at all.

Miss Jinnah's nomination caught the ruling party unaware. They knew that the opposition had been "hobnobbing" with Miss Jinnah, and of her avowed views on such crucial issues as fundamental rights, direct vote, and parliamentary democracy, which she gave vent to time and again; but they felt that old, frail and somewhat broken in health as she was, she would refuse all overtures from the opposition. What did she stand to gain by "playing into the hands of these discredited" leaders? Since her brother's demise, she had been almost looked upon as *Khatoon-i-Pakistan* (The First Lady of Pakistan) and *Madar-i-Millat* (Mother of the Nation). And she had filled the role of an elderly mother calling the erring children to the right track whenever the occasion demanded with singular distinction and grace. Would she, then, give up this "lofty eminence" in favor of the rough and tumble world of active politics? Would she, at 71, subject herself to a long, arduous election campaign? No sensible person in her position, it was felt, would by her own volition, condescend to become the center of a bitter, gruelling controversy, and that when she was to be pitted against a man of the stature of President Ayub. These considerations led the ruling party to assume that she would refuse the nomination. They even sent emissaries to her—and some PML leaders publicly appealed to her "good sense" to keep herself away from the impending political controversy.

The reaction to her acceptance varied with the political orientation of the commentators. Phrases such as "unfortunate," "most sorrowful," "tragic," and "a cover for self-seekers and power-hunters" contrasted with such as "a great historic decision," "the conscience of the people," and "a great challenge to those among us who dream and crave for the establishment of a clean political and moral order."

In any case, soon after Miss Jinnah's crucial decision, the political scene in Pakistan underwent a sudden and sweeping change: it gave nerve and verve to the opposition; anti-Ayub sentiment, thus far silent out of either fear or expediency, became vocal almost overnight. The opposition's confidence was further bolstered by the courts' decisions declaring the government's ban on the Jamaat-i-Islami illegal and the West Pakistan Loudspeaker Ordinance void. This led most of the intellectuals, student and workers' organizations and the bar associations almost without exception to come out openly in favor of Miss Jinnah. The list of opposition adherents was formidable and impressive in terms of both numbers and intellect and social status, as well as professional, middle and working class background.

It was a measure of the change in the political landscape of Pakistan that during the next three months strikes, demonstrations and protest rallies swept the country from one end to the other. There were strikes by jute workers throughout East Pakistan for 53 days, erupting in serious riots in the Khalishpur industrial area (Khulna); by the Chittagong port workers; by West Pakistan transport workers, paralyzing communications throughout the province; and by Bannu woolen mills' workers in the Frontier. Strike notices were served by the East Pakistan Railway Employees' League and the Karachi Electric Supply Corporation employees. A new labor front called the East Pakistan Workers' Council was launched in October and a 15-point program was formulated. Secondary school teachers in East Pakistan and primary school teachers in West Pakistan went on strike. And, above all, students' grievances, whether genuine or supposed, erupted into a strike throughout the western province, so intense in character that the government was, for the first time, forced to close down all educational institutions for an indefinite period in early December 1964. Pandora's box, it seemed, had been broken wide open.

When the opposition launched its campaign on October 1, there was some skepticism that it would continue the whole way. But the teeming, tumultuous receptions Miss Jinnah received all the way from Peshawar to Karachi in her eight-day tour of West Pakistan put heart into the opposition camp, and made it increasingly bold, vocal and determined. The welcome she received during her week-long East Pakistan tour was even more frantic: whole towns and villages came out to demonstrate their "smothering affection." The Green Arrow, East Pakistan's fastest express train, which carried her from Dacca to Chittagong, crawled along at the rate of seven miles an hour; it took more than 28 hours to cover the 196-mile journey, normally covered in seven hours. Everywhere the most characteristic feature of her receptions was their spontaneity and sincerity. The tour, however, ended on a sad note: Nazimuddin, the architect of the COP and the inspiration behind Miss Jinnah's candidacy, died as a result of campaign fatigue on October 22. This setback seemed to unnerve even the fiery, determined campaigner, but only for the moment. Nazimuddin's exit doubtless affected the COP's chances at the polls, but since the campaign had got off to a good start, the newly found party was saved from a premature collapse.

Initially, Ayub seemed altogether unconcerned with what the opposition was doing or saying. During August and September, his references to the COP and its nine-point program were scant and fleeting, but instead emphasized the need for "economic and political stability with a strong center . . . for Pakistan's forward march" and argued that the Moghul dynasty's downfall in the subcontinent had resulted from a weakening of the central government after Aurangzeb. But the unexpected response to his rival's call finally forced him to undertake an equally determined campaign in person.

The Manifestos

The election manifestos of the two candidates may be briefly noted here. Miss Jinnah's manifesto, the COP's nine-point program, called for the achievement of a fully democratic constitution; the direct election of the national and provincial assemblies, and full legislative and budgetary powers for them; a federal parliamentary structure with built-in provincial autonomy consistent with the integrity of Pakistan and parity at the center; curtailment of the presidential powers; separation of the judiciary from the executive and the supreme courts' right to determine the constitutional validity of laws; the withdrawal of the ban on political parties; release of all political detenus and repeal of all repressive laws. With respect to foreign policy, Kashmir, minorities, administrative reforms, inter and intra-wing developmental disparity, and Islamic content, it did not differ much from Ayub's manifesto.

Despite the adoption of a manifesto by the PML in the previous March, Ayub thought it expedient to issue his own personal manifesto.[1] . . .

The analysis of their respective manifestos by the two rivals was interesting. Ayub characterized the COP's program as a "bundle of lies," a string of "catchy slogans based on sentiments of parochialism, regionalism and petty issues." On the other hand, Ayub's manifesto was dubbed an "election bluff." His pragmatic approach, it was said, in effect meant nothing but "a superimposed constitution or an ordinance issued as fundamental law." He had "already practiced his pragmatism by rejecting the reports of the Constitution and Franchise Commissions." The omission of any reference to the method by which the people's will would be ascertained was denounced and a referendum on the question of direct polls demanded.

More caustic was Miss Jinnah's comment. Referring to Ayub's promise to safeguard "the basic rights" of the people under the rule of law, she asked whether the law he had in mind was the one that he would "ordain, promulgate and proclaim" as he had "been doing during the last six years"; "his armory" consisted of nothing but laws such as "the Press Ordinance, externment laws, Security Acts, and a host of other laws." She even accused him of "lack of faith in the people" and dubbed him "a dictator," who was "now trying to wear the garb of a democrat."

Voting Procedure

Under the Pakistan constitution, the voters delegate their right to choose the President and members of the national and provincial assemblies to 80,000 representatives—the "basic democrats" who form the electoral college. The electorate is divided into 80,000 tiny constituencies each consisting of about 200–600 voters. Once these members of the electoral college (MECs) are elected, the voters have little hold over them with regard to their choice of presidential and assembly candidates, whatever their promises and predilections at the time of their own elections. Hence the PML's decision not to give tickets to the contestants at this basic tier, but to "own the person who wins the election"; the COP, on the other hand, did—perhaps to demonstrate its strength as well as to exert moral pressure on those elected on its ticket. In these circumstances, the preferences of the MECs were unknown until they had actually cast their votes.

[1] For the full text of Ayub Khan's manifesto, see Reading No. 76, pp. 437–440.

The elections to this lowest tier were held in West Pakistan from October 31 to November 9 and in East Pakistan from November 10 to 19. About 2,725 candidates were elected unopposed in West Pakistan, and some 2,123 in the east wing; the rest of the seats were contested, usually by more than two candidates. In Karachi, for instance, 5,575 candidates filed nomination papers for 1,569 seats; in Dacca 2,158 nominations were received for 692 seats; in Lahore district 11,506 nominations were filed by 7,291 candidates for 2,313 seats; and in Peshawar the candidates for 192 seats totalled over a thousand. Over 100,000 nominations were filed for the 40,000 seats in East Pakistan. A large number of candidates chose to disguise their political affiliation, thus avoiding indicating whether they supported President Ayub or Miss Jinnah. Even as the polling progressed, it was alleged that the procedure for the MECs' elections had "built-in loopholes, permitting large scale bogus voting and all manner of corrupt practices." The COP had earlier challenged the voters' lists, and had demanded the holding of elections in a particular city, town or district on a single day to avoid bogus voting. Its 34-page White Paper, listing ten specific charges and demanding a judicial inquiry headed by a High Court judge, was brushed aside as an alibi to cover its failure at the polls. Even so, it was difficult in the end to say how each party had fared; both claimed an overwhelming majority of seats.

Nominations for the presidency were called for on November 22 and this set off another bitter controversy between the two rivals and their parties. The 72-hour notice given for the filing of nominations was considered insufficient and an attempt to "obstruct" the opposition. The COP's fears that the government planned to screen out Miss Jinnah gained strength when it was learned that three members of Ayub's own cabinet—in addition to Ayub, Miss Jinnah and two other minor candidates—had filed nomination papers. Under the constitution only four candidates including the sitting President (who could contest a second term without being subjected to the screening process) can contest the election. Hence, even if the two minor candidates withdrew, the remaining five would still necessitate screening by the assemblies—in which case the immense PML majorities in the assemblies could screen out Miss Jinnah.

It was this that led the opposition to challenge the eligibility of President Ayub to contest the elections, charging that as a Field Marshal in the Army, he held an office of profit and was, thus, subject to the prohibition on such candidacies in Article 115 of the constitution. The government's notification that he had retired from service with effect from February 16, 1960 was disputed at length: the COP even threatened to move the courts in the matter. In the end, however, Miss Jinnah was saved from the screening process by the withdrawal of the three ministers, while Ayub was saved from a court reference with regard to his eligibility.

The penultimate stage in the election campaign was the holding of the ten "confrontation" meetings to enable the candidates to project their views before the electors, in crowds of between 4,000 and perhaps 10,000. Miss Jinnah demanded a direct confrontation with Ayub but, under the procedures, the candidates did not meet each other but came in turn. She walked out of the first Rawalpindi meeting, proferring a series of charges against the administration and the Election Commission, which were stoutly refuted.

These meetings were important because a candidate's success at the polls, in the ultimate analysis, depended upon his ability to influence the MECs. The PML which had discreetly decided, on the one hand, against the issuance of tickets at this tier, and, on the other, upon "owning" the successful candidates, now made an all-out effort to attract COP supporters. Appeals were made to their good sense, their patriotism, even their self-interest. They were repeatedly told, for instance, that they were the "custodians of this [Basic Democracy] system" and that it was their "responsibility to guard it against those" who were out to "destroy" it and their "position in it."

On this point the opposition's stand was somewhat awkward. Their leaders had in the past bitterly railed against this system, calling it a "base" democracy, designed to rob the people of their right to directly elect their representatives to the assemblies. During the campaign, however, they had somewhat changed their stand, repeatedly assuring the basic democrats that though they would no longer form the electoral college, they would be more than adequately compensated by the conferment of greater powers in the local self-government sphere and by being released from the present tutelage of the executive. These assurances, in turn, led to charges of insincerity, *volte face* and opportunism, designed to mislead the MECs. Ayub repeatedly told them that once deprived of their present electoral rights, they would be reduced "to a mere instrument of local-government." And, to be sure, such appeals paid Ayub huge dividends. It was also a measure of the "enlightened self-interest" of at least some of the basic democrats that during the projection meetings they repeatedly enquired about the emoluments they would get and the powers they would wield, in case of their election.

The Issues

The presidential contest was not merely a contest between two individuals; it was a contest between two ways of life of which they had become the most outstanding symbols. It was, by any standard, a battle of giants, and the debate was long, bitter, sometimes even bordering on personal abuse and slander, but all the time providing a memorable lesson in political education and awakening.

There have been few elections in which the alternatives before the electors were so sharply opposed—and focussed. The issues as presented by Ayub and Miss Jinnah were, indeed, in terms of black and white, with no shades of grey in between—"stability versus chaos" and "democracy versus dictatorship." Ayub protested that dictators did not give constitutions nor hold elections, much less go begging for votes. But the fiery septuagenarian retorted that "the so-called constitution" was "promulgated by one man, made and administered by one man, who can appoint himself, dismiss himself, and go on pension whenever he likes as if Pakistan is an absolute monarchy."

Ayub asserted that his system ensured stability within and without, but Miss Jinnah retorted that what was desired was stability through a system and not through a person: "the stability of a country was not jeopardized by a change of government"; nor did it "depend on one man or a handful of persons." On the contrary, it "originates from the people" who "are the real foundation of a stable system." Ayub, on his part, asserted that the country would be "demolished" if the opposition won.

The opposition adopted a united front approach in order to exploit the dissatisfied elements in the country. Hence its slogan of "democracy versus dictatorship." "Give me votes and I will give you democracy," said Miss Jinnah repeatedly. This approach was meant to make the people believe that the opposition stood for unfettered democracy; Ayub for unbridled autocracy. But diametrically opposite was the ruling party's strategy. Not only did it characterize the Ayub government as a democracy suited to Pakistani conditions, but it was determined to deflect the election campaign into side issues which were bound ultimately to hurt the opposition cause.

The most crucial among these was India. The occasionally favorable Indian comments, understandable in view of India's traditional hostility to every government in Pakistan, was assiduously and continuously exploited by PML spokesmen to prove that the Indians desired a change in Pakistan because of their fear of Ayub and their hope of political instability in Pakistan following Miss Jinnah's victory. The opposition was even accused of wanting to "disarm Pakistan and sell it out to India." India's armed strength, which was three times Pakistan's in 1960, had, thanks to western military aid, increased to five times Pakistan's; a vigorous and skillful leadership was therefore indispensable to frustrate recurring Indian designs, and such leadership could be provided by Ayub alone.

Secondly, the National Awami party's association with the COP was interpreted by the PML to mean that the opposition stood for the disintegration of Pakistan. The NAP, it may be remembered, supports the dismemberment of One Unit in West Pakistan, complete provincial autonomy and two economies. Bhashani has often been charged with holding East Pakistan secession views; Khan Abdul Ghaffar Khan, another top NAP leader, is well-known for his advocacy of "Pakhtoonistan." For some inexplicable reason, Ghaffar Khan chose, during the election period, to visit Kabul as a state guest, where he was greeted with, in Pakistani views, the anathemic title of "Quaid-i-Pakhtoonistan" (the supreme leader of Pakhtoonistan). All this provided grist to the PML's propaganda mills. Miss Jinnah's repeated assurances that all controversial issues such as the One Unit would be decided by the national assembly in case of her election, could not and did not dispel the doubts created in the public mind.

Midway through the campaign, Miss Jinnah, in the course of a rebuttal of the government's claims of success in the foreign affairs' sphere, charged it with "incompetence" in failing to restrain the United States, which was once claimed as "Pakistan's best friend," from giving aid to India. This remark was pounced upon to infer that Miss Jinnah and her supporters must be the lackeys of the State Department. In spite of several clarifications, this refrain was kept up uninterrupted, and some ministers even went to the extent of accusing the opposition of "getting assistance from foreign countries to dislodge the present regime." The Americans, it was alleged, were underwriting the opposition campaign in West Pakistan while the Indians were footing the bill in the East Wing.

Provincial issues did not figure much in the campaign. Miss Jinnah had largely confined herself to national issues, but others did not. In a bid, perhaps, to exploit East Pakistani sentiment, Governor Monem Khan even accused the opposition of having failed to nominate an East Pakistani as its candidate. The Commerce Minister charged that Miss Jinnah had failed to donate to the East Pakistani cyclone sufferers from funds at her disposal. An opposition leader, on the other hand, accused the government of failure to take effective measures for flood control in the east and a host of other things, although the Ayub government had gone out of the way to meet East Pakistani grievances in respect of development and inter-wing parity.

But the one issue that loomed large throughout the entire campaign and may have deflected considerable votes, especially in conservative and rural areas, against Miss Jinnah was whether a woman could become the head of an avowedly Islamic state. The fundamentalist Jamaat-i-Islami, one of the opposition components, argued that she could under extraordinary circumstances, but a crop of *ulama* and *mashaikh* (religious dignitaries) conferences, soon after Miss Jinnah's nomination, issued *fatwas* (religious decrees) against a woman becoming the head of a Muslim state. These decrees received wide publicity through speeches, statements, leaflets, pamphlets and posters. "Is there no man," asked Monem Khan in disgust, "who can become the head of the state?" In the heat of the controversy, however, it was altogether forgotten that the issue has far deeper consequences, moral as well as social, than what a mere election fight signified. Nor was it remembered that Muslim history includes several women as head of state or commander of armies, and also that no Pakistani has ever demurred to the election of women legislators, the appointment of women ministers and ambassadors, or to Pakistan's acceptance of a woman as the head of the Commonwealth.

And what about their *prima donna,* this high priestess of the opposition? She was "a venerable person," no doubt, but in allowing these elements "to hide behind her to promote their designs and disrupt the country," she had made herself "a tool" in the hands of these "condemned politicians." In easy instalments, but with mounting vehemence, she was accused of a great many things: of "ambition," of considering Pakistan her "personal property," of being "old, recluse and weak-minded," of articulating "what was whispered in her ears," of lacking "experience in statecraft," and, to top it all, of not making "the grade," even "if a bottom standard was set." How, then, "would she run the country" if returned to power? And, to the immense joy of Ayub's supporters, Miss Jinnah's somewhat laconic answers at the projection meetings seemed to confirm some of these allegations.

Miss Jinnah's troubles did not, however, end there. The opposition's demand for a caretaker government, for access of its candidate to the state-owned radio (which the President could freely use), for the reduction in the number of polling stations (especially in the west wing which had 218 stations, with some having only about 18–60 electors), and for the appointment of polling and presiding officers entirely from the judiciary, or, alternately, from the teaching profession, were refused for one reason or another. Its meage financial resources inhibited the opposition from preaching its message in the countryside through leaflets, pamphlets, posters and newspaper ads (to counter PML's extensive publicity), or even to buy enough jeeps for electioneering purposes. The 64 jeeps sanctioned by the government in West Pakistan were considered insufficient for 218 polling stations, some of them in areas inaccessible by air or rail routes. And the opposition charges of the "kidnapping, coercion and arrests all over the country" of its voters, polling agents, workers and supporters mounted high in the last three days before the elections. There were no end to counter-charges either. Thus, tension, nervousness, even suspicion hung heavily in the air when the electors, having listened to the last-minute frantic appeals urging them to vote "fearlessly," conscientiously and "with faith in the destiny of the nation," went to the polls on January 2, 1965.

The Elections

The results gave Ayub a clear, convincing, even thumping victory, and the opposition was stunned by the crushing defeat. Ayub secured 49,951 (62.7%) of the 79,700 votes cast, and Miss Jinnah 28,691 (36%); Ayub's majority of 21,260 votes was formidable by any standard. West Pakistan gave Ayub a massive 28,939 (73.3%) and Miss Jinnah a meager 10,257 (26.7%), whereas Ayub received 21,012 votes (52.9%) in the east wing and Miss Jinnah 18,434 (46.5%). She carried only three of the country's sixteen divisions by meager majorities: Chittagong, Dacca and Karachi. The "dummy" candidates, Kamal and Bashir, polled a total of 183 and 64 votes respectively, and another 810 votes were declared invalid.

Ayub's 73.3% vote in the west was understandable: he secured the almost unanimous support of the 3,282 nominated members in tribal areas in the Frontier and Baluchistan (about 9% of the total west wing votes); about 75% of the votes in Sind where Foreign Minister Bhutto, along with local landlords, wields immense influence; and a like majority in the Punjab which stood to lose by the possible dismemberment of One Unit in case of an opposition victory. But more surprising was his absolute majority in East Pakistan which was expected to go overwhelmingly in Miss Jinnah's favor. This underlines the success of the rural works programs in the east wing. In addition, most of its 20% minority vote, and the entire refugee vote went to bolster Ayub's gains. The Ayub regime was thus saved from "an ominous identification" with the west wing, and eastern separatism was scotched—at least for a long while.

In effect the vote meant that while the cities generally went with Miss Jinnah, Ayub's massive hold in rural areas was indisputable. Miss Jinnah's strength came from the protest vote of the professional and middle class in urban areas which generally consider Ayub's administration as being "altogether too paternal, concerned no doubt, to give the peasant a better deal, but distrusting any involvement in public affairs by those who are politically mature" and who feel their "democratic instincts . . . frustrated by the insistence on a 'basic' democracy designed for the limited horizon of the uneducated."

Ayub's victory meant a vote in favor of continuing stability and against an uncertain parliamentary democracy, so fiercely advocated by the opposition—an opposition which, in spite of a "common enemy," could not altogether curb their petty and personal jealousies (East Pakistan NAP's lukewarm attitude throughout the campaign even led to charges of "betrayal" by Mujibur Rahman). But perhaps the largest single factor in the President's victory was the fact that in voting for Ayub "the electors were voting for themselves." Miss Jinnah's first indiscrete suggestion that they were the "creatures" of the President, and the opposition leaders' pledge to denude them of their crucial voting rights, were kept dangling before them all the while. In addition, about two-fifths of those elected were sitting basic democrats who, having enjoyed the benefits of the system, were averse to their curtailment. Above all, Miss Jinnah had perforce to fight Ayub under his own system and under his rules; worse still, she was fighting, not for an office, but to demolish one.

President Ayub interpreted the heavy vote in his favor "as an expression of the instinct of self-survival in a society choosing orderly progress rather than chaotic regression," as an approval of both his internal and external policies as well as a mandate for his system and constitution. He thanked those millions who had voted him to power, but had also a kind word for those who had opposed him, especially for Miss Jinnah who "fought the elections according to her own lights" and for whom he bore "no personal grudge." The vanquished could not afford to be so charitable, especially when she felt "cheated" by the "fool-proof" system devised by her opponent. She levelled a series of charges, questioned the impartiality and fairness of the elections, but was "grateful to those thirty thousand electors who had the courage to stand by their conviction and have voted according to their conscience in spite of all kinds of pressure." She renewed her earlier pledge to continue to work for the restoration of the sovereignty of the people and true democracy in the country.

This means that the opposition, if and when it recovers from this setback, may renew its attack on the Basic Democracy system which, in its view, "is calculated to make it immensely difficult to overturn a government." But Ayub would be the last person to compromise on this basic feature of his constitution, which, he believes, makes adult franchise and democracy meaningful at this stage of Pakistan's development. Both parties are equally vehement, but what could the opposition do except to rail against the system occasionally? More deeply entrenched than ever by the recent vote, President Ayub is in no mood to listen to opposition demands. Time is, one would suspect, on his side, and he can consolidate his position all the more. But there is also an opportunity for him to use the next five years to enhance his popularity by conciliating the opposition to the extent he thinks fit. In any case, much of the criticism against the system would disappear if the major parties make it a rule to issue party tickets to the candidates at the lowest tier and they, on their part, hold fast to their election pledges in presidential and assembly voting.

All told, the elections were not only an exciting, but an educative affair as well. The point is that they were held at all: this was something in Pakistan's dismal history. Some of the allegations levied by both parties might better have been left unsaid; neither President Ayub nor Miss Jinnah deserved some of the epithets cast against them by each other and by their respective supporters. The scars will remain for some time, but it is to Miss Jinnah's credit that she never let the campaign degenerate into parochial, provincial, and petty issues as usually happens in multi-racial, multi-lingual and economically disparate societies; in that way, her candidacy has helped national integration, rather than disintegration. It is another thing whether the political dialogue initiated during last fall will continue.

75 • Sharif al-Mujahid: *The Assembly Elections in Pakistan* *

Compared to the recent Presidential elections, the assembly elections in Pakistan were relatively unexciting for some very obvious reasons. Under the Pakistan Constitution, the President is the central, if not the sole, repository of all power: besides being the executive head and the commander of the armed forces, he enjoys substantial powers in the field of legislation as well. The (uni-

* *Asian Survey,* Vol. 5, No. 11 (November 1965), pp. 538–551. By permission.

cameral) National Assembly is neither so powerful nor so influential in the formulation of national policies as the U.S. Congress, not to speak of legislatures in the parliamentary system.

The Assembly's control of the purse is limited: its sanction is required only for the "new expenditures" in the annual budget statement (which forms a very small part). Presidential appointments and decisions, and ministerial actions are beyond its control. The procedure for circumventing the President's veto on bills passed by it is extremely difficult and circuitous. Constitutional amendments call for a two-thirds majority with the presidential concurrence and a three-fourths majority without such concurrence. In such a situation, the President still has the power to refer the matter to referendum by the electoral college or dissolve the Assembly and seek re-election himself. Although the question as to who would wield power for the next five years had been settled in the Presidential elections, no government likes to face a hostile legislature all the time, much less resort to special emergency provisions to circumvent the roadblocks in the path of governmental legislation put up by such a legislature. Hence the hope of the ruling Pakistan Muslim League party (PML) was to pick up at least two-thirds of the seats in the Assembly and the equally determined efforts of the Combined Opposition Party (COP) were to deny the ruling party such a comfortable majority.

Notwithstanding the stake of both the parties in the composition of the new National Assembly, the elections failed to arouse major interest, chiefly because the outcome of the Presidential elections had, for good or ill, seemingly cast the die. Ayub's victory had more than recouped the sagging morale of the ruling PML, effectively checkmated the fastgathering momentum of the opposition and, most importantly, seriously affected its morale. Whereas the PML was going from one resounding victory to another, the opposition was floundering in one defeat after another, moving in the course of this from demoralization to despair.

The opposition's gloom in the wake of the Presidential defeat could be traced largely to the fact that the opposition not only became a victim of its own propaganda, but had succumbed in some measure to the propaganda of its rival as well. High-sounding claims by rival groups are a normal feature of elections everywhere, especially in a country like Pakistan where public leaders seem to consider tall claims and strong words an adequate substitute for concrete action. Towards the end of the campaign, the opposition, in view of the unexpected popular upsurge for its cause, on the surface had reason to be confident. A close upset victory seemed conceivable. There were some hard cold facts about Pakistan politics, however, which should not have been ignored. Ayub had to win not only because of his achievements but, more important, because of the 1962 Constitution. The 80,000 members of the Electoral College (MECs) had good reason not only to be grateful to him but also to protect their political stake in national life and their crucial role in channelling local development activities (the Third Plan allocates Rs. 2,500 million for rural works programs during the next five years).

Hence, it was extraordinary that in a mere three months of campaigning and in the face of numerous handicaps, the opposition mustered 36% of the votes of the electoral college against a well-entrenched President operating under a strong presidential system and with some very special political rules. It was, indeed, almost a miracle—even if the COP's charges of election malpractices were to be dismissed as highly exaggerated.

To believe that it would win was tragic enough for the COP, but more devastating was its acceptance of the ruling party's argument that its defeat in the Presidential election was "crushing." A five-to-three defeat might be described as decisive but not altogether paralyzing; similarly, a 62.7% victory could be termed convincing but not a "landslide," especially when 4.5% of the votes came from the nominated tribal MECs. Indeed, it was no mean achievement to obtain the support of three-eighths of the electorate, especially under the Basic Democracy (BD) system. From an election by acclamation, or by 90% to 95% vote (as was predicted by governmental spokesmen) to a 62.7% victory was a big comedown. The Field-Marshal, moreover, had been obliged to shed some of his "Olympian paternalism" for a "more popular posture." These were positive gains. Above all, the five-to-three vote signified that the country wanted to engage in critical discussion and thought rather than conformism. An imaginative and forward-looking leadership could have successfully exploited these facts into future victories. In brooding over its defeat for too long, however, the opposition lost the psychological political initiative to its formidable rival. And once the psychological initiative was lost, its momentum was lost, its confidence gave way to a feeling of its own helplessness and the hopelessness of the cause it espoused. Nothing could be more tragic for an opposition party.

That the opposition was in a quandary became evident all the more when the COP met in Karachi in the third week of January to take stock of the political situation and decide upon two crucial issues: viz, (1) the 'one command-one party' formula and the establishment of "an Alliance for Freedom and Democracy" under Miss Jinnah's "inspiring leadership"; and (2) to contest or boycott the coming Assembly elections. The East Pakistan National Democratic Front (NDF), launched immediately after the promulgation of the 1962 Constitution, and headed by Nurul Amin, a former East Pakistan Chief Minister, and comprising several top-notch political leaders, had consistently stood for uniting the "democratic forces" in the country under one unified command to carry on the "struggle for democracy till it is fully achieved"; now it renewed its call for the immediate self-dissolution of all political organizations, parties, and groups to pave the way for "partyless unity" under one banner. Over this 'one command-one party' formula, opinion at the Karachi COP Conference was sharply divided. The middle-of-the-road Muslim League Council (CMF) and the center-right Nizam-i-Islam Party (NIP) largely favored such an arrangement, the center-left Awami League (AL) was noncommittal, but the extreme-left National Awami Party (NAP) and the extreme-right Jamaat-i-Islami (JI) were vehemently opposed to any proposals for self-dissolution. This was chiefly because, being more ideological and cohesive than the other groups, they, while desiring a more democratic climate in the country to enable them to preach their ideology more freely (and hence their adhesion to the COP), did not expect to capture power in the near future and could not afford to loosen their hold over their comparatively fewer but more disciplined and dedicated adherents. Instead, they favored the formulation of a minimum program for the restoration of democracy, to which all parties could agree without having to dissolve themselves. Thus the COP's electoral alliance could not be transformed into a more permanent and cohesive organization and program.

In reality, however, relatively little thought seems to have been given to this crucial issue. The Conference was primarily occupied in a long and somewhat acrimonious debate over whether or not to fight the impending elections. While the

CML was adamant on boycotting them, the East Pakistan-based AL and NAP were determined to contest the elections. The AL in West Pakistan was not concerned, and the West Pakistan NAP was largely for a boycott. Chaudhri Muhammad Ali (NIP) and Maulana Maududi (JI), initially flexible on the issue, were soon won over to the boycott idea. Thus the pro-participation and pro-boycott groups were largely divided along provincial lines.

The pro-boycott group felt that the elections were bound to be "flagrantly rigged" and that they should "not be partners in a farce worse than the last." They had no faith not only in the BD system, but also in the present MECs who could be "intimidated," "coerced," and "bribed." Besides, since not more than 10 to 15 per cent of the members would be returned, it would be infinitely better to boycott the elections than to provide anaemic opposition which could scarcely be in a position to block official bills.

The clamor by the more radical in this group for a "mass movement for democracy" in preference to the "frustrated attempts" at the polls could not receive much support for obvious reasons. If the component parties and leaders were not prepared to curb their personal and party ambitions in favor of a unified command, how could they produce a towering personality to rally and hold them together? Miss Jinnah's talents included a single-minded dedication to the goal of restoring parliamentary democracy and national prestige; an undaunted and razor-sharp tongue; and a "savage contempt" for the present regime. These were all useful assets for such a campaign, but her advanced age, poor health, and, above all, her disgust at the opposition's agonizing indecision and the mutual squabbles among its components, ruled out such role for her. Nor was there a mass base for a civil disobedience movement which could survive the onslaught of a well-entrenched government, armed with a host of restrictive laws including Section 144 (prohibiting the assembly of more than four men) and the loudspeaker ordinance.

The press also was beyond the opposition's reach, at least in West Pakistan. The government-sponsored National Press Trust owns eleven large dailies in English, Urdu, and Bengali in the two areas of Pakistan. Both the radio and the more important national news agency are government-owned. If the opposition seemed unnerved by an election defeat, overawed by the ugly Karachi riots in the wake of the victory celebrations, and cowed by the alleged arrests of about "500 political workers" in East Pakistan, how could it sustain a semi-constitutional agitation in the face of such adamant forces?

On the other hand, the pro-participationists maintained that legislatures formed the most important forum for the constitutional struggle for democracy and that a party would become inert and lifeless if it failed to utilize this forum. The function of a political party was not solely to capture power but to educate public opinion, which purpose, in the context of the Pakistani situation, could more fully be achieved by sending members to assemblies. To boycott the elections would not only mean conceding defeat without a fight, but would also amount to a gross betrayal of the 28,691 MECs who fearlessly voted for Miss Jinnah. With a little more campaigning, it was argued, the opposition could get about 40% of the seats in East Pakistan, which had given Miss Jinnah a 46.5% vote.

After protracted and fruitless deliberations for five days, the COP conference decided, chiefly at the insistence of the AL and NAP, to meet again in Dacca five days later, with a view to enabling the members to study the trends in East Pakistan and hold consultations with leaders there. Two more days of debate and the presence of the opposition members of the National Assembly (MNAs), then meeting in Dacca, clinched the issue; the COP finally decided to contest the elections in spite of its skepticism as to whether they would be "fair and impartial."

The Karachi and Dacca conferences had put a serious strain on the COP's unity: at one time it was even feared that this political and moral crisis might well destroy it. This did not happen, but the inherent weaknesses in its structure came fully into the open. Naturally, the government spokesmen deftly exploited this situation to further damage the opposition image. Half-hearted and inordinately delayed decisions are injurious to any cause. Still, a decision, arrived at through a long process of discussion and persuasion could, by no stretch of the imagination, be termed as a sign of "political bankruptcy"; instead, it denoted a critical and democratic temper. Paradoxically though, while the COP leaders were accused of being quarrelsome, wavering, indecisive and irresolute for not coming to a quick decision, when the COP decision did come, it was characterized as a "dirty game."

In any case, because of its preoccupation with the contest-or-boycott issue, the COP could not seriously challenge the delimitation of constituencies which was announced by the Election Commission on January 7. The opposition alleged that the redistricting of constituencies went against considerations of contiguity, compactness, homogeneity and easy communication, and was done in such a way as to cut into opposition majority areas in order to neutralize its hold over them. In Chittagong, for instance, the redistricting, it was pointed out, disrupted "the common affinity of the people of the various areas," besides creating "bottlenecks to the opposition by geographical readjustment of zones." Old constituencies like Miserserai and Sitakund were broken up, the former being connected with Fatikchhari which has no direct means of communication with Miserserai either by land or water routes, with connections possible only if one travelled some 50 miles across other constituencies. Many other charges of unfair gerrymandering were issued, including some relating to Karachi itself. These objections were heard by the Election Commission and redressed in some cases.

National Elections

Nominations for the NA were called for February 16, withdrawals were allowed till February 26, and elections were announced for March 21. Some 672 candidates (East Pakistan 312; West Pakistan 360) filed nomination papers for the 150 seats. Aspirants for the six reserved women seats were to be elected later by the new MNAs. Sixteen candidates in the West and two in the East ran unopposed, all PML nominees, except for one independent in West Pakistan. After withdrawals, 419 candidates contested the remaining 132 seats.

Of the 476 aspirants for PML tickets, some of those refused official tickets stood as "independent" candidates in spite of repeated appeals and threats, leading to the expulsion of 37 members (West 21; East 16) for violating party discipline. The PML contested 146 seats excluding the four seats in the tribal areas whose representatives, to be named by the (government-nominated) jirgas, could join any party after elections; several leading industrialists, businessmen, and landlords were among its nominees. The COP contested 25 seats in the West, and, in collaboration with the NDF, 71 seats in the East. Independent candidates totalled 148 (West 71; East 77).

During the assembly elections, President Ayub maintained the sobriety, restraint, and largely forget-and-forgive attitude which was characteristic of his victory broadcast on January 2. Affirming that his opponents, too, had "served the cause of democracy," he had on that occasion called for the subsidence of "the passion and prejudice generated by the elections." In subsequent weeks, the President pursued two, somewhat different, tactics. On the one hand he called for an end to "all controversies" over the constitution (he interpreted his election as President as "a vote of confidence" in the constitution) and he insisted that in "a democracy, the verdict of the majority has got to be accepted"). On the other hand, he urged that a sharp distinction be made between "political opposition" and "political enmity" if the opposition wished to "build up a healthy democratic set-up in the country." Political enmity, he argued, might lead to "civil war" and democratic institutions such as elections were meant to prevent civil war. These appeals were well-timed, not only because of the grotesque Karachi riots and the post-election fracas at a number of places in East Pakistan, but, more important, because the opposition seemed serious about boycotting the elections and adopting the radical but unpredictable course of mass agitation.

It was, however, noticeable that while Ayub himself was calling for restraint and political rapprochement, other PML spokesmen and dignitaries seemed to be vengeful. Some very provocative statements were made by the ruling party's functionaries and Ministers (who perhaps were anxious to demonstrate their utility to the President and his Party by talking big). The East Pakistan Muslim League passed a series of "shocking" resolutions which went directly against the spirit and theme of the President's repeated appeals. Among other things, they called for the reintroduction of nominations to all tiers of the BDs (with a view to making the elected BDs subservient to official functionaries); action against four Bengali opposition newspapers for "spreading falsehood and perjury" and also against the government contractors, license, and permit holders who had proved "to be more disloyal" during the Presidential elections; and for setting up a high-powered body (consisting of government officials)—and not a *judicial* commission as demanded by the opposition—to inquire into the conduct of the government officials who allegedly campaigned and canvassed for the opposition candidates. The third demand, remarked a Dacca daily, "lent color" to the charge of "the rule of the vested interests;" it asked in disgust: "Does it mean that about half, if not more of the population of the country should be treated as second-class citizens because they did not support the government politically?"

The Issues

The debate in the Assembly elections was a poor second to that in the Presidential contest; it was limited in scope, intensity, and duration. Ayub was certainly anxious to get a two-third majority in the House, but he did not bother to campaign too much for the party except by issuing appeals from his Presidential post, transforming his receptions into "campaign meetings." His participation, however limited, was yet resented by the opposition which wanted him to make a clear distinction between his position as head of the state and as party chief. Otherwise, they argued, it created the unmistakable impression that the MECs of the government were fully behind the PML.

The PML's appeal and strategy rested on two or three main themes: prestige abroad, political stability and economic development at home, and the "political bankruptcy" of the opposition in not forging a united front. Since the vote for Ayub in the Presidential elections was a vote for stability and progress, the MECs, argued Ayub, would do well to vote the PML, thereby strengthening his hands in his efforts "to build up Pakistan as a welfare state," but, all the same, they should elect "honest," "efficient," and "patriotic" people.

The elaboration of this theme was left to his numerous lieutenants. Foreign Minister Bhutto argued that the elections were not between personalities but between two political parties representing different political ideologies, and that political stability could be ensured only if an absolute majority of the PML were elected to the National Assembly. After all, the PML was the only organized, well-disciplined party "with a pragmatic approach to national problems" and a well-defined program "to make the country an Islamic welfare state"; it was the only organization "which could guarantee the protection of the legitimate rights of the people and continue its benevolent policies under the dynamic leadership of President Ayub." The people had demonstrated their "unique sense of wisdom," "political sagacity and love for the country" in the presidential elections, and chosen the path of "progress and prosperity"; would they now be misled by opposition slogans and empty promises, and commit harakiri? The sole purpose of the COP in begging for votes was to undo the BD system ultimately; hence, it was in the interest of the MECs themselves not to commit suicide by supporting the opposition.

To the East Pakistani electors, the appeal was more specific. The emphasis was on the economic stakes they had in a PML victory. They had complete control over the Rs. 300 million annual rural works program; in the Third Plan (1965-70), the province has been allocated Rs. 2,000 million more than its Western counterpart with a view to close the existing economic disparity by 5%; the successful implementation of the Plan was, therefore, far more vital to the East than to the Western wing of the nation. Hence there were frequent references to the Plan in the pronouncements of the East Pakistani leaders.

Contrasted with this was the general emphasis in the West on the rise of the country's prestige abroad, this argument having been so timely buttressed by Ayub's successful visit to China in February. Favorable comments on Pakistan's foreign policy, political stability, and economic development appearing abroad were frequently invoked and reproduced extensively in the daily press.

As against these issues, the opposition had nothing concrete to offer except their platform of an unfettered democracy. For the intelligentsia, this could well be an end in itself, but perhaps not for the MECs, especially of the rural areas, whose vision could not but be limited, whose interests were more local and personal than national and altruistic, and whose understanding of abstract principles and theories was obviously meager.

The opposition campaign also suffered from several other handicaps. First, it did not believe in the BD system; it distrusted the MECs for their "unpredictability"; in addition, its terrible lack of organization forced individual candidates to organize their campaign personally and entirely on their own. Finally, it was difficult for the five COP components and the NDF to prepare an agreed list for all the constituencies; at one stage the NAP in the East and the JI in the West almost broke away from the COP parliamentary boards over the issue of tickets to their own party candidates. Some of the seats were ultimately left open, enabling more than one opposition candidate to contest them, and this proved disastrous for the COP cause in East Pakistan. But for the indefatigable efforts of Chaudhri Muhammad Ali (NIP), who, since the untimely demise of Nazimuddin, had done the utmost to keep the opposition united, the COP would perhaps not have survived this new crisis.

The Elections

Even as the elections approached, the COP demanded the withdrawal of Section 144 and loudspeaker restrictions, and the cancellation of warrants against political workers, in order to create a "climate of freedom," so essential for elections. In a country where the newspapers are beyond the reach of the illiterate masses, and the radio beyond that of the parties, political meetings are the only means through which campaign issues can be brought before the public. Hence the ban on public meetings and processions amounted to "a drastic denial of the democratic process." The absence of a public airing of various views made the "quiet cajoling" of the MECs and "whispering" the principal methods of electioneering. This, in turn, encouraged the MECs, now supremely conscious of their political importance, to resent any public interference in their "privilege" and "discretion" to vote the candidate they deemed fit.

During the last week, large-scale arrests of MECs and opposition leaders and workers throughout West Pakistan were alleged. It was charged that 80 MECs, together with a former provincial minister and another COP leader in the Jhang-Muzaffargarh area were jailed. Also reportedly arrested were 18 workers in Karachi itself, including some aides of Baqi Baluch. (Baqi Baluch was seriously injured in an assassination attempt by unknown gunmen in Lahore last January—the bullets instead killed a local journalist.) Harassment of workers, raiding of opposition election camps by rivals without hindrance, coercion and intimidation were frequently alleged. Chaudhri Muhammad Ali who visited Montgomery, Jhang, and Lyallpur districts, charged that "it was the police who were fighting the election with police methods."

Charges of utilizing official machinery and pressure tactics in "wooing the MECs" were frequent in the East as well. The PML, in collaboration with the government, was accused of using "the carrot and stick method," circle officers and government transport, and of getting officials to issue invitations to the MECs to attend election meetings scheduled to be addressed by the President, Governors, Ministers, and political functionaries. The PML, on its part, charged the COP of intimidating and misleading the MECs.

Thus it was, again, in an atmosphere of charges and counter-charges, that the MECs proceeded to elect the MNAs on March 21. The results gave the PML a thumbing majority: 120 seats. The opposition secured 15 seats (COP 10; NDF 5) in East Pakistan, and one in the West. The rest were independents, including the former leader of the opposition and the son of the former opposition leader, Mian Iftikharuddin. The most unexpected victory was that in the West, of Miss Jinnah's Election Agent, Hasan A. Shaikh, who routed Siddique Dawood—a leading industrialist, sitting MNA and the PML treasurer—by a convincing margin. One unusual feature of the elections was the large number of tied seats—three of them prestige seats. One Minister and 24 sitting MNAs lost their seats. Although the

PML won 80% of the seats, it secured only 54.8% (East 49.64%; West 61.31%) of the votes cast, the opposition a little more than 25% (34% in the East), the rest being gained by the "independents."

Had the NA elections been held simultaneously with the Presidential contest, the results would obviously have been much different than was the case. The results were all the more complicated because of the crop of "independents" who not only prevented a straight fight between the PML and the COP in more than half the constituencies, but also allowed some of the PML nominees to win by a minority vote. The COP's initial indecision about contesting the polls, their later squabbles over preparing an agreed list, the recrudescence of the AL-NAP rivalry in the East, and, above all, their folly in declaring some of the safer constituencies open (enabling more than one opposition candidate to contest them), had played havoc with their fortunes. In the Chittagong area, for instance, despite getting majority votes cumulatively in four of the five constituencies and majority votes in two constituencies, the opposition lost all the seats.

The PML hailed the massive electoral victory in glowing terms, from the President downward. Sabur Khan, leader of the House in the NA, on the other hand, considered the opposition's failure to capture more seats "a tragedy," since it would not be able to raise serious discussion through an adjournment motion which required the support of at least 20 members. Demoralized all the more, the opposition felt that it had "won morally by exposing the inherent weakness of the indirect system of election"; this exposure was, however, poor consolation for its misfortunes.

Provincial Elections

With the pattern of the future clearly decided in the presidential and NA polls, the provincial assembly (PA) elections excited much less interest. The NA results had justified the worst fears of the anti-participationists: to take part in the PA elections was, therefore, considered "an exercise in futility." The country, the COP contended, was being taken, step by step, towards "naked authoritarianism," in defiance of the people's mandate and popular sentiments. Hence, it should explore other ways to prepare the country for the ultimate restoration of "the birthright of democracy to the people." Thus, while the party as such should disassociate itself from the provincial polls, individual members could contest on their own, if they so wished. Few opposition candidates offered themselves in West Pakistan either as "independents" or under their own respective party labels. In East Pakistan, however, the opposition parties, at the district level, contested 81 seats, and supported the "independents" in the rest.

In West Pakistan, a total of 779 candidates filed nomination papers, 47 PML and pro-PML "independent" candidates were returned unopposed, and 99 seats were contested. In the East, about 900 candidates filed nomination papers, two PML candidates were returned unopposed, and 670 finally contested 148 seats. The PML expelled a total of 138 "renegades" (East 99; West 39), who were "duping the people by posing as Muslim League candidates."

As against the NA elections, provincial and local issues alone mattered in the PA elections. With the opposition irretrievably demoralized, the over-confident PML did not bother to campaign to any extent. In addition, most of the old-timers who were experienced campaigners, had retired from the central and provincial cabinets on March 23 (when Ayub began his second term), and since their status seemed to depend entirely on their cabinet posts, they went into complete silence.

Significantly, in spite of a live front on the Rann of Kutch in the West and a devastating cyclone in the East (both of which should have normally deflected some vote in the favor of the government), the PML did poorly. West Pakistan gave the PML 96 seats, the independents 49 seats, and the JI one seat. Among the independents, at least four were opposition candidates. The ruling party secured 11,834 votes (48.78%) in a total of 24,425 votes cast; the "independents" and opposition together bagged 12,425 votes (51.22%). In the East, the PML failed to gain an absolute majority: it secured only 66 seats; 58 went to "independents" and 23 to the opposition (AL 11; NAP 4; NDF 3; CML 3; JI 1; NIP 1). Of the 37,233 votes cast, the PML secured some 14,144 votes (38%), the opposition parties 5,863 (16.33%), and the "independents" (about half of whom were backed by the opposition) 16,284 votes (45.35%).

The voting trend during the PA elections indicated that the voters were more influenced by individuals rather than by party labels and programs. It is not, however, without significance that the "independents," largely supported by the opposition, secured 51.22% votes in the West, and the "independents" and the opposition together obtained 61.7% in the East. While East Pakistan returned about 20 expelled Leaguers in the West, it was mostly the "independents" without any party affiliation who defeated the official PML candidates in 49 constituencies.

The emergence of a formidable phalanx of "independents" in the provincial legislatures has created a ticklish problem. Whereas, under the Political Parties' Act, crossing of the floor by party members is prohibited (in which case they would have to resign their seats and seek re-election), these "independents" are free to cross the floor any time they like and according to the whim of the moment. Nobody yet seems to know how to resolve this disturbing feature of the new assemblies. Governor Monem Khan, perhaps in view of the depleted PML strength in the East Pakistan Assembly, hopes that some of these "independents" will eventually join the PML.[1] But the question still remains whether an independent member can join the party whose official candidate he has defeated. Would this not violate the spirit of the Political Parties' Act, besides amounting to betraying the electors who had rejected that party at the polls?

The tiny, 16-member opposition in the NA, led by Nurul Amin, is undaunted, alert and, in terms of its quality and parliamentary wit, quite formidable. It took the Assembly nine hours to pass the first clause of the Constitution (Third Amendment) Bill, and the bill itself was passed after the opposition had staged a walk-out.

Of all the trends that have emerged from the Presidential and Assembly elections, two are most dominant. While, on the one hand, a majority of the electoral college favor the present regime, its members, on the other, are extremely unpredictable on some matters. They gave a massive 62.7% vote to the PML in the presidential polls, 54.8% in the national and 42.25% in the provincial. This shows that, while President Ayub is more popular than his party, the MECs consider it their

[1] PML's official policy in this regard was outlined when its new Secretary-General, Bhutto, said that "independents and others outside the Muslim League will find that the doors of this organization are not bolted" (*Dawn*, May 18, 1965). This was in conformity with the earlier PML decision to adopt the winners in the basic democracies' elections.

privilege to vote the way they like, although in all the elections it was repeatedly emphasized by both the governmental and opposition spokesmen that the contest was not between personalities but between parties. This erratic voting behavior shows flexibility on the part of at least one-third of the MECs based upon theories of "discretion" and "conscience." They have not proved to be as "honest," as "conscientious," as "responsible," and as "patriotic" as President Ayub thought they would be.

It is not usually remembered that the BD system was devised at a time when Ayub not only stood for a "partyless democracy" but when he was also vehemently against the revival of political parties. To turn the basic democrats (BDs) into an electoral college was an afterthought. Since President Ayub supports, as his manifesto signifies, a pragmatic approach to problems, it might not be too "heretical" to pinpoint the need for certain reforms in the BD system in the light of its operation during the last three elections. To suggest, as some opposition leaders do, that the indirect system of election (because of the simple reason of its being indirect) is always or altogether undemocratic is basically erroneous. Even so, the present system could perhaps be made more democratic.

First, the "license" given to the MECs to vote according to their own "discretion" or "conscience" (which, at least in one-third of the cases, does not seem to be a consistent discretion or conscience), might well be withdrawn. If the members of National and Provincial Assemblies cannot have a separate conscience of their own, apart from that delegated to them by a majority of their electors, why should the MECs who, by all accounts, are largely inferior to these MNAs and MPAs in terms of their education, intelligence, breadth of vision, comprehension of issues, and on other accounts, be allowed the privilege of voting according to their own "conscience"? If the crossing of the floor by a party member is outlawed under the 1962 Constitution, should not the same apply to the MECs on whom devolves the tremendous responsibility of electing the country's rulers? This, in turn, would require that the major parties intending to contest the Presidential and/or Assembly elections should, by statute, be made to issue tickets at the basic tier rather than resorting to the convenient course of adopting the winner in a particular constituency. Contesting the BD elections on a party ticket alone would enable the MECs to get a clear mandate from the people as to their choice. And the MECs should be made to carry out this mandate rather than be left free to be deflected by their own "discretion"—and perhaps their "interest"—which, in any case, can be no substitute for the electors' mandate.

And even as the MNAs and MPAs vote openly and publicly on various measures under discussion, so these MECs should be made to vote on the President or members of the Assemblies openly and publicly and not by secret ballot—to obviate the possibility of a betrayal of their commitments to their own electors. But all this would be possible only if facilities for the demonstration and exertion of public opinion (through unrestricted public meetings, processions, and other means) are not curbed.

In any case, such a procedure would not only promote public morality and a sense of responsibility among the BDs, but would also make the system above criticism as being undemocratic. Without this prerequisite at the basic level, however, the growth of a healthy political atmosphere and of well-organized parties in the nation will be difficult if not impossible.

Let us summarize. The last three elections have been extremely instructive, deepening the political consciousness in the country. In the light of the lessons learned during these elections, the PML is being reorganized in a more systematic way, but the opposition continues to remain in doldrums. Its despair lies in the multiplicity of its components, and the personal ambitions of some of their leaders, which have thus far prevented their merger into one or two composite parties. This chaotic proliferation of political parties was chiefly responsible not only for bringing the parliamentary system into disrepute, but also for wrecking it from within, thus facilitating the military take-over in October 1958. Now, it has wrecked the COP as well.

COP misfortunes during the past year could be traced chiefly to its inability to resolve the Hamletian dilemma: 'to be or not to be!' First, it was whether to contest the Presidential contest or not; then the National Assembly elections; still later, the provincial ones. And now the most ticklish, but crucial question is: to merge or not. Three elections defeats, one more shattering than the other, should have normally roused the opposition from its immobility, but indications in this direction thus far are feeble and scant. In any case, if and when this "miracle" of a single opposition front takes place, it will still be difficult to discover an acceptable leader, except Miss Jinnah who, since last fall, is considered as a leader in her own right, rather than merely being one by virtue of the accident of her birth.

As for President Ayub, nobody is likely to challenge him seriously for a long while. Although the present quiescent political situation can be expected to change after the elder "politicians," debarred from participation in the country's political life, are released from their EBDO-cage in January 1967, there is scant doubt that Ayub will run for a third term—of course, at the request of the Assemblies—and under present conditions at least, would probably win. Not only time and tide, but even age seems to tilt the balance against the opposition stalwarts.

76 • Mohammad Ayub Khan: *Election Manifesto, 1965* *

The following manifesto is a political document, produced by Ayub Khan during the 1964–65 elections as a kind of political platform. Like most such documents, it promises all things to all men; nevertheless, a careful reading of it will give one an insight into Pakistan's political hopes and aspirations. A summary of the manifesto of the Combined Opposition parties is to be found in the first selection of this Section Five.

I believe that Allah, in His infinite mercy, created Pakistan to give the Muslims of these regions a homeland in which to mould their lives in accordance with the fundamental principles and the spirit of Islam;. .

* *Pakistan Perspective* (Washington, D. C.: Embassy of Pakistan, n.d.), pp. ix–xiii. By permission. This manifesto was issued on the eve of the Presidential election in Pakistan, January 1965.

that Pakistan is destined to play a glorious role in the history of mankind and in particular in the advancement and progress of Muslims all over the world;

that the will of the people is supreme in all matters of the State;

that democracy provides the surest means of securing the fullest participation of the people in the affairs of their country;

that whatever the institutional form democracy may take in Pakistan, it must be based on pragmatism rather than dogmatism and must safeguard the basic right of the people to freedom of speech, freedom of association and freedom of assembly under the rule of law;

that the people of Pakistan must themselves determine the form of government which should be established consistent with the ideological basis of the country and the fundamental need for preserving the sovereignty, security and unity of the country;

that the people of Pakistan must move, as fast as possible, into the age of science and technology, while steadfastly preserving the basic tenets of their faith, in order to attain a higher standard of living;

that all class distinctions should disappear and Pakistanis should live and prosper as a model community symbolizing Islamic brotherhood and equality of man;

that there must be complete equality of opportunities available to all citizens of Pakistan;

that Pakistan should develop into a welfare state where basic necessities are available to all.

I maintain that the reforms such as the land reforms, educational reforms, constitutional reforms and administrative reforms introduced during the last six years are aimed at freeing the society from the shackles of past domination, and elimination of class tensions and conflicts;

that further progress, in pursuit of the beliefs I have enunciated, would be possible only if we develop sufficient self-reliance to study our own problems and to solve them in our own way;

that only an enlightened approach based on practical realism rather than dominated by theorization, will help us to shed retrograde and antiquated traditionalism and usher in an era of true liberation: political, cultural, social, economic and intellectual;

that in all material and economic matters our attitude should not be doctrinaire but one dictated by the basic requirements of the situation;

that Pakistan's sovereignty and unity as a nation can be guaranteed only by a strong Center capable of providing full provincial autonomy without allowing centrifugal forces to re-assert themselves;

that in our dealings with other countries the determining factor must always be the interest of Pakistan and that we must always endeavor to enlarge the areas of understanding and friendship with other countries, particularly those who are our neighbors;

that we must work toward the establishment of world peace and human happiness and strive in all possible ways to save mankind from the horrors of war.

I undertake to maximize the utilization of national resources; to provide for the widest possible and most equitable distribution of wealth;

to adopt all practical means to raise the income of the common man so as to reduce the disparity between the rich and the poor;

to ensure that the burden of taxation is distributed in a fair and equitable manner;

to eliminate cartels and monopolies;

to rationalize the land revenue system so as to give a fair deal especially to the small land-holder;

to adopt all practical measures to prevent the recurrence of floods in East Pakistan and to provide, as far as possible, adequate facilities for the rehabilitation of those affected by this menace;

to adopt all such measures as may be necessary to control water-logging and salinity in West Pakistan and to reclaim affected areas as far as possible;

to ensure the stability of the prices of goods used by the common man and to prevent inflation to the extent possible;

to take steps for the rehabilitation of homeless people and to provide better housing facilities;

to ensure that improvement in the standard of living of the people is not neutralized by unbalanced increase in population;

to associate local people in the administration of their affairs and to transfer gradually such functions as may be possible to the Basic Democracies;

to expand further the scope of rural works program in financial as well as functional terms;

to build up a strong rural community capable of looking after its own needs;

to provide greater educational facilities as envisaged in the Outline of the Third Five-Year Plan;

to work out a code of ethics for the press and to establish a voluntary machinery within the press itself to regulate effectively its conduct according to the code;

to take further measures to root out corruption in all branches of the Administration and to raise the standard of efficiency in the public services;

to take expeditious steps to achieve parity between the two wings of the country in the light of the constitutional provisions and to ensure that the pace of progress of the various regions of West Pakistan, as a single indivisible Unit, is increased further to bring about a balanced pattern of growth throughout the country;

to provide growing facilities for cultural integration and for the promotion of original and creative thinking;

to advance the ideology of Muslim nationalism which will enable Pakistan to serve as a strong base for collaboration with other Muslim countries of the world;

to support all liberal causes and to provide whatever assistance may be possible to such people or communities as may be in bondage or under the yoke of colonialism, imperialism or any other form of domination;

to continue to strive for the right of self-determination for the people of Jammu and Kashmir, and for its exercise in accordance with the UNCIP [United Nations Commission for India and Pakistan] resolutions and to provide all moral support to the freedom fighters of Kashmir;

to provide full protection and safeguards to minorities in Pakistan and to ensure for them equal opportunities, rights and privileges.

I urge for Patience. Growth and development need time and not all the benefits can be secured by one generation. We have to work not only for ourselves but also for those who will follow us, and the thought that most of the benefits of our efforts may be reaped by the coming generations should be the mainstay of our effort;

for Faith. We must have faith in ourselves and in our destiny, and whatever the community might embark upon should be a source of pride and satisfaction to all of us;

for Moderation. Reforms should be undertaken in a missionary and not in a vainglorious spirit. The objective should be to produce a better arrangement rather than to destroy an existing arrangement;

for National Outlook. We cannot afford to think in terms of provinces or regions. The economic advancement which we have already achieved has taken us to a stage where further progress will depend on our ability to evolve a national outlook, a national vision and to secure national unity;

for Hard Work. Empty slogans and fond hopes will get us nowhere. It is only through hard work undertaken in a selfless spirit and in the service of the community that we can achieve results.

It is in an endeavor to reach the objectives which I have outlined above that I am seeking re-election to the office of the President of Pakistan. My sole aim is to establish the sovereignty of the people and to work for the progress of Pakistan and the happiness and prosperity of the people of Pakistan.

MOHAMMAD AYUB KHAN

Bibliography

COMMUNIST CHINA

Adams, Ruth, ed., *Contemporary China.* New York: Random House (Vintage Books V-340), 1966.

Barnett, A. Doak, *Cadres, Bureaucracy, and Political Power in Communist China.* New York: Columbia University Press, 1967.

———, *China After Mao.* Princeton, N.J.: Princeton University Press, 1967.

Blaustein, Albert P., ed., *Fundamental Legal Documents of Communist China.* South Hackensack, N. J.: Rothman, 1962.

Blum, Robert, *The United States and China in World Affairs,* ed. by A. Doak Barnett. New York: McGraw-Hill, 1966.

Boorman, Howard L., ed., "Contemporary China and the Chinese," *The Annals of the American Academy of Social and Political Science,* Vol. 321 (January 1959).

———, A. Eckstein, P. E. Mosely, and B. Schwartz, *Moscow-Peking Axis: Strengths and Strains.* New York: Harper, 1957.

Bowie, Robert R., and John K. Fairbanks, eds., *Communist China, 1955–1959: Policy Documents with Analysis.* Cambridge, Mass.: Harvard University Press, 1962.

Brandt, Conrad, Benjamin Schwartz, and John K. Fairbank, eds., *A Documentary History of Chinese Communism.* Cambridge, Mass.: Harvard University Press, 1952.

Brzezinski, Z. K., *The Soviet Bloc: Unity and Conflict,* rev. ed. Cambridge, Mass.: Harvard University Press, 1967.

Chao, K. C., "Economic Planning and Organization in Mainland China: A Documentary Study (1949–1957)," 2 vols. (mimeo.), *Chinese Economic and Political Studies.* Cambridge, Mass.: Harvard University Press, 1959–60.

Cheng, J. Chester, ed., *The Politics of the Chinese Red Army.* Stanford, Calif.: Hoover Institution, 1966.

The China Quarterly (articles in).

Chen, Theodore H. E., ed., *The Chinese Communist Regime: Documents and Commentary.* New York: Praeger, 1967.

Gittings, John, *The Role of the Chinese Army.* London and New York: Oxford University Press, 1967.

Granqvist, Hans, *The Red Guard, A Report on Mao's Revolution,* trans. by E. J. Friis. New York: Praeger, 1967.

Griffith, William E., *The Sino-Soviet Rift.* Cambridge, Mass.: M.I.T. Press, 1964.

Halperin, Morton H., *China and the Bomb.* New York: Praeger, 1965.

Hinton, Harold C., *Communist China in World Politics.* Boston: Houghton Mifflin, 1966.

Houn, Franklin, W., *A Short History of Chinese Communism.* Englewood Cliffs, N. J.: Prentice-Hall (Spectrum Book S-166), 1967.

Hsieh, Alice L., *Communist China's Strategy in the Nuclear Era.* Englewood Cliffs, N. J.: Prentice-Hall (Spectrum Book S-32), 1962.

Jan, George P., ed., *Government of Communist China.* San Francisco: Chandler, 1966.

Lewis, John W., *Leadership in Communist China.* Ithaca, N. Y.: Cornell University Press, 1963.

———, ed., *Major Doctrines of Communist China.* New York: Norton, 1964.

Liu, W. T., ed., *Chinese Society under Communism: A Reader.* New York: Wiley, 1967.

North, Robert C., *Moscow and Chinese Communists.* Stanford, Calif.: Stanford University Press, 1953.

Rubinstein, Alvin Z., *Communist Political Systems.* Englewood Cliffs, N. J.: Prentice-Hall, 1966.

Schram, Stuart R., *The Political Thought of Mao Tse-tung.* New York: Praeger, 1963.

Schurmann, Franz, *Ideology and Organization in Communist China.* Berkeley: University of California Press, 1966.

———, and Orville Schell, eds., *The China Reader: Communist China, Revolutionary Reconstruction and International Confrontation, 1949 to the Present.* New York: Random House, 1967.

Tang, Peter S. H., *Communist China Today,* Vol. I, 2nd ed. rev. Washington, D. C.: Research Institute on the Sino-Soviet Bloc, 1961.

U.S. Senate, Committee on Government Operations (86th Cong., 1st Sess.), *National Policy Machinery in Communist China.* Washington, D. C.: Government Printing Office, 1959.

Zagoria, Donald S., *The Sino-Soviet Conflict, 1956–1961.* Princeton, N. J.: Princeton University Press, 1962.

JAPAN

Baerwald, H. H., *The Purge of Japanese Leaders under the Occupation.* University of California Publications in Political Science, Vol. 8. Berkeley: University of California Press, 1959.

Borton, Hugh, *et al., Japan Between East and West.* New York: Harper, 1957.

Burks, Ardath, W., *The Government of Japan.* New York: Crowell, 1961.

Cole, Allan B., *Japanese Society and Politics: The Impact of Social Stratification and Mobility on Politics.* Boston University Studies in Political Science. Boston: Boston University Press, 1956.

———, and Naomichi Nakanishi, eds., *Japanese Opinion Polls with Socio-Political Significance, 1947–1957.* Medford, Mass.: The Fletcher School of Law and Diplomacy, Tufts University, 1959. (Available from University Microfilms, Inc., Ann Arbor, Michigan.)

———, George O. Totten, and Cecil H. Uyehara, *Socialist Parties in Postwar Japan.* New Haven: Yale University Press, 1966.

Colton, Kenneth E., and Hattie K. and George O. Totten, eds., "Japan Since Recovery of Independence," *The Annals of the American Academy of Political and Social Science,* Vol. 308 (November 1956).

Feis, Herbert, *Contest Over Japan.* New York: Norton, 1967.

Fukutake, Tadashi, *Man and Society in Japan.* Tokyo: University of Tokyo Press, 1962.

Government Section, Supreme Commander for the Allied Powers, *Political Reorientation of Japan: September 1945 to September 1949,* 2 vols. Washington. D. C.: Government Printing Office, 1949.

Ike, Nobutaka, *Japanese Politics.* New York: Knopf, 1957.

Langdon, Frank, *Politics in Japan.* Boston: Little, Brown, 1967.

Linebarger, P. M. A., D. Chu, and A. W. Burks, *Far Eastern Governments and Politics: China and Japan.* New York: Van Nostrand, 1954.

Maki, John M., *Court and Constitution in Japan: Selected Supreme Court Decisions, 1948–60.* Seattle: University of Washington Press, 1964.

———, *Government and Politics in Japan: The Road to Democracy.* New York: Praeger, 1962.

Maruyama, Masao, *Thought and Behaviour in Modern Japanese Politics,* ed. by Ivan Morris. London and New York: Oxford University Press, 1963.

Matsumoto, Y. S., *Contemporary Japan: The Individual and the Group.* Philadelphia: American Philosophical Society, 1959.

McNelly, Theodore, *Contemporary Government of Japan.* Boston: Houghton Mifflin, 1963.

Mendel, Douglas H., Jr., *The Japanese People and Foreign Policy.* Berkeley: University of California Press, 1961.

Morris, Ivan, *Nationalism and the Right Wing in Japan.* London and New York: Oxford University Press, 1960.

Olson, Lawrence, *Dimensions of Japan.* New York: American Universities Field Staff, 1963.

Packard, George R., *Protest in Tokyo: The Security Treaty Crisis of 1960.* Princeton, N. J.: Princeton University Press, 1966.

Passin, Herbert, ed., *The United States and Japan.* The American Assembly. Englewood Cliffs, N. J.: Prentice-Hall, 1966.

Quigley, H. S., and J. E. Turner, *The New Japan: Government and Politics.* Minneapolis: University of Minnesota Press, 1956.

Scalapino, Robert A., *Democracy and the Party Movement in Prewar Japan: The Failure of the First Attempt.* Berkeley: University of California Press, 1953.

———, *The Japanese Communist Movement, 1920–1966.* Berkeley: University of California Press, 1967.

———, and Junnosuke Masumi, *Parties and Politics in Contemporary Japan.* Berkeley: University of California Press, 1962.

Steiner, Kurt, *Local Government in Japan.* Stanford, Calif.: Stanford University Press, 1965.

Tsuneishi, Warren M., *Japanese Political Style: An Introduction to the Government and Politics of Modern Japan.* New Haven, Conn.: Yale University Press, 1966.

Van Adouard, E. J. L., *Japan: From Surrender to Peace.* New York: Praeger, 1954.

Von Mehren, A. T., ed., *Law in Japan: The Legal Order in a Changing Society*. Cambridge, Mass.: Harvard University Press, 1963.

Ward, Robert E., and Dankwart Rustow, eds., *Political Modernization in Japan and Turkey*. Princeton, N. J.: Princeton University Press, 1964.

INDIA

Austin Granville, *The Indian Constitution*. Toronto: Oxford University Press, 1966.

Bailey, F. G., *Politics and Social Change: Orissa in 1959*. Berkeley: University of California Press, 1963.

———, *Tribe, Caste, and Nation*. Manchester: Manchester University Press, 1966.

Braibanti, R., and J. J. Spengler, eds., *Administration and Economic Development in India*. Durham, N. C.: Duke University Press, 1963.

Brass, Paul R., *Factional Politics in an Indian State: The Congress Party in Uttar Pradesh*. Berkeley: University of California Press, 1965.

Brecher, Michael, *Nehru: A Political Biography*. New York: Oxford University Press, 1959. Abridged edition. Boston: Beacon Press, 1962.

———, *Nehru's Mantle*. New York: Praeger, 1966.

Brown, D. Mackenzie, *Indian Thought from Manu to Gandhi*. Berkeley: University of California Press, 1958.

———, *Indian Thought from Ranade to Bhave*. Berkeley: University of California Press, 1961.

DeBary, W. T., *Sources of the Indian Tradition*. New York: Columbia University Press, 1958.

Gandhi, Mahatma, *An Autobiography: The Story of My Experience with Truth*. Boston: Beacon Press, 1957.

Harrison, S. S., *India: The Most Dangerous Decade*. Princeton, N. J.: Princeton University Press, 1960.

Isaacs, H. R., *India's Ex-Untouchables*. New York: John Day, 1964.

Lamb, B. P., *India: A World in Transition*. New York: Praeger, 1962.

Menon, V. P., *The Integration of the Indian States*. New York: Macmillan, 1956.

———, *The Transfer of Power in India*. Princeton, N. J.: Princeton University Press, 1957.

Morris-Jones, W. H., *The Government and Politics of India*. London: Hutchinson University Press, 1964.

Nair, Kusum, *Blossoms in the Dust: The Human Factor in Indian Development*. New York: Praeger, 1962.

Nehru, Jawaharlal, *The Discovery of India*. New York: Anchor Books, 1960.

———, *Toward Freedom*. Boston: Beacon Press, 1958.

Orenstein, Henry, *Gaon: Conflict and Cohesion in an Indian Village*. Princeton, N. J.: Princeton University Press, 1965.

Palmer, N. D., *The Indian Political System*. Boston: Houghton Mifflin, 1961.

Park, R. L., *India's Political System*. Englewood Cliffs, N. J.: Prentice-Hall, 1967.

———, and I. Tinker, eds., *Leadership and Political Institutions in India*. Princeton, N. J.: Princeton University Press, 1959.

Rosen, George, *Democracy and Economic Change in India*. Berkeley: University of California Press, 1966.

Rudolph, L. I., and S. H. Rudolph, *The Modernity of Tradition: Political Development in India.* Chicago: University of Chicago Press, 1968.
Smith, Donald E., *India as a Secular State.* Princeton, N. J.: Princeton University Press, 1963.
Srinivas, M. N., *Caste in India.* New York: Asia Publishing House, 1961.
Weiner, Myron, *Party Building in a New Nation: Indian National Congress.* Chicago: University of Chicago Press, 1968.
———, *The Politics of Scarcity: Public Pressure and Political Response in India.* Chicago: University of Chicago Press, 1961.
———, ed., *State Politics in India.* Princeton, N. J.: Princeton University Press, 1967.

PAKISTAN

Abbott, Freeland, *Islam and Pakistan.* Ithaca, N. Y.: Cornell University Press, 1968.
Ayub Khan, Mohammad, *Friends Not Masters.* New York: Oxford University Press, 1967.
Aziz, Ahmad, *Islamic Modernism in India and Pakistan: 1857–1964.* London: Oxford University Press, 1967.
Binder, Leonard, *Religion and Politics in Pakistan.* Berkeley: University of California Press, 1961.
Boliths, Hector, *Jinnah: Creator of Pakistan.* London: John Murray, 1954.
Callard, Keith, *Pakistan: A Political Study.* New York: Macmillan, 1958.
Chaudhri, G. W., *Democracy in Pakistan.* Dacca: Green Book House, 1963.
Chaudhri, Muhammad Ali, *The Emergence of Pakistan.* New York: Columbia University Press, 1967.
Feldman, Herbert, *Revolution in Pakistan.* London: Oxford University Press, 1967.
Goodnow, H. F., *The Civil Service of Pakistan.* New Haven, Conn.: Yale University Press, 1964.
Hakim, Khalifa Adbul, *Islamic Ideology.* Lahore: Institute of Islamic Culture, 1953.
Husain, A. F. A., *Human and Social Impact of Technological Change in Pakistan,* 2 vols. Dacca: Oxford University Press, 1956.
Ikram, S. M., *History of Muslim Civilization in India and Pakistan.* Lahore, Ashraf, 1961.
———, *Modern Muslim India and the Birth of Pakistan.* Lahore: Ashraf, 1965.
———, *Muslim Civilization in India.* New York: Columbia University Press, 1964.
Khurshid, Ahmad, ed. and trans., *Islamic Law and Constitution,* by Syed Abul 'Ala Maudoodi. Karachi: Jama'at-i-Islami, 1955.
———, ed., *Studies in the Family Law of Islam,* 2nd ed. Karachi: Chiragh-i-Rah, 1961.
Malik, Hafeez, *Moslem Nationalism in India and Pakistan.* Washington, D. C.: Public Affairs, 1963.
Mushtaq, Ahmad, *Government and Politics in Pakistan,* 2nd ed. Karachi: Pakistan Publishing House, 1963.
Pakistan Historical Society, *History of the Freedom Movement,* 2 vols., Karachi: Pakistan Historical Society, 1957.

Palmer, Norman D., *South Asia and United States Policy*. Boston: Houghton Mifflin, 1966.

Papanek, Gustav F., *Pakistan's Development*. Cambridge, Mass.: Harvard University Press, 1967.

Qureshi, Ishtiaq Husain, *The Muslim Community of the Indo-Pakistan Subcontinent, 610–1947: A Brief Historical Analysis*. 's-Gravenhage: Mouton, 1962.

Sayeed, Khalid B., *Pakistan: The Formative Phase*. New York: Institute of Pacific Relations, 1960.

———, *The Political System of Pakistan*. Boston: Houghton Mifflin, 1967.

Smith, Wilfred Cantwell, *Islam in Modern History*. Princeton, N. J.: Princeton University Press, 1955.

———, *Modern Islam in India*. London: Gollancz, 1946.

Tinker, Hugh, *India and Pakistan: A Political Analysis*. New York: Praeger, 1962.

Von Vorys, Karl, *Political Development in Pakistan*. Princeton, N. J.: Princeton University Press, 1965.

Wilcox, Wayne A., *Pakistan: The Consolidation of a Nation*. New York: Columbia University Press, 1963.